Globalization

and

INTERNATIONAL TRADE POLICIES

World Scientific Studies in International Economics

(ISSN: 1793-3641)

Published

Vol. 1 Cross-Border Banking: Regulatory Challenges
edited by Gerard Caprio, Jr (Williams College, USA), Douglas D. Evanoff (Federal Reserve Bank of Chicago, USA) & George G. Kaufman (Loyola University Chicago, USA)

Vol. 2 International Financial Instability: Global Banking and National Regulation
edited by Douglas D. Evanoff (Federal Reserve Bank of Chicago, USA), George G. Kaufman (Loyola University Chicago, USA) & John Raymond LaBrosse (Int'l Assoc. of Deposit Insurers, Switzerland)

Vol. 3 Risk Management and Value: Valuation and Asset Pricing
edited by Mondher Bellalah, Jean-Luc Prigent, Annie Delienne (Université de Cergy-Pontoise, France), Georges Pariente, Olivier Levyne, Michel Azaria (Institut Supérieur de Commerce, ISC Paris, France) & Jean-Michel Sahut (ESC Amiens, France)

Vol. 4 The Rules of Globalization (Case Book)
edited by Rawi Abdelal (Harvard University, USA)

Vol. 5 Institutions and Gender Empowerment in the Global Economy
edited by Kartik Roy (University of Queensland, Australia), Hans Blomqvist (Swedish School of Economics and Business Administration, Finland) & Cal Clark (Auburn University, USA)

Vol. 6 Globalization and Systemic Risk
edited by Douglas D. Evanoff (Federal Reserve Bank of Chicago, USA), David S. Hoelscher (International Monetary Fund, USA) & George G. Kaufman (Loyola University Chicago, USA)

Vol. 7 Fostering Monetary and Financial Cooperation in East Asia
edited by Duck-Koo Chung (North East Asia Research Foundation, South Korea) & Barry Eichengreen (University of California, Berkeley, USA)

Vol. 9 Globalization and International Trade Policies
by Robert M Stern

Forthcoming

Vol. 8 Challenges of Economic Development in the Middle East and North Africa Region
by Julia C Devlin

9 World Scientific Studies in International Economics

Globalization and International Trade Policies

Robert M. Stern
University of Michigan, USA

World Scientific
NEW JERSEY · LONDON · SINGAPORE · BEIJING · SHANGHAI · HONG KONG · TAIPEI · CHENNAI

Published by

World Scientific Publishing Co. Pte. Ltd.
5 Toh Tuck Link, Singapore 596224
USA office: 27 Warren Street, Suite 401-402, Hackensack, NJ 07601
UK office: 57 Shelton Street, Covent Garden, London WC2H 9HE

British Library Cataloguing-in-Publication Data
A catalogue record for this book is available from the British Library.

GLOBALIZATION AND INTERNATIONAL TRADE POLICIES
World Scientific Studies in Internaitonal Economics — Vol. 9

ISBN-13 978-981-270-013-1
ISBN-10 981-270-013-7

Typeset by Stallion Press
Email: enquiries@stallionpress.com

Printed in Singapore by B & Jo Enterprise Pte Ltd

Preface and Acknowledgments

This volume is a collection of mostly coauthored papers dealing with issues of globalization; analysis of multilateral, regional, and bilateral trading arrangements; services trade; and trade and labor standards. All of the papers have previously been published in a variety of academic journals, books, and reports. Their inclusion in this volume is intended to enhance the understanding and analysis of many of the most important current and historical issues of international trade and trade policy that have engaged my attention and my coauthors over the years. I wish in particular to express my thanks to my coauthors and to dedicate this volume to them.

I am grateful to Judith Jackson for her careful and painstaking assistance in preparing many of the original manuscripts and in overseeing their inclusion in this volume. I would also like to thank Yvonne Tan Hui Ling for her assistance with publication arrangements.

Robert M. Stern
Ann Arbor, Michigan
December 3, 2007

Contributors

Andrew G. Brown, Wellfleet, MA; formerly Director in the Department of Economic and Social Affairs, United Nations.

Drusilla K. Brown, Associate Professor of Economics, Tufts University, USA.

Alan V. Deardorff, John W. Sweetland Professor of International Economics and Professor of Economics and Public Policy, Department of Economics and Gerald R. Ford School of Public Policy, University of Michigan, USA.

Kyoji Fukao, Professor, The Institute of Economic Research, Hitotsubashi University, Japan.

Kozo Kiyota, Associate Professor, Faculty of Business Administration, Yokohama National University, Japan; and Visiting Associate Professor of Economics, 2006–2008, Gerald R. Ford School of Public Policy, University of Michigan, USA.

Toshihiro Okubo, Research Associate, Institute for Political and Economic Governance and The Manchester Regional Economics Center, University of Manchester, UK.

Robert M. Stern, Professor of Economics and Public Policy (Emeritus), Department of Economics and Gerald R. Ford School of Public Policy, University of Michigan, USA.

Contents

Chapter 1

Introduction and Overview

Robert M. Stern

I. Introduction

This book brings together a collection of papers that Robert M. Stern and his coauthors have written and that have been published over the years in academic journals, books, and reports. The collection addresses a variety of issues pertinent to the global trading system. One group of papers deals with globalization in terms of what the public needs to know about this phenomenon and the role of the World Trade Organization (WTO), whether some countries may be hurt by globalization, how global market integration relates to national sovereignty, and how and whether considerations of fairness are and should be dealt with in the global trading system and WTO negotiations. A second group of papers consists of analytical and computational modeling studies of multilateral, regional, and bilateral trading arrangements and negotiations from a global and national perspective for the United States and other major trading countries. The remaining papers include an empirical analysis of barriers to international services trade and the consequences of liberalization, and issues of international trade and labor standards.

The book can serve the interests of upper-level undergraduates, postgraduates, academics, researchers, and policy-makers in international trade and trade policy. Each paper in the chapters that follow has been edited to some extent but still contains all of the essential details as originally published. At the end of each chapter, there is a series of study questions that may be used for teaching purposes by faculty members and students.

Brief summaries of the chapters that comprise the volume are provided below. Given the length and complexities of the chapters, these summaries should be helpful in guiding the reader in focusing attention on the particular topics and issues that are of greatest interest and concern. Also, at the end of each chapter, there are suggested further readings listed that provide up-to-date treatment of the relevant subject matter in the chapter that the reader will find helpful.

II. Overview

Part I. *Globalization*

Chapter 2 — "What the Public Should Know about Globalization and the World Trade Organization," with Alan V. Deardorff, *Review of International Economics*, 2002.

This chapter reviews the essentials of economic globalization, as well as the major institution that has recently gotten much of the credit and blame for it, the World Trade Organization (WTO). It first defines globalization, which is just the increasing economic integration of the world economy. It then asks who gains and loses from globalization, drawing primarily upon economic theory to identify its benefits and costs, and who within and among the world's economies get them. The discussion concludes by asking briefly what can and should be done about globalization.

The second half of the chapter turns to the WTO, which was the focus of so much negative attention at its Seattle meeting in December 1999. For it too, it is first asked what the WTO is, trying to clarify several misperceptions about what it does and why. It is then asked what groups gain and lose from the WTO, some simply as a byproduct of its role in facilitating globalization, but others from particular WTO rules and procedures. This leads to the controversies that raged in Seattle in November 1999. The Seattle events are described as they have been described to us by those who were there at the time. The chapter concludes with what might be done to change both the WTO itself and the public's perceptions of it.

Chapter 3 — "Globalization's Bystanders: Does Trade Liberalization Hurt Countries That Do Not Participate?" with Alan V. Deardorff, *World Development*, August 2006, 34(8).

This chapter uses trade theory to examine the effects of trade liberalization on countries that do not participate in it. These include both countries that fail to participate in multilateral trade negotiations, and also countries that lie outside of preferential trading arrangements such as free trade areas. The analysis suggests that, while it is theoretically possible for excluded countries to gain, through improved terms of trade, from trade liberalization, several reasons suggest that they are more likely to lose.

Chapter 4 — "Global Market Integration and National Sovereignty," with Andrew G. Brown, *The World Economy*, March 2006, 29(3).

This chapter first traces the evolution of the global trading system from the 19th century to the present-day GATT/WTO arrangements, calling attention to the key roles of reciprocity and non-discrimination. It is noted how the system is now challenged by the new paradigm of global market integration. Then considered is the recent plethora of free trade agreements (FTAs), including those between industrial and developing countries, and their uneasy relationship with a multilateral system based on non-discrimination. Thereafter, the boundaries of the WTO are defined, and there is an examination of how the potential expansion of these boundaries may result in the over-extension and weakening of the effectiveness and influence of the WTO.

Chapter 5 — "Concepts of Fairness in the Global Trading System," with Andrew G. Brown, *Pacific Economic Review*, August 2007, 12(3).

This chapter first establishes why some conception of fairness is inherent in a system of trade rules and procedures that is voluntary. The different criteria implicitly used in assessments of fairness are then explored. First considered is the operational idea of reciprocal gains in market access — long embodied in GATT/WTO negotiations. It is observed that reciprocity is less important in the actual outcomes than in the rhetoric of bargaining. Considered next are the economists' criteria of efficiency as defined in welfare terms or in terms of productivity growth, and note their limited bearing on the idea of fairness. Focusing first on relations among the developed economies, the broader idea of fairness as equality of opportunity is addressed. This idea embraces not only reciprocity in market access but also equality in the supporting rules affecting market access. Disparate national conceptions of fairness can be bridged only when differences in national forms of business organization or in preferences for public goods do not intervene. The question of fairness in relations among countries at very different levels of development is next addressed. The meaning of distributive justice in trade relations is first explored, and then how far it is realized in present arrangements for market access. Thereafter considered is the question of fairness for developing countries in the rules affecting market access. The analysis of criteria is completed with some comments on procedural justice affecting both developed and developing countries in such matters as dispute settlement and trade defense measures. The findings are summarized in a final section together with suggested implications pertinent to the Doha Development Round negotiations.

Part II. *Analysis of Multilateral, Regional, and Bilateral Trading Arrangements*

Chapter 6 — "Multilateral Trade Negotiations and Preferential Trading Arrangements," with Alan V. Deardorff, in Alan V. Deardorff and Robert M. Stern (eds.), *Analytical and Negotiating Issues in the Global Trading System*, University of Michigan Press, 1994.

This chapter begins with a discussion of the principles of the General Agreement on Tariffs and Trade (GATT), followed by a brief history of the main characteristics of the GATT negotiating rounds and an assessment of their accomplishments. The chapter then addresses how preferential trading arrangements are accommodated within Article XXIV of the GATT Articles of Agreement and proceeds to a discussion of the characteristics and consequences of existing preferential arrangements and a comparison of the advantages and limitations of multilateralism and preferential arrangements. Thereafter, a comparative advantage framework is introduced for the purpose of undertaking a theoretical analysis of the welfare effects of the expansion of preferential trading blocs. Finally, there is a discussion of some implications for the design of trading blocs with the objective of enhancing world economic welfare.

Chapter 7 — "An Overview of the Modeling of the Choices and Consequences of U.S. Trade Policies," with Alan V. Deardorff, in Alan V. Deardorff and Robert M. Stern (eds.), *Constituent Interests and U.S. Trade Policies*, University of Michigan Press, 1998.

This chapter provides the context for the theme of a conference, "The Representation of Constituent Interests in the Design and Implementation of U.S. Trade Policies," which was held at the University of Michigan in 1996. It first reviews the normative and political economy approaches to the modeling of trade policies. The normative approach is the basis for the traditional analysis of the welfare effects of trade and the choice of policies designed to correct distortions in the economy and to achieve first-best optima. The political economy approach provides an analytical framework for understanding of the choices made by policy-makers in a political setting in response to the lobbying and related activities of producing interests. The major limitations of these approaches are identified and then discussed in what Dixit (1996) has referred to as the "transaction-cost approach," which may provide a middle-ground between the other approaches and permit the analysis of some hitherto imperfectly understood issues of trade policy. There is also a brief discussion of the empirical literature pertinent to the normative and political economy approaches.

Thereafter, a sketch of the main features of the U.S. trade-policy process is provided, focusing in particular on the roles played by the agencies of government together with the important constituent interest groups in the U.S. economy. Each of the modeling approaches are then considered and how they can be interpreted in the representation of the behavior and interactions of the different constituencies. Setting the modeling issues aside, it is also asked what can be learned from the past half-century of U.S. trade policy experiences. It is observed that there has been a distinctive movement towards more liberal and open trade in the United States and elsewhere in the period being considered. There is a final discussion of the implications of the interplay of the different modeling approaches for research and policy in light of the observations about the ways in which trade liberalization and increased openness have evolved.

Chapter 8 — "Issues of Manufactures Liberalization and Administered Protection in the Doha Round," with Alan V. Deardorff, *Global Economy Journal*, December 2005, 5(4).

This chapter focuses especially on the positions that the developing countries should take in their own interests on the issues of manufactures liberalization and administered protection in the Doha Development Agenda negotiations. A series of recommendations are set forth with supporting arguments:

- For market access, both developed and developing countries should commit to reducing their most restrictive trade barriers, using a formula approach with limited exceptions.
- Negotiated tariff reductions should be phased in over a period of ten years in equal incremental installments.

- Adjustment assistance should be provided by a system of wage insurance and subsidized by transfers from developed countries.
- The rules for safeguards, countervailing duties, and anti-dumping should be redrafted to focus their use on cases of legitimate economic justification and to discourage their use as protectionist devices.
- The U.S. and EU should devise and implement a program of comprehensive but declining import restrictions on imports from China consistent with China's terms of WTO accession and eliminated by 2008.
- WTO rules governing Preferential Trading Arrangements should be revised to ensure that they contribute to the liberalization and simplification of the multilateral trading system.
- Preference-granting countries should provide assistance to countries experiencing the erosion of preferences due to multilateral liberalization.
- The WTO system of dispute resolution should remain in place.
- Special and differential assistance, if granted, should not exempt countries from the provisions for their own market liberalization.

Developing countries should participate actively and constructively in the negotiations to further their own interests. Developing countries may be at a disadvantage in the negotiating process, due to their resource limitations and inexperience in negotiations. Offsetting such disadvantages, however, are their large numbers and the compelling case for meeting their needs. What is needed is leadership and cooperation as, for example, with the Group of 20 and other coalitions, together with willingness to listen and be flexible on the part of their developed country counterparts.

Chapter 9 — "An Assessment of the Economic Effects of the Menu of U.S. Trade Policies," with Kozo Kiyota, *Global Economy Journal*, December 2005, 5(4).

In this chapter, the Michigan Model of World Production and Trade is used to calculate the aggregate welfare and sectoral employment effects of the menu of U.S. trade policies. The menu of policies encompasses the various preferential U.S. bilateral and regional FTAs negotiated and in process, unilateral removal of existing trade barriers by the United States, its FTA partner countries, and global (multilateral) free trade. The welfare impacts of the FTAs on the United States are shown to be rather small in absolute and relative terms. The sectoral employment effects are also generally small, but vary across the individual sectors depending on the patterns of bilateral liberalization.

The welfare effects on the FTA partner countries are shown to be mostly positive though generally small, but there are some indications of potentially disruptive employment shifts in some partner countries. The results further suggest that there would be trade diversion and detrimental welfare effects in some non-member countries/regions. It also appears that, while FTA partners may gain from the bilateral FTAs, they may be adversely affected because of overlapping "hub-and-spoke" arrangements due to other discriminatory FTAs that have been negotiated.

The welfare gains from both unilateral trade liberalization by the United States and from global (multilateral) trade liberalization are shown to be rather substantial and more uniformly positive for all countries/regions in the global trading system as compared to the welfare gains from the bilateral FTAs analyzed.

The issue then is whether the WTO member countries will be able to overcome their divisiveness and indecisions and bring the Doha Round multilateral negotiations to a successful conclusion. The computational results suggest that the menu choice appears to be clear.

Chapter 10 — "Trade Diversion under NAFTA," with Kyoji Fukao and Toshihiro Okubo, in Robert M. Stern (ed.), *Japan's Economic Recovery: Commercial Policy, Monetary Policy, and Corporate Governance*, Edward Elgar Publishing, 2003.

In this chapter, a theoretical framework is developed for analyzing how tariff preferences in the NAFTA may affect U.S. imports from Canada and Mexico. Using trade and tariff information at the 2-digit and 4-digit levels of the Harmonized System, our econometric analysis has suggested that there may be trade diversion especially in U.S. imports of textiles and apparel products from Mexico. Evidence based on other studies suggests that these imports have come at the expense especially of Asian suppliers.

The research and some of the other studies noted demonstrate the importance of commodity disaggregation in analyzing the effects of preferential trading arrangements. There is also a strong case to be made for analyzing how foreign direct investment and outsourcing interact with tariff preferences in influencing patterns of trade and specialization in member and non-member countries in preferential trading arrangements.

Chapter 11 — "Some Economic Effects of the Free Trade Agreement between Tunisia and the European Union," with Drusilla K. Brown and Alan V. Deardorff, in Ahmed Galal and Bernard Hoekman (eds.), *Regional Partners in Global Markets: Limits and Possibilities of the Euro-Med Agreements*, London and Cairo: Centre for Economic Policy Research and Egyptian Center for Economic Studies, 1997.

This chapter uses a specially constructed version of the Michigan Brown–Deardorff–Stern Computational General Equilibrium (CGE) Model of World Production and Trade to estimate the potential economic effects on the Tunisian economy that may result from the free trade agreement (FTA) between Tunisia and the European Union (EU) that was concluded in July 1995. The static welfare benefits for Tunisia of the FTA are found to range from slightly negative to somewhat positive, depending on what is assumed about inter-sectoral capital mobility in Tunisia. Further, depending on the length of time allowed for the phasing in of the FTA, Tunisia could experience significant adjustment problems in connection with the inter-sectoral movements of labor and capital that the FTA would induce. Finally, while the computational scenarios are subject to the difficulties of integrating foreign direct investment (FDI) into a CGE trade modeling framework, it is concluded that the FDI inflows into Tunisia that might result from the

FTA would not materially increase Tunisian economic welfare. These results suggest therefore that Tunisia may not have much to gain economically from the FTA. Reducing its trade barriers multilaterally and reinforcing these actions with further liberalization of its foreign investment policies and maintenance of macroeconomic and political stability might in the end be the best path for Tunisia to follow.

Chapter 12 — "A North American Free Trade Agreement: Analytical Issues and a Computational Assessment," with Drusilla K. Brown and Alan V. Deardorff, *The World Economy*, January 1992.

This chapter seeks to identify some important issues arising in the analysis of a NAFTA and to provide a computational assessment of some of the economic effects involved. While the various experiments conducted are not exhaustive of all the possible changes that might be negotiated in connection with a NAFTA, they are nonetheless indicative of the order of magnitude on trade, output, number of firms, factor returns, and employment that could result from trilateral trade liberalization and increased investment.

Overall, the computational results suggest that the formation of a NAFTA will have positive benefits for all countries involved on several accounts, as follows:

- The participating countries all enjoy an increase in aggregate welfare.
- Although the inclusion of Mexico erodes some of Canada's benefits under the US-Canada FTA, the effect is minuscule.
- The wage gap between the United States and Mexico will narrow, thereby reducing the incentive for illegal immigration. However, the real wage in the United States still rises as a result of trade liberalization.
- A NAFTA will have beneficial scale effects in all three countries.
- A reduction in barriers against foreign direct investment in Mexico will stimulate new capital formation, which has the beneficial effects of alleviating poverty in Mexico by raising the

marginal product of labor and raising the average product of both capital and labor by increasing the scale of production in Mexico.

- The inflow of capital into Mexico may come primarily from outside the NAFTA, not from the United States, suggesting the fear that US firms will relocate production in Mexico may be largely unfounded.
- There appears to be relatively little inter-sectoral factor reallocation in the United States especially, so that the associated relocation costs are likely to be small.
- While there are negative effects on the rest of the world, they appear to be relatively small.

Chapter 13 — "Computable General Equilibrium Estimates of the Gains from U.S.–Canadian Trade Liberalization," with Drusilla K. Brown, in David Greenaway, Thomas Hyclak, and Robert J. Thornton (eds.), *Economic Aspects of Regional Trading Arrangements*, London: Harvester Wheatsheaf, 1989.

This chapter provides some estimates of the economic effects of the U.S.-Canada Free Trade Agreement that was negotiated in 1986–87 and implemented beginning in 1989. The focus is primarily on bilateral tariff elimination, although some attention is given to the removal of non-tariff barriers. The many qualitative aspects of the FTA are not included in the computational analysis. The computational model used has a variety of features of imperfect competition that distinguish it from the more commonly used model that assumes perfect competition, constant returns to scale, and national product differentiation.

The computational results suggest that the FTA will be beneficial to both Canada and the United States. National income may be increased in Canada by 1%–2% and by less than 1% for the United States. The far-reaching changes in the rules and procedures governing bilateral trade and investment relations would be likely to reduce the uncertainty of policies and lower costs of transactions. The rest of the world is also likely to benefit from the FTA.

Chapter 14 — "The Effects of the Tokyo Round on the Structure of Protection," with Alan V. Deardorff, in Robert E. Baldwin and Anne O. Krueger (eds.), *The Structure and Evolution of Recent U.S. Trade Policy*, Chicago: University of Chicago Press for the National Bureau of Economic Research, 1984.

This chapter presents a computational analysis of the protective effects of the changes in tariffs and NTBs that were negotiated in the Tokyo Round of multilateral trade negotiations that were completed in 1979–1980. The analysis is based on the Michigan Model of World Production and Trade. The focus is on the changes in value added by sector for the major industrialized and developing countries that participated in the Tokyo Round negotiations. The chief findings were as follows:

- The change in per unit value added (CPVA) as calculated by the model provided substantially different information about the structure of protection as compared to using nominal tariffs or effective rates of protection. The CPVA calculation was more closely related to the flows of changes in protection than the other measures.
- The Tokyo Round reduced protection most in those sectors that were previously most protected, although the pattern of protection remained substantially unaltered from what it was previously.
- The greatest benefits of the Tokyo Round would be felt in the sectors with the greatest export interests, reflecting the fact that the pattern of tariff reductions was quite similar across countries.
- There was no evidence that levels of protection were more uniform as a result of the Tokyo Round, protection was not becoming any more or less cascaded against imports of final goods, or that the Tokyo Round was biased against the interests of the major developing countries.

Part III. *Services Trade*

Chapter 15 — "Empirical Analysis of Barriers to International Services Transactions and the Consequences of Liberalization," with Alan V. Deardorff, in Aaditya Mattoo, Robert M. Stern, and Gianni Zanini (eds.), *Handbook of International Trade in Services*, New York and Oxford: Oxford University Press and the World Bank, 2008.

This chapter begins with a conceptual framework for understanding international services transactions and the barriers that may affect them. There follows a discussion of the characteristics of services barriers, and we provide some examples of barriers for the banking sector and for foreign direct investment in services sectors. Next, there is a discussion of methods of measurement of services barriers, including frequency measures and indexes of restrictiveness, price-effect and quantity-effect measurements, gravity-model estimates, and financial-based measurements. In each case, information and examples are provided of how the measurements are constructed and an evaluation of their merits and limitations. The appendix contains brief summaries of studies that have used these methods. Thereafter, there is a discussion of how the various measurements can be used in assessing the economic consequences of the liberalization of services barriers. Since this chapter is designed for instructional purposes, it concludes with a presentation of guideline principles and recommended procedures for measuring services barriers and assessing the consequences of their liberalization.

Part IV. *International Trade and Labor Standards*

Chapter 16 — "Pros and Cons of Linking Trade and Labor Standards," with Drusilla K. Brown and Alan V. Deardorff, in Douglas Nelson (ed.), *The Political Economy of Policy Reform: Essays in Honor of J. Michael Finger*, Elsevier, 2004.

Some advocates of labor and environmental rights have asked that these issues also be taken over by the WTO and that they be enforced by the same mechanism that it uses for policing trade policies. This chapter reviews the arguments for and against such integration in the case of labor standards. The debate is first put into context by reviewing the issues and the events that have led to the current situation. Next considered are the arguments in favor of putting labor standards into the WTO and then the arguments against doing so. Finally, advice is offered to developing countries as to the position that they should take in this debate, and how more broadly they should deal with this and other issues in the forthcoming WTO multilateral trade negotiations.

Chapter 17 — "The Effects of Multinational Production on Wages and Working Conditions in Developing Countries," with Drusilla K. Brown and Alan V. Deardorff, in Robert E. Baldwin and L. Alan Winters (eds.), *Challenges to Globalization*, University of Chicago Press, 2004.

This chapter assesses the evidence regarding the effects of multinational production on wages and working conditions in developing countries. It is motivated by recent controversies concerning whether multinational firms in developing countries exploit workers by paying low wages and subjecting them to substandard conditions. First addressed are the efforts of activist groups, universities, and colleges in the "Anti-Sweatshop" Campaign in the United States, the social accountability of multinational firms, and the role of such international institutions as the International Labor Organization and World Trade Organization in dealing with labor standards and trade. It is then considered conceptually how foreign direct investment might affect host-country wages. Available theories yield ambiguous predictions, leaving the effects to be examined empirically. It is therefore important to review empirical evidence on multinational firm wages in developing countries, and the relationship between foreign direct investment and labor rights. This evidence indicates that multinational firms routinely provide higher wages and better working conditions than their local counterparts, and they are typically not attracted preferentially to countries with weak labor standards.

Chapter 18 — "U.S. Trade and Other Policy Options and Programs to Deter Foreign Exploitation of Child Labor," with Drusilla K. Brown and Alan V. Deardorff, in Magnus Blomström and Linda Goldberg (eds.), *Topics in Empirical International Economics: A Festschrift in Honor of Robert Lipsey*, University of Chicago Press, 2001.

There is a growing theoretical and empirical literature concerning the causes and consequences of child labor. The objective of this chapter is to evaluate the policy initiatives targeted at child labor in light of the newly emerging theoretical argumentation and empirical evidence. The focus in particular is on programs to address child-labor practices, and an attempt is made to evaluate these programs, given the empirical evidence concerning the primary determinants of when and why children work. Throughout, it is found to be instructive to evaluate the policies that have been adopted with the intent of reducing overall child labor in terms of the impact they are likely to have on the welfare of children.

Chapter 19 — "Labor Standards and International Trade," INTAL, *Integration and Trade*, May/June 1999.

This chapter explores the wide disparity of views on issues of international labor standards and the available options for addressing the issues involved. Labor standards are multi-faceted and may vary from country to country depending on the stage of development, per capita income, and political, social, and cultural conditions and institutions. It may be difficult therefore to distinguish unambiguously so-called core labor standards from other labor standards that will depend on given national circumstances. A review of the theoretical and empirical analysis of labor standards suggests that there are no compelling grounds on which to support the international enforcement and harmonization of labor standards. It is argued accordingly that the World Trade Organization is not the appropriate international institution to deal with issues of international labor standards. Rather, the International Labor Organization is the preferred multilateral forum to monitor and help developing countries to improve their labor standards. In the final analysis, the policies of the United States and other industrialized countries should be directed to maintaining open markets and encouraging the economic growth of their developing country trading partners. This is the surest way to achieve higher labor standards since there is pervasive historical evidence that standards are improved as per capita incomes increase.

Part I

GLOBALIZATION

Chapter 2

What the Public Should Know about Globalization and the World Trade Organization*

Alan V. Deardorff and Robert M. Stern†

I. Introduction

The term "globalization" has only recently become commonplace, yet trade economists like us have been studying and teaching about it for decades, even centuries. The institution of the World Trade Organization (WTO) has only recently come to exist, yet legal experts on international trade have been studying and teaching for almost half a century about its predecessor, the GATT, as well. In both cases, specialists in international trade have argued the benefits, but also acknowledged the costs, of international economic integration and

* Published in *Review of International Economics*, 10(3), August 2002, pp. 404–423. Reprinted with permission from Blackwell Publishing.

† We have benefited greatly from conversations with the economic and legal scholars who participated in a meeting at the Georgetown University Law Center on January 28, 2000. We also had useful comments from our students, from participants at a conference in Delphi, Greece, May 2000, where this was presented, and from an anonymous referee.

the institutions that facilitate it. Yet until recently ours was a specialty that only a few paid attention to, especially in the United States where the size of domestic markets seemed to render the rest of the world of only secondary importance. Only in the 1990s did America begin to wake up to the significance of world markets and institutions. By the end of the decade, at the Seattle ministerial meeting of the WTO in December 1999, a host of voices were raised against both. This has turned our academic specialty from obscure to reviled in barely a moment. In this paper we try to set the record straight.

Our purpose is to clarify, for both globalization and the WTO, what they are and what they mean to the world. We do not primarily intend to be advocates of either, and we will acknowledge and explain both the costs and benefits of both. But inevitably, having spent our careers consistently finding the benefits to outweigh the costs, we will conclude that here. Yes, there are those who lose from world markets and institutions, and some of them are understandably opposed when these intrude into their lives. But overall, we agree with almost all others who have looked at these issues carefully and objectively (and many, admittedly, who have not), that the vast majority of people in the world are ultimately made better off by the spread of global markets and the efforts of the WTO to keep those markets reasonably free. To be sure, there are problems that need to be addressed, and we will mention them too and possible solutions for them. But even in their current imperfect form, the WTO and the open international markets that it has fostered are far better for the world economy than the alternatives that would likely arise if they were disbanded and reversed.

Our paper will be in two parts, the first on globalization and the second on the WTO. In both, we will first define and document the phenomena at issue, then identify the major groups who benefit and lose from their effects. Much of this discussion, especially for globalization, will inevitably repeat what trade economists have been saying about trade for two centuries, for the issues are not new. However, they have taken new forms in recent years, and the WTO has likewise expanded the institutional scope of its predecessor, the GATT, in ways that also need to be addressed. In particular, events in Seattle raised many issues that had only recently been seen in discussions of international trade, and we will do our best to describe what these were and what actually happened in Seattle. In both parts of the paper, we will conclude with some discussion of what the options are for action, if any, and what we believe should be done. The paper concludes with a final section that tries in much briefer form to answer the question of our title, listing what we believe to be the most important things that the public should know about globalization and the WTO.

II. Globalization

What Is It?

Everybody is writing about globalization these days, and the word means different things to different people. We take it to mean the increase in international transactions in markets for goods, services, and some factors of production, plus the growth and expanded scope of institutions that straddle national borders — including firms, governments, international institutions, and nongovernmental organizations (NGOs). At the most basic level, globalization is growth of international trade. But it is also the expansion of much else, including foreign direct investment (FDI), multinational corporations (MNCs), integration of world capital markets and resulting financial capital flows, extraterritorial reach of government policies, attention by NGOs to issues that span the globe, and the constraints on government policies imposed by international institutions. All of this has fostered an increasing sense of helplessness among many who feel that their lives and their economic options are being determined not by themselves, or even by their countrymen and their own governments, but by external forces over which they have no control. Residents of small countries may have experienced this long ago, but in the United States and other large countries, this is a new experience, and for many it is disagreeable.

Evidence of globalization is not hard to find, although the surprise may be that the current wave of globalization is not the first.

In many ways, the world economy reached a peak of globalization just before World War I, when trade and FDI attained what were then unprecedented levels that are still quite remarkable given the technologies that were available for transportation and communication. But the current wave of globalization has far surpassed that of a century ago.

Figure 1 shows one indicator of the growth of trade over the last half century. Measured as an index of the ratio of world exports to world GDP (1990 = 100), the graph shows that this ratio increased fairly steadily through the early 1970s. It then stalled until the mid-1980s, when its growth resumed, and it grew especially fast in the mid-1990s. By 1998 it was more than three times what it was in 1950.[1]

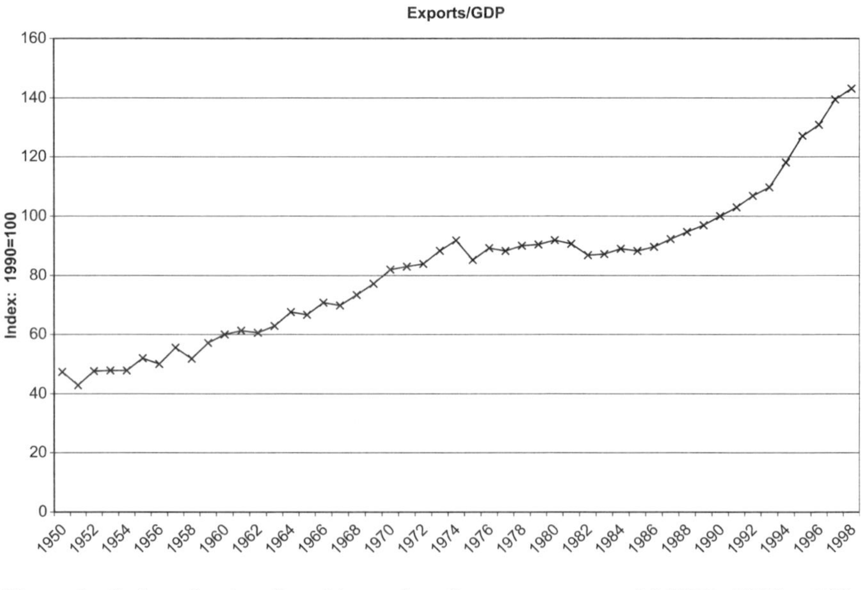

Figure 1. Index of ratio of world merchandise exports to world GDP, 1990 = 100. *Source*: WTO, International Trade Statistics, 1999.

[1] There has also been a significant growth of services trade, as documented in the WTO, *International Trade Statistics*.

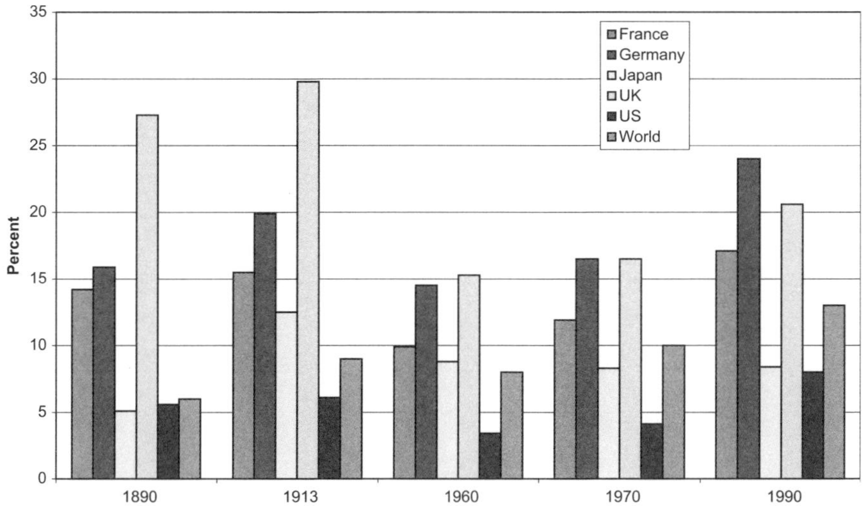

Figure 2. Ratio of merchandise exports to GDP for major countries and the world, selected years 1890–1990.

Source: Crafts (2000), Table 2.1, p. 26.

A longer perspective is shown in Figure 2, which graphs merchandise exports over GDP in selected years from 1890 to 1990 for several countries and the world. The earlier peak in 1913 is evident, and for Japan and the U.K., exports remained below 1913 in 1990. This graph also shows the considerable variation, even among large countries, in the relative importance of international trade.

Increased international capital flows have been most pronounced in portfolio investment, which, like trade, displayed an earlier peak prior to World War I. Figure 3 shows foreign assets as a percent of world GDP for selected years. The pre-WWI levels were not reached again until around 1980, after which they grew threefold by 1995. We do not have exactly comparable information on FDI or the presence of MNCs in the world economy, although information reported by Crafts (2000) shows that both were also important in 1914. The real stock of FDI relative to world GDP rose by 59% from 1960 to 1995. Thus, at least in the second half of the 20th century, both international trade and international capital flows of various kinds were

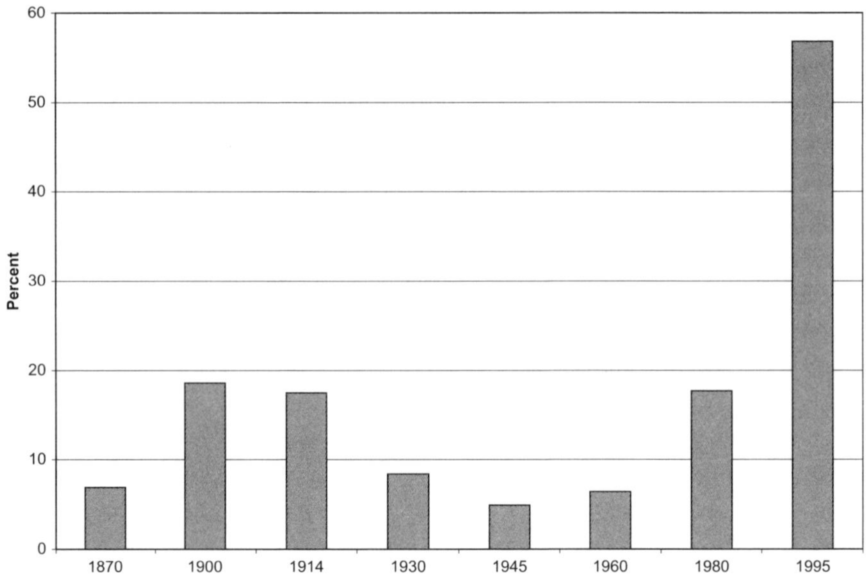

Figure 3. Ratio of foreign assets to world GDP, selected years 1870–1995.
Source: Crafts (2000), Table 2.3, p. 27.

increasing steadily, and this is much of what has come to be called globalization.[2]

What has caused these changes? Two obvious reasons are technology and policy. Improvements in both transportation and communication have increased globalization in all markets, trends that may be accelerating today with the Internet. Policies, in contrast, have alternated direction over the years, restricting international transactions and mobility after World War I, then opening up after World War II.

Figure 4 reports average tariffs on manufactures for several major industrialized countries for selected years. Before World War I, tariffs were fairly high, becoming even higher in the 1930s. After World War II they were brought down gradually, mostly through

[2] There has *not* been a comparable increase in international labor mobility, which also reached a peak just before WWI.

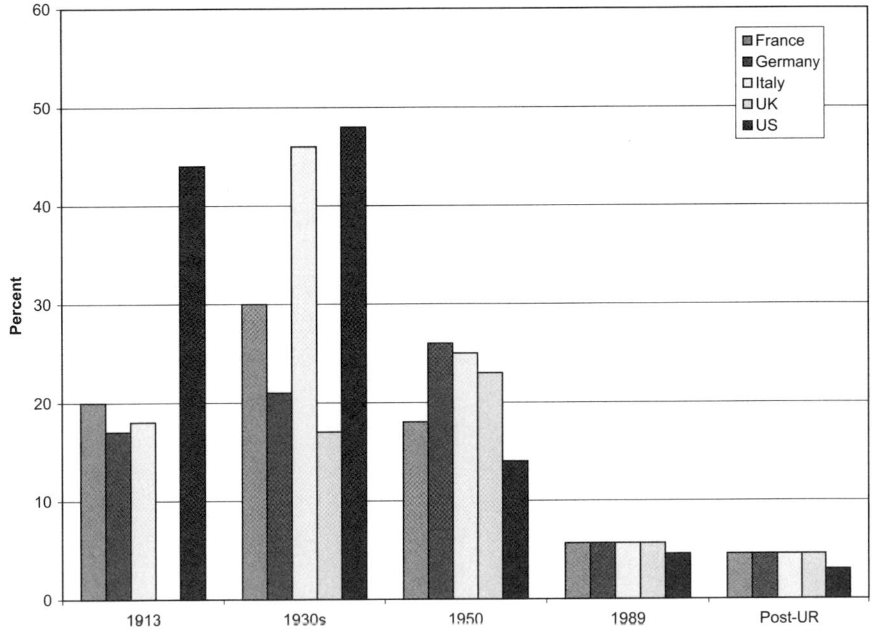

Figure 4. Average tariffs on manufactures, selected years 1913–post-Uruguay Round. *Source*: Crafts (2000), Table 2.4, p. 28.

GATT negotiations, and today they are almost negligible in most manufacturing sectors for these countries. Not reported are tariffs in less developed countries (LDCs), which remained high much longer and are still large compared to those in Figure 4. However LDC tariffs too were substantially reduced, often unilaterally, starting at various times in the 1980s. Developed-country tariff reductions have been partially offset by nontariff barriers (NTBs), especially in the 1980s,[3] but nonetheless it seems clear that much of the substantial growth of international trade was due to reduced policy barriers to trade.[4]

[3] See Deardorff (1991). Note, however, that most NTBs in developed countries are scheduled to be eliminated by 2005.

[4] An exception, however, is agriculture, which is still subject to relatively high tariffs and other restraints.

Is this, then, all there is to globalization — increased trade and capital flows caused by improved technology and reduced policy barriers? Not really. Other aspects of economic life have also become globalized. Governments are increasingly sensitive to policies used by other countries. NGOs look increasingly beyond borders, either because their issues are intrinsically global (the hole in the ozone layer), or because they view their causes to be of worldwide importance (human rights). Corporations increasingly operate across national borders, and have grown to sizes that dwarf some countries, achieving leverage over national governments that may free the companies from control. Again, all of these changes had counterparts in the 19th century, but that does not make their importance today any less.

Finally, the designers of the post-war institutions explicitly envisioned the need for countries to cooperate, and sometimes to sacrifice narrow national interests for the greater good. These institutions have been very successful, at least in expanding their own power and importance. The World Bank, the IMF, and now perhaps the WTO have reached the size that they can grow on their own momentum. Some find these changes gratifying; others find them threatening. And all are part of globalization.

Whom Does It Help and Whom Does It Hurt?

At its core, globalization means that international markets are becoming more integrated. Such integration has been the subject of international trade theory for two centuries, and economists have a good understanding of its effects. In this section, we review these insights from trade theory.

Static Effects of Trade

Who gains from trade? The first answer is consumers. That is, everybody in a country stands to gain from trade in their role as consumers of goods and services. For many reasons — including comparative advantage, economies of scale, increased competition, and access to a greater variety of products — a country's average consumer, with an average income, is better off with trade than without.[5] That is, the average person's income will buy a larger, more desirable bundle of goods and services with trade than without, increasing their material standard of living. This proposition, called the "gains from trade," has been shown theoretically in all sorts of economic models. With only a few exceptions — which economists generally view as unlikely to reverse the broad conclusion in practice — it applies to all countries comparing trade to not trading at all. The argument extends to further degrees of openness, as well as to other kinds of openness such as international movement of capital. Thus, the fundamental case for trade and globalization is that it raises the average person's standard of living.[6]

However, this benefit applies to the average person, with average income. Income is not equally distributed, and trade may not benefit everybody. A fundamental result of trade theory, the Stolper–Samuelson (SS) Theorem, identifies winners and losers from trade in terms of the national abundance and scarcity of factors of production, such as labor and capital, from which they derive their incomes. Owners of abundant factors tend to gain more than average from trade, while owners of scarce factors are made unambiguously worse off.[7] More general models allow for additional sources of gain from trade and suggest that even owners of scarce factors may gain, in which case

[5] This statement is literally correct only if the word "average" refers to the simple arithmetic mean of incomes — that is, total income divided by total population. Given the very skewed distribution of income, this does *not* necessarily mean that the majority of consumers are better off, since in principle the rich could enjoy a disproportionate share of the gains. However, in practice the vast majority of consumers are likely to gain from trade, the losers being only the small minority whose incomes fall disproportionately due to direct competition from imports.

[6] These conclusions are, strictly speaking, theoretically valid only for countries that are too small to influence world prices with changes in their trade. For large countries, the "optimal tariff" is positive, allowing them to benefit somewhat at the world's expense. While this argument might apply to a country the size of the United States, we believe that U.S. levels of protection in sectors where it is highest are well above this "optimal" level, and in any case this argument for protection bears scant resemblance to what opponents of globalization have in mind.

[7] See Stolper and Samuelson (1941).

SS says only that they gain less than average. But the possibility remains that they actually lose.

So trade theory tells us that, indeed, there may be losers as well as gainers from trade and globalization. Who are the losers? In the United States, with its abundance of capital, education, and land, the scarce factor is clearly labor. Not that we have a small labor force — we do not. But we have even more of everything else. In this relative sense, we are especially scarce in those workers without a great deal of education, what we will simply call labor. Therefore, trade theory tells us that the group in the United States most likely to lose from globalization, or at best to gain less than everyone else, is labor. This is hardly a surprise. Growing opposition to globalization by organized labor shows that they are well aware of this. The surprise may be that economists, who tend to favor trade, would agree. But we do.

It follows from this, too, that trade is likely to increase income inequality in advanced countries. Because labor has lower income than those with income from other sources, and because trade lowers the relative wage, it tends to make the poor relatively poorer. Leaving aside the legitimate question of whether an increased return to some other factors, such as the return to education, may actually increase the opportunity to escape poverty by becoming skilled, we therefore expect in the short run at least that globalization will increase inequality in rich countries like the United States. Empirical studies, reviewed e.g. in Freeman (1995), confirm that increased trade accounts for a portion (although much less than half) of the increased inequality observed in the United States since 1980.

Why, then, do we claim that there are gains from trade? Because we are confident from both theory and experience that the winners gain more than the losers lose, enough so that policy could potentially compensate them, leaving everyone better off. In the long run, with some mobility across population groups and with programs to permit the whole population to share in the country's income, most people can expect to be better off with trade than without.[8]

[8] Also in the long run, economic well-being depends most on how rapidly countries grow. Here the role of trade is less well understood, but in recent decades countries have grown more rapidly with trade than without. See below.

SS also applies to LDCs, but there the scarce factor is different. Being poor, LDCs are the mirror image of the United States, with labor abundant and most other factors scarce, especially capital and education. These belong to the elite, who therefore lose from trade, according to SS. Labor in LDCs will gain. Since labor in LDCs is far poorer than labor in developed countries, globalization can be expected to reduce income inequality worldwide, even while it may increase inequality within rich countries.

Are there other gainers and losers from trade, besides the owners of abundant and scarce factors? Yes, and many of them are obvious. Due to trade, some industries expand and others contract. Many people are invested in "industry specific" capital, human and/or physical, in particular industries — skills and equipment that are useful only within an industry. These people gain or lose along with their industries, and some can find the basis for their livelihoods destroyed, a serious cost that public policy can usually only partially acknowledge. For some, these costs continue for months or even years, as they relocate, retrain, reinvest, and otherwise readjust. Others, especially those later in life, may never recover. Trade theory does not in any way dismiss these costs as unimportant or even as smaller than other gains. Economists therefore usually favor only gradual movement toward freer trade, so that these adjustment costs can be accommodated within the routine ups and downs of markets.[9]

Nonetheless, owners of contracting-industry specific factors are a major source of concern in response to globalization. These include, for example, American owners and workers in textile and apparel firms, India's skilled workers in steel mills that were built as it attempted self-sufficient industrialization, and Mexico's small farmers of corn (maize) who now compete with more productive farms in the Midwest United States. These are only a few of the many groups throughout the world who have reason to be leery of globalization because of their dependence on industry-specific factors.

---

[9] In Brown, Deardorff and Stern (1992), for example, we estimated the employment reallocation effects of the NAFTA for the United States, and found them to be much smaller than the normal turnover within U.S. industries in one year.

It is not only whole industries that expand and contract due to trade. Within an industry, particular firms also win and lose, and firms that have prospered in a protected domestic market may not be the same ones that do well in a globalized economy. Anticipating in advance the identities of winners and losers may be impossible, but once the process is underway, particular firms will try to speed it up or slow it down, depending on how well they deal with its competitive pressures.

Dynamic Effects of Trade

This discussion of gains and losses by particular firms and by specific factors is appropriate primarily to the short run, because in the longer run, people relocate, retrain, and otherwise readjust to changing circumstances. Gains and losses to abundant and scarce factors, in contrast, last longer, continuing even after factors have moved from failing firms and contracting industries into new and expanding ones. However, this is not the end of the story. Over even longer time horizons, the total of a country's factors changes with economic growth. It is reasonable to ask, then, who gains and loses from trade in the *very* long run, as sizes of countries and their rates of economic growth may change.

An easy answer to who gains and loses from trade in the very long run is: "Not us." Keynes said that in the long run we are all dead, and he was probably right. Thus whoever may be the long run gainers and losers from globalization, they will be subsequent generations, not ourselves. That makes it harder to predict how they will fare, since we know less about them than we do about ourselves. In a dynamic economy like the United States, the owners of tomorrow's capital, land, and human capital may not be the descendents of those who own these factors today. Therefore, even without economic growth, our best bet for helping future generations is to maximize total income. Globalization does exactly that. Therefore, we have some confidence that "everyone" in future generations will benefit from it.

Allowing for economic growth, this conclusion becomes still more likely, although the theoretical basis for it is less certain than the aggregate gains from trade in the shorter run. Economists do not in fact have a solid theoretical grasp of how trade affects economic growth, perhaps because growth itself is less well understood than the economics of static markets. Instead, there exist a variety of models of growth, and even more ideas of how trade may interact with growth. Some predict only that trade permits a country to grow larger than it otherwise would; others suggest that trade lets countries grow faster indefinitely. And there are also models where trade may be bad for growth.

But empirical evidence is much clearer that trade and globalization are good for growth. For half a century, most countries that have minimized trade have failed to grow, while those that have stressed exports have done much better. After a few successful countries demonstrated the benefits of trade for growth — especially the "four tigers" of Hong Kong, Singapore, South Korea, and Taiwan — other countries opened their markets and grew faster as well. This process has had setbacks, but few economists today doubt that open markets are beneficial for growth, even if we do not entirely know why.

If so, the case is even stronger that, in the very long run, entire populations gain from globalization. Those who are hurt by trade in the short run may lose relative to others. But because they will have a smaller slice of a larger pie, they may well be better off absolutely. That will surely be true if trade permits countries not just to grow to larger size, but to continue growing at faster rates indefinitely. In that case, globalization and trade are beneficial for everyone who will ultimately be alive.

Effects of International Capital Flows

All of our discussion so far refers to the gainers and losers from trade. To a great extent, the gainers and losers from international capital flows are the same, since capital tends to flow in response to the same market forces as trade. There is, however, the added proviso that those who are internationally mobile tend to do better than those who are not. Dani Rodrik (1997) has stressed that, in a globalized economy where some groups are mobile and others are not, those who can move tend to benefit at the expense of others. In the last half century, capital has become increasingly mobile, while labor has not. We therefore expect some additional tendency for labor to lose, and capital to gain, from globalization.[10]

This may account in part for a widely held perception that globalization is mostly for the benefit of large corporations, as argued by Lori Wallach (2000) of the NGO Public Citizen. It is certainly true that large corporations often (but not always) prosper in the international environment, and those small corporations who also prosper become large as a result. This is partly due to their ability to shift operations around the world to wherever makes the most economic sense. If they do this well, their stockholders gain. Of course, the larger the corporation the more likely is its stock to be widely held, including in the retirement funds of workers. Therefore, the gains that accrue to capital accrue in part to those workers who manage to save during their working years.

Capital mobility has another quite different implication, however, that has little to do with returns to factors of production. Financial capital often takes very short-term forms, and it is highly liquid — able to move quickly into and out of a country or a currency in response to speculative expectations. Such movements generate another class of winners and losers: those who bet correctly and incorrectly on changes in financial markets. More important, however, are other victims of short-term capital flight. When expectations turn against a country or its currency, the resulting capital outflow batters many of those within the country. Borrowers default, banks become insolvent, credit to finance exports dries up, and the damage spreads through domestic markets causing recession that hurts much of the

[10] Capital gains most if it starts in a capital abundant country and can earn more by going abroad, but this is just an example of factor abundance at work. The point here is different. Mobile capital, even in capital scarce countries, stands to gain from the potential to move, and this is an advantage that immobile labor lacks. This is most important in imperfectly competitive factor markets where the division of profits and rents depends on the bargaining power of the participants. Mobile capital, by threatening to move abroad, can reach a more favorable contract with immobile labor.

population regardless of their apparent exposure to foreign markets. This is the story of the Asian crisis of 1997, but it had happened before, and will probably happen again. The harm here is a byproduct of globalization, but also of the prosperity that globalization has previously contributed to via capital inflows.

Other Effects of Globalization

This completes our list of those gainers and losers from globalization. But the discussion would be incomplete without mentioning several additional benefits and costs.

On the side of benefits, many say that globalization has reduced inflation. Inflation rates in many countries are low, and inflationary pressures have so far been restrained even where unemployment rates are also low. Some attribute this to a "new economy," in which technology and global markets together restrain firms from raising prices. If this continues and if it truly is a byproduct of globalization, then the lower inflation rate and the associated lower sustainable rate of unemployment benefit almost everyone.

Another possible benefit of globalization is an increased rate of technological progress and productivity growth. The slowdown in productivity growth that began in the mid-1970s appears to have reversed in the late 1990s, although it is too soon to know whether this is permanent. Here too, some argue that increased international competition has forced firms to innovate and to economize on labor, increasing productivity, and that this may be a lasting benefit of globalization. We see even less evidence to support this conclusion than the previous one, but it deserves mention.

Finally, globalization affects local cultures, causing changes that are sometimes admired, sometimes deplored. International trade, travel, and capital flows have exposed people everywhere to the products and sometimes the customs of other countries. This is evident in the United States, for example with the variety of national cuisines now available in restaurants and supermarkets. The same is happening even more in reverse, although many are unhappy to see it. U.S. culture is spreading throughout the globe through trade, especially U.S.

exports of movies, music, and television programs. Young people around the world are adopting American styles of dress, music, and behavior, to the dismay of some of their elders and of those who fear the loss of their own cultural traditions. As economists, we are reluctant to discount the choices made freely by consumers anywhere. But cultures are public goods, and fragile ones at that. Globalization may bring cultures into conflict, and new policies for protecting them may be needed.

What Should be Done about Globalization?

We have heard it said that globalization has so much momentum that it cannot be stopped. We disagree. Unforeseen events, and even deliberate policies with unforeseen consequences, could conceivably reverse the process of globalization, just as World War I and the Great Depression did once before. There is little reason to believe that the world is now immune from the sorts of worldwide disruptive events that have wracked it twice before within the last century.[11] If such occur, much will depend on the wisdom and expertise of the world's leaders and their efforts to repair and restore the institutions of the world economy afterwards.

It is also conceivable that public policy could change direction and reverse globalization more deliberately. The institutions of the global economy — the World Bank, IMF, and WTO — would be incapacitated if the United States or Europe withdrew support, and considering recent controversies, this could happen. Without them, especially the WTO, the world could descend into a trade war or a series of competitive devaluations and tariff increases, just as in the 1930s. These were *not* irrational acts by uninformed policymakers, acts that we would not repeat today. Instead, like the uncooperative

---

[11] Actually, there is one reason for hope, and it is globalization itself. Those who designed the post-war international institutions at Bretton Woods in the 1940s were not just seeking economic prosperity for the world. They hoped that trade and other forms of economic integration would make wars less likely in the future. Of course, the globalization at the beginning of the century had failed to serve that purpose.

strategies in the Prisoners' Dilemma of game theory, they were rational individual responses to situations. Without some mechanism for international cooperation, the same could easily happen again.

While we believe that the benefits outweigh the costs for both trade and FDI, we are less sure of the free movement of financial capital. The disruption and hardship caused by recent financial crises could perhaps have been avoided through better policies and decisions on the part of governments and international organizations, but a case can also be made for limited restriction on international movement of short-term capital. This is not our area of expertise, and we are reluctant to take a position on it. We merely note that smart people disagree on this issue, and leave it at that.

Aside from financial capital markets, then, what policies should be pursued with regard to globalization? As we have said, we believe that globalization has been largely a good thing, with the benefits exceeding the costs. Therefore we certainly do not want to see any reversal of direction, or a return to protection. Since most of the costs of globalization are costs of adjustment, analogous costs would arise again if we moved back in the other direction. Indeed, given the progress toward global and efficient markets, continued liberalization may be less painful than what has come before. In any case, we favor continuing liberalization of both trade and direct investment.

Many of the concerns of those who oppose globalization are legitimate, however, and should not be ignored. National governments and international institutions must address their concerns, assisting those who lose most from globalization wherever they can without undermining the process. How this can best be done deserves greater study and perhaps experimentation, but programs of adjustment assistance, wage insurance, and retraining should be considered.

III. The WTO

What Is It?

The World Trade Organization, created in 1995, is the successor to, and incorporates within it, the GATT — the General Agreement on

Tariffs and Trade — which was a treaty among western market economies at the end of World War II. Member countries agree to rules about when they may increase trade barriers, especially tariffs, in order to prevent them using trade policies that harm other countries. The GATT was also a forum for negotiation to reduce trade barriers. Presumably the WTO will do this as well, although it has not yet. The GATT oversaw eight rounds of multilateral trade negotiations, culminating in the Uruguay Round that created the WTO. The WTO also took on issues that GATT had not covered, including trade in services, tariffication in agriculture, and intellectual property protection.[12]

The most important change in the WTO, compared to the GATT, may be its dispute settlement mechanism (DSM). The GATT permitted countries to complain against other countries for violating its rules. Each complaint was handled by a "panel" of experts who issued a report that, if adopted unanimously by GATT members, would require the offending party to either change its behavior or be subject to sanctions. However, unanimity meant that the offending party could block a report, in effect giving every country veto power over findings against itself. The surprise was that this ever worked at all, which it did.

The WTO reversed this bias, requiring instead a unanimous decision to block a report, and it therefore made the DSM much more effective. It also made other improvements, including the right to appeal. The intent was to provide viable enforcement for WTO rules, and it appears to have worked. The DSM has been used much more often than under the GATT, both by and against a wide range of countries, as shown in Table 1. Just as important, large countries (the U.S.) have stopped going outside the GATT with their most important complaints.

Inevitably, however, the DSM has not worked to everyone's satisfaction. The WTO restricts policies that harm other countries, not only deliberately, but also inadvertently, as when policy restricts the options of another country's citizens. A contentious example was

[12] There are many good sources of information about the GATT and WTO. See, for example, Deardorff (1997).

Table 1. WTO disputes: Consultation requests, January 1, 1995 to March 23, 2000.

Complaints by	Respondents					
	United States	Japan	European Com.[a]	Oth. Ind. Countries	Dev./ Emerging	Total[b]
United States	—	5	25	7	24	61
Japan	4	—	—	—	3	7
European Communities	16	6	—	5	25	52
Other Industrialized Countries	5	1	5	3	12	26
Developing/Emerging Economies	17	—	17	1	25	60
Total[b]	43	11	47	16	89	206

Notes: [a] Includes complaints against the European Communities (EC) as well as individual EC member countries. [b] Totals reflect individual cases involving more than one country requesting consultation with respondent.

Source: World Trade Organization, "Overview of the State-of-Play of WTO Disputes," http://www.wto.org./wto/dispute/bulletin.htm, March 23, 2000.

the "shrimp-turtle" case. A U.S. law protected sea turtles from death in the nets of shrimp fishermen by prohibiting imports of shrimp caught without "turtle exclusion devices" (TEDs). Since it is impossible to tell from looking at a shrimp how it was caught, the law restricted imports from certain countries. These took the case to the WTO, which decided against the United States. In effect, this decision struck down U.S. law, an intrusion into sovereignty that offended environmentalists and others. There have been other, similar examples.

The potential of the WTO to intrude in national affairs was also increased by its expanded coverage. The GATT was limited to trade in goods, even excluding certain sectors such as agriculture and textiles/apparel. The latter was covered instead by the GATT-sanctioned Multi-Fibre Arrangement (MFA), restricting developing-country exports to developed countries. The WTO changed all that, or at least it promises to. The Uruguay Round scheduled the elimination of the MFA, though the most difficult liberalization is postponed ("backloaded") ten years. First steps were also taken in agriculture, converting existing NTBs to tariffs (tariffication) so as later to negotiate them downward. And trade in services was covered in a parallel agreement to the GATT, the General Agreement on Trade in Services (GATS).

The WTO also expanded to new areas. Most prominent and effective is its TRIPS (Trade Related Intellectual Property) Agreement covering intellectual property — primarily patents, copyrights, and trademarks. In addition, the WTO includes (as the GATT had before, actually) some small ways that countries may use trade policies for environmental purposes. However, the one area — much discussed — where the WTO has *not* been extended is labor standards and rights. Despite many in developed countries who favor using trade policies for this purpose, resistance from the developing world, as well as from corporations who employ labor there, has prevented it from even being discussed.

Whom Does It Help and Whom Does It Hurt?

With its expanded role, the WTO will affect many groups. But fundamentally it is still, like the GATT, a force for increased trade, and thus for much of globalization. The WTO has not, yet, done much on international capital movements, although its agreement on financial services will lower transactions costs for movements of financial capital. But it has done much to facilitate international trade. Those who gain and lose from the WTO, then, are also those who gain and lose from globalization.

Therefore, all that we said above applies here as well, about gains and losses to abundant and scarce factors, to industry-specific factors, and to factors unable to move or retrain. Because the WTO extends to previously excluded sectors — textiles, apparel, agriculture, and services — those principles will apply especially strongly to them. For example, developed-country textile workers, who have been protected for decades, have particular reason now to be concerned, if indeed the MFA will disappear. Developing-country textile workers have corresponding reason to be hopeful.[13]

More generally, however, the WTO has an important institutional role beyond just fostering trade: to constrain countries from using trade policies that will hurt each other and themselves. Without such constraints, two things would guide countries' uses of trade policies. First, large countries would be able to use policies to gain at small countries' expense. Second, weak and misguided governments would be able to use policies to benefit themselves and their "cronies." The WTO, with its rules and its DSM for enforcement, deters both. It protects weak countries from strong countries, and also weak countries from themselves. This is true especially for poor countries. Thus, even though the WTO was mostly designed by rich countries and even corporations, its greatest beneficiaries may well be in the developing world.

Who loses from the WTO? Again, some of the losers are simply those who lose most from trade, and here we must point again to relatively unskilled labor in developed countries. It makes perfect sense that organized labor in developed countries should be skeptical of the

---

[13] For owners of textile firms it is more complicated. Developed-country firms may move production abroad. Some developing-country firms have prospered, using export licenses under the MFA to make extraordinary profits.

benefits from the WTO, for theory predicts that greater trade will indeed hurt their members, at least relatively.

Aside from these effects of globalization itself, the rules of the WTO will also hurt those who would wish to break them. If there are large countries that seek to use their economic size at other countries' expense, then they will be frustrated by the WTO. Fortunately, we see little evidence in recent decades that the most powerful countries have sought to do this.

More likely losers, therefore, are those who seek to use trade policy for other legitimate purposes but run afoul of the WTO, as in the shrimp-turtle case. Those who seek to halt environmental degradation naturally wish to use trade policies to pursue their aims, since few other policies work across borders. Yet to do so risks violating the strictures of the WTO. Environmentalists have therefore sometimes been hamstrung by WTO rules, and they believe that they — or the environment — are hurt by the WTO.

It is true that the WTO makes the objectives of environmentalists harder to attain. Policies impose costs, and some are borne by other countries when one country unilaterally uses trade policies for environmental purposes. The WTO gives those costs more weight than if countries could act alone. This means that a lower level of environmental protection will result when these costs are factored in. This is as it should be, however, since global policy decisions should be based on global costs and benefits, including all aspects of all people's lives, not just the environment or one country. Environmentalists, whose role is narrower, will indeed make less progress when their interests are balanced against those of others.

Environmentalists might say, "Fine, but the WTO does not just balance other interests against the environment; it rules the environment out of court. All we want is for environmental concerns to be heard in the WTO." In fact, the WTO does include several environmental clauses, so even here the question is one of balance. How much role should environmental concerns play in justifying trade policies? Arguably, the current system has not done badly. The problem with using trade policies for environmental and other purposes is that they too easily push the cost onto others. The WTO has forced their advocates to find fairer ways to achieve those purposes. For example, the shrimp-turtle brouhaha led, more quietly, to shrimp fishermen being equipped with TEDs at developed country expense. We would say that this was the right solution all along.

There are other issues, besides the environment, whose advocates wish to use trade policies, including human rights and labor standards. For both, the United States especially has used trade policies in the past, against non-WTO members like China, and in our implementation of preferential trading arrangements. Some see the WTO as an enemy of human rights and labor standards. That conclusion is way too strong, but as with the environment, as the WTO interferes with policies that would otherwise be available to pursue these ends, the ends themselves will not be attained as fully.

In the case of human rights, the WTO does permit some use of trade policies, such as the economic sanctions that were used against Rhodesia in 1965 and against South Africa in 1985. Formally, these were permitted under GATT Article XXI, based on actions under the United Nations Charter for purposes of peace and security.[14] The WTO does not permit unilateral sanctions for human rights, however.

In the case of labor standards and labor rights, the issue is more complex, partly because it is so difficult to separate the moral from the economic, and partly because of different views of what labor standards mean economically.[15] Some labor standards, such as the prohibition of slave labor and exploitative child labor, are clearly moral issues. Others, such as a minimum wage, are economic. And still others, such as working conditions and child labor with the approval of caring parents, are somewhere in between. Where to draw the line, and who should draw it, are hard to say.[16]

Economically, most labor standards affect the cost of labor, even when not explicitly about wages. But their effects depend on how one

---

[14] See Jackson and Davey (1986, p. 917).

[15] The line between human rights and labor standards is not always clear. The right to organize and a safe workplace are both on most lists of labor standards, but they might also be regarded as human rights.

[16] For more on labor standards see Brown, Deardorff, and Stern (1996, 2000).

believes that wages are determined. From the perspective of competitive markets, which guides most economists on this issue, labor standards are mostly about the remuneration of labor in poor versus rich countries, and higher labor standards in the former primarily benefit the latter, putting developing country workers out of work. Another view, however, is that all labor remuneration is at the expense of capital, so that higher labor standards merely reduce profits. In economics, this second view makes most sense if employers have market power, something that globalization is in fact likely to undermine. But not everyone believes market economics, especially non-economists, and there are plenty of subscribers to this second view among opponents of the WTO. In their view, by excluding labor standards as a basis for trade policy, the WTO helps capitalists and hurts workers, everywhere. But modern economics suggests that only developed-country workers may be hurt, while the true beneficiaries of the WTO are the developing-country workers whom labor standards are ostensibly meant to help.

The latter view, which we share, is voiced prominently by economists and by most leaders of developing countries. They perceive labor standards, when enforced by trade sanctions, as thinly disguised protection for developed-country labor. The WTO excludes labor standards as part of its broader role of protecting the weak from the strong. We agree with the position taken at the 1996 GATT Ministerial Meeting in Singapore that issues of labor standards should be handled in the International Labor Organization, although we also favor some increase in that organization's resources and effectiveness.

Other Objections to the WTO

Even among those who think the WTO has it right on environment and labor standards, however, the WTO does nonetheless have flaws. One is its lack of transparency. The proceedings of the DSM panels are secret, and the panelists get information only from governments. Some regard this mechanism as non-democratic, and they fear its capture by corporations with financial stake in the outcome. They would like interested NGOs to be able to provide input to the process, and perhaps to have the panelists themselves selected by a process that NGOs could influence.

The complaint about non-democratic procedures is ironic, since the WTO works by consensus among mostly democratic governments, whereas NGOs are by definition self-appointed special interests. More important, however, is a concern from developing countries, that opening the DSM to public scrutiny and influence would cause its capture by precisely these special interests, at developing-country expense.

Nonetheless, even defenders of the WTO are coming to see the DSM's secrecy as counterproductive. It is also inconsistent with other WTO procedures, which have always been open if anyone cared to look at them. Therefore, many say the DSM should permit NGOs and others to file "friend-of-the-court briefs." Some also argue that a more permanent body should replace the panels themselves, instead of being assembled case-by-case. If so, then greater public input to selection of that body might be natural.

Another concern has long been that a few rich countries dominate the WTO, developing countries having little role. This is true in spite of — or even because of — its formal reliance on consensus. With 140 member countries,[17] consensus is not practical, and therefore a smaller group has typically sought agreement among themselves, then come to the larger group for approval. This smaller group, named the "green room group" after the room in which they have sometimes met at WTO headquarters in Geneva, has been assembled on an ad hoc basis by the Director General and has included both developed and developing countries based on their interest in the issues being addressed.[18] However, many developing countries — especially smaller ones — have been excluded and were not formally represented, not by design because there was no design,

[17] As of November 30, 2000, according to the WTO website in May 2001.

[18] Our information comes from personal communication with Rufus Yerxa, who participated in these meetings on behalf of the United States during the Uruguay Round. He lists almost twenty countries as having been present in the green room, including a handful of developing countries such as Brazil, India, and Nigeria.

but by default. Exactly how to change this is not clear, but it must be changed.

As already noted, a common objection to the WTO is that it overrules domestic laws. This is true, for that is its purpose. The GATT was a treaty among countries to prevent them from using certain laws and policies that would adversely affect each other. The WTO continues that purpose. However, while the original GATT dealt only with tariffs, over time the GATT/WTO has expanded to many other policies, such as environmental laws, whose main purposes are not international. Critics object that the WTO undermines domestic policies, not just tariffs. Countries might well want to reconsider membership if these new restrictions are too onerous. Had the WTO existed for 50 years without the opportunity to withdraw, this might be a big concern. However, since all members joined only six years ago, it would be surprising if many were now to pull out.

A troubling feature of the WTO for many is that countries may not restrict imports based upon the process by which they were produced. The WTO permits countries to exclude goods deemed harmful to health or the environment, for example, but only based on observable characteristics of the products themselves. In practice countries often want to exclude imports that were produced by a process that has harmed the environment, has violated labor standards or human rights, has adverse health consequences for consumers, or may be otherwise undesirable. These are often legitimate concerns, and if the process could be inferred from a product characteristic at the border, the WTO might permit their exclusion. But without that, exclusion must be based on the country where they were produced and some judgment about practices there. This runs the risk of excluding products that did not use the offending process, and also of undermining a producing country's legitimate comparative advantage.

A final concern of many WTO critics is that it is dominated by large corporations. This is true and probably inevitable, since it is large corporations that do most trade. Corporations have both the incentive and the resources to influence policies, and they do, both within countries and internationally. This means that the WTO has elements that would not be there without corporate lobbying, and some of these elements are undesirable. For example, anti-dumping statutes are economically nonsensical and pernicious, and yet the GATT has always permitted them, for the obvious reason that many corporations want them. More recently, in response to corporate lobbying, the Uruguay Round added intellectual property rights to the WTO, in spite of strong resistance from developing countries that ultimately was overcome by the promise of market opening in textiles and apparel.[19]

The WTO, then, is not a perfect organization. It could be improved, but many of its flaws will inevitably remain, because they are there in response to political realities. Overall, it seems clear to us that the WTO serves an extremely useful purpose and that it serves it surprisingly well.

One indication that the WTO is not too far off the mark comes from its opponents. Although they share unhappiness with the WTO, some say that it does too much, others that it does too little. Environmentalists usually complain that it does too much, ruling against national efforts to improve the environment, and they want it weakened or destroyed so that national policies can proceed unhindered. Labor activists, on the other hand, complain that it does too little, not enforcing labor standards around the world. They want the WTO to take on more issues, and interfere more with national policies.

What Happened in Seattle?

All this is background for the events surrounding the WTO ministerial meeting in Seattle in December 1999. Ministerial meetings are held regularly, every two years in a different location, but the purpose of this particular meeting was well known: to agree on the parameters of a new round of negotiations. This did not happen. The meeting attracted protestors, and these demonstrated in the streets of Seattle

---

[19] And despite arguments that they had no more business in the WTO than labor rights. See Deardorff (1990).

and even prevented the opening session. The negotiators nonetheless did have extensive discussions, but they failed to reach agreement and left Seattle empty-handed.

One issue is, why? The protestors naturally took credit for derailing the new round and stopping the WTO in its tracks. However, most of those who were involved in the negotiations say that the protests had little to do with the failure.

The first problem was that the countries of the WTO had failed to agree beforehand on an agenda for these meetings. They had met at WTO headquarters in Geneva for months, trying to reach agreement, but they failed even then, long before the Seattle protests. The ministerial meeting nonetheless went ahead, but it was crippled by this failure in the preparations, which in turn was due both to bad luck and to the depth of the disagreements dividing the participants.

The bad luck was that the United States was distracted by its talks with China on terms of entry to the WTO. These negotiations had been expected to finish long before, but were instead delayed by the accidental bombing of the Chinese embassy in Belgrade. The negotiations with China were stalled, then continued, and finally concluded just shortly before the WTO ministerial. This prevented the United States from making all of the efforts that were needed to reach agreement on an agenda.

But agreement might have been elusive anyway. Large differences divided the participants, including whether even to discuss certain issues. In agriculture, the United States and LDCs sided with other agricultural exporters wanting to push ahead with negotiations. The European Union and Japan wanted nothing to do with that. The EU was however on the side of the United States on another issue: labor standards. Both wanted at least to talk about them in a new round, while LDCs, as noted here, were firmly opposed. LDCs, EU, and Japan sided together, against the United States, on anti-dumping. They wanted to reopen negotiations on this, in hopes of restricting the increasing use of these policies, but the United States refused. Finally, LDCs were unhappy with the backloading of the textile agreement and wanted to renegotiate the timetable, feeling that they had gotten very little market access in return for their acceptance of the TRIPS agreement. Here too, the United States and EU refused. On all of these issues, one of the parties did not want them even discussed.

There also were other problems encountered in Seattle. The United States, as host of the meeting, was pushing for a new round that would include many issues and proceed rapidly, perhaps causing some countries to feel they were being railroaded. Key players in the negotiations were new to their jobs, including especially Mike Moore, who had been installed as Director General of the WTO only a short time before. Finally, the desire for further multilateral liberalization may have been diminished by many countries' participation in various regional agreements, such as NAFTA, Mercosur, and the various free trade agreements of the EU.

Meanwhile, the protestors were gathered in unprecedented abundance. They included representatives of U.S. labor unions, labor rights activists, environmental groups, human rights advocates, and anti-corporate interests. Their disruption of the meeting was confined to conventional forms of protest, such as picketing, chanting, and blocking streets. However, the event and publicity also attracted a group of self-described anarchists. They had no particular interest in trade or the WTO, but were bent only on destruction, and they made news and enemies by throwing rocks and breaking windows. This drew more attention than peaceful protest ever would have, but it is not clear what effects it really had.

Toward the end of the week of meetings, with the negotiations making little progress, President Clinton arrived in Seattle and made a speech that seems to have derailed them completely. Previously, the United States and EU had both hoped to insert labor rights into the negotiations, but only in a small way. They tried to persuade the developing countries that the issue would only be discussed, not negotiated, and that there certainly would not be any use of trade sanctions in pursuit of labor rights. Whether this could have succeeded is unclear, but in any case, Clinton's speech explicitly mentioned using trade sanctions to enforce labor rights. From then on, developing country opposition hardened, even to discussion, and it became clear that no agreement on an agenda for a new round would be reached.

As we said, the protestors take credit for this failure, while the negotiators say that the protestors made little difference. We do not know who is right, and perhaps nobody does. It does seem that Clinton's speech was the final straw that prevented agreement, and he may have been influenced by the protests. On the other hand, even if he was responding to the protests, he may have decided that the meetings were going to fail anyway, and thus opted to collect political points for Al Gore from the opportunity. Or his first priority may have been permanent normal trade relations (PNTR) with China, and he did not want to anger labor further until after the election. We have no way of knowing.

It should be noted, however, that a failure of trade negotiations is hardly unprecedented. In the early 1980s, the United States also failed to initiate a new round, at another ministerial meeting. Later, with the Uruguay Round underway, negotiations collapsed several times, with no apparent hope of being restarted. Nonetheless they did, and the round eventually concluded successfully. It is therefore quite possible that what was not accomplished in Seattle will happen later, at another time and place.

What to Do?

What are the possible next steps, for those who support the WTO?[20] What can they (we) do? The most obvious option is simply to continue along the path already laid out in the Uruguay Round negotiations, which specified negotiations (the "built-in agenda") that must be pursued under that agreement. That is happening. Indeed, less informed protestors must have wondered, on February 8, 2000,

[20] For those who oppose it, the choices are working to cause its demise or working to change it. The first might best be accomplished by getting the United States to withdraw, perhaps by putting pressure on Congress. The second might ultimately happen in response to continued protests, although it would help if the protesters could agree on what they want.

when the *Wall Street Journal* headlined "WTO Will Launch Talks to Lower Trade Barriers," just how this could happen. This is *not* the new round that failed in Seattle, but only a scheduled review of barriers in agriculture and services. But it is good that countries are once again talking.

Perhaps most important for WTO supporters, however, would be to pursue any changes on which they and opponents can agree. This could increase support for the WTO. Many would favor improved transparency in the operations of WTO panels, and a greater effort on the part of the WTO and its friends to explain itself to the public. Indeed, this paper is an effort in the latter direction.

Some supporters of the WTO may also favor, or at least accept, greater participation by NGOs. If that participation is limited to the filing of friend-of-the-court briefs, which dispute settlement panels could choose to read or not as they see fit, then this might open up the process without unduly weighting it in favor of those with the most resources.[21] However, we still prefer that NGOs express their views through duly constituted national governments. If greater transparency serves better to inform the NGOs of what is being addressed in WTO discussions and DSM panels, then they should have no difficulty using governments to convey their views and the often valuable information that they can provide.

There is, however, one area where we definitely favor greater participation in the WTO. Developing countries must become more formally represented in WTO decision-making. Exactly how to do this, we do not know. Perhaps it could be a steering committee with both permanent members from the large developed countries and a rotating set of representatives from small and poor countries. It will not be easy to choose these representatives fairly. But it must be done, if the WTO is to move ahead in a world where developing countries play ever more important economic roles.

---

[21] A recent Appellate Body decision has permitted such input to the DSM.

IV. Conclusion

In this conclusion, we try to distill what we have said into a list of the essentials:

On Globalization:

1. Globalization refers to the most recent expansion of global trade, together with expanding flows of real and financial capital across national borders.
2. Globalization increases average real incomes in all countries, but within countries the gains are shared unequally and some may lose.
3. Losers from globalization include owners of scarce factors, as well as those in contracting industries, if they cannot easily change their location, skills, or industry of employment.

On the WTO:

4. The WTO was formed by governments for the purpose of promoting globalization and preventing countries from doing harm with their trade policies.
5. Those who gain most from the WTO are those who gain from globalization, especially small, poor countries who would be most hurt by nationalistic trade policies.
6. The WTO limits those who would use trade policies for other goals, including environment, labor standards, and human rights, forcing them to pursue their objectives at less cost to other countries.
7. The WTO provides a dispute settlement mechanism that has been quite effective, but its operation has been less transparent than it could be.
8. The WTO operates by consensus, but its large membership makes that process unwieldy and exclusionary in practice, leaving many developing countries especially without a voice.

On Seattle:

9. The December 1999 protests at the Seattle ministerial heightened public awareness of globalization and the WTO, perhaps contributing to the failure to initiate a new trade round.
10. The more basic reason for the Seattle failure was the disagreements that divide major participants on agriculture, labor standards, anti-dumping, and market access in textiles and apparel.

Study Questions

1. What is globalization? How it is measured, and how has it changed in the past century or more?
2. Whom does globalization help or hurt? What are the static effects of trade? Dynamic effects? What are the effects of international capital flows? Other effects of globalization?
3. What should be done about globalization?
4. What is the role and structure of the WTO? What are its main activities? Whom does the WTO help or hurt? Other objections to the WTO?
5. What happened in Seattle in December 1999? What has happened concerning the WTO since?
6. What should be done about the WTO?

References

Brown, Drusilla K., Alan V. Deardorff, and Robert M. Stern. 1992. "A U.S.-Mexico-Canada Free Trade Agreement: Sectoral Employment Effects and Regional/Occupational Employment Realignments in the United States," in National Commission for Employment Policy, *The Employment Effects of the North American Free Trade Agreement: Recommendations and Background Studies*, Special Report, October.

Brown, Drusilla K., Alan V. Deardorff, and Robert M. Stern. 1996. "International Labor Standards and Trade: A Theoretical Analysis," in Jagdish Bhagwati and Robert Hudec (eds.), *Fair Trade and Harmonization: Prerequisites for Free Trade?*, Cambridge, MA: MIT Press, pp. 227–280.

Brown, Drusilla K., Alan V. Deardorff, and Robert M. Stern. 2000. "U.S. Trade and Other Policy Options and Programs to Deter Foreign Exploitation of Child

Labor," forthcoming in Magnus Blomström and Linda Goldberg (eds.), *Topics in Empirical Research: A Festschrift in Honor of Robert E. Lipsey*, University of Chicago Press.

Crafts, Nicholas. 2000. "Globalization and Growth in the Twentieth Century," International Monetary Fund, Research Department, Working Paper WP/00/44, March.

Deardorff, Alan V. 1990. "Should Patent Protection Be Extended to All Developing Countries?" *The World Economy* 13 (December), pp. 497–507.

Deardorff, Alan V. 1991. "Trade Policy of the Reagan Years," in Anandi P. Sahu and Ronald L. Tracy (eds.), *The Economic Legacy of the Reagan Years: Euphoria or Chaos?*, New York: Praeger Publishers, pp. 187–203.

Deardorff, Alan V. 1997. "An Economist's Overview of the World Trade Organization," in Korea Economic Institute, *The Emerging WTO System and Perspectives from Asia*, Joint U.S.-Korea Economic Studies, Vol. 7.

Freeman, Richard B. 1995. "Are Your Wages Set in Beijing?" *Journal of Economic Perspectives* 9 (Summer), pp. 15–32.

Jackson, John H. and William J. Davey. 1986. *Legal Problems of International Economic Relations*, 2nd Edition, St. Paul, Minn.: West Publishing Co.

Rodrik, Dani. 1997. *Has Globalization Gone Too Far?* Washington, D.C.: Institute for International Economics.

Stolper, Wolfgang and Paul A. Samuelson. 1941. "Protection and Real Wages," *Review of Economic Studies* 9, pp. 58–73.

Wallach, Lori. 2000. "Lori's War," interview with Lori Wallach, *Foreign Policy*, Spring.

Suggested Further Reading

Academic Consortium on International Trade (http://www.fordschool.umich.edu/rsie/acit/).

Bhagwati, Jagdish. 2007. *In Defense of Globalization*. Oxford and New York: Oxford University Press.

Black, Sandra E. and Elizabeth Brainerd. 2004. "Importing Equality? The Impact of Globalization on Gender Discrimination," *Industrial and Labor Relations Review* 57(4), pp. 540–559.

Burtless, Gary, Robert Lawrence, Robert Litan, and Robert Shapiro. 1998. *Globaphobia: Confronting Fears About Open Trade*. Washington, DC: Brookings Institution, Progressive Policy Institute, Twentieth Century Fund.

Stiglitz, Joseph E. 2006. *Making Globalization Work*. New York: W.W. Norton.

Wolf, Martin. 2004. *Why Globalization Works*. New Haven: Yale University Press.

Chapter 3

Globalization's Bystanders: Does Trade Liberalization Hurt Countries That Do Not Participate?*

Alan V. Deardorff and Robert M. Stern†

I. Introduction

Globalization has many meanings, and many effects. Here we will focus on only one of each: globalization as the reduction in barriers to international trade, and its effect on the countries that, for whatever reason, do not themselves participate in that process. It is often observed by proponents of globalization that, while not all countries have prospered during the recent upsurge in global integration, most of the countries that have failed to prosper, especially in Africa, have been distinctive in the extent to which they have remained relatively closed off from world markets. The supposed implications are that these countries, had they embraced trade liberalization, would have done better, and that, while trade liberalization by others has perhaps

* Reprinted from *World Development*, Vol. 34, No. 8, pp. 1419–1429, © 2006, with permission from Elsevier.
† We have benefited from comments by participants in the UNU/WIDER meeting, and especially those of Ryes Jenkins and from an anonymous referee.

not helped these countries due to their own reluctance to participate, it has not hurt them either. They have only hurt themselves.

In this chapter we use the tools of international trade theory to examine especially the second of these implications. How has trade liberalization by the larger part of the world's economy affected those countries that have not participated? Have they, perhaps, benefited from trade liberalization in spite of their outsider status, as free riders? Or have they instead been harmed by trade liberalization, made worse off than if trade liberalization had not occurred?

For the sake of argument, we will divide the world's countries into just two types: the "included" countries and the "excluded." The included countries are those that have substantially lowered their barriers to international trade, perhaps as part of the trade liberalization fostered by the General Agreement on Tariffs and Trade (GATT) and now the World Trade Organization (WTO), and/or perhaps through preferential trading arrangements (PTAs) such as the European Union (EU) and the North American Free Trade Agreement (NAFTA). The excluded countries are those that have stayed out of PTAs and have either failed to join the GATT/WTO or who have joined but have taken such advantage of the provision for "special and differential treatment" that their trade barriers have remained high. For the most part, these excluded countries have remained in that category through their own choice (their governments', that is) and not because the included countries would not have welcomed their participation in trade liberalization.

In principle, presumably, a country could cut itself off completely from world markets, and thus achieve an extreme form of this excluded status. From the perspective of the analysis here, such a country could not be hurt by globalization, since it would not be aware of it, except perhaps through non-economic mechanisms that we will not examine, such as trans-border pollution. Instead, the excluded countries that we will consider are engaged to some extent with world markets, exporting and importing at a moderate rate that is subject to trade barriers that are high, but that are not all prohibitive. It is the fact that they trade at all that makes them vulnerable to the effects of trade liberalization by others, since it may change their terms of this trade. Indeed, it is the effect of trade liberalization on an excluded country's terms of trade that will be the sole concern of this paper, and we will examine this effect through several quite standard theoretical models of international trade. There are, of course, other ways that a country could potentially be affected by another country's trade liberalization, other than through the terms of trade. But these other mechanisms are less well understood both theoretically and empirically, so we will only say a few words about them, in the concluding section of the paper.

In Section II we take our first two passes at the question by using one of the oldest tools of international trade theory: the offer curve. From this we will see first how an excluded country might easily be expected to benefit, not lose, from trade liberalization by other countries. But on more careful inspection, the same tool will suggest that such a benefit is conditional on the relative extent of liberalization by two subsets of the other countries: those who export the same good as the excluded country, and those who import it. Indeed, much depends on the degree to which the included countries reduce their tariffs on the good or goods of export interest to the excluded country.

In Section III, instead of simply taking as given the tariff cuts of included countries, we then ask in which sectors these tariff cuts are likely to occur. A simple "political economy" model suggests that tariffs are not likely to be cut on the products that excluded countries happen to export, thus making it more likely that they will lose from trade liberalization by other countries. This theoretical result is of course motivated by the common observation that developing countries today face higher tariffs than developed countries, a fact that, on this interpretation, can be attributed to the developing countries' own collective choice to exclude themselves from trade liberalization.

In both of Sections II and III we assume that, when included countries do lower their tariffs on particular goods, they do it on imports from all other countries, even the excluded ones. That is, this trade liberalization is done, in the WTO's language, on an MFN (most favored nation) basis. This is of course required by the WTO for imports from any countries that are themselves members of the WTO, and in fact, although it is not required, it seems to be fairly commonly done even for most excluded countries that are not members. The United States, for example, gives MFN status to almost every country in the world, even though it does not have to do this under WTO rules.[1] The results in Sections II and III, therefore, show that excluded countries may be hurt by trade liberalization of other countries, even though they remain subject to the same tariffs as everybody else.

In fact, however, they do not. Increasingly in recent years, countries who wish to participate in trade liberalization have done so not just through the MFN liberalization of the WTO, but also through PTAs negotiated among pairs or small groups of countries. In Section IV, therefore, we examine the additional harm that is likely to be done to excluded countries if a significant part of trade liberalization takes this form.

In Section V we conclude by trying to extract some policy implications from all of this. Since nothing in our analysis contradicts the traditional presumption from trade theory that trade liberalization is beneficial for the world as a whole, we certainly would not conclude that this aspect of globalization should be stopped, or even slowed down. But the harm that it may do to excluded countries needs to be recognized, and greater efforts need to be made to deal with it. The most obvious way to do that, of course, would simply be to include these countries more fully in trade liberalization.

II. When Can a Country Free Ride?

The simplest analysis of the effect of one country's liberalization on another is provided by offer curves. Suppose there are two countries, A and E, where E will be the "excluded country" throughout the analysis in this section. Both countries produce and trade two goods, X and Y. If E exports good X, then its offer curve is something like

[1] There are only two or three exceptions, including Cuba and North Korea. MFN status for China was of course a matter of annual controversy before China joined the WTO, but in practice, in spite of threats to withdraw it, China regularly had its MFN status renewed.

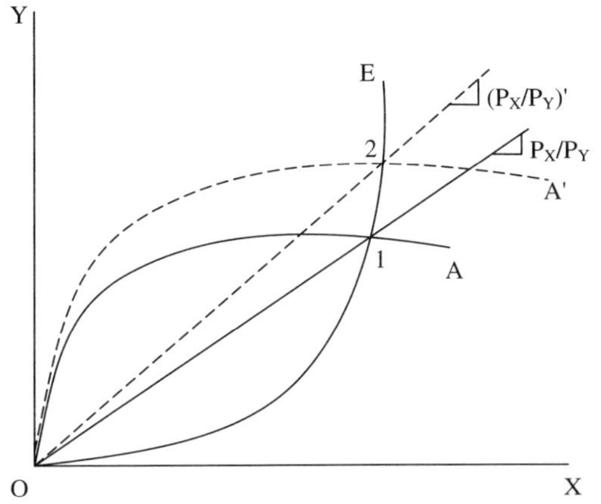

Figure 1. The excluded country, E, gains when the rest of world, A, liberalizes.

OE in Figure 1, showing the quantities of X that it is willing to export in exchange for various quantities imported of good Y. The slope of any line from the origin to the curve is the relative price of good X. The curve OE indicates that country E will import more of good Y only if it gets a higher relative price for its export of good X, or equivalently, if it pays a lower relative price for its import of good Y. The curve also suggests that a higher relative price of X will elicit more exports from country E, although from the curvature it is possible that beyond some point a further increase in price will cause exports to fall. The reason is that a rise in the relative price of X is an improvement in country E's terms of trade, implying that its real income rises, and it may choose to use this income to consume more of both goods, thus possibly exporting less. In any case, it is this improvement in the terms of trade that we will be looking for, to see whether country E may benefit from liberalization elsewhere.

If E were itself engaged in free trade, then we could easily use trade indifference curves[2] to indicate the level of welfare within country E, since these would be tangent to any price line from the origin

[2] See Meade (1952).

where it crosses the offer curve. However, since our interest is in a country that certainly does not have zero tariffs, this cannot be done. Nonetheless, because a tariff reduces a country's imports below what would be optimal, a rise in its terms of trade that permits it to import more will always improve its welfare. Therefore it will be enough, in order to infer effects on country E's welfare, to see what happens to its terms of trade.

In Figure 1, country E engages in trade with a single other country, A, which is an exporter of the other good, Y. Initially country A, like E, has a tariff on its imports of good X. Then, for whatever reason (perhaps because it newly recognizes the gains from trade), it reduces that tariff. The effect, familiar from offer-curve analysis, is to shift A's offer curve outward, away from the origin, as shown, to OA′. Equilibrium moves from point 1 to point 2 in the figure, and the terms of trade of the excluded country E improve. Thus, the excluded country benefits from country A's liberalization.

Of course, if the world really contained only these two countries, then one might wonder whether country A would really liberalize to this extent, since the improvement in E's terms of trade is a worsening of A's. For this reason country A, if it were sensible, might not reduce its tariff to zero, since doing so would cause it to forego some of the benefits of levying a monopoly tariff, which, given country E's continuing protection, there is no reason for it not to use. But if A previously had a tariff above the monopoly level, then it could gain by a tariff reduction, and country E, as shown, would gain along with it. In any case, as we now consider a world with a larger number of countries, such monopoly-tariff considerations become less relevant.

For the two-country case is hardly what we want to see. In practice, our excluded country confronts a large world of a great many countries, all of whom may be liberalizing. If we can think of the foreign offer curve, OA, as representing the aggregate of all those countries, then Figure 1 suggests a much more relevant gain for the excluded country E as a free rider on global liberalization. It must of course be true that, since E is an exporter of good X, the rest of the world must in aggregate be a net importer of good X, and therefore the world's offer curve does indeed look something like OA.

Since trade liberalization by any country must cause its offer curve to expand outward, Figure 1 may seem to guarantee that, in fact, excluded countries can only gain from the rest of the world's liberalization.

That is not the case, however. While it is true that individual country offer curves expand with their liberalization, and it is also true that any group of countries may be represented by an aggregate offer curve that is, in effect, their sum, it is *not* true that trade liberalization by those countries necessarily expands the aggregate offer curve outward. Suppose, for example, that the rest of the world consists of just two countries, one that exports Y and the other that imports it. If the latter imports less than the former exports, the offer curve of the two together will look like OA in Figure 1. But if now only the second of these two countries were to lower its tariff (on Y, since that is what it imports), it would import more Y and thus reduce, not expand, the amount that the two together export. The aggregate offer curve would shift inward.

To correctly identify the effect of liberalization on world markets, then, we need to separate countries with different trade patterns. This is done in Figure 2, where for convenience we now take the excluded country E to be very small compared to others, as suggested

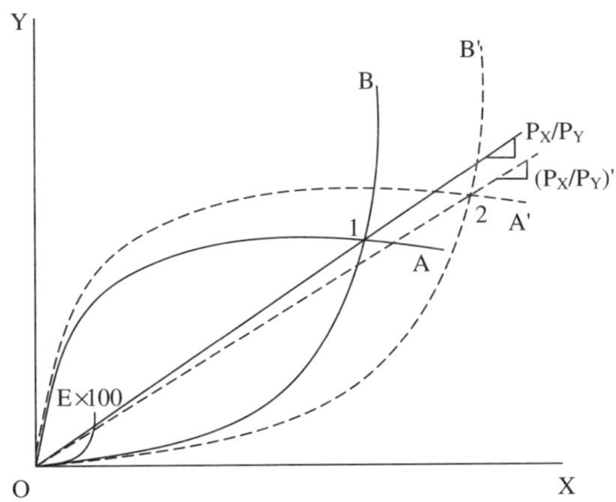

Figure 2. The excluded country, E, loses when other exporters of X (Country B) liberalize more than other importers of X (Country A).

by drawing its offer curve, OE, 100 times actual size. The rest of the world then consists of two countries, A that exports Y and B that exports X. In the initial equilibrium at point 1, world prices are determined (since country E is negligibly small) by the offer curves OA and OB. Now, as A and B both reduce their tariffs, both offer curves expand outward by some amounts, perhaps to OA′ and OB′, and the new equilibrium is at point 2. As drawn, the terms of trade of country E worsens. It is hurt by the rest of the world's liberalization.[3]

What determines this result? Most simply, country E (as an exporter of X) will be hurt if, at initial prices, those countries that are also net exporters of X expand their trade more than those countries that are net importers of X. This in turn depends, though only in part, on the sizes of the two groups of countries' tariff reductions. If the X-exporters, whose relevant tariffs are on Y, reduce their tariffs more than the Y-exporters, whose relevant tariffs are on X, then other things equal we may expect country E to lose. Conversely, in order for country E to free ride on others' liberalization, it needs greater reductions in tariffs on what it exports than on what it imports. This is not exactly right, even in this simple two-goods case, since countries may differ for various reasons in the extent to which their quantities of trade respond to tariff reductions. But as a first approximation in ignorance of these other determinants of trade, what matters is these two sets of tariff reductions.

It is obvious why the excluded country gains from others' reductions in their tariffs on its exports. These cause increases in demand for its export good on world markets and thus increase its world price. But why do other countries' tariff cuts on its imports matter at all? The answer is that these tariff cuts cause world prices of the imports to rise, reducing what the excluded country can get in exchange for its exports. In a two-goods model, there really is no difference between a rise in export prices and fall in import prices, and the same

[3] If country E were not small, then its supply and demand in the international market would have to be taken into account in determining the new equilibrium world price. This would not change the conclusion, however, since this would only reduce the size of the change in price, not reverse its direction.

is true with many goods if one looks at appropriate indexes of the prices of both. However, in the real world people seldom do look at such indexes, and the public and political perception of the effects of export prices and import prices may be quite different. We will look next at a model that allows for this.

III. Which Tariffs Will Fall with Multilateral Liberalization?

The point of this section is to argue what may seem obvious: that countries that do not themselves participate in tariff liberalization are likely to find that other countries do not reduce tariffs on their exports. Obvious or not, this does not follow easily from the simple welfare economics of tariffs, which says that the gain to importing countries from lowering their own tariffs does not depend on whether other countries do. Except for terms-of-trade motivations in large countries — which some, though not all, regard as implausible motivators for trade policies — the rest-of-world will always benefit from lowering its tariffs on a country's products, even if that country keeps its own tariffs high. Of course, the same reasoning implies that we should already see tariffs close to zero in most of the world, which we do not, and which we certainly did not see prior to the liberalizations undertaken under the GATT/WTO.

To answer this question, then, we must have some sort of model of the political economy of trade policy. Such models have been built and increasingly refined in the trade literature, with early efforts by Findlay and Wellisz (1982), Mayer (1984), and Hillman (1989), whose approaches were then integrated successfully by Grossman and Helpman (1994). For the purpose here, however, a much simpler framework will suffice, one that could perhaps be viewed as a simplification of the Grossman and Helpman model.

The true welfare effects of a tariff reduction include the following, as a simple partial equilibrium model would suggest: a gain to domestic consumers; a loss (of tariff revenue) to the domestic government; a loss to import-competing domestic producers; and — if the size of the importing country is large enough for the tariff cut to raise the world price of the good — a gain to foreign producers and a loss to foreign consumers. In a world where the tariff was the only prior distortion, it is well known that the sum of these effects must be positive — that is, the world as a whole gains from a tariff cut. The importing country alone also gains if it is small enough that the world price is unaffected, but it may not gain if the worsening of its terms of trade outweighs the efficiency gain.

All of this may be beside the point, however, if political forces favor some constituencies over others, as seems to be the case given that virtually all countries, and especially many small ones, have had positive and often quite high tariffs throughout history. The political economy literature explains this by allowing producers to exert special influence on trade policy, by one means or another. Grossman and Helpman, in particular, model producers as contributing financially to incumbent politicians in return for their providing or maintaining tariff protection. The politicians, in turn take account of both the contributions that they receive and also broad economic welfare in making their policy decisions.

Here, however, we will assume instead that policy makers in most countries are concerned *only* about producer welfare, ignoring completely any gains or losses to consumers and, in most cases, ignoring also any effects of tariff revenues. This could perhaps be justified along the lines of Grossman and Helpman as an extreme case of putting all weight on the contributions that politicians receive. However it could also be motivated less cynically by observing that the gains and losses to producers, very much including their employees, are much easier to see than the gains and losses to consumers. Also, because they tend to be concentrated on small groups in the population, the severity of effects on producers is evident, while the effects on individual consumers may be dismissed as too small to worry about. As for also ignoring tariff revenues, that would be a dubious assumption in a country where tariffs provide the bulk of government revenues, and we will bring it back into the analysis for such countries below. But in advanced countries with many other (and more efficient) revenue generating opportunities, it seems plausible that these revenues might also play only a negligible role.

In order to incorporate this simple assumption into a correspondingly simple model, we follow Grossman and Helpman in assuming that preferences are "quasi-linear" so that, except in a numeraire sector in which we always assume free trade, demand in each country for each good depends only on its price relative to the numeraire. And we go even further than Grossman and Helpman on the production side. They assumed specific factors in each sector, with labor mobile among sectors. We assume that *all* factors are specific, so that output in each sector in each country is simply fixed. We also follow Grossman and Helpman in assuming that all goods are only final goods, so that there are no imported intermediate inputs. That is an important limiting assumption, as we will note.

Suppose, then, that there are C countries, $c = 1,\ldots,C$, and $G + 1$ goods, $g = 0,1,\ldots,G$, with good zero the aforementioned numeraire. All countries share the same demand functions for the non-numeraire goods, $D_{gc} = 1 - p_{gc}$, $g = 1,\ldots,G$, so that trade patterns depend only on differences across countries in exogenous production levels. These take either of two values, a low value $\bar{X}_g$ in countries that will be importing the good, and a high value $\bar{\bar{X}}_g$ in countries that will be exporting it.

Although we will assume there is some trade, even before any liberalization, it is worth noting the autarky prices that would follow from these production levels and demands: Countries with low production have a high autarky price, denoted $\tilde{p}_g = 1 - \bar{X}_g$, while countries with high production have a low autarky price, $\tilde{\tilde{p}}_g = 1 - \bar{\bar{X}}_g \leq \tilde{p}_g$. Let $\bar{S}_g^C = \{c \mid X_{gc} = \bar{X}_g\}$ be the set of all countries with low production of good g, and $\bar{N}_g^C \left(\sum_{c \in \bar{S}_g^C} 1\right)$ be the number of those countries; define $\bar{\bar{S}}_g^C$, $\bar{\bar{N}}_g^C$ analogously. And let $\bar{S}_c^G = \{g \mid X_{gc} = \bar{X}_g\}$ be the set of all goods that country c produces in small quantity; $\bar{N}_c^G$ the number of those goods; and $\bar{\bar{S}}_c^G$, $\bar{\bar{N}}_c^G$ analogously.

Initially, we let all countries have the same *ad valorem* tariff on a good, t_g^0, which is assumed small enough to permit trade: $t_g^0 < (\tilde{p}_g - \tilde{\tilde{p}}_g)/\tilde{\tilde{p}}_g$. In the initial equilibrium denoted "0", exporters receive a world price p_g^{W0} while importers pay a higher importer's price, $p_g^{M0} = (1 + t_g^0)\, p_g^{W0}$, both of which are determined by the requirement that demands, at these prices, add up to production:

$$\bar{\bar{N}}_g^C(1 - p_g^{W0}) + \bar{N}_g^C(1 - (1 + t_g^0)p_g^{W0}) = \bar{\bar{N}}_g^C \bar{\bar{X}}_g + \bar{N}_g^C \bar{X}_g, \tag{1}$$

from which

$$p_g^{W0} = \frac{\bar{\bar{N}}_g^C \tilde{\tilde{p}}_g + \bar{N}_g^C \tilde{p}_g}{C + t_g^0 \bar{N}_g^C}. \tag{2}$$

Now consider the possibility of all countries moving to free trade, denoted "F", in all sectors. The world price — given by (2) but with t_g^0 replaced by zero — is then simply the average of the two autarky prices with weights equal to the fraction of countries with each. Relevant to the choice — of whether or not to make this move to free trade — is the change in producer welfare. Since production is fixed, this is simply

$$\Delta\pi_{gc}^F = (p_g^{WF} - p_{gc}^0)X_{gc}, \tag{3}$$

where p_{gc}^0 and X_{gc} are to be replaced by p_g^{W0} and $\bar{\bar{X}}_g$ for an exporter and by p_g^{M0} and $\bar{X}_g$ for an importer. Letting

$$\delta_{gc} = \begin{cases} 1 & \text{if } c \in \bar{S}_g^C \\ 0 & \text{if } c \in \bar{\bar{S}}_g^C \end{cases} \tag{4}$$

indicate that country c imports good g, it turns out that

$$\Delta\pi_{gc}^F = \frac{p_g^{WF} X_{gc}^0 t_g^0}{C + t_g^0 \bar{N}_g^C}(\bar{N}_g^C - \delta_{gc} C). \tag{5}$$

Thus, as one would expect, looking only at producers' welfare, the move to free trade in one sector causes exporters to gain and importers to lose.[4] It is easily confirmed, however, that the sum of these changes across all countries is positive, simply because individual exporters produce more than individual import-competitors. Summing (5) across all countries yields:

$$\sum_{c} \Delta\pi_{gc}^{F} = \frac{p_g^{WF} t_g^0 \bar{N}_g^C \bar{\bar{N}}_g^C}{C + t_g^0 \bar{N}_g^C} (\bar{\bar{X}}_g - \bar{X}_g) > 0. \tag{6}$$

Thus, even from the perspective of producers alone, the world as a whole benefits from a move to free trade.

Individual countries may not gain in this sense, however. Certainly they lose in particular sectors if they are importers and a positive tariff is reduced, since that hurts their competing producers. It is true that if positive tariffs are reduced by all countries in all sectors, then a country is likely to have export-sector producers who gain at the same time that import-competing producers lose. But there is no guarantee that the gain to the former is larger, for a given country, than the loss to the latter. In an extreme case, a country could be an importer of every good other than the numeraire, in which case it would have no producers who gain. And even if we require a plausible mix of export and import sectors outside the numeraire, if a country happens to export only in sectors with a large number of other exporting countries, then its exporters will gain little from the liberalization. Thus there may well be countries that stand to lose, from this producers-only perspective, from a multilateral move to free trade. Such countries would presumably not participate in such a move.[5]

---

[4] If we allowed for traded intermediate inputs, it would not be this simple. A local producer could benefit from a tariff cut on its input.

[5] In addition, the assumption here that governments care only about producers, and not even about their own revenues, is particularly questionable in poor countries where tariff revenues may bulk large in government budgets. Such countries, even if their export-sector producers would gain more from liberalization than their import-competitors would lose, might opt out of liberalization for that reason.

Thus an actual liberalization, if it occurs in this framework, is likely to include only a subset of the world's countries: a group of countries for whom MFN[6] tariff reductions benefit their export-sector producers more than they harm their import-competing producers. Of course, by not including tariff reductions by countries outside that group, the gains to the former are likely to be smaller than if all countries had moved together to free trade. But this may be offset by the included group simply not reducing tariffs on products that its members do not export.

Note that in this framework, a country would never unilaterally reduce its tariffs.[7] To do so would provide no benefit at all to its exporters, and only harm its import competitors. So for MFN liberalization to occur, countries must find others who are willing to reduce their tariffs as well, so as to create benefits for their exporters. Whether such willing participants can be found is uncertain. It depends on the patterns of comparative advantage across countries.

Suppose, to take a simple example where limited liberalization can succeed, that there are two or more goods that importing countries do not produce at all. Then a group of countries who export different ones of these goods will necessarily benefit, as producers, if they agree to reduce tariffs on these goods alone, since the export-sector producers in each will gain from the others' tariff reductions, and they will not have any import-competing producers who will lose. Thus we know that there may exist a group of countries that will willingly reduce their tariffs on a set of goods. On the other hand, suppose that all countries but one are importers of all goods except the numeraire, on which by assumption all have zero tariffs. Then there will not exist any group of countries willing to reduce tariffs at all.

The important point, however, is the following. Suppose that there does exist a set of countries, S^C, that would be willing to reduce tariffs on a set of goods, S^G. And suppose that any good within S^G is exported only by countries not in S^C. Then producers in the countries

[6] We will look at preferential agreements in the next section.

[7] Again, this need not be the case if there are traded intermediate inputs. Indeed, a tariff on any input that is only imported and not produced domestically would be eliminated based on the interests of producers that use it.

of S^C will gain at least as much by excluding that good from S^G as by including it, and they will gain strictly more if any of them produce this good. Thus in this model we should not expect multilateral liberalization by a subset of the world's countries, if it occurs, to include goods that are exported only by countries outside that group. Again, of course, this would not be the case if consumer welfare were taken fully into account.[8]

If the outside countries export goods that are also exported by some of the inside countries, then producers in the latter would lose if these goods were removed from S^G. Their governments might still accept this exclusion, however, if they have other export producers who gain sufficiently.

The conclusion from this section, then, is that excluded countries are *not* likely to benefit from MFN liberalization by other countries, simply because these other countries are not likely to reduce tariffs on the goods of greatest export interest to the excluded countries. Somewhat ironically, this would not be the case if a particular excluded country were very similar, in its pattern of trade, to the countries that are liberalizing. But it is certain to be true if the excluded countries are distinctly different from the included ones, as perhaps by being less economically developed.

One might wonder how large these adverse effects may be. Unfortunately we are not in a position to answer that question for the countries where it is most relevant, where a detailed study of their particular exports and imports would be needed, together with estimates of the effects of liberalization on corresponding prices. A hint of what might be found, however, can be obtained from studies of trade liberalization using computable general equilibrium (CGE) models. In Brown, Deardorff, and Stern (2003), for example, we calculated the effects of the Uruguay Round tariff reductions on the terms of trade of some twenty countries and groups of countries. We found that while the terms of trade improved for most developed parts of the world, terms of trade worsened in most of the developing world,

[8] On the other hand, allowing the government to care about tariff revenues would only make the point stronger.

including declines of about one percent in India, Sri Lanka, the rest of South Asia, and the Philippines.

IV. Preferential Trade Liberalization

So far we have considered only MFN liberalization. But an increasing amount of trade liberalization in recent years has taken the form of PTAs. In these arrangements, as required by the WTO, the liberalization is typically more extreme, with tariffs reduced further and on more goods than may be covered in a multilateral WTO agreement. They are, however, discriminatory. Countries that are not part of a particular PTA continue to be subject to what are still called the MFN tariffs of the PTA countries, although the MFN name is now insidiously misleading. Countries outside a PTA are not being treated as well as the "most favored nation" at all, but instead have their exports to countries within the PTA taxed at a higher rate than is applied to exports from other member countries.

The literature on PTAs, starting with Viner's (1950) analysis of customs unions and continuing today, emphasizes the positive and negative effects that arise from "trade creation" and "trade diversion." This seems to suggest that if the former somehow outweighs the latter, then the PTA is beneficial. That may be true for the countries inside the PTA, and perhaps even for the world as a whole. But it is very unlikely to be true for the countries that remain outside the PTA. For them trade creation is largely irrelevant, while trade diversion represents a loss. That is, when a PTA causes a member country to import from a partner rather than from an outside country, that constitutes a fall in demand for the product of the outside country. If the affected trade flow is large enough to matter at all, then this will cause a fall in the world price of the imported good and a worsening of the terms of trade of the outside country.

This does not have to happen. PTAs can take several forms, in particular with regard to the tariffs that the countries levy on trade from outside. If these tariffs are low enough, then the countries of the PTA may continue to trade with the rest of the world as much as they did before. Kemp and Wan (1976), for example, showed that a customs union could set a common external tariff that would keep net imports of every good from the rest of the world unchanged, thus assuring no impact at all on the well-being of the rest of the world.[9] However, if external tariffs are not changed when the PTA is formed, as is usually the case in a free trade area (FTA), then the fact that the preferences favor trade with partners over trade with outside countries suggests that trade with the rest of the world is likely to fall.

If that happens, then the effect on the excluded countries is exactly like Figure 1 in reverse. That is, the collective offer curve of the countries of the FTA before it is formed is OA′, and formation of the FTA shifts it inward to OA, causing a worsening of the excluded country's terms of trade.

Even with an FTA and unchanged external tariffs, this is not a necessary outcome, although it seems far more likely than the alternative. For example, in a two-goods model, suppose that the FTA includes countries A and B which import goods X and Y respectively over positive tariffs. When they eliminate these tariffs on trade with each other, at the initial world price each will import from the other instead of from the outside world, as long as each can supply all of the other's needs at a price differing from the world price by less than the tariff. If this is the case, then whatever may have been the two-countries' combined trade with the world before the FTA, this trade shrinks to zero in its presence. Only if the countries differ in size by enough that one of them cannot meet the other's demands at such a price will the two together continue to trade with the world at the initial price. And even then it is likely that their combined net trade will shrink.[10,11]

---

9 Panagariya and Krishna (2000) showed a similar result for free trade areas.

10 However, this does not seem to be inevitable. In analysis not included here, it appears to be possible to construct a case where opposite income effects in the two FTA countries cause an increase in their net trade with the world.

11 Another case would have both of the FTA members importing the same good from the world. If their tariffs are the same, then the FTA has no effect on this trade. But if their tariffs are different, then as pointed out by Richardson (1995), the high-tariff country will import as much as possible from the low-tariff country, which will expand its imports to replace those of the high-tariff country. In this case, too, net trade of the two may expand since, in effect, the tariff of the high-tariff country is rendered irrelevant.

Thus, while exceptions do seem to be possible, on the whole it appears that preferential liberalization is even more likely to be harmful than multilateral liberalization to those countries that do not participate in it. Note that this does not require that trade diversion somehow outweigh trade diversion, but only that it occur at all. The same conclusion can also be obtained by different means in different models. Brown, Kiyota, and Stern (2005), for example, used a CGE model to calculate the effects of a Free Trade Agreement of the Americas and found that the elimination of tariffs on manufactures in such an FTA would improve the welfare of all the participating countries and regions but lower welfare in all but two of the sixteen non-participating countries and regions that were included in their model. Using a different economic mechanism, Chang and Winters (2002) argue (and support empirically, with data from MERCOSUR) that preferential liberalization favoring one of two Bertrand competitors will cause the unfavored firm to lower its export price. No doubt there are many other mechanisms that could work as well.

V. Conclusion

This analysis suggests that, although it is not inevitable, it is strongly likely that excluded countries will be hurt by trade liberalization undertaken by other countries. It may be true that, if tariff reductions are MFN on products that are selected at random, then an excluded country has as good a chance of gaining from them as of losing. But MFN tariff reductions have not in practice been in randomly selected sectors, but rather in sectors in which the tariff-reducing countries stand most to gain as exporters. Thus, MFN tariffs are unlikely to be cut on products that are primarily exported by the excluded countries. Furthermore, much of the trade liberalization that has occurred in recent years has been preferential, not MFN. While preferential liberalization usually covers (almost) all products, its discriminatory nature means that it tends to divert trade away from excluded countries and thereby makes them worse off by moving their terms of trade against them.

The models here have focused only on these terms-of-trade effects because these are well understood and amenable to static analysis. There may well be other, perhaps more important, effects than these that should be considered, but it seems likely that they would act in the same direction. Consider, for example, the "dynamic gains from trade" that are often mentioned augmenting the benefits from trade as in Baldwin (1992). One such source of dynamic gains might arise from economies of scale that allow some industries' costs to fall over time as they expand production. To the extent that other countries' trade liberalization reduces demand for an excluded country's exports, this will undermine not only its terms of trade but also its ability to take advantage of such dynamic scale economies in export industries. Or consider the alternative possibility that technology flows follow trade flows, permitting countries to tap into the technological advances that are occurring in other countries, as in Coe and Helpman (1995). Here too, if excluded countries find their trade with such countries reduced, they may suffer an ever widening gap between their technologies and those at the frontier. No doubt other mechanisms could be suggested as well that lie outside the simple models looked at here, but it seems likely that all would build on sources of gain from trade that are lost when excluded countries have their volumes of trade reduced.

Note that these losses from trade liberalization occur only because the excluded countries do, in fact, trade. The effects analyzed here all work through the terms of trade, and a country would be immune from them if it did not trade at all. But this is no reason not to trade, for these losses all represent a reduction of their gains from trade, not a reduction of welfare to below what it would have been in autarky. Thus, the excluded countries would be ill-advised to exclude themselves even further from world markets as a means of avoiding these losses. It won't work.

Nor is it a reason for trade liberalization itself to be restrained, at least not in its MFN manifestation. As should be clear from this analysis, the reason that excluded countries may lose from trade liberalization is that the liberalization does not go far enough, not that it goes too far. It is the exclusion of some sectors and/or some exporting countries from the benefits of tariff cuts that creates a bias against excluded countries.

Thus, the best chance of avoiding these losses to excluded countries is simply not to exclude them. Or, if they cannot be persuaded to participate, we need to find a mechanism for cutting tariffs that will work across all sectors instead of favoring only the export sectors of the participating countries.

The current multilateral trade negotiations of the Doha Development Agenda show promising signs of doing exactly this. Developing countries are playing a more active role than ever before, at least in pressing the developed countries to reduce trade barriers in sectors of export interest to them. At the same time, developed countries are insisting that the developing countries also participate more than they have before by reducing their own tariffs. If both of these outcomes can be achieved, developing countries — at least those who participate — will stand to gain substantially. Even those countries that remain outside the WTO may gain from this, to the extent that tariffs are reduced on their exports as well.

Preferential liberalization, in the form of proliferating FTAs, poses a more difficult problem. If this proliferation does not abate, there are only two ways that an excluded country may hope to avoid being harmed by it. One is to join in and negotiate FTAs of its own with as many partners as it can. Unfortunately, the poorer a country is, the less likely it is that others will have any interest in negotiating with it. And even if FTAs were to be formed including all possible pairings or groupings of countries, the administrative complications of conforming to all of their rules would put the poorest countries at a disadvantage.

The other route toward lessening the harm from preferential liberalization, as it affects excluded countries, is for nondiscriminatory liberalization to render preferences meaningless. If MFN tariffs were all zero, then any FTA would be both unnecessary and ineffective. Thus, the best cure for the side effects of preferential trade liberalization is nondiscriminatory trade liberalization.

Study Questions

1. Globalization refers here to the reduction of barriers to international trade and the effects on participating countries. While many countries have prospered from globalization, this is not the case for much of Africa that has remained relatively closed off from world markets. To what extent have globalization's bystanders hurt themselves by not participating in globalization or been benefited/harmed by trade liberalization?
2. How are the included/excluded countries defined, and how are these countries affected by liberalization and changes in the terms of trade?
3. With two countries, how are offer curves derived and the terms of trade measured? How are changes in tariffs and the terms of trade determined? Can the excluded country gain from trade liberalization of its trading partner? Under what conditions may the aggregate offer curve shift inward?
4. With two large countries and an aggregate of small countries, can the small country aggregate experience worsened terms of trade? By focusing only on producers' welfare, why do exporters gain from trade liberalization? How are import-competing producers affected? Will countries benefit from unilateral liberalization? How will excluded countries be affected if there are tariff reductions on goods not of interest to them? Is there any evidence of such effects?
5. How are excluded countries likely to be affected by preferential trading arrangements?
6. What are the potential impacts of dynamic economies of scale and technological change that may occur with trade liberalization? How can trade liberalization be designed to benefit excluded countries?

References

Baldwin, Richard E. 1992. "Measurable Dynamic Gains from Trade," *Journal of Political Economy* 100, pp. 162–174.

Brown, Drusilla K., Alan V. Deardorff, and Robert M. Stern. 2003. "Computational Analysis of Multilateral Trade Liberalization in the Uruguay Round and Doha

Development Round," in Aaditya Mattoo and Robert M. Stern (eds.), *India and the WTO*, Washington, D.C.: World Bank and Oxford University Press, pp. 13–46.

Brown, Drusilla K., Kozo Kiyota, and Robert M. Stern. 2005. "Computational Analysis of the Free Trade Area of the Americas (FTAA)," Discussion Paper No. 528, Research Seminar in International Economics, University of Michigan, February 5.

Chang, Won and L. Alan Winters. 2002. "How Regional Blocs Affect Excluded Countries: The Price Effects of MERCOSUR," *American Economic Review* 92(4), pp. 889–904.

Coe, David T. and Elhanan Helpman. 1995. "International R&D Spillovers," *European Economic Review* 39 (May), pp. 859–887.

Findlay, R. and S. Wellisz. 1982. "Endogenous Tariffs, the Political Economy of Trade Restrictions, and Welfare," in Jagdish Bhagwati (ed.), *Import Competition and Response*, Chicago: University of Chicago Press.

Grossman, Gene M. and Elhanan Helpman. 1994. "Protection for Sale," *American Economic Review* 84 (September), pp. 833–850.

Hillman, Arye L. 1989. *The Political Economy of Protection*, London: Harwood.

Kemp, Murray C. and Henry Y. Wan, Jr. 1976. "An Elementary Proposition Concerning the Formation of Customs Unions," in Murray Kemp, *Three Topics in the Theory of International Trade: Distribution, Welfare, and Uncertainty*, Amsterdam: North Holland.

Mayer, Wolfgang. 1984. "Endogenous Tariff Formation," *American Economic Review* 74, pp. 970–985.

Meade, James Edward. 1952. *A Geometry of International Trade*, London: Unwin Brothers Ltd.

Panagariya, Arvind and Pravin Krishna. 2000. "On Necessarily Welfare-Enhancing Free Trade Areas," *Journal of International Economics* 57, pp. 353–367.

Richardson, Martin. 1995. "Tariff Revenue Competition in a Free Trade Area," *European Economic Review* 39, pp. 1429–1437.

Viner, Jacob. 1950. *The Customs Union Issue*, New York: Carnegie Endowment for International Peace.

Suggested Further Reading

Harrison, Ann (ed.). 2006. *Globalization and Poverty*. Chicago: University of Chicago Press.

Hertel, Thomas W. and L. Alan Winters (eds.). 2006. *Poverty & the WTO: Impacts of the Doha Development Agenda*. Washington, D.C.: Palgrave Macmillan and the World Bank.

Hoekman, Bernard and Marcelo Olarreaga (eds.). 2007. *Global Trade and Poor Nations.* Washington, D.C.: Brookings Institution Press.

Newfarmer, Richard (ed.). 2006. *Trade, Doha, and Development: A Window into the Issues.* Washington, D.C.: The World Bank.

Winters, L. Alan. 2002. "Trade Policies for Poverty Alleviation," in Bernard Hoekman, Aaditya Mattoo, and Philip English (eds.), *Development, Trade, and the WTO: A Handbook.* Washington, D.C.: The World Bank.

Chapter 4

Global Market Integration and National Sovereignty*

Andrew G. Brown and Robert M. Stern†

I. Introduction

In this paper, we focus on areas of potential conflict arising in the World Trade Organization (WTO) from the pursuit of global market integration in a world comprised of separate nation-states. We recognize the persuasive economic logic in enlarging market access by means of reducing barriers to trade and investment in goods and services and by conforming domestic regulatory practices to promote economic efficiency. But, as we will argue, the unfettered advocacy of global market integration that has become so ardently pursued by the major industrialized countries may be misguided. It undermines the multilateral principles of reciprocity and non-discrimination and gives insufficient attention to the immense diversity among countries in political, economic, and social conditions and in policy aims. Unless this diversity is taken into account, there may be considerable strains

* Published in *The World Economy*, 29(3), March 2006, pp. 257–279. Reprinted with permission from Blackwell Publishing.

† Helpful comments on an earlier version of our paper were received from an anonymous referee, Juan Carlos Hallak, Bernard Hoekman, and Marina Whitman.

placed on the WTO as the arbiter and enforcer of the rules and procedures for trade liberalization that are at the heart of the multilateral trading system.

To provide some historical perspective on the foregoing issues, in Section II following, we briefly trace the evolution of the global trading system from the 19th century to the present-day GATT/WTO arrangements. We call attention particularly to the opposing paradigms — the cosmopolitan and the national — underlying many issues that comprise the agenda of trade negotiations and that may place stress on the trading system. In Section III, we consider the recent plethora of free trade agreements (FTAs), including those between industrial and developing countries, and their uneasy relationship with a multilateral system based on non-discrimination. In Section IV, we identify what we see as the boundaries of the WTO and consider how the expansion of these boundaries may result in the over-extension and weakening of the effectiveness and influence of the WTO. Section V concludes.

II. The Global Trading System: Yesterday and Today

> "I don't think they play at all fairly," Alice began in a rather complaining tone, "and they all quarrel so dreadfully one can hardly hear oneself speak — and they don't seem to have any rules in particular; at least, if there are, no one attends to them..." (Lewis Carroll, *Alice's Adventures in Wonderland*, p. 112)

To a reader in the 19th century, that might well have seemed a fair description of global trading relations at the time rather than of a game of croquet in the Queen of Hearts court. It was only in the course of the 19th century that the beginnings of some order, as we know it today, began to emerge. Industrialization was taking hold in several countries, and it generated an intensified search for foreign markets and sources of supply. Governments in Europe were faced with calls to lower tariff barriers on imported inputs and to negotiate reductions in tariffs protecting foreign markets. But in a nationalistic world of vying states — as it still is today — governments were not about to ease access to their markets in the absence of some quid pro quo.

The way forward was found in the adoption of two instruments of policy — reciprocity and non-discrimination — which set off a wave of trade liberalization. These two ideas enabled countries to surmount their innate distrust of each other and to engage in mutually beneficial, and generalized, reductions in tariff barriers. Reciprocity — meaning contingent and equivalent concessions — assuaged the fear of governments that they might not be receiving at least as much from others as they were giving themselves, and non-discrimination reassured them that they were enjoying the same treatment as had been won by other competing states. Neither of these ideas was a sudden intellectual invention; they had long been known in human affairs. But their application to trade relations was comparatively new and did much to advance global trade liberalization.

Historians usually identify the signing of the Anglo-French Treaty of 1860 as the landmark that signaled the new era of trade relations. Besides the need for a political gesture of friendship, the immediate cause of the signing of the Treaty was a decision by the French government to follow Britain's policy of trade liberalization. The French leaders were persuaded at the time by the popular, but mistakenly simplistic and mono-causal, belief that Britain's superior industrial performance owed much to its free trade policy. However, in undertaking to reduce tariffs on British manufactures, the French government sought some concession from Britain in order to win the support of its export interests in getting the lower tariffs passed through parliament. Although Britain had already nailed the flag of free trade to its mast — and firmly, but exceptionally, believed that others in their own interest should also reduce their tariffs unilaterally — it accommodated the French political need.[1] Further, when other European countries anxiously sought comparable access to the French market, France offered them the same tariff rates that it had set for Britain. The inclusion of such a most-favored-nation (MFN) clause in commercial treaties thereafter became common practice among the European states. It also had the advantage of preventing treaties from

[1] For a full account of the Anglo-French negotiations, see Hinde (1987). For a history of multilateral trade relations over the period 1850 to 2000, see Brown (2003).

being in a constant state of flux with tariff schedules being repeatedly renegotiated bilaterally.

What emerged in industrializing Europe from the struggle of countries to gain market access for their exports of manufactured goods was a network of bilateral, commercial treaties linked together through the MFN clause. While this was a step toward more predictable trade relations, however, the system was not notable for its stability. Apart from Britain — which adhered with almost religious fervor to free trade — most European countries found their treaty obligation hard to live with. After a drift toward freer trade in the 1850s and 1860s, most countries later assumed more protectionist stances. Commercial treaties were frequently denounced or renegotiated, and some lengthy and bitter trade wars broke out. Still, while every country valued the freedom to make unilateral decisions about its national trade barriers, all were driven reluctantly to accept constraints on their behavior in order to gain access to others' markets.

The outbreak of WWI and the political upheaval engendered in its aftermath disrupted trade relations for some years. Nevertheless, in the peace conferences following the war, the avowed goal of governments was to restore the pre-1914 order in international monetary, financial and trade relations. But economic conditions militated against a restoration of the minimal levels of mutual trust necessary for agreements. In the unstable monetary conditions of the early 1920s, countries engaged in currency depreciations that were seen by others as competitive and that, in line with economic thinking of the time, made the negotiation of tariff reductions pointless. For a while, in the later 1920s, restoration of the gold standard made the outlook appear more hopeful for trade relations. But the differences in tariff levels between the high and low tariff countries were sizable, and governments could not agree on a common formula for tariff cutting. The onset of the Depression and the early responses to it, with tariff increases and currency devaluations, put an end to any hopes for more normal trade relations.

Some countries, led by Germany, resorted to bilateral barter or clearing arrangements that were necessarily discriminatory. Others, like Britain, sought to revive trade through the creation of preferential trading areas. In these circumstances of worldwide inadequacies in domestic demand, trade relations largely ceased to be conducted within a multilateral framework based on non-discrimination.

It is notable that the United States played virtually no part in the evolution of trade relations before WWI and remained largely aloof from international trade affairs in the inter-war years. American manufacturing and marketing skills had become internationally evident as early as the 1890s, but the United States remained for many years principally an exporter of primary commodities. It was fortunate that agricultural exports generally met with low trade barriers before WWI, so there were few restraints on the U.S. pursuit of a high tariff policy on imported manufactures. Indeed, the U.S. Congress could then interpret reciprocity as the negotiation of reductions in foreign tariffs under the threat of increases in American tariffs. MFN treatment was also offered only conditionally so that to qualify for a new MFN tariff rate, all trading partners had to offer equivalent tariff reductions.

However, by the 1920s the interest of U.S. manufacturing industries in foreign markets had grown substantially with the share of manufactures having risen to nearly two-thirds of total exports. A latecomer in the world of trade relations, it was only then that the United States began gradually to accommodate itself to the accepted international norms. With the adoption of the Fordney–McCumber Tariff Act in 1922, the principle of unconditional MFN treatment was adopted. And in 1934, the passage of the Reciprocal Trade Agreements Act made reciprocity — understood as equivalence in concessions — the accepted means of gaining improved access to foreign markets.

The New Era of the General Agreement on Tariffs and Trade (GATT) and the World Trade Organization (WTO)

After WWII, when the United States launched its grand design to establish an orderly multilateral framework for international monetary, financial and trade relations, the ideas of non-discrimination and reciprocity again became central to the global arrangements for trade.

But now, they were formally embodied in a multilateral agreement, the GATT. Two factors reinforced the great importance given by U.S. policy makers at the time to the principle of non-discrimination. One was the conviction of Secretary of State Cordell Hull that the trade discrimination practiced internationally in the 1930s exacerbated the bitter political rivalries in a period that had finally terminated in war. The other was the more commercial reason that U.S. manufacturers particularly resented the British imperial preferences erected in the early 1930s.

The ideas of non-discrimination and reciprocity have contributed substantially to the progressive reduction of trade barriers among the core industrial countries, including North America, Western Europe, and Japan, since WWII. These core countries, until very recently, dominated trade relations within the framework of the GATT/WTO, and their central focus was on the reduction of industrial tariffs. In earlier years, these tariff reductions were negotiated bilaterally on a reciprocal basis, and later, reciprocity was expressed in the adoption of a common tariff formula that replaced or supplemented bilateral negotiations. In principle, the core countries likewise adhered largely to non-discrimination in their trade with each other. But, in practice, they deviated substantially in the 1970s and 1980s by resorting to measures outside the framework of the GATT. These measures mainly took the form of voluntary export restraints or orderly marketing agreements. While their incidence fell more on Japan and some of the newly industrializing countries in East Asia and elsewhere, this evasion of GATT rules became so prevalent that it seriously undermined the respect for the system on which its existence depended. It was partly for this reason that governments during the Uruguay Round agreed to eschew these practices and so reaffirm adherence to non-discrimination.

Thus, up to and even including the Uruguay Round (1986–1993), it could be fairly said that the ideas of reciprocity and non-discrimination largely shaped international trade relations. But events brought about changes during and after the Uruguay Round. Reciprocity lost some of its relevance and clarity as a guiding principle; and, in the face of the proliferation of free trade areas (FTAs), non-discrimination in trade relations among states appeared to fade into the background.

Reciprocity and the Changing Character of Trade Negotiations

Two changes taking place during and since the Uruguay Round have muddied the nature of reciprocity as an idea guiding multilateral trade relations. The first is that, at the behest of the industrial countries, the content of trade negotiations has been substantially broadened; and the second is that the developing countries — thanks largely to their emergence as significant exporters of manufactures — have become influential participants in these negotiations.

Among the major industrial countries, the negotiation of improved market access for service industries and for capital remained based on a clear recognition of reciprocity. Countries agreed to a mutual widening of markets, yielding potential advantage to producers and investors on all sides. In this regard, even the new agreement on the protection of intellectual property rights (IPRs) only reaffirmed a mutually advantageous form of cooperation that had long been in place.

For the developing countries, however, the question of reciprocity was more complex and uncertain. Developing countries had earlier sought a special status within the GATT, claiming that the industrial countries should reduce their trade barriers to the developing countries in line with the principle of non-discrimination, but without reciprocity by the developing countries. The exceptional status of the developing countries was taken further in the 1970s when the industrial countries introduced the Generalized System of Preferences; and it was also given formal recognition during the Tokyo Round in the late 1970s when clauses relating to special and differential treatment were incorporated into the GATT. Further, particular groups of developing countries have been given additional, preferential access to industrial countries' markets. The other side of the coin was that the industrial countries felt free to disregard the spirit of the GATT whenever it proved politically expedient to do so. They did not hesitate to practice extensive discrimination against specific exports from developing countries, most egregiously when they imposed restrictions on textiles and apparel in the 1960s that burgeoned into the MFA.

Before the launching of the Uruguay Round, however, these unequal relations had begun to change. Many developing countries had made progress in modernizing their economies through industrialization; and they were all influenced, in varying degree, by the worldwide shift in beliefs about economic policy that, among other things, favored more outward-oriented growth. Indeed, several developing countries had unilaterally lowered their trade barriers and most had become members of, or sought membership in, the GATT.

During and after the Uruguay Round, some "rebalancing" in trade relations began to take place, though it remains highly controversial whether the negotiations satisfied the condition of reciprocity. While developing countries generally did not fully reciprocate in tariff reductions, they agreed, in principle, to the opening up of market access to service industries and to limitations on the conditions that could be imposed on FDI. These were both concessions that appeared to largely benefit producers and investors in the industrial countries. When the new international rules on IPRs were added to the list, the grounds for questioning the reciprocal character of the negotiations appeared substantial to many observers.

But there is another and less obvious reason why the idea of reciprocity has lost much of its clarity. This is because the Uruguay Round also gave weight to rules — like those relating to subsidies and FDI — that, while certainly bound up with issues of market access, also impinged directly on domestic policies and practices. Together with revisions of domestic laws and regulations required by the liberalization of the service industries, these initiated what some commentators have dubbed the "deeper integration" of markets. They marked the beginning of a new development in trade relations in which actual or proposed WTO rules could penetrate more deeply into the management of national economic and social affairs.[2]

[2] See Whitman (2004) for a discussion of the issues involving the deeper integration of markets, including pertinent references to the writings of Sylvia Ostry and others.

Some of the issues later raised by the industrial countries for inclusion in the Doha Round bore the same stamp.

While some developing countries may have tacitly accepted these changing rules, others have voiced serious misgivings. As in all countries, the desire to protect entrenched domestic interests for internal political reasons has doubtless been an active consideration. But there are other, more valid reasons. Of central concern are the limitations that these changes imposed on the development policies that these countries were pursuing. Since the early years after WWII, most developing country governments have — as discussed more fully in Section IV — used their powers to establish national firms in non-traditional sectors. They have created investment opportunities for the domestic business community (or political elite) through the use of a range of measures including tariffs, subsidies in one form or another, quantitative restrictions, and limitations on foreign investment. There is considerable concern accordingly that the freedom to pursue such development policies has been jeopardized by some of the rules adopted in the Uruguay Round.

Some of these new rules were apparently extending the principle of national treatment beyond its traditional, and limited, meaning through added restrictions on the freedom of governments to discriminate in favor of national firms by means of domestic measures. In effect, the leading WTO member governments were collectively seeking to create an international framework of rules and procedures within which their own markets could be more closely integrated with each other. It was, in more popular terms, to establish a "level playing field" in which the firms of each country would ideally compete everywhere on the same terms. The incipient framework drew on the ideas that guided the industrial countries in the management of their own domestic markets, and in particular, on those of the leading power, the United States.

This represents a new paradigm in trade relations. It is advocated by those who lean toward a cosmopolitan view of the global economy, one that sees the emergence of an increasingly integrated world market governed by common rules that regulate transactions in this single market. It is a view that coincides with exporting interests, and especially those of multinational corporations. But almost all countries also have national aims that they are not willing to surrender in order to accommodate their trading partners. Some of these aims are rightly dismissed by cosmopolitan proponents as essentially being obstructive rent-seeking activities, agricultural protectionism and antidumping measures being cases in point. But, as we argue later, there is a global diversity in aims and policies. Many of these aims and policies have deep roots in national societies, and they should therefore be afforded legitimacy. This is a reality that is reflected in the historically more familiar view of the world as composed of separate nation-states, each with its own national market. In this view, it is for each country to decide — in the light of its own social norms and economic aims — how far it wants to adjust its own domestic laws and practices in order to accommodate its trading partners and to gain a comparable adjustment from them.[3] It is a view that has long been the basis for achieving the reciprocal liberalization of trade.

III. Non-Discrimination and Free Trade Arrangements

The idea of non-discrimination has been seriously threatened by the recent proliferation of bilateral or regional free trade arrangements (FTAs).[4] While preferential arrangements existed long before the global trading system came into being and have complemented it ever since, the recent increase in the number of these arrangements has been nothing less than extraordinary. The WTO has reported (www.wto.org) that, by its definition, there were 250 regional trade agreements that had been notified, and that the number could rise to 300 by the end of 2005. The number may thus have roughly trebled since the WTO was first established in 1995.

To understand how this has happened, we should recall the statesmanship of the United States after WWII when it used its unparalleled power to establish a new international, monetary, financial and trading

[3] See Whalley (2005) for a perceptive analysis of how different social values might interact and change in the process of increasing international economic interdependence.

[4] See Srinivasan (2005) and Sutherland *et al.* (2004, pp. 19–28) for discussion of the erosion of non-discrimination.

system. At the heart of U.S. trade policy lay the conviction that an open, non-discriminatory system was in its own best interests and the world at large. Thus, in the early post-war decades, U.S. trade policy conformed well with the theory of hegemonic stability.[5] Confident in its power of command, the United States willingly provided the world with the public good of non-discrimination.

The first doubts in the United States about its confident role as a hegemonic leader in the economic sphere came in the 1970s when it abandoned the Bretton Woods regime of fixed exchange rates. This perception of loss in status was greatly augmented in the 1980s as Japan appeared to challenge U.S. leadership in such industries as semi-conductors, computers, electronics, and automobiles, and as the domestic mix of tight money and fiscal expansion led to dollar appreciation and an unparalleled trade deficit. The Reagan administration sought to counter rising protectionist sentiment by launching the Uruguay Round of multilateral trade negotiations, but the slow pace of progress did little to alter the more nationalist mood of the U.S. Congress. It was only another symptom of the changed outlook that, when the European Community (EC) sought to move forward in the later 1980s from a customs union to a common market through its Single Market program, this was widely misinterpreted in the United States as the emergence of "Fortress Europe."

These circumstances fanned a new U.S. interest in regional and bilateral trade agreements as an alternative to multilateralism and non-discrimination in order to gain greater foreign market access. The first major outcome of this new direction was the Canada–U.S. Trade Agreement of 1988. The U.S. interest, however, went further than its immediate neighbor, when President Reagan raised the vision in 1988 of a Free Trade Area of the Americas, an idea reiterated by President George H. W. Bush in 1990. When Mexico proposed that it should join the United States and Canada in forming a North American free trade area, it was welcomed; and the Clinton administration completed the negotiations after taking office in 1993. In the

[5] For an exposition and critique of the theory, see Keohane (1984). For a recent reassessment of the theory, see Pigman (2002).

early 1990s, the United States further extended this interest to the Pacific basin when it joined the forum for Asia-Pacific Economic Cooperation (APEC). A vigorous program of negotiating new FTAs was launched by the new Bush administration in 2001 with small developing countries in Africa, Asia, and Latin America.

EC actions in the 1990s did nothing to counter this trend towards greater regionalism, as both geo-political events and its own regional interests pushed the EC in the same direction. With the end of Soviet domination in 1989, a new political ambition of a pan-European union involving Central and Eastern Europe was created, and it welcomed formerly neutral members of EFTA into its fold. The EC, however, did not stop at the borders of Europe, as it entered into bilateral FTA negotiations with several of these countries around the Mediterranean region.. More recently, the EU has concluded FTAs with Mexico, Chile and South Africa and initiated negotiations with MERCOSUR.

It was the conduct of these leading trading powers that encouraged the proliferation of FTAs in the late 1990s and early 2000s. Any lingering fears among EU and U.S. policy makers that these arrangements might have systemic risks had largely evaporated by the early 1990s. The risk — often expressed in the late 1980s — that three huge mutually exclusive trading blocs centered around the EU, the United States, and (more hypothetically) Japan, might emerge, no longer seemed to have much substance. After all, the main thrust of post-war trade liberalization has been the reductions of trade barriers among the major industrial countries themselves; and it is in no small part a consequence of such liberalization that commercial relations among these countries have become increasingly interlocked. Much of their trade is intra-industry; the sales of affiliates in each other's territory exceed their exports to each other; much of their FDI goes toward each other; and they are intertwined through an extensive network of mergers, alliances, licensing arrangements, and other business relations. Their degree of commercial and economic interdependence thus militates strongly against any possibility of their raising barriers against each other in order to form more exclusive trading areas with their FTA partners. Further, in instances where the major industrial countries might have viewed each other's actions as intended to gain a sheltered market in a third country, they have been able to counter such possible rivalry by negotiating parallel agreements themselves, thereby taking out the sting of trade diversion of the bilateral or regional FTAs. FTAs thus apparently offer a way of making easy, if modest, additional gains in market access and can also coincidentally serve as useful instruments of foreign policy for the leading trading powers.

Other countries elsewhere have followed suit. FTAs among groups of developing countries have, of course, long existed and have usually been intended to widen markets among neighboring countries in the process of industrialization. But the late 1990s and early 2000s saw an exceptional burst of activity among both more and less industrialized countries. Japan, so long an upholder of the principle of non-discrimination, entered into bilateral negotiations with several countries in Asia and Latin America; and so also did South Korea. China, followed by Japan, proposed the formation of a larger FTA with the ASEAN countries. Similarly, with a new-found interest in enlarging its foreign market access, India established an FTA with neighboring countries (SAFTA), signed FTAs with Singapore and Thailand, and proposed a free trade link with ASEAN. Further, the ASEAN members formed an FTA in 2003, while MERCOSUR sought to enlarge its membership in its surrounding region. African countries also formed several sub-regional trading groups. This listing of recent developing countries' FTA initiatives is certainly incomplete, but it is indicative of the new activity.

The Systemic Effects of FTAs

In international trade relations, the countries of the world have always searched for some balance between the propensity to exchange commercial preferences with political or economic allies and the simultaneous desire to safeguard commercial transactions from arbitrary political interventions by other governments. Since WWII, an effective balance has been maintained by adherence to the idea of non-discrimination — even if honored as often in the breach as in the observance. As a consequence, the momentum toward progressive reduction in multilateral trade barriers has been sustained. At no time have the industrial countries sought to form exclusionary trading areas either by raising their own margins of preference or by persuading their trading partners to do so.

Within this largely benign environment, it is quite plausible to argue that the lowering of trade barriers within FTAs is contributing positively to global trade liberalization; and history may well prove this right. That some of the very large developing countries — like Brazil, China and India — have been forming FTAs, only adds to the positive momentum, especially when we recall that trade among developing countries themselves encounters high trade barriers.

But it remains true that FTAs are a slow, messy and inefficient way of progressing toward greater global trade liberalization. Though FTAs may generally enhance the economic welfare of FTA partners — at least in static terms — they also cause trade diversion from third countries and can thus generate inefficiencies as well as exacerbate global trade tensions. FTAs, moreover, require separate rules of origin for different arrangements, a situation that Jagdish Bhagwati has famously described as producing a "spaghetti bowl" of overlapping regulations. FTAs also create a vested interest in the preservation of preferences and in resistance to multilateral trade liberalization.

Further, recent FTAs between industrial and developing countries have some even larger deficiencies. First, the balance of bargaining power greatly favors the industrial countries, opens the door to a relationship of dependency, and constrains the developing countries in pursuing independent economic policies. Second, the arrangements fail to address some central issues in global trade relations — notably, agricultural protection and antidumping rules — where the participation of all the industrial countries is essential for progress. This latter point, indeed, touches on the still broader reason why FTAs are not a possible substitute for multilateralism. While roughly half of global trade is now conducted within the framework of FTAs, it is the global trading system that governs both trade relations among the long dominant economic powers of the EU, United States and Japan, and the relations of these powers with the newly emerging growth poles in world trade like Brazil, China and India.

IV. Establishing the Boundaries of the WTO

As already noted, world trade liberalization made great strides after WWII on the basis of the two major pillars of multilateralism: reciprocity and non-discrimination (MFN). Until the Uruguay Round (1986–1993), the periodic GATT negotiations focused on the reduction of external trade barriers to make gains in reciprocal and non-discriminatory market access. During and since the UR, these underpinnings of the multilateral system have lost their primacy. In the course of the UR, there was an extension of trade rules, directed most notably toward the liberalization of domestic markets for services and investment and toward the protection of IPRs. Following the conclusion of the UR, efforts were made to include the so-called Singapore issues of competition, investment, government procurement, and trade facilitation on the agenda of the WTO Doha Development Agenda negotiations. Attempts have also been made to incorporate labor and environmental standards into the WTO. All of these developments reflect the idea, not simply of promoting trade liberalization among separate national markets, but of furthering global market integration through the convergence of national market regulations. In some degree, the breakaway from non-discrimination through the proliferation of FTAs only accentuates the movement away from trade liberalization based on reciprocal gains in market access.

In our judgment, the existing and proposed extensions of the WTO into domestic rule making may be misguided. We view the central role of the WTO as facilitating commercial relations among its member nations. The WTO should therefore not be an instrument to shape national markets and institutions so that they will conform to some idealized model of how a global economic system should work. There are boundaries to the extent to which WTO disciplines can, or should, superimpose themselves on commercial conduct in national markets.

The Boundaries to the WTO Regime

To clarify the appropriate scope of the WTO, Table 1 provides a categorization of the various actual or proposed disciplines of the regime. These include: (1) core disciplines; (2) disciplines that may require modification to take legitimate national interests into account; (3) preferential trading arrangements that do not inhibit

Table 1. The boundaries to the WTO regime.

Core disciplines

- Most favored nation (MFN) treatment
- Market access based on reciprocity
- Prohibition of quantitative import restrictions
- Customs valuation and procedures
- Transparency (especially in standards)
- Safeguards
- Antidumping
- Dispute settlement

Present disciplines requiring modification to take legitimate national interests into account

- Domestic subsidies
- TRIMS
- TRIPS
- Government procurement

Preferential trading arrangements that do not inhibit global trade (Article XXIV)

- Customs unions
- Free trade arrangements
- Sectoral arrangements
- Developing country preferences

National regulations for health, safety, and consumer protection

- Countries set their own national standards, without protectionist intent

National regulations wholly beyond WTO boundaries

- Labor and environmental standards
- Regulations affecting service industries exempt from market access negotiations
- Competition policy

global trade; (4) national regulations involving health, safety, and consumer protection; and (5) national regulations that lie wholly beyond WTO boundaries. While not included explicitly, allowance needs to be made under the foregoing disciplines/boundaries for provision of Special and Differential treatment to low income or least developed countries.

In considering the WTO boundaries, there are two conditions to bear in mind: (1) the positive economic nationalism that legitimately motivates most governments to pursue policies that are sincerely believed will improve the material well-being of their populations and sustain their social cohesion; and (2) the institutions surrounding national markets that are embedded in social mores and the particular structure of business organization. When WTO rules and procedures are pushed beyond the boundaries set by these conditions, they may sour trade relations and erode the general consent to the core disciplines on which the effectiveness of the WTO rests.

To expand further on the application of WTO boundaries, we now elaborate on the interpretation of these conditions,[6] addressing subsequently how the WTO "playing field" may be best delineated and the role of the WTO in dealing with preferential trading arrangements.

Economic Nationalism

Economic nationalism is widely used as a pejorative term, manifests itself frequently in international economic relations and policies and is usually rightly denounced by trade specialists as a regression into mercantilism. There is a long history of beggar-thy-neighbor policies in international economic affairs, and the guardians of economic rationality are justly wary of nationalist rhetoric. But that should not blind them to the reality that nationalist sentiment is a powerful force that also has positive economic consequences. The great revolution in rising expectations, which first began within some western countries in

[6] Issues of delimiting the WTO boundaries are also addressed in Hoekman (2002, 2004, 2005) and Sutherland *et al.* (2004, pp. 61–72).

the 18th and 19th centuries, has since swept around the world; and politically vocal people everywhere expect that their own national governments will take measures to improve their material well-being. Though the great majority of countries now have capitalist systems, beliefs about how governments could best accomplish this purpose vary widely; and they have changed within countries over time. But what has remained ever present is the responsibility that peoples place on their governments — as the highest political authority in their societies — to seek gains in national well-being. As illustrated below, such economic nationalism sets limits that have to be respected in multilateral rule making.

Domestic Subsidies and Industrial Policies

Among today's established industrial countries, governments broadly see themselves as fulfilling their responsibility if able to maintain technological leadership — at least in some sectors — or, at worst, not to fall behind others in the endless race toward economic betterment. Accepting that private enterprises should make most economic decisions in response to market prices, they see their responsibility largely as the support of education, provision of infrastructure, and promotion of general scientific and technological research and development. Such economic nationalism has been reflected in the WTO mainly through its rules on subsidies. While government subsidies to individual firms or industries are often seen as contraventions of "fair" trade because they may distort market prices, subsidies of general research and development are not so viewed. The lines between specific and general subsidies are, however, not always clear-cut. For example, in very large-scale industries like the aircraft industry, EU subsidization of the Airbus and U.S. defense procurement favoring Boeing have been an ongoing source of bilateral friction. Yet, until recently, the EU and U.S. policies have broadly remained in place, although they are now under challenge in the WTO dispute settlement procedure, albeit with an uncertain outcome. Other manifestations of economic nationalism stem from cross-border mergers and acquisitions that may threaten the independence of national corporations regarded as "national champions." But they have so far not been constrained in this area by the WTO since it has no agreement on competition policy.

Most developing country governments have been no less powerfully motivated by economic nationalism. In the earlier post-war years, indeed, the sense of national pride — enhanced by new-won independence — occasioned widespread nationalization of foreign enterprises and stressed the development of nationally-owned enterprises. While most governments have since shed their hostility toward foreign investment, they have not lost their determination to foster the expansion of a rising indigenous industrial sector. Countries that have made substantial progress in industrialization have generally made extensive use of policies intended to provide inducements to, and financial and technical support for, national firms to encourage expansion of production and introduction of new products and processes. By such means, they have sought to benefit from learning spillovers, and to overcome coordination failures that might otherwise impede their economic growth. However, such policies — pursued on the nationalist grounds that they promote indigenous development and evidently effective in the circumstances — are perhaps not consistent with the rules of the GATT/WTO as these rules now stand. But it is noteworthy that national policies have for the most part been considered to lie within the purview of governments and have not been challenged in the GATT/WTO.

Our position accordingly is that efforts to restrict domestic subsidies that constrain industrial policies should be carefully circumscribed in the WTO.

TRIMS and TRIPS

In the UR negotiations, agreements on "trade related" investment measures (TRIMS) and IPR (TRIPS) protection were incorporated into the WTO. These are clear examples of the extension of international rule making into areas of domestic policy.

The TRIMS Agreement fell short of what its sponsors — mainly the United States — sought. They had hoped for an agreement on foreign investment that, when taken together with GATS (which accorded foreign investors the right of establishment in service industries), would succeed in gaining less restricted access to the markets of other countries for their corporate investors. They also hoped that, once their investors had been granted access, such foreign investment would enjoy full national treatment. These aims were not realized. However, developing countries had to accept some restrictions on their freedom to apply conditions on FDI. They were no longer permitted to impose local content requirements on foreign enterprises to mandate their meeting particular levels of local procurement, or stipulate that foreign enterprises meet trade-balancing requirements. Underlying TRIMS is an evident conflict between the legitimate economic nationalism of developing countries in pursuing measures intended to advance their own development and the commercial interests of multinational corporations.

The TRIPS Agreement addresses long-standing issues of foreign piracy and counterfeiting of patents, copyrights and trademarks that have always been of concern to the owners of these IPRs. In the earlier stages of their own industrialization, the now industrialized countries were generally neglectful of foreign owned IPRs. Freewheeling imitation and reverse engineering of foreign products and processes were principal means of gaining new technology (Chang, 2002). However, as these countries themselves began to generate technological innovations, they acquired an interest in the reciprocal recognition of IPRs. What TRIPS accomplished was an extension of such mutual recognition to all WTO members. For a great many developing countries, however, the element of reciprocity has been largely absent from the agreement, since they have had few IPRs for which they might seek recognition abroad. On the other hand, the agreement has restricted their freedom to copy and apply new technologies at will. Further, utilization of new technologies patented elsewhere will require payment of royalties or fees, implying a transfer of financial resources from poor to rich countries.

Defenders of the new discipline point to the potentially beneficial development effects. Their argument is that, as the rights of patent holders are now more secure, corporations may be more willing to set up production in countries where they formerly feared that their patented processes would be surreptitiously stolen and copied. But against this is the check that the discipline imposes on the unrestrained transfer of technology. WTO members have, at least, recognized this in the special provisions agreed to in regard to pharmaceutical patents and the treatment of HIV/AIDS, malaria and tuberculosis.[7]

It is our contention that the TRIMS and TRIPS Agreements may well lie outside the appropriate boundaries for many WTO developing country members. We would argue accordingly that the broader investment measures that were part of the Singapore agenda should be permanently shelved. We would also argue that the transition period for TRIPS conformance be made open-ended for developing countries until such time as they themselves will benefit — both internally and through the reciprocal recognition of rights — by implementing the domestic laws and institutions needed to carry out the enforcement procedures of the Agreement.

Government Procurement

In the course of the Tokyo Round in the late 1970s, a plurilateral agreement on government procurement was negotiated to become effective in 1981, with a number of industrial country signatories. There are presently 28 signatory governments. The agreement was designed to make the procedures and practices of government procurement more transparent and nondiscriminatory as between domestic and foreign suppliers. The emphasis is on tendering practices and covers both designated national and local government entities, with specified threshold values for the contracts involved. While the number of signatory countries has expanded, it is noteworthy that comparatively few developing countries have become signatories. The reason apparently is that the procurement agreement

---

[7] A well informed and balanced assessment of IPRs and development is provided in the report of an international group of experts appointed by the U.K. government (Commission on Intellectual Property Rights, 2002).

is viewed as being overly intrusive in challenging the rights of governments to maintain control over the award of contracts and programs for public procurement.

We recognize that existing procurement policies in many countries may be inefficient, costly, and subject to rent seeking, so that measures to reform these policies may therefore be in a country's national interest. But it is not clear why such reform should be carried out under WTO auspices, especially since a substantial amount of public procurement may stem from pursuit of a variety of social and political objectives and programs that are at the foundations of domestic government policies and may only tangentially be trade related. It is not surprising therefore that many developing countries have remained opposed to inclusion of government procurement, one of the Singapore issues, as part of the Doha Development Agenda negotiations.

Markets and Institutions

It is obvious that national markets function within a framework of laws, regulations, and more informal, but well embedded, practices; and that the framework differs widely among countries. Some obvious forces that account for the differences are the social mores of each country, its political institutions, and the particular forms of organization of its firms and industries as its capitalist system has evolved. These have never prevented transactions across national frontiers. So long as traders share some core similarities in modes of commercial conduct, they have been able to trade advantageously with each other. It has been enough that they share respect for private property rights and contractual arrangements, and that they accept some judicial procedure for resolving disputes. But in a world of nation-states, traders have also found that the differences in laws, institutions and social practices may impede their access to foreign markets. This has driven the search in the GATT/WTO for common rules that would ensure greater similarity in competitive conditions. Firms in the leading economic powers have deemed dissimilarities from their own national conditions to give rise to "unfair" competition and have called for a "level playing field." This has been powerfully supported, at the intellectual level, by an idealized neo-classical model of markets that presupposes universal institutional conditions associated historically with the development of capitalism in the United States or Britain.

There are, however, limits on the extent to which nations can be expected to conform to multilaterally established rules that may challenge their own social mores or forms of business organization. To be effectively applied at home, rules have to be compatible with the prevailing beliefs and practices within which the domestic market functions. Rules that are in conflict will not be accepted or, if formally accepted, will not be enforced or will be enforced only weakly. Certainly, some distinction has to be drawn here between laws, regulations and practices that are deeply embedded and those that lie more on the surface or merely benefit rent seekers. Cumbersome and outmoded customs procedures, for instance, may not reflect any deeply held beliefs, and their reform may be impeded only by bureaucratic inertia. There is no objective test by which to determine where the line lies, but we can cite some reforms proposed as appropriate for the WTO that, in our view, exceed the proper boundaries.

Competition Policy

Competition policy is a case in point in which the diversity in forms of business organization among countries limits the possibility or desirability of common rules. There are many variants of capitalism as it has evolved in the unique political, social, and economic circumstances of each country. Perhaps two of the most striking circumstantial differences are the relation between the state and private enterprises and the interrelations among firms themselves. In most English-speaking industrial countries, for example, the relationship between private enterprises and government has historically been more adversarial and arms length in comparison with the more cooperative relation in many other countries. Likewise, there are many differences in the competitive or cooperative relations among firms that are socially regarded as acceptable. These give rise to differences in market practices that can be seen by foreign producers as impediments to trade.

An example of what we have in mind is the Structural Impediments Initiative that was prominent in U.S.-Japan relations in the 1980s and 1990s, and that involved U.S. pressure on Japan to change long-standing business practices and institutions that allegedly constrained access of U.S. exports and FDI in the Japanese market. The WTO was involved in two prominent cases dealing with U.S. access to Japan's domestic market in automobiles and film. The United States decided to drop the automobiles complaint and was on the losing side of the WTO dispute settlement decision to deny the Kodak film complaint. In retrospect, the U.S. actions may have been ill advised to begin with. It also appears that the Japanese government instituted measures on its own in recognition of the national need for institutional and policy reform in a number of sectors.

Arguments similar to the foregoing can be applied to developing countries. In our view accordingly, competition policy lies outside the appropriate boundaries of the WTO regime.

Labor Standards

Labor standards are another case in point. There have been strong political pressures to seek the incorporation of labor standards in the WTO. We need not rehearse the familiar arguments of the representatives of labor and of social activists about the exploitation of low wage labor in developing countries or recall the counterarguments about the weakness of the broader economic rationale underlying the labor and social activists' position. It is enough to note that the case for inclusion of labor standards in the WTO rules, on grounds of economic welfare, is widely regarded as very weak, both in logic and empirically. It is widely held that the best contribution that the WTO can make to raising labor standards is accordingly to facilitate the expansion of world trade since, almost everywhere, as economic growth has taken place and incomes have risen, working conditions have sooner or later improved. Nonetheless, the proponents favoring inclusion of labor standards in trade agreements have been powerfully reinforced by their claim to the high moral ground in arguing that, whatever the economic consequences, it is morally wrong to condone poor labor standards in other countries.

No one would contest the right of individuals or groups to advocate the norms of their society or to call for economic sanctions when the most egregious violations of human rights are being committed. In the present context, however, the issue is whether industrial nations, by virtue of their power, should, as a condition of trade, insist that other countries respect particular labor standards that they themselves value and that are interwoven with the levels of individual and social well-being, which, thanks to their long history of economic growth, they now enjoy.

Many developing countries see this demand as presumptuous and politically self-serving, as the governments of industrial countries appear to be placating domestic groups that either represent sectional interests or are not well informed. But there is a more pragmatic reason for rejection of this position, which is that it is very likely to be ineffective. The transplant of social norms from one society to another is exceedingly difficult to accomplish. Everywhere, changes in domestic regulations embodying new norms of behavior take place in response to demands from coalitions of politically influential groups within the country. External leverage applied through trade threats may possibly tilt the balance in favor of reform, but by itself will rarely bring about any lasting change in prevailing social beliefs and practices. What the inclusion of rules about labor standards in the WTO would most likely accomplish is its entrapment in disputes about policies that countries regard as wholly domestic affairs.

Environmental Standards

Many of the arguments just made concerning labor standards apply to domestic environmental standards, which will depend on prevailing social beliefs and practices and differences in per capita incomes between nations. In our view, just as with labor standards, the determination of environmental standards should therefore lie outside the boundaries of the WTO.

Health and Safety Standards and Consumer Protection

Another problematic policy area for the WTO is the range of measures that governments may design and implement with regard to health and safety standards and consumer protection. In this connection, EU policies regarding imports of hormone-treated beef and products containing genetically modified organisms (GMOs) provide an apt illustration of the limits of WTO policies. The issues here concern the rights of nations to establish their own national health and safety standards, including the restriction of imports deemed to contravene national standards. We recognize that standards can be and have been used for protectionist purposes, and that there may not always be a firm scientific basis to warrant certain standards. But so long as governments believe it is in the national interest to protect public health, the right to do so should be respected. Depending on how scientific evidence evolves, governments may then decide over time to moderate their restrictions, as, for example, the EU has been doing recently with GMOs. This suggests accordingly that the rules and decisions of the WTO should not be rigidly applied in cases in which public health is at issue, and there is lacking a consensus regarding the available scientific evidence for the production and processing of the products involved.

The Playing Field

So, if we accept the limits described above, how is the WTO's playing field to be defined? The role of the WTO is to provide a framework in which governments can negotiate and monitor the reduction of impediments to trade that serve no larger purpose than the protection of sectional interests within individual countries. Such impediments cannot be legitimately defended on the kinds of grounds discussed above. They serve only to lower economic efficiency within the countries in which they are practiced and deprive producers in other countries of wider market access. The world abounds in these impediments, and their gradual reduction is the *raison d'etre* of the WTO. Drawing the line between these impediments and those that have larger purposes is the task of the WTO rules.

As already mentioned, agricultural impediments illustrate this point. Even if, for example, as the EU, Japan, and other nations assert, the subsidization of agriculture has broad social as well as economic aims, it is an inefficient way of accomplishing the social purposes as well as meeting economic needs. The economic case against agricultural subsidization as serving sectional interests and lowering national efficiency appears to be well founded. A similar case can be made against the resort to antidumping measures that are the policy of choice by protectionist interests in developed countries and have become increasingly widespread in developing countries.

Sectional interests are, of course, everywhere and governments are rarely independent of them. For individual governments, trade negotiations based on reciprocity have the advantage that they pit export interests against sectional protectionist interests. Negotiations force governments that want wider market access abroad to liberalize at home. It is a great benefit of the WTO that, in bringing countries together around the negotiating table, pressures are openly and internationally placed on protectionist domestic interests.

Many issues are not clear-cut and rules can never be drawn that are always unambiguous or that foresee changing circumstances. A mechanism for dispute settlement is consequently essential, but it should not be called upon to adjudicate on policy issues. Its business is the interpretation of existing rules, not the formation of policy. So, in the rules making process, it is important that new rules should enjoy widespread consent.

Free Trade Agreements

We need finally to consider how the WTO boundaries should be defined with respect to FTAs. As discussed above, FTAs often manifest the "real politik" that motivates nation-states in pursuing national self-interest in their external relations. Many FTAs that have been negotiated involve neighboring countries that already trade extensively with each other, so that there has been comparatively little trade diversion, except perhaps in some labor-intensive sectors such as textiles and clothing.

Except for U.S. FTAs, most other FTAs are confined mainly to the bilateral removal of tariffs and quotas. U.S. FTAs are more invasive in seeking to extend the integration of markets to cover many non-trade issues and to impose conformity with U.S. institutions and policies. Nonetheless, FTA members are still bound by WTO rules, which may help to explain why we have not witnessed the formation of major trading blocs as was postulated might occur. It may be the case furthermore that FTAs are becoming generalized as both large and small countries are seeking to expand their arrangements to help offset preferences provided in previously negotiated FTAS. But there are some large countries like Brazil, China, and India that are latecomers to the FTA process and are not likely to become partners in FTAs with the major industrialized countries. It may well turn out then that these large developing countries will become bulwark supporters of the WTO multilateral system.

There is, however, some role for the WTO to play in encouraging the greater openness of existing FTAs by expanding FTA membership, thereby moving the trading system closer to multilateralism. It might thus become possible to dispense with the rules of origin and remove the distortions that have been created by the many overlapping FTAs that now exist. Continuing pursuit of multilateral trade negotiations will also serve to erode preferential trade margins incorporated into FTAs and offer countries greater benefits than they may obtain from FTAs.

V. Conclusion

In this paper, we have reviewed the development of the present-day global trading system. We have noted that the success of the GATT system prior to the Uruguay Round (UR) was based on the twin pillars of reciprocity and non-discrimination. But during and since the conclusion of the UR, there has been a pronounced shift toward the pursuit of conformity in domestic regulatory policies and institutions covering a variety of institutions, business practices, and social mores.

In our judgment, the expansion of the boundaries of the WTO into domestic areas may be misguided.

Countries cooperate with each other through the WTO in order to benefit mutually from international specialization. To this end, they negotiate reductions in trade barriers and agree on supporting rules of conduct to verify compliance. Businesses, after all, have a legitimate concern that reductions negotiated on their behalf should not be effectively annulled by domestic measures later taken by trading partners. But this does not mean that the WTO should be taken as a vehicle for the dissemination of values or economic beliefs that are not widely shared. The criterion of success for WTO rules is that they should be widely, and willingly, accepted as necessary to promote mutually advantageous trade relations. If this is not so, the cooperation on which the system rests is vitiated.[8]

To be sure, there are strong differences in views about where the WTO boundaries should lie. But too much energy can be poured unproductively into debate about the boundaries. Within the WTO boundaries, there is great scope for further multilateral action to lower trade barriers and widen markets. There are many trade barriers that do not bear close scrutiny as rational measures either from a national or an international viewpoint. They can neither be defended as measures integral to national growth or development policies nor embedded in social values or in the long-standing structure of business organization. Unbiased analysis would reveal that they are no more than the abuse of governmental powers to protect special interests.

But where does the drive to confront these interests and remove the protectionist barriers come from? In recent decades in the developing world, it has come sometimes from governments committed to a radical shift in economic policies that have privatized and deregulated at home and liberalized external trade. More generally, over time, in both industrial and developing countries, it has come incrementally through pressures from their own export interests to negotiate for improvements in market access abroad. Reciprocity has

[8] We elaborate further on this point in Brown and Stern (2005).

demanded, however, that countries face up to at least some of their own protectionist interests and remove barriers.

Thus, reciprocity in the reduction of barriers to trade in goods and services remains the key to further trade liberalization. There are many other actions that the WTO can, and does, take to facilitate trade and smooth trade relations. But its task should not be the integration of national markets into one grand global market. By the same token, the rise of FTAs has been eroding the principle of non-discrimination. While market forces and particularly the resistance of some of the major emerging economies may gradually result in restoration of respect for non-discrimination, the WTO could play a key role in convincing the countries that are parties to FTAs to change the nature and structure of these arrangements to move the trading system closer to the multilateral ideal and to continue pursuit of multilateral trade negotiations that will benefit countries even though preferential margins will be eroded.

Study Questions

1. Define reciprocity and non-discrimination (Most-Favored-Nation/MFN). What are the historical origins of these trade-policy instruments? What happened to international trading relations in the period between WWI and WWII? What was "conditional" MFN as used by the United States and why was this policy changed?
2. What was the purpose of the General Agreement on Tariffs and Trade (GATT) after WWII? How well did the GATT achieve its objectives? How did the WTO come to be formed, and how does it differ from the GATT? What has caused the broadening of the agenda of multilateral trade negotiations? How have developing countries been treated under the GATT and WTO? Why has reciprocity lost much of its clarity?
3. What is the meaning of a "level playing field" in international trade relations? What is the "cosmopolitan" view of the global economy? What is the "national sovereignty" view?
4. When and why did U.S. policy shift away from multilateralism towards regional and bilateral trade agreements? The EC and

Japan? Emerging market economies and developing economies? Why haven't the major industrial countries — United States, EU, and Japan — formed competing preferential trading blocs? Are free trade agreements (FTAs) a stumbling block or a positive movement towards global trade liberalization? How may FTAs constrain developing countries?

5. Are the existing and proposed extensions of the WTO into domestic rule making misguided? What are the boundaries or disciplines that comprise the WTO regime? What is the significance of economic nationalism and institutions embedded in social mores and the structure of business organization? How do the following issues fit within the WTO boundaries: domestic subsidies and industrial policies; TRIMS and TRIPS; government procurement; competition policy; labor standards; environmental standards; and health and safety standards and consumer protection?
6. How should the WTO "playing field" be defined? Should agricultural protection, antidumping, and other protectionist actions be dealt with in the WTO negotiations and rule making? What is the role of WTO dispute settlement? How should the proliferation of FTAs be addressed?
7. How successful has trade liberalization been in the past 50 years in the GATT system? What are the future prospects for reciprocity and non-discrimination as the keys to further trade liberalization?

References

Brown, A.G. 2003. *Reluctant Partners: A History of Multilateral Trade Cooperation, 1850–2000* (Ann Arbor: The University of Michigan Press).

Brown, A.G. and R.M. Stern. 2005. "Concepts of Fairness in the Global Trading System," in process.

Carroll, L. 1946. *Alice's Adventures in Wonderland* (London: Penguin Group).

Chang, H.J. 2002. *Kicking Away the Ladder: Development Strategy in Historical Perspective* (London: Anthem Press).

Hinde, W. 1987. *Richard Cobden: A Victorian Outsider* (New Haven and London: Yale University Press).

Hoekman, Bernard. 2002. "Strengthening the Global Trade Architecture for Development: The Post-Doha Agenda," *World Trade Review* 1:23–45.
Hoekman, Bernard. 2004. "Overcoming Discrimination Against Developing Countries: Access, Rules and Differential Treatment," Centre for Economic Policy Research, Discussion Paper No. 2694 (October).
Hoekman, Bernard. 2005. "Operationalizing the Concept of Policy Space in the WTO: Beyond Special and Differential Treatment," *Journal of International Economic Law* 8:405–424.
Keohane, R.O. 1984. *After Hegemony: Cooperation and Discord in the World Political Economy* (Princeton, New Jersey: Princeton University Press).
Pigman, G.A. 2002. "Hegemony Theory, Unilateral Trade Liberalization and the 1996 US Farm Bill," in P.K. O'Brien and A. Clesse (eds.), *Two Hegemonies: Britain 1846–1914 and the United States 1941–2001* (Aldershot, England and Burlington, VT: Ashgate Publishing Limited).
Srinivasan, T.N. 2005. "Nondiscrimination in GATT/WTO: Was There Anything to Begin With and Is There Anything Left?" *World Trade Review* 2:69–95.
Sutherland, Peter (Chairman) *et al.* 2004. *The Future of the WTO: Addressing Institutional Challenges in the New Millennium* (Geneva: WTO).
Whalley, John. 2005. "Globalization and Values," CESifo Working Paper Series No. 1441 (April).
Whitman, Marina v.N. 2004. "From Trade Liberalization to Economic Integration: The Clash between Private and Public Goods," in Jacob Ryten (ed.), *The Sterling Public Servant: A Global Tribute to Sylvia Ostry* (Montreal & Kingston: McGill-Queen's University Press).

Suggested Further Reading

Preeg, Ernest H. 1995. *Traders in a Brave New World: The Uruguay Round and the Future of the International Trading System*. Chicago: University of Chicago Press.
Rodrik, Dani. 2007. *One Economics, Many Recipes: Globalization, Institutions, and Economic Growth*. Princeton, NJ: Princeton University Press.

Chapter 5

Concepts of Fairness in the Global Trading System*

Andrew G. Brown and Robert M. Stern[†]

I. Introduction

How are we to assess the fairness of the global trading system as embodied in the GATT/WTO? Views about what constitutes fairness differ widely, and there is surely no incontrovertible yardstick. But can we be clearer about the criteria that are appropriate and what they mean in more operational terms?

Some would say that fairness is hardly a relevant idea in trade relations. There are the anti-globalization advocates who view the trading system as being dominated by powerful governments and corporations whose main concern is to enhance national interests and

* Published in *Pacific Economic Review*, 12(3), August 2007, pp. 293–318. Reprinted with permission from Blackwell Publishing.
† We wish to thank Dan Ciuriak, John Curtis, Alan Deardorff, Kimberly Elliott, Patrick Low, the conference participants, K.C. Fung, and members of the University of Michigan Research Seminar in International Economics for helpful comments on an earlier version of the paper. We wish also to thank Judith Jackson for typing and editorial assistance.

corporate profits to the possible detriment of the less fortunate within their own societies or the societies of poorer nations; they find capitalism to be inherently unfair. There are others who, though accepting the capitalist system, take a realpolitik view of trade relations. They share a view long ago expressed by Thucydides (1934) in describing how the much weaker Melians were called upon by the powerful Athenians to surrender their city. The councilors of Melos appealed for fair treatment, but the Athenian ambassadors replied that "...right, as the world goes, is only a question between equals in power, while the strong do what they can and the weak suffer what they must."

We do not accept either of these views. We take capitalism as the institutional basis of the trading system, and we do not find the realpolitik view to be an accurate portrayal of modern trade relations. The developed countries that — until recently — dominated GATT/WTO negotiations have observed "right" by claiming to adhere, in principle, to reciprocity, Most-Favored-Nation (MFN) treatment, and national treatment in their trade relations. Though there have been some large differences in political and economic power, the stronger nations have not behaved in the manner portrayed by Thucydides; for, trade relations among modern nation-states have not been based on military conquest but rely on cooperation secured through diplomatic persuasion.

The system of cooperation works within a skeletal framework of norms. The framework, however, leaves ample room for differences of views about fairness relating to such matters as the market access arrangements of trading partners, or their commercial practices, or even their different social standards as these affect trade. It is fairness in this context of inter-governmental trade relations, now greatly expanded to include numerous developing countries, that we address here.

We should note that our focus means that we do not directly address one other aspect of fairness relating to trade policies, namely, the internal distributional effects of these policies. It is certainly an important matter for domestic public policy that trade negotiations give rise to winners and losers within national economies. In this paper, we assume that these distributional issues will influence the negotiating stances of governments and affect their perceptions of fairness. In this way, they are part of our discussion of fairness in intergovernmental trade relations.

We take as a premise that, since membership in a system of cooperation like the GATT/WTO is voluntary, its rules and procedures rest on mutual consent. In the context of discussing fairness, this is a crucial characteristic. That is, unless there is a consensus about the fairness of the rules and procedures in the trading system, countries will not willingly abide by them indefinitely. Fairness is therefore an element in the existence and functioning of the system.

Such a system of cooperation is, to be sure, only approximated in reality. The powerful are more able to press for the adoption of rules and procedures that suit them, while the weak are more often obliged to compromise. It can be argued that, since participation is voluntary, no country need accept the negotiated outcomes if it believes that these run counter to its interests. But that is not necessarily so, since rejection would entail withdrawal from membership in the GATT/WTO altogether. A country would then lose all the rights embodied in the GATT/WTO regime, such as MFN treatment and the protections afforded by the dispute-settlement mechanism. Thus, there may be circumstances in which a country may emerge worse off from a round of negotiations, yet to find it has no choice but to accept the worsened status. Nevertheless, it remains true that, if ideas of fairness are seriously and persistently violated, the cooperation on which the system rests will be threatened and the system thereby undermined.

We do not explore the microfoundations of fairness, something that is addressed in the experimental and game- and negotiation-theory literature.[1] We believe that, while the judgments of individuals or nations in matters affecting them have inescapably a self-serving bias, they can all recognize that fairness appears to be met when certain

[1] See, for example, Carraro *et al.* (2005) for a review and synthesis of bargaining theory, negotiation theory, and the theory of fair division.

conditions are satisfied — like reciprocity in bargaining situations or equality of treatment in the application of common rules.[2]

In what follows, we argue that fairness in the global trading system can best be assessed in terms of two criteria: equality of opportunity and distributive equity. It should be understood that we do not advance equality of opportunity as a high moral principle. It is an instrumental criterion to be valued for its consequences, namely that it facilitates the reaching of inter-governmental agreements that protect and enhance the mutually advantageous trading system. Distributive equity can also be argued — somewhat more tendentiously — to be an instrumental criterion. That is, in correcting for the disadvantageous initial conditions faced by poorer countries, it is ensuring that all can respond to a legal, or formal, notion of equality of opportunity. For many of us, however, there is also a deontological element in the criterion insofar as we accept it as a moral obligation and do not insist upon it because of its advantages to ourselves. The problem that confronts us in this paper thus lies in defining these criteria in more concrete and operational terms.

It should be noted that we do not include the economists' yardstick of efficiency as a criterion of fairness. Efficiency is pertinent to the extent to which global resources are being used optimally. But no nation is likely to subscribe willingly to successive trade agreements

[2] In an interesting and insightful paper, Suranovic (2000) has classified these conditions into seven principles divided between "equality fairness" and "reciprocity fairness". Equality fairness includes non-discrimination fairness, distributional fairness, and golden rule fairness. Reciprocity fairness includes positive reciprocity fairness, negative reciprocity fairness, privacy fairness, and maximum benefit fairness. Suranovic describes each of these conditions in detail and provides examples in the context of international trade. Narlikar (2006) interprets fairness to mean legitimacy of process and equity of outcomes in the context of the GATT/WTO. She traces the shifts in attitudes of developing countries towards the GATT/WTO in terms of how the balance between these two concepts has changed. Her idea of fairness as a composite resembles our framework, but there remain difficulties of integrating them. Risse (2005) analyzes considerations of fairness that stem from the trading relationships among countries that reflect differences in comparative advantage, levels of income, and social institutions.

that leaves it worse off, no matter the gain in global welfare. The efficiency yardstick is, however, important in choosing among alternative ways of fulfilling the conditions of fairness. And the analysis of alternatives may in itself alter the perception of fairness that influences agreements. We should nevertheless be aware that the yardstick of efficiency pervades much of the commentary on the global trading system, and — ambiguous though it also is — may tend to overshadow considerations of fairness.

For the purpose of our discussion, we classify the agreements of the global trading system into four categories: commitments dealing directly with market access, such as tariff schedules and service agreements; rules that support market-access commitments by preventing the use of other domestic measures that nullify or impair the commitments or by facilitating the flow of trade; rules dealing with the use of measures to defend against alleged "unfair" trade or with dispute-settlement procedures; and rules dealing with the governance of the system. We define and illustrate the application of our criteria to the first three categories. We say nothing in this paper on the last category though it also raises large issues of fairness.

In Section II following, we review the yardstick of efficiency in order to put it into perspective in the context of a discussion of fairness. In Section III, we discuss equality of opportunity in market access. In Section IV, we ask what distributive equity means in relation to market access. In Section V, we turn to equality of opportunity in regard to supporting rules. In Section VI, we briefly discuss procedural justice, which is a special case of equality of opportunity. In Section VII, we consider fairness in the context of the Doha Round, commenting briefly on the views of Stiglitz and Charlton (2004, 2005) and presenting views of our own, particularly on market access arrangements between developed and developing countries. Section VIII concludes.

II. The Efficiency Criterion

For political leaders and their trade diplomats, bargaining to win gains in market access has been at the core of trade negotiations, and this is what ideas of fairness have turned around. For economists, however, this has not conformed with their way of thinking about rational behavior. Defining rationality as the maximization of utility, they find gains in market access an unsatisfactory standard in that it fails to capture fully the welfare benefits arising from trade negotiations. That is, it focuses largely on the liberalization of export markets and not on the effects of trade liberalization as a whole.[3]

For many economists — borrowing from welfare theory — a practically acceptable criterion of fairness would be that the trade negotiations result in a more efficient global economy. Greater efficiency is defined as a movement toward Pareto optimality, and in the context of international trade, that state would be reached when no country can be made better off without some other being made worse off. If, however, the losing countries can be compensated by the gaining countries, still leaving the latter with some net benefit, this would qualify as an improvement in efficiency. This compensation rule is an important qualification in international trade since gains in allocative efficiency made by individual countries may be offset by losses arising from terms-of-trade effects. However, beyond this compensation rule, the efficiency criterion does not concern itself with the distribution among countries of the welfare benefit that accrues from the trade negotiations. It is a utilitarian view of fairness which says that, so long as no country gains at the expense of any other, no country has rational grounds for resisting multilateral trade liberalization.

For most non-economists (as well as for some economists), a criterion that does not address the distributional issue appears quite strange; it seems to be evading a central aspect of fairness (a facet that is discussed below). Within the logic of general equilibrium analysis,

[3] Wonnacott and Wonnacott (2005) have argued that economists have tended to fall into the opposite error of focusing too much on the gains from unilateral import liberalization, neglecting the gains that come from the reduction of foreign trade barriers through reciprocal tariff negotiations. This is misleading since, as they demonstrate, reciprocal tariff negotiations are economically superior to unilateral tariff reductions. The former provides added benefits that the latter cannot. Moreover, while both yield favorable efficiency gains, potentially unfavorable changes in the terms of trade have to be taken into account.

however, the issue seems less relevant. Since the reasoning is that efficiency gains result from trade liberalization, the gains accruing to each country are determined, at least in part, by the country's own action in liberalizing its import trade. If it is within a country's own power to enhance its benefit from trade, the question of fairness among countries does not arise. It is true, however, that each country is affected by the others in so far as failure by the others to liberalize deprives it of the benefit of the expansion of its export industries. Thus, the one concern that the criterion has with the distribution of gains turns on the relative gains that countries make in gaining greater access to export markets.

Though many economists might generally admit that the criterion does not address the issue of the distribution of benefits among countries, they would still defend its value. They would argue that, in defining the conditions under which optimal output can be realized, it makes a major contribution to the assessment of policy measures affecting the functioning of markets. Its central theorem is that, provided certain restrictive assumptions are met, Pareto optimality would be realized when a state of equilibrium is reached in a perfectly competitive market; and so any movement toward this state constitutes a gain. Thus, most economists unhesitatingly support reductions in trade barriers as positive in their effects. They might admit that, because of the political economy of trade relations, the application of such a yardstick of efficiency to the outcome of multilateral trade negotiations may not be a sufficient answer to the question of fairness. But it does seem entirely reasonable that *some* assessment of the effects of the negotiations on the performance of markets is a relevant part of the overall judgment.

Disregard of the distributional issue is not the only criticism that can be leveled against this efficiency criterion. It derives from a theoretical model of the market economy that abstracts from many aspects of reality. Even when accepted on its own limited terms, it has to be qualified by recognition that market failures take place. In the context of international trade, it has long been accepted, for instance, that protection of infant industries on grounds of externalities is, at least in principle, a legitimate exception. Further, still within its own terms of static equilibrium analysis, the criterion disregards the costs of adjustment to a new state of equilibrium that follow from trade liberalization. These can be of no small importance. It is one characteristic of many economies — especially of those in the process of development — that they suffer from major structural rigidities arising from poorly functioning markets and institutional deficiencies. Adjustments to changes in market conditions can take many years. This is especially true of agriculture. Thus, for example, in response to lower-cost imports of foreign food, peasant farmers growing staple crops for subsistence and sale may be forced to abandon their land and join the ranks of the underemployed in the cities. Reemployment of the land may have to wait years for sufficient improvements in the rural infrastructure and institutions — such as the marketing arrangements, transport, farm-extension services, or the reform of land ownership — before more productive, and competitive, farming can reemerge. In poor economies with large pools of labor, both land and labor may thus remain idle for many years. Potential output may be lost and, what is perhaps worse, the erosion in the structure of rural society may endanger social cohesion.

The criterion of efficiency is also vulnerable to major criticism because it derives from static equilibrium analysis. It defines efficiency in terms of optimal resource allocation and not in terms of the long-term rate of growth in output. If efficiency is redefined to include the long-term increase in output resulting from productivity growth and resource accumulation, the policy prescriptions derived from static analysis may not remain the same. There is unfortunately much less agreement within the economics profession about the policy prescriptions appropriate for economic growth than for optimum allocative efficiency, so the issue is debatable. It is certainly quite possible that there are large overlaps in the policy measures that would improve both static and dynamic efficiency. Economists have pointed to the effects that measures to improve resource allocation may also have on economic growth — the spur of greater competition, for instance, or exploitation of economies of scale, or the knowledge spillovers that come from links with international markets.[4] It seems

[4] The relationships between trade and growth are analyzed in the pioneering work by Grossman and Helpman (1993).

quite plausible in reality that there may be substantial fusion of the trade measures affecting both static and dynamic efficiency when trade relations are being considered among economies that are at similar levels of technological advancement, have well functioning markets and comparable, supporting market institutions.

But for most developing countries (perhaps leaving aside small countries), whatever the positive effects of foreign trade and investment on economic growth, it seems unexceptional to assert that the pace of such growth depends primarily on the performance of domestic producers. There has to be a body of (private or public) entrepreneurs able and willing to organize new productive enterprises in response to sufficient incentives and supported by a stable framework of legal, financial and technical institutions. But domestic policies, including trade policies, that take account of the need to promote a growing cadre of domestic entrepreneurs, to encourage diversification and to realize the externalities that generate increasing returns, are likely to diverge from those that focus on the improvement of allocative efficiency. The former may argue for discrimination in favor of domestic producers, whereas the latter is neutral on the issue.

Thus, even accepting the utilitarian foundation of the criterion of efficiency, it does not provide an unassailably reliable and clear-cut guide to policy. Market failures have to be allowed for, and a dynamic definition does not lead to the same policy prescriptions. But as a surrogate criterion for fairness in the global trading system, its utilitarian basis constitutes a more fundamental flaw. In his critique of utilitarianism, Rawls (1971) noted that the idea of "the greatest good for the greatest number" is not compatible with forms of social cooperation entered into by equals for mutual advantage. All participants expect some benefit and none seek the greatest good of the greatest number. Without reciprocity, the voluntary cooperation does not take place.[5]

Despite the uncertain intellectual basis for the conventional criterion of efficiency, its prescription in support of free trade has a strong

---

[5] Amartya Sen (1988) has offered an extensive critique of the efficiency criterion. See, for example, his lectures "On Ethics and Economics."

visceral attraction for a great many economists. We suggest that the reason lies not solely in the logic of the equilibrium analysis from which it is deduced but in a broader belief based on two observations, one empirical and one historical. First, it embodies the simple, but irrefutable, truth — so persuasively enunciated by Adam Smith — that specialization raises living standards, and since "the division of labor is limited by the extent of the market," barriers to trade are inherently suspect. Second, it is consistent with the historical observation that capitalist enterprise, operating in ever expanding markets, has appeared to be the most effective way of raising the income and wealth of nations. For many, the outcome appears sufficient justification for the criterion.

III. Equality of Opportunity and Market Access

For the developed countries at least, the principles embodied in the GATT/WTO — reciprocity, MFN treatment, and national treatment — appear to have provided a working guide to fairness. They have been forged from long historical experience and have proved their value in promoting trade relations. They therefore deserve great respect. However, none is free from ambiguities or easy to define in operational terms. Perhaps the principle of MFN treatment is the least ambiguous though its clarity is now under heavy attack as the number of bilateral trade agreements, all presented ostensibly as free trade arrangements, has multiplied.[6] National treatment is fraught with disagreements about its interpretation and application, as we discuss later in the section on equality of opportunity and supporting rules. What we focus on here is the use of reciprocity as a guide to fairness.

Reciprocity

The notion of reciprocity appears operationally important because it assuages the nationalist sentiment that all states harbor and that could

[6] We do not comment further here on the relation between these bilateral arrangements and the fairness of the global trading system though the erosion of MFN treatment clearly does harm to the perception of fairness.

otherwise prevent them from gaining the improved market access that they want for their exports. Evidently, no government, unless convinced of the benefits of unilateral trade liberalization, is willing to be accused of giving away more to other states than it receives.[7] Indeed, it has sometimes been politically important for trade negotiators to claim at home that the concessions received in multilateral trade negotiations are greater than the concessions granted. Were this in some objective sense a reality, trade negotiations might have taken place much more infrequently since they would have amounted to a zero-sum game. But, within the clerisy constituted by the trade negotiators from different nations, this large political obstacle has been surmounted by adoption of equivalence as a conventional basis for mutual concessions.

The convention of reciprocity has undoubtedly played a large role in the history of trade relations. In bilateral trade negotiations, negotiators have often directly compared, product by product, the size of the tariff cuts and the volume of trade involved in order to assure themselves of equivalence. But this certainly is not an exact and faithful characterization of multilateral trade negotiations witnessed in the more recent past. Finger, Reincke and Castro (2002) demonstrated this very clearly for the Uruguay Round. In the tariff negotiations, they found no evidence that countries had sought to negotiate equivalent gains in market access if equivalence is understood in any precise, quantitative sense. Comparing changes in *ad valorem* tariffs (using $dT/(1+T)$ as a meaningful measure), they found for their sample that the tariff reductions given and received by individual countries did not correspond. For example, India and South Korea gave their trading partners reductions that amounted to 6.16 percent and 5.99 percent while the reductions they received were 1.22 percent and 1.87 percent. Moreover, when the tariff cuts for the sample of countries were multiplied by the value of the imports or exports to

[7] There may, however, be other motives for participation in a global trade agreement. Some governments, for instance, may welcome participation because it allows them to overcome internal opposition to the opening up of domestic markets. This might make them less insistent on full reciprocity.

which the cuts applied — a measure of the gains in market access — numerous countries recorded large imbalances. This lack of equivalence might, of course, have been lessened or made greater if we could include the potential gains in market access resulting from the liberalization of trade in services, and from the revisions or introduction of several rules that affected market access.

Nonetheless, it can reasonably be argued that, in recent negotiations among the developed countries, a rough sense of equivalence could be perceived to have guided them even if there was no close accounting of the gains in market access. In each of the major areas of negotiation, the mutual concessions among these countries were roughly comparable. In tariffs, for example, though the average reduction was not exactly the same, the differences were not large (since tariff levels were already low). Likewise, in the service industries, what negotiators sought was national treatment in each other's markets, and it could well be argued that, since firms in all these countries were more or less equally able to make gains in the others' markets, the potential gains in market access were comparable. Much the same could also be said of the changes made in rules such as technical barriers to trade, which affect market access.

However, this kind of judgment cannot be so readily made in regard to the outcome of the Uruguay Round negotiations affecting trade relations between the developed and developing countries. There was neither the same symmetry in the different trade measures on which the trade partners made concessions, nor could it be assumed that the supply responses to the reductions in similar measures would be roughly comparable. The most dramatic gain for the developing countries was purportedly the agreement gradually to dismantle the Multi-Fiber Arrangement (MFA). In return, these countries undertook to lower or bind their tariffs, remove quotas, open up their service industries to some degree, and abide by new or revised rules for such matters as subsidies, foreign direct investment (FDI), and intellectual property. In some of these areas of negotiation, such as the service industries or the new or revised trade rules, the gains in market access clearly favored the developed countries. Were these offset by a possible excess of gains accruing to the developing countries that arose from the mutual reduction or removal of tariffs and quotas by all countries? It is evidently extremely difficult to form a judgment and all the more difficult if we add in both the financial transfers implied by the agreement on intellectual property rights — though not a market-access issue at all — and the back-loading of the removal of the MFA quotas. Thus, with regard to the relations between developed and developing countries as reflected in the Uruguay Round outcomes, the criterion of equivalence in market access gains seems to recede into a fog of uncertainty.

Does this mean then that the criterion is useless? This does not appear to be so. In the earlier stages of multilateral trade negotiations, at least in relations among themselves, the developed countries have in the past adopted common formulae for tariff reductions and agreed on the inclusion or exclusion of other negotiable items on the basis of expected reciprocal benefits. It is when negotiations advanced to more concrete and specific levels that the attention of negotiators appears to have shifted from the issue of inter-country equivalence to an internal accounting of the political value or cost of the concessions gained and granted. At that point, there is no particular reason to expect any correspondence between the inter-country equivalence implied in the initial framework for negotiations and the political balance sheet drawn up at home. Even so, Finger, Reincke and Castro (2002) found that in the final stages of negotiations on tariff reductions, delegations still sought to assure themselves that all parties had made their "appropriate contributions."

Again, however, the initial usefulness of the criterion appears to have worked out much less satisfactorily in the Uruguay Round when relations between developed and developing countries are considered. The large differences among these groups of countries in industrial structures and in inherited trade policies (not to mention disparities in bargaining power) made for substantial differences in the content of the bargains struck. So, compared with the bargain struck among developed industrial countries, there was evidently less comparability in the negotiated changes in measures and more uncertainty about the outcomes measured in terms of the consequent expansion in exports.

Still, understood as rough equivalence, the criterion remains important. It counters the nationalist sentiment that can breed mutual mistrust and impede trade cooperation. For such cooperation, it is important that states perceive themselves as being treated as equal, and independent, entities. In so far as the gains in market access can be measured, there is an objective means of assuring every state that it has been so treated. But it has to be admitted that there is great difficulty in translating the criterion into measurable trade outcomes. It is only expected equality of opportunity, not equality of outcome, that can be the basis of negotiations among market economies. And if the outcome, does not correspond at all to expectations, the sense of fairness is not fulfilled.

Initial Conditions

Even if equivalent gains in market access could be realized in the rounds of multilateral trade negotiations, that would not assure countries of equality of opportunity in regard to market access. Countries enter into negotiations with many differences in the level and profile of their trade barriers, and equivalent reductions in trade barriers do not eliminate these differences. However, successive rounds of negotiations narrow the absolute differences and may eventually render them unimportant. This has been happening among the developed countries since WWII in non-agricultural goods and has begun more recently in some services.

But between the developed and developing countries, large differences persist. As has long been pointed out, there are biases in the trade barriers of developed countries against the exports of developing countries. The most obvious instance is the array of measures that restrict trade in agricultural products. Certain labor-intensive manufactures, most notably textiles and apparel, face relatively high tariffs. Tariff escalation by the degree of processing of primary products likewise appears directed against products in which developing countries have a comparative advantage. That these kinds of barriers introduce an overall bias into the developed countries' MFN trade policies appears to be borne out by the measure of trade restrictiveness constructed by the IMF and World Bank (IMF and World Bank, 2004). The measure covers some of the more important trade barriers — MFN tariffs, core non-tariff barriers (NTBs), domestic agricultural subsidy schemes, and the major preferential programs. As Hoekman (2004, p. 14) notes, when the preferential programs of developed countries are left out of the calculations, the measure indicates that low-income developing countries (as defined by the World Bank) would face greater barriers to their exports to OECD countries than would other exporters from developed countries.[8]

On the other side of the coin, it is also a fact that, among developing countries, trade barriers on non-agricultural goods and services remain high across-the-board. Over the last twenty years or so, numerous countries have unilaterally lowered their tariffs on manufactures, lessening the disparity in existing trade barriers. Some countries bound all their tariffs during the Uruguay Round but many bound only some. Whether the coverage was complete or not, the great majority set their bound rates at levels that were substantially higher than their current, applied rates. So, many countries have accepted only limited formal obligations in granting market access.

The gradual lessening of these embedded biases in trade barriers of both developed and developing countries is a condition of realizing fuller equality of opportunity in market access.

IV. Distributive Equity and Market Access

Does fairness demand that equality of opportunity in market access be modified, in some degree, to satisfy distributive equity? There are at least two grounds for supporting this position.

One derives from a sense of moral obligation to the poor. The great disparity in levels of living among countries and the very large numbers of people living in extreme poverty have convinced many that the governments of rich countries have a responsibility to assist the poor countries in alleviating their poverty. The most visible

[8] It should also be remembered that many of the OECD countries trade on a duty free basis with each other as members of the EU or NAFTA.

expression of this obligation is the provision of aid. But since foreign trade is widely seen to play a part in economic betterment, it is identified as another means of pursuing the same end.

It can also be argued that equality in market access will not be realized so long as some countries are unable to take advantages of the opportunities created by negotiations. The global trading system presupposes the operation of freely competitive markets in which firms in the participating countries respond to new opportunities. But a number of poor countries do not yet have such well functioning markets and merit favorable treatment to strengthen their capacity to exploit new opportunities.[9]

But what does distributive equity mean in the context of the global trading system? It is familiarly associated with the redistribution of income or wealth, but that clearly does not apply here. Though some Third World advocates argued otherwise in past decades, the trading system today is not seen as a vehicle for resource transfers. It is an arrangement for promoting commercial relations among firms and individuals in different countries that are expected to be mutually advantageous. In our view, distributive equity only acquires meaning in this context if the trading system contributes to accelerating the economic development of the poorer countries. This may be accomplished in one, or both, of two ways.

It is through gains in access to foreign markets that the domestic market can be enlarged and that specialization can be enhanced, leading to such possible beneficial consequences for growth as learning, economies of scale, and technological improvements. More controversially, it is also through protection of domestic markets that, at least in the earlier phases of development, domestic firms (whether nationally or foreign owned) can be induced to establish, to expand and eventually to become competitive with their larger, technologically more advanced foreign competitors. But how far individual

[9] Wealthy countries may, of course, have other motives for assistance to developing countries. They may want to promote development in order to limit uncontrolled immigration across borders, or to combat terrorism, or, more broadly, to exercise political influence. But these do not raise the issue of distributive equity.

countries can gain access to other countries' markets and how far they can gain their consent to protect their own markets, are matters that have to be settled in their relations with other countries.[10] Thus, the requirement of distributive equity in the global trading system is presumably that the development of poor countries should be favored through the common pursuit of measures that accord their firms preferred status in their foreign or domestic markets or both.

In practice, developed countries have offered favorable access to their markets through their several non-reciprocal preferential programs.[11] Under the Generalized System of Preferences (GSP), the developed countries have provided developing countries with preferential access to their markets since the 1970s. In addition, both the U.S. and EU operate other, still more favorable, schemes for particular groups of countries, such as the countries of Sub-Saharan Africa under the U.S. African Growth and Opportunity Act (AGOA) or the EU's Cotonou Agreement that favors the African, Caribbean, and Pacific (ACP) former colonies. Further, the developed countries generally provide still more extensive preferences to the least developed countries.[12]

---

[10] True, we cannot exclude the fact that countries may independently benefit from unilateral reductions in trade barriers and that, indeed, this may be an integral part of their growth strategy. Thus, viewing trade benefits solely in terms of national economic growth does not necessarily provide a comprehensive definition of all the benefits from trade. But it is part of a comprehensive definition and does raise the issue of equity.

[11] These preferential measures are sometimes discussed as though they were a means of redistributing current income generated by trade to developing countries. A criticism of preferential programs is, for instance, that the rent is sometimes captured by importers in the developed countries. But if the intent of the measure is to promote development, what matters is not the effect on the current distribution of trade income but the effect on production and exports in the developing country. Some long-standing preferential arrangements, however, clearly no longer serve any development purpose and are no more than mechanisms for income transfers. The arrangement covering the exports of a few developing countries under the Sugar Protocol of the EU is an example.

[12] For a review of the literature on the benefits of preferences for developing countries, see Hoekman and Ozden (2005).

These preferential schemes have been of some value, though often less than expected. Their product coverage is quite extensive, ranging in 2001 from over 60 percent of dutiable imports into the Quad countries from GSP beneficiaries to 100 percent for imports into the EU from least developed countries under its Everything But Arms scheme once the scheme is fully implemented, according to UNCTAD (2003). Measured as a discount on the MFN rate, the tariff preference also sounds quite large. Mattoo and Subramanian (2004) calculate that, under the GSP scheme of the Quad countries, tariffs are roughly 50 percent below those applied under the MFN, and more under the other schemes. However, in some schemes, the actual use of these preferences falls far short of their potential use. According to UNCTAD (2003, p. 5), under the Quad's GSP schemes, less than 40 percent of the covered imports actually entered the importing countries at the preferential rates.[13] One possible reason for this lack of use is that exporters found the transaction costs of the certification process too heavy in relation to the saved preferential margin. That is, despite the large discount on the MFN rate, the margin is, in fact, only some 2 to 4 percent on average, according to Mattoo and Subramanian (2004, p. 397). A more common speculation is that exporters were unable to comply with rigorous rules of origin.

The conclusion we draw is that, while the schemes have surely benefited individual producers, their impact on the overall export performance of countries is an open question. The fact that some 60 percent of the products listed under the Quad's GSP schemes were exported without the inducement of a preferential margin suggests that the schemes may have played only a minor role in assisting the export growth of developing countries in general. The main impetus may have come from internal economic growth, structural change, and export-oriented policies.

---

[13] We should note, however, that the fragmentary evidence, in UNCTAD (2003, p. 6), does seem to indicate that exporting firms in the least developed countries have responded more fully to the inducement, having recorded higher utilization rates. Preferential margins were, of course, higher and perhaps rules of origin were less onerous.

Much more controversial is the question whether distributive equity demands that the global trading system should also allow developing countries freedom to apply preferential measures in support of firms within their own domestic markets. Responses turn on the causal beliefs held about the effectiveness of protectionist measures in assisting national development. There is ample empirical evidence that the highly protectionist, import-substituting policies pursued by a number of countries in earlier post-war decades were often detrimental to sustained development. The policies encouraged the emergence of inherently high cost industries, contributed to biases in domestic cost structures that impeded export growth, and sheltered domestic enterprises from competition and the need to innovate. Greater openness has tended to be associated with higher economic growth. However, this criticism of inward-looking policies does not demonstrate that protectionist measures, as part of an array of domestic policies, are ineffective in contributing to the development of emerging countries. The recognition of the value of protection in fostering the establishment of new industries has a long tradition. In providing protection from foreign competition, protection may allow time for new firms to learn and to overcome scale disadvantages.[14]

These differences in causal beliefs are not likely to be resolved any time soon. Practically, the persuasiveness of the one view or the other depends a great deal on the specific circumstances of the individual country under consideration. Countries vary so enormously in their economic size and stage of economic development that any sweeping generalization may justifiably be suspect. This being so, any agreement on how the global trading system can fairly address the issue, is only possible if the differences in causal beliefs are accommodated. This means that the multilateral trade rules should make adequate allowance for the use by countries of protectionist measures that are defensible as developmental policies.

---

[14] The industrial policies pursued by countries like Japan and South Korea in the early phases of their modernization bear out the effectiveness of this approach in the right circumstances. For an insightful empirical and historical study of industrial policy in several developing countries, see Amsden (2001).

V. Equality of Opportunity in Supporting Rules

Developed Countries

Reciprocally negotiated reductions in the principal trade barriers are supported by other rules like those relating to customs procedures, the application of sanitary or phytosanitary standards, technical barriers to trade, the use of quantitative restrictions, and subsidies. Some of these rules partly serve to enhance market access in that they facilitate trade and reduce transactions costs. But they also meet the need of trading partners to reassure themselves that the value of the negotiated concessions on direct trade barriers would not be emasculated by other domestic regulations or practices. Underlying the formation of these rules has again been the criterion of equality of opportunity. Countries have sought equivalent treatment. Along with the procedures for dispute settlement and the use of measures against "unfair" trade, these constitute the rules of the game and are of great instrumental value in promoting a system of cooperation in which trade can flourish.

The process of rule formation has been, and continues to be, a fluid one. Since the GATT was first ratified after World War II, many of the original rules have been repeatedly revisited and revised, and there have been numerous additions to the rules. Most commentators would doubtless agree that countries are now more assured of equitable treatment than was the case fifty years ago; there is less evasion of the formal market-access commitments than there was. But, reflecting the diverse circumstances of member countries, every step forward has been made in the face of often strongly held differences of views on what constitutes a fair rule. Progress has been possible when countries have been able to bridge the gap in their different perceptions of fairness. Their perceptions have not necessarily merged, but they have been sufficiently close to make possible mutual accommodations for the sake of the greater trade cooperation from which they all benefit.

Political obstructionism motivated by a self-interested bias has, of course, not been absent in limiting rule formation. Despite no large differences of perception about fairness, agreement on some seemingly straightforward matters has sometimes been slow to reach. In the 1950s, for example, European countries complained about the so-called American selling price method of customs valuation that the United States used for some chemical products based on the domestic price of an equivalent product. This issue was apparently resolved during the Kennedy Round (1964–1967) in which agreement was reached on the use of customs valuation that would assure equal treatment. But the U.S. Congress refused to ratify the agreement, ostensibly on the grounds that the U.S. administration had exceeded its negotiating mandate.[15] It was not until the Tokyo Round (1973–1979) that a more uniform method of customs valuation was incorporated in the rules, as Destler (1986, p. 63) has noted.

The difficulty in arriving at rules widely regarded as fair also sometimes stems less from large differences in normative beliefs about fairness than from the technical complexity of the issue. Every national market functions within a framework of norms, laws, institutions and more informal customs that both facilitate and restrict market-driven transactions. While there are certainly some strong, but broad, similarities among the advanced market economies, as, for instance, in commercial laws, the differences in more specific practices are legion. Technical barriers to trade are one such instance, and the agreement reached during the Tokyo Round on these barriers was rightly regarded as a significant accomplishment. While recognizing the right of countries to set their own standards in matters like health, the environment, and consumer safety, the agreement encouraged countries to move toward internationally agreed standards that would facilitate the flow of trade. At the same time, by requiring greater transparency in national inspection and certification procedures, it lessened fears that technical standards would be manipulated to discriminate against traded products. The benefits of the agreement were expected to be reciprocal and therefore accepted as equitable.

---

[15] It was this experience that led to the introduction in the 1970s of the "fast track" procedure under which the U.S. Congress would have an up or down vote on the entire package of a trade negotiation submitted to it by the Executive Branch of the U.S. Government.

Its test, however, has lain entirely in whether the specific standards applied by individual countries to particular categories of products are seen as fair by others. (The beef hormone case to be discussed in a later section on procedural justice is one instance of disagreement.)

Agreement about the fairness of proposed rules is always more difficult, and sometimes impossible, to reach when the rules address issues embedded more deeply in national preferences for public goods. It has always been recognized, for instance, that subsidies could nullify or impair the market-access commitments made by countries in trade negotiations, and that some discipline to define the impermissible was needed. But virtually all countries have made, and still make, extensive use of subsidies in support of a wide range of social and economic purposes. These run from income support for farmers to the rationalization of failing industries to the development of technologically more advanced enterprises. In the commercial sphere, the differences among countries in the use of subsidies are in large part linked to the relation between the state and private enterprise that has evolved over time. The United States, at least over the last 25 years, has emphasized reliance on market-determined decisions, and in the Uruguay Round negotiations, it sought a broad definition of what constituted a subsidy and a narrow definition of subsidies that were not "actionable" under the GATT/WTO. Most of the other developed countries as well as developing countries wanted a more restricted definition of subsidies and a more inclusive set of non-actionable subsidies. Reluctant compromises were made for the sake of reaching some agreement, but it is doubtful if the participants are fully reconciled to all aspects of the agreement, particularly with regard to the possible abuses in using countervailing duties.

The more it is the case that proposed trade rules impinge on different national preferences for social and economic policy, the more difficult it is to agree on their fairness. The preferences may be rooted in strongly held, but different, normative or causal beliefs that make it extremely difficult, or impossible, for countries to agree on what constitutes equality of opportunity. But these preferences cannot be disregarded in rule-making if the system is to be judged fair.

They thus set limits on the extent to which trade rules can intrude into national economies.

Developing Countries

As noted, developed countries have been able to arrive at supporting rules when their different conceptions of fairness in the matters addressed have converged sufficiently to make the rules mutually acceptable. The specific terms of their agreements on different issues have, in their eyes, satisfied the condition of equality of opportunity. Until recently, developing countries have been weak and peripheral actors in such rule making, and it cannot be said that their conceptions of fairness have played a comparably influential role. The rules have emerged largely from negotiations among the developed countries, and they have tended to suit their circumstances. Not surprisingly, many developing countries have accordingly complained that the rules have been designed with insufficient regard for their particular policy preferences or their distinctively different institutional conditions.

Some proponents of universal application of the rules have argued that most of the obligations placed on developing countries are, in any event, welfare-enhancing since they modernize legal and administrative systems and promote the integration of the countries into the global economy. This judges the rules by the economists' efficiency criterion and, whether the assertion is true or not, it implies an approach that is not consistent with the character of the WTO as a system of rules based on consent given voluntarily.

It is not, of course, practicable that, in a complex, cooperative arrangement like the global trading system, every country should agree to every rule. Consensus has to be reached, and it is right that the world's largest traders should exercise the most influence. But reasonable attention to all differing views and interests is a precondition of voluntary compliance.

For many developing countries, a major criticism of some of the rules generated by the Uruguay Round has been that they place constraints on their development policy options. Rules of conduct governing the use of some domestic policy instruments, which are primarily intended to protect market-access commitments from nullification or impairment, have appeared to clash with the use of these instruments in pursuit of national development. We have already mentioned the subsidy rules, which will be discussed further below. But a similar concern applies to the agreement on investment (TRIMS), which placed other restrictions on national development policies, particularly in prohibiting import content requirements designed to promote backward linkages as a condition of inward FDI.[16]

It is evident that many developing countries face a quandary in regard to such issues. On the one hand, from a global viewpoint, it appears entirely reasonable that these countries should subscribe to rules that protect the market-opening commitments they have made in furtherance of their own trade objectives. On the other hand, many do not want to forego the use of such domestic policy instruments for national development. The appropriate line of division between trade and development measures has not yet been satisfactorily drawn in the WTO agreements.[17]

The Agreement on TRIPS, was, of course, a particularly egregious instance of a new condition being introduced into the trading system of rules and procedures without sufficient consultation among countries and without an adequate basis of common consent. Taken by itself, the Agreement lacked for many countries any clear evidence of reciprocal benefit — and, indeed, the benefit by any count was negative for some. Further, until later modified, it rode rough shod over the public goods preferences of many countries for the health of their

---

[16] Investment again figured among the Singapore issues proposed for the Doha Development Round as did government procurement, which may be another instrument of development policy, but these issues were later dropped, following the September 2003 WTO Cancun Ministerial Meeting.

[17] In rule formation during the Uruguay Round, the developed countries introduced the idea that, if a policy measure was trade related, it was a legitimate subject for rule formation. That was perhaps consistent with the aim of global market integration but far too all-inclusive. For developing countries, a better rule of thumb would be whether the domestic policy measures cause material injury to a trading partner.

populations. Proposals to incorporate labor or environmental standards into the WTO rules, with the intent of using trade measures to enforce compliance, have likewise been seen by many developing countries as an intrusion into the conduct of their own social policies. Though often subscribing voluntarily to international conventions on labor or environmental standards, they do not accept that the global trading system should be used as an indirect means of enforcement. Moreover, they fear that the incorporation of such standards would be open to protectionist abuse.

Many developing countries have also complained that there has been insufficient appreciation of the practical problems that they face in implementation of new rules. It has, for instance, often proved burdensome for developing countries to have to comply with technical standards that are established by the developed countries and that require progressively more complex certification and testing procedures.

The WTO has recognized these practical problems in some degree by the provisions attached to rules that allow for special and differential treatment (SDT). However, the mostly time limited exemptions with usually modestly longer times for least developed countries have appeared unrealistic for many countries.

It has generally been feasible for many countries, especially those long established as nations and with central bureaucracies capable of supporting a functioning market economy, to conform to the common rules, if given sufficient time to draft new domestic laws, revise administrative procedures and train staff. However, for numerous others, mostly small and poor countries without long histories as independent states and with weak central bureaucracies, or extremely small states whose size gives rise to large administrative diseconomies, implementation of some of the rules has confronted them with tasks that are both administratively and financially onerous and often rank low in their list of domestic priorities. Finger and Schuler (2000) have pointed out, for instance, that to conform to the WTO prescribed method of customs valuation, countries must first have in place an effective and modernized customs administration, and that is often not the case. An extensive overhaul of the existing customs administration thus becomes a prerequisite of conforming to the WTO rules.

In our view, realism demands a franker recognition by WTO members that there are a number of countries whose state institutions or economic size do not equip them to undertake fully all the obligations of the multilateral trading system. And it is equally only realistic to acknowledge that the development of the needed range of institutions will often take, not years, but decades. Hoekman, Michalopoulos and Winters (2004) have proposed that the countries qualifying for exemption should be composed of those that meet certain broad criteria like per capita income, institutional capacity, or economic scale; it would include all the least developed countries together with some other poor countries penalized by small size. These countries are capable of complying with core rules relating to MFN treatment, tariff binding obligations, the eschewal of quantitative restrictions, dispute settlement procedures, and trade-remedy measures. But any demand that they comply with all rules dissociates rule-making from reality.

An objection to the view just expressed is that it would be politically difficult in the setting of a multilateral agency, where decisions are made by consensus, to agree on the qualifying countries. The difficulty comes, not in adding countries to the qualifying list, but in excluding or graduating them from the list. Keck and Low (2005) discuss other proposals that refine the criteria and make them rule-specific. This approach does not alter the need for political decisions, but in diffusing the decision-taking among a number of rules, it might lessen the political difficulty. On the other hand, it envisages a more laborious process. In this context, it is also worth noting that it has proved feasible for the UN to establish, and periodically review, its list of least developed countries.[18] Moreover, what is at stake for other

[18] First established in 1971, the list contained 25 countries, and it now numbers 50. The reasons for the increase appear to have been several; these include the broadening and refinement of the criteria, improvements in data, the absence of sustained economic growth, or the actual worsening of economic circumstances in some countries. Failure to graduate countries appears to have played only a minor role in enlarging the list (UNCTAD, 2003).

members of the WTO in agreeing to a list of countries that might err on the side of generosity, is very minor. The importance of these countries in world trade is miniscule. In their analysis of the role of these countries in the Doha Round, Mattoo and Subramanian (2004) drew up a list of 62 countries whose combined share in world imports of goods and services was a mere 1.1 percent.

VI. Procedural Justice

Though broad agreement may be reached on the fairness of the adopted rules, this does not assure agreement on the fairness of their application. Conflicting parties may have quite different interpretations of the rules, being influenced not only by raw self-interest but also by their particular normative and causal beliefs. Whichever way contested rules are applied, they are not likely to satisfy all the affected parties. All that can be accomplished is to ensure that the procedures for interpretation and application of the rules are themselves fair. A number of the WTO's rules and agreements are, in fact, designed and implemented with the objective of establishing such procedural justice not only in dispute settlement, but also in such other matters as measures dealing with unfair trade and the negotiating process.

Most would agree that the dispute settlement machinery established as part of the Final Act of the Uruguay Round has generally worked well. A number of developing countries have successfully used the machinery, and it has proved important in resolving disputes among the leading trading nations. The task of adjudication is, however, a delicate and difficult one, for the adjudicators have to be careful not to go beyond the consensus views on what constitutes fairness. For example, in the EU-U.S. dispute over the EU ban on imports of genetically modified (GM) foods, the semi-judicial process was called upon to define the line between commercial activity and collective preferences. In order to accommodate differences among countries in their collective preferences for health and safety standards, the WTO rules allow countries to ban imports that do not conform to the standards that they have set for themselves. However, because of the fear that countries could abuse these rules for protectionist purposes, it was also agreed during the Uruguay Round that any restrictions imposed on health grounds should be scientifically defensible. In the case of the GM foods, the EU argued in support of its imposition of a ban on imports that there was insufficient scientific evidence that the foods did not harm human health. The U.S. response was that there was no evidence of harm to human health. Thus, their disagreement was not on the scientific evidence but on a difference in assessment of risk. This is a normative difference that precludes the emergence of a shared view on what is fair, although assessments of risk may change over time as new scientific evidence becomes available.[19]

Provided the dispute-settlement bodies stay within the spirit of the agreed rules, the fairness of the dispute-settlement machinery then turns on whether its procedures are equitable. One apparent inequity that many have pointed out is the asymmetry between large and small countries in their capacity to penalize any failure to comply with a judgment. If a small country is authorized by the Dispute Settlement Body to raise tariffs on goods from a much larger trading partner, this does not have the same effect as in the reverse case. The experience is, however, that the larger countries have not been encouraged to ignore dispute settlement rulings. They have evidently been willing to conform to rules of conduct that they have agreed to as fair in past negotiations.[20] A practically more important inequity, discussed by Hoekman and Mavroidis (2000), for many of the smallest and poorest countries is their inability to utilize the dispute-settlement process because of their lack of legal and informational resources.

When we turn to measures to defend against alleged "unfair" trade, the problems are different. It has long been recognized in trade agreements that trading partners should have the freedom to

---

[19] The turtle/shrimp dispute raised still subtler issues of the boundary between commercial activities and collective preferences.

[20] That is, they are recognizing the value of cooperation when the game is endlessly repetitive.

set aside their trade obligations unilaterally under certain circumstances. Thus, the WTO Agreements permit member countries to take action against predatory pricing, the subsidization of imported goods, or import surges. The difficulty is that the freedom is open to abuse — as frequently happens when domestic producers exploit the provisions to obtain protection for their industries. The provisions are especially vulnerable to such abuses since they rely on administrative decisions within the importing countries for their application. While efforts were made during the Uruguay Round to specify more carefully the criteria and procedures that countries were obliged to adhere to in considering defensive action, it remains a fact that the semi-judicial function is carried out by the administrative authorities in the importing countries. Still more exact specification of the criteria and procedures to be applied under the Agreements could further narrow the scope for administrative discretion in their application, but some room for interpretation would inescapably remain. What would do still more to enhance procedural fairness would be the transfer of the semi-judicial function to more independent bodies.

VII. Fairness and the Doha Round

Having reviewed at some length the different concepts of fairness that in our view are of paramount importance, we now consider how the issues of fairness can be applied in the context of the Doha Round. We begin by discussing the principles of fairness that Stiglitz and Charlton (2004) recommend to be applied in the Doha Round and that have attracted considerable attention. Thereafter, we draw upon the two concepts of fairness — equality of opportunity and distributive equity — with reference to their applicability to the Doha Round negotiations.

Stiglitz and Charlton Principles of Fairness

Stiglitz and Charlton (2004) have proposed a set of principles of fairness that they argue should provide a framework for the ongoing

Doha Development Round negotiations.[21] They state (p. 11) that: "It seems self-evident that:

1. Any agreement should be assessed in terms of its impact on development; items with a negative effect on development should not be on the agenda.
2. Any agreement should be fair.
3. Any agreement should be fairly arrived at.
4. Any agreement should be limited in scope."

The first principle calls for the use of general equilibrium incidence analysis to be carried out under WTO auspices to determine how countries are affected by different proposals for trade liberalization. The point is to determine which policies maximize the welfare gains for developing countries in particular. The second principle involves a "fairness constraint," such that the outcome of any liberalization agreement provides a larger share of aggregate benefits to the poorer countries, net of domestic efficiency effects due, for example, to reduction or removal of domestic subsidies such as agricultural supports. The third principle of "procedural" fairness refers to the openness, transparency, and conduct of the negotiation process and dispute-settlement resolution. It includes the design of the negotiating agenda and dispute-settlement procedures in ways to attain greater symmetry of power and information among both developed and developing WTO member countries. The fourth principle calls for limiting the scope of issues comprising the negotiating agenda and avoiding unwarranted intrusions into national sovereignty.

---

[21] It is noteworthy in this connection that when he was Senior Vice-President and Chief Economist at the World Bank, Stiglitz (2000) favored the principles of "fairness" and "comprehensiveness." However, he did not then spell out what he meant by fairness. He interpreted comprehensiveness to cover a wide variety of issues of potential benefit to developing countries, including what later have become referred to as the "Singapore issues." More recently, Charlton and Stiglitz (2005) have set forth a narrower scope of the priorities that they recommend for the Doha negotiations, with an emphasis on achieving greater market access for developing country exports.

In discussing their first principle, Stiglitz and Charlton (2004) and Charlton and Stiglitz (2005) cite the widespread use of computable general equilibrium (CGE) models that are designed to provide estimates of the potential welfare effects of alternative negotiating options. While they consider CGE modeling results as suggestive, they note that most of these models are comparative static in construction and typically do not take into account adjustment costs and potential dynamic effects of liberalization on productivity, flows of FDI, and changes in capital formation, all of which may be growth enhancing. Granting these qualifications about the present state of the art in CGE modeling and taking into account the lack of data on the trade barriers and domestic economic structure of most poor countries especially, we consider it unlikely that the Stiglitz–Charlton first principle of using modeling focused on developing country interests can be achieved in the short period of time to be covered by the Doha negotiations.

The Stiglitz–Charlton first and second principles appear to be a combination of the efficiency criterion with an emphasis on the welfare gains to be assessed by modeling efforts together with an application of the principle of distributive equity. The principle of distributive equity presumably enters in by analyzing alternative negotiating options that are focused on enhancing developing country welfare. But this fails to recognize that the criterion of efficiency is defective as a yardstick of fairness in the global trading system. Equality of opportunity, not maximum benefit as defined in general equilibrium analysis, is the condition that would collectively satisfy fairness, modified in some degree by recognition of distributive equity. Gains in static welfare are affected by these arrangements, but the optimization of static welfare — or its distribution among countries — cannot be used to determine what a fair set of arrangements should be.[22] Further, as we have argued, distributive equity in global trading arrangements appears to make more sense if understood as a means of

[22] Srinivasan (2005) provides a critique of the various writings and proposals of Stiglitz and Charlton. As he notes (p. 12): "...it is not obvious why the *share* of benefits from an agreement that accrues to poorer countries necessarily has to rise for it to be fair.

promoting development through the provision of preferential treatment at home or abroad to the firms of poorer countries.

The Stiglitz–Charlton third and fourth principles are less problematic, being similar to what we have discussed under the headings of procedural justice and the limitations imposed on equitable supporting rules by the need to respect differences in national social and economic beliefs and practices.

Achieving Equality of Opportunity and Distributive Equity in the Doha Round

We have presented our interpretation of fairness under the heading of two criteria: equality of opportunity and distributive equity. At the present time, it cannot be said that the global trading system corresponds closely to these two criteria, and there is ample scope for improvement in the Doha Round. Some of the rules supporting market access, as we have indicated earlier, do not sufficiently accommodate different national conditions, institutions or policy preferences to be generally accepted as fair, even when taken as a package. Procedural justice is also far from having been reached. However, we will confine our remaining comments to the primary issue of fairness in the market-access arrangements prevailing between developed and developing countries.[23]

Equality of opportunity in the negotiation of gains in market access is a definition of reciprocity. We have noted earlier that reciprocity has served well enough in past negotiations among developed countries but that, when applied to negotiations between developed and developing countries in the Uruguay Round, it appeared to be a very vague and uncertain criterion. The reason was that, whereas for the developed

---

[23] It is an anomaly of the present arrangements that removal of some of the existing distortions could seriously penalize some small countries. The reduction of subsidies and trade barriers to agricultural products is likely to have adverse effects on a number of countries that now enjoy preferred access to developed country markets or benefit from subsidized food imports. For some small countries, heavily dependent on a single export crop, the consequences may be particularly severe. The most elementary notion of fairness dictates some form of compensation.

countries, the criterion could be applied within each of the sectors or issues on which mutual concessions were negotiated, between developed and developing countries there was much less symmetry in the sectors and issues being negotiated, and large trade-offs were made across them. This is unfortunate since fairness can be more readily assessed when negotiations relate to like sectors or issues. However, so far as market-access negotiations are concerned, some bargaining across sectors is inescapable — though there could possibly be merit in striving for reciprocity within sectors.[24] Still, there would be some gain in clarity if the fairness of market-access negotiations were assessed separately from those relating to rule-making and procedural justice. As we have already argued, other standards of fairness apply to the latter.

A move to adhere more closely to market-access gains, of course, does not address the biases inherent in preexisting trade barriers or the great disparity in national economic conditions that give rise to the call for distributive equity. There is, as we have noted, a recognized bias in the trade barriers of developed countries against many of the products in which the developing countries have a comparative advantage. Developed countries can claim that the bias is offset by their non-reciprocal preferential programs and by the less-than-full reciprocity that they concede to developing countries in tariff negotiations. We suggest, however, that both fairness and efficiency would be better served if, over time, the bias in trade barriers were progressively removed while developing countries, apart from the low-income and least developed countries, moved closer toward full reciprocity.

An alternative to removal of the bias in developed countries' trade barriers is to make their non-reciprocal preferential programs larger and more effective. But it is highly improbable that these programs are ever likely to be made a more extensive instrument of promoting development in most developing countries. The successful export performance of a number of these countries alone militates against their more extensive use. Moreover, if the rationale of these programs is to encourage the formation and expansion of export-oriented firms and

---

[24] An obvious example in services is the right to make temporary transfers of low-cost labor in order to fulfill construction contracts.

not to transfer income to developing countries, then the programs seem largely relevant for low-income and least developed countries in the early stages of diversifying their production and exports. These programs have, in addition, undesirable characteristics when measured by the efficiency criteria. They generate inefficiencies in diverting trade from the lowest-cost producers, and they create overlapping rules of origin. Further, they are not necessarily stable, since they are extended unilaterally and can be arbitrarily withdrawn. In comparison with multilateralism, weaker countries are less protected from the use (or abuse) of trade measures by the powerful for non-trade aims.

We can also ask whether less-than-full reciprocity in tariff negotiations best serves the criterion of distributive equity if that is taken to mean favorable treatment of developing countries in order to promote their development. Developing countries appear to have been deterred from full reciprocity in part because of their belief that they should be able to protect their domestic production more than developed countries both for infant-industry reasons and because of the limitations on their capacity to adjust. There are good arguments, however, in moving toward full reciprocity, not least of which is that larger tariff cuts would encourage trade with other developing countries. But concerns about infant industries and sensitive lines of production also need to be taken into account if some weight is to be given to distributive equity. This might be accomplished by more specific measures than less-than-full reciprocity in across-the-board tariff cuts. For example, exclusion of a proportion of tariff lines from the tariff-cutting formula as proposed by India at one stage, makes more specific provision for branches of production that countries may continue to want to protect. On agriculture, a similar proposal has been made that certain "special products," mostly crops of subsistence of semi-subsistence smallholders, should be excluded from liberalization measures.[25]

[25] The protection of agriculture is, as we have suggested, something of a special case. The costs of adjustment to agricultural liberalization can be heavy in many developing countries, even threatening social cohesion. Particularly when staple crops are affected, there may be grounds for protection that are not developmental in the familiarly understood sense.

Another, still more specific measure would be revision of the rules governing the ability of countries to alter their tariff commitments on infant-industry grounds. GATT/WTO rules have long allowed countries to break their bound tariff commitments on these grounds, but the relevant part of Article (XVIII A) has been largely unused. This was mostly because, when the need arose, it was possible to invoke balance-of-payments reasons for breaching commitments, though the obligation to compensate affected trading partners for the losses sustained from raising tariffs has surely been an added deterrent. With conditions for use on balance-of-payments grounds made more rigorous, the issue of compensation comes to the fore. It is a highly restrictive condition, and it is accordingly difficult to say that the rule provides significant freedom to developing countries in the use of tariffs as a development measure. One possible solution would be waiver of the commitment under specified circumstances, possibly providing for a permissible number of waivers over a ten-year period. This is not far removed from the provisions in the present Agreement on Safeguards in which the protection of injured industries may be instituted in developing countries for a period of up to ten years.

The rules on subsidies and countervailing measures would similarly require revision. The present Agreement recognizes, in general terms, that domestic subsidies may play an important role in the economic development programs of developing countries. This, however, is not explicitly allowed for in the operational provisions of the Agreement. Domestic subsidies that may be challenged by trading partners include any that nullify or impair the benefits they are accorded through the binding of tariffs; and this again gives developing countries an incentive not to bind their tariffs or not to lower them. A provisional clause in the Agreement defined "actionable subsidies" to include subsidies such as those for regional development within countries or to support the implementation of environmental regulations, but it contained no reference to developmental subsidies. The clause was allowed to lapse in 2000, and its replacement would be the opportunity for a more development-oriented definition.

VIII. Conclusion

Any attempt to define fairness in global trade relations should teach a certain humility. Even if we could transcend the self-serving bias inherent in the judgment of all interested parties, there is still no conclusive and incontrovertible way of assessing fairness. We have suggested a framework composed of two criteria: equality of opportunity and distributive equity. Equality of opportunity is realized when there is reciprocity among countries in the reduction of trade barriers, when they adhere to MFN treatment, when the biases in initial conditions are removed, when the rules supporting market access are not only seen as equivalent but are also consistent with national preferences within countries, and when procedural justice is respected in such matters as dispute settlement and the use of trade-remedy measures. Equality of opportunity, however, has to be modified in some degree to allow for distributive equity — understood as the promotion of development. In this framework, the criterion of efficiency is not a primary yardstick of fairness, but it is relevant in choosing among ways in which fairness can be realized.

We have noted that, in market-access negotiations, reciprocity is of most value in realizing fairness, when negotiations are confined to like sectors or sub-sectors; it becomes more difficult to assess fairness when negotiations are more comprehensive. But in assessing fairness, a clear distinction should at least be drawn between market-access negotiations — to which reciprocity applies — and other rule-making issues — for which other standards of fairness are relevant. We have also noted that the substance of supporting rules and the introduction of new rules face limits posed by the diversity that exists among countries in their aims and conditions. Rules will only be regarded as fair if they respect the different, but strongly-held, national preferences.

We have argued that, in the context of the global trading system, distributive equity has meaning only in one particular sense. It has to be understood that the global trading system is not a vehicle for income transfers but an arrangement for furthering mutually advantageous commercial relations among countries. Since trade can help promote the development of the poorer countries, the relevant consideration is the effect of the system in doing so. Distributive equity thus turns around the question of whether the trading system gives preference to the efficient growth of production in the poorer nations through sales in foreign or domestic markets.

At present, the bias in the trade barriers of developed countries against goods and services in which developing countries may have a comparative advantage is only modestly offset by the non-reciprocal preferential arrangements that are in force. However, apart from those that apply to the least developed and other mostly small and poor countries, these preferential arrangements are not likely to be improved. Developing countries generally would, in any case, probably benefit more from a progressive reduction in the bias in developed countries' trade barriers. If this were accompanied by the embrace of fuller reciprocity in tariff reductions on their part, they would move into a more equal partnership with the developed countries in the global trading system. With the rise of the large, industrially more advanced countries like Brazil, China, India and South Africa as significant trading partners, that would seem the likely course of future events anyway. But many developing countries still have great poverty and are not going to shed their developmental status for many years. As we see it, the WTO rules should fully recognize this status by assuring them the option to use specific developmental measures.

Study Questions

1. Why must there be consensus about the fairness of the rules and procedures in the global trading system? Where does fairness come in? What are the meaning and significance of equality of opportunity, distributive equity, and efficiency? How do internal distributional issues relate to inter-governmental trade relations? What are the four types of agreements of the global trading system?
2. Why is the criterion of efficiency so important in the context of trade negotiations, and what does it have to do with fairness? What are the main criticisms of the criterion of efficiency? Does the criterion of fairness provide a reliable and clear-cut guide to policy?

3. What are the principles embodied in the GATT/WTO: reciprocity, most-favored-nation (MFN), and national treatment? What do they have to do with fairness? How is market access defined, measured, and equivalence determined in trade negotiations? In what sense were the Uruguay Round negotiations unbalanced? What is the difference between expected equality of opportunity and equality of outcome?
4. Does fairness demand that equality of opportunity in market access be modified to satisfy distributive equity? What does distributive equity mean in the global trading system? How important have been the trade preferences granted by the U.S. and EU? To what extent should multilateral trade rules allow the use of protectionist measures for development purposes?
5. What purposes do rules fulfill in global trade? What determines the fairness of rules and agreement on such rules? How are developing countries affected by the rules that have been adopted? Should allowance for acceptance of rules be made for particular developing countries?
6. What is procedural justice, and how can it be achieved? What is the role of dispute settlement? What are the issues involved in using measures to deal with alleged unfair trade?
7. What are the principles of fairness set forth by Stiglitz and Charlton to provide a framework for the Doha Round negotiations? How applicable are these principles?
8. How can equality of opportunity in relation to market access and reciprocity be achieved in the Doha Round negotiations? Should market-access negotiations be assessed within sectors or across sectors and distinguished from negotiations involving rule making and procedural justice? How should the bias in developed country trade barriers be addressed in the negotiations? Should developed countries' non-reciprocal preferential programs be expanded? Is multilateralism preferable for developing countries?
9. Should developing countries be permitted to use measures for infant-industry protection or be exempted from full reciprocity? How can intra-developing country trade be encouraged? Should domestic subsidies for developmental purposes be allowed?

10. What are the objectives for realization of equality of opportunity among countries? How may equality of opportunity be modified to achieve distributive equity to promote development? How should the criterion of efficiency be applied? Should the global trading system be a vehicle for income transfers to developing countries? How will countries like Brazil, China, India, and South Africa influence the design and impacts of the multilateral negotiations? What policies should be applied to the least developed countries?

References

Amsden, Alice D. 2001. *The Rise of the Rest: Challenges to the West from Late Industrializing Economies.* New York: Oxford University Press.

Carraro, Carlo, Carmen Marchiori and Alessandra Sgobbi. 2005. "Advances in Negotiation Theory: Bargaining, Coalitions and Fairness," Fondazione Eni Enrico Mattei, Nota di Lavoro 66, 2005 (May).

Charlton, Andrew H. and Joseph E. Stiglitz. 2005. "A Development-Friendly Prioritization of Doha Round Proposals," *The World Economy* 28, pp. 293–312.

Destler, I.M. 1986. *American Trade Politics: System Under Stress.* Washington, DC: Institute for International Economics, and The Twentieth Century Fund.

Finger, Michael J. and Philip Schuler. 2000. "Implementation of Uruguay Round Commitments: The Development Challenge," *The World Economy* 23, pp. 511–524.

Finger, Michael J., Ulrich Reincke, and Adriana Castro. 2002. "Market Access Bargaining in the Uruguay Round: Rigid or Relaxed Reciprocity?" in Jagdish Bhagwati (ed.), *On Going Alone: The Case for Relaxed Reciprocity in Freeing Trade.* Cambridge: MIT Press.

Grossman, Gene M. and Elhanan Helpman. 1993. *Innovation and Growth in the Global Economy.* Cambridge, MA: MIT Press.

Hoekman, Bernard. 2004. "Dismantling Discrimination against Developing Countries: Access, Rules and Differential Treatment," Discussion Paper Series No. 4694, Centre for Economic Policy Research, London.

Hoekman, Bernard and Caglar Ozden. 2005. "Trade Preferences and Differential Treatment of Developing Countries: A Selective Survey," World Bank Policy Research Working Paper No. 3566 (April).

Hoekman, Bernard, Constantine Michalopoulos and L. Alan Winters. 2004. "Special and Differential Treatment of Developing Countries in the WTO: Moving Forward After Cancun," *The World Economy* 27, pp. 481–506.

Hoekman, Bernard and Petros C. Mavroidis. 2000. "WTO Dispute Settlement, Transparency and Surveillance," *The World Economy* 23, pp. 527–542.

International Monetary Fund and World Bank. 2004. *Global Monitoring Report.* Washington, DC.

Keck, Alexander and Patrick Low. 2005. "Special and Differential Treatment in the WTO: Why, When and How?" in Simon J. Evenett and Bernard M. Hoekman (eds.), *Economic Development and Multilateral Trade Cooperation.* London and Washington, DC: Palgrave/McMillan, CEPR, and World Bank.

Mattoo, Aaditya and Arvind Subramanian. 2004. "The WTO and the Poorest Countries: The Stark Reality," *World Trade Review* 3, pp. 385–407.

Narlikar, Amrita. 2006. "Fairness in International Trade Negotiations," *The World Economy* 29, pp. 1005–1028.

Rawls, John. 1971. *The Theory of Justice.* Cambridge, MA: Harvard University Press.

Risse, Mathias. 2005. "Fairness in Trade," Conference on Political Economy of Fairness and Globalization, Tulane University (April).

Sen, Amartya. 1988. *On Ethics and Economics.* London and Cambridge, MA: Blackwell.

Srinivasan, T.N. 2005. "Doha Round of Multilateral Negotiations and Development," in process.

Stiglitz, Joseph E. 2000. "Two Principles for the Next Round or, How to Bring Developing Countries in from the Cold," *The World Economy* 23, pp. 437–454.

Stiglitz, Joseph E. and Andrew Charlton. 2004. "The Doha Round of Trade Negotiations: An Agenda to Promote Development and Facilitate Adjustment," Commonwealth Finance Ministers Meeting, Provisional Agenda Item 7, FMM(04)15, St Kitts & Nevis, September 28–29.

Stiglitz, Joseph E. and Andrew Charlton. 2005. *Fair Trade for All.* New York: Oxford University Press.

Suranovic, Steven M. 2000. "A Positive Analysis of Fairness with Applications to International Trade," *The World Economy* 23, pp. 283–308.

Thucydides. 1934. *The Peloponnesian Wars.* New York: The Modern Library.

UNCTAD. 2003. *Trade Preferences for LDCs: An Early Assessment of Benefits and Possible Improvements.* UNCTAD/ITCD/TSB/2003/8, Geneva.

Wonnacott, Paul and Ronald Wonnacott. 2005. "What's the Point of Reciprocal Trade Negotiations? Exports, Import and Gains from Trade," *The World Economy* 28, pp. 1–20.

Suggested Further Reading

Brown, Andrew and Robert M. Stern. 2005. "Achieving Fairness in the Doha Development Round," *Global Economy Journal,* Vol. 5(4).

Brown, Andrew G. and Robert M. Stern. 2007. "Issues of Fairness in International Trade Agreements," *Margin — The Journal of Applied Economic Research* 1(1), pp. 1–22.

Brown, Andrew and Robert M. Stern. 2008. "Issues of Fairness in WTO Dispute Settlement," in James C. Hartigan (ed.), *Trade Disputes and the Dispute Settlement Understanding of the WTO: An Interdisciplinary Assessment.* Elsevier, Frontiers of Economics and Globalization.

Kapstein, Ethan B. 2006. *Economic Justice in an Unfair World: Toward a Level Playing Field.* Princeton: Princeton University Press. Reviewed by Bernard Hoekman, *Journal of Economic Literature*, September 2007, pp. 753–755.

Part II

ANALYSIS OF MULTILATERAL, REGIONAL, AND BILATERAL TRADING ARRANGEMENTS

Chapter 6

Multilateral Trade Negotiations and Preferential Trading Arrangements*

Alan V. Deardorff and Robert M. Stern†

I. Introduction

For some years now, there has been a growing feeling in the United States and other major trading countries that their interests are not being well served by reliance on multilateral trade negotiations carried out under the auspices of the General Agreement on Tariffs and Trade (GATT). There has been considerable interest accordingly in seeking

*Reprinted with permission from Alan V. Deardorff and Robert M. Stern, eds., *Analytical and Negotiating Issues in the Global Trading System*, Ann Arbor: University of Michigan Press, 1994, Chapter 2, pp. 27–94.

† The research underlying this chapter was supported in part by a grant from the Ford Foundation to the Institute of Public Policy Studies at The University of Michigan for a program of research on trade policy. Helpful comments on earlier versions of the chapter were received from members of the Research Seminar in International Economics at The University of Michigan, Jon D. Haveman, James A. Levinsohn, Ronald W. Jones, Gary R. Saxonhouse, Bernard M. Hoekman, Carsten Kowalczyk, and various conference participants. We wish to thank Judith Jackson and Tonia Short for typing and editorial assistance.

the benefits of freer trade by means of preferential bilateral/plurilateral trading arrangements of various kinds. The purpose of this chapter is to investigate these issues.

To put multilateralism and preferential arrangements in historical perspective, it is important to recall that bilateral and plurilateral deals and arrangements have always been an important part of the trade policy environment,[1] and have coexisted with multilateralism from the start. In this connection, we may note that, beginning in 1934, U.S. tariff authority was transferred from the Congress to the Executive Branch in accordance with the Reciprocal Trade Agreements Act (RTAA). As Winters (1990, p. 1289) has remarked, this was done in an effort to offset the detrimental effects of the Smoot–Hawley Act of 1930 that had increased U.S. tariff rates to historic highs and engendered foreign retaliatory actions against U.S. exports. The idea was that foreign markets for U.S. exports might be opened if the United States in turn was ready to make concessions to open its own market. Under the authority of the RTAA, the United States completed twenty bilateral trade agreements between 1934 and 1939. As Winters (1990, p. 1290) notes, the bilaterally negotiated tariff reductions were relatively small. But what was important here was that all the agreements provided for unconditional most-favored-nation (MFN) treatment. This was necessary to insure that an individual negotiating country would receive the benefits of whatever further tariff reductions might later be negotiated between the United States and other countries.

Bilateral reciprocity combined with MFN was subsequently adopted as the *modus operandi* of the GATT, and, as we will discuss below, there have been significant elements of bilateralism in all of the GATT negotiations from 1947 to the present. Thus, while we often think of the GATT as a system based on multilateralism, this may not give due recognition to the role that bilateralism has played in the system. A further manifestation of bilateralism in the GATT was the

---

[1] The scope of bilateral arrangements is in fact much greater than implied here if account is taken of the many "friendship, commerce, and navigation" treaties and the bilateral investment treaties that have been negotiated over a long period of time. In addition, there are numerous sectoral agreements in existence.

inclusion of Article XXIV relating to the formation of customs unions and free trade areas. We will note in our later discussion that a substantial number of preferential trading arrangements have in fact been set up within the GATT system, and that Article XXIV has been largely ineffective in overseeing and disciplining these arrangements. What all of this suggests then is that the current world trading system is best described as a coexistence of multilateralism and bilateral/plurilateral arrangements. It is apparent therefore that nations have not opted for a purely multilateral system. The question then is whether this mixture of trading arrangements may be conducive or detrimental to world economic welfare.

The chapter proceeds as follows. We begin in Section II with a discussion of the principles of GATT. In Section III, we present a brief history of the main characteristics of the GATT negotiating rounds and an assessment of their accomplishments. Section IV is devoted to how preferential trading arrangements are accommodated within Article XXIV of the GATT Articles of Agreement and to a discussion of the characteristics and consequences of existing preferential arrangements. In Section V, we discuss more generally the advantages and limitations of multilateralism and preferential arrangements. In Section VI, we undertake a theoretical analysis of the welfare effects of the expansion of preferential trading blocs using a comparative advantage framework. We conclude in Section VII with some implications for the design of trading blocs with the objective of enhancing world economic welfare.

II. The Principles of GATT[2]

The haphazard history of trade policy prior to World War II, including both unilateral protectionism and bilateral deals to undo that protectionism, led after the war to the formation of the GATT. A very strong case can be made that the GATT has had a profound and

---

[2] There are many excellent discussions of the principles and functioning of the GATT, including Baldwin (1987), Bhagwati (1990a,b, 1991), Finger (1979), Jackson (1989), Jackson and Davey (1986), Patterson (1989), Winters (1990), and Wolf (1987).

beneficial influence on the global trading system. Since World War II, the GATT has provided a consensual framework of rules and procedures for the efficient conduct of international trade. In addition, it has served as a negotiating forum in which major reductions in trade barriers have been agreed upon and carried out. The two main pillars or guiding principles of the GATT are well known: *nondiscrimination* and *reciprocity.*

The principle of nondiscrimination means essentially that a nation's trade policies are applied in a uniform and like manner to all of its trading partners. Individual nations or groups of nations are therefore not to be singled out for special preferential or punitive treatment as the case might be. For the principle of nondiscrimination to work effectively, nations must act cooperatively and seek to enhance world welfare. This would rule out aggressive or exploitative behavior that is designed to benefit individual nations or groups of nations at the expense of others. In the event of disputes between GATT signatories, the presumption is that there would be impartial adjudication. The interests of small nations especially would therefore be protected against the possibly detrimental actions of larger and more powerful nations.

The principle of reciprocity is more pragmatic in character and arises from the idea that trade liberalization should be viewed in a cooperative context in which countries will exchange concessions on a reciprocal basis. However, the principle of reciprocity does not necessarily rule out unilateral liberalization. Rather, as already noted, reciprocity stems in large measure from the efforts of the United States, especially during the 1930s, to use reductions in U.S. trade barriers as an inducement to get its trading partners to do likewise. Narrowly conceived, reciprocity implies that concessions will be balanced bilaterally, and this is in fact how trade liberalization was effected during the 1930s. Under the GATT, particularly prior to the Kennedy Round in 1963–1967, negotiations were primarily bilateral. But what is crucially important is that the GATT embodies the Most-Favored-Nation (MFN) principle, so that any concessions that may be negotiated bilaterally are then automatically extended to all other GATT member nations. The GATT system can thus be viewed as a multilateral system in which there is nondiscrimination and reductions in trade barriers are made generally available to all countries that adhere to MFN.[3]

The GATT is intended to foster transparency of trade policy measures. This has been most evident in the legal binding of tariff rates by GATT member nations and efforts to reduce these bound rates by negotiation. Transparency has also been an objective with regard to the use of nontariff measures of various kinds. Greater transparency will thus facilitate international transactions by consumers and business firms.

The GATT focus on the reduction and removal of trade barriers and fostering transparency can be achieved most effectively in what Bhagwati (1990b) has called a "fix rule trading regime." This means a regime in which trade is guided by a set of rules governing access to markets, that is, rules that permit markets to operate in such a way that the actions of private transactors will serve to enhance economic efficiency and welfare. This is to be distinguished from a "fix quantity rule trading regime," in which trade is managed more directly by government authority establishing quantitative targets for exports and imports without regard necessarily to the effects that managed trade may have on efficiency and welfare.

III. A Brief History of GATT Negotiating Rounds[4]

As indicated in Table 1, there have been eight rounds of GATT negotiations since 1947. In the first GATT round (Geneva 1947), there

[3] Krugman (1991b, 1992a) asserts that the GATT is based on what he calls principles of "enlightened mercantilism." He refers to this as "GATT-think" whose basic principles are: (1) exports are good; (2) imports are bad; and (3) other things equal, an equal increase in imports and exports is good. He concludes nonetheless that the trading system has been well served by the principles of GATT-think. The reason is that GATT-think captures important political realities in terms of the way in which the interests of exporting firms are played off as a counterweight against the interests of import-competing firms. Seen in this light, reciprocity and MFN become the "hidden logic" in the GATT system as the prime vehicles for achieving the dismantling of trade restrictions and thus promoting the benefits of freer trade.

[4] The discussion here draws especially on Finger (1979) and Winters (1990).

Table 1. GATT negotiating rounds.

GATT Round	Counties Participating	Trade Affected (Billions of $)	Average Depth of Cut[a]	U.S. Tariff Reductions		
				Import Coverage[b]	Bilateral[c]	Multilateral[d]
1. Geneva, 1947	23	$10.0	35%	56%	n.a.%	84%
2. Annecy, 1949	33	n.a.	37	6	35	39
3. Torquay, 1951	34	n.a.	26	15	58	64
4. Geneva, 1956	22	2.5	15	20	74	80
5. Dillon, 1960–1961	45	4.9	20	19	69	96
6. Kennedy, 1965–1967	48	40.0	44	64	n.a.	91
7. Tokyo, 1973–1979	99	155.0	34[e]	n.a.	n.a.	n.a.
8. Uruguay, 1986–1994	100	n.a.	n.a.	n.a.	n.a.	n.a.

[a]Weighted by dutiable imports.
[b]Imports subject to tariff reductions as a percentage of total dutiable imports.
[c]Share of imports subject to a tariff reduction coming from the individual country receiving that concession.
[d]Share of imports subject to a tariff reduction coming from all countries participating in the negotiating round.
[e]Weighted by total imports.

Sources: Adapted from Finger (1979, pp. 424–425), Jackson and Davey (1986, pp. 324–325), Deardorff and Stern (1986, p. 49), and Winters (1990, p. 1291).

were 23 participating countries and $10 billion of trade affected by tariff concessions. For the United States in particular, concessions covered 56 percent of total dutiable imports, and, as Finger (1979, p. 423) notes, tariff reductions plus tariff bindings covered 78 percent of total imports. The next two negotiating rounds (Annecy 1949 and Torquay 1951) mainly involved newly acceding countries to the GATT, and in this sense these rounds can be considered as a completion of the first round. Once tariff bindings were effected, the Geneva (1956), Dillon (1960–1961), and Kennedy (1963–1967) Rounds then focused almost entirely on tariff reductions. There were 48 countries involved in the Kennedy Round and $40 billion of trade covered by tariff concessions. While tariff reductions also figured importantly in the Tokyo Round (1973–1979), the primary focus by then was on nontariff measures. The Uruguay Round (1986–1994) is the eighth negotiating round. It involved some 100 participating countries and had a large agenda, including negotiations on: trade barriers; sectoral liberalization (e.g., agriculture and textiles and apparel); GATT rules, procedures, and the functioning of the GATT system; and "new" issues (intellectual property rights, trade-related investment measures, and services).

All of these multilateral rounds might suggest that the world shifted abruptly after World War II from bilateral deals to a system of purely multilateral cooperation. Such was not the case, however. As Winters (1990) notes, the negotiations themselves were completely bilateral in the early GATT rounds, and their multilateral implication arose solely from the requirement of MFN. In an effort to deal with problems of free riding, the negotiated concessions were lumped into a single package and were provisional until the overall agreement was completed and signed. This was intended to provide a means of assessing the reciprocity of concessions. In addition, efforts were made to maximize the benefits of the liberalization for the negotiating parties. Finger (1979) refers to this as *internalization*, and it is measured as the imports subject to tariff reductions as a percentage of all dutiable imports on either a bilateral or multilateral basis. In order to maximize the degree of internalization, countries negotiated on a product-by-product, *principal supplier* basis, meaning that concessions were to be exchanged bilaterally on goods for which the two countries were each other's major suppliers. The importance of internalization can be seen in Table 1, where it apparently became increasingly difficult to select goods for negotiating purposes in the successive rounds. That is, the import coverage of U.S. tariff reductions decreased from 56 percent in the Geneva Round (1947) to 19 percent in the Dillon Round (1960–1961). At the same time, the bilateral internalization ratio in the Dillon Round grew to 69 percent and the multilateral ratio to 96 percent.

Given the obvious limitations of the product-by-product, principal-supplier approach in the Dillon Round, it was decided in the Kennedy Round to adopt an across-the-board form of tariff negotiation whereby tariff rates were to be reduced by a fixed percentage according to an agreed formula, with exemptions to be negotiated for industries that were deemed too sensitive to liberalize. It is evident from Table 1 that the import coverage of U.S. tariff reductions in the Kennedy Round was increased substantially as compared to the Dillon Round, and that the degree of multilateral internalization remained relatively high. This is noteworthy in view of the fact, as Winters (1990) points out, that the tariff negotiations still had a pronounced bilateral orientation. In addition to its tariff negotiations, the Kennedy Round agenda was intended to include negotiations on NTBs and agriculture and to give special attention to developing country exports. It was also decided to forego reciprocal concessions on the part of developing countries. As Winters (1990) and others have noted, the Kennedy Round did not succeed to any important extent in reducing existing NTBs, and the agricultural negotiations failed. It also appeared that the only developing countries to gain significantly in the Kennedy Round were those that did make reciprocal concessions, so that the "special and differential treatment" of developing countries was of questionable value to them.

The principle of across-the-board linear reductions of tariff rates with exemptions was continued in the Tokyo Round, again involving a significant element of bilateralism. But the Tokyo Round dealt primarily with the rules of the GATT system, including technical standards, customs valuation, import licensing and quantitative restrictions, safeguards, subsidies and countervailing duties, antidumping, government procurement, and civil aviation. The Tokyo Round constituted therefore a marked departure from earlier rounds in view of its focus on GATT rules and procedures. Since these are "constitutional" matters, they clearly do not lend themselves to quantitative assessment and to bilateral quid pro quo concessions. It also means that it is difficult to achieve consensus on the design and scope of the specific negotiating items, and, accordingly, that the negotiations may be protracted and nettlesome if there are significant disagreements among the major participants.

The United States led an effort to launch the eighth round of GATT negotiations at the GATT Ministerial Meeting in 1982, but this meeting was apparently badly timed in view of the ongoing world recession, and there were important disagreements about the agenda that was tabled. As already noted, the Uruguay Round was subsequently initiated in 1986. It is unquestionably the most far reaching of all the GATT rounds to date. The Uruguay Round has fourteen individual negotiating groups dealing with trade barriers, sectoral issues, GATT rules and procedures, and new issues. As Winters (1990) notes, it has an even stronger orientation towards "constitutional" matters than was the case in the Tokyo Round. It also seeks to address the difficult issues of agricultural subsidy programs, reaffirms the continuation of the special and differential treatment for most developing countries, and leaves the questions of the choice of formulae for reductions in tariffs and NTBs to be decided in the course of the negotiations.

The Uruguay Round was scheduled for completion in December 1990, but the negotiations were suspended because the United States and the Cairns Group of other major agricultural exporting countries considered the offer by the European Community (EC) to reduce its agricultural subsidies to be unacceptably small. The Uruguay Round negotiations were later resumed, but their completion was still contingent on whether the EC would make agricultural concessions that the major agricultural exporters were willing to accept. This means that the rest of the Uruguay Round negotiating agenda was being held in abeyance.

The experience of the GATT negotiating rounds is instructive with regard to the successes achieved and also the problems that have been encountered. First, it is clear that the tariff rates of the major industrialized countries have been reduced to relatively low levels, and, as a consequence, that tariffs on the whole no longer constitute major barriers to trade for these countries. Even though there has been a distinct bilateral orientation in the tariff negotiations, the degree of multilateralization of the tariff concessions has been substantial. Second, it is also clear that NTBs have not been reduced to any significant extent, although some reductions may be possible if the Uruguay Round were concluded on a positive note. Third, the Uruguay Round is the first time that issues of agricultural subsidies have been squarely faced on an international level. It comes as no surprise that the depth of domestic opposition to reductions in these subsidies was profound, given that the subsidies were in place for decades and that agricultural incomes depend heavily on them. It is perhaps regrettable that many other important issues were being held hostage to the agricultural negotiations, but it is arguable that the stakes in agricultural liberalization may be potentially greater as compared to these other issues. Finally, beginning with the Tokyo Round and continuing in the Uruguay Round, there has been a pronounced shift towards negotiations covering the rules and procedures of the GATT system. Many aspects of these rules and procedures touch directly on domestic policies in the major trading countries/blocs, so that there are bound to be important differences in the design and implementation of these policies and in the role that interest groups may play when it comes to making changes in policies.

The combination of the impasse in the agricultural negotiations and the pronounced shift towards negotiations on "constitutional" issues may be interpreted as testimony to the difficulties associated with multilateralism as efforts are being made to bring about changes in longstanding domestic policies in the major countries/blocs. It is in this light that the prospects for negotiating preferential arrangements seem appealing. In order to be able to evaluate the case to be made for preferential arrangements, it will first be useful to examine how these arrangements are handled within the GATT and to examine the characteristics and consequences of the important arrangements that have been implemented since World War II.

IV. Preferential Trading Arrangements and the GATT

GATT Article XXIV

In drafting the Articles of Agreement of the GATT, some allowance had to be made for preferential arrangements. The presumption was that such arrangements might be welfare enhancing provided certain criteria were met.[5] The details are set out in Article XXIV of the GATT, which is entitled "Territorial Application-Frontier Traffic-Customs Unions and Free Trade Areas." This Article is reproduced in the Appendix.

Article XXIV:4 states that:

> The contracting parties recognize the desirability of increasing freedom of trade by the development, through voluntary agreements, of closer integration between the economies of the countries parties to such agreements. They also recognize that the purpose of a customs union or of a free-trade area should be to facilitate trade between the constituent territories and not to raise barriers to the trade of other contracting parties with such territories.

It is further stated in Article XXIV:5(a),(b),(c) that "... the duties and other regulations of commerce ... shall not be higher or more restrictive than ... prior to the formation ..." of the customs union or free-trade area (FTA) and that the arrangement is to be concluded "within a reasonable length of time." The GATT is to be provided (Article XXIV:7(a)) with information pertaining to the arrangement in order that reports and recommendations can be made as deemed

[5] Bhagwati (1992a) suggests a three-fold rationale for inclusion of Article XXIV in the GATT: (1) full integration of trade among a subset of countries would give the bloc a quasi-national status that would be consistent with the single-nation MFN obligation towards other GATT members; (2) removal of all barriers would preclude special and more limited preferential arrangements; and (3) the formation of a trading bloc might further the achievement of freer trade on a global basis.

appropriate, and compensatory adjustments may be sought if rates of duty are increased (Article XXIV:6). Finally, Article XXIV:8(a), (b) states that "... the duties and other restrictive regulations of commerce ... are [to be] eliminated on substantially all the trade between the constituent territories in products originating in such territories."[6]

An indication of the major preferential arrangements that have been implemented between 1947 and 1991 is given in Table 2, which is adapted from Whalley (1991). A more detailed list of the 69 preferential agreements of various kinds and subsequent amendments thereto notified to the GATT between 1947 and 1988 is given in Schott (1989), who notes (pp. 24–25) that only four agreements were explicitly deemed to be compatible with Article XXIV and that no agreement was found to be incompatible.[7] This is not to say that criticisms of preferential arrangements have been absent in GATT deliberations. But it appears nonetheless that the GATT member countries have sidestepped whatever discipline might have been justified with respect to particular arrangements that did not meet the criteria of Article XXIV.[8]

Having described the GATT provisions for preferential arrangements and the lack of any effective surveillance of them, it is of interest to consider some characteristics and consequences of some of the most noteworthy existing arrangements.

---

[6] See Jackson and Davey (1986, p. 457) for a list of some of the problems of legal interpretation arising from the language of Article XXIV.

[7] See also the listings of regional and preferential trading arrangements in de la Torre and Kelly (1992, pp. 8, 9, 11, and 12) and Fieleke (1992, pp. 4–5).

[8] According to Patterson (1989, p. 361): "The effective destruction of Article XXIV as a serious restraint on FTA and customs unions began in earnest when the European Community was examined and subjected to very extensive debate under these provisions in 1957–1958. No agreement was reached as to the legal question of whether the EC satisfied the requirements of Article XXIV. Apart from political considerations, which dictated a tolerant attitude on the part of some, including the United States, the participants in these discussions concluded that the EC was going to go forward as set out in the Treaty of Rome, and if it were formally found to be 'illegal,' the GATT as an institution would be mortally wounded." See also the discussion of the role of GATT in influencing regional arrangements in Bhagwati (1992a) and Finger (1992).

Table 2. Major preferential trading arrangements, 1947–1991.

1947	Article XXIV included in GATT. Allows formation of customs unions and free trade areas under certain conditions.
1957	Treaty of Rome established the European Economic Community. A customs union involving Belgium, Luxembourg, France, the Netherlands, Germany, and Italy. Treaty went into force 1 January 1958.
1959	Stockholm Convention established the European Free Trade Association (EFTA) to go into effect 1 July 1960. Members included Austria, Denmark, Norway, Portugal, Sweden, Switzerland, and the United Kingdom.
1960	Montevideo Treaty established the Latin American Free Trade Association (LAFTA) comprising Argentina, Brazil, Chile, Colombia, Ecuador, Mexico, Paraguay, Peru, and Uruguay.
1960	Central American Common Market (CACM) formed. Included Costa Rica, El Salvador, Guatemala, Honduras, and Nicaragua.
1963	Yaoundé Convention between the EEC and former French, Belgian, and Italian colonies in Africa. Gives these countries preferential access to the EC and set up the European Development Fund.
1965	Australia and New Zealand formed a free trade area.
1965	Canada and the United States sign Automobile Products Trade Agreement (Auto Pact).
1967	East African Community formed. Included Kenya, Tanzania, and Uganda.
1967	ASEAN formed. Included Brunei, Indonesia, Malaysia, Philippines, Singapore, and Thailand.
1969	Andean Pact formed. Included Bolivia, Chile, Colombia, Ecuador, Peru, and Venezuela.
1969	Yaoundé Convention extended.
1973	European Community enlarged to include Britain, Ireland, and Denmark.
1975	Yaoundé Convention superseded by Lomé Convention. Extended preferential arrangements to include former colonies of Britain and widened to include countries in the Caribbean and Pacific.
1983	Australia and New Zealand formed Closer Economic Relationship to provide for a free trade agreement.
1984	United States implements Caribbean Basic Economic Recovery Act to extend duty-free treatment to 21 beneficiary countries in the region for 12 years.
1985	United States–Israel Free Trade Area Agreement enters into force. Over a 10-year period, all tariffs between the two countries to be eliminated.

(*Continued*)

Table 2. (*Continued*)

1986	Portugal and Spain join the European Community. Single European Act signed to provide for full European integration in 1992.
1989	Canada-U.S. Free Trade Agreement enters into force. Under agreement all items should be traded duty-free between the two countries by 1998.
1990	EC and EFTA undertake discussions on a European Economic Area which would provide for freer movement of goods, services, capital, and people between the two associations.
1990	United States announces "Enterprise for the Americas" initiative to explore a hemisphere-wide free trade zone involving countries of North, Central, and South America.
1991	United States, Mexico, and Canada enter discussions on a North American free trade area.

Source: Adapted from Whalley (1991).

Characteristics and Consequences of Preferential Arrangements

A great deal of analytical attention has been devoted over the years to the economic issues posed by preferential arrangements, but it would take us too far afield to review these issues in detail. For our purposes here, a convenient summary of the issues is provided in Wonnacott and Lutz (1989, pp. 69–70), who identify several considerations that relate in particular to the likelihood of trade creation or trade diversion and therefore to whether world economic welfare may be increased or lowered as the result of a preferential arrangement.[9] They note that the ratio of trade creation to trade diversion will depend on whether:

1. The tariffs of outside countries are high and the initial tariffs of member countries are also high. In this case, the formation of a preferential arrangement is not likely to be trade diverting since

[9] See de Melo, Panagariya, and Rodrik (1992) for a review and extension of the pertinent literature dealing with: (1) the welfare effects of trading blocs; (2) the role of economies of scale, factor mobility, and tariff revenues; and (3) institutional considerations. See also de la Torre and Kelly (1992, pp. 3–6) and Saxonhouse (1992).

there would not be a great deal of trade with outside countries. By the same token, the welfare effects of the preferential arrangement would be enhanced if the member-country tariffs on imports from outside countries were subsequently set at low rates.

2. The prospective member countries are already major trading partners and are close geographically.
3. There are important differences in comparative advantage among the member countries.

In addition, they argue that a preferential arrangement is most likely to be viable if the member countries are at similar levels of development and the division of gains from the preferential arrangement can be achieved without major economic and political disagreement. In this connection, Schott (1991, pp. 2–3) emphasizes the importance of the sustainability of the trading relationships among the member countries and the compatibility of their laws and regulations governing trade flows among themselves and with third countries.

It is interesting in light of the foregoing considerations to examine Table 3, adapted from Wonnacott and Lutz (1989, p. 76), which lists the important preferential arrangements that have been established and the changes in trade patterns that have occurred. The eight arrangements are classified into two groups according to the changes in internal trade prior to and after the arrangement was put in place.[10] Wonnacott and Lutz draw a number of conclusions about the experiences of the preferential arrangements listed:

1. The preferential arrangements in the first group, in which internal trade increased, generally followed an across-the-board approach to the freeing of internal trade, whereas the second group followed primarily a product-by-product approach. In the latter case, except for the ASEAN, there was a decline in external trade.

---

[10] It will be noted that Table 3 does not include the entry of Greece, Portugal, and Spain into the EC, the 1983 Closer Economic Relationship between Australia and New Zealand, and the 1985 U.S.-Israel and 1989 U.S.-Canada FTAs. Also, it does include arrangements that are no longer in force.

Table 3. Trade patterns of preferential trading blocs (percentage of combined GDP of member nations).

Association and Time Period[a]	Internal Trade			External Trade			Total Trade		
	Base	Later	Change	Base	Later	Change	Base	Later	Change
Readily apparent increases in internal trade									
Central American Common Market (CACM)[b]	1.8	10.0	8.2	33.4	33.2	−0.2	35.2	43.2	8.0
European Community (EC6)[c]									
1953–1957/1963–1967	8.1	13.1	5.0	20.0	17.9	−2.1	28.1	31.0	2.9
1953–1957/1968–1972	8.1	17.2	9.1	20.0	18.3	−1.7	28.1	35.5	7.4
European Community (EC9)[d]									
1968–1972/1978–1982	17.6	24.3	6.7	17.9	24.0	6.1	35.5	48.3	12.8
European Free Trade Association (EFTA)[e]									
1955–1959/1965–1969	6.9	8.7	1.8	30.1	27.4	−2.7	37.0	36.1	−0.9
Andean Pact[f]									
1964–1968/1974–1978	0.9	2.4	1.5	30.5	38.2	7.7	31.4	40.6	9.2

(*Continued*)

Table 3. (*Continued*)

Association and Time Period[a]	Internal Trade			External Trade			Total Trade		
	Base	Later	Change	Base	Later	Change	Base	Later	Change
No obvious effect on internal trade									
Association of Southeast Asian Nations (ASEAN)[g]	7.0	7.8	0.8	37.5	49.9	12.4	44.5	57.7	13.2
New Zealand–Australia FTA									
1961–1965/1971–1975	1.7	1.8	0.1	28.6	24.8	–3.8	30.3	26.6	–37.0
Latin American Free Trade Area (LAFTA)[h]	1.6	1.6	0.0	19.0	13.1	–5.9	20.6	14.7	–5.9
East African Community (EAC)[i]	6.3	3.9	–2.4	35.6	34.5	–1.1	41.9	38.4	–3.5

[a]Except for EAC and ASEAN, the base period precedes establishment of the regional association. For EAC and ASEAN (both established in 1967), bilateral trade data from the period preceding establishment are not available.
[b]Members include: Costa Rica, El Salvador, Guatemala, Honduras, and Nicaragua.
[c]Members include: Belgium, France, W. Germany, Italy, Luxembourg, and the Netherlands.
[d]Members include: EC6 plus Denmark, Ireland, and United Kingdom.
[e]Members include: Austria, Denmark, Finland, Norway, Sweden, Switzerland, and United Kingdom.
[f]Members include: Bolivia, Chile, Colombia, Ecuador, Peru, and Venezuela.
[g]Members include: Brunei, Indonesia, Malaysia, the Philippines, Singapore, and Thailand.
[h]Members include: Argentina, Brazil, Chile, Colombia, Ecuador, Mexico, Paraguay, and Uruguay.
[i]Members include: Kenya, Tanzania, and Uganda. EAC effectively came to an end in 1977.
Source: Adapted from Wonnacott and Lutz (1989, p. 76) and based on IMF, *Direction of Trade*.

The substantial increases in internal trade and comparatively small declines in the external trade of the European Community (EC) are especially noteworthy.

2. There is an apparently positive relationship between the expansion of internal trade and the similarity of development and economic structure, which is also suggestive of the fact that similar economies like those in Western Europe tend to be each other's best customers. Geographical proximity does not appear to be a controlling factor in all situations, as suggested particularly in the different experiences of the Central American Common Market and the East African Community.

The conclusions regarding the EC experience coincide with those of Schott (1991), who observes (pp. 4–5) that the "EC has substantially succeeded in promoting the integration of its member economies" and that "intra-EC trade has far outpaced the growth of exports to third markets." Further, he notes (p. 6) that the multilateral system has been able to accommodate the continuing integration of the European market and evolution of a strong regional trading bloc. Schott also examines the emerging North American trading bloc, which was not included in Table 3. As he notes, both Canada and Mexico conduct about two-thirds of their export and import trade with the United States as well as being large-scale recipients of U.S. foreign direct investment. While there are many similarities between the Canadian and U.S. economies in terms of their economic structure, level of development, and compatibility of their trade regimes, this is of course much less true in comparison to Mexico. But when account is taken of the far reaching unilateral economic reforms and liberalization achieved by Mexico in recent years and the commitment of the Mexican government to continue its policy reforms, the prospects for a successful North American trading bloc appear to be favorable despite the differences between Mexico and the United States and Canada.[11] Further, Schott judges that a North American

[11] For a computational analysis of a North American Free Trade Agreement, see Brown, Deardorff, and Stern (1992).

Free Trade Area (NAFTA) is likely to be compatible with the multilateral trading system insofar as U.S. trade especially will continue to be directed very substantially to markets outside of North America and all three NAFTA nations will look to the multilateral system to expand their trading opportunities and to provide a framework for governing their trade relations.

This brief review of existing preferential trading arrangements suggests that the most successful and durable arrangements have been those involving the already advanced industrialized regions in Western Europe and North America.[12] Preferential arrangements among developing countries have in contrast not been particularly successful and often not durable, especially because they have often been designed with import-substitution objectives in mind.[13] It is also noteworthy that Japan and the Asian newly industrializing countries (NICs) are not members of any *de jure* trading bloc. While it is conceivable that an Asian trading bloc might be formed in the future, it seems like a long way off, since, as Schott (1991, p. 14) notes, the countries in the Asia/Pacific region are very widely dispersed geographically, have rather different levels of development and different trade policies and regulatory regimes, and do not have a strong commitment to regionalism. This latter point is most compelling since a great deal of the international trade and investment of Japan and the other Asian countries relates to other parts of the world, especially the United States and Western Europe.

The conclusion that can be drawn from all of this is that the multilateral system has been able to accommodate a series of preferential arrangements over the past three decades, and it is arguable that the arrangements involving the advanced industrialized countries especially have been welfare enhancing on the whole both to the member

[12] This statement should apply as well to the Closer Economic Relationship between Australia and New Zealand.

[13] For more detailed and up-to-date empirical analyses of the experiences of developed and developing countries with preferential trading arrangements, see de Melo, Panagariya, and Rodrik (1992), de la Torre and Kelly (1992), Fieleke (1992), Irwin (1992), Nogues and Quintanilla (1992), Whalley (1992), and Winters (1992).

countries and to the outside world. Further, it is especially noteworthy that there has been a continuing commitment to multilateralism on the part of the same countries that have participated in these preferential arrangements, given that extra-bloc trade has usually remained important to them. This suggests that the powerful trading blocs and individually powerful trading nations have found it in their interest to adhere to an essentially cooperative form of international behavior rather than seeking to achieve benefits through exploiting their market power in trade.

V. The Advantages and Limitations of Multilateralism and Preferential Arrangements[14]

Having briefly examined the experiences of the GATT negotiating rounds and the characteristics and consequences of preferential arrangements within the GATT system, it is interesting next to juxtapose multilateralism and preferential arrangements and seek to identify their respective advantages and limitations. This discussion is not intended to answer which is necessarily better since, as already mentioned, the two are complementary in many respects. We nonetheless hope that our discussion may serve to identify the major elements of choice and compatibility between multilateralism and preferential arrangements and provide a basis for insuring that the international trading system will function to enhance world welfare.

The Case for Multilateralism

Trade liberalization can be undertaken unilaterally, and there are many instances when unilateral liberalization has in fact been carried out. But governments may often feel constrained by domestic interest groups who are opposed to unilateral liberalization. A case can be

[14] The discussion in this section is based especially on Baldwin (1987), Bhagwati (1990a,b, 1992a,b), Finger (1979), Hoekman (1991), Jackson (1989), Krugman (1991b, 1992a,b), Patterson (1989), Nogues (1990), Schott (1989, 1991), Whalley (1991), Winters (1990), Wolf (1987), and Yarbrough and Yarbrough (1986).

made accordingly for multilateral liberalization, as Finger (1979) and others have pointed out, on an economy-wide and reciprocal basis. This permits a balancing of the interests of consumers and exporting firms and workers who will benefit from multilateral liberalization against the interests of import-competing firms and workers who may experience displacement.[15] The presumption is that the benefits of liberalization will far outweigh the costs so that it should be possible, at least in principle, to devise a tax-subsidy arrangement or some other type of income redistribution so that in effect the gainers can compensate the losers.[16]

As already stated, the GATT system is premised on the desirability of cooperative behavior among nations. This is necessary so that the economic benefits derived from multilateral liberalization can be realized. If the system works effectively, there would be political benefits as well, insofar as nations would act in harmony and would avoid the introduction of exploitative trade policy measures and thus forestall possible retaliatory actions by aggrieved trading partners.

In a world of nation-states, it is obvious that issues of national sovereignty and national interest will be of great importance. When trade disputes arise, it is inevitable that their reconciliation will require appropriate policy changes by governments. Since individual nations have agreed to certain obligations and have been guaranteed certain rights as a condition of their membership in the GATT, their acceptance of GATT dispute settlements will of necessity lead to overriding the opposition of domestic interest groups. In this way, national autonomy and sovereignty have to be superseded in order to enhance global welfare.

As already noted in our discussion, it is important to recognize that there is leeway in the existing multilateral trading system for

---

[15] This is the "hidden logic" that has made GATT successful according to Krugman (1991b, 1992a) in spite of the seeming mercantilistic principles (GATT-think) that he identifies as underlying the GATT.

[16] Finger (1979) characterizes multilateral liberalization as a public good since it has the properties of being nonexclusive and nonrival. That is, because of MFN, access to markets is available to all foreign exporters (nonexclusion), and there is no limit on the amount of goods that any foreign supplier(s) or nation(s) can export (nonrivalness).

nations to take actions or enter into agreements on a bilateral or plurilateral basis insofar as there are situations in which welfare enhancing mutual interests can be pursued on this more limited basis. In evaluating these actions, what is important is whether or not they are detrimental to third countries. Indeed, as we have already noted, Article XXIV of the GATT permits preferential trading arrangements to be carried out, although subject to the qualification that such arrangements should not reduce world welfare. In this respect, the GATT system should be flexible enough to accommodate a variety of trading arrangements, but with the proviso mentioned that such arrangements not be detrimental to world welfare.

Role and Authority of the GATT in a Changing World Economy

Before discussing the litany of criticisms of multilateralism, it is important to realize that the world trading system is in continuous flux, being subjected to a variety of both long- and short-term economic and political influences. Some of these influences affect all nations in common, while others will have differential impacts on particular nations and sectors. What this means is that the role and authority of an institution like the GATT must be able to cope with changing conditions.

Since the GATT is premised on a consensual framework, its ability to function and exercise authority is derived from the support that its members provide to it. The United States has played the central leadership role in the GATT since its inception, championing the cause of multilateralism and providing the initiative and momentum for the convening and completion of the successive GATT negotiating rounds. U.S. influence has waned in recent years, however, as the EC and Japan especially and some of the major developing countries have become economically more important and powerful in the global trading system. Some observers believe that a watershed in U.S. influence dates especially from the failed GATT Ministerial Meeting in 1982 when the U.S.-designed agenda for a new round of negotiations was rebuffed. In retrospect, the call for a new GATT round at a time when the world was experiencing the most severe recession since the 1930s may have been ill advised.

In any case, the rhetoric of U.S. trade policy has since been changed, with an expressed readiness to consider and actually carry to conclusion bilateral and plurilateral negotiating options at the same time that the multilateral option is also to be pursued. Indeed, there appears to be both a carrot and a stick at work here, insofar as the United States is saying that it will pursue the more limited negotiating options unless other major trading countries/blocs show a greater willingness to support multilateral liberalization. To date, neither the EC nor Japan has been willing to assume a leadership role in global negotiations, and the smaller industrialized countries are not important enough to make their influence felt. Some of the major developing countries have become more vocal and involved in the GATT, but these countries have been reluctant, at least formally, to give up whatever advantages they believe to have been derived from special and differential treatment in the past.[17]

The position of the United States in the global trading system during the 1980s was also markedly affected by the macroeconomic imbalance and associated deficits on trade and current account that occurred with dollar appreciation. Given the increased import penetration and problems with exporting that were experienced and the inability to achieve fiscal tightening, pressures in the U.S. Congress grew substantially for import protectionism to ward off allegedly "unfair trade" actions and for activism backed by threats of import restrictions designed to open foreign markets. Japan in particular has been singled out because of its substantial and enduring bilateral trade surplus with the United States. This has reinforced the notion that Japanese policies and domestic institutions are different than those in the other major countries and that Japan does not abide by the same rules and practices of its trading partners. Richardson (1991) has remarked that these interventionist pressures seem to have abated somewhat in the early 1990s, although it is possible that they could reemerge.

Our point is that the support for multilateralism and the GATT system was strongest when the United States played the dominant

---

[17] This could be changing though, especially in the light of the often far reaching unilateral liberalization that has been carried out in many countries.

leadership role. This now seems to have changed, and other major countries/blocs have thus far been slow to fill the void.[18] Moreover, it appears to be especially difficult to effect multilateral trade liberalization at a time when major countries are experiencing significant macroeconomic imbalances.

Criticisms of Multilateralism and Advantages of Preferential Arrangements

Having discussed the case for multilateralism and the international economic environment in which the GATT must function, we can now consider a number of important criticisms that have been levied against multilateralism and the GATT. They include:

1. The more countries that are involved in a multilateral negotiation, the more difficult and time consuming it will be to draw up a negotiating agenda and to conduct and conclude a negotiation.[19] In view of the numerous parties involved in a GATT negotiation and the size and complexity of the negotiating agenda, individual countries/blocs may find themselves less able to focus on issues that concern them directly. It is possible furthermore that there may be foot dragging and a tendency for negotiating results to reflect the "lowest common denominator" of the countries participating in the negotiation. These difficulties can presumably be avoided in negotiating preferential arrangements in which fewer countries are involved and the negotiating agenda can be more readily agreed upon.
2. Because of MFN, concessions may be granted to individual countries without there being any quid pro quo. Free riding may thus

---

[18] Of course, it may not be absolutely necessary to have a single country or regional bloc to serve a hegemonic role, but our reading of historical experience suggests that it can indeed make an important difference in the effectiveness of the trading system.

[19] See Table 1 for details on country participation and the length of time of the individual negotiating rounds.

occur, unless steps are taken to make concessions conditional as, for example, was done with certain Tokyo Round codes that apply only to signatory nations. The problem is all the more serious because special and differential treatment was extended to developing countries beginning in the 1960s, with the consequence that these countries were exempted from making reciprocal concessions. Bilateral/plurilateral arrangements may therefore be appealing as a way of limiting free riding.

3. The GATT system of dispute settlement has not worked well, especially since an effective enforcement mechanism is lacking. Furthermore, the GATT rules are inadequate in important respects. For example, it has proven difficult to resist the introduction of nontariff restrictive measures of various kinds and to effectively constrain the use of domestic and export subsidies that impact directly on trade.
4. The GATT has also been too narrowly focused on trade in goods and has not dealt effectively with issues that lie outside the Articles of Agreement. Examples here include the "new" issues of services and trade related intellectual property rights and investment measures that were belatedly placed on the agenda of the Uruguay Round negotiations, and environmental issues that promise to become increasingly important. This suggests that bilateral or plurilateral negotiations can be more focused and tailored to specific circumstances.
5. Asymmetries exist with respect to the influence of large as compared to medium-size and small countries. Large countries may believe that the GATT system ties their hands because of the nondiscrimination and MFN principles, and, accordingly, that their national economic and political interests would be better served in bilateral or plurilateral negotiations that are designed to protect their domestic firms and/or to open foreign markets to their exporters. Medium-size and small countries, on the other hand, while recognizing the benefits of MFN, if their trade is predominantly with a single large trading country or bloc, may believe that they can get better and more assured access to its

market by means of preferential trading arrangements rather than through multilateral negotiations.[20]

Criticisms of Preferential Trading Arrangements

Having articulated the various criticisms of multilateralism and arguments in support of preferential trading arrangements, we now call attention to a number of limitations of preferential arrangements, as follows:

1. Perhaps the chief concern over preferential trading arrangements is that they may be detrimental to world welfare because of the trade diverting effects that may result and because of the exploitative tariff behavior that the formation of large trading blocs may engender. However, as we have already indicated, there is no presumption that preferential arrangements need be welfare reducing. Indeed, we will show in our theoretical discussion below that the expansion of preferential arrangements may well constitute a move toward freer trade in some circumstances. Also, the formation of trading blocs need not in itself lead to exploitative behavior if there is a strong sense of commitment to international cooperation among governments in the design and implementation of trade policies and to the removal of trade barriers.[21] Of course, nothing can be guaranteed one way or the

[20] We should note that a word of clarification is in order here, lest the foregoing remarks be interpreted to the effect that bilateral/plurilateral negotiations need be harmful particularly to nonmember countries. This will not be the case when bilateral/plurilateral negotiations succeed in achieving greater liberalization than would be possible in a multilateral negotiation and nonmembers are able to share in the benefits.

[21] Using a political economy framework, Krugman (1992b) argues that a small number of large regional blocs may actually enhance global welfare by facilitating the bargaining process internationally, promoting greater liberalization within individual blocs, eliminating the need for a hegemon, and accommodating institutional differences. For criticism of Krugman's views, see especially Bergsten (1991) and Bhagwati (1992a).

other. It will depend on the circumstances. Nonetheless, it might be argued that this agnostic conclusion is fraught with danger. That is, there is a case to be made that the world needs a strong multilateral system with effective rules and discipline to avoid the formation of welfare reducing trading blocs and to constrain their potentially exploitative behavior.

2. Critics of multilateralism have pointed to the slowness and cumbersomeness of GATT negotiations and thus to the greater comparative ease of bilateral/plurilateral negotiations. This favorable view of preferential arrangements has been questioned, however, by a number of proponents of multilateralism. For example, Schott (1989) argues that, while the GATT rounds typically last for several years, the serious and definitive negotiations are concentrated within a relatively short period of time. Also, most of the actual negotiations involve a limited number of the major trading countries/blocs. In contrast, Schott cites some specific drawbacks of preferential arrangements, including: (a) an inability or unwillingness to address NTBs and other problems more related to the multilateral system (e.g., subsidies); (b) difficulties in reconciling quid pro quo demands; (c) identifying which sectors are to be liberalized at a faster or slower pace than others or not at all; (d) elaborating detailed and potentially costly rules of origin; and (e) the need in any event to cover in detail the same issues as in a multilateral negotiation and to reconcile possible divergences of rights and obligations between multilateral and preferential arrangements. Further, if existing preferential arrangements are to be extended to additional countries, a whole new set of negotiations may be required each time another member is to be admitted. A case can be made therefore that it is misleading and even false to believe that it may be relatively easy to negotiate preferential trading arrangements.
3. We mentioned above that the United States appears to have used the prospect of its entering into preferential arrangements as a means of inducing other major trading countries/blocs to pursue the multilateral option. It is not at all clear, however,

whether this can be a successful strategy. The argument is especially problematic if the United States were in fact to enter into such preferential agreements. In that event, this could be interpreted by other countries as a signal that the United States was abandoning its unqualified support and preference for multilateral liberalization. Support for multilateralism might also be eroded in any case if a large part of the available negotiating effort and expertise were shifted to the preferential option. Furthermore, once a preferential arrangement is created, it may become dominated by vested interests who feel threatened by, and will thus oppose, multilateral liberalization. It is possible, finally, that the creation of a number of separate trading blocs could heighten international policy conflicts and frictions.

VI. Theoretical Analysis of the Welfare Effects of the Expansion of Trading Blocs

Having set out the advantages and limitations of both multilateralism and preferential arrangements, suppose now that the proliferation of preferential trading arrangements, in the form of FTAs or something similar, is inevitable. Is there anything that we can say theoretically about what this may portend for the welfare of the world?

There are many issues to be considered here, but we will confine our attention to only one: Is a world of a small number of trading blocs significantly inferior to a world of free trade? We say "significantly inferior" because it seems safe to assume that a world of perfectly free trade will never be reached by any mechanism. Experience suggests that multilateral negotiations can at best reduce trade barriers to low levels, but they cannot eliminate them. Since FTAs by definition reduce external barriers to zero within the included countries and do not presumably maintain or introduce intra-bloc barriers, it is potentially the case that a world of trading blocs, with each bloc forming an FTA, could raise world welfare closer to its free trade level than multilateral negotiations. In that case, the world of blocs would not look altogether bad.

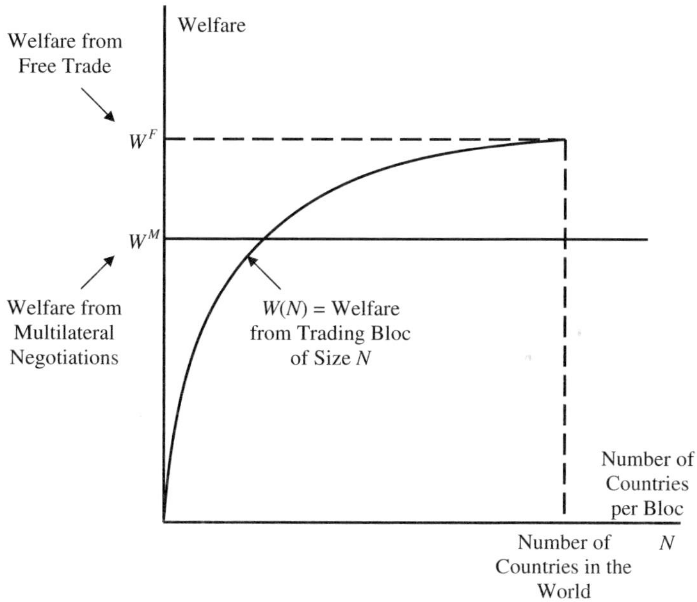

Figure 1. World welfare with trading blocs and multilateral negotiations.

To illustrate this possibility in simple terms, imagine that we could measure welfare of a country or the world as a function of the size of trading blocs. Suppose, as we will discuss below, that world welfare rises rapidly as bloc size rises at first, then levels off and approaches the free trade level, W^F, as bloc size approaches the world as a whole, as drawn in Figure 1. Then if multilateral negotiations can only achieve a level of welfare somewhere short of the free trade level, as at W^M in Figure 1, there is a point beyond which blocs are large enough to yield a higher welfare than multilateral negotiations. Of course, it remains to be seen whether the effect of bloc size on welfare shown in Figure 1 can be correct.[22]

[22] The assumption in Figure 1 is that the time path of welfare is monotonic as trading blocs increase in size. Krugman (1991a) and Bhagwati (1992a) suggest that there could be other paths in which world welfare would not consistently rise.

The Krugman Argument

Krugman (1991a,b, 1992b) has addressed this question directly.[23] He examines a model of a large number of countries, each of which produces a distinctive good and each of which initially levies its optimal tariff on all imports. He then computes world welfare as these countries are combined into various numbers of equal sized trading blocs, each with zero tariffs internally, and each revising their external tariffs to remain optimal against goods from outside the bloc. While no general result can be obtained from this model, Krugman finds computationally that world welfare declines as the number of blocs decreases (and countries are therefore combined into ever larger FTAs) until the number of blocs reaches three. World welfare then increases as the number of blocs is reduced still further to two, and it increases even more with the move to worldwide free trade in a single bloc. That is, world welfare is at a minimum when the number of blocs is three. Krugman therefore concludes in the context of his model that bilateralism is generally undesirable, since the formation of FTAs would reduce world welfare at almost every stage.

This is an ingenious argument. It is based, however, on a model that stacks the cards against bilateralism. In an alternative framework one might easily conclude that the formation of FTA trading blocs would be beneficial and that a world of a small number of blocs, even three, might be about as good as one could ask for.

A distinctive feature of Krugman's model is that the firms in each country are assumed to produce goods that are distinct from those

[23] There is of course a large and venerable literature on the welfare effects of customs unions and free trade areas, including what determines whether particular combinations of countries forming trading blocs will raise or lower welfare. In addition to extensive discussions of trade creation and trade diversion, perhaps the most notable contribution is Kemp and Wan's (1976) demonstration that any grouping of countries into a customs union can be welfare improving, both for them and for the world as a whole, given a suitable selection of their common external tariff. None of this literature, however, seems to bear directly on the issue here of the welfare effects of the size of trading blocs. For a recent analytical survey of pertinent theory relating to the welfare effects of trading blocs, see especially de Melo, Panagariya, and Rodrik (1992). See also Kennan and Riezman (1990) and Kowalczyk (1989, 1990, 1992).

produced by all other firms. This product differentiation allows him the simplicity of a single-sector monopolistic-competition model, and thus the kind of clean and simple theorizing that one has learned to expect from Krugman. However, the assumption also means that the countries of Krugman's model are subject to something very like the Armington assumption, which is that each country's products are imperfect substitutes for those of all other countries. This, we believe, is largely responsible for Krugman's results.

The Armington assumption has a long history in the construction of computable general equilibrium models of international trade.[24] However, for some purposes, and especially for modeling the welfare effects of trade barriers, it has become increasingly recognized that the Armington assumption places an idiosyncratic stamp upon results.[25] In the context of FTAs and trading blocs, the Armington assumption seems especially likely to yield peculiar implications. First, the Armington assumption makes it important for any country to import from every other country, since each has something unique to provide. This means that an extreme form of trading blocs in which blocs do not trade at all with each other would be welfare disasters. That is, depending on the functional form of the utility function, welfare would be either very low or infinitely low. This is not necessarily wrong, of course, but we find it rather implausible that each country's welfare should depend so sensitively on access to the products of each and every other country in the world.

Second, the Armington assumption increases the importance of trade diversion, as compared to trade creation, and therefore increases the likelihood that a preferential arrangement will be welfare reducing. Since this may be counter intuitive, the point requires some explanation.

As usually explained, trade diversion might seem to be impossible in a world of differentiated products. The classic description of

---

[24] See, for example, Whalley (1985) and subsequent work based on Whalley's model by Harrison and Rustrom (1991) and Nguyen, Perroni, and Wigle (1991).

[25] Brown (1987) in particular has analyzed critically the implications of relying on the Armington assumption.

trade diversion is the switch away from a low-cost external supplier of a good to a higher-cost supplier of the same good within an FTA. Since with differentiated products the same good is not available from different countries, this simple form of trade diversion is not possible. In addition, Krugman's model does not have differences in costs, and this too would seem to rule out trade diversion as usually described.

However, a more general definition of trade diversion would not involve identical products, and it would not require any particular differences in costs. Any time there is substitution away from one good in favor of another as a result of distorted price signals that incorrectly reflect costs, there will tend to be a welfare reduction.[26] If the two goods are both imported, then this substitution may usefully be labeled as trade diversion, for the welfare loss is from the same source as in the simpler, more familiar example.

Product differentiation in Krugman's model assures that any expansion of an FTA, short of subsuming the entire world, will involve such trade diversion. As long as any countries remain outside the union, there will be substitution away from their products when the FTA lowers the consumer prices of the products produced by new members of the FTA. Since the products of these two groups of countries previously faced the same tariffs, their relative prices within the FTA had been undistorted, and they become distorted by the FTA. Thus trade diversion necessarily occurs in Krugman's model, no matter how large the FTA becomes.

There is trade creation too, of course, as substitution also occurs away from previously protected domestic goods and towards imports from new members of the FTA. However, it is easy in Krugman's model for trade diversion to dominate trade creation.

To see why, suppose that the welfare effects depend only on the number of goods for which there is trade creation and trade diversion.

[26] Although this is not certain, just as trade diversion by the narrower definition is not necessarily welfare worsening. See Kowalczyk (1990) for a recapitulation of this argument.

In a world of many countries, when only two of these form an FTA, there is creation of trade for the goods produced by the partners, but diversion of trade away from all of the goods produced by all other countries. Since the number of the latter countries, and therefore goods, is much larger than the number of countries and goods in the FTA, it is not surprising that diversion outweighs creation. Then, as the FTA is made larger and larger, the number of countries inside the FTA — and hence the amount of trade creation — grows, while the number of countries still outside the FTA shrinks. But even when one enlarges the FTA to include one-third of the world (the three-bloc case), there are still two-thirds of the world's products from which trade is being diverted, and only one-third for which trade is being created. Again, then, it is not surprising that each enlargement of the FTA up to this point lowers welfare and that the three-bloc case is the worst possible. Only when the goods and countries included in a bloc become as numerous as the goods and countries outside does trade creation finally have a reasonable chance of dominating trade diversion, and only then does the FTA raise welfare.

As this explanation is intended to suggest, then, the assumptions of complete product differentiation and the consequent exaggerated importance of each country and each country's goods for every other country's consumers may introduce a bias against the possibility that an FTA will be beneficial.

One other feature of the Krugman model should also be mentioned, since it may well contribute to his results even if it does not drive them. In his first paper on this subject, Krugman (1991a) assumes that trading blocs maintain optimal tariffs against the rest of the world at all times. In part because of the high degree of product differentiation just discussed, these optimal tariffs tend to rise as bloc size increases, contributing to the welfare loss for the world as a whole. In a more recent analysis, however, he questions the usefulness of this assumption and replaces it with a constant external tariff in his calculations. The conclusion that world welfare is minimized with either three or two blocs survives. Therefore, while the assumption of an optimal tariff may have exacerbated the welfare losses in the earlier analysis, it seems not to have caused them. The assumption of product differentiation instead seems to play the more important role.[27]

A Comparative Advantage Approach

As an alternative, suppose that trade among countries conforms more to the traditional model of comparative advantage. That is, all countries are capable of producing the same list of goods, but they differ in their abilities to do so either because of differences in technology or differences in factor endowments.[28] The effect of an FTA on world welfare then depends, we will argue first, on the differences among countries that join to form the FTA. Furthermore, as long as countries choose as partners others with whom enough differences in comparative advantage exist, they will tend to capture for themselves a significant portion of the gains from trade that would be available from a move to complete free trade by the world. In such cases, it may well be that the majority of the gains from trade that would be possible with worldwide free trade can be captured by a group of trading blocs. The blocs would only need to be large enough and to include countries with a sufficiently divergent variety of comparative advantages.[29]

Unfortunately, we are not able to make these points with any great generality. However, we can illustrate them by means of simple examples, and that will be our approach.

---

[27] It is also noteworthy that Krugman (1991a,b, 1992b) qualifies his analysis by noting that trade diversion may be lessened if the trading blocs consist of countries that are "natural" trading partners who would trade to a very large extent with each other in the absence of the formation of a trading bloc. While there may be some merit to this point, we have noted above that geographic proximity may not necessarily be a controlling factor. Bhagwati (1992a) makes a similar point and also notes that relatively high substitution elasticities between nonmember and member country goods could prove detrimental to welfare.

[28] We abstract from considerations of imperfect competition and increasing returns to scale. More will be said on this below.

[29] The welfare gains would thus come mainly from an expansion of interindustry trade, and there would be presumably (transitional) costs of adjustment.

A Four-Country Example

Consider first a four-country version of the simple two-good Ricardian trade model that has been used for two centuries to illustrate the concept of comparative advantage.[30] Let the countries have identical preferences and labor endowments, and let unit labor requirements for producing the two goods, X and Y, be also the same in countries 1 and 2 and in countries 3 and 4, but differ between the two pairs of countries. That is, let countries 1 and 2 have a comparative advantage in good X relative to countries 3 and 4.

We will consider only the extremes of free trade and autarky to make our point. Suppose that prohibitive tariffs initially exist in all four countries, and that we now consider opening pairs of the four countries to free trade, thus forming trading blocs. It makes a great difference which pairs of countries we choose to form a bloc. If countries 1 and 2 were to form an FTA, they would not in fact trade with each other since their autarky prices are the same. They would gain nothing from trade. If countries 1 and 3 were to form an FTA, however, they would indeed trade and gain from trade exactly as in the traditional two-country model. Thus it is only if countries with different comparative advantages join in an FTA that there can be trade creation, and only then are there gains from formation of the FTA.[31]

This example also illustrates our other point that worldwide free trade may not be necessary. In this example, with identical preferences and labor endowments and only two different sets of technologies, the worldwide free trade equilibrium is identical to the equilibrium that will be attained if any pair of countries with different technologies form an FTA, save only for size. That is, the equilibrium world price with free trade is also the equilibrium price within an FTA formed by, say, countries 1 and 3, and the quantities produced and consumed within each country are also the same. Only the total outputs are different, being twice for four countries what they are for two.

---

[30] The example works just as well with Heckscher–Ohlin assumptions.

[31] We assume here and in what follows that there are zero domestic barriers within any given country that would inhibit intra-bloc trade.

Thus, in this very special case, all of the gains from trade that can be achieved with worldwide free trade can also be achieved in two completely separate trading blocs, so long as each bloc includes countries with different technologies. This illustrates the point that trading blocs can in principle approximate (and in this case equal) the welfare levels of complete free trade.

In a more general model, one would not expect to find blocs equaling the welfare of free trade, but a tendency in this direction does seem likely. It seems plausible that blocs would in general achieve levels of welfare that are between autarky and free trade, being closer to the latter the larger are the blocs and the more diverse in terms of technologies represented. With only four countries we cannot capture much of this, but we can capture a part of it — and also foreshadow our next examples — by looking at blocs in terms of expected values.

Suppose in the four-country model that we are to form two blocs of two countries each, but that the composition of the blocs is to be decided randomly. What are the levels of welfare associated with two blocs in this sense, and how do they compare to autarky and complete free trade? The answer depends on what random mechanism is used for selecting blocs.

Let each possible pattern of blocs be equally likely. There are three such patterns: (1,2)(3,4), (1,3)(2,4), and (1,4)(2,3). Of these only the first has the countries staying at autarky levels of welfare, while the other two have the countries attaining free trade levels. Thus, the formation of two random blocs yields an expected gain in welfare that is two-thirds that of free trade.

To be a bit more formal in preparation for the next example, assume there are two types of countries in this four-country case. Let countries 1 and 2 be type A and countries 3 and 4 be type B. Let the welfare attained by a country of type i when it trades in an FTA including countries of types $j,k,l,\ldots$, be denoted w^i_{jkl}. Thus w^A_A is the autarky welfare of a country of type A, w^A_{AB} is the welfare of a country of type A in an FTA with a country of type B, and so on.

Now let $W(I)$ be the level of expected world welfare associated with an equal number of blocs of size *I*. In the four-country example, the only possibilities are $I = 1$ (autarky), 2 (two blocs) and 4 (free trade). Adding up over the four countries one can obtain world autarky welfare as

$$W(1) = 2w_A^A + 2w_B^B,$$

and free trade welfare as

$$W^F = W(4) = 2w_{AB}^A + 2w_{BA}^B.$$

The world gains from free trade are then

$$G^F = G(4) = W(4) - W(1) = 2\left(w_{AB}^A + w_A^A\right) + 2\left(w_{BA}^B + w_B^B\right).$$

The expected welfare for a country of type *A* from two randomly chosen blocs is $(1/3)w_A^A + (2/3)w_{AB}^A$ and there is a similar expression for a country of type *B*. Therefore, expected world welfare with two blocs is

$$W(2) = 2\left[(1/3)w_A^A + (2/3)w_{AB}^A\right] + 2\left[(1/3)w_B^B + (2/3)w_{BA}^B\right].$$

Comparing to $W(1)$, the expected gain in world welfare from two blocs is then

$$\begin{aligned} G(2) &= W(2) - W(1) \\ &= 2\left[(1/3)w_A^A + (2/3)w_{AB}^A\right] + 2\left[(1/3)w_B^B + (2/3)w_{BA}^B\right] - 2w_A^A - 2w_B^B \\ &= (2/3)G^F. \end{aligned}$$

What this says is that the expected gain from forming two trading blocs, with the composition of the blocs randomly selected, is two-thirds of the gain that would arise from a single bloc, or free trade. That is, trading blocs do, on average, generate more than half of the gains from free trade.

A Six-Country Example

To allow for a slightly richer array of possibilities than the four-country model, now consider six. Again let there be just two goods and two technologies, so that the countries are of only two types, *A* and *B*, now with three of each. In addition to the extremes of autarky and free trade, there are now the possibilities of three blocs with two countries each, and of two blocs with three countries each. The two-country blocs have the same possibilities for welfare as before, but the three-country blocs do not: a country can join with zero, one, or two other countries of the same type as itself.

Levels of world welfare under autarky and free trade are the same as before, except that there are now six countries instead of three:

$$W(1) = 3w_A^A + 3w_B^B,$$
$$W^F = W(6) = 3w_{AB}^A + 3w_{AB}^B.$$

This gives a world gain from free trade of

$$G^F = G(6) = 3\left[w_{AB}^A + w_{AB}^B - w_A^A - w_B^B\right].$$

With blocs of two countries, there are fifteen ways that the six countries can be distributed across three blocs. In only six of these do all three blocs have one country of each type, so that they all attain the same welfare as under free trade. In the remaining nine, one bloc has two type-*A* countries, one has two type-*B*, and one has one of each. This leads to an expected world welfare of

$$W(2) = (2/5)\left[3w_{AB}^A + 3w_{AB}^B\right] + (3/5)\left[2w_A^A + 2w_B^B + w_{AB}^A + w_{AB}^B\right],$$

and an expected gain from trade of

$$G(2) = (3/5)G^F.$$

Thus with more countries, blocs of two countries still produce more than half the benefit of free trade, but the expected gain is somewhat smaller than in the four-country case.

With two blocs of three countries, there are ten ways that the six countries can be distributed across the blocs. One of those ways has all three type-A countries in one bloc and all three type-B in the other, leading to autarky levels of welfare in both. In the nine other ways that the two blocs can appear, each bloc has two countries from one type and one from the other. Expected welfare is therefore:

$$W(3) = \left(\frac{1}{10}\right)\left[3w_A^A + 3w_B^B\right] + \left(\frac{9}{10}\right)\left[2w_{AAB}^A + w_{AAB}^B + w_{ABB}^A + w_{ABB}^B\right].$$

Interpretation of this expression does not lead to anything as simple as the other cases, and we will not try to carry it further here. It seems likely, though we have not been able to prove it, that it involves higher expected welfare than $W(2)$.

This example has one additional feature that would appear in a more general case but did not appear in the four-country case. It is quite possible for a country to achieve a level of welfare higher than worldwide free trade by joining an FTA. Consider a country of type A in an FTA with two other countries of type B, an "ABB" FTA in the notation used above. In a competitive model without increasing returns to scale, the free-trade equilibrium price in any group of countries is a weighted average of the autarky prices of the separate countries, the weights depending on the sizes of the countries. Thus, the equilibrium price in an ABB FTA will be closer to the autarky price of the type B countries than will the equilibrium price under free trade where there are equal numbers of countries of the two types. Since the welfare of any country increases with the difference between the equilibrium price and its own autarky price, it follows that the type-A country is better off in the ABB FTA than it would be under free trade:

$$W_{ABB}^A > W_{AB}^A.$$

A Many-Country Case

As our final example, we consider a many-country case where comparative advantage is more generally defined in terms of relative autarky prices and may therefore reflect differences in technologies and/or factor endowments. Suppose the world consists of $M + 1$ countries, numbered $i = 0,1,\ldots,M$. Let these countries have, in general, different autarky prices but be otherwise identical in the following sense: each produces and consumes two goods, and their excess supplies of good 1 are

$$ES^i(p) = p - q^i,$$

where p is the price of good 1 in terms of the numeraire good 2, and q^i is the only parameter of this excess supply function that we allow to differ across countries. Since in autarky, q^i is the autarky price of good 1 in country i.[32]

In addition to the autarky prices, one can also derive the world free-trade equilibrium price, p^F, from

$$\sum_{i=10}^{M} ES^i(p^F) = 0$$

as

$$p^F = \frac{1}{M+1}\sum_{i=10}^{M} q^i,$$

which is simply the average of the autarky prices.[33]

[32] Note the assumption that price, p, appears in this function with a coefficient of one. What is important here is that each country has the same coefficient, indicating that behavior of both producers and consumers at the margin is identical across countries, and also that countries are in some sense equal in size (else a large country would have a much larger quantity response to a change in price than a small country). It is not important that the common coefficient happens to be one, which could always be assured by appropriate choice of units. A somewhat more general formulation would permit a different coefficient on p for each country. This would add complexity, and would also invalidate the result to be derived, without some additional assumption. Such an additional assumption will be suggested in a footnote below.

[33] If countries have different coefficients on price in their excess supply functions, then this becomes a weighted average with those coefficients serving as weights.

Suppose that country 0 were to contemplate joining a trading bloc of some N other countries in addition to itself. If those N countries were $i = 1,...,N$, then the resulting equilibrium bloc price, $p^{0,N}$, would be

$$p^{0,N} = \frac{1}{N+1}\sum_{i=0}^{N} q^i = \frac{1}{N+1} q^0 + \frac{N}{N+1} p^N, \tag{1}$$

where p^N is the equilibrium bloc price for countries $1,\ldots,N$ (without country 0). That is, if country 0 joins the bloc it will face an equilibrium price that is a weighted average of its own autarky price and that of the bloc excluding itself, the weight on the latter being larger the more countries are in the bloc. But suppose that, instead of the participants in the bloc being known, country 0 will join a bloc with N other randomly selected countries. In that case its equilibrium bloc price will still be given by Equation (1), but the equilibrium price of the N-bloc, p^N, will be random. Since Equation (1) is linear, the expected equilibrium price for the bloc of $N+1$ countries will be given in terms of the expected equilibrium price for the N-bloc:

$$Ep^{0,N} = \frac{1}{N+1} q^0 + \frac{N}{N+1} Ep^N \tag{2}$$

To calculate Ep^N, let $c(N)$ be the number of possible N-country blocs that can be formed out of the M countries $1,...,M$. If each is equally likely, then

$$\begin{aligned} Ep^N &= \frac{1}{c(N)} \sum_{j=1}^{c(N)} p^{Nj} \\ &= \frac{1}{c(N)} \sum_{j=1}^{c(N)} \frac{1}{N} \sum_{i=1}^{N} q^{Nj}, \end{aligned}$$

where is p^{Nj} the equilibrium bloc price for the jth possible bloc of size N, and h_{ji} is the index of the ith country in that jth bloc. This is a simple average of all the autarky prices $q^1,\ldots,q^M$, with each one repeated by the number of blocs in which it appears. Since each p^{Nj} bloc is equally likely and all possible blocs are represented in this summation, each autarky price q^i for $i = 1,\ldots,M$, must appear the same number of times in this summation, and thus have equal weight. Thus,

$$Ep^N = \frac{1}{M}\sum_{i=1}^{M} q^i = p^M,$$

which is just the equilibrium bloc price for the bloc of all M countries other than country 0. That is, the expected equilibrium price for a bloc of N countries chosen randomly from a larger group of M countries is just the equilibrium price for the M countries themselves as a bloc.[34] Substituting this into Equation (2), the result for a randomly selected bloc of size $N + 1$ including country 0 is therefore

$$Ep^{0,N} = \frac{1}{N+1} q^0 + \frac{N}{N+1} p^M. \tag{3}$$

This result is illustrated in the top panel of Figure 2. The horizontal axis measures the number of countries in a bloc in addition to country 0, while the vertical axis measures various prices. The autarky price in country 0, q^0, is shown as lower than the equilibrium bloc price for all countries excluding zero, p^M. As the above equation indicates, the expected equilibrium bloc price for a bloc of

---

[34] This is the result we need, and it was in order to get it that we assumed the countries to be identical in such a strong way. If countries instead have different coefficients on price in their excess supply functions, it will not in general be true. (To see this, simply consider $N = 1$ and $M = 2$, with one country having a much larger coefficient and hence a large influence on the equilibrium price. The expected price in a one-country randomly chosen bloc is halfway between their two autarky prices, while the equilibrium price for the two together is much closer to the autarky price of the high-coefficient country.) The result can nonetheless be salvaged if the coefficients are uncorrelated with the autarky prices.

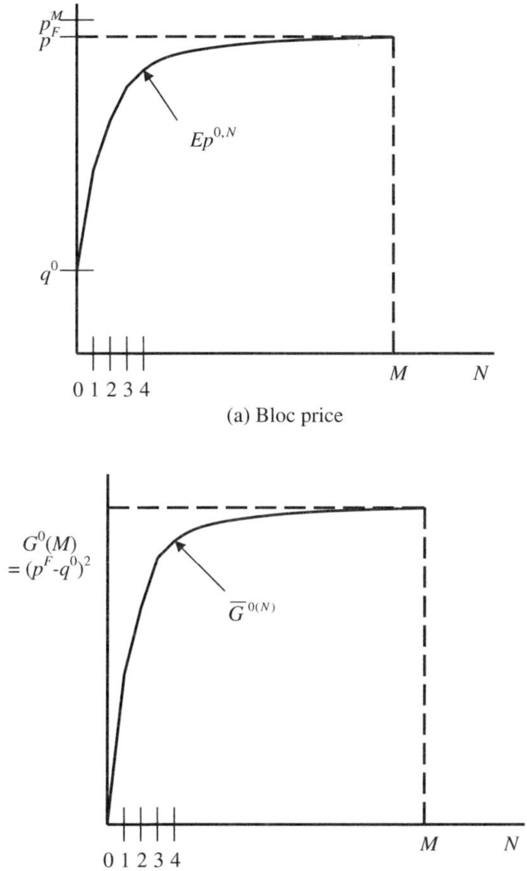

(a) Bloc price

(b) Country welfare

Figure 2. Expected bloc price and country welfare with trading blocs.

country 0 plus N other randomly selected countries rises to halfway between q^0 and p^M for $N = 1$ and continues thereafter to approach p^M. The graph stops at $N = M$, where the free trade price p^F is reached just short of p^M.

The bottom panel of Figure 2 gives information about the welfare of country 0 in these various circumstances. The welfare of a country is given by its indirect utility function, which in this case takes the simple form[35]

$$V^i(p) = (p - q^i)^2.$$

Letting $G^0(N)$ be the expected gain in welfare of country 0 from entering into a bloc with N other randomly selected countries,

$$G^0(N) = EV^0(p^{0,N}) \geq V^0(Ep^{0,N}) = (Ep^{0,N} - q^0)^2 \equiv \bar{G}^0(N), \qquad (4)$$

using the convexity of $V(\bullet)\bar{G}^0(N) = V^0(Ep^{0,N})$.

Thus the bottom panel of Figure 2 graphs as a function of N, taking $Ep^{0,N}$ as given by Equation (3) from the top panel. From the inequality in Equation (4), this graph provides a lower bound on the gain to country 0 from entering into blocs of various sizes. This graph illustrates the conclusion discussed throughout this section of the chapter: that much of the gains from free trade can be achieved, in this case for an individual country, by entering into FTA trading blocs of larger and larger size.

The curve $\bar{G}^{0(N)}$ in Figure 2 provides only a lower bound for the expected gains from entering into blocs of various sizes for a particular country. We are not able to place an upper bound on this gain, which could extend well above the curve and even above the level of welfare in free trade. Indeed, one can easily find cases where the expected welfare for a country from entering into a bloc that includes only part of the world will be higher than its welfare from free trade. Suppose in a world of many countries that one of them has an autarky price equal to the free-trade price. Then it has nothing to gain from free trade at all. But by entering into trading blocs with only part of the world, it is quite likely to meet a bloc price that

[35] This is obtained by integrating the excess supply function above, and normalizing on a level of welfare of zero in autarky.

differs from its autarky price, and therefore enjoy greater welfare. Thus, for a particular country, it is quite possible that trading blocs are better than free trade.

This cannot be the case for the world as a whole, however. We know from the literature on the gains from trade that world welfare cannot be larger with trade barriers than without, and will usually be smaller. Therefore, the upper bound on world welfare is given by free trade. Since the lower bound can be obtained by adding together vertically curves like $\bar{G}^{0(N)}$ in Figure 2, the world expected gains from trading blocs of various sizes are indeed constrained to lie between a curve like $W(N)$ in Figure 1 and the horizontal line shown for free trade, just as we surmised earlier.

Tariffs

Our discussion in this section has assumed that tariffs were always either prohibitive or zero. This may seem to be an important limitation in a world where actual tariffs are mostly neither of these. Furthermore, by excluding non-zero, non-prohibitive tariffs we have ruled out any possibility of trade diversion: with previously prohibitive tariffs there was no trade to be diverted by the formation of an FTA. Finally, this assumption has also made it unnecessary for us to consider the distinction between an FTA and a customs union: our FTAs continue to charge prohibitive tariffs against the rest of the world, and it therefore does not matter whether those tariffs are the same or not.

All of this seems to suggest that our analysis cannot be of much relevance. However, we would argue that our main result of the potential desirability of trading blocs can only be enhanced by now allowing for trade to occur over nonzero tariffs. As long as FTAs continue to involve zero tariffs internally, the presence of some trade externally can only raise welfare as compared to what it would have been in the prohibitive tariff case that we examined. Since we argued that expected welfare rises with the size of trading blocs and approaches the free-trade level as the blocs become large, the even higher welfare of blocs that do trade externally must have at least the second of these properties as well.[36]

Extensions and Caveats

The analysis here has included only three very simple examples. There are many directions in which it would be desirable to go with this, and it is premature to suggest that we know what such extensions would yield. However, these results do seem sufficient to at least raise the possibility that trading blocs may be welfare improving, and even that they may approach the level of welfare that could have been attained by free trade.

However, the examples here are at the opposite extreme from the model of Krugman, in the sense that they stack the cards in favor of trading blocs just as his model stacks them against. This suggests that an important consideration is whether in fact most trade is driven by differences in comparative advantage, as in the examples here, or by other considerations such as the product differentiation that drives Krugman's model. In a world where comparative advantage dominates and countries act cooperatively rather than noncooperatively in their trade policies, trading blocs of diverse countries may not be so bad.

Similarly, the examples here have assumed constant returns to scale and perfect competition. If instead there are increasing returns to scale and/or imperfect competition of various sorts, the argument here would have to be modified and possibly weakened. As long as trading blocs are too small to permit minimum efficient scale in many industries, or too small to permit a reasonable amount of competition, enlarging the blocs will increase welfare more than in the case considered here for these additional reasons. If this process can be

[36] Haveman (1992) has developed a model of trading blocs that encompasses comparative advantage and positive (optimal) tariffs that apparently negates this conclusion and reinforces Krugman's conclusion that the formation of trading blocs will be detrimental to world welfare as the number of blocs increases to two rather than three as in Krugman's model. In Haveman's model, however, this result does depend on the assumption that external tariffs are levied optimally at each stage.

completed while the blocs still encompass only a fraction of the world, then these effects strengthen our argument, since welfare will rise with bloc size even more rapidly when blocs are still small. On the other hand, if the entire world market is needed to surpass minimum efficient scale in many industries, or to permit a satisfactory level of competition, then these effects could conceivably turn our concave function into a convex one. In that case, any division of the world into trading blocs could fall well short of free trade in terms of welfare.

Note, finally, that the conclusion of our theoretical discussion is that a group of trading blocs, if they are large enough, can approximate the level of welfare that may be feasibly attainable from a multilateral system. However, it is also clear that if such blocs are too small and if the trade between them is too limited, then the gains we have described will not be achieved. In terms of our Figure 1, blocs must be sufficiently large to bring us up the curve to the free trade level, or else barriers to trade will be detrimental to world welfare. Therefore, our analysis argues in favor of trading blocs only if they are sufficiently large and only if they collectively encompass the entire world.

It is quite possible that a multilateral system of controls would be needed to assure that blocs do achieve this size and comprehensiveness, as well as to prevent the blocs from increasing levels of protection among themselves. Thus, as we will elaborate further in the concluding section, we do not view this simple theoretical analysis as undermining the case for GATT or for multilateral oversight of trade policy. We would only suggest on the basis of this analysis that trading blocs might have a legitimate place in a multilateral system, and that their presence should not be taken as necessary evidence that the gains from multilateral trade are being foregone.

VII. Implications for the Design of Trading Blocs to Enhance World Welfare

From our institutional and historical discussion, it appears that preferential arrangements are an inevitable part of the world trading system. From our theoretical discussion, it appears that such arrangements are not necessarily the economic disasters that they have sometimes been supposed to be. It remains therefore to examine how the multilateral trading system should accommodate preferential arrangements, since it evidently must, in order to assure that their presence does not undermine other desirable features of the multilateral system and in order if possible to assure that they yield the greatest benefits and the fewest costs for the world as a whole. In this concluding section, therefore, we make several suggestions for how the multilateral trading system should be structured to this end.[37]

1. The GATT should recognize bilateral arrangements as an intrinsic part of any multilateral system, and not treat them as exceptions to the rule only to be tolerated. At present, in spite of Article XXIV, there is a tendency to regard new preferential arrangements as undermining the legitimacy of the GATT, and as long as they are treated that way they will indeed have that effect. Instead, much as the IMF came to accommodate the existence of flexible exchange rates in the 1970s, the GATT must accommodate preferential arrangements so that their presence will be seen as contributing to the system rather than tearing it apart.
2. The requirement, already embodied in Article XXIV, that new preferential arrangements should not lead to an increase in the level of protection, must be strengthened and enforced. In fact, the evidence does not suggest that such arrangements have historically added significantly to the level of protection, so it should not be too difficult to enforce such a requirement. But, where cases can be brought to the GATT of violations of Article XXIV, they should be encouraged. That will not only serve in a minor way to restrain protectionism. But it will serve in a more major way to enhance the role of the GATT *vis-à-vis*

[37] See also Bhagwati (1992a,b) and Whalley (1991) for related suggestions concerning the role and treatment of preferential arrangements within the multilateral system.

such preferential arrangements and make it clear that the two can and should coexist.[38]

3. Language should be added to the GATT encouraging the formation of preferential arrangements where they are most likely to be beneficial to the countries involved and to the world. On the basis of comparative advantage, the GATT should favor arrangements that combine countries with large, rather than small, differences in factor endowments and technologies. In particular, the GATT should encourage the inclusion of less developed countries within preferential arrangements, not involving only other developing countries like themselves, but involving also developed countries with whom they can benefit the most from trade.
4. Finally, and perhaps most importantly, the GATT should insist that preferential arrangements should have ways of accommodating new members, and that all countries (or at least all GATT members) should have access to joining some trading bloc, somewhere in the world. It will indeed be a disaster, politically as well as economically, if the formation of preferential trading arrangements leads not to an entire world of trading blocs, but rather to a world of blocs that include only the rich countries and a handful of their favored neighbors. Developments so far in Europe and America suggest a surprising and encouraging willingness to extend preferential treatment beyond the borders of the developed world. It remains to be seen whether this willingness will cease once the developed countries have acquired a comfortable buffer between themselves and the rest of the Third World. The GATT could and should play an important role in preventing this from happening.

---

[38] It is essential here, as Bhagwati (1992a,b) and others have stressed, that measures be taken to constrain the use of antidumping measures and voluntary export restraints. The limitation of these measures is of course desirable in its own right and is ostensibly being dealt with in the Uruguay Round negotiations. The improvements here would then presumably carry over to the enforcement of Article XXIV.

Appendix

GENERAL AGREEMENT ON TARIFFS AND TRADE
Article XXIV
Territorial Application–Frontier Traffic–Customs Unions and Free Trade Areas

1. The provisions of this Agreement shall apply to the metropolitan customs territories of the contracting parties and to any other customs territories in respect of which this Agreement has been accepted under Article XXVI or is being applied under Article XXXIII or pursuant to the Protocol of Provisional Application. Each such customs territory shall, exclusively for the purposes of the territorial application of this Agreement, be treated as though it were a contracting party; *Provided* that the provisions of this paragraph shall not be construed to create any rights or obligations as between two or more customs territories in respect of which this Agreement has been accepted under Article XXVI or is being applied under Article XXXIII or pursuant to the Protocol of Provisional Application by a single contracting party.
2. For the purposes of this Agreement a customs territory shall be understood to mean any territory with respect to which separate tariffs or other regulations of commerce are maintained for a substantial part of the trade of such territory with other territories.
3. The provisions of this Agreement shall not be construed to prevent:

   (a) Advantages accorded by any contracting party to adjacent countries in order to facilitate frontier traffic;
   (b) Advantages accorded to the trade with the Free Territory of Trieste by countries contiguous to that territory, provided that such advantages are not in conflict with the Treaties of Peace arising out of the Second World War.

4. The contracting parties recognize the desirability of increasing freedom of trade by the development, through voluntary agreements,

of closer integration between the economies of the countries parties to such agreements. They also recognize that the purpose of a customs union or of a free-trade area should be to facilitate trade between the constituent territories and not to raise barriers to the trade of other contracting parties with such territories.

5. Accordingly, the provisions of this Agreement shall not prevent, as between the territories of contracting parties, the formation of a customs union or of a free-trade area or the adoption of an interim agreement necessary for the formation of a customs union or of a free-trade area; *Provided* that:

   (a) With respect to a customs union, or an interim agreement leading to the formation of a customs union, the duties and other regulations of commerce imposed at the institution of any such union or interim agreement in respect of trade with contracting parties not parties to such union or agreement shall not on the whole be higher or more restrictive than the general incidence of the duties and regulations of commerce applicable in the constituent territories prior to the formation of such union or the adoption of such interim agreement, as the case may be;

   (b) With respect to a free-trade area, or an interim agreement leading to the formation of a free-trade area, the duties and other regulations of commerce maintained in each of the constituent territories and applicable at the formation of such free-trade area or the adoption of such interim agreement to the trade of contracting parties not included in such area or not parties to such agreement shall not be higher or more restrictive than the corresponding duties and other regulations of commerce existing in the same constituent territories prior to the formation of the free-trade area, or interim agreement, as the case may be, and not to raise barriers to the trade of other contracting parties with such territories;

   (c) Any interim agreement referred to in sub-paragraphs (a) and (b) shall include a plan and schedule for the formation of such a customs union or of such a free-trade area within a reasonable length of time.

6. If, in fulfilling the requirements of sub-paragraph 5(a), a contracting party proposes to increase any rate of duty inconsistently with the provisions of Article II, the procedure set forth in Article XXVIII shall apply. In providing for compensatory adjustment, due account shall be taken of the compensation already afforded by the reductions brought about in the corresponding duty of the other constituents of the union.
7. (a) Any contracting party deciding to enter into a customs union or free-trade area, or an interim agreement leading to the formation of such a union or area, shall promptly notify the CONTRACTING PARTIES and shall make available to them such information regarding the proposed union or area as will enable them to make such reports and recommendations to contracting parties as they may deem appropriate.
   (b) If, after having studied the plan and schedule included in an interim agreement referred to in paragraph 5 in consultation with the parties to that agreement and taking due account of the information made available in accordance with the provisions of sub-paragraph (a), the CONTRACTING PARTIES find that such agreement is not likely to result in the formation of a customs union or of a free-trade area within the period contemplated by the parties to the agreement or that such period is not a reasonable one, the CONTRACTING PARTIES shall make recommendations to the parties to the agreement. The parties shall not maintain or put into force, as the case may be, such agreement if they are not prepared to modify it in accordance with these recommendations.
   (c) Any substantial change in the plan or schedule referred to in paragraph 5(c) shall be communicated to the CONTRACTING PARTIES, which may request the contracting parties concerned to consult with them if the change

seems likely to jeopardize or delay unduly the formation of the customs union or of the free-trade area.

8. For the purposes of this Agreement:

(a) A customs union shall be understood to mean the substitution of a single customs territory for two or more customs territories, so that

(i) duties and other restrictive regulations of commerce (except, where necessary, those permitted under Articles XI, XII, XIII, XIV, XV and XX) are eliminated with respect to substantially all the trade between the constituent territories of the union or at least with respect to substantially all the trade in products originating in such territories, and,

(ii) subject to the provisions of paragraph 9, substantially the same duties and other regulations of commerce are applied by each of the members of the union to the trade of territories not included in the union;

(b) A free-trade area shall be understood to mean a group of two or more customs territories in which the duties and other restrictive regulations of commerce (except, where necessary, those permitted under Articles XI, XII, XIII, XIV, XV and XX) are eliminated on substantially all the trade between the constituent territories in products originating in such territories.

9. The preferences referred to in paragraph 2 of Article I shall not be affected by the formation of a customs union or of a free-trade area but may be eliminated or adjusted by means of negotiations with contracting parties affected. This procedure of negotiations with affected contracting parties shall, in particular, apply to the elimination of preferences required to conform with the provisions of paragraph 8(a)(i) and paragraph 8(b).

10. The CONTRACTING PARTIES may by a two-thirds majority approve proposals which do not fully comply with the requirements of paragraphs 5 to 9 inclusive, provided that such proposals lead to the formation of a customs union or a free-trade area in the sense of this Article.
11. Taking into account the exceptional circumstances arising out of the establishment of India and Pakistan as independent States and recognizing the fact that they have long constituted an economic unit, the contracting parties agree that the provisions of this Agreement shall not prevent the two countries from entering into special arrangements with respect to the trade between them, pending the establishment of their mutual trade relations on a definitive basis.
12. Each contracting party shall take such reasonable measures as may be available to it to ensure observance of the provisions of this Agreement by the regional and local governments and authorities within its territory.

Study Questions

1. To what extent have multilateralism and preferential arrangements coexisted? What have been the roles of bilateral reciprocity combined with Most Favored Nation (MFN) treatment in the GATT? What is GATT Article XXIV?
2. What are the core principles of the GATT: nondiscrimination and reciprocity? In what sense is the GATT a "fix rule trading regime"?
3. What were the main accomplishments of the GATT negotiating rounds?
4. What are the principal features of GATT Article XXIV? What are the essential characteristics and consequences of preferential arrangements? What have been the most successful and durable preferential trading arrangements?
5. What is the case for multilateralism? How did the role and authority of the GATT adapt to a changing world economy? What are the criticisms of multilateralism and advantages of

preferential arrangements? What are the criticisms of preferential arrangements?

6. Is a world of a small number of trading blocs significantly inferior to a world of free trade? What are the characteristics and limitations of Krugman's model of trading blocs? What are the economic effects of trading blocs whose membership consists of countries with differences in their comparative advantage?
7. In what ways might the multilateral trading system be designed to accommodate preferential arrangements?

References

Baldwin, Robert E. 1987. "Multilateral Liberalization," in J. Michael Finger and Andrzej Olechowski (eds.), *A Handbook on the Multilateral Trade Negotiations.* Washington, D.C.: The World Bank.

Bergsten, C.F. 1991. "Commentary on Paul Krugman, 'The Move Toward Free Trade Zones'," in Federal Reserve Bank of Kansas City, *Policy Implications of Trade and Currency Zones.* Kansas City: Federal Reserve Bank of Kansas City.

Bhagwati, Jagdish N. 1990a. "Departures from Multilateralism: Regionalism and Aggressive Unilateralism," in David Greenaway (ed.), "Policy Forum: Multilateralism and Bilateralism in Trade Policy: Editorial Note," *Economic Journal* 100, pp. 1304–1317.

Bhagwati, Jagdish N. 1990b. "Multilateralism at Risk: The GATT is Dead. Long Live the GATT," *The World Economy* 13, pp. 149–169.

Bhagwati, Jagdish. 1992a. "Regionalism and Multilateralism: An Overview," in Jaime de Melo and Arvind Panagariya (eds.), *New Dimensions in Regional Integration.* New York: Cambridge University Press, forthcoming.

Bhagwati, Jagdish N. 1992b. "The Threats to the World Trading System," in Robert M. Stern (ed.), "Symposium on Issues for the Global Economy in the 1990s," *The World Economy* 15, pp. 443–456.

Bhagwati, Jagdish. 1995. "U.S. Trade Policy: The Infatuation with Free Trade Areas," in Bhagwati Jagdish and Andre D. Krueger (eds.), *The Dangerous Drift to Preferential Trade Agreements.* Washington, D.C.: American Enterprise Institute for Public Policy Research.

Brown, Drusilla K. 1987. "Tariffs, the Terms of Trade and National Product Differentiation," *Journal of Policy Modeling* 9, pp. 503–526.

Brown, Drusilla K., Alan V. Deardorff, and Robert M. Stern. 1992. "A North American Free Trade Agreement: Analytical Issues and a Computational Assessment," *The World Economy* 15, pp. 11–29.

Deardorff, Alan V. and Robert M. Stern. 1986. *The Michigan Model of World Production and Trade: Theory and Applications.* Cambridge: MIT Press.

de la Torre, Augusto and Margaret R. Kelly. 1992. *Regional Trade Arrangements*, Occasional Paper 93. Washington, D.C.: International Monetary Fund.

de Melo, Jaime, Arvind Panagariya, and Dani Rodrik. 1992. "Regional Integration: An Analytical and Empirical Overview," in Jaime de Melo and Arvind Panagariya (eds.), *New Dimensions in Regional Integration.* New York: Cambridge University Press, forthcoming.

Fieleke, Norman S. 1992. "One Trading World, or Many: The Issue of Regional Trading Blocs," *New England Economic Review*, May/June, pp. 3–20.

Finger, C. Michael. 1992. "GATT's Influence on Regional Arrangements," in Jaime de Melo and Arvind Panagariya (eds.), *New Dimensions in Regional Integration.* New York: Cambridge University Press, forthcoming.

Finger, J. M. 1979. "Trade Liberalization: A Public Choice Perspective," in Ryan C. Amacher, Gottfried Haberler, and Thomas D. Willett (eds.), *Challenges to a Liberal Economic Order.* Washington, D.C.: American Enterprise Institute.

Harrison, Glenn W. and E.E. Rustrom. 1991. "Trade Wars, Trade Negotiations and Applied Game Theory," *Economic Journal* 101, pp. 420–435.

Haveman, Jon D. 1992. "Some Welfare Effects of Dynamic Customs Union Formation," in process.

Hoekman, Bernard M. 1991. "Multilateral Trade Negotiations and the Coordination of Commercial Policies," in Robert M. Stern (ed.), *The Multilateral Trading System: Analysis and Prospects for Negotiating Change.* Ann Arbor: University of Michigan Press, forthcoming.

Irwin, Douglas A. 1992. "Multilateral and Bilateral Trade Policies in the World Trading System: An Historical Perspective," in Jaime de Melo and Arvind Panagariya (eds.), *New Dimensions in Regional Integration.* New York: Cambridge University Press, forthcoming.

Jackson, John H. 1989. *The World Trading System: Law and Policy of International Economic Relations.* Cambridge: MIT Press.

Jackson, John H. and William J. Davey. 1986. *International Economic Relations*, Second Edition. St. Paul: West Publishing Co.

Kemp, Murray C. and Henry Wan, Jr. 1976. "An Elementary Proposition Concerning the Formation of Customs Unions," *Journal of International Economics* 6, pp. 95–97.

Kennan, John and Raymond Riezman. 1990. "Optimal Tariff Equilibria with Customs Unions," *Canadian Journal of Economics* 23, pp. 70–83.

Kowalczyk, Carsten. 1989. "Trade Negotiations and World Welfare," *American Economic Review* 79, pp. 552–559.

Kowalczyk, Carsten. 1990. "Welfare and Customs Unions," National Bureau of Economic Research, Paper No. 3476. Cambridge: NBER.

Kowalczyk, Carsten. 1992. "Paradoxes in Integration Theory," *Open Economies Review* 3, pp. 51–59.

Krugman, Paul R. 1991a. "Is Bilateralism Bad?" in Elhanan Helpman and Assaf Razin (eds.), *International Trade and Trade Policy*. Cambridge: MIT Press.

Krugman, Paul. 1991b. "The Movement Toward Free Trade Zones," in Federal Reserve Bank of Kansas City, *Policy Implications of Trade and Currency Zones*. Kansas City: Federal Reserve Bank of Kansas City.

Krugman, Paul. 1992a. "Does the New Trade Theory Require a New Trade Policy?" in Robert M. Stern (ed.), "Symposium on Issues for the Global Economy in the 1990s," *The World Economy* 15, pp. 423–441.

Krugman, Paul. 1992b. "Regionalism vs. Multilateralism: Analytical Notes," in Jaime de Melo and Arvind Panagariya (eds.), *New Dimensions in Regional Integration*. New York: Cambridge University Press, forthcoming.

Ludema, Rodney D. 1991. "On the Value of Free-Trade Areas in Multilateral Negotiations," in process.

Nguyen, Trien T., Carlo Perroni, and Randall M. Wigle. 1991. "The Value of a Uruguay Round Success," *The World Economy* 14, pp. 359–374.

Nogues, Julio. 1990. "The Choice Between Unilateral and Multilateral Trade Liberalization Strategy," *The World Economy* 13, pp. 15–26.

Nogues, Julio and Rosalinda Quintanilla. 1992. "Latin America's Integration and the Multilateral Trading System," in Jaime de Melo and Arvind Panagariya (eds.), *New Dimensions in Regional Integration*. New York: Cambridge University Press, forthcoming.

Patterson, Gardner. 1989. "Implications for the GATT and the World Trading System," and "Comments" by John Whalley, in Jeffrey J. Schott (ed.), *Free Trade Areas and U.S. Trade Policy*. Washington, D.C.: Institute for International Economics.

Richardson, J. David. 1991. "U.S. Trade Policy in the 1980s: Turns and Roads Not Taken," National Bureau of Economic Research, NBER Working Paper No. 3725 (June). Cambridge: NBER.

Saxonhouse, Gary. 1992. "Trading Blocs, Pacific Trade and the Pricing Strategies of East Asian Firms," in Jaime de Melo and Arvind Panagariya (eds.), *New Dimensions in Regional Integration*. New York: Cambridge University Press, forthcoming.

Schott, Jeffrey J. 1989. "More Free Trade Areas?" in Jeffrey J. Schott (ed.), *Free Trade Areas and U.S. Trade Policy*. Washington, D.C.: Institute for International Economics.

Schott, Jeffrey J. 1991. "Trading Blocs and the World Trading System," *The World Economy* 14, pp. 1–18.

Whalley, John. 1985. *Trade Liberalization Among World Trading Areas*. Cambridge: MIT Press.

Whalley, John. 1991. "Harnessing the New Regionalism," in process.

Whalley, John. 1992. "Regional Trade Arrangements in North America: CUSTA and NAFTA," in process.

Winters, L. Alan. 1990. "The Road to Uruguay," in David Greenaway (ed.), "Policy Forum: Multilateralism and Bilateralism in Trade Policy: Editorial Note," *Economic Journal* 100, pp. 1288–1303.

Winters, L. Alan. 1992. "The European Community: A Case of Successful Integration," in Jaime de Melo and Arvind Panagariya (eds.), *New Dimensions in Regional Integration.* New York: Cambridge University Press, forthcoming.

Wolf, Martin. 1987. "Why Trade Liberalization is a Good Idea," in J. Michael Finger and Andrzej Olechowski (eds.), *A Handbook on the Multilateral Trade Negotiations.* Washington, D.C.: The World Bank.

Wonnacott, Paul and Mark Lutz. 1989. "Is There a Case for Free Trade Areas?" and "Comments" by Isaiah Frank and Martin Wolf, in Jeffrey J. Schott (ed.), *Free Trade Areas and U.S. Trade Policy.* Washington, D.C.: Institute for International Economics.

Yarbrough, Beth V. and Robert M. Yarbrough. 1986. "Reciprocity, Bilateralism, and Economic Hostages: Self-Enforcing Agreements in International Trade," *International Studies Quarterly* 30, pp. 7–21.

Suggested Further Reading

Bhagwati, Jagdish. 1993. "Regionalism and Multilateralism: An Overview," in Jaime de Melo and Arvind Panagariya (eds.), *New Dimensions in Regional Integration.* Cambridge: Cambridge University Press.

Bhagwati, Jagdish, Pravin Krishna, and Arvind Panagariya. 1999. *Trading Blocs: Alternative Approaches to Analyzing Preferential Trading Agreements.* Cambridge: MIT Press.

Ethier, Wilfred J. 1998. "Regionalism in a Multilateral World," *Journal of Political Economy* 106(6), pp. 1214–1245.

Krishna, Pravin. 1998. "Regionalism and Multilateralism: A Political Economy Approach," *Quarterly Journal of Economics* 113(1), pp. 227–250.

Limao, Nuno. 2006. "Preferential vs. Multilateral Trade Liberalization: Evidence and Open Questions," *World Trade Review* 5(2), pp. 155–176.

Preeg, Ernest H. 1970. *Traders and Diplomats: A History and Analysis of the Kennedy Round of Negotiations Under the GATT.* Washington, D.C.: The Brookings Institution.

Chapter 7

An Overview of the Modeling of the Choices and Consequences of U.S. Trade Policies*

Alan V. Deardorff and Robert M. Stern

I. Introduction

This chapter is designed to provide the context for the theme of a conference entitled "The Representation of Constituent Interests in the Design and Implementation of U.S. Trade Policies," which was held at the University of Michigan in November 1996. In Section II, we first review the normative and political economy approaches to the modeling of trade policies. The normative approach is the basis for the traditional analysis of the welfare effects of trade and the choice of policies designed to correct distortions in the economy and to achieve first-best optima. The political economy approach provides an analytical framework for understanding of the choices made by policy makers in a political setting in response to the lobbying and related activities of producing interests. We identify

* Reprinted with permission from Alan V. Deardorff and Robert M. Stern, eds., *Constituent Interests and U.S. Trade Policies*, Ann Arbor: University of Michigan Press, 1998, pp. 29–52.

the major limitations of these approaches and then discuss what Dixit (1996) has referred to as the "transaction-cost approach," which may provide a middle-ground between the other approaches and enable us to address some hitherto imperfectly understood issues of trade policy. We also include in Section II a brief discussion of the empirical literature pertinent to the normative and political economy approaches.

In Section III, we provide a sketch of the main features of the U.S. trade-policy process, focusing in particular on the roles played by the agencies of government together with the important constituent interest groups in the U.S. economy. We then consider how each of the modeling approaches can be interpreted in its representation of the behavior and interactions of the different constituencies. Setting the modeling issues aside, we also ask what can be learned from the half-century of U.S. trade policy experiences after World War II, and we observe that there has been a distinctive movement towards more liberal and open trade in the United States and elsewhere during this period.

In Section IV, we conclude with some summary remarks and discuss the implications of the interplay of the different modeling approaches for research and policy in light of our observation about the ways in which trade liberalization and increased openness have evolved.

II. Issues of Policy Design and Choice

Economic theories have traditionally been divided into two categories, positive and normative, the former attempting to describe what is, the latter what ought to be. Analyses of economic policies, such as international trade policies, have similarly been of these two types. Normative analysis of trade policies has included, for example, theories of the optimal tariff; while positive analysis, since it must describe the behavior of policy makers, has typically been labeled the political economy of trade policy. In this section we will briefly review these two strands of literature. Then we will discuss the approach to policy analysis, dubbed by Dixit (1996) as the "transaction-cost" approach, and examine what it may say for the design of international economic policy.

The Normative Approach to Policy Making

The normative approach to policy making has a very long history in the field of trade policy, extending back to the earliest writings of Smith and Ricardo on the desirability of free trade. Normative analysis starts with a conception (often implicit) of a social welfare function of the Bergson–Samuelson variety, which is built up from the utility functions of individuals. In other cases, normative conclusions are motivated only by a Pareto efficiency criterion, that is, that no opportunities remain unexploited that would improve the welfare of one individual without harming another. On these bases, trade theorists have established some now classic results:

- That free trade is Pareto optimal for the world as a whole;
- That free trade is Pareto optimal for a country whose domestic markets are not distorted, provided that the country is too small to influence its terms of trade;
- That a large country can optimally exploit its power over the terms of trade, and therefore over its trading partners, by levying a positive tariff, provided however that other countries do not respond in kind;
- That while trade intervention may be welfare improving even for a small country if distortions exist within it, a better policy will always deal more directly with those distortions.

Distortions here refer to all manner of departures from the norm of perfect competition that has provided the benchmark for optimality in a closed economy since the work of Arrow and Debreu. A short list of such distortions would include: externalities, positive or negative, across consumers and/or producers; market power on the part of buyers and/or sellers that enables them to influence prices; policies that intervene in markets causing differences in the prices faced by different consumers and/or producers; and noneconomic objectives that enter the social welfare function with or without appearing in individual utility functions. Any of these will give rise to the potential for benefit from some sort of policy that itself introduces another distortion. Ideally, such a policy should be designed either to correct or offset the distortion by making the policy-induced distortion equal and opposite to the distortion being corrected. Trade policies, because they distort prices faced by both producers and consumers, are almost always suboptimal and often welfare worsening. As we suggested some years ago in Deardorff and Stern (1987), use of trade policy is like "doing acupuncture with a fork" since no matter how well you aim the first prong (distortion), the other will cause unwanted damage. The one exception is the terms of trade argument for a large country, where the failure of individual producers and consumers to internalize their country's effect on the terms of trade distorts both of their decisions equally.

A critical issue in any normative policy analysis, however, trade or otherwise, is the distribution of income. If the income distribution matters to society, as it surely must, then one could include it in the above list of distortions, with the implication that the first-best policy for dealing with it would be one that directly redistributes income without itself introducing other unwanted distortions. Such a policy would be a system of lump-sum taxes and transfers, defined as payments that do not depend on any behavior that is in the control of those affected. In the static world of Arrow–Debreu general equilibrium, where either time does not exist or where all transactions to the end of time are contracted in advance, such a policy is easy to define. In the real world, however, it is impossible both to base such payments on observables that are truly outside the control of the individuals whose income is to be altered, and to have the resulting payments do any good in improving the income distribution. Most obviously, basing payments on observed income will induce both payers and recipients to deliberately earn less income, so as to alter the payments in their favor. Therefore, the prescription of using a first-best policy for redistributing income is not helpful.

In the field of public finance, there is a large literature dealing accordingly with "optimal taxation," attempting to identify how best to use the necessarily distorting tax policy tools that are available. In the field of international trade, the issue of income distribution has been dealt with primarily by arguing that, in this case, trade policies are not even second best. Dixit and Norman (1980, 1984) have shown that removal of trade policies can be accompanied by changes in commodity (consumer) taxes and subsidies in such a way as to leave all consumers at least as well off as before. A corollary is that any desired change in income distribution can be achieved better by using commodity taxes and subsidies than by using trade policies, even though the former are themselves only second best since they too provide incentives to alter behavior.

These strong implications of normative analysis of trade policies are viewed by some as rather troubling, since they prescribe policies that are so at variance with what we see being used in the world. The only first-best use of trade policy that the normative analysis allows is to improve the terms of trade. This motivation would suggest at best, however, that trade would be restricted only by large countries, whereas we typically observe the largest trade barriers used in developing countries, many of which are economically quite small. At the same time, normative analysis provides hardly any rationale at all for policies that promote trade, rather than restricting it, although the new trade theory has identified certain special cases where subsidies to trade may be welfare improving for strategic reasons. Therefore, the normative analysis identifies as optimal a world that is so far from what we actually observe that one may wonder about its relevance, and even its accuracy.

The Political Economy Approach to Policy Making

In part because of dissatisfaction with normative theory as a means of understanding actual international trade policies, the political economy approach has been developed by a variety of authors over the last two decades especially. This literature has taken the positive approach of trying to *explain what is, not necessarily what ought to be*, and that has meant modeling the political process in some fashion along with the economics of trade. Since this literature has been ably surveyed several times, for example by Rodrik (1995) and by Helpman (1995), rather than duplicate their efforts, we will simply provide a short overview, based largely on their contributions.[1]

The unified treatment that characterized the normative approach has not been possible for the political economy models, largely because there is no consensus model of the political process. Instead, various authors have identified different features of the political environment and political processes to stress in their modeling, and they have consequently obtained a corresponding variety of conclusions. The five principal types of model are listed in Table 1, which has been adapted mainly from Rodrik (1995) and Helpman (1995). The first two of these model types attempt explicitly to model the political electoral process, along with the economics. The last three, on the other hand, deal more abstractly with political forces, assuming that lobbyists and/or policy makers set political contributions and/or levels of protection to maximize their own welfare given the action of the other group. In effect, they model protection as the result of an equilibrium between supply and demand for protection along the lines outlined by Baldwin (1982).

The most straightforward modeling of the political determinants of protection was done by Mayer (1984), who explicitly modeled a simple political environment in which tariffs are selected by direct democracy, that is, by majority vote. Letting the level of protection be voted on directly means that it will be set to favor the median voter. By combining this assumption with a standard model of international trade (Mayer considered both a Heckscher–Ohlin (H-O) model and a specific factors (SF) model), Mayer was able to predict tariffs based on the distribution of ownership of factors of production. Unfortunately, if factors are narrowly owned while consumer interests are broad, this approach predicts counter-factually that tariffs will be nonexistent, or even negative. In the H-O model, if labor ownership is broad while capital ownership is concentrated, the model delivers protection on the labor intensive good, which seems more plausible.

[1] Both surveys provide ample references to the literature that can be consulted for more detailed analysis and discussion.

Table 1. Types of political economy models of trade policy.

Modeling Approach	Author(s)	Who Sets Tariffs?	How It Works	Protection Depends on
Median-voter approach (Direct democracy)	Mayer (1984)	Median voter: by selecting tariff that maximizes that voter's welfare	Population derives income from industries, possibly protected. They vote on level of tariff, which therefore maximizes the income of the median voter	+ median voter's share of ownership + number of people in industry + size of sector – elasticity of import demand
Campaign contributions approach (Electoral competition)	Magee–Brock–Young (1989)	Politicians and lobbyists jointly: parties select tariffs to benefit their associated factor, while lobbyists contribute to their probability of election	Elections depend on contributions. Factor owners contribute to precommitted political parties to maximize their earnings	Outcome of Nash game

(*Continued*)

Table 1. (*Continued*)

Modeling Approach	Author(s)	Who Sets Tariffs?	How It Works	Protection Depends on
Tariff-formation function approach	Findlay–Wellisz (1982)	Industries: by spending resources on lobbying and optimizing on the given tariff-formation function	Tariff assumed to depend directly on resources spent on lobbying. All individuals maximize their incomes	+ relative effectiveness of pro- vs. anti-protection dollars – number of people in industry + size of sector – elasticity of import demand
Political support function approach	Hillman (1989)	Policy makers: by selecting tariffs to maximize given political support function	"Political support" depends on industry profits and efficiency. Policy makers maximize political support	– weight of efficiency in political support + size of sector – elasticity of import demand
Political contributions approach	Grossman–Helpman (1994)	Politicians: to maximize objective function defined on contributions and welfare	Single incumbent chooses policy to maximize contributions and economic welfare. Industry (specific factor) lobbyists offer optimal contributions contingent on policies	– number of people in industry – weight attached to welfare + size of sector – elasticity of import demand

Source: Adapted from Rodrik (1995) and Helpman (1995).

And if a small cost of voting is added to the SF model, decision can be taken away from the median voter and a broad pattern of protection favoring specific factors can emerge. However, the approach suffers in all cases from the unreality of the assumption that individual tariffs are determined by majority vote, which is virtually never the case in practice.

Magee, Brock, and Young (1989) (MBY) sought greater realism in modeling the electoral process by assuming representative democracy. To the 2 × 2 × 2 H-O trade model they added two political parties, one favoring free trade and the other protection, plus two lobbying groups, representing the interests of the two factors of production. Parties announce their intended levels of protection in their political platforms, adjusting these levels to maximize their probabilities of election given the contributions they expect from lobbyists responding to those platforms. Lobbyists then set their optimal contributions in response. This model has much greater realism than the direct democracy model, but it is much weaker in its ability to yield clear implications. It is, for example, the only approach from which Helpman was unable to derive a clean expression for the level of protection, as reported in the final column of Table 1, where it is noted only that protection depends on the Nash equilibrium of a game.[2] Furthermore, the attempt at greater realism is perhaps inevitably unsuccessful, since it can never capture the full richness of what actual political parties and lobbying groups are able to do, or how their interaction results in an electoral outcome.

An alternative approach, therefore, has been to focus not on the actual mechanics of the political process and its methods of making decisions, but rather to model the larger forces that interact in producing policy outcomes and the ways that participants in the process deal with these forces. The first such example actually predated Mayer's (1984) direct democracy model, and was provided by Findlay

[2] That is, equilibrium is defined as levels of protection for each party that are optimal given the level of protection provided by other party. However, it is apparently not possible to solve for this equilibrium in an explicit form comparable to the formulas obtained from the other models.

and Wellisz (1982). They subsumed the entire policy-making process into a black box, so to speak, that translated lobbying expenditure into tariffs. This "tariff formation function" was then the basis for optimization by owners of sector-specific factors, who would choose their levels of lobbying to maximize the net benefits to them of securing protection.

A second such approach was, in a sense, the mirror image of the tariff formation function approach. Hillman (1989) started instead from a "political support function," which in effect translated the tariff provided by a policy maker into the level of political support that it would receive in return. This, then, was another black box, this time on the industry side, although Hillman did assume that the support arising due to the profits generated by the tariff would be tempered by a loss of political support in other dimensions due to the tariff's induced economic inefficiency. Thus here it is the policy maker, not the industry, who optimizes, balancing the political gains from providing protection against the political losses from inefficiency, both of which were embodied in the political support function.

Just as the tariff formation function approach focused on the decision to demand protection, leaving the supply of protection unexplained, the political support function approach focuses on the supply of protection, leaving the demand for it unexplained. These two approaches were therefore complementary, and it was natural that the next step would combine them. This was the contribution of Grossman and Helpman (1994).[3]

In this "political contributions approach," the lobbying expenditures of Findlay–Wellisz become direct payments, but instead of contributing to the campaigns of political parties as in MBY, the Grossman–Helpman industries make payments directly to policy makers already in office. Also, the contributors stipulate that their payments are in return for protection — in fact, they offer an entire schedule of payments to the policy makers, stating the amounts that they will contribute as functions of the protection provided.

[3] Feenstra and Bhagwati (1982) also modeled supply and demand for protection interactively, as a game between labor and government.

The policy makers, in turn, make optimal choices from these schedules, which were themselves determined optimally by the industries. In effect, then, the political contributions approach combines the tariff formation function and the political support function, each however now being derived as the optimal response to the other.

At the present time, the political contributions approach of Grossman and Helpman is the state-of-the-art in the political economy of trade policy, and it has indeed proven to be a useful and versatile analytical framework. Its authors have succeeded in applying the approach not only to the original problem of explaining tariffs, but also to explaining competition and cooperation in tariff setting, the politics of free trade areas, and other issues.

These political economy models have moved us well beyond the limited understanding of international trade policies that we had before they were developed. We now can see a variety of reasons why the political process yields outcomes that economists view as suboptimal. Furthermore, that understanding has been embodied in an analytical framework where we can observe the tradeoffs of competing interests and even predict, to an extent, how the political and economic systems will respond to changes in the conditions that they face.

As for explaining the level of protection itself, most of these approaches yield predictions of what considerations will lead to more or less protection. Helpman (1995) expressed each of the above approaches to political economy in a unified modeling framework and was able to derive the explicit tariff formulas that were predicted by four of the five approaches. The implications of these tariff formulas in terms of what motivates protection are listed in the final column of Table 1. It is interesting that the approaches all agreed on the (positive) importance of both industry size as well as inelasticity of demand in giving rise to protection for a sector. Each approach also has its own distinctive parameters that influence protection, while the approaches disagree on the role of the number of people in an industry in determining its protection.

On the other hand, there still exist a number of issues that are unexplained by any of these political economy models. This, in fact, was the theme of Rodrik (1995), who noted several such gaps in the theory. These were:

Why is international trade not free? The models explain why governments intervene in the economy, which is in order to alter the distribution of income in favor of certain interests. But they do not explain why intervention in trade is the tool used for this purpose, except by assuming that it is the only tool available. We know from the normative approach to trade policy that trade intervention is not first-best for this purpose, and optimizing governments and/or industry interests could therefore gain more of whatever they are seeking by using other policies. Thus, if those other policies were included in the political economy models, they would imply that trade of small countries would be free. Rodrik reviews several papers that have provided partial but rather specialized answers to this question. He concludes (p. 1476) that "a sufficiently general and convincing explanation for this phenomenon has yet to be formulated."

Why are trade policies universally biased against trade? Even with only trade policies admitted into the models as tools, many of them have the unfortunate implication that trade should be subsidized as often as it is taxed. That is, the same considerations that lead a government to favor an import-competing industry with a tariff should lead it to favor export industries with export subsidies. Yet this is clearly not the case in the real world, where explicit export subsidies are confined primarily to agriculture, while tariffs and other trade restrictions have been applied pretty much across the board for industrial products. One answer to this is to point to the GATT prohibition against export subsidies, but this seems only to beg the question, since the GATT prohibition (against export subsidies but not against tariffs) remains unexplained. Rodrik finds only a handful of explanations for the bias against trade in the literature, the most successful in his view being a combination of history (that tariffs were the best or only way that early governments had to generate revenues) and some model of persistence, or bias in favor of the status quo.

What are the determinants of the variation in protection levels across industries, countries and time? Here there has been more work done, both empirical and theoretical, and indeed part of the motivation for the political economy literature on trade policy has been to explain or illuminate some of the empirical work that preceded it. But while reviewing with approval some efforts to explain what has been observed empirically, Rodrik's assessment (p. 1482) is that "these empirical regularities overlap only imperfectly with the results of the theoretical literature." We shall have more to say on this below.

The Transaction-Cost Approach to Policy Making

While it seems clear that the normative approach to policy making suffers from its failure to incorporate political considerations that in fact prevent optimal policies from being undertaken, the political economy approach perhaps goes too far in the other direction. With all policies being determined endogenously, there is no scope for policy analysis itself to make any contribution. That is, the same model that tells us that the policy makers will use tariffs to protect special interests also tells us that it is useless to ask them to do otherwise. They are, at least in the models that address their behavior explicitly, already behaving optimally given their incentives and constraints. They are already taking into account, to the extent they are willing, any effects on the broader social welfare that we might tell them about. Indeed, if there really were a role for scholars to play in formulating policy, a proper political economy model should already have incorporated those scholars into the model. There seems accordingly to be no scope for analysts of policy to contribute to the improvement of the world economy, except perhaps by diligently carrying out their assigned role as information providers.

A possible escape from this conundrum is provided by the literature on public choice, of which the political economy approach to policy making is really a part. Buchanan and Tulloch (1962) and later writings by Buchanan and others distinguished between the individual policies made by policy makers and the framework, or constitution, within which those policy makers operate. As Dixit (1996) puts it, there is a distinction between *policy acts* and *policy rules.* Policy acts are determined endogenously by policy makers interacting with other interests and within the framework of constraints and incentives that the policy rules provide, and it is therefore useless to try to change those acts at that level. But the policy rules are set less frequently and from behind a "veil of uncertainty" as to how the rules will affect those who set the rules. The proper role for policy analysis is therefore to inform the setting of the rules. Thus, for example in the context of the Grossman–Helpman political economy model of trade policy, it is pointless to tell the policy makers that tariffs benefit industries at the expense of consumers. They already know that, and they are taking it into account when they balance the contributions they receive against the general interest. However, one could still press for a revision of the rules that would, say, make contributions more difficult, or that would enhance the incentive for policy makers to respond to social welfare. Unfortunately, constitutions are seldom rewritten, and therefore if the only hope for improving public policy is through that channel, an idealistic advocate of improved public policy might be forgiven for being discouraged.

Dixit (1996), however, has argued for a middle-ground between the normative analysis and the more positive political economy approach. He argues first that the distinction between policy acts and policy rules is too extreme. On the one hand, policy rules are never really formulated behind a complete veil of uncertainty. Framers of a constitution always have clear ideas of where their own interests lie, at least in the short run, and they cannot be expected to ignore those interests in formulating the rules that they themselves will live by. At the same time, many individual policy acts have implications for future policy rules, as they may influence precedents or expectations of future policies. At both levels, then, makers of both policy rules and policy acts will typically have both some degrees of freedom for working in the public interest, but also some stake in the outcome themselves that limits their degrees of freedom in other dimensions. Policy making is in fact, Dixit argues, an ongoing process that occurs in real time and that blends both the private incentives of the policy makers to respond to special and general interests, together with an evolution of the rules of policy that gradually may change those incentives.

While this may seem very confusing and imprecise, Dixit suggests a fruitful way to sort out how policy is constrained, but that may nonetheless guide that evolution. This is to focus on "transaction costs." He defines these as any distortions in the political and/or economic environments that interfere with the direct pursuit of the optima that a normative analysis might identify. These include things like uncertainty and asymmetric information, incomplete contracts, agency problems,[4] bounded rationality, and no doubt many others. The proper role for policy analysts, then, is not to tell policy makers what to do (the policy acts) on an ongoing basis, or to wait for infrequent opportunities to revise the entire constitution of policy. Rather, they should be watching for opportunities that arise more frequently to make changes in the rules of policy, and their recommendations should be formulated against the backdrop of the transaction costs that may already be evident in the kinds of policy rules that are currently in place. That is, they should be looking for changes in rules and procedures that allow the economic and political systems to deal more effectively with transaction costs. These changes may be only small and incremental, but on occasion they may involve or lead to regime changes that are sizable in scope.

Dixit gives only one formal example of how this might work. He builds a model of common agency, in which multiple principals are served by a single agent whom they attempt to influence for their own benefit. With the acts of the agent only imperfectly observable by the principals, they will in general be unable to motivate a first-best outcome for all concerned, even if they were to act together. The reason is the problem of moral hazard that routinely arises in such cases, reflecting a tradeoff between efficiency and risk sharing, and this is one example of a transactions cost. An additional transaction cost is also present here, however, if the principals cannot act together. Acting independently, and even if each cares only about a separate dimension of the agent's behavior, they nonetheless will provide

[4] This refers to the problems that arise when one individual, the agent, acts on behalf of another, the principal. The problem is for the principal to devise a system of incentives that will induce the agent to act in the principal's interest.

incentives to the agent to skimp on their service of other principals, in order to get more for themselves. The result is even worse than the second-best outcome that could have been achieved had they acted together. Dixit shows, however, that if principals can be prevented from penalizing the service to other principals, perhaps by removing their access to information about that service, then the principals acting separately will do better than even the second-best outcome they could have achieved together. That is, in this context in which an agent provides separate services for multiple principals, the principals will be better served if each is *not* told what the agent has done for others, as compared to all having full information. This is an example, albeit rather abstract, in which it would serve no purpose to instruct the agent simply to implement a first-best policy, since the agent cannot be expected to ignore the incentives coming from the principals. But a change in the framework of policy, in this case changing the information that is available to the principals, is both possible and may be agreed upon, since it permits a more efficient outcome that can benefit all and that none will have the means or incentive to undermine.

In this view, institutional arrangements that condition policy choices should be viewed as "coping mechanisms" for dealing with transaction costs, and they should be judged not on whether they yield first-best outcomes but rather on whether they do better than alternative arrangements that are available for the same purpose. Thus in Dixit's example above, the underlying transaction costs, which arise first from moral hazard and second from the presence of multiple principals, make a first-best outcome impossible. Allowing each of the multiple principals independently to lobby the agent may be far from optimal, but as a means of coping with these transaction costs it may nonetheless be better than alternatives that, say, might neglect the interests of many of these principals altogether. On the other hand, once it has been discovered by means of economic analysis that this particular coping mechanism can be improved upon by restricting the information available to the principals, it becomes possible to improve the coping mechanism. And note that such an improvement may not need to wait for a complete overhaul of the policy regime such as might accompany a new constitution.[5] Rather, coping mechanisms can be modified in both small and large ways, and in real time, as either the system or our understanding of it evolve.

What does all of this have to do with trade policy? Here, alas, we are on our own, since Dixit's book does not address the questions that we would most like his approach to answer for our purpose here. The closest he comes to applying his transaction-cost approach to trade policy is a thoughtful discussion of the international trading system in the second half of the twentieth century, from the GATT to the WTO. He uses transaction costs, for example, to explain the presence of exceptions in the GATT and WTO rules on tariff bindings. Without the safeguards clause, which permits countries to raise tariffs when a surge of imports causes major damage to a domestic competing industry, the GATT would be unable to sustain its cooperation in the face of its Prisoners' Dilemma incentives to defect. Dixit also discusses other features of the GATT and WTO rules, such as the treatments of textiles, agriculture, and nontariff barriers, all of which he sees as coping mechanisms but not especially good ones.

Dixit does not address the questions that Rodrik identified as being unanswered by the political economy approaches to trade policy, and we may ask whether the transaction-cost approach offers any better hope of resolving them. We will focus only on the first two of Rodrik's three questions: Why is international trade not free? And why are trade policies universally biased against trade? Interpretations of these questions, in light of the political economy literature, might be: Why do policy makers redistribute income by taxing imports instead of (more efficiently) subsidizing production? And why do they also seem to favor import-competing industries over export industries, taxing imports but not subsidizing exports?

---

[5] That of course depends on what the existing constitution says. In the example, if the existing constitution mandates freedom of information, then the needed change to restrict the principals' knowledge of each others' benefits might require a constitutional change. For while it is in their collective interests to restrict information, each individually would have an incentive to seek that information given the freedom to do so.

A simple, and hardly new, answer to both of these questions is that tariffs on imports are much less well understood by the public (and perhaps also by the policy makers and their constituents) than are subsidies. A subsidy to production is clearly a hand-out, and the public understands that. Even when a subsidy is provided not by direct payment but by a tax break, the public understands that as well. But the benefits from a tariff (or quota) on imports may not be viewed as accruing directly to the industry that benefits, even though as economists we understand that the effect is the same as if it did. On the contrary, a tariff on imports may be viewed as mattering most directly only for foreign producers, and even its effect on domestic consumers is not always fully appreciated by the lay public. Furthermore, the beneficiary from a tariff appears to be the government, which collects the revenue, a fact that even adversely affected consumers might perceive as offsetting some of their loss (as indeed it does). Thus, the fact that a tariff has all of the effects (and more) of a subsidy to domestic producers is something that the producers may figure out, but that the rest of the citizenry may find difficult to comprehend. Similarly, regarding the bias against trade, while a government may protect its import-competing industries without complete public understanding, a similar attempt to assist export industries with a subsidy will be understood at once. Therefore, both of Rodrik's questions can possibly be answered by noting the difficulty of the public's understanding the true effects of tariffs in contrast to the ease of understanding the effects of subsidies.

As far as we can see, this explanation of patterns of policy assistance does not fit well into any political economy approach to policy. But it may well fit within the transaction-cost approach. Problems of incomplete and asymmetric information have already been mentioned as sources of transaction costs, as well as the need for policy institutions to find ways of coping with them. Those problems had to do with knowing what a particular economic agent was doing. Here we are stressing a different kind of incomplete information: the incomplete understanding of economic cause and effect that characterizes a potentially important part of the public. This is a transaction cost as much as the others, and like the others it has led to coping mechanisms.[6]

One such coping mechanism is simply education. Over the last half century, the message of economists about the effects of trade policy has been repeated in schools, in the press, and even occasionally (though not recently) in presidential debates. It may be argued that this has been in part responsible for the remarkable reduction in tariffs that has been achieved over this period. Of course, this occurred in conjunction with another coping mechanism, the GATT and the rounds of multilateral trade negotiation that it sponsored. As already noted, Dixit sees the history of the GATT as a good example of coping with transaction costs, which he identified as Prisoners' Dilemma incentives that would otherwise characterize trade policy in the absence of GATT-sponsored cooperation. But we would argue that the GATT, and now the WTO, has been a mechanism also of coping with public ignorance about trade policy. And it truly has been an exercise of coping with the cost, not removing it, for the rule of the GATT has not so much been to educate the public about the true effects of trade as to instill instead a sense of international obligation that may have some of the same effect. We return to this point at the end of Section III.

Of course, no coping mechanism is perfect, and this has been true in spades of the GATT success in bringing down tariffs. To some extent, as the public has come to recognize the adverse effects of tariffs, attention has merely shifted to trade policy tools that are even less comprehensible, such as quotas, voluntary export restraints, and government-to-government political pressures. The increasing resort to NTBs as tariffs have fallen is well documented, although their overall quantitative significance has not been definitively measured.[7] Our own view is that the decline in tariffs has done far more good than the harm caused by the NTBs that have replaced them. But the rise of

[6] As noted in Table 3 below, Krueger (1996) suggests a number of examples of simple arguments favoring protection that achieve public acceptance even though the protection may be detrimental to consumer welfare.

[7] See Deardorff and Stern (1996) for an analysis of methods of measuring NTBs.

NTBs has meant that the informational transactions costs in trade policy that remain will be more difficult to cope with than those we have faced previously.

Empirical Evidence

Our discussion thus far has focused on the conceptual aspects of the different approaches to the modeling of trade policy. In this connection, it may be useful to supplement this discussion with reference to some of the pertinent empirical literature and methodology used.

The Normative Approach

A variety of empirical methods have been used to study the cost of protection or subsidies and its counterpart, the reduction/removal of these policies. These methods include: (1) partial equilibrium estimates by commodity group/sector, based primarily on assumed values of demand and supply elasticities; (2) partial equilibrium industry studies using econometric analysis; and (3) computable general equilibrium (CGE) model simulations. These studies typically yield estimates of the welfare effects of tariffs and NTBs of various kinds, with varying degrees of precision depending on the assumptions used especially in choosing or estimating the critical elasticity parameters and different market structures.

Illustrative studies include: (1) Hufbauer and Elliott's (1994) partial equilibrium estimates of the cost of U.S. protection by sector; (2) review of measurement of NTBs by Deardorff and Stern (1996); (3) econometric analysis of the U.S. auto sector by Berry, Levinsohn, and Pakes (1995); and (4) Martin and Winters (1996), which contains several CGE analyses of the effects of the Uruguay Round negotiations. While these different types of studies have certain methodological limitations, they are nonetheless useful in calling attention to the orders of magnitude of the welfare effects of existing trade policies and changes in these policies. They can serve accordingly as a kind of benchmark in determining how significant the departures from first-best optima may be. Of course, there will still remain a need to understand why these trade policies are used in the political context and what their impact will be through time as coping mechanisms may or may not come into play.

The Political Economy Approach

There is a very substantial empirical literature that has sought to explain the determinants of trade policy. These include both regression-type studies and case studies of the experiences of individual countries and sectors. Many of these studies have related to U.S. trade policy, although some cross-country studies have been done as well. Rodrik (1995) surveys many of the pertinent regression studies, while Krueger (1996) contains case studies of a number of important U.S. sectors that have been the object of U.S. trade-policy actions. Some of the key findings and hypotheses that emerge from the various studies are summarized in Tables 2 and 3.

As already mentioned, Rodrik notes (p. 1480) that there has not been a very close link between the theoretical and empirical research, and that the empirical research has thus often been designed in an intuitive rather than rigorous manner. From the final column in Table 1, industry size and employment would appear to be important theoretically, although the expected sign of employment is not the same for all the models. However, the actual evidence summarized in Table 2 appears to emphasize many other factors that are not represented directly in the different modeling approaches. Much the same can be said about many of the key hypotheses derived from the U.S. case studies summarized in Table 3. This is not to deny the accomplishments of the formal political economy models described in Table 1. But it suggests nevertheless that these models provide but a limited understanding of what in fact are the main determinants and consequences of trade policy in the United States and other countries.

III. Representation of Constituent Interests

In this section, we first discuss the main features of the U.S. trade-policy process and then interpret this process in the light of the

Table 2. Summary of key results of empirical studies of the determinants of protection.

1. Protection across industries

- Protection received by an industry is higher when:
    - it is a labor-intensive, low-skill, low-wage industry;
    - it has high import penetration, has experienced an increase in import penetration, or has been in decline;
    - it produces consumer goods rather than intermediate goods;
    - it engages in little intra-industry trade;
    - its customers are not highly concentrated.
- There is mixed evidence on whether high levels of industry concentration result in greater protection.
- Tariffs and NTBs may be complements.

2. Protection across countries or institutional contexts

- Average tariff rates tend to decrease as capital-labor ratios increase.
- Poor countries tend to tax agriculture while rich countries subsidize it.
- NTBs are higher in countries that are economically large, have higher unemployment rates, have larger average size and smaller average number of parliamentary constituencies, and use proportional representation as their electoral system (subject to the degree of autonomy of party leaders).
- In U.S. antidumping proceedings, the determination of dumping depends on technical factors while the determination of injury is more political and is affected by industry concentration, size, and employment.

3. Protection over time in the United States

- The average tariff level tends to rise in recessions.
- Historically, Republicans have tended to raise tariffs and Democrats to reduce them.
- The delegation of tariff setting to the Executive Branch has resulted in the lowering of tariffs and reduced susceptibility to narrow pressure groups.
- There may be higher levels of protection when the political parties are divided between the Executive Branch and the Congress.

4. Protection over time in developing countries

- In a deep economic crisis, when economy-wide macroeconomic reforms are introduced, it may be easier to introduce trade-policy reforms as well.

Source: Adapted from Rodrik (1995, pp. 1480–1487).

Table 3. Summary of key political economy hypotheses based on case studies of U.S. sectoral trade policies.

1. **U.S. economic and political interests are not effectively served by protectionism.** The interests of final consumers are not taken into account. No consideration is given to the effects of protection on the costs to other industries. Protection introduced in periods of recession tends to remain in place.
2. **Simple rather than complex arguments are most effective in obtaining industry protection.** Considerations of "fairness," "equity," job loss, the "need" for an industry, and maintenance of incomes are often invoked in seeking protection.
3. **Political clout is crucial in obtaining protection.**
4. **Institutions may be designed to constrain protection**, as for example, in NAFTA and the Uruguay Round agreement in which protection is to be phased out over time.
5. **Protection may not actually help protected sectors because of offsetting market-induced responses and technological change.**
6. **Protection is more likely when there is unanimity among the firms involved.** User industries appear generally unwilling to oppose protection that raises their input costs.
7. **Effective lobbying and organization of interest groups are important determinants of protection.**
8. **Past protection can be expected to lead to future protection.** History matters.

Source: Adapted from Krueger (1996, pp. 431–441).

modeling approaches just discussed. We consider thereafter what can be learned about the design and consequences of U.S. trade-policy experiences in the past half century since the end of World War II.

Structure of the U.S. Trade-Policy Process

In Figure 1, we present a schematic overview of how the U.S. trade-policy process is structured and its various functions. This will of course be very familiar to trade specialists. Nonetheless, it will be helpful in clarifying the subsequent discussion of the advantages and limitations of the different modeling approaches. The top part of the figure depicts the Executive Branch, Congress, and the main

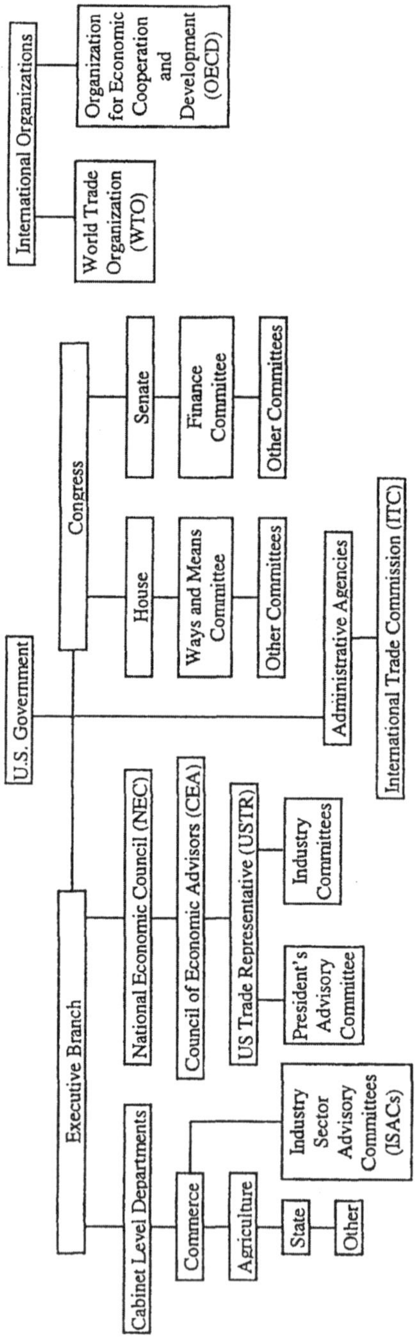

Figure 1. Structure of the U.S. trade-policy process.

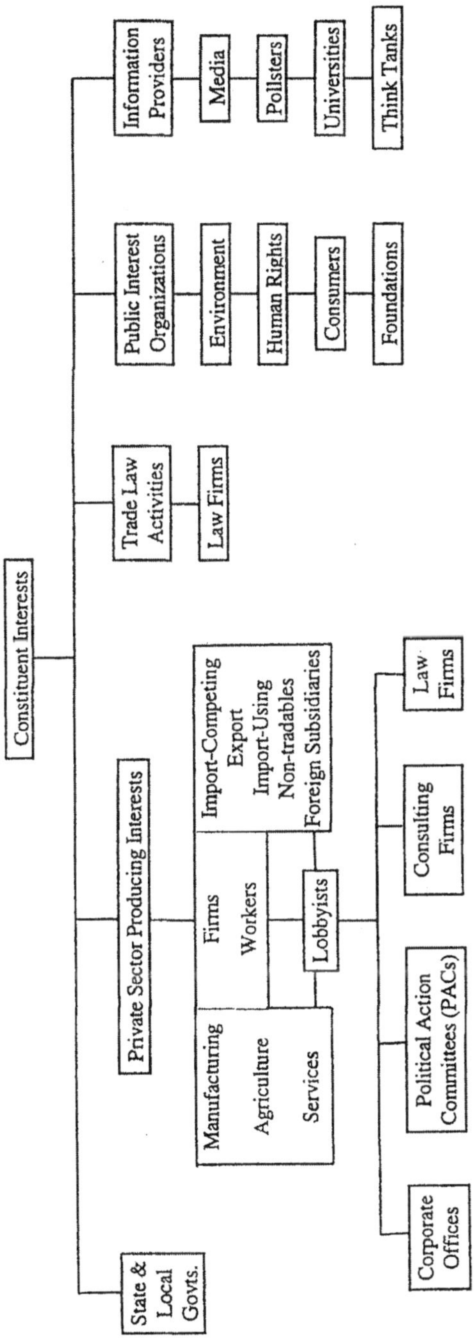

Figure 1. (*Continued*)

administrative agency, the International Trade Commission (ITC), which investigates especially alleged violations of U.S. trade laws. We also show membership in the World Trade Organization (WTO), which is the bridge between U.S. domestic trade laws and their international counterparts as embodied in the WTO charter. The locus of U.S. trade policies is centered in the Executive Branch, in particular in the Office of the U.S. Trade Representative (USTR), which was established in the 1960s in an effort to concentrate in a single agency the responsibilities for decision making on trade matters and international trade negotiations that previously had been carried out on an interagency basis at the cabinet level. The National Economic Council was established by the Clinton Administration in 1993 and presumably provides recommendations on the overall directions of U.S. trade policies. The Council of Economic Advisors (CEA) dates from the period immediately following World War II, and it provides information and analytical evaluations of all aspects of U.S. economic policies, both domestic and international. One of the three CEA members typically is an academic specialist in international trade and finance. The USTR maintains close working relations with firms and labor organizations by means of the so-called Industry Sector Advisory Committees (ISACs) that are especially active in periods of international trade negotiations. The USTR also works closely with the pertinent Congressional committees that deal with issues of trade policy.

In the U.S. Congress, the two most important committees involved in the trade-policy process are the House Ways and Means Committee and the Senate Finance Committee. Other congressional committees also deal often with trade issues when these issues bear upon their policy domains. But traditionally the Ways and Means and Finance Committees play the major roles in the trade-policy process because of their authority over tax and expenditure decisions. The division of authority on trade issues between the Executive Branch and the Congress has of course been discussed extensively over the years. In this connection, it seems fair to say that, during the period since World War II, the Executive Branch played the decisive role until the early 1970s, and that since then the Congress has become much more active in defining the trade-policy agenda and the design of trade policies.

In the bottom part of Figure 1, we depict the array of constituent interests who are affected by trade policies and who in turn may influence the choice and design of trade policies by means of political contributions to candidates and parties, facilitating legal actions on behalf of trade clients, advocacy of the public interest, and providing information on trade and related issues to the branches and agencies of government and to the other constituent interests noted.

We typically associate efforts to influence trade policies with the activities of private-sector producing interests. These interests embrace both firms and workers across the economic spectrum, including agriculture, manufacturing, and services. This is not to say, however, that these sectoral activities share common objectives, since the producing interests may differ depending upon their position in the economy, that is, whether they are import-competing, export, or nontradable sectors, and the degree of foreign ownership and operation. Furthermore, the ways in which sectoral influences are expressed may stem directly from the firms and workers themselves or through a variety of organizations, including sectoral associations, organized labor, political action committees (PACs), and specialized lobbying, consulting, and legal firms. We also designate a separate category of law firms that specialize in the provision of legal services in connection with the administration of the trade laws on behalf of their clients. While we have not had the opportunity to gather evidence on the lobbying and related expenditures and other activities of private-sector producing interests, it is our impression that these interests account for the major share of the resources designed to influence trade policy. But there are other constituent interests to consider as well.

Thus we indicate a category that represents the public interest, including organizations that specialize in providing information and that seek to influence government policies relating especially to the environment, human rights, and consumer choice and welfare. These public-interest organizations have grown increasingly in number and size especially since the 1970s and have given voice to concern about the ways in which U.S. trade and other economic policies impact on the environment and on economic, social, and political conditions both in the United States and in other nations. Many of these groups were especially active in the NAFTA debate in 1992–1993, and they have continued to be involved in many current trade policy issues. These public-interest organizations are by no means uni-dimensional, in the sense that some may promote a policy agenda favoring economic efficiency and growth, while others may take more absolutist positions that place much less emphasis on economic efficiency and growth as ends in themselves and greater emphasis on social and political objectives. We also include foundations in the public-interest category. They provide financial support to some of the advocacy organizations and especially to academic institutions and "think tanks" that we depict as information providers. Foundation support can serve both the general public interest as well as special interests.

The final category shown in Figure 1 refers to information providers. These include print, broadcast, and electronic media that gather and disseminate economic and other information to government and to the various constituencies noted and that may pursue particular economic policy objectives depending on their target audiences. Academic institutions also serve as providers of information on trade and other economic policies, both through classroom teaching and through the dissemination of theoretical and applied economic research. We include here as well think tanks that specialize in economic research, some of which parallels what goes on in academic institutions, but which commonly involves some particular policy orientation dependent in large measure on the sources of funding.

It is difficult to determine without further study how important and effective the different constituent interests may be in influencing trade policy. Nonetheless, it is evident from Figure 1 that the trade-policy process is a complex structure involving a host of agents and principals. The branches and agencies of government provide the impetus for trade-policy initiatives that are intended to serve the public interest as well as to cater to special interests by implementing protectionist measures that restrict import trade and by furnishing subsidies that are designed to expand exports. While our discussion has been focused on trade policy, we should also mention that the agencies of government and constituent interests are involved in policy activities that affect inward and outward foreign direct investment (FDI), banking, and portfolio investment, all of which may have a direct or indirect bearing on trade and trade policies. It is important to emphasize in any case that there is a continuous interaction between the agents of government and the multitude of principals who comprise the constituent interest groups noted. It is interesting in this light now to consider how the trade-policy process is represented in the different modeling approaches that were discussed in the preceding section.

Modeling U.S. Trade Policies

We have distinguished three modeling approaches to U.S. trade policies: (1) the normative approach based on a social welfare function; (2) the positive approach based on political economy; and (3) the transaction-cost approach that is a middle-ground between the foregoing two approaches. We shall discuss each of these in turn using the framework in Figure 1.

Normative Approach

As already discussed, the normative approach to trade policy assumes that the government has an objective function whose arguments include welfare maximization and optimal resource allocation under conditions of perfect competition. For a system like this to operate successfully, there is a need for a government that in itself works perfectly and that is capable of implementing policies that will achieve its welfare maximization and efficiency goals. Whether and how governments can in actuality be organized and operated to attain the conditions of this first-best world is not dealt with in this normative modeling approach. On the theoretical level at least, it is required that the government be omniscient and behave, so to speak, as a beneficent dictator. But what remains unclear in these circumstances is why governments will be created to begin with and, if they are created, what the rules may be that will guide their policy choices. The normative approach thus seems to take the existence of perfect government for granted and interprets its role in policy making as implementing the prescriptions of the normative approach for the general benefit of society.

In terms of our Figure 1, it is as if the Executive Branch can play an omniscient and beneficent role. But given the structure of the U.S. Government noted in the figure, together with the variety and complexity of the constituent interests, it might appear that a leap of imagination is required to make the normative approach viable. This is all the more true once account is taken of the possible violations of one or more of the modeling assumptions noted above. It might be argued nonetheless that it may not be necessary to model the structure of the trade-policy process in detail. This will be the case especially if policy makers are guided by welfare and efficiency objectives in formulating and executing trade policies. If so, the normative approach can provide the framework for evaluation of alternative policies based on the conventional welfare analysis that is familiar to trade economists.

Clearly, however, this may be stretching things, because the normative approach does not explain why governments choose the trade policies that they do, especially when these policy choices are so frequently at variance with first-best optimal criteria. It is for this reason that so much attention has been devoted to the political economy approach to which we now turn.

Political Economy Approach

As noted above, the political economy approach is especially valuable insofar as it enhances the understanding of the forces that shape the choice and design of trade policies. What the different political economy models have in common is that they give greater weight to some individuals and interest groups than to others in determining policy choices overall. Welfare considerations thus either do not enter at all in the policy process or enter only alongside distributional considerations. In terms of our Figure 1, trade policy choices will be influenced both in the Executive Branch and in the Congress especially, whereas the investigatory power of the ITC is based mainly on the facts and legal interpretations embodied in U.S. trade laws as they were formulated in those other branches. According to the political economy approach, the private-sector producing interests, together with the trade law actions of legal firms acting in their behalf, are the driving forces determining the trade policy choices of government. There is also scope for international actions since policy choices may be interdependent particularly in the cases of large countries and trading blocs.

Because the political economy approach focuses primarily on the influence of producer interests in determining policy choices and electoral politics, Figure 1 suggests that there are some potentially important interests that this approach does not take sufficiently into account. These include the variety of public interest and advocacy organizations, especially those that are concerned with issues of trade and the environment, human rights, and other noneconomic, trade-related objectives such as the fostering of democratic political and social institutions. This applies also to the role played by information providers. In essence, then, the political economy approach is incomplete and needs to be adapted to make allowance for those other constituent group activities. But what is perhaps the main limitation of the political economy approach is that, because it is not concerned with the pros and cons of alternative trade policies, it offers no guidance to policy makers in choosing among the available policy alternatives. As already stressed, this is what the normative approach seeks to accomplish. The question then is whether or not Dixit's transaction-cost approach provides a useful middle-ground between the other two approaches.

The Transaction-Cost Approach

To understand issues of trade and other economic policies, the transaction-cost approach emphasizes that society is comprised of numerous agents acting on behalf of numerous principals and carrying out numerous policies in real time. Our Figure 1 is thus helpful in calling attention to the multiplicity of constituent groups who care about what government does and who seek to influence its policy choices. Unless we take this broad view, it appears to us difficult to comprehend the choice and outcome of trade policies. An amalgam of the normative and political economy approaches is therefore essential. To help accomplish this end, we need especially to study how the different constituencies are organized and how they intersect with each problem in the trade-policy process. One way to do this is to consider particular trade policy changes and their economic effects over time. It would be essential in this regard to identify the transaction costs at issue that stand in the way of achieving first-best results and at the same time to consider the coping mechanisms that are operative. These coping mechanisms will be indicative of the success or failure of the government in reducing transaction costs by its policy actions and associated efforts on the part of both the government and different constituent groups to mitigate the consequences of both market and political failures. We shall return to these matters in our concluding section, but, before doing so, it might be worthwhile to put our modeling discussion aside and to consider what can be learned from observation of the overall experiences of U.S. trade policies in the past half century.

What Can Be Learned from the U.S. Trade-Policy Experiences in the Fifty Years Since World War II?

In reflecting on the U.S. trade-policy experiences in the half century since the end of World War II, it is useful to consider these experiences within the transaction-cost framework as involving the interplay between the forces of trade liberalization and protectionism/export subsidies as a dynamic process occurring in real time. It is beyond the scope of our paper to review the quantitative dimensions of the post-World War II effects of U.S. trade policies. Nonetheless, our reading of the literature and assessment of the actual outcomes of the trade-policy process strongly suggest on balance that the U.S. economy has been subject to a distinctive liberalizing orientation and resultant overall improvement in economic welfare, even when changes in income distribution are taken into account. If our interpretation is correct, it appears that the coping mechanisms involved in U.S. trade policies have been sufficiently powerful so as to reduce transaction costs over time. We realize of course that not everyone would accept this conclusion, citing especially the frequent resort to nontariff protectionism in the past two decades or more and the long-standing restrictions applied especially to trade in agricultural products and apparel.

But granting this, the general orientation of U.S. domestic and trade policies in favor of market-based outcomes and the lowering of U.S. and foreign trade barriers has in our judgment ruled the day. As noted in our earlier discussion, this has been reinforced by the existence and influence of the General Agreement on Tariffs and Trade (GATT), which provided the context and authority for trade liberalization and nondiscrimination for GATT members by means of the GATT articles of agreement and the periodic multilateral trade negotiations that have taken place, most recently with conclusion of the Uruguay Round negotiations and creation of the WTO in 1994. U.S. leadership has without question been the driving force in helping to reduce tariff barriers as well as trying to address the problems created by NTBs. This process has of course been far from perfect, but, in our view, the outcome has nevertheless been highly beneficial to the major industrialized and developing countries involved in the global trading system. The increasing tendency in recent years in many newly industrializing countries and in the former socialist economies to reduce and remove barriers to domestic production and trade and to move towards market-based resource allocation has thus far served to reinforce the liberalizing orientation of the global economic system.

We cannot say with certainty of course whether the movement towards increased liberalization will be continued in the future. But it appears to us to be a reasonable working assumption that this will be the case. Our view here is colored by the prospect of a stronger international body represented by the newly created WTO that has put in place what promises to be a more effective dispute settlement mechanism. It will clearly require time and experience to determine whether the WTO can fulfill its expectations. Much will depend on how the major actors in the global system respond and whether they will use the WTO to fend off special interests domestically that may seek to influence national policies that contravene WTO rules and obligations. There is also the issue of whether the spread of regional trading arrangements will help or hinder the liberalizing process. In our view, regionalism is likely to turn out to be a liberalizing force, especially insofar as it leads smaller countries to lock in the reduction of domestic and external barriers in exchange for market access. The key here will be whether this can be done in a welfare enhancing manner.

A final consideration that deserves mention is the important role played by international investment in the global economy. It has been the case that restrictions on international capital flows among the major industrialized countries especially have been markedly reduced in the past half century. This is evidenced by the significant narrowing of interest differentials, which can be taken as a sign of increased efficiency in the functioning of international financial markets. These markets have also witnessed many innovations by international financial institutions that have been reflected in changes in their organizational structure and increases in the kinds of international financial instruments available to market participants. The tendency of international financial markets to move closer to conditions of perfect international capital mobility is really quite remarkable, even given the downside of possibly excessive exchange-rate volatility in today's floating rate system and problems of domestic monetary management that some countries have encountered.

Equally important have been the substantial increases in foreign direct investment and the associated trade accounted for by multinational corporations (MNCs). While most FDI is carried out by MNCs operating among the group of major industrialized countries, there have been sizable movements of FDI to the newly industrializing countries, especially in East and Southeast Asia and also in Latin America. What is so important about FDI is that it serves to foster more efficient international allocation of resources and the transfer of technology. Again, FDI may have its downside, but this pales in comparison to the truly significant benefits that MNCs have brought about.

We conclude this section by emphasizing how powerful the forces of liberalization of international trade and international investment have been in the past half century for the United States and other countries in the global economic system. The question at hand then is how we can relate this experience to the modeling of trade policy that has been the subject of our preceding discussion.

IV. Conclusions and Implications for Research and Policy

In broad terms what our discussion reveals is a history of far more intervention in international trade than can be explained by the normative approach to analysis of trade policy, yet also a reasonably steady and quite substantial movement towards more open markets and more liberal trade in the past half century. The political economy approach to trade policy has provided important insights into why it is that the prescriptions of normative analysis often fail to be observed. But it has so far neglected to incorporate various constituent interests other than producing interests who appear to have played important roles in the U.S. trade policy process. Furthermore, the political economy approach alone seems ill-equipped to explain the steady movement toward freer trade that has occurred.

Staiger (1995) provides an interesting model of gradual trade liberalization that results when producer interests are gradually eroded over time. What happens is that early partial liberalization causes the specific factors in protected sectors to depreciate and migrate elsewhere, and this makes further future liberalization politically feasible. Here, political economy helps to explain the pace of liberalization, but it does not explain why it occurs at all, which depends in Staiger's model on an assumed "political will" to liberalize.

Our conjecture, following these various lines of research but especially Dixit's discussion of transaction costs, is that this "political will" may be found in the ongoing efforts of the many interested actors in the economy to cope with the transactions costs that have led to protection in the first place. Focusing only on producer interests, and especially those who compete with imports, has enabled the political economy approach to explain protection. But that approach will have to incorporate additional interests, including not only other producers but also many of the other interests that we identified in Figure 1, if it is to explain more fully why these political forces result in protection rather than other more direct policies of income redistribution and, especially, if it is to explain the overall movement toward more liberal trade that we have witnessed in the post-World War II period.

We speculated earlier that one of the transaction costs that may explain protection is the difficulty that the public has in understanding the true effects of trade and other policies. If that is true, then the movement towards more liberal trade may be the result of increasingly successful efforts on the part of many of the interests in Figure 1 to cope with this lack of understanding. In the long run, one of the most important constituent interests in U.S. trade policy may be our very selves!

Study Questions

1. What are the normative and political economy approaches to the modeling of trade policies? What is the transaction-cost approach? What are the insights and limitations of the different approaches?
2. What are the empirical methods that have been used in implementing studies of the different approaches to the modeling of trade policies? What are the principal findings of these studies?
3. How can the structure of the U.S. trade-policy process be characterized? Who are the major constituent interest groups involved? To what extent are the different approaches to modeling trade policies helpful in understanding U.S. experiences? What is the outlook for the future of U.S. trade policies?

References

Baldwin, Robert E. 1982. "The Political Economy of Protection," in Jagdish Bhagwati (ed.), *Import Competition and Response*, Chicago: University of Chicago Press.

Berry, Steven, James Levinsohn, and Ariel Pakes. 1995. "Voluntary Export Restraints on Automobiles: Evaluating a Strategic Trade Policy," in process, January 30.

Buchanan, James M. and Gordon Tulloch. 1962. *The Calculus of Consent.* Ann Arbor, MI: University of Michigan Press.

Deardorff, Alan V. and Robert M. Stern. 1987. "Current Issues in U.S. Trade Policy: An Overview," in Robert M. Stern (ed.), *U.S. Trade Policies in a Changing World Economy.* Cambridge, MA: MIT Press, Chapter 2, pp. 15–68.

Deardorff, Alan V. and Robert M. Stern. 1996. *Measurement of Nontariff Barriers*, report prepared for the Organization of Economic Cooperation and Development.

Dixit, Avinash K. 1996. *The Making of Economic Policy: A Transaction-Cost Politics Perspective.* Cambridge, MA: MIT Press.

Dixit, Avinash K. and Victor Norman. 1980. *Theory of International Trade.* London: Cambridge University Press.

Dixit, Avinash K. and Victor Norman. 1984. "Gains from Trade without Lump-Sum Compensation," *Journal of International Economics* 21, pp. 111–122.

Feenstra, Robert C. and Jagdish N. Bhagwati. 1982. "Tariff Seeking and the Efficient Tariff," in Jagdish Bhagwati (ed.), *Import Competition and Response.* Chicago: University of Chicago Press.

Findlay, R. and S. Wellisz. 1982. "Endogenous Tariffs, the Political Economy of Trade Restrictions, and Welfare," in Jagdish Bhagwati (ed.), *Import Competition and Response.* Chicago: University of Chicago Press.

Grossman, Gene M. and Elhanan Helpman. 1994. "Protection for Sale," *American Economic Review* 84, pp. 833–850; reprinted in Alan V. Deardorff, James Levinsohn, and Robert M. Stern (eds.), *New Directions in Trade Theory.* Ann Arbor, MI: University of Michigan Press.

Helpman, Elhanan. 1995. "Politics and Trade Policy," Discussion Paper No. 1269, Centre for Economic Policy Research, London (November).

Hillman, Arye L. 1989. *The Political Economy of Protection.* London: Harwood.

Hufbauer, Gary C. and Kimberly A. Elliott. 1994. *Measuring the Costs of Protection in the United States.* Washington, D.C.: Institute for International Economics.

Krueger, Anne O. 1996. *The Political Economy of American Trade Policy.* Chicago: University of Chicago Press.

Magee, Stephen P., William A. Brock, and Leslie Young. 1989. *Black Hole Tariffs and Endogenous Policy Formation.* Cambridge, MA: MIT Press.

Martin, Will and L. Alan Winters. 1996. *The Uruguay Round: Widening and Deepening the World Trading System.* New York: Cambridge University Press.

Mayer, Wolfgang. 1984. "Endogenous Tariff Formation," *American Economic Review* 74, pp. 970–985.

Rodrik, Dani. 1995. "Political Economy of Trade Policy," in G. Grossman and K. Rogoff (eds.), *Handbook of International Economics, Vol. III.* Amsterdam: North-Holland.

Staiger, Robert W. 1995. "A Theory of Gradual Trade Liberalization," in Alan V. Deardorff, James Levinsohn, and Robert M. Stern (eds.), *New Directions in Trade Theory*. Ann Arbor, MI: University of Michigan Press.

Suggested Further Reading

Gawande, Kishore. 2006. "The Structure of Lobbying and Protection in U.S. Agriculture," in Simon J. Evenett and Bernard M. Hoekman (eds.), *Economic Development & Multilateral Trade Cooperation*. Washington, DC: Palgrave Macmillan and the World Bank.

Gawande, Kishore and Pravin Krishna. 2004. "The Political Economy of Trade Policy: Empirical Approaches," in E. Kwan Choi and James Harrigan (eds.), *Handbook of International Trade*, Volume 2. Oxford: Blackwell.

Gawande, Kishore, Pravin Krishna, and Michael J. Robbins. 2006. "Foreign Lobbies and U.S. Trade Policy," *Review of Economics and Statistics* 88, pp. 563–571.

Goldberg, Pinelopi and Giovanni Maggi. 1999. "Protection for Sale: An Empirical Investigation," *American Economic Review* 89, pp. 1135–1155.

Chapter 8

Issues of Manufactures Liberalization and Administered Protection in the Doha Round*

Alan V. Deardorff and Robert M. Stern

I. Introduction

The Doha Round of multilateral trade negotiations in the World Trade Organization (WTO) has been billed from the start as the "Doha Development Agenda (DDA)," with the promise in the Doha Ministerial Declaration to "place [developing countries'] needs and interests at the heart of the Work Programme adopted in this Declaration."[1] The reason for this emphasis was in part the perception that previous rounds had neglected the interests of developing countries or, in the case of the Uruguay Round, had brought developing countries on board with promises that were misleading or not likely to be kept. After the December 1999 Seattle and the September 2003

* Article reprinted with permission from the publisher, The Berkeley Electronic Press, C2005. Originally published in the *Global Economy Journal*, available at http://www.bepress.com/gej/vol5/iss4/7/.

[1] WTO (2001, para. 2).

Cancún Ministerial Meetings, in which negotiations floundered in part on the conflicting objectives of developed and developing countries, there is a question of whether and how the DDA negotiations will be able to achieve the objectives set forth in the November 2001 Doha Declaration especially from the standpoints of the developing countries.

In this paper we address what we believe to be the most important issues in the Doha Round involving manufactures liberalization and administered protection. Our analysis and recommendations are based primarily on the understanding of the economics of international trade that has been developed over the last two centuries and is widely taught in the universities of the world, and also on the research in recent years dealing with specific aspects of trade negotiations in general and of the Doha Round in particular.

It is important to emphasize that developing countries are a diverse group, and that any change in policy may be beneficial for some of them while it hurts others. This is inevitable, and should be attended to by institutions other than the WTO that are capable of providing country-specific assistance. The WTO itself must provide a structure within which countries can prosper, and that is what our recommendations are directed toward.

Since our paper is intended to be a quick and accessible read for those involved in or attempting to influence the negotiations, we present it in the form of recommendations, buttressed by only the briefest of explanations and references to the literature. Those who seek a more complete discussion can consult that literature. In our discussion to follow, we focus especially on the positions that we believe the developing countries should take in their own interests on the issues of manufactures liberalization and administered protection. We hope that, if the expressed intent of the Doha negotiations to foster economic development is more than window dressing, negotiators for the industrialized countries too will favor these positions, even when they may run counter to some of the domestic interests that they represent.

II. Market Access

RECOMMENDATION 1: Both developed and developing countries should commit to reducing their most restrictive trade barriers, including the elimination of all quotas and the substantial reduction of their highest import tariffs, and also the rationalization of tariff escalation and rules of origin[2] that are biased against developing country exports.

ARGUMENT: For various reasons, the highest trade barriers that exist today are predominately on imports of the products most readily exported by developing countries, in particular apparel. Because these products tend to be labor intensive, such barriers undermine the ability of developing countries to pursue their comparative advantage as labor-abundant countries, thus adding to the already massive handicaps that these countries often bear. At the same time, the trade barriers in the developing countries themselves are often more restrictive than those in the developed countries and cover a much wider variety of products. These barriers also interfere with the abilities of the developing countries to trade with each other. And more importantly, they impose costs both on their own industrial users and on final consumers of these products. Like any meaningful liberalization, reducing these trade barriers will stimulate strong resistance in the countries that commit to do it. But efforts should be focused on overcoming that resistance, and perhaps on providing compensation to those domestic interests who will be hurt by it, rather than on resisting the liberalization itself. It is such resistance to liberalization that has led the world to its current regime of trade that, although it is liberal to an unprecedented degree, nonetheless remains restricted in

[2] Escalation is the common pattern of higher tariffs on processed goods than on semi-processed goods and inputs, a pattern that creates effective protection on final goods that is higher than nominal protection and that makes it particularly difficult for developing countries to expand into final-goods production. Rules of origin are necessary in free trade areas (FTAs), in which the member countries retain different external tariffs, in order to determine whether a good qualifies for tariff-free treatment within the FTA. These rules take many forms and often discriminate against developing countries.

those industries most important to the export success of developing countries.

RECOMMENDATION 2: Tariff cuts are best accomplished by means of a tariff-cutting formula that all countries apply in almost all sectors, with only a limited number of exceptions. Although the choice of formula is less important than the vigor with which it is applied, a formula that cuts large tariffs more than small ones has several advantages over a formula that cuts all tariffs equally. In addition, some countries may want to completely eliminate those tariffs that are already very small, rather than just making them smaller, but that can be left to the discretion of countries to decide on their own and need not be incorporated into the formula.

ARGUMENT: The use of a formula for tariff cuts has become standard procedure in multilateral trade rounds ever since the membership in the GATT reached a point where exclusively bilateral negotiated tariff cuts, extended to others on a most-favored-nation (MFN) basis, became too cumbersome and tended to exclude those countries that were too small or too poor to attract others to negotiate with them. Given the particular need in the Doha Round to include developing countries in the tariff-cutting process, use of a formula is necessary.

The simplest formula would be a proportional cut in all tariffs by some percentage, and that would not be a bad thing, since it would move the world unambiguously in the direction of freer trade. However, a formula such as the Swiss formula from the Tokyo Round, which cuts large tariffs more than small ones, has certain advantages.[3] One is that, for a given average tariff reduction, the formula reduces the dispersion of tariff rates across countries and sectors, and this is likely to be beneficial for country and world welfare. A second advantage is that the distortionary effect of a tariff tends to rise quadratically with its size, so that the welfare benefits of reducing large tariffs are larger than reducing small ones. And finally, a third advantage is that

[3] See Francois *et al.* (2004) for a more detailed discussion of alternative tariff-cutting formulae.

routine use of such formulae in trade rounds reduces the disincentive for countries to cut tariffs unilaterally between rounds.

Because the welfare costs of tariffs rise quadratically with their size, the welfare benefits of eliminating tariffs that are already very small are negligible. There is therefore no need for the multilateral system to require that such small tariffs be reduced to zero. But this ignores the administrative costs of administering tariffs, which for very small tariffs may be larger than the tariff revenue. It is therefore in the interests of countries even from the narrow perspective of their budgets to eliminate such tariffs. Because of this, it seems that the decision to do so can be left up to them.

III. Implementation

RECOMMENDATION 3: It is customary and appropriate to allow countries several years in which to implement any commitments they make that will entail difficulties of adjustment. This is true of tariff reductions, and may be especially so for developing countries that commit to significant reductions in their highest tariffs. A period of ten or even fifteen years to accomplish this adjustment would not be excessive. However, it is essential that this not be simply a delay of tariff reductions, but rather an extended period during which tariffs are reduced regularly and predictably, so that markets may anticipate the needed adjustments and undertake them in advance. A simple scheme would require that all negotiated tariff reductions be phased over a period of ten years in ten equal incremental reductions.

ARGUMENT: Tariff reductions inevitably require some reallocation of resources out of the protected import competing sectors. This reallocation is both costly and painful, since it normally responds to market signals that reduce wages, employment, and profits of incumbent industries. By slowing this process down, some of the adjustment can be accommodated within the normal turnover of the industry, reducing some of these costs substantially. More importantly, when it is made clear well in advance that these adjustments will have to take place, workers and firms can redirect their energies toward expanding sectors and avoid some of these costs completely. But this requires that the tariff reductions be expected and believed.

A tempting option here is simply to postpone the tariff reductions in their entirety to the end of a phase in period, as was largely done, in effect, with import quotas in the Uruguay Round Agreement on Textiles and Clothing. The problem here is that, without experiencing any liberalization early in the phase in period, those who will be affected may come to doubt that adjustment will be needed, or even that tariffs will actually be reduced. By reducing them in equal increments throughout the phase in period, the realistic need for adjustment should become evident.

Recommendation 4: Some form of adjustment assistance should be provided to workers and firms in developing countries who are displaced by imports as a result of tariff reductions. A suitable program would consist of wage insurance, and should be subsidized by transfers from developed countries.

Argument: The need for adjustment assistance for workers and firms displaced by trade has been recognized in developed countries for several decades. The need is if anything greater in developing countries, where workers and firms have fewer resources of their own to serve as a cushion. The need is especially severe when the required adjustment includes relocation of workers from rural to urban areas. Trade adjustment assistance has a long but not very illustrious history in the developed world, where programs have more often helped workers to *not* adjust than to adjust, and programs in developing countries will need to avoid these pitfalls. The approach that is now most often recommended by economists, though so far seldom used, would be a system of wage insurance that temporarily replaces a portion of any decline in wages that a trade-displaced worker experiences in moving into alternative employment.[4] This will work within the manufacturing sector, but it will often not work for agricultural workers whose previous wage is difficult to ascertain. For the latter, wage insurance could be based on an assumed benchmark agricultural wage.

[4] See Kletzer (2004).

IV. Administered Protection

Recommendation 5: The rules for administered protection — safeguards, countervailing duties, and anti-dumping — should be redrafted to focus their use on cases of legitimate economic justification, but to discourage their use as protectionist devices that limit market access.

Argument: It is widely acknowledged among economists that most if not all uses of anti-dumping laws, and many uses of safeguard and countervailing duty laws, are not justified by inappropriate or harmful behavior on the part of foreign exporters.[5] Rather, these uses of administered protection have become the tools of choice for industries seeking protection for conventional (self-interest) reasons in a world where legislated protection is constrained by the GATT/WTO.[6] Unfortunately, even though the amount of trade covered by actual administered protection is small compared to trade covered by MFN tariffs and other barriers, the threat of action under these laws is pervasive and affects trade much more widely. This threat, even where no actions are taken, discourages trade and fosters collusion among world suppliers, thereby reducing world welfare. Like so many trade barriers, the costs of administered protection may be especially severe for developing countries that are often its targets. These costs include not only the usual production and consumption costs of trade restrictions, but also the costs of participating in the legal proceedings involved. Even more unfortunately, the trend today seems to be for developing countries to enact such laws of their own, thus not only further restricting their own trade, but also wasting their

---

[5] Appropriate uses of these laws would include: facilitating adjustment to injurious import surges (safeguards); offsetting the distortionary effects of those subsidies that are not themselves corrections for market distortions (countervailing duties); and prevention of dumping that is plausibly predatory — that is, dumping intended to secure a dominant market position and permit later price increases (anti-dumping). See Deardorff (1987, 1989), and Finger and Zlate (2005).

[6] See Deardorff and Stern (2005) for an "Introduction and Overview" to a symposium of papers marking A Centennial of Antidumping Legislation and Implementation.

own resources on the administration of these laws. Some means needs to be found to reverse this trend, perhaps by limiting the criteria in the WTO for action under these various forms of administered protection.

Recommendation 6: The U.S. and EU should devise and implement a program of comprehensive but declining import restrictions on exports from China, consistent with the negotiated terms of China's WTO accession and leading steadily and predictably to the elimination of these restrictions by 2008.

Argument: The negotiations of China's WTO accession correctly anticipated that large trade flows might result and lead to market disruptions requiring some form of safeguards protection. What was not anticipated, it seems, was the suddenness with which trade would expand and the political and economic disruptions that would be caused, not just by the trade itself but also by the policy responses to it. This has been disruptive not just for China and the U.S./EU, but also for other developing countries whose exports compete with China's. To minimize these disruptions and uncertainties, we recommend that policies be put in place that will be more predictable, so that both exporters and importers in all of these countries can go on about their business with greater confidence.

V. Preferential Arrangements

Recommendation 7: WTO rules governing the formation of Preferential Trading Relationships (PTRs) should be revised to insure that they contribute to the liberalization and simplification of the multilateral trading system.

Argument: Article XXIV of the GATT was drafted when PTRs were envisioned as a small number of largely isolated groups of countries, rather than the proliferation of overlapping free trade areas and customs unions that we see today. Free trade areas especially, with their complex rules of origin and with their tendency to be formed between pairs of countries, contribute to a trading system that discourages the multilateral sourcing of supply chains that constitutes much of the promise of modern technology and globalization. Furthermore, many PTRs today are negotiated in overlapping "hub and spoke" arrangements that limit trade among the spokes, and these spokes are most often occupied by developing countries, so that trade patterns among them are distorted. What is needed is an amendment to Article XXIV that would govern the expansion of the membership in these arrangements, as well as the relationships among overlapping PTRs, so as to assure that their proliferation moves the world toward, and not away from, more liberal world trade.[7]

RECOMMENDATION 8: Although it is hard to see how this can be a part of any multilateral agreement, countries that have granted trade preferences that are now being undermined by multilateral liberalization should recognize that they have an obligation to assist those countries whose preferences are eroded. That assistance should be included in the programs of adjustment assistance discussed above, but the responsibility for funding that assistance should rest with the former preference-granting country.

ARGUMENT: Trade preferences extend the effects of tariff protection to suppliers in the preferred country, typically a neighbor state or former colony with a special relationship to the preference-granting country. The effect of extending that protection is to foster the existence and expansion of the protected industry, up to a level at which its costs are above comparable producers on world markets by the amount of the preference. That margin is an indication of how painful it will be for these suppliers when the preference is removed, but it is also a measure of how much demanders in the preference-granting country have been paying, implicitly, in subsidy to the favored producers. When multilateral tariffs are reduced and these preferences are eroded, the gain to these demanders and to their country is larger

[7] See Bhagwati *et al.* (1999) for several analyses of whether regionalism helps or hinders the progress toward multilateral liberalization. After comparing multilateral and regional liberalization scenarios, we — in Brown *et al.* (2003, p. 827) — conclude that "realization of the very significant benefits of multilateral liberalization may be jeopardized by pursuing these [regional] arrangements."

than this subsidy, and they should be able to provide at least this much to assist adjustment.

VI. Dispute Resolution

Recommendation 9: We recommend no changes in the WTO system of dispute resolution.

Argument: The system established in the Uruguay Round is far from perfect, and it is easy to cite aspects of it that do not work well. Numerous suggestions have been tabled that might improve it, and we are sympathetic to many of them. However, there does not yet seem to be anything close to a consensus in favor of any of these, and until there is, we favor leaving well enough alone. The WTO mechanism is certainly succeeding in one sense: countries are using it. And while they do not always abide by the decisions that emerge from that mechanism, the outcomes are respected in enough cases to sustain the system. Countries that ignore its rulings at least accept that they are in violation and may be the target of authorized retaliation.

VII. Special Treatment

Recommendation 10: The Doha Round should provide "special and differential treatment" of developing countries, and especially of the least developed countries, but this treatment should entail assistance with bearing the costs and fulfilling the obligations of the agreement, *not* exemption from the provisions for their own market liberalization.

Argument: The phrase "special and differential treatment" in the old GATT too often meant exempting developing countries from liberalizing their own trade. The phrase appears again in the Doha Declaration, though without specifying what it will mean in this case.[8] It is to be hoped that, this time around, it will not mean continued protection, but rather acknowledgement of the adjustment costs of liberalization and a plan to provide assistance with bearing those costs. Such assistance is likely to include longer periods of time to

[8] WTO (2001, para. 44).

comply with WTO rules, but it must also include financial and technical assistance.

VIII. Conclusion

This paper has touched only on what we take to be the major issues affecting developing countries in the Doha Round, and then only with regard to manufactures liberalization and administered protection. There are many other issues of importance to them, and the issues addressed here also involve many details that we have not been able to include. It is essential that developing countries participate actively and constructively in the negotiations to further their own interests. They cannot rely on the best intentioned developed countries to do this for them, since these countries will inevitably find themselves making compromises in favor of their own interests and in response to powerful pressures from their constituents. Developing countries are at a disadvantage in the negotiating process, due to their resource limitations, and in many cases due also to their inexperience in negotiations. Offsetting these disadvantages, however, are their large numbers and the compelling case that can be made for meeting their needs. What is needed is leadership and cooperation on their part, and a willingness to listen and be flexible on the part of their developed country counterparts.

With regard to the former, we find encouraging the emergence at Cancún of what is now called the Group of 20 developing countries, even though it may have contributed at the time to the collapse of the negotiations. With regard to the latter, it is also encouraging that the U.S. and EU, in the two years since the Cancún impasse, have agreed to some of the steps that they resisted at that time. Further progress will require that both groups, the developing countries very definitely included, be willing to back off from positions on which they have, until now, been intransigent.

Study Questions

1. How have trade rounds neglected the interests of developing countries? What are the recommendations offered for promoting

market access by means of lowering trade barriers? Should a formula be used for tariff reductions? Over what periods of time should tariff reductions be implemented, and what sorts of adjustment assistance may be desirable?

2. What changes should be made in the rules for administered protection? What policies should the U.S. and EU adopt regarding imports from China? How should the WTO rules governing preferential trading arrangements be revised? What should be done about preference erosion for developing countries? How effective is the WTO system of dispute resolution? To what extent should developing countries be given special and differential treatment? How can the developing countries be proactive in the Doha Round and best promote their interests?

References

Bhagwati, J., Krishna, P. and Panagariya, A. (eds.) 1999. *Trading Blocs: Alternative Approaches to Analyzing Preferential Trade Agreements.* Cambridge, MA: MIT Press.

Brown, D. K., Deardorff, A. V. and Stern, R. M. 2003. "Multilateral, Regional and Bilateral Trade-Policy Options for the United States and Japan," *The World Economy* 26(6), pp. 803–828.

Deardorff, A. V. 1987. "Safeguards Policy and the Conservative Social Welfare Function," in Kierzkowski, H. (ed.), *Protection and Competition in International Trade*, Blackwell.

Deardorff, A. V. 1989. "Economic Perspectives on Dumping Law," in Jackson J. H. and Vermulst, E. A. (eds.), *Anti-Dumping Law and Practice: A Comparative Study*, pp. 23–39. Ann Arbor: The University of Michigan Press.

Deardorff, A. V. and Stern, R. M. 2005. "Introduction and Overview, Symposium on a Centennial of Antidumping Legislation and Implementation," *The World Economy* 28(5), pp. 633–640.

Finger, J. M. and Zlate, A. 2005. "Antidumping: Prospects for Discipline from the Doha Negotiations," *Journal of World Investment and Trade* 6(4), pp. 531–552.

Francois, J., Martin, W. and Manole, V. 2004. "Choosing Formulas for Market Access Negotiations: Efficiency and Market Access Considerations," manuscript, January 29.

Kletzer, L. G. 2004. "Trade-Related Job Loss and Wage Insurance: A Synthetic Review," *Review of International Economics* 12(5), pp. 724–748.

World Trade Organization. 2001. "Ministerial Declaration," adopted November 14, WT/MIN(01)/DEC/1.

Suggested Further Reading

Anderson, Kym and Will Martin (eds.). 2006. *Agricultural Trade Reform & the Doha Development Agenda*. Washington, DC: Palgrave Macmillan and the World Bank.

Deardorff, Alan V., Robert M. Stern, and John Whalley. 2007. "Reviving the Doha Round: The Agenda for the Developing Countries," in *Monitoring Trade Policy: A New Agenda for Reviving the Doha Round*, Policy Monitoring Paper 1, Kiel Institute for the World Economy and Centre for Economic Policy Research (CEPR).

Evenett, Simon J. 2007. "Reciprocity and the Doha Round Impasse: Lessons for the Near Term and After," *Aussenwirtschaft*, IV.

Hoekman, Bernard. 2008. "The General Agreement on Trade in Services: Doomed to Fail? Does it Matter?" *Journal of Industry, Competition, and Trade* 8, pp. 295–318.

Chapter 9

An Assessment of the Economic Effects of the Menu of U.S. Trade Policies*

Kozo Kiyota and Robert M. Stern

I. Introduction

In this paper, we present a computational analysis of the economic effects of the menu of U.S. trade policies. The menu encompasses the various U.S. bilateral and regional free trade agreements (FTAs) that have been negotiated in recent years and the negotiations currently in process, unilateral removal of existing trade barriers by the United States and its FTA partner countries, and global (multilateral) free trade. The analysis is based on the Michigan Model of World Production and Trade. The Michigan Model is a multi-country/multi-sector computable general equilibrium (CGE) model of the global trading system that has been used for over three decades to analyze the economic effects of multilateral, regional, and bilateral

* Article reprinted with permission from the publisher, The Berkeley Electronic Press, C2005. Originally published in the *Global Economy Journal*, available at http://www.bepress.com/gej/vol5/iss4/22/.

trade negotiations and a variety of other changes in trade and related policies.

In Section II following, we present a brief description of the main features and data of the Michigan Model. The results of the computational analysis of the U.S. FTAs are presented in Section III. In Section IV, we consider the cross-country patterns of the welfare effects of the various FTAs. In Section V, we provide a broader perspective on the FTAs that takes into account the effects of the unilateral and multilateral removal of trade barriers by the United States and its FTA partner countries, and other countries/regions in the global trading system. Section VI provides a summary and concluding remarks.

II. The Michigan Model of World Production and Trade

Overview of the Michigan Model

The version of the Michigan Model that we use in this paper covers 18 economic sectors, including agriculture, manufactures, and services, in each of 22 countries/regions. The distinguishing feature of the Michigan Model is that it incorporates some aspects of trade with imperfect competition, including increasing returns to scale, monopolistic competition, and product variety. A complete description of the formal structure and equations of the model can be found on line at www.Fordschool.umich.edu/rsie/model/.

Interpreting the Modeling Results

To help the reader interpret the modeling results, it is useful to review the features of the model that serve to identify the various economic effects to be reflected in the different applications of the model. Although the model includes the aforementioned features of imperfect competition, it remains the case that markets respond to trade liberalization in much the same way that they would with perfect competition. That is, when tariffs or other trade barriers are reduced in a sector, domestic buyers (both final and intermediate) substitute toward imports and the domestic competing industry contracts production while foreign exporters expand. Thus, in the case of multilateral liberalization that reduces tariffs and other trade barriers simultaneously in most sectors and countries, each country's industries share in both of these effects, expanding or contracting depending primarily on whether their protection is reduced more or less than in other sectors and countries.

Worldwide, these changes cause increased international demand for all sectors. World prices increase most for those sectors where trade barriers fall the most. This in turn causes changes in countries' terms of trade that can be positive or negative. Those countries that are net exporters of goods with the greatest degree of liberalization will experience increases in their terms of trade, as the world prices of their exports rise relative to their imports. The reverse occurs for net exporters in industries where liberalization is slight — perhaps because it may already have taken place in previous trade rounds.

The effects on the welfare of countries arise from a mixture of these terms-of-trade effects, together with the standard efficiency gains from trade and also from additional benefits due to the realization of economies of scale. Thus, we expect on average that the world will gain from multilateral liberalization, as resources are reallocated to those sectors in each country where there is a comparative advantage. In the absence of terms-of-trade effects, these efficiency gains should raise national welfare measured by the equivalent variation for every country,[1] although some factor owners within a country may lose, as will be noted below. However, it is possible for a particular country whose net imports are concentrated in sectors with the greatest liberalization to lose overall, if the worsening of its terms of trade swamps these efficiency gains.

[1] The equivalent variation is a measure of the amount of income that would have to be given or taken away from an economy before a change in policy in order to leave the economy as well off as it would be after the policy change has taken place. If the equivalent variation is positive, it is indicative of an improvement in economic welfare resulting from the policy change.

On the other hand, although trade with imperfect competition is perhaps best known for introducing reasons why countries may lose from trade, actually its greatest contribution is to expand the list of reasons for gains from trade. Thus, in the Michigan Model, trade liberalization permits all countries to expand their export sectors at the same time that all sectors compete more closely with a larger number of competing varieties from abroad. As a result, countries as a whole gain from lower costs due to increasing returns to scale, lower monopoly distortions due to greater competition, and reduced costs and/or increased utility due to greater product variety. All of these effects make it more likely that countries will gain from liberalization in ways that are shared across the entire population.[2]

The various effects just described in the context of multilateral trade liberalization will also take place when there is unilateral trade liberalization, although these effects will depend on the magnitudes of the liberalization in relation to the patterns of trade and the price and output responses involved between the liberalizing country and its trading partners. Similarly, many of the effects described will take place with the formation of bilateral or regional FTAs. But in these cases, there may be trade creation and positive effects on the economic welfare of FTA-member countries together with trade diversion and negative effects on the economic welfare of non-member countries. The net effects on economic welfare for individual countries and globally will thus depend on the economic circumstances and policy changes implemented.

In the real world, all of the various effects occur over time, some of them more quickly than others. However, the Michigan Model is static in the sense that it is based upon a single set of equilibrium

---

[2] In perfectly competitive trade models such as the Heckscher–Ohlin Model, one expects countries as a whole to gain from trade, but the owners of one factor — the "scarce factor" — to lose through the mechanism first explored by Stolper and Samuelson (1941). The additional sources of gain from trade due to increasing returns to scale, competition, and product variety, however, are shared across factors, and we routinely find in our CGE modeling that both labor and capital gain from multilateral trade liberalization.

conditions rather than relationships that vary over time. The model results therefore refer to a time horizon that depends on the assumptions made about which variables do and do not adjust to changing market conditions, and on the short- or long-run nature of these adjustments. Because the supply and demand elasticities used in the model reflect relatively long-run adjustments and it is assumed that markets for both labor and capital clear within countries,[3] the modeling results are appropriate for a relatively long time horizon of several years — perhaps two or three at a minimum. On the other hand, the model does not allow for the very long-run adjustments that could occur through capital accumulation, population growth, and technological change. The modeling results should therefore be interpreted as being superimposed upon longer-run growth paths of the economies involved. To the extent that these growth paths themselves may be influenced by trade liberalization, therefore, the model does not capture such effects.

Benchmark Data

Needless to say, the data needs of this model are immense. Apart from numerous share parameters, the model requires various types of elasticity measures. Like other CGE models, most of our data come from published sources.

The main data source used in the model is "The GTAP-6.0 Database" of the Purdue University Center for Global Trade Analysis Project, as adapted from Dimaranan and McDougall (2005). The reference year for this GTAP database is 2001. From this source,

[3] The analysis in the model assumes throughout that the aggregate, economy-wide, level of employment is held constant in each country. The effects of trade liberalization are therefore not permitted to change any country's overall rates of employment or unemployment. This assumption is made because overall employment is determined by macroeconomic forces and policies that are not contained in the model and would not themselves be included in a negotiated trade agreement. The focus instead is on the composition of employment across sectors as determined by the microeconomic interactions of supply and demand resulting from the liberalization of trade.

we have extracted the following data, aggregated to our sectors and countries/regions[4]:

- Bilateral trade flows among 22 countries/regions, decomposed into 18 sectors. Trade with the rest-of-world (ROW) is included to close the model.
- Input-output tables for the 22 countries/regions, excluding ROW.
- Components of final demand along with sectoral contributions for the 22 countries/regions, excluding ROW.
- Gross value of output and value added at the sectoral level for the 22 countries/regions, excluding ROW.
- Bilateral import tariffs by sector among the 22 countries/regions.
- Elasticity of substitution between capital and labor by sector.
- Bilateral export-tax equivalents among the 22 countries/regions, decomposed into 18 sectors.

The monopolistically competitive market structure in the non-agricultural sectors of the model imposes an additional data requirement of the numbers of firms at the sectoral level, and there is need also for estimates of sectoral employment.[5] The employment data, which have been adapted from a variety of published sources, will be noted in tables below.

The GTAP-6.0 database has been projected to the year 2005, which is when the Uruguay Round liberalization will have been fully implemented. In this connection, we extrapolated the labor availability in different countries/regions by an average weighted population growth rate of 1.2% per annum. All other major variables have been projected, using an average weighted growth rate of GDP of 2.5%.[6] The 2005 data

---

[4] Details on the sectoral and country/region aggregation are available from the authors on request.

[5] Notes on the construction of the data on the number of firms and for employment are available from the authors on request.

[6] The underlying data are drawn from World Bank sources and are available on request. For a more elaborate and detailed procedure for calculating year 2005 projections, see Hertel and Martin (2000) and Hertel (2000).

have been adjusted to take into account two major developments that have occurred in the global trading system since the mid-1990s. These include: (1) implementation of the Uruguay Round negotiations that were completed in 1993–1994 and were to be phased in over the following decade; and (2) the accession of Mainland China and Taiwan to the WTO in 2001.[7] We have made allowance for the foregoing developments by readjusting the 2005 scaled-up database for benchmarking purposes to obtain an approximate picture of what the world may be expected to look like in 2005.[8] In the computational scenarios to be presented below, we use these re-adjusted data as the starting point to carry out our liberalization scenarios for the U.S. bilateral FTAs and for the accompanying unilateral and global free trade scenarios.

The GTAP 6.0 (2001) base data for tariffs and the estimated tariff equivalents of services barriers are broken down by sector on a global basis and bilaterally for existing and prospective FTA partners of the United States in Table 1. The post-Uruguay Round tariff rates on agriculture, mining, and manufactures are applied rates and are calculated in GTAP by dividing tariff revenues by the value of imports by sector.

The services barriers are based on financial data on average gross (price-cost) margins constructed initially by Hoekman (2000) and

---

[7] The tariff data for the WTO accession of China and Taiwan have been adapted from Ianchovichina and Martin (2004). In addition to benchmarking the effects of the Uruguay Round and China/Taiwan accession to the WTO, Francois *et al.* (2005) benchmark their GTAP dataset to take into account the enlargement of the European Union (EU) in 2004 to include ten new member countries from Central and Eastern Europe and some changes in the EU Common Agricultural Policies that were introduced in 2000. Our EU and EFTA regional aggregate includes the 25-member EU, but the benchmark data were not adjusted to take into account the adoption of the EU common external tariffs by the new members. Because of data constraints, we have not made allowance for the Information Technology Agreement and agreements for liberalization of financial and telecommunication services following conclusion of the Uruguay Round.

[8] See Anderson and Martin (2005), who use a model developed at the World Bank that benchmarks their GTAP 6.0 data to 2015 for computational purposes.

Table 1. Post-Uruguay Round tariff rates by sector for the United States (percent).

	Global	Singapore	Australia	Morocco	SACU	Thailand	Korea	FTAA				
								Canada	CAC	Chile	Mexico	South America
Agriculture	0.9	0.1	1.2	0.1	1.2	0.4	0.4	0.0	0.4	0.9	0.0	2.2
Mining	0.0	0.0	0.1	0.0	0.0	0.0	0.0	0.0	0.0	0.0	0.0	0.0
Food, Beverages & Tobacco	2.0	1.2	1.7	3.2	3.8	1.4	4.7	0.0	3.0	1.4	0.0	2.1
Textiles	5.5	9.3	6.6	7.1	6.3	8.7	10.6	0.0	6.8	11.4	0.0	7.7
Wearing Apparel	10.0	13.8	10.8	10.5	12.1	13.6	13.8	0.0	10.7	11.5	0.0	12.7
Leather Products & Footwear	7.3	5.6	4.1	3.6	0.2	7.7	8.4	0.0	4.1	6.7	0.0	6.6
Wood & Wood Products	0.2	0.2	0.4	0.2	0.0	0.0	0.4	0.0	0.0	0.2	0.0	0.3
Chemicals	1.6	3.2	1.0	0.0	0.2	1.1	3.0	0.0	0.8	0.1	0.0	0.9
Non-metallic Min. Products	3.1	5.2	2.9	0.9	0.0	1.4	2.1	0.0	0.0	0.6	0.0	2.6
Metal Products	1.0	1.9	0.3	0.7	0.1	0.5	1.9	0.0	0.0	0.5	0.0	0.6
Transportation Equipment	1.1	0.5	1.4	0.1	0.0	0.0	2.3	0.0	0.0	1.1	0.0	0.1
Machinery & Equipment	0.6	0.2	1.1	0.0	0.0	0.1	0.5	0.0	0.0	0.2	0.0	0.7

(*Continued*)

Table 1. (*Continued*)

	Global	Singapore	Australia	Morocco	SACU	Thailand	Korea	FTAA				
								Canada	CAC	Chile	Mexico	South America
Other Manufactures	1.2	1.3	0.9	0.0	0.1	0.3	4.1	0.0	0.4	0.1	0.0	1.3
Elec., Gas & Water	0.0	0.0	0.0	0.0	0.0	0.0	0.0	0.0	0.0	0.0	0.0	0.0
Construction	9.0	9.0	9.0	9.0	9.0	9.0	9.0	0.0	9.0	9.0	0.0	9.0
Trade & Transport	27.0	27.0	27.0	27.0	27.0	27.0	27.0	0.0	27.0	27.0	0.0	27.0
Other Private Services	31.0	31.0	31.0	31.0	31.0	31.0	31.0	0.0	31.0	31.0	0.0	31.0
Government Services	25.0	25.0	25.0	25.0	25.0	25.0	25.0	0.0	25.0	25.0	0.0	25.0

Note: Central America and Caribbean (CAC) members include Costa Rica, Dominican Republic, El Salvador, Guatemala, Honduras, and Nicaragua, and are to be included in the FTAA.

Sources: Adapted from Francois and Strutt (1999); Brown *et al.* (2002); and Dimaranan and McDougall (2005).

adapted for modeling purposes in Brown *et al.* (2002). The gross operating margins are calculated as the differences between total revenues and total operating costs. Some of these differences are presumably attributable to fixed costs. Given that the gross operating margins vary across countries, a portion of the margin can also be attributed to barriers to FDI. For this purpose, a benchmark is set for each sector in relation to the country with the smallest gross operating margin, on the assumption that operations in the benchmark country can be considered to be freely open to foreign firms. The excess in any other country above this lowest benchmark is then taken to be due to barriers to establishment by foreign firms.

That is, the barrier is modeled as the cost-increase attributable to an increase in fixed cost borne by multinational corporations attempting to establish an enterprise locally in a host country. This abstracts from the possibility that fixed costs may differ among firms because of variations in market size, distance from headquarters, and other factors. It is further assumed that this cost increase can be interpreted as an *ad valorem* equivalent tariff on services transactions generally. It can be seen in Table 1 that the constructed services barriers are considerably higher than the import barriers on manufactures. While possibly subject to overstatement, it is generally acknowledged that many services sectors are highly regulated and thus restrain international services transactions.

For the United States, the highest import tariffs for manufactures are recorded for textiles, wearing apparel, and leather products & footwear, both globally and bilaterally. The values and shares of U.S. exports and imports are broken down by sector according to origin and destination in Tables 2–3 on a global basis as well as for FTA partners. Employment by sector is indicated for the United States and its FTA partners in Table 4.

III. Computational Analysis of U.S. Free Trade Agreements

As already noted, the United States has signed or is currently in the process of negotiating a number of bilateral FTAs. These include the

Table 2. Value of U.S. sectoral exports by destination and origin, 2001 (millions of U.S. dollars).

Value	Global	Singapore	Australia	Morocco	SACU	Thailand	Korea	FTAA				
								Canada	CAC	Chile	Mexico	South America
Agriculture	31,488	79	85	103	43	390	1,883	3,542	684	23	4,032	1,475
Mining	6,435	35	35	22	26	30	246	1,370	15	10	281	505
Food, Beverages & Tobacco	29,107	199	266	43	63	185	1,150	4,624	789	94	3,518	1,361
Textiles	12,625	64	94	18	25	53	165	2,529	1,578	45	3,724	1,183
Wearing Apparel	5,116	25	27	4	7	11	34	389	1,135	12	1,290	803
Leather Products & Footwear	1,930	16	14	0	4	30	96	148	48	5	342	168
Wood & Wood Products	28,076	188	458	17	112	146	560	8,759	632	93	4,365	1,469
Chemicals	102,913	3,247	2,109	30	522	779	2,771	19,864	1,827	486	14,607	7,948
Non-metallic Min. Products	13,890	157	322	16	101	88	461	3,269	119	78	1,349	999
Metal Products	33,490	317	219	5	88	166	1,013	10,604	261	69	6,239	1,357
Transportation Equipment	110,075	3,858	1,888	31	1,083	1,095	3,029	35,001	496	372	12,154	4,217
Machinery & Equipment	279,309	10,311	4,628	79	963	1,918	12,131	45,107	2,618	1,408	34,627	16,995
Other Manufactures	14,710	182	236	2	63	134	245	1,769	394	59	1,028	654
Elec., Gas & Water	732	12	6	0	2	4	16	245	2	1	16	41
Construction	2,739	1	2	0	2	12	4	14	17	0	1	19
Trade & Transport	62,203	771	1,145	59	343	403	2,057	1,783	366	350	756	1,999
Other Private Services	109,632	1,496	1,063	90	339	701	2,793	4,170	519	188	1,147	2,909
Government Services	44,252	409	571	255	225	276	780	1,094	238	141	715	1,951
Total	888,720	21,367	13,167	777	4,013	6,421	29,435	144,281	11,736	3,435	90,191	46,054

(*Continued*)

Table 2. (*Continued*)

Percent	Global	Singapore	Australia	Morocco	SACU	Thailand	Korea	FTAA				
								Canada	CAC	Chile	Mexico	South America
Agriculture	100.0	0.3	0.3	0.3	0.1	1.2	6.0	11.3	2.2	0.1	12.8	4.7
Mining	100.0	0.5	0.5	0.3	0.4	0.5	3.8	21.3	0.2	0.2	4.4	7.9
Food, Beverages & Tobacco	100.0	0.7	0.9	0.1	0.2	0.6	4.0	15.9	2.7	0.3	12.1	4.7
Textiles	100.0	0.5	0.7	0.1	0.2	0.4	1.3	20.0	12.5	0.4	29.5	9.4
Wearing Apparel	100.0	0.5	0.5	0.1	0.1	0.2	0.7	7.6	22.2	0.2	25.2	15.7
Leather Products & Footwear	100.0	0.9	0.7	0.0	0.2	1.6	4.9	7.7	2.5	0.3	17.7	8.7
Wood & Wood Products	100.0	0.7	1.6	0.1	0.4	0.5	2.0	31.2	2.2	0.3	15.5	5.2
Chemicals	100.0	3.2	2.0	0.0	0.5	0.8	2.7	19.3	1.8	0.5	14.2	7.7
Non-metallic Min. Products	100.0	1.1	2.3	0.1	0.7	0.6	3.3	23.5	0.9	0.6	9.7	7.2
Metal Products	100.0	0.9	0.7	0.0	0.3	0.5	3.0	31.7	0.8	0.2	18.6	4.1
Transportation Equipment	100.0	3.5	1.7	0.0	1.0	1.0	2.8	31.8	0.5	0.3	11.0	3.8
Machinery & Equipment	100.0	3.7	1.7	0.0	0.3	0.7	4.3	16.1	0.9	0.5	12.4	6.1
Other Manufactures	100.0	1.2	1.6	0.0	0.4	0.9	1.7	12.0	2.7	0.4	7.0	4.4
Elec., Gas & Water	100.0	1.6	0.8	0.1	0.3	0.5	2.2	33.4	0.3	0.1	2.2	5.6
Construction	100.0	0.1	0.1	0.0	0.1	0.4	0.2	0.5	0.6	0.0	0.1	0.7
Trade & Transport	100.0	1.2	1.8	0.1	0.6	0.6	3.3	2.9	0.6	0.6	1.2	3.2
Other Private Services	100.0	1.4	1.0	0.1	0.3	0.6	2.5	3.8	0.5	0.2	1.0	2.7
Government Services	100.0	0.9	1.3	0.6	0.5	0.6	1.8	2.5	0.5	0.3	1.6	4.4
Total	100.0	2.4	1.5	0.1	0.5	0.7	3.3	16.2	1.3	0.4	10.1	5.2

Source: GTAP 6.0 adapted from Dimaranan and McDougall (2005).

Table 3. Value of U.S. sectoral imports by destination and origin, 1997 (millions of U.S. dollars).

Value	Global	Singapore	Australia	Morocco	SACU	Thailand	Korea	FTAA				
								Canada	CAC	Chile	Mexico	South America
Agriculture	20,644	35	207	32	80	432	53	4,582	1,792	887	3,750	2,977
Mining	69,789	0	322	81	170	28	2	16,971	108	196	8,285	12,109
Food, Beverages & Tobacco	34,790	58	1,771	29	125	2,185	245	7,860	962	828	2,841	2,561
Textiles	30,961	154	66	5	249	874	1,607	2,376	2,436	6	3,932	1,175
Wearing Apparel	50,788	213	44	104	302	1,689	1,805	1,438	4,374	17	6,122	3,136
Leather Products & Footwear	22,480	8	27	7	24	770	211	169	27	2	526	1,883
Wood & Wood Products	63,362	185	103	6	97	609	516	30,720	215	698	4,513	2,205
Chemicals	108,578	1,192	422	36	383	992	2,026	20,041	1,118	317	3,719	5,024
Non-metallic Min. Products	20,054	3	65	3	52	461	191	2,860	68	22	2,012	1,700
Metal Products	64,781	75	1,108	5	2,291	490	2,138	16,056	171	949	4,841	4,398
Transportation Equipment	191,656	183	709	2	428	173	7,403	53,987	70	17	23,094	4,176
Machinery & Equipment	373,201	13,336	932	95	371	5,881	17,704	39,869	1,149	29	65,698	3,949
Other Manufactures	57,287	67	182	5	592	1,491	972	1,633	184	9	1,802	845
Elec., Gas & Water	2,104	2	13	1	11	4	5	1,563	6	1	17	55
Construction	764	2	2	3	1	6	3	5	9	0	4	5
Trade & Transport	82,987	791	1,758	365	578	1,427	1,333	2,221	810	261	1,086	1,897
Other Private Services	69,873	1,761	762	102	139	492	1,304	2,394	512	137	602	1,941
Government Services	20,736	196	426	256	125	77	739	582	230	44	120	899
Total	1,284,834	18,261	8,917	1,136	6,019	18,080	38,257	205,326	14,242	4,420	132,964	50,937

(*Continued*)

Table 3. (*Continued*)

Percent	Global	Singapore	Australia	Morocco	SACU	Thailand	Korea	FTAA				
								Canada	CAC	Chile	Mexico	South America
Agriculture	100.0	0.2	1.0	0.2	0.4	2.1	0.3	22.2	8.7	4.3	18.2	14.4
Mining	100.0	0.0	0.5	0.1	0.2	0.0	0.0	24.3	0.2	0.3	11.9	17.4
Food, Beverages & Tobacco	100.0	0.2	5.1	0.1	0.4	6.3	0.7	22.6	2.8	2.4	8.2	7.4
Textiles	100.0	0.5	0.2	0.0	0.8	2.8	5.2	7.7	7.9	0.0	12.7	3.8
Wearing Apparel	100.0	0.4	0.1	0.2	0.6	3.3	3.6	2.8	8.6	0.0	12.1	6.2
Leather Products & Footwear	100.0	0.0	0.1	0.0	0.1	3.4	0.9	0.8	0.1	0.0	2.3	8.4
Wood & Wood Products	100.0	0.3	0.2	0.0	0.2	1.0	0.8	48.5	0.3	1.1	7.1	3.5
Chemicals	100.0	1.1	0.4	0.0	0.4	0.9	1.9	18.5	1.0	0.3	3.4	4.6
Non-metallic Min. Products	100.0	0.0	0.3	0.0	0.3	2.3	1.0	14.3	0.3	0.1	10.0	8.5
Metal Products	100.0	0.1	1.7	0.0	3.5	0.8	3.3	24.8	0.3	1.5	7.5	6.8
Transportation Equipment	100.0	0.1	0.4	0.0	0.2	0.1	3.9	28.2	0.0	0.0	12.0	2.2
Machinery & Equipment	100.0	3.6	0.2	0.0	0.1	1.6	4.7	10.7	0.3	0.0	17.6	1.1
Other Manufactures	100.0	0.1	0.3	0.0	1.0	2.6	1.7	2.9	0.3	0.0	3.1	1.5
Elec., Gas & Water	100.0	0.1	0.6	0.1	0.5	0.2	0.2	74.3	0.3	0.0	0.8	2.6
Construction	100.0	0.2	0.3	0.4	0.1	0.8	0.4	0.7	1.2	0.0	0.6	0.6
Trade & Transport	100.0	1.0	2.1	0.4	0.7	1.7	1.6	2.7	1.0	0.3	1.3	2.3
Other Private Services	100.0	2.5	1.1	0.1	0.2	0.7	1.9	3.4	0.7	0.2	0.9	2.8
Government Services	100.0	0.9	2.1	1.2	0.6	0.4	3.6	2.8	1.1	0.2	0.6	4.3
Total	100.0	1.4	0.7	0.1	0.5	1.4	3.0	16.0	1.1	0.3	10.3	4.0

Source: GTAP 6.0 adapted from Dimaranan and McDougall (2005).

Table 4. Employment by sector, 2001: United States and FTA partners (number of workers and percent of employment).

Workers (thousand)	United States	Singapore	Australia	Morocco	SACU	Thailand	Korea	FTAA				
								Canada	CAC	Chile	Mexico	South America
Agriculture	3,559	0.1	478	5,228	5,011	19,659	2,421	481	6,891	863	7,518	29,303
Mining	616	1	73	63	329	46	20	207	48	83	135	1,583
Food, Beverages & Tobacco	2,155	21	219	309	215	118	333	295	1,597	299	1,923	4,713
Textiles	845	2	44	189	73	134	425	79	229	39	603	1,603
Wearing Apparel	616	12	47	372	126	235	262	86	1,029	29	207	2,303
Leather Products & Footwear	92	1	13	41	32	15	95	13	119	25	195	623
Wood & Wood Products	2,236	38	226	80	215	44	364	520	585	144	710	2,349
Chemicals	2,717	56	119	127	173	52	559	291	666	150	1,269	2,855
Non-metallic Min. Products	724	8	50	123	78	39	162	66	211	34	398	1,027
Metal Products	3,120	55	199	84	216	69	520	324	264	109	607	996
Transportation Equipment	2,246	52	102	55	90	26	539	322	92	27	824	445
Machinery & Equipment	5,335	221	158	74	187	58	1,468	480	590	47	1,030	1,130
Other Manufactures	519	4	17	1	26	23	81	42	102	3	70	376
Elec., Gas & Water	1,529	13	74	46	140	118	65	136	290	38	207	212
Construction	10,406	153	730	804	1,457	2,016	1,786	929	2,381	491	2,547	9,247
Trade & Transport	39,104	810	3,090	2,333	3,234	9,571	8,109	5,301	6,792	1,700	13,389	32,627
Other Private Services	18,105	431	1,557	143	1,448	948	2,581	2,670	1,296	480	1,599	3,890
Government Services	52,786	164	2,706	1,706	6,741	3,987	4,520	4,448	6,754	1,785	8,070	52,560
Total	146,711	2,043	9,901	11,779	19,791	37,157	24,311	16,691	29,937	6,347	41,301	147,841

(*Continued*)

Table 4. (*Continued*)

Percent	United States	Singapore	Australia	Morocco	SACU	Thailand	Korea	FTAA				
								Canada	CAC	Chile	Mexico	South America
Agriculture	2.4	0.0	4.8	44.4	25.3	52.9	10.0	2.9	23.0	13.6	18.2	19.8
Mining	0.4	0.0	0.7	0.5	1.7	0.1	0.1	1.2	0.2	1.3	0.3	1.1
Food, Beverages & Tobacco	1.5	1.0	2.2	2.6	1.1	0.3	1.4	1.8	5.3	4.7	4.7	3.2
Textiles	0.6	0.1	0.4	1.6	0.4	0.4	1.7	0.5	0.8	0.6	1.5	1.1
Wearing Apparel	0.4	0.6	0.5	3.2	0.6	0.6	1.1	0.5	3.4	0.5	0.5	1.6
Leather Products & Footwear	0.1	0.1	0.1	0.3	0.2	0.0	0.4	0.1	0.4	0.4	0.5	0.4
Wood & Wood Products	1.5	1.9	2.3	0.7	1.1	0.1	1.5	3.1	2.0	2.3	1.7	1.6
Chemicals	1.9	2.8	1.2	1.1	0.9	0.1	2.3	1.7	2.2	2.4	3.1	1.9
Non-metallic Min. Products	0.5	0.4	0.5	1.0	0.4	0.1	0.7	0.4	0.7	0.5	1.0	0.7
Metal Products	2.1	2.7	2.0	0.7	1.1	0.2	2.1	1.9	0.9	1.7	1.5	0.7
Transportation Equipment	1.5	2.5	1.0	0.5	0.5	0.1	2.2	1.9	0.3	0.4	2.0	0.3
Machinery & Equipment	3.6	10.8	1.6	0.6	0.9	0.2	6.0	2.9	2.0	0.7	2.5	0.8
Other Manufactures	0.4	0.2	0.2	0.0	0.1	0.1	0.3	0.2	0.3	0.0	0.2	0.3
Elec., Gas & Water	1.0	0.6	0.7	0.4	0.7	0.3	0.3	0.8	1.0	0.6	0.5	0.1
Construction	7.1	7.5	7.4	6.8	7.4	5.4	7.3	5.6	8.0	7.7	6.2	6.3
Trade & Transport	26.7	39.6	31.2	19.8	16.3	25.8	33.4	31.8	22.7	26.8	32.4	22.1
Other Private Services	12.3	21.1	15.7	1.2	7.3	2.6	10.6	16.0	4.3	7.6	3.9	2.6
Government Services	36.0	8.0	27.3	14.5	34.1	10.7	18.6	26.6	22.6	28.1	19.5	35.6
Total	100.0	100.0	100.0	100.0	100.0	100.0	100.0	100.0	100.0	100.0	100.0	100.0

Sources: ILO website (2005); Taiwan Government website (2005); UNIDO (2005); and World Bank (2005).

agreements with Chile and Singapore approved by the U.S. Congress in 2003; agreements with Central America and the Dominican Republic (CAFTA), Australia, Morocco, and Bahrain approved in 2005; and ongoing negotiations with the Southern African Customs Union (SACU), Andean Countries (Bolivia, Colombia, Ecuador, and Peru), Panama, Thailand, Korea, and the Free Trade Area of the Americas (FTAA).[9] As we note in Brown *et al.* (2004, 2005a,b), the United States has a myriad of objectives in pursuing FTAs, including increased market access and shaping the regulatory and political environment in FTA partner countries to conform to U.S. principles and institutions. By the same token, the FTA partners are attracted by the preferential margins for U.S. market access and opportunities to improve their economic efficiency and to design and implement more effective domestic institutions and policies.

We present below some results of the analysis of the following FTAs, which are denoted as:

USCHFTA	U.S.-Chile FTA
USSGFTA	U.S.-Singapore FTA
USCAFTA	U.S.-Central America FTA
USAUSFTA	U.S.-Australia FTA
USMORFTA	U.S.-Morocco FTA
USSACUFTA	U.S.-Southern African Customs Union FTA
USTHFTA	U.S.-Thailand FTA
USKORFTA	U.S.-Korea FTA
FTAA	Free Trade Area of the Americas

Data constraints do not permit the analysis of the U.S. FTAs with the Andean countries, Bahrain and other countries in the Middle East, and Panama.

Our reference point is the post-Uruguay Round 2005 database together with the post-Uruguay Round tariff rates on agricultural products and manufactures and the specially constructed measures of

---

[9] See the USTR website (www.ustr.gov) for more information on the variety of U.S. FTAs completed or in process.

services barriers described above. Four scenarios have been carried out for each FTA: (A) removal of agricultural tariffs[10]; (M) removal of manufactures tariffs; (S) removal of services barriers; and (C) combined removel of agricultural and manufactures tariffs and services barriers, denoted by USCHFTA-C, etc. The results for the separate removal of the agricultural, manufactures, and services barriers and for the sectoral effects on exports, imports, and gross output are available on request.

We should emphasize that our computational analysis does not take into account other features of the various FTAs, which do not lend themselves readily to quantification. These other features cover E-commerce, intellectual property, labor and environmental standards, foreign direct investment, government procurement, trade remedies, dispute settlement, and the development of new institutional and cooperative measures. By the same token, because of data constraints, we have not made allowance for rules of origin and special preferences that may be negotiated as part of each FTA and that could be designed for protectionist reasons to limit trade.

USCHFTA-C: U.S.-Chile Free Trade Agreement — The U.S.-Chile FTA was approved by the U.S. Congress in 2003. The estimated global welfare effects are indicated in Table 5. Global welfare increases by $7.6 billion, with U.S. welfare increasing by $6.3 billion (0.1% of GNP) and Chile's welfare by $1.4 billion (1.7% of GNP).[11] The sectoral results for the United States are shown in Table 6 and indicate small absolute and percent changes in employment across the U.S. sectors. The sectoral employment effects for Chile are indicated in Table 7 and show relatively large employment increases in agriculture, wood & wood products, metal products,

---

[10] The bilateral FTA scenarios in this section make no allowance for reductions in agricultural export subsidies and agricultural production subsidies, which are excluded from bilateral negotiations and fall within the scope of the multilateral negotiations.

[11] The estimated effects on aggregate exports/imports, terms of trade, and real returns to capital and labor for this and all other FTAs to be analyzed in what follows are available from the authors on request. Changes in bilateral trade flows by country/region of origin and destination are also available.

Table 5. Global welfare effects of bilateral negotiating options for the United States (billions of dollars and percent of GNP).

Billions of Dollars	US-Chile	US-Singapore	US-CAC	US-Australia	US-Morocco	US-SACU	US-Thailand	US-Korea	FTAA
Japan	0.0	0.5	−0.5	−0.6	0.1	−0.0	−0.1	0.5	−1.0
United States	6.3	17.0	11.8	18.6	8.2	9.0	15.2	29.1	62.4
Canada	0.0	0.1	−0.3	−0.1	0.0	0.0	0.0	0.4	5.3
Australia	−0.0	0.0	−0.1	5.1	0.0	0.0	0.0	0.2	−0.1
New Zealand	−0.0	0.0	−0.0	0.0	0.0	0.0	0.0	0.0	−0.0
EU and EFTA	−0.1	1.7	−2.5	−0.5	0.3	−0.1	0.2	1.5	−5.3
Hong Kong	−0.0	−0.0	−0.1	−0.0	0.0	−0.0	−0.0	0.1	−0.0
China	−0.0	0.1	−0.4	−0.2	0.0	−0.0	−0.2	1.2	−0.3
Korea	−0.0	0.1	−0.1	−0.2	0.0	−0.0	−0.0	13.1	−0.3
Singapore	0.0	2.5	−0.0	−0.0	0.0	0.0	−0.0	0.0	−0.0
Taiwan	0.0	−0.0	−0.1	−0.1	0.0	−0.0	−0.0	0.0	−0.2
Indonesia	−0.0	0.0	−0.1	0.0	0.0	−0.0	−0.1	0.1	−0.2
Malaysia	−0.0	−0.4	−0.0	−0.0	0.0	−0.0	−0.1	0.1	−0.1
Philippines	0.0	−0.0	−0.1	−0.0	0.0	−0.0	−0.0	0.0	−0.1
Thailand	−0.0	−0.1	−0.1	−0.0	0.0	−0.0	5.2	0.0	−0.1
Rest of Asia	0.0	0.1	−0.5	−0.1	0.0	−0.0	−0.1	0.1	−0.6
Chile	1.4	0.0	−0.0	0.0	0.0	0.0	0.0	0.0	3.4
Mexico	0.0	0.0	−0.2	−0.1	0.0	0.0	−0.0	0.2	8.4
Central America and the Caribbean (CAC)	0.0	−0.0	5.1	−0.0	0.0	−0.0	−0.0	0.1	7.4
South America	−0.1	0.1	0.3	−0.0	0.0	0.0	−0.0	0.4	36.2
Morocco	−0.0	0.0	−0.0	−0.0	1.2	−0.0	0.0	0.0	−0.0
Southern African Customs Union (SACU)	−0.0	0.0	−0.0	−0.0	0.0	1.6	−0.0	0.0	−0.1
Total	7.6	21.6	12.1	21.8	9.9	10.5	19.8	47.3	114.6

(*Continued*)

Table 5. (*Continued*)

Percent	US-Chile	US-Singapore	US-CAC	US-Australia	US-Morocco	US-SACU	US-Thailand	US-Korea	FTAA
Japan	0.0	0.0	–0.0	–0.0	0.0	0.0	0.0	0.0	–0.0
United States	0.1	0.1	0.1	0.1	0.1	0.1	0.1	0.2	0.5
Canada	0.0	0.0	–0.0	–0.0	0.0	0.0	0.0	0.0	0.6
Australia	0.0	0.0	–0.0	1.1	0.0	0.0	0.0	0.0	–0.0
New Zealand	0.0	0.0	0.0	0.0	0.0	0.0	0.0	0.0	–0.0
EU and EFTA	0.0	0.0	–0.0	0.0	0.0	0.0	0.0	0.0	–0.1
Hong Kong	0.0	–0.0	–0.0	–0.0	0.0	0.0	–0.0	0.1	–0.0
China	0.0	0.0	–0.0	–0.0	0.0	0.0	–0.0	0.1	–0.0
Korea	0.0	0.0	–0.0	–0.0	0.0	0.0	–0.0	2.5	–0.1
Singapore	0.0	2.4	–0.0	–0.0	0.0	0.0	–0.0	0.1	0.0
Taiwan	0.0	0.0	–0.0	–0.0	0.0	0.0	–0.0	0.0	–0.1
Indonesia	0.0	0.0	–0.1	0.0	0.0	0.0	–0.0	0.1	–0.1
Malaysia	0.0	–0.4	–0.0	–0.0	0.0	0.0	–0.1	0.1	–0.1
Philippines	0.0	–0.1	–0.1	–0.0	0.0	0.0	–0.0	0.0	–0.1
Thailand	0.0	–0.0	–0.1	–0.0	0.0	0.0	3.6	0.0	–0.1
Rest of Asia	0.0	0.0	–0.1	–0.0	0.0	0.0	–0.0	0.0	–0.1
Chile	1.7	0.0	–0.0	0.0	0.0	0.0	0.0	0.0	4.1
Mexico	0.0	0.0	–0.0	–0.0	0.0	0.0	0.0	0.0	1.1
Central America and the Caribbean (CAC)	0.0	0.0	3.9	–0.0	0.0	0.0	–0.0	0.1	5.6
South America	0.0	0.0	0.0	0.0	0.0	0.0	0.0	0.0	2.3
Morocco	0.0	0.0	–0.0	0.0	2.8	0.0	0.0	0.0	–0.0
Southern African Customs Union (SACU)	0.0	0.0	–0.0	0.0	0.0	1.0	–0.0	0.0	–0.1

Table 6. Sectoral employment effects of bilateral negotiating options for the United States (number of workers and percent of employment).

Number of Workers	US-Chile	US-Singapore	US-CAC	US-Australia	US-Morocco	US-SACU	US-Thailand	US-Korea
Agriculture	(287)	531	6,023	(85)	988	284	2,191	32,782
Mining	(45)	196	264	405	91	51	170	(338)
Food, Beverages & Tobacco	(144)	(77)	664	(920)	127	45	128	2,243
Textiles	(15)	(137)	(6,917)	403	118	(490)	(1,905)	(4,264)
Wearing Apparel	(57)	(145)	(7,196)	298	(33)	(298)	(2,089)	(3,756)
Leather Products & Footwear	(7)	63	266	75	4	34	(577)	(232)
Wood & Wood Products	(148)	142	577	302	78	116	216	(664)
Chemicals	8	316	593	1,167	131	210	669	(698)
Non-metallic Min. Products	29	145	217	370	96	84	241	24
Metal Products	(277)	1,015	1,077	1,158	87	467	806	(2,537)
Transportation Equipment	14	914	619	1,616	77	915	1,021	(3,195)
Machinery & Equipment	825	4,524	3,113	3,728	*111*	482	1,791	(4,180)
Other Manufactures	26	335	557	567	28	106	433	270
Elec., Gas & Water	(17)	(25)	93	26	14	20	44	111
Construction	(39)	(351)	(60)	(166)	(17)	36	(54)	(850)
Trade & Transport	(237)	(3,111)	(376)	(8,472)	(1,711)	(1,847)	(5,079)	(7,596)
Other Private Services	(100)	(3,341)	792	(1,404)	(9)	306	567	(899)
Government Services	469	(994)	(305)	931	(247)	(520)	1,427	(6,218)

(*Continued*)

Table 6. (*Continued*)

Percent	US-Chile	US-Singapore	US-CAC	US-Australia	US-Morocco	US-SACU	US-Thailand	US-Korea
Agriculture	−0.0	0.0	0.2	0.0	0.0	0.0	0.1	0.9
Mining	−0.0	0.0	0.0	0.1	0.0	0.0	0.0	−0.1
Food, Beverages & Tobacco	−0.0	0.0	0.0	−0.0	0.0	0.0	0.0	0.1
Textiles	0.0	−0.0	−0.8	0.1	0.0	−0.1	−0.2	−0.5
Wearing Apparel	−0.0	−0.0	−1.2	0.1	−0.0	−0.1	−0.3	−0.6
Leather Products & Footwear	−0.0	0.1	0.3	0.1	0.0	0.0	−0.7	−0.3
Wood & Wood Products	−0.0	0.0	0.0	0.0	0.0	0.0	0.0	−0.0
Chemicals	0.0	0.0	0.0	0.0	0.0	0.0	0.0	−0.0
Non-metallic Min. Products	0.0	0.0	0.0	0.1	0.0	0.0	0.0	0.0
Metal Products	−0.0	0.0	0.0	0.0	0.0	0.0	0.0	−0.1
Transportation Equipment	0.0	0.0	0.0	0.1	0.0	0.0	0.1	−0.1
Machinery & Equipment	0.0	0.1	0.1	0.1	0.0	0.0	0.0	−0.1
Other Manufactures	0.0	0.1	0.1	0.1	0.0	0.0	0.1	0.1
Elec., Gas & Water	0.0	0.0	0.0	0.0	0.0	0.0	0.0	0.0
Construction	0.0	0.0	0.0	0.0	0.0	0.0	0.0	−0.0
Trade & Transport	0.0	−0.0	0.0	−0.0	0.0	0.0	−0.0	−0.0
Other Private Services	0.0	−0.0	0.0	−0.0	0.0	0.0	0.0	0.0
Government Services	0.0	0.0	0.0	0.0	0.0	0.0	0.0	−0.0

Table 7. Sectoral employment effects for the US FTA partner countries (number of workers and percent of employment).

Number of Workers	US-Chile	US-Singapore	US-CAC	US-Australia	US-Morocco	US-SACU	US-Thailand	US-Korea
Agriculture	3,114	(1)	(207,012)	200	(28,610)	(5,204)	(166,217)	(105,568)
Mining	315	(22)	(5,940)	(1,211)	(889)	(1,406)	(1,417)	100
Food, Beverages & Tobacco	244	(557)	(36,977)	1,677	(2,872)	(904)	(1,601)	(4,419)
Textiles	20	112	97,644	(112)	(4,185)	3,303	10,916	34,349
Wearing Apparel	112	1,758	392,213	(123)	(2,686)	25,823	22,112	37,050
Leather Products & Footwear	(2)	(45)	(3,011)	(107)	(747)	(197)	1,905	5,929
Wood & Wood Products	1,378	(880)	(15,526)	(767)	(124)	(907)	(778)	868
Chemicals	232	(1,721)	(15,726)	(1,571)	(639)	(912)	(823)	2,087
Non-metallic Min. Products	(34)	(247)	(9,451)	(516)	(791)	(546)	(810)	(549)
Metal Products	959	(2,627)	(19,923)	(2,788)	150	(2,471)	(2,278)	3,798
Transportation Equipment	(127)	(1,582)	(8,143)	(1,491)	(195)	(1,765)	(406)	8,139
Machinery & Equipment	(1,421)	(10,134)	(66,601)	(2,995)	(66)	(2,172)	(1,154)	3,415
Other Manufactures	(14)	(97)	(5,539)	(182)	(3)	(326)	(195)	1,123
Elec., Gas & Water	147	(16)	1,767	(146)	58	(510)	382	263
Construction	413	64	(7,334)	(503)	482	(2,218)	4,831	(394)
Trade & Transport	960	4,479	(48,492)	9,988	40,613	382	161,135	10,586
Other Private Services	1,212	11,998	(10,818)	2,867	388	(5,074)	(1,860)	(2,304)
Government Services	(7,508)	(482)	(31,132)	(2,219)	115	(4,897)	(23,746)	5,527

(*Continued*)

Table 7. (*Continued*)

Percent	US-Chile	US-Singapore	US-CAC	US-Australia	US-Morocco	US-SACU	US-Thailand	US-Korea
Agriculture	0.4	−1.3	−3.0	0.0	−0.6	−0.1	−0.9	−4.4
Mining	0.4	−2.9	−12.2	−1.7	−1.4	−0.4	−3.0	0.5
Food, Beverages & Tobacco	0.1	−2.9	−2.3	0.8	−1.0	−0.4	−1.4	−1.3
Textiles	0.1	5.5	43.7	−0.3	−2.2	4.7	8.3	7.6
Wearing Apparel	0.4	15.6	37.8	−0.3	−0.7	21.6	9.5	14.1
Leather Products & Footwear	−0.0	−3.7	−2.5	−0.8	−1.9	−0.7	12.7	6.1
Wood & Wood Products	1.0	−2.3	−2.6	−0.3	−0.2	−0.4	−1.7	0.2
Chemicals	0.2	−3.0	−2.3	−1.3	−0.5	−0.5	−1.5	0.4
Non-metallic Min. Products	−0.1	−2.9	−4.5	−1.0	−0.7	−0.7	−2.1	−0.3
Metal Products	0.9	−4.8	−7.6	−1.4	0.2	−1.1	−3.3	0.7
Transportation Equipment	−0.5	−3.0	−9.2	−1.5	−0.4	−1.9	−1.6	1.5
Machinery & Equipment	−3.0	−4.6	−11.4	−1.9	−0.1	−1.2	−2.0	0.2
Other Manufactures	−0.5	−2.4	−5.3	−1.1	−0.2	−1.2	−0.9	1.4
Elec., Gas & Water	0.4	−0.1	0.6	−0.2	0.1	−0.4	0.3	0.4
Construction	0.1	0.0	−0.3	−0.1	0.1	−0.2	0.2	−0.0
Trade & Transport	0.1	0.6	−0.7	0.3	1.7	0.0	1.7	0.1
Other Private Services	0.3	2.8	−0.8	0.2	0.3	−0.4	−0.2	−0.1
Government Services	−0.4	−0.3	−0.5	−0.1	0.0	−0.1	−0.6	0.1

trade & transport, and other private services, and relatively large employment declines in machinery & equipment and government services. These employment changes for Chile suggest the extent of labor market adjustments that may occur as a result of the FTA.

USSGFTA-C: U.S.-Singapore Free Trade Agreement — The welfare effects of a U.S.-Singapore FTA, which was approved by the U.S. Congress in 2003, noted in Table 5, indicate an increase in global welfare of $21.6 billion, with U.S. welfare rising by $17.0 billion (0.1% of GNP) and Singapore's welfare by $2.5 billion (2.4% of GNP). In Table 6, the sectoral employment effects for the United States are relatively small, whereas in Table 7, for Singapore, there are relatively large sectoral employment increases in textiles, wearing apparel, and services, and declines in most other sectors. These sectoral changes suggest sizable employment adjustments for Singapore that may occur in the FTA with the United States.

USCAFTA-C: U.S.-Central America Free Trade Agreement — The U.S.-CAFTA was approved by the U.S. Congress in 2005. The estimated global welfare effects of the CAFTA shown in Table 5 indicate a rise of $12.1 billion, U.S. welfare increases by $11.8 billion (0.1% of GNP) and the welfare of the aggregate of Central America and the Caribbean (CAC) increases by $5.1 billion (3.9% of GNP).[12] It can also be seen that the CAFTA is apparently trade diverting for most of the non-member countries/regions shown. The sectoral employment effects for the United States, noted in Table 6, indicate that the employment declines are concentrated in textiles and wearing apparel and are comparatively small as a percent of employment in these sectors, –0.8% and –1.2%, respectively. The sectoral employment changes for the CAC are shown in Table 7. The increases are quite large in textiles and wearing apparel, and there are employment declines in most of the other sectors, as the expansion of the relatively

[12] The GTAP 6.0 data refer to a CAC aggregate and do not provide separate data for the five Central American countries and the Dominican Republic that comprise the CAFTA. It is noted in Brown, Kiyota, and Stern (2005b) that the CAFTA countries account for a substantial proportion of CAC trade so that using CAC data may be a reasonable approximation for modeling purposes.

labor-intensive industries attracts workers from the rest of the economy. These results thus suggest that the CAFTA may result in significant worker displacement in the process of adjustment brought about by elimination of the import barriers.

USAUSFTA-C: U.S.–Australia FTA — The U.S.-Australia FTA was approved in late 2004 and took effect at the beginning of 2005. It can be seen in Table 5 that global welfare rises by \$21.8 billion, U.S. welfare by \$18.6 billion (0.1% of GNP), and Australian welfare by \$5.1 billion (1.1% of GNP). There are many instances of trade diversion for non-partner countries. The sectoral effects for the United States in Table 6 show small employment changes, while the positive employment changes for Australia in Table 7 are concentrated in food, beverages & tobacco, trade & transport, and other private services, and there are negative effects across all the other sectors ranging from –0.3% to –1.9% of sectoral employment.

USMORFTA-C: U.S.-Morocco FTA — The U.S.-Morocco FTA was approved in 2005. As noted in Tables 2–3, U.S. trade in goods and services with Morocco is rather small. By far the largest proportions of Morocco's trade are with the EU and EFTA. The global welfare increase from the U.S.-Morocco FTA indicated in Table 5 is \$9.9 billion, with welfare increases by \$8.2 billion (0.1% of GNP) for the United States, and \$1.2 billion (2.8% of GNP) for Morocco. The U.S. sectoral employment changes noted in Table 6 are negligible. For Morocco, in Table 7, the largest employment increases are in trade & transport, and the largest declines in agriculture, food, beverages & tobacco, textiles, and apparel. The welfare and employment effects of the U.S.-Morocco FTA are thus seen to be fairly small.

USSACUFTA-C: U.S.-Southern African Customs Union FTA — The effects of the U.S.-SACU FTA, which is currently being negotiated, are indicated in Table 5, and show an increase of \$10.5 billion in global welfare, \$9.0 billion (0.1% of GNP) for the United States, and \$1.6 billion (1.0% of GNP) for the SACU members combined. In Table 6, there are indications of negligible sectoral employment impacts for the United States. In Table 7, the employment increases for SACU are concentrated in textiles and wearing apparel and are negative across the remaining sectors as labor is attracted towards the labor-intensive sectors.

USTHFTA-C: U.S.-Thailand FTA — The U.S.-Thailand FTA is currently being negotiated. In Table 5, the global welfare increase is $19.8 billion, a $15.2 billion (0.1% of GNP) increase for the United States, and a $5.2 billion (3.6% of GNP) increase for Thailand. There is evidence of pervasive trade diversion. The sectoral employment changes for the United States noted in Table 6 are negligible. For Thailand, in Table 7, the largest employment increases are concentrated in textiles and wearing apparel, construction, and trade & transport, and there are employment declines especially in agriculture, mining, food, beverages & tobacco, several capital-intensive manufactures, other private services, and government services. Some of the percentage employment effects are relatively large.

USKORFTA-C: U.S.-Korea FTA — The negotiation of a U.S.-Korea FTA is currently in process. In Table 5, global welfare is shown to increase by $47.3 billion, U.S. welfare by $29.1 billion (0.2% of GNP), and Korea's welfare by $13.1 billion (2.5% of GNP). The sectoral employment effects on the United States are small, whereas some of the employment effects are substantial in absolute terms although rather small in percentage terms.

FTAA-C: Free Trade Area of the Americas — Discussions have been ongoing for several years to create a Free Trade Area for the Americas (FTAA).[13] Since the country detail in our model does not include the individual members of the FTAA, we have chosen to approximate it by combining the United States, Canada, Mexico, and Chile with an aggregate of Central American and Caribbean (CAC) and an aggregate of other South American nations. The welfare effects of the FTAA are indicated in Table 5 and amount to $114.6 billion globally, $62.4 billion (0.5% of GNP) for the United States, $5.3 billion (0.6% of GNP) for Canada, $8.4 billion (1.1% of GNP) for Mexico, $3.4 billion (4.1% of GNP) for Chile, $7.4 billion (5.6% of GNP) for the CAC, and $36.2 billion (2.3% of GNP) for the

---

[13] For details on the FTAA negotiations, see the website of the Office of the United States Trade Representative (www.ustr.gov).

aggregate of other South American countries. There is some evidence of trade diversion, in particular for Japan and the EU/EFTA. The sectoral employment effects for the United States, indicated in Table 8, show relatively small employment declines in mining, textiles and wearing apparel, transportation equipment, and trade & transport, and increases in all other sectors. The sectoral employment effects for Canada are also small, whereas the employment changes for Mexico, Chile, the CAC, and other South American countries are noteworthy. This suggests that the developing countries covered in the FTAA would experience more employment adjustments than the United States and Canada.

IV. Hub and Spoke Effects of the U.S. FTAs

In the discussion of the U.S. bilateral FTAs in the preceding section, it was noted that there were indications of negative welfare effects for a number of non-member countries/regions. It is well known theoretically that preferential trading arrangements may result in both trade creation, which is welfare enhancing, and trade diversion, which will reduce welfare as trade is shifted from lower to higher cost sources of supply. But there is another consideration, which is that bilateral FTAs are based on the "hub-and-spoke" arrangement, with the United States representing the hub and with separate spokes connecting the bilateral FTA partners to the hub. In negotiating these bilateral FTAs, no account is taken of the effects that they may have on non-members, even though there may be a bilateral FTA with one or more of the non-members. As more and more bilateral FTAs are negotiated, the spokes of the FTAs may thus emanate out in many different and overlapping directions, with resulting distortions of global trade patterns. That is, this combination of varying preferences among different and overlapping FTAs may lead to greatly increased transactions costs for firms and the undermining of the most-favored–nation (MFN) principle of non-discrimination that is at the heart of the multilateral trading system. These effects of the proliferation of FTAs are what Bhagwati refers to as "spaghetti-bowl" effects.

Table 8. Sectoral employment effects for the FTAA member countries (number of workers and percent of employment).

Number of Workers	United States	Canada	Chile	Mexico	CAC	South America
Agriculture	9,675	2,717	12,264	(18,395)	(241,554)	158,734
Mining	(979)	(664)	(2,819)	(116)	(5,753)	25,836
Food, Beverages & Tobacco	10	441	720	(4,401)	(49,231)	8,765
Textiles	(10,056)	(1,299)	359	(1,513)	102,334	48,397
Wearing Apparel	(9,343)	(815)	(86)	(1,995)	410,491	66,471
Leather Products & Footwear	(486)	(130)	(33)	(1,738)	1,388	32,314
Wood & Wood Products	1,292	653	2,779	968	(19,169)	(22,626)
Chemicals	2,857	(401)	196	6,988	(11,364)	(18,685)
Non-metallic Min. Products	788	(89)	(206)	778	(12,341)	(2,315)
Metal Products	26	(807)	1,769	2,077	(21,151)	3,395
Transportation Equipment	(1,667)	(397)	(75)	7,307	(9,885)	7,282
Machinery & Equipment	9,916	(426)	2,452	3,580	(56,652)	(14,875)
Other Manufactures	2,073	(67)	35	(32)	(3,350)	(3,173)
Elec., Gas & Water	52	(47)	303	127	1,968	264
Construction	(372)	(59)	(165)	267	(7,729)	(22,151)
Trade & Transport	(5,368)	2,217	(7,600)	9,117	(33,826)	(48,275)
Other Private Services	739	(556)	716	(811)	(6,855)	(5,060)
Government Services	842	(272)	(10,609)	(2,209)	(37,320)	(214,299)

(*Continued*)

Table 8. (*Continued*)

Percent	United States	Canada	Chile	Mexico	CAC	South America
Agriculture	0.3	0.6	1.4	−0.3	−3.5	0.5
Mining	−0.2	−0.3	−3.4	−0.1	−11.8	1.6
Food, Beverages & Tobacco	0.0	0.2	0.2	−0.2	−3.1	0.2
Textiles	−1.2	−1.7	0.9	−0.3	45.8	3.0
Wearing Apparel	−1.5	−1.0	−0.3	−1.0	39.6	2.9
Leather Products & Footwear	−0.6	−1.0	−0.1	−0.9	1.2	5.3
Wood & Wood Products	0.1	0.1	1.9	0.1	−3.3	−1.0
Chemicals	0.1	−0.1	0.1	0.6	−1.7	−0.7
Non-metallic Min. Products	0.1	−0.1	−0.6	0.2	−5.8	−0.2
Metal Products	0.0	−0.3	1.6	0.3	−8.0	0.3
Transportation Equipment	−0.1	−0.1	−0.3	0.9	−11.2	1.6
Machinery & Equipment	0.2	−0.1	5.2	0.3	−9.7	−1.3
Other Manufactures	0.4	−0.2	1.2	−0.1	−3.2	−0.9
Elec., Gas & Water	0.0	−0.0	0.8	0.1	0.7	0.1
Construction	0.0	−0.0	−0.0	0.0	−0.3	−0.2
Trade & Transport	−0.0	0.0	−0.5	0.1	−0.5	−0.2
Other Private Services	0.0	−0.0	0.2	−0.1	−0.5	−0.1
Government Services	0.0	−0.0	−0.6	−0.0	−0.6	−0.4

An indication of the trade diversion associated with the U.S. FTAs and the overlapping of the spokes involved is shown in the left-hand side of Table 9, which has shaded cells indicating cases of positive welfare effects and white cells indicating cases of negative welfare effects. Altogether, 9 FTAs are shown, although there is some double counting insofar as the U.S.-CAC and U.S.-Chile bilateral FTAs are encompassed in the FTAA. In any event, it seems evident from Table 9 that trade diversion and negative welfare effects are pervasive. Thus, while partner-FTA countries may gain directly from their FTAs, as indicated by "X" in the table, they may be adversely affected by other FTAs that have been negotiated.

The global results of the bilateral FTAs in Table 5 suggest that the negative welfare effects on non-members may be rather small in both absolute terms and as a percent of GNP. But, as mentioned in our earlier discussion, because of data limitations, our results do not reflect the potential welfare declines due to rules of origin and other discriminatory arrangements built into the bilateral FTAs. On the other hand, we do not allow for increased inflows of foreign direct investment into the partner countries or the effects of improvements in productivity and increased capital formation. Unfortunately, we are not in a position to assess these potential benefits. But it seems clear from our computational results that the welfare increases from the FTA removal of trade barriers are fairly small on the whole. Pending further analysis, we therefore conclude that there is reason to be concerned about the trade diversion and overlapping spoke effects of bilateral FTAs.

V. Welfare Effects of Unilateral Free Trade and Global Free Trade

In this section, we ask how the welfare of the United States, its FTA partners, and other countries/regions in the global trading system would be affected if it were feasible to adopt unilateral free trade or global free trade on a non-discriminatory (MFN) basis as compared to the adoption of discriminatory bilateral FTAs. The detailed results by country/region are indicated in Table 10, and the results for the

Table 9. Welfare effects of bilateral FTAs and unilateral and global free trade.

	Bilateral FTAs									Unilateral Free Trade									Global FT
	1	2	3	4	5	6	7	8	9	10	11	12	13	14	15	16	17	18	
	US-CHL	US-SGP	US-CAC	US-AUS	US-MOR	US-SACU	US-THA	US-KOR	FTAA	US	SGP	AUS	MOR	SACU	THA	KOR	CHL	CAC	
1 Japan																			X
2 US	X	X	X	X	X	X	X	X	X	X									X
3 Canada									X										X
4 Australia				X								X							X
5 New Zealand																			X
6 EU and EFTA																			X
7 Hong Kong																			X
8 China																			X
9 Korea								X								X			X
10 Singapore		X									X								X
11 Taiwan																			X
12 Indonesia																			X
13 Malaysia																			X
14 Philippines																			X
15 Thailand							X								X				X
16 Rest of Asia																			X
17 Chile	X								X								X		X
18 Mexico									X										X
19 CAC			X						X									X	X
20 South America									X										X
21 Morocco					X								X						X
22 SACU						X								X					X
No. of Positive Effects	10	16	3	5	22	9	8	22	6	20	22	22	22	22	22	21	22	22	22

Notes: 1) Shaded cells indicate countries with positive welfare effects, while white cells indicate countries with negative welfare effects.
2) "X" indicates unilateral free trade countries.

Table 10. Welfare effects of unilateral and global free trade.

Billions of Dollars	Unilateral Free Trade									Global Free Trade
	United States	Singapore	Australia	Morocco	SACU	Thailand	Korea	Chile	CAC	
Japan	11.0	0.7	4.6	1.1	1.2	6.7	6.0	1.0	3.0	312.0
United States	368.8	1.6	1.8	2.8	2.5	6.3	12.1	1.5	4.5	591.0
Canada	–9.8	0.2	0.2	0.3	0.2	0.6	1.4	0.2	0.4	46.8
Australia	4.5	0.1	4.3	0.2	0.1	0.7	1.3	0.0	0.2	28.5
New Zealand	1.1	0.0	0.7	0.0	0.0	0.1	0.2	0.0	0.1	8.6
EU and EFTA	133.5	3.4	3.6	7.6	6.5	10.9	22.4	2.5	6.7	840.0
Hong Kong	9.3	0.2	0.1	0.1	0.1	0.9	1.3	0.1	0.3	47.7
China	3.0	0.2	1.1	0.2	0.4	1.4	–2.3	0.2	0.5	145.6
Korea	4.3	0.1	1.0	0.2	0.3	0.8	37.1	0.3	0.9	78.4
Singapore	2.1	1.1	0.1	0.1	0.1	0.9	0.7	0.0	0.1	17.6
Taiwan	3.9	0.1	0.4	0.1	0.3	1.0	0.7	0.1	0.1	56.3
Indonesia	2.3	0.1	0.4	0.0	0.1	0.5	0.9	0.0	0.1	25.0
Malaysia	4.3	0.7	0.3	0.1	0.1	1.9	1.2	0.1	0.2	38.0
Philippines	0.8	0.1	0.1	0.0	0.0	0.4	0.3	0.0	0.0	11.4
Thailand	2.0	0.2	0.3	0.1	0.2	14.3	0.3	0.0	0.1	25.8
Rest of Asia	8.9	0.2	0.7	0.1	0.4	0.9	1.4	0.1	0.2	66.7
Chile	0.8	0.0	0.0	0.0	0.0	0.1	0.3	4.6	0.1	9.0
Mexico	–8.5	0.1	0.1	0.2	0.2	0.3	0.9	0.1	0.4	54.4
Central America and the Caribbean (CAC)	3.4	0.0	0.0	0.0	0.0	0.1	0.6	0.1	6.3	16.4
South America	5.2	0.3	0.1	0.5	0.4	1.0	1.7	1.0	0.8	106.7
Morocco	0.7	0.0	0.0	2.4	0.0	0.0	0.1	0.0	0.0	5.0
Southern African Customs Union (SACU)	0.8	0.0	0.1	0.2	8.9	0.2	0.2	0.0	0.1	11.3
Total	552.3	9.5	20.1	16.3	22.2	50.1	88.5	12.1	25.1	2,542.1

(*Continued*)

Table 10. (*Continued*)

Percent	Unilateral Free Trade									Global Free Trade
	United States	Singapore	Australia	Morocco	SACU	Thailand	Korea	Chile	CAC	
Japan	0.2	0.0	0.1	0.0	0.0	0.1	0.1	0.0	0.1	5.9
United States	2.9	0.0	0.0	0.0	0.0	0.1	0.1	0.0	0.0	4.6
Canada	−1.1	0.0	0.0	0.0	0.0	0.1	0.2	0.0	0.1	5.1
Australia	1.0	0.0	0.9	0.0	0.0	0.2	0.3	0.0	0.1	6.3
New Zealand	1.7	0.0	1.1	0.1	0.1	0.2	0.3	0.0	0.2	13.5
EU and EFTA	1.2	0.0	0.0	0.1	0.1	0.1	0.2	0.0	0.1	7.6
Hong Kong	4.7	0.1	0.0	0.0	0.1	0.4	0.6	0.1	0.1	24.0
China	0.2	0.0	0.1	0.0	0.0	0.1	−0.2	0.0	0.0	9.9
Korea	0.8	0.0	0.2	0.0	0.1	0.2	7.0	0.1	0.2	14.8
Singapore	2.1	1.1	0.1	0.1	0.1	0.9	0.7	0.0	0.1	17.3
Taiwan	1.1	0.0	0.1	0.0	0.1	0.3	0.2	0.0	0.0	15.7
Indonesia	1.3	0.1	0.2	0.0	0.1	0.3	0.5	0.0	0.1	13.5
Malaysia	4.0	0.6	0.3	0.1	0.1	1.8	1.1	0.1	0.2	34.8
Philippines	0.9	0.1	0.1	0.0	0.1	0.5	0.3	0.0	0.0	12.6
Thailand	1.3	0.1	0.2	0.1	0.1	9.8	0.2	0.0	0.1	17.7
Rest of Asia	0.9	0.0	0.1	0.0	0.0	0.1	0.2	0.0	0.0	6.8
Chile	1.0	0.0	0.0	0.0	0.0	0.1	0.3	5.5	0.1	10.9
Mexico	−1.1	0.0	0.0	0.0	0.0	0.0	0.1	0.0	0.1	6.9
Central America and the Caribbean (CAC)	2.6	0.0	0.0	0.0	0.0	0.1	0.4	0.0	4.8	12.3
South America	0.3	0.0	0.0	0.0	0.0	0.1	0.1	0.1	0.1	6.9
Morocco	1.7	0.0	0.0	5.4	0.1	0.1	0.2	0.0	0.1	11.6
Southern African Customs Union (SACU)	0.5	0.0	0.1	0.1	5.7	0.1	0.1	0.0	0.1	7.2

U.S. bilateral FTAs and the FTAA, unilateral liberalization, and global free trade are summarized for the United States and its FTA partner countries/regions in Table 11. Unilateral free trade adopted by the United States would increase U.S. welfare by $368.8 billion (2.9% of GNP), which is more than three times greater than the U.S. welfare gains from the bilateral FTAs combined. If there were global (multilateral) free trade, U.S. welfare would be increased by $591.0 billion (4.6% of GNP). There are also clear indications that, except for Singapore and Australia, the FTA partner countries would generally gain more from the adoption of unilateral free trade by the United States as compared to the partner-country gains from their bilateral FTAs. Furthermore, the FTA partner countries would generally gain even more if they adopted unilateral free trade and especially if there were global free trade. These benefits are clearly reflected in the predominance of the shaded cells in the right-hand side of Table 9.

VI. Summary and Conclusions

In this chapter, we have used the Michigan Model of World Production and Trade to calculate the aggregate welfare and sectoral employment effects of the menu of U.S. trade policies. The menu of policies encompasses the various preferential U.S. bilateral and regional FTAs negotiated and in process, unilateral removal of existing trade barriers by the United States, its FTA partner countries, and global (multilateral) free trade. The welfare impacts of the FTAs on the United States are shown to be rather small in absolute and relative terms. The sectoral employment effects are also generally small, but vary across the individual sectors depending on the patterns of bilateral liberalization.

The welfare effects on the FTA partner countries are shown to be mostly positive though generally small, but there are some indications of potentially disruptive employment shifts in some partner countries. The results further suggest that there would be trade diversion and detrimental welfare effects in some non-member countries/regions. It also appears that, while FTA partners may gain from the bilateral

Table 11. Summary results: Welfare effects.

	Bilateral FTA					Unilateral/Global free trade		
	US Hub		Spokes		World	Country		World
	Bill. $	% of GNP	Bill. $	% of GNP	Bill. $	Bill. $	% of GNP	Bill. $
Bilateral FTA/Unilateral free trade								
United States	115.30	0.89				368.8	2.9	552.3
Chile	6.3	0.05	1.4	1.7	7.6	4.6	5.5	12.1
Singapore	17.0	0.13	2.5	2.4	21.6	1.1	1.1	9.5
Australia	11.8	0.09	5.1	1.1	12.1	4.3	0.9	20.1
CAC	18.6	0.14	5.1	3.9	21.8	6.3	4.8	25.1
Morocco	8.2	0.06	1.2	2.8	9.9	2.4	5.4	16.3
SACU	9.0	0.07	1.6	1.0	10.5	8.9	5.7	22.2
Thailand	15.2	0.12	5.2	3.6	19.8	14.3	9.8	50.1
Korea	29.1	0.23	13.1	2.5	47.3	37.1	7.0	88.5
Regional free trade								
FTAA	62.4	0.48	60.7		114.6			
Global free trade								
United States						591.0	4.6	
Chile						9.0	10.9	
Singapore						17.6	17.3	
Australia						28.5	6.3	
CAC						16.4	12.3	2542.1
Morocco						5.0	11.6	
SACU						11.3	7.2	
Thailand						25.8	17.7	
Korea						78.4	14.8	

FTAs, they may be adversely affected because of overlapping "hub-and-spoke" arrangements due to other discriminatory FTAs that have been negotiated.

The welfare gains from both unilateral trade liberalization by the United States and from global (multilateral) trade liberalization are shown to be rather substantial and more uniformly positive for all countries/regions in the global trading system as compared to the welfare gains from the bilateral FTAs analyzed.[14] The issue then is whether the WTO member countries will be able to overcome their divisiveness and indecisions and bring the Doha Round multilateral negotiations to a successful conclusion. Our computational results suggest that the menu choice of policy options is clearly in favor of multilateral liberalization.

Study Questions

1. What are the main features and data of the Michigan Model of World Production and Trade that is used for computational purposes? What are elements of imperfect competition that are included in the model? What is the time horizon of the model analysis and computational results? How are services barriers measured in the model?
2. What are the computational results for the various FTAs that are analyzed for the U.S., partner countries, rest of world, and the world as a whole? What is meant by the "hub and spoke effects" of the U.S. FTAs? To what extent is there evidence of trade diversion in the various FTAs?
3. What are the welfare effects of unilateral free trade and global free trade for the U.S., its FTA partners, the rest of world, and the world as a whole? What is the optimal menu of U.S. trade policies?

[14] See Brown *et al.* (2005b) for sensitivity analysis of introducing alternative parameters in the model and the resulting welfare impacts of global free trade.

References

Anderson, K. and Martin, W. 2005. "Agricultural Trade Reform and the Doha Development Agenda." *The World Economy* 28(9), pp. 1301–1328.

Bhagwati, J. and Panagariya, A. 1996. "Preferential Trading Areas and Multilateralism — Strangers, Friends, or Foes?" in J. Bhagwati and A. Panagariya (eds.), *The Economics of Preferential Trade Agreements*, Washington, DC: American Enterprise Institute.

Brown, D. K., Deardorff, A. V., and Stern, R. M. 2002. "CGE Modeling and Analysis of Multilateral and Regional Negotiating Options," in Stern, R. M. (ed.), *Issues and Options for U.S.–Japan Trade Policies*, Ann Arbor: University of Michigan Press.

Brown, D. K., Kiyota, K., and Stern, R. M. 2004. "Computational Analysis of the U.S. FTA with the Southern African Customs Union (SACU)." Research Seminar in International Economics, University of Michigan, Working Paper No. 508 (July).

Brown, D. K., Kiyota, K., and Stern, R. M. 2005a. "Computational Analysis of the Free Trade Agreement of the Americas (FTAA)." *North American Journal of Economics and Finance* 23, pp. 153–185.

Brown, D. K., Kiyota, K., and Stern, R. M. 2005b. "Computational Analysis of the U.S. FTAs with Central America, Australia, and Morocco." *The World Economy* 28(10), pp. 1441–1490.

Dimaranan, B. V. and McDougall, R. A. 2005. *Global Trade, Assistance, and Protection: The GTAP 6r Data Base.* West Lafayette, IN: Center for Global Trade Analysis, Purdue University, forthcoming.

Francois, J. and Strutt, A. 1999. "Post-Uruguay Round Tariff Vectors for GTAP Version 4," Erasmus University, manuscript.

Francois, J., van Meijl, H., and van Tongeren, F. 2005. "Trade Liberalization in the Doha Development Round." *Economic Policy* 20, pp. 349–391.

Hertel, T. W. 2000. "Potential Gains from Reducing Trade Barriers in Manufacturing, Services and Agriculture." *Federal Reserve Bank of St. Louis Review* 82, pp. 77–99.

Hertel, T. W. and Martin, W. 2000. "Liberalizing Agriculture and Manufactures in a Millennium Round: Implications for Developing Countries." *The World Economy* 23(4), pp. 455–469.

Hoekman, B. 2000. "The Next Round of Services Negotiations: Identifying Priorities and Options." *Federal Reserve Bank of St. Louis Review* 82, pp. 31–47.

Ianchovichina, E. and Martin, W. 2004. "Economic Impacts of China's Accession to the WTO," in D. Bhattasali, S. Li, and W. Martin (eds.), *China and the WTO: Accession, Policy Reform, and Poverty Reduction Strategies*, Washington, DC: Oxford University Press and the World Bank.

International Labor Organization (ILO). 2005. LABORSTA (http://laborsta.ilo.org/cgi–bin/brokerv8.exe).

Stolper, W. and Samuelson, P. A. 1941. "Protection and Real Wages." *Review of Economic Studies* 9, pp. 58–73.

Taiwan Government. 2005. (www.stat.gov.tai/bs2/2005YearBook.pdf).
United Nations Industrial Development Organization (UNIDO). 2005. *UNIDO Industrial Statistics Database 2005 at the 3-digit Level of ISIC (Revision 2)* on CD-ROM. Geneva: UNIDO.
World Bank. 2005. *World Development Indicators on CD-ROM.* Washington, DC: World Bank.

Suggested Further Reading

Brown, Drusilla K., Kozo Kiyota, and Robert M. Stern. 2006. "Computational Analysis of the Menu of U.S.-Japan Trade Policies," *The World Economy* 29, pp. 669–676.
Brown, Drusilla K., Kozo Kiyota, and Robert M. Stern. 2008. "An Analysis of a U.S.-SACU Free Trade Agreement," *World Development* 36, pp. 461–484.
Kiyota, Kozo and Robert M. Stern. 2007. *The Economic Effects of a Korea–U.S. Free Trade Agreement.* Washington, DC: Korea Economic Institute, April.
Michigan Model of World Production and Trade (http://www.fordschool.umich.edu/rsie/model/).
Schott, Jeffrey J. (ed.). 2004. *Free Trade Agreement: U.S. Strategies and Priorities.* Washington, DC: Institute for International Economics.

Chapter 10

Trade Diversion Under NAFTA*

Kyoji Fukao, Toshihiro Okubo and Robert M. Stern

I. Introduction

Prior to and since the inception of the North American Free Trade Agreement (NAFTA) in January 1994, there has been a great deal of interest in policy and academic circles about the impact that NAFTA might have on the trade and economic welfare of the NAFTA members — Canada, Mexico, and the United States — and nonmembers. In this chapter, we investigate the effects of NAFTA on trade diversion at a highly disaggregated level of commodity detail. The rationale for this approach is that the creation of a preferential trading arrangement like NAFTA involves the interplay of the removal of the differential structure of tariffs between member countries and the maintenance of these national tariffs with respect to nonmembers. In addition, we know that rules of origin were designed to provide special preferences for selected sectors in the NAFTA to the possible detriment of nonmembers.

* Reprinted with permission from Robert M. Stern (ed.), 2003, *Japan's Economic Recovery: Commercial Policy, Monetary Policy and Corporate Governance*, Chapter 2, Cheltenham, UK and Northampton, MA, USA: Edward Elgar, pp. 21–61.

We begin in Section II with a brief review of the complexities of distinguishing the effects of NAFTA from the myriad of other forces at work before and following the inception of NAFTA. We also discuss the approaches and conclusions of some pertinent studies of the effects of NAFTA. In Section III and the Appendix, we present the theoretical model that provides the basis for our analysis and the framework for our econometric investigation and a description of the data. Our empirical results are reported in Section IV. Conclusions and implications for further research are presented in Section V.

II. NAFTA in Context and a Review of the Literature

If we were able to do a controlled experiment, we would want to compare the economic situation before and after NAFTA was created. Unfortunately, in the social sciences, the ability to construct a controlled experiment is typically hampered because other things are happening that will serve to confound the design and interpretation of the experiment. Thus, for example, as Krueger (2000, pp. 762–765) has noted, there are a number of difficulties that arise in evaluating the effects of NAFTA. These include: (1) anticipation beginning in 1990 that negotiations would lead to creation of NAFTA; (2) the phasing out of NAFTA tariffs over a 10–15 year time period beginning in 1994; (3) trade liberalization being undertaken elsewhere at the same time that NAFTA was being implemented; (4) continuing responses to Mexico's unilateral trade liberalization initiated in the late 1980s; and (5) the real appreciation of the Mexican peso from 1987–1994 and subsequent depreciation in the course of Mexico's financial crisis in late 1994.[1] Given all of the foregoing currents of change, it is by no means an easy matter to isolate the effects of NAFTA. Nonetheless, some efforts have been made that are worthy of attention.

Gould (1998) used a gravity-model approach in determining how NAFTA may have affected the growth of North American trade.

[1] See Lustig (2001) for a review of Mexico's economic performance and policies since 1980.

The model is estimated in log first differences with aggregated bilateral trade flows on a quarterly basis for 1980 through 1996 and measures of real GDP, GDP price deflators, real exchange rates, and dummy variables to represent changes in the trade regimes during the period involved. His empirical results suggest that, in its first three years: (1) NAFTA may have stimulated the growth of U.S. aggregate exports to Mexico but not U.S. imports from Mexico; (2) U.S. bilateral trade into Canada and Canadian-Mexican trade were not affected by NAFTA; and (3) trade diversion was probably negligible.

Krueger (1999b, 2000) examined the changing patterns of trade flows and noted that the trade relationships among the NAFTA countries intensified considerably in the 1990s. But she did not find much evidence that imports from the rest of the world declined as intra-NAFTA trade increased. Krueger also concluded that tariff differentials for U.S. imports from Mexico and East Asia did not appear to have changed dramatically. Further, she conducted a "shift in share" analysis and found that the increase of Mexico's share in its trade with the United States was not much different than with the rest of the world, reflecting both the impact of Mexico's unilateral liberalization and the peso depreciation after 1994. Finally, on the basis of fitting some gravity equations, she found little evidence that trade patterns had been significantly altered by preferential trading arrangements, although the results did suggest that NAFTA countries imported less than predicted from nonmember countries.[2] On the basis of the foregoing, Krueger concluded that NAFTA was almost certainly trade-creating rather than trade-diverting.

---

[2] For a more comprehensive study of preferential trading arrangements using a gravity-model approach, see Soloaga and Winters (2001). They find no evidence of trade diversion for NAFTA. Coughlin and Wall (2000) use a gravity-model approach in analyzing how NAFTA has changed the pattern of exports of U.S. states to foreign geographic destinations. See also Karemara and Ojah (1998) for a gravity-model analysis comparing the trade impacts for selected manufactures for the ASEAN members and NAFTA. Their data for NAFTA end in 1993, however, so that they do not capture the trade effects following the inception of NAFTA in 1994.

In some earlier work, Krueger (1993, 1999a) called attention to the importance of rules-of-origin (ROO) as protectionist devices in free trade agreements. In this connection, James and Umemoto (1999, 2000) focused attention on the restrictive ROO affecting especially market access in NAFTA for textiles and wearing apparel from East Asia. On the basis of examining changes in market shares prior to and following the implementation of NAFTA, they concluded that there was *prima facie* evidence of trade diversion. They also examined changes in trade shares of footwear and electrical machinery, which were also subject to ROO in the NAFTA, and concluded that there was little evidence of trade diversion in footwear and none in the case of electrical machinery. James and Umemoto present a model of ROO, but they do not implement this model in their empirical analysis of changes in trade shares.

Burfisher *et al.* (2001) provide a useful survey of the impact of NAFTA on the United States that covers both macroeconomic issues and structural adjustments. They point out the fallacies in much of the macroeconomic discussion related to NAFTA involving the effects on U.S. labor markets, the balance of trade, aggregate employment effects, and the effects of the peso crisis. With regard to structural adjustments, they focus on agricultural transition, the rationalization of automobile production and parts, and the effects of ROO on textiles and apparel. They note that intra-NAFTA trade in agricultural products has risen, and there is evidence that Mexico has taken steps to liberalize its agricultural policies and to lock in these reforms. Prior to NAFTA, Mexico had significant distortions in its automobile sector, and, with NAFTA, these distortions were phased out. In negotiating NAFTA, it was specified that vehicles should have a 62.5 percent North American content. In response to the phase-out of the Mexican restrictions and implementation of the ROO, Burfisher *et al.* cite evidence of significant rationalization effects in the production of autos and parts that have benefited the North American auto industry. However, they do not address the question of whether trade diversion has occurred. Finally, with regard to textiles and apparel,

Burfisher *et al.* conclude that there is rather clear evidence of trade diversion especially *vis-à-vis* East Asia, which corresponds to what James and Umemoto (1999, 2000) found in their research as noted above.

Arndt and Huemer (2001) provide graphical analyses of the changes in the dollar value of U.S. exports and imports and the shares accounted for by Canada, Mexico, and Japan on a quarterly basis from 1990-I to 2001-II. Since the inception of NAFTA in 1994, Mexico has displaced Japan as the second largest market for U.S. exports, while Canada's share of U.S. exports has remained relatively unchanged. What is more striking is that Mexico's share of U.S. imports has risen from around 8 percent in 1994 to 12 percent in 2001, while Japan's share has fallen from about 18 percent to 12 percent in this same period. Arndt and Huemer also depict changes in U.S. imports and import shares at the industry level for motor vehicles, television sets, and textiles and apparel. They show that Mexico apparently increased its share of U.S. imports of automobiles at the expense of Japan; its share of U.S. television imports at the expense of China, Japan, Korea, and Taiwan; and its share of U.S. imports of textiles and apparel at the expense of China and other Asian suppliers. Finally, Arndt and Huemer provide graphical evidence of the importance of foreign outsourcing from the United States to Mexico especially and to Canada for motor vehicles, television sets, and textiles and apparel. While this outsourcing predates NAFTA, they show that there has been a significant increase in U.S. exports of components to and imports of end products from its NAFTA partners since 1994. Arndt and Huemer conclude accordingly that NAFTA has had a significant impact on intra-North American trade through the combination of discriminatory tariff reductions resulting in trade diversion and through increased outsourcing that reflects the reorganization and relocation of production and the exchange of component inputs and end products.

By far the most ambitious and comprehensive study of the trade effects of NAFTA is Romalis (2001), which came to our attention after we had completed our own study. Setting out a conceptual framework, Romalis develops reduced-form equations in which the shares of U.S. imports of commodities sourced from Canada or Mexico depend on the tariff preferences under NAFTA extended to the two countries. He makes allowance for the time varying effects of tariff preferences as well as control measures for commodity and industry characteristics. Working at the 8-digit Harmonized System (HS) level, he tracks U.S. bilateral trade with Canada and Mexico for 6874 commodities annually from 1989 to 2000 and constructs the preferential tariff rates that apply to these commodities. Based on his regression results, he finds that NAFTA has had a significant effect on U.S. imports from Canada and especially from Mexico. Further, he finds no statistical evidence of trade creation in analyzing the growth of U.S. imports of the commodities covered. Romalis concludes therefore that NAFTA has been primarily trade diverting.

We turn now to our own research, which, as mentioned, will focus on a disaggregated level for selected manufactured goods, using a version of the gravity model that may serve to identify the presence or absence of trade diversion as the consequence of NAFTA. Our work is related to what James and Umemoto and Arndt and Huemer have done descriptively in intra-NAFTA trade and is in the same spirit as Romalis insofar as we use an explicit theoretical model and econometric analysis to try to identify the forces at work that have affected NAFTA's trade.

III. Conceptual Framework and Empirical Implementation

The Model

In order to illustrate the effects of NAFTA, we focus on how it may have affected the shares of member and non-member countries in U.S. imports at a detailed commodity level. For this purpose, we develop a partial-equilibrium trade model of differentiated-product industries under monopolistic competition with N countries. The model is patterned after earlier work along these lines by Helpman and Krugman (1985), Markusen (1986), and Bergstrand (1989).

The technical details of the model are set out in the Appendix to the chapter.

As indicated in the Appendix, the conceptual basis for the empirical analysis to be carried out is given by Equation (1):

$$\begin{aligned}\ln(s_{z,n,1}(t)) = \lambda_{z,n} - \lambda_{z,1}\left(\ln(w_n(t)) - \sum_{i=2}^{N} s_{z,i,1}^{0}\ln(w_i(t))\right) \\ - \lambda_{z,2}\left(\ln(T_{n,1}(t)) - \sum_{i=2}^{N} s_{z,i,1}^{0}\ln(T_{z,i,1}(t))\right) \\ + \lambda_{z,3}v_{z,n,1}^{0}\left(\ln(T_{n,1}(t)) - \sum_{i=2}^{N} s_{z,i,1}^{0}\ln(T_{z,i,1}(t))\right) \\ + \varepsilon_{z,n}(t), \qquad (1)\end{aligned}$$

where $s_{z,n,j}$, w_n, and $T_{z,n,j}$ denote the percentage of imports from country n in U.S. total imports of industry z products, country n's wage rate, and one plus the tariff and tariff equivalent of non-tariff barriers of U.S. imports used in the output by industry z in country n. $v_{z,n,j}$ is the percentage of exports of industry z products from country n to the U.S. in total products of industry z in country n. $\lambda_{z,n}$ depends on country-specific factors such as distance from the United States and each county's endowment of industry-specific production factors. $\varepsilon_{z,n}(t)$ is the usual error term.

The equation implies that the U.S. import share of country n is a decreasing function of country n's relative wage rate and U.S. trade barriers against country n. Moreover, the creation of NAFTA will reduce U.S. imports from non-member countries. Equation (1) implies that this trade-diversion effect will be greater, if the initial share of Mexico and Canada in U.S. imports is large (higher $s_{z,n,1}$ for n = Mexico and Canada) or if the U.S. initially is a very important destination for Mexico's and Canada's exports (higher $v_{z,n,1}$ for n = Mexico and Canada). As shown in the Appendix, the three elasticity values $\lambda_{z,1}$, $\lambda_{z,2}$, and $\lambda_{z,1}$ are positive. Using panel data, we can estimate the above equation as a fixed-effect model.

Empirical Implementation

As stated, our objective is to evaluate the trade-diversion effects from the creation of NAFTA in the U.S. import market on the basis of our theoretical model. For this purpose, we use a fixed-effect panel analysis for manufactured commodities at the Harmonized System (HS) 2-digit level from 1992 to 1998. Data for 1998 were the latest comprehensive data available at the time of writing (May 2001). Our regressions cover the entire spectrum of U.S. manufactured goods imports, for HS 30 to HS 99, for the domain of U.S. trading partners.

We derived the following equation for regression analysis from Equation (1):

$$\begin{aligned} \ln(s_{z,n,1}(t)) = a_0 &+ a_{z,1}\ln(w_n(t)) + a_{z,2}\ln(T_{n,1}(t)) \\ &+ a_{z,3}v^0_{z,n,1}\ln(T_{n,1}(t)) \\ &+ \sum_n a_{z,n,4} COUNTRYDUM_{z,n} \\ &+ \sum_t a_{z,t,5} TIMEDUM_{z,t}(t) + \varepsilon_{z,n}(t). \end{aligned} \qquad (2)$$

The dependent variable is the natural logarithm of each country's import share in the U.S. market for each commodity in each year.[3] On the right-hand side, the first independent variable is the natural logarithm of wage rates in each year in each exporting country. We approximated each exporting country's wage rates by its GDP per capita in U.S. dollars. The second independent variable is the natural logarithm of one plus U.S. tariff rates against each exporting country.

---

[3] When one country's import share is zero, we treated it as a missing observation. Therefore, our data are an unbalanced panel. If there were some variables that strongly affect the chances for observation (non-zero imports) but not the outcome under study, it would be more appropriate to take account of the sample-selection process by estimating a selection model, such as Heckman (1979). But in our case, there seems to be no such variable. So we did not take account of sample-selection bias. For more detail on this issue, see Manning *et al.* (1987).

The third independent variable is the product of the percentage of exports of the commodity from each country to the United States in total exports of this country in 1991 and the natural logarithm of one plus tariff rates toward each export.[4] Based on our theoretical model, we expect negative signs for the coefficients of these three variables.[5] In order to control country-specific factors that are not included in independent variables, such as distance from the United States and each country's endowment of industry-specific production factors, we use country dummies. The time dummies stand for macro shocks such as changes in average U.S. tariff rates against all the countries and changes in world GDP.

The import shares are calculated from the HS 2-digit import data in U.S. Census Bureau, *U.S. Imports of Merchandise on CD-ROM* and *U.S. Imports History on CD-ROM.* GDP per capita data are from the *World Development Indicators on CD-ROM 2000* (World Bank). Percentages of each country's exports of each commodity to the United States in total exports of this country are taken from Statistics Canada, *World Trade Analyzer.* Data on bilateral tariff rates are taken from the *TRAINS* dataset of UNCTAD.[6] The data at the 2-digit level are compiled by taking a weighted average of 6-digit HS tariff rates, using U.S. import shares of each 6-digit HS commodity in 1991 as weights.

---

[4] In addition, we considered U.S. NTBs. We used frequency measure of U.S. NTBs in 1993 at the HS 4-digit level, obtained from OECD, *Indicators of Tariffs and Non-Tariff Trade Barriers 1997.* We assumed that U.S. NTBs against all the countries were identical and constant until 1993, and that the NTBs against Canada and Mexico became zero after 1994. Therefore, our NTB variables were almost identical with the NAFTA dummy variables. As a consequence, we do not report below the results using the NTB measures.

[5] The question arises as to whether using import shares as the dependent variable is the best way of getting at trade diversion. That is, changes in import shares may be influenced by a variety of structural factors on both the supply and demand sides that are not being taken into account in the model. We had considered constructing a structural model, but time, resource, and data constraints prevented us from doing so.

[6] Data on tariff rates are available at 6-digit HS for 1993, 1994, 1996, and 1998. We have used 1993 tariff rates for 1992. Tariff rates for 1995 and 1997 are calculated as the average of 1994 and 1996 and 1996 and 1998, respectively.

As we will report in the next section, $a_{z,3}$, the estimated coefficients of the product of the percentage of exports of the commodity from each country to the United States in total exports of this country in 1991 and the natural logarithm of one plus tariff rates toward each export, are not significant and do not have the expected negative sign in many commodities. Because of this we have also estimated the following equation, which does not include this variable:

$$\begin{aligned}\ln(s_{z,n,1}(t)) = a_0 &+ a_{z,1}\ln(w_n(t)) + a_{z,2}\ln(T_{n,1}(t)) \\ &+ \sum_n a_{z,n,4} COUNTRYDUM_{z,n} \\ &+ \sum_t a_{z,t,5} TIMEDUM_{z,t}(t) + \varepsilon_{z,n}(t). \qquad (3)\end{aligned}$$

Both reductions in tariff rates among NAFTA countries and removal of NTBs might have trade-diversion effects. In order to check this, we replaced the tariff variables with a NAFTA dummy in Equation (4) below. The NAFTA dummy takes value one for Canada and Mexico after the creation of NAFTA in 1994. In order to take account of the fact that NAFTA trade barriers are phased out gradually over time, we also used a lagged NAFTA dummy in Equation (5), which takes value one for Canada and Mexico after 1995:

$$\begin{aligned}\ln(s_{z,n,1}(t)) = a_0 &+ a_{z,1}\ln(w_n(t)) + a_{z,2} NAFTADUM_n(t) \\ &+ \sum_n a_{z,n,4} COUNTRYDUM_{z,n} \\ &+ \sum_t a_{z,t,5} TIMEDUM_{z,t}(t) + \varepsilon_{z,n}(t). \qquad (4)\end{aligned}$$

$$\begin{aligned}\ln(s_{z,n,1}(t)) = a_0 &+ a_{z,1}\ln(w_n(t)) \\ &+ a_{z,2} LAGGEDNAFTADUM_n(t) \\ &+ \sum_n a_{z,n,4} COUNTRYDUM_{z,n} \\ &+ \sum_t a_{z,t,5} TIMEDUM_{z,t}(t) + \varepsilon_{z,n}(t). \qquad (5)\end{aligned}$$

We expect positive signs for coefficients of the NAFTA dummy and the lagged NAFTA dummy.

Equations (2)–(5) are estimated by OLS with fixed effects with a correction for first-order autocorrelation in the disturbances. It should be noted that there is a possibility that industries defined by HS 2-digit codes might be too broad and include too many commodities with different characteristics. To take this into account, we have also estimated the above equations for selected industries at the HS 4-digit level from 1992 to 1998.

IV. Empirical Results

As mentioned above, we estimated regression equations for the HS 2-digit U.S. imports of manufactured goods for the period 1992–1998. There were 70 sets of regressions that were run. It turned out that the coefficients of the tariff rates were statistically significant in 15 of the 70 cases. The results for these 15 cases are reported in Table 1.[7] The results for the other 45 cases are available from the authors on request.[8]

For the 15 commodities noted in Table 1, the coefficients of tariff rates were negative and significant at the 5 percent level in either Equations (2) or (3). In most cases, these coefficients were generally greater than 20. When this coefficient takes a value 20, it means that a 5 percent reduction of U.S. tariff rates on imports from one country will double that country's share in U.S. total imports. Therefore, our results suggest that tariff rates have significant effects on U.S. trade in the case of these commodities.

We should note that for a substantial number of commodities, such as pharmaceutical products and electric machinery, U.S. tariff

[7] The estimated coefficients of GDP, country dummies, and time dummies are not reported because of space limitations but are available from the authors on request.

[8] The coefficients of the NAFTA dummies and lagged NAFTA dummies were either insignificant or had unexpected signs in most cases. Only in the cases of HS 43 (Furskins), HS 50 (Silk), and HS 60 (Knitted or Crocheted Fabrics) were the lagged NAFTA dummies positive and significant at the 5 percent level.

Table 1. Statistically significant regression results for HS 2-digit manufactured commodities.

HS Code	Definition	Equation 1			Equation 2		Equation 3		Equation 4	
		Tariff t-value	Share* Tariff t-value	No. of Obs F-value	Tariff t-value	No. of Obs F-value	Nafta Dummy t-value	No. of Obs F-value	Lagged Nafta t-value	No. of Obs F-value
30	Pharmaceutical Products	−35.43	−31.68	366	−17.57	538	0.37	632	0.46	632
		(−3.13)	(−0.39)	2.25	(−1.78)	1.11	(0.44)	1.51	(0.61)	1.53
37	Photographic or	−38.10	−466.37	306	−16.57	537	−0.07	588	0.02	588
	Cinematographic Goods	(−2.23)	(−2.14)	3.45	(−1.68)	1.52	(−0.09)	0.85	(0.03)	0.85
44	Wood and Articles of Wood;	−69.71	181.05	636	−43.89	814	−0.27	834	−0.20	834
	Wood Charcoal	(−3.93)	(1.22)	4.03	(−2.93)	2.92	(−0.46)	1.97	(−0.37)	1.96
45	Cork and Articles of Cork	−183.42	254.84	139	−11.17	680	−0.10	755	−0.02	755
		(−4.50)	(0.90)	3.62	(−0.75)	0.26	(−0.14)	0.46	(−0.03)	0.46
46	Mfr of Straw, Esparto etc.;	−17.07	82.79	351	−3.48	668	−0.36	670	−0.29	670
	Basketware & Wickerwork	(−1.98)	(3.26)	2.09	(−0.65)	1.72	(−0.56)	1.70	(−0.50)	1.69
49	Printed Books, Newspapers etc;	−330.47	156.36	483	−203.63	721	0.13	789	0.17	789
	Manuscripts etc	(−3.72)	(0.40)	2.66	(−3.35)	2.25	(0.22)	0.85	(0.30)	0.86
51	Wool & Animal Hair, including	−91.60	43.55	358	−10.06	663	0.53	664	0.64	664
	Yarn & Woven Fabric	(−3.73)	(3.21)	2.79	(−1.36)	1.44	(0.74)	1.28	(0.98)	1.33
52	Cotton, including Yarn and	−35.17	46.93	502	−31.52	715	0.91	716	1.06	716
	Woven Fabric Thereof	(−1.10)	(0.59)	1.79	(−2.85)	2.15	(1.06)	1.25	(1.36)	1.34

(*Continued*)

Table 1. (*Continued*)

HS Code	Definition	Equation 1			Equation 2		Equation 3		Equation 4	
		Tariff t-value	Share* Tariff t-value	No. of Obs F-value	Tariff t-value	No. of Obs F-value	Nafta Dummy t-value	No. of Obs F-value	Lagged Nafta t-value	No. of Obs F-value
60	Knitted or Crocheted Fabrics	−89.64	86.33	377	−10.49	584	1.17	585	1.43	585
		(−3.56)	(2.58)	4.40	(−1.24)	4.44	(1.45)	4.50	(1.94)	4.72
62	Apparel Articles and Accessories,	−56.69	65.50	678	−8.57	927	0.16	928	0.21	928
	Not Knit, etc.	(−2.86)	(2.55)	2.29	(−1.37)	6.76	(0.22)	6.53	(0.31)	6.54
66	Umbrellas, Walking-Sticks,	−12.92	45.99	376	−12.80	573	0.32	637	0.40	637
	Riding-Crops etc. Parts	(−1.61)	(1.25)	0.91	(−2.42)	1.79	(0.36)	1.20	(0.50)	1.22
79	Zinc and Articles Thereof	−64.66	29.62	256	−20.09	568	−0.14	586	−0.07	586
		(−1.96)	(0.77)	1.33	(−1.29)	1.44	(−0.17)	1.09	(−0.09)	1.09
82	Tools, Cutlery etc. of	−31.37	−12.65	434	−5.26	640	0.26	659	0.20	659
	Base Metal & Parts Thereof	(−2.90)	(−0.16)	1.52	(−0.89)	0.93	(0.39)	0.86	(0.33)	0.86
85	Electric Machinery etc.; Sound	−26.60	218.66	650	−13.75	855	0.02	881	0.19	881
	Equip; TV Equip; Pts	(−2.67)	(1.86)	2.69	(−1.83)	4.06	(0.02)	3.78	(0.29)	3.79
90	Optic, Photo etc.,	−11.46	−2.78	583	−17.36	755	0.14	778	0.09	778
	Medical or Surgical	(−1.76)	(−0.08)	1.49	(−3.67)	4.28	(0.23)	2.23	(0.16)	2.23
	Instruments etc.									

Table 2. U.S. tariff rates: Selected HS 2-digit commodities.

HS Code	Definition	Year	U.S. Tariff Rates %	
			On Imports from Canada	On Imports from Mexico
46	Mfr of Straw, Esparto etc.;	93	0.00	3.01
	Basketware & Wickerwork	96	0.00	0.00
51	Wool & Animal Hair,	93	11.03	15.75
	including Yarn & Woven Fabric	96	1.01	3.23
52	Cotton, including Yarn and	93	4.57	8.98
	Woven Fabric Thereof	96	0.88	2.65
60	Knitted or Crocheted Fabrics	93	6.66	13.33
		96	1.33	4.55
62	Apparel Articles and Accessories,	93	6.70	12.93
	Not Knit etc.	96	1.23	3.19
79	Zinc and Articles Thereof	93	2.01	2.69
		96	0.35	0.00

rates on imports from Canada and Mexico were negligible even before 1994. In these cases, we cannot argue that NAFTA had a significant trade-diversion effect. Table 2 shows U.S. tariff rates on imports of the fifteen commodities from Canada and Mexico in 1993 and 1996. For six of the fifteen categories, indicated in boldface, U.S. tariff rates on imports from either Canada or Mexico were greater than 2.5 percent in 1993. Probably we can infer relatively large trade-diversion effects in these uses.

To clarify matters in more detail, Figure 1 shows U.S. tariff rates on imports from Canada, Mexico, and the rest of the world and the two NAFTA country shares in U.S. imports for each of these 6 commodities. It would appear that for textiles and apparel products, which include HS 51 Wool & Animal Hair, including Yarn & Woven Fabric, HS 52 Cotton, including Yarn and Woven Fabric Thereof, HS 60 Knitted or Crocheted Fabrics, and HS 62 Apparel Articles and Accessories, Not Knit etc., U.S. tariff rates towards Canada and Mexico were reduced considerably after 1994. On the other hand,

HS 46 Mfr of Straw, Esparto etc.; Basketware & Wickerwork

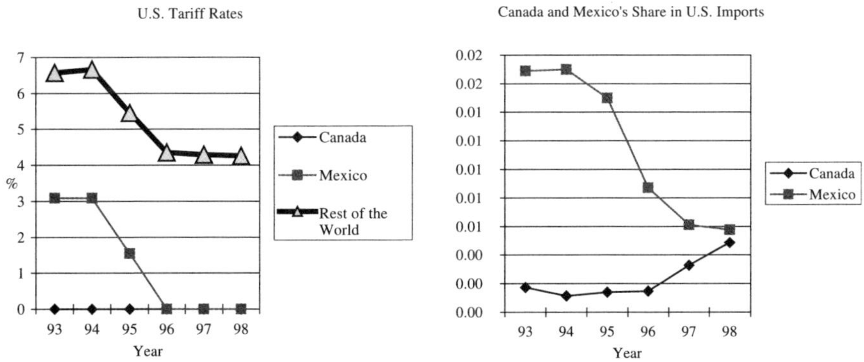

HS 51 Wool & Animal Hair, including Yarn & Woven Fabric

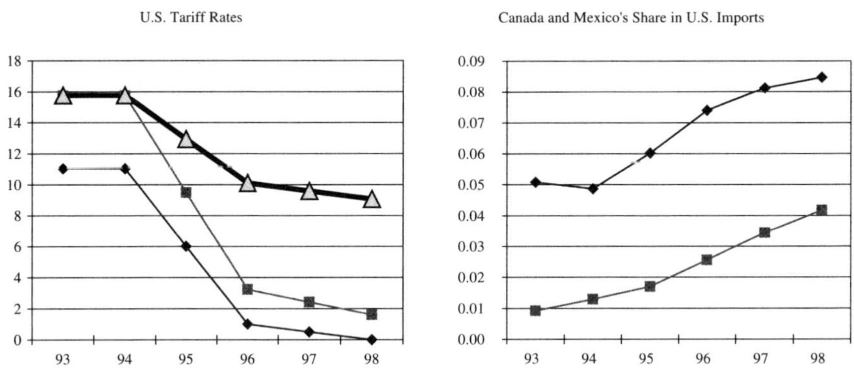

HS 52 Cotton, including Yarn and Woven Fabric Thereof

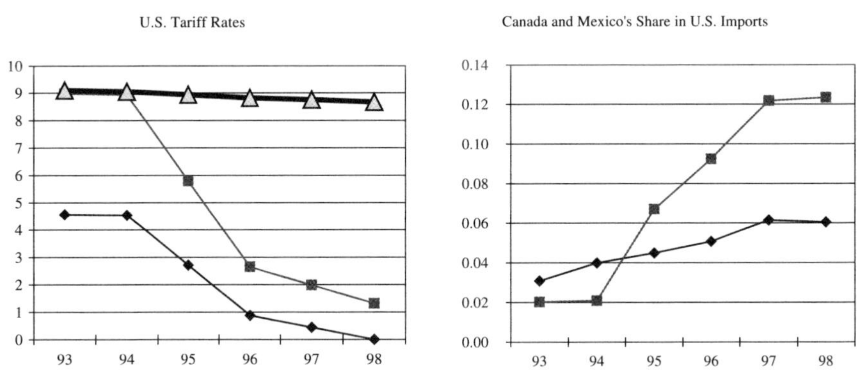

Figure 1. U.S. tariff rates and imports: Selected HS 2-digit commodities.

HS 60 Knitted or Crocheted Fabrics

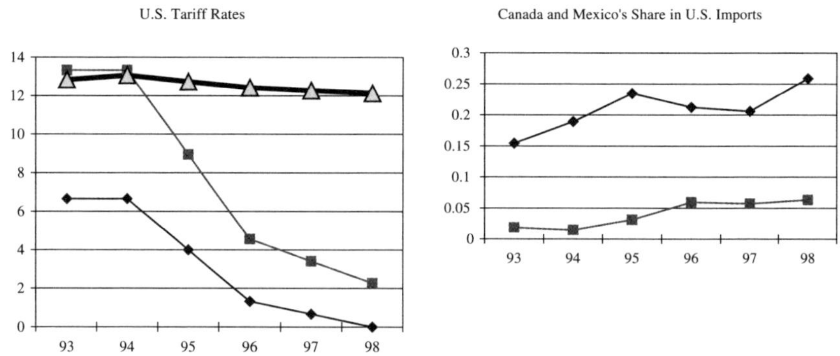

HS 62 Apparel Articles and Accessories, Not knit etc.

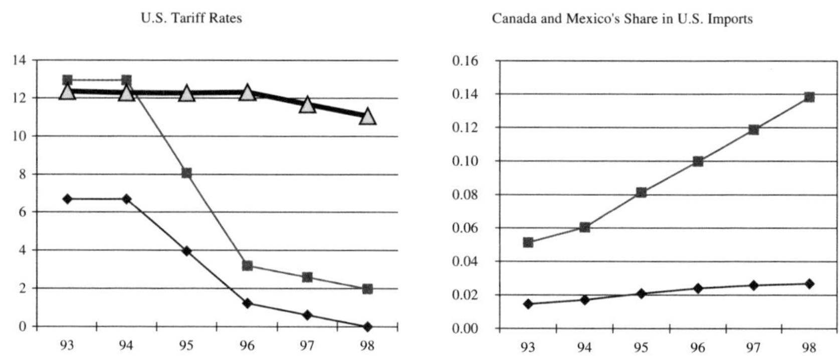

HS 79 Zinc and Articles Thereof

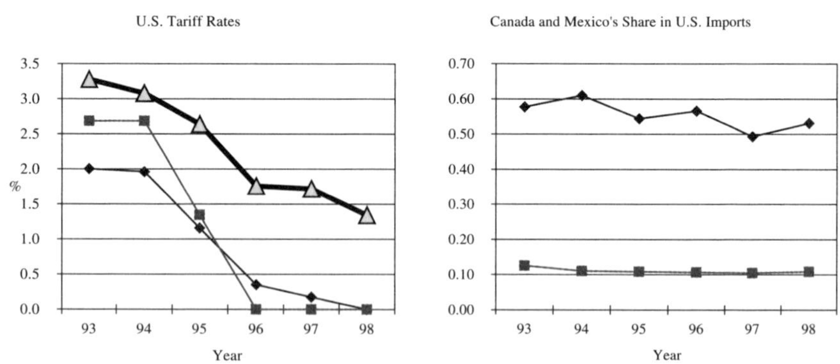

Figure 1. (*Continued*)

U.S. tariff rates toward the other countries remained relatively high during the period. Reflecting these discriminatory tariff cuts, the shares of Canada and Mexico in U.S. imports increased substantially. For the other two commodity categories, HS 46 Mfr of Straw and HS 79 Zinc, although U.S. tariff rates toward Canada and Mexico were reduced after 1994, the tariff rates towards the other countries were also reduced in a parallel fashion. We do not observe therefore substantial increases in the Canadian or Mexican shares in U.S. imports in these two cases. We conclude therefore, based on Figure 1 and our regression results in Table 1, that the creation of NAFTA had significant trade-diversion effects on U.S. imports mainly in the cases of textile and apparel products.

As already mentioned in the previous section, it is possible that commodities defined by HS 2-digit codes might be too broad and include too many commodities of different characteristics to permit rigorous analysis. To take this into account, we have also estimated our equations for selected commodities at the HS 4-digit level from 1992 to 1998. The commodities have been selected following James and Umemoto (1999, 2000), who focused on such labor-intensive goods as textiles, apparel, leather products and footwear, and electronic products. We also include motor cars and vehicles since these were subject to a rule of origin as noted earlier. The specific 4-digit commodities that we selected are as follows:

HS 4202 Travel Goods, Handbags, Wallets, Jewelry Cases, Etc.
HS 6002 Knitted or Crocheted Fabrics, NES
HS 6109 T-Shirts, Singlets, Tank Tops, Etc., Knit or Crochet
HS 6115 Pantyhose, Socks & Other Hosiery, Knit or Crochet
HS 6401 Waterproof Footwear, Rubber or Plastic, Bond Sole
HS 8529 TV Receivers, Incl. Video Monitors & Projectors
HS 8703 Motor Cars & Vehicles for Transporting Persons

In order to take account of the fact that NAFTA tariffs are being phased out gradually over time, we also used a lagged NAFTA dummy, which takes the value one for Canada and Mexico after 1995. In the case of automobile trade, the United States had already liberalized its imports from Canada prior to NAFTA. To take account of this, we used a Mexico dummy, which takes the value one for Mexico after 1994 for regressions for "motor cars and vehicles."

Before evaluating the regression results, we provide in Figures 2 and 3 an overview of U.S. tariff rates and imports from NAFTA and non-NAFTA countries for the seven commodities defined by HS 4-digit code that we have selected. For almost all commodities, Canada and Mexico received substantial tariff margins of preference after NAFTA, and it can be seen that NAFTA tariffs were phased out gradually over time. We should further note that tariff rates were very low in the case of machinery. It appears from Figure 2 that in the cases of apparel, such as "T-shirts" and "socks," and machinery, such as "TV receivers" and "motor vehicles," Mexico increased its share in U.S. imports more substantially than Canada. Canada gained more in "travel goods" and "waterproof footwear."

The regression results are reported in detail in Table 3 and summarized in Table 4. It is evident that both tariff rates and the NAFTA dummies are significant in general. For "travel goods" and "motor cars and vehicles," neither variable is significant.[9] For "socks," only the NAFTA dummy is significant. For "TV receivers," only tariff rates are significant. For many commodities, GDP per capita is insignificant or has an unexpected positive sign.

It thus appears from these more disaggregated results that NAFTA has resulted in significant trade diversion especially in textiles, apparel, and some footwear products. Since U.S. tariff rates were relatively low in the cases of "motor cars and vehicles" and "TV receivers" and since foreign direct investment and outsourcing may be important in these industries, the changes in import shares noted may reflect these determinants more than changes in tariff rates, which are the focus of our model.

---

[9] Probably, we obtained insignificant results in the case of "travel goods" because this category covers too many different types of commodities.

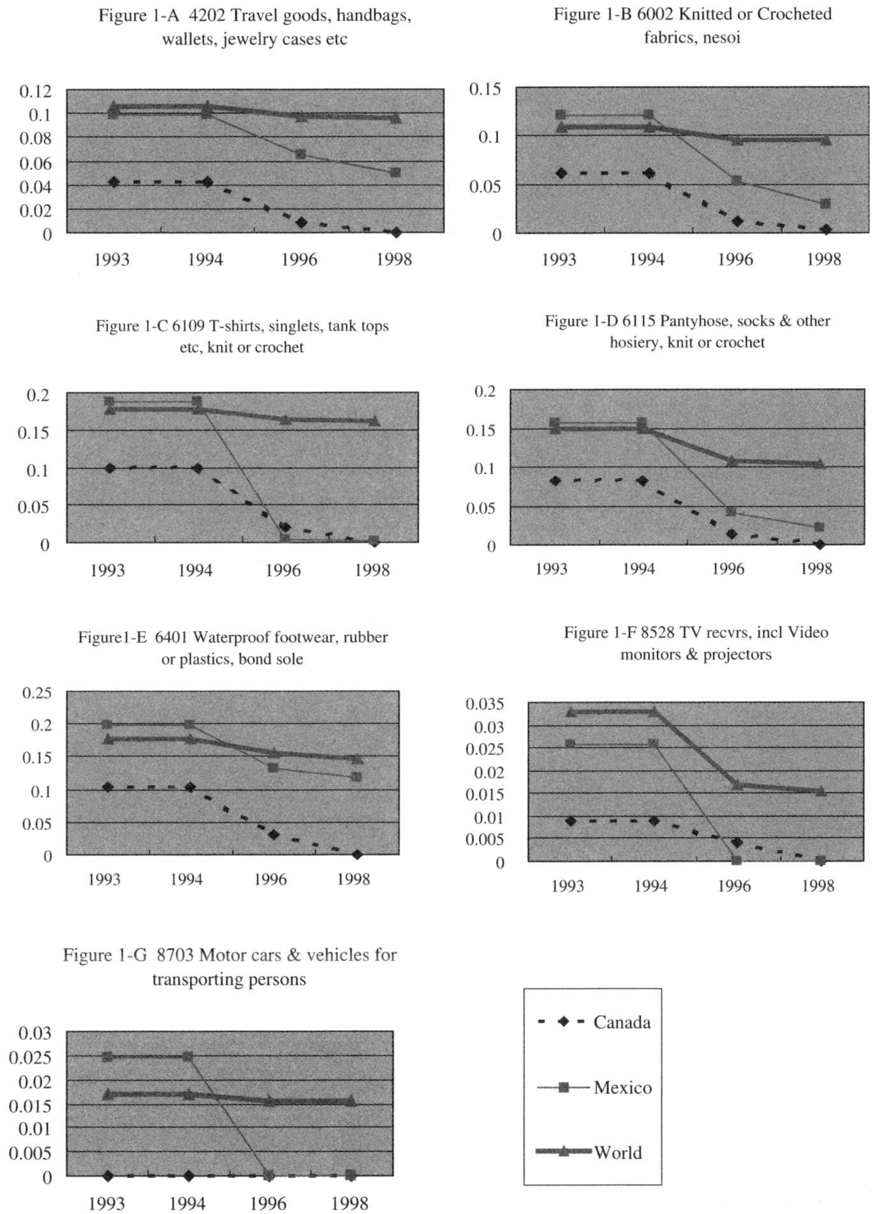

Figure 2. U.S. tariff rates: Selected HS 4-digit commodities.

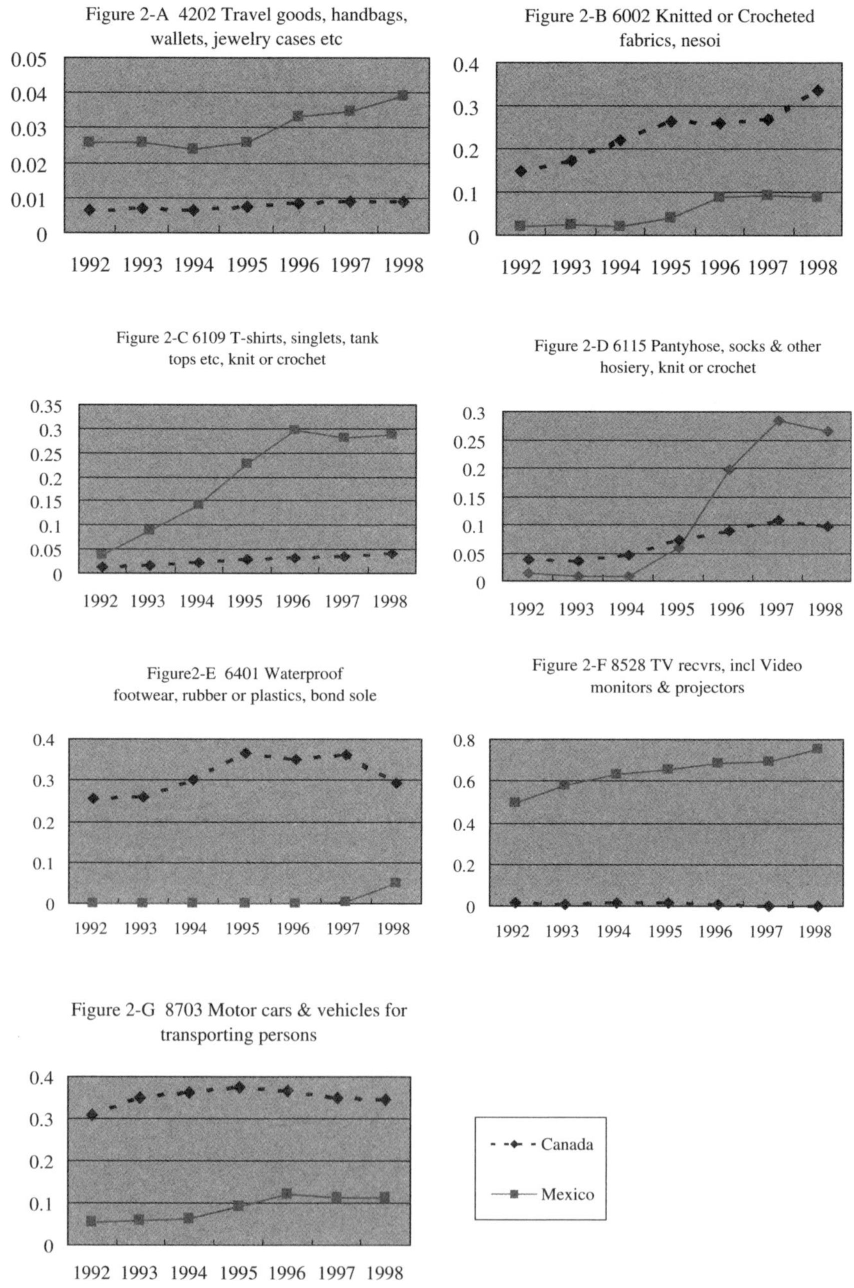

Figure 3. U.S. imports: Selected HS 4-digit commodities.

Table 3. Regression results: Selected HS 4-digit commodities.

HS 4202	TRAVEL GOODS, HANDBAGS, WALLETS, JEWELRY CASES ETC
HS 6002	KNITTED OR CROCHETED FABRICS, NESOI
HS 6109	T-SHIRTS, SINGLETS, TANK TOPS ETC, KNIT OR CROCHET
HS 6115	PANTYHOSE, SOCKS & OTHER HOSIERY, KNIT OR CROCHET
HS 6401	WATERPROOF FOOTWEAR, RUBBER OR PLASTICS, BOND SOLE
HS 8528	TV RECVRS, INCL VIDEO MONITORS & PROJECTORS
HS 8703	MOTOR CARS & VEHICLES FOR TRANSPORTING PERSONS

[ ]: t-value — Country Dummies are omitted
** 5% significant — Time dummies (t1=1992, t2=1993, t3=1994, t4=1995, t5=1996, t6=1997)
* 10% significant

(*Continued*)

Table 3. (*Continued*)

HS 4202 TRAVEL GOODS, HANDBAGS, WALLETS, JEWELRY CASES ETC						
# of Regressions	1	2	3	4	5	6
Const	−8.619 [−40.33]**	−9.502 [−84.73]**	−8.583 [−32.73]**	−9.595 [−54.01]**	−9.667 [−73.03]**	−9.668 [−73.13]**
GDP per capita	−0.225 [−0.38]	1.079 [2.01]**	−0.642 [−0.73]	0.87 [1.04]	0.902 [1.08]	0.925 [1.10]
Tariff	15.072 [0.85]	10.06 [0.8]	15.263 [0.85]	7.207 [0.57]		
Share*tariff	−22.778 [−0.78]		−24.12 [−0.83]			
t1			0.149 [0.67]	0.018 [0.08]	0.035 [0.16]	0.033 [0.15]
t2			0.131 [0.68]	0.097 [0.5]	0.114 [0.59]	0.114 [0.59]
t3			0.037 [0.22]	0.131 [0.76]	0.143 [0.84]	0.151 [0.88]
t4			0.146 [0.87]	0.257 [1.56]	0.263 [1.60]	0.262 [1.59]
t5			0.026 [0.16]	0.028 [0.18]	0.028 [0.17]	0.027 [0.17]
t6			0.032 [0.2]	−0.091 [−0.57]	−0.092 [−0.57]	−0.091 [−0.57]
Nafta					0.341 [0.50]	
Nafta(Lag)					0.46 [0.74]	
# of Obv.	570	733	570	733	733	733
R-squared	0.002	0.009	0.0046	0.019	0.018	0.019
F-statistics	0.3	2.79	0.24	1.38	1.37	1.41

(*Continued*)

Table 3. (*Continued*)

HS 6002 KNITTED OR CROCHETED FABRICS, NESOI						
# of Regressions	1	2	3	4	5	6
Const	−5.34 [−4.72]**	−6.437 [−5.51]**	−5.908 [−4.7]**	−7.588 [−6.16]**	−7.741 [−6.25]**	−7.631 [−6.14]**
GDP per capita	1.708 [1.27]	1.125 [0.83]	0.731 [0.5]	−0.336 [−0.23]	−0.215 [−0.14]	−0.08 [−0.05]
Tariff	−52.04 [−3.06]**	−20.367 [−3.06]**	−61.01 [−2.48]**	−18.708 [−2.59]**		
Share*tariff	55.107 [1.45]		70.903 [1.41]			
t1			0.209 [0.75]	0.395 [1.61]	0.61 [2.54]**	0.613 [2.56]**
t2			−0.195 [−0.71]	−0.107 [−0.44]	0.128 [0.55]	0.132 [0.57]
t3			−0.445 [−1.61]	−0.269 [−1.12]	−0.075 [−0.32]	−0.028 [−0.12]
t4			−0.42 [−1.64]*	−0.279 [−1.14]	−0.166 [−0.68]	−0.161 [−0.66]
t5			−0.167 [−0.69]	−0.226 [−0.93]	−0.16 [−0.66]	−0.153 [−0.63]
t6			−0.036 [−0.15]	−0.257 [−1.08]	−0.212 [−0.89]	−0.207 [−0.86]
Nafta					1.19 [1.62]	
Nafta(Lag)						1.218 [1.8]*
# of Obv.	385	421	385	421	421	421
R-squared	0.054	0.029	0.0887	0.0627	0.05	0.05
F-statistics	5.79	4.98	3.25	2.68	2.15	2.23

(*Continued*)

Table 3. (*Continued*)

HS 6109 T-SHIRTS, SINGLETS, TANK TOPS ETC, KNIT OR CROCHET						
# of Regressions	1	2	3	4	5	6
Const	−7.183 [−31.83]**	−8.046 [−141.60]**	−7.817 [−27.57]**	−8.592 [−66.01]**	−8.642 [−66.74]**	−8.641 [−66.82]**
GDP per capita	−0.306 [−0.26]	0.0029 [0.05]	−0.072 [−0.64]	−0.063 [−1.15]	−0.065 [−1.18]	−0.066 [−1.19]
Tariff	−55.47 [−1.82]*	−5.547 [−1.40]	−13.84 [−0.45]	−3.976 [−1.05]		
Share*tariff	83.197 [1.51]		1.224 [0.02]			
t1			0.779 [3.42]**	0.902 [4.86]**	0.937 [5.04]**	0.935 [5.04]**
t2			0.733 [3.23]**	1.016 [5.60]**	1.056 [5.82]**	1.055 [5.82]**
t3			0.468 [2.12]**	0.794 [4.44]**	0.801 [4.50]**	0.831 [4.66]**
t4			0.419 [1.87]*	0.605 [3.34]**	0.606 [3.35]**	0.606 [3.35]**
t5			0.214 [0.96]	0.326 [1.82]*	0.325 [1.82]*	0.325 [1.82]*
t6			−0.189 [−0.86]	0.021 [0.12]	0.017 [0.10]	0.017 [0.10]
Nafta					1.712 [2.18]**	
Nafta(Lag)						1.655 [2.31]**
# of Obv.	367	776	367	776	776	776
R-squared	0.02	0.003	0.1062	0.0915	0.097	0.098
F-statistics	2.01	0.99	3.87	7.87	8.37	8.45

(*Continued*)

Table 3. (*Continued*)

HS 6115 PANTYHOSE, SOCKS & OTHER HOSIERY, KNIT OR CROCHET						
# of Regressions	1	2	3	4	5	6
Const	−7.13 [−6.74]**	−6.3 [−5.61]**	−8.339 [−6.64]**	−6.982 [−5.22]**	−6.764 [−5.08]**	−6.921 [−5.20]**
GDP per capita	0.307 [0.22]	1.487 [1.30]	−1.173 [−0.68]	0.856 [0.61]	1.139 [0.82]	0.958 [0.69]
Tariff	−1.821 [−0.17]	−0.821 [−0.11]	−4.556 [−0.42]	−1 [−0.13]		
Share*tariff	−10.394 [−1.05]		−8.286 [−0.83]			
t1			0.414 [1.39]	0.195 [0.78]	0.249 [1.00]	0.236 [0.95]
t2			0.245 [0.92]	0.117 [0.47]	0.179 [0.73]	0.161 [0.66]
t3			0.26 [0.91]	0.235 [0.93]	0.244 [0.98]	0.238 [0.95]
t4			−0.08 [−0.24]	0.008 [0.03]	0.025 [0.10]	0.058 [0.23]
t5			0.184 [0.62]	0.045 [0.17]	0.065 [0.25]	0.052 [0.20]
t6			−0.324 [−1.12]	−0.143 [−0.55]	−0.123 [−0.48]	−0.135 [−0.52]
Nafta					1.757 [2.18]**	
Nafta(Lag)						1.283 [1.75]*
# of Obv.	328	454	328	454	454	454
R-squared	0.008	0.005	0.0403	0.013	0.026	0.022
F-statistics	0.63	0.84	1.1	0.57	1.17	0.96

(*Continued*)

Table 3. (*Continued*)

HS 6401 WATERPROOF FOOTWEAR, RUBBER OR PLASTICS, BOND SOLE						
# of Regressions	1	2	3	4	5	6
Const	−5.269 [−4.73]**	−6.399 [−5.53]**	−4.325 [−3.57]**	−4.555 [−3.42]**	−4.679 [−3.46]**	−5.259 [−3.95]**
GDP per capita	−0.946 [−0.45]	0.119 [0.06]	−2.571 [−1.05]	−3.43 [−1.44]	−3.93 [−1.67]*	−3.036 [−1.31]
Tariff	−38.18 [−3.23]**	−20.49 [−3.28]**	−33.19 [−2.62]**	−12.79 [−1.86]*		
Share*tariff	−65.39 [−1.26]		−55.47 [−1.05]			
t1			0.355 [0.72]	0.772 [1.72]*	1.084 [2.56]**	1.083 [2.62]**
t2			−0.254 [−0.56]	0.277 [0.67]	0.646 [1.7]*	0.675 [1.82]*
t3			0.002 [0.00]	0.54 [1.39]	0.746 [2.02]**	0.902 [2.48]**
t4			−0.019 [−0.05]	0.443 [1.15]	0.617 [1.64]*	0.627 [1.71]*
t5			−0.826 [−2.26]**	−0.742 [−2.19]**	−0.681 [−2.01]**	−0.684 [−2.07]**
t6			−0.393 [−1.05]	−0.13 [−0.37]	−0.107 [−0.31]	−0.098 [−0.29]
Nafta					1.48 [1.5]	
Nafta(Lag)						2.788 [3.28]**
# of Obv.	199	238	199	238	238	238
R-squared	0.114	0.057	0.1442	0.1744	0.138	0.178
F-statistics	6.37	5.4	3.36	3.64	3.47	4.69

(*Continued*)

Table 3. (*Continued*)

8528 TV RECVRS, INCL VIDEO MONITORS & PROJECTORS						
# of Regressions	1	2	3	4	5	6
Const	−7.927 [−20.19]**	−8.599 [−80.08]**	−8.109 [−14.09]**	−8.869 [−28.39]**	−9.097 [−40.89]**	−9.086 [−40.96]**
GDP per capita	0.346 [0.19]	−0.208 [−0.12]	0.28 [0.15]	−0.138 [−0.08]	−0.322 [−0.18]	−0.409 [−0.23]
Tariff	−89.61 [−3.22]**	−51.08 [−2.68]**	−83.96 [−1.87]*	−32.48 [−1.05]		
Share*tariff	99.218 [1.66]*		96.675 [1.52]			
t1			0.532 [1.25]	0.68 [1.72]*	0.887 [2.58]**	0.875 [2.56]**
t2			−0.139 [−0.33]	0.003 [0.01]	0.212 [0.64]	0.201 [0.60]
t3			0.213 [0.51]	0.341 [0.9]	0.574 [1.86]*	0.556 [1.79]*
t4			0.184 [0.43]	0.253 [0.65]	0.507 [1.63]	0.509 [1.64]*
t5			0.276 [0.84]	0.149 [0.48]	0.142 [0.46]	0.143 [0.46]
t6			0.108 [0.33]	0.121 [0.39]	0.133 [0.43]	0.132 [0.43]
Nafta					−0.139 [−0.16]	
Nafta(Lag)						−0.341 [−0.42]
# of Samples	281	320	281	320	320	320
R-squared	0.046	0.03	0.0647	0.0489	0.045	0.045
F-statistics	3.52	3.62	1.62	1.48	1.34	1.36

(*Continued*)

Table 3. (*Continued*)

8703 MOTOR CARS & VEHICLES FOR TRANSPORTING PERSONS						
# of Regressions	1	2	3	4	5	6
Const	−8.617 [−8.73]**	−10.58 [−26.49]**	−8.518 [−2.41]**	−10.65 [−24.17]**	−10.52 [−24.42]**	−10.53 [−24.46]**
GDP per capita	0.251 [2.03]**	0.276 [2.13]**	0.251 [2.01]**	0.261 [1.97]**	0.255 [1.92]*	0.254 [1.92]*
Tariff	−72.9 [−0.51]	39.727 [1.63]	−28.94 [−0.06]	36.401 [1.48]		
Share*tariff	51.06 [0.29]		−2.787 [0.00]			
t1			−0.429 [−0.64]	0.131 [0.46]	0.18 [0.62]	0.183 [0.64]
t2			−0.467 [−0.7]	0.223 [0.8]	0.268 [0.94]	0.271 [0.96]
t3			−0.236 [−0.36]	0.155 [0.57]	0.181 [0.67]	0.217 [0.79]
t4			−0.497 [−1.18]	0.1 [0.38]	0.113 [0.43]	0.113 [0.43]
t5			−0.847 [−2.59]**	−0.312 [−1.12]	−0.318 [−1.13]	−0.319 [−1.14]
t6			−0.418 [−1.26]	0.028 [0.1]	0.027 [0.10]	0.027 [0.10]
Nafta					0.548 [0.79]	
Nafta(Lag)						0.61 [0.96]
Mexico						
# of Samples	173	278	173	278	278	278
R-squared	0.038	0.035	0.0926	0.0567	0.049	0.05
F-statistics	1.75	3.55	1.43	1.44	1.23	1.28

(*Continued*)

Table 3. (*Continued*)

# of Regressions	7
Const	−10.79 [−24.14]**
GDP per capita	0.261 [1.99]**
Tariff	54.569 [2.02]**
Share*tariff	
t1	0.18 [0.63]
t2	0.27 [0.96]
t3	0.143 [0.53]
t4	0.096 [0.37]
t5	−0.311 [−1.12]
t6	0.029 [0.11]
Nafta	
Nafta(Lag)	
Mexico	1.679 [1.59]
# of Samples	278
R–squared	0.069
F–statistics	1.57

Table 4. Summary of regression results of Table 3.

Commodities		Tariff	NAFTA or NAFTA(Lag)
HS 4202	TRAVEL GOODS, HANDBAGS, WALLETS, JEWELRY CASES ETC		-
HS 6002	KNITTED OR CROCHETED FABRICS, NESOI	**	*
HS 6109	T-SHIRTS, SINGLETS, TANK TOPS ETC, KNIT OR CROCHET	*	**
HS 6115	PANTYHOSE, SOCKS & OTHER HOSIERY, KNIT OR CROCHET	-	**
HS 6401	WATERPROOF FOOTWEAR, RUBBER OR PLASTICS, BOND SOLE	**	**
HS 8528	TV RECVRS, INCL VIDEO MONITORS & PROJECTORS	**	-
HS 8703	MOTOR CARS & VEHICLES FOR TRANSPORTING PERSONS	-	-

* Significant at 10 percent level.
** Significant at 5 percent level.
- Not significant.

V. Conclusions and Implications for Further Research

In this chapter, we have developed a theoretical framework for analyzing how tariff preferences in the NAFTA may affect U.S. imports from Canada and Mexico. Using trade and tariff information at the 2-digit and 4-digit levels of the Harmonized System, our econometric analysis has suggested that there may be trade diversion especially in U.S. imports of textiles and apparel products from Mexico. Evidence based on other studies suggests that these imports have come at the expense especially of Asian suppliers.

Our research and some of the other studies that we have noted demonstrate the importance of commodity disaggregation in analyzing the effects of preferential trading arrangements. There is also a strong case to be made for analyzing how foreign direct investment and outsourcing interact with tariff preferences in influencing patterns of trade and specialization in member and non-member countries in preferential trading arrangements.

Appendix. Partial-Equilibrium Trade Model of Differentiated-Product Industries under Monopolistic Competition with *N* Countries

In this Appendix we present a theoretical foundation of our empirical model. It is assumed that there are Z industries and N countries. Each firm produces a differentiated product. Let $H_{z,n}$ denote the number of firms in country n's industry z. $H_{z,n}$ is endogenously determined. All households have identical preferences. The utility-maximization problem of a representative household in importing country j is:

$$\max \prod_{z=1}^{Z} \left(\sum_{n=1}^{N} \sum_{h=1}^{H_{z,n}} c_{z,n,h,j}^{\frac{\theta_z - 1}{\theta_z}} \right)^{\eta_z \frac{\theta_z}{\theta_z - 1}},$$

subject to

$$\sum_{z=1}^{Z} \sum_{n=1}^{N} \sum_{h=1}^{H_{z,n}} p_{z,n,h} T_{z,n,j} \Omega_{z,n,j} c_{z,n,h,j} = Y_j, \tag{A.1}$$

where $c_{z,n,h,j}$ denotes country j's consumption of output by industry z's firm h in country n. θ_z is the elasticity of substitution (>1) between the output of different firms in industry z. η_z denotes the expenditure share of industry z's output in total expenditure. $p_{z,n,h}$ is the f.o.b. price of firm h's output of country n's industry z. $T_{z,n,j}$ is one plus the tariff and tariff equivalent of non-tariff barriers of country j's imports used in the output by industry z in country n. $\Omega_{z,n,j}$ is the c.i.f./f.o.b. factor (>1) to ship output of industry z from country n to county j. Finally, Y_j represents country j's national income.

Using utility maximization, we can derive country *j*'s demand function for the output by firm *h* in industry *z* in country *n*:

$$c_{z,n,h,j} = \frac{1}{\sum_{n=1}^{N} H_{z,n}} \left(\frac{p_{z,n,j}\Omega_{n,j}T_{z,n,j}}{p_{z,j}} \right)^{-\theta_z} \frac{\eta_Z \Upsilon_j}{p_{z,j}}, \tag{A.2}$$

where $p_{z,j}$ denotes country *j*'s price index of industry *z*'s output. $p_{z,j}$ is defined as:

$$p_{z,j} = \left\{ \frac{\sum_{n=1}^{N} \sum_{h=1}^{H_{z,n}} \left(p_{z,n,h}\Omega_{n,j}T_{z,n,j}\right)^{1-\theta_z}}{\sum_{n=1}^{N} H_{z,n}} \right\}^{\frac{1}{1-\theta_z}}. \tag{A.3}$$

Next we formulate the profit-maximization behavior of firm *h* in industry *z* in country *n*. We assume that there are three factors of production: capital, labor, and sector-specific production factors. In our model, the comparative advantage of each country is determined by the endowment pattern of these sector-specific and non-specific production factors. Each firm in industry *z* produces a differentiated product in a market of monopolistic competition, using the three factors of production, labor (L), capital (K), and the industry-specific factor (Q_z). The production technology used in a particular industry *z* is identical for all firms in that industry. The technology function takes a linear form, yielding the following production function:

$$\sum_{j=1}^{N} c_{z,n,h,j} = \frac{1}{\alpha_z^{\alpha_z} \beta_z^{\beta_z} \gamma_z^{\gamma_z}} K_{z,n,h}^{\alpha_z} L_{z,n,h}^{\beta_z} Q_{z,n,h}^{\gamma_z}. \tag{A.4}$$

The left-hand side denotes the total output of firm *h*. We assume constant variable costs ($\alpha_z + \beta_z + \gamma_z = 1$). The firm also incurs fixed costs:

$$\delta_z = \frac{1}{\alpha_z^{\alpha_z} \beta_z^{\beta_z} \gamma_z^{\gamma_z}} K_{z,n,h,f}^{\alpha_z} L_{z,n,h,f}^{\beta_z} Q_{z,n,h,f}^{\gamma_z}, \tag{A.5}$$

where $K_{z,n,h,f}$, $L_{z,n,h,f}$, and $Q_{z,n,h,f}$ denote the factor inputs required for the continuation of production.

Firm h's profit-maximization problem is:

$$\max p_{z,n,h}\left(\sum_{j=1}^{N} c_{z,n,h,j}\right) - w_n(L_{z,n,h} + L_{z,n,h,f}) - r_n(K_{z,n,h} + K_{z,n,h,f}) - q_{z,n}(Q_{z,n,h} + Q_{z,n,h,f}),$$

subject to Equations (A.4) and (A.5), where w_n, r_n, and $q_{z,n}$ are country n's wage rate, rental price of capital, and price of the industry-specific factor.

From cost-minimization conditions, we can derive the following marginal-cost function:

$$MC_{z,n,h} = r_n^{\alpha_z} w_n^{\beta_z} q_{z,n}^{\gamma_z}. \tag{A.6}$$

Fixed cost is expressed by:

$$FC_{z,n,h} = \delta_z r_n^{\alpha_z} w_n^{\beta_z} q_{z,n}^{\gamma_z}. \tag{A.7}$$

From profit-maximization conditions, we can derive:

$$p_{z,n,h} = \frac{\theta_z}{\theta_z - 1} MC_{z,n,h}. \tag{A.8}$$

We assume that new firms can freely enter industry z, and the following zero-profit condition holds in equilibrium:

$$\left(\frac{\theta_z}{\theta_z - 1} - 1\right) MC_{z,n,h} \sum_{j=1}^{N} c_{z,n,h,j} = FC_{z,n,h}. \tag{A.9}$$

Using Equations (A.6) and (A.7), we can simplify the zero-profit condition as:

$$\frac{1}{\theta_z - 1}\sum_{j=1}^{N} c_{z,n,h,j} = \delta_z. \tag{A.10}$$

We assume that since industry z is small in each country, the wage rate and the rental price of capital are exogenously determined. The price of the industry z-specific production factor, $q_{z,n}$, is determined by the market-equilibrium condition. Using Equations (A.6), (A.7), and cost-minimization conditions, we can express firm h's demand for the industry z-specific factor as:

$$Q_{z,n,h} = \frac{\gamma_z}{q_{z,n}} r_n^{\alpha_z} w_n^{\beta_z} q_{z,n}^{\gamma_z} \left\{ \left(\sum_{j=1}^{N} c_{z,n,h,j} \right) + \delta_Z \right\}. \tag{A.11}$$

From zero-profit condition (A.10) and factor-demand function (A.11), we get the market-equilibrium condition for the sector z-specific production factor:

$$Q_{z,n} = H_{z,n} Q_{z,n,h} = \frac{\gamma_z}{q_{z,n}} r_n^{\alpha_z} w_n^{\beta_z} q_{z,n}^{\gamma_z} \theta_z \delta_z H_{z,n}, \tag{A.12}$$

where $Q_{z,n}$ denotes the exogenously determined endowment level of the sector z-specific factor in country n. We assume that $Q_{z,n}$ is constant over time. The equilibrium price level of the sector z-specific factor in country n is expressed by:

$$q_{z,n} = \left(\frac{\gamma_z \delta_z \theta_z}{Q_{z,n}} r_n^{\alpha_z} w_n^{\beta_z} H_{z,n} \right)^{\frac{1}{\alpha_z + \beta_z}}. \tag{A.13}$$

The number of firms in country n's industry z is implicitly determined by the zero-profit condition (A.10). Using demand function (A.2) and Equation (A.13), the zero-profit condition (A.9) can be expressed by:

$$\delta_z = \frac{1}{\theta_z - 1}\left\{\sum_{j=1}^{N} \frac{1}{\sum_{n=1}^{N} H_{z,n}} \left(\frac{\Omega_{n,j} T_{z,n,j}}{p_{z,j}}\right)^{-\theta_z} \frac{\eta_Z \Upsilon_j}{p_{z,j}}\right\}$$
$$\times \left(\frac{\theta_z}{\theta_z - 1} r_n^{\alpha_z} w_n^{\beta_z} q_{z,n}^{\gamma_z}\right)^{-\theta_z}$$
$$= \frac{1}{\theta_z - 1}\left\{\sum_{j=1}^{N} \frac{1}{\sum_{n=1}^{N} H_{z,n}} \left(\frac{\Omega_{n,j} T_{z,n,j}}{p_{z,j}}\right)^{-\theta_z} \frac{\eta_Z \Upsilon_j}{p_{z,j}}\right\}$$
$$\times \left\{\frac{\theta_z^{\frac{1}{\alpha_z+\beta_z}}}{\theta_z - 1} r_n^{\frac{\alpha_z}{\alpha_z+\beta_z}} w_n^{\frac{\beta_z}{\alpha_z+\beta_z}} \left(\frac{\gamma_z \delta_z}{Q_{z,n}} H_{z,n}\right)^{\frac{\gamma_z}{\alpha_z+\beta_z}}\right\}^{-\theta_z} . \qquad \text{(A.14)}$$

We assume that $Q_{z,n}$ and the c.i.f./f.o.b. factor (>1) to ship industry z's output from country n to country j, $\Omega_{z,n,j}$, are constant over time. By taking the natural logarithm and differentiating both sides of the equation over time, we get:

$$G(H_{z,n}) = -\frac{\alpha_z + \beta_z}{\gamma_z} \sum_{j=1}^{N} v_{z,n,j} G(T_{z,n,j})$$
$$+ \frac{(\theta_z - 1)(\alpha_z + \beta_z)}{\theta_z \gamma_z} \sum_{j=1}^{N} v_{z,n,j} G(p_{z,j})$$
$$+ \frac{\alpha_z + \beta_z}{\theta_z \gamma_z} \sum_{j=1}^{N} v_{z,n,j} G(\Upsilon_j) - \frac{\alpha_z}{\gamma_z} G(r_n)$$
$$- \frac{\beta_z}{\gamma_z} G(w_n) - \frac{\alpha_z + \beta_z}{\theta_z \gamma_z} G(H_z), \qquad \text{(A.15)}$$

where $G(x)$ denotes the growth rate of variable x; $v_{z,n,j}$ is the percentage of exports of industry z products from country n to country j in total products of industry z in country n; and H_z is the total number of industry z firms in the world.

Next we consider how trade barriers affect the U.S. import share of U.S. trade partners in our model. We treat the United States as country 1. Let $s_{z,n,j}$ denote the percentage of imports from country n in country j's total imports of industry z products:

$$s_{z,n,j} = \frac{p_{z,n,h}\Omega_{z,n,j}H_{z,n}c_{z,n,h,j}}{\sum_{i\neq j} p_{z,i,h}\Omega_{z,i,j}H_{z,i}c_{z,i,h,j}}. \tag{A.16}$$

The growth rate of country n's share in total U.S. imports of industry z products is expressed by:

$$\begin{aligned} G(s_{z,n,1}) &= G(p_{z,n,h}) + G(H_{z,n}) + G(c_{z,n,h,1}) \\ &\quad - \sum_{i=2}^{N} s_{z,i,1}(G(p_{z,i,h}) + G(H_{z,i}) + G(c_{z,i,h,1})). \end{aligned} \tag{A.17}$$

We assume that international capital movements always equalize the rental price of capital across countries. Using Equations (A.2), (A.8), (A.13), and (A.17), we get:

$$\begin{aligned} G(s_{z,n,1}) &= -\mu_{z,1}\left(G(w_n) - \sum_{i=2}^{N} s_{z,i,1}G(w_i)\right) \\ &\quad - \mu_{z,2}\left(G(T_{n,1}) - \sum_{i=2}^{N} s_{z,i,1}G(T_{z,i,1})\right) \\ &\quad + \mu_{z,3}\left(G(H_{z,n}) - \sum_{i=2}^{N} s_{z,i,1}G(H_{z,i})\right), \end{aligned} \tag{A.18}$$

where $\mu_{z,1}$, $\mu_{z,2}$, and $\mu_{z,3}$ take positive values. Using Equation (A.15), we get:

$$\begin{aligned}
&G(H_{z,n}) - \sum_{i=2}^{N} s_{z,i,1} G(H_{z,i}) \\
&= -\frac{\alpha_z + \beta_z}{\gamma_z}\left(\sum_{j=1}^{N} v_{z,n,j} G(T_{z,n,j}) - \sum_{i=2}^{N} s_{z,i,1} \sum_{j=1}^{N} v_{z,i,j} G(T_{z,i,j})\right) \\
&\quad + \frac{(\theta_z - 1)(\alpha_z + \beta_z)}{\theta_z \gamma_z}\left(\sum_{j=1}^{N} v_{z,n,j} G(p_{z,j}) - \sum_{i=2}^{N} s_{z,i,1} \sum_{j=1}^{N} v_{z,i,j} G(p_{z,j})\right) \\
&\quad + \frac{\alpha_z + \beta_z}{\theta_z \gamma_z}\left(\sum_{j=1}^{N} v_{z,n,j} G(Y_j) - \sum_{i=2}^{N} s_{z,i,1} \sum_{j=1}^{N} v_{z,i,j} G(Y_j)\right) \\
&\quad + \frac{\beta_z}{\gamma_z}\left(G(w_n) - \sum_{i=2}^{N} s_{z,i,1} G(w_i)\right). \qquad \text{(A.19)}
\end{aligned}$$

The calculation of the complex terms of Equation (A.19) is beyond the scope of this paper. In order to simplify our analysis we set the following assumptions: (1) compared with changes in U.S. trade policy, trade policies in other countries did not have a significant effect on the number of firms in industry z of the country they trade with; and (2) all firms in industry z have similar sales destination patterns, that is, $(v_{z,i,1}, v_{z,i,2}, v_{z,i,3}, \ldots, v_{z,i,N}) = (v_{zji,1}, v_{zj,2}, v_{zji,3}, \ldots, v_{z,j,N})$ for all i and j. Under assumption (1), the first term on the right-hand side of Equation (A.19) is approximated by:

$$-\frac{\alpha_z + \beta_z}{\gamma_z} v_{z,n,1}\left(G(T_{z,n,1}) - \sum_{i=2}^{N} s_{z,i,1} G(T_{z,i,1})\right).$$

The second and the third terms are negligible under assumption (2). Therefore we get:

$$G(s_{z,n,1}) = -\lambda_{z,1}\left(G(w_n) - \sum_{i=2}^{N} s_{z,i,1}G(w_i)\right)$$
$$-\lambda_{z,2}\left(G(T_{n,1}) - \sum_{i=2}^{N} s_{z,i,1}G(T_{z,i,1})\right)$$
$$+\lambda_{z,3}\, v_{z,n,1}\left(G(T_{n,1}) - \sum_{i=2}^{N} s_{z,i,1}G(T_{z,i,1})\right). \qquad (A.20)$$

Integrating the above equation over time, we have Equation (1) that provides the basis for our empirical analysis:

$$\ln(s_{z,n,1}(t)) = \lambda_{z,n} - \lambda_{z,1}\left(\ln(w_n(t)) - \sum_{i=2}^{N} s_{z,i,1}^{0}\ln(w_i(t))\right)$$
$$-\lambda_{z,2}\left(\ln(T_{n,1}(t)) - \sum_{i=2}^{N} s_{z,i,1}^{0}\ln(T_{z,i,1}(t))\right)$$
$$+\lambda_{z,3}v_{z,n,1}^{0}\left(\ln(T_{n,1}(t)) - \sum_{i=2}^{N} s_{z,i,1}^{0}\ln(T_{z,i,1}(t))\right)$$
$$+\varepsilon_{z,n}(t). \qquad (1)$$

$\lambda_{z,n}$ depends on country-specific factors such as $Q_{z,n}$. $\varepsilon_{z,n}(t)$ is the usual error term. The three elasticity values $\lambda_{z,1}$, $\lambda_{z,2}$, and $\lambda_{z,3}$ are complicated functions of the parameters, such as θ_z (the elasticity of substitution between the output of different firms) and γ_z (the income share of the industry z-specific factor). But it can be shown that these values are increasing functions of θ_z and decreasing functions of γ_z.

Study Questions

1. What are the difficulties that arise in evaluating the effects of NAFTA? What do previous studies suggest have been the

trade effects of NAFTA? Has there been evidence of trade diversion or trade creation? What have been the effects of rules of origin?

2. What are the principal features of a gravity model and the adaptation of this model being applied for econometric investigation? What data have been used in the empirical analysis? What do the empirical results suggest at the 2-digit and 4-digit levels of the commodity classifications used?

References

Arndt, Sven and Alex Huemer. 2001. "North American Trade After NAFTA: Parts I and II," *Claremont Policy Briefs*, Issue No. 01-01 and 01-02, Claremont Graduate University, April and July.

Bergstrand, Jeffrey H. 1989. "The Generalized Gravity Equation, Monopolistic Competition, and the Factor Proportions Theory of International Trade," *Review of Economics and Statistics* 71, pp. 143–153.

Burfisher, Mary E., Sherman Robinson, and Karen Thierfelder. 2001. "The Impact of NAFTA on the United States," *Journal of Economic Perspectives* 15, pp. 125–144.

Coughlin, Cletus C. and Howard, J. Wall. 2000. "NAFTA and the Changing Pattern of State Exports," Working Paper 2000-029, Research Division, Federal Reserve Bank of St. Louis (October).

Gould, David M. 1998. "Has NAFTA Changed North American Trade?" Federal Bank of Dallas, *Economic Review*, First Quarter, pp. 12–23.

Heckman, James. 1979. "Sample Bias as a Specification Error," *Econometrica* 47, pp. 153–162.

Helpman, Elhanan and Paul Krugman. 1985. *Market Structure and Foreign Trade*. Cambridge: MIT Press.

James, William E. and Masaru Umemoto. 1999. "Rules of Origin and the Competitive Position of Asian Textiles and Apparel Producers in the North American Market," ICSEAD Working Paper Series, Vol. 99-1 (January).

James, William E. and Masaru Umemoto. 2000. "NAFTA Trade with East Asia: Rules of Origin and Market Access in Textiles, Apparel, Footwear, and Electrical Machinery," *ASEAN Economic Bulletin* 17, pp. 293–309.

Karemara, David and Kalu Ojah. 1998. "An Industrial Analysis of Trade Creation and Diversion Effects of NAFTA," *Journal of Economic Integration* 13, pp. 400–425.

Krueger, Anne O. 1993. "Free Trade Agreements as Protectionist Devices: Rules of Origin," National Bureau of Economic Research, Working Paper 4342.

Krueger, Anne O. 1999a. "Are Preferential Trading Agreements Trade-Liberalizing or Protectionist?" *Journal of Economic Perspectives* 13, pp. 105–124.

Krueger, Anne O. 1999b. "Trade Creation and Trade Diversion under NAFTA," National Bureau of Economic Research, Working Paper 7429 (December).

Krueger, Anne O. 2000. "NAFTA's Effects: A Preliminary Assessment," *The World Economy* 23, pp. 761–775.

Lustig, Nora. 2001. "Life is Not Easy: Mexico's Quest for Stability and Growth," *Journal of Economic Perspectives* 15, pp. 85–106.

Manning, W. G., N. Duan, and W. H. Rogers. 1987. "Monte Carlo Evidence on the Choice Between Sample Selection and Two-Part Models," *Journal of Econometrics* 35, pp. 59–82.

Markusen, James. 1986. "Explaining the Volume of Trade: An Eclectic Approach," *American Economic Review* 76, pp. 1002–1011.

Romalis, John. 2001. "NAFTA's Impact on North American Trade," in process.

Soloaga, Isidro and L. Alan Winters. 2001. "Regionalism in the Nineties: What Effect on Trade?" *North American Journal of Economics and Finance* 121, pp. 1–29.

Suggested Further Reading

Cadot, Olivier *et al.* 2006. *The Origin of Goods: Rules of Origin in Free Trade Agreements*. New York: Oxford University Press.

Kunimoto, Robert and Gary Sawchuck. 2006. "NAFTA Rules of Origin," in John M. Curtis and Aaron Sydor, eds., *NAFTA @ 10*, Trade Policy Research, Special Edition, Foreign Affairs and International Trade Canada. Ottawa: Minister of Public Works and Government Services Canada.

Romalis, John. 2007. "NAFTA's and CUSFTA's Impact on International Trade," *Review of Economics and Statistics* 89, pp. 416–435.

Chapter 11

Some Economic Effects of the Free Trade Agreement between Tunisia and the European Union*

Drusilla K. Brown, Alan V. Deardorff and Robert M. Stern

I. Introduction

In this chapter, we use a specially constructed version of the Michigan Brown–Deardorff–Stern (BDS) Computational General Equilibrium (CGE) Model of World Production and Trade to estimate some potential economic effects on the Tunisian economy that may result from the free trade agreement (FTA) between Tunisia and the European Union (EU) that was concluded in July 1995. The BDS CGE model provides measures of the effects that the FTA may have on the trade, output, and employment in the goods and services sectors for Tunisia and its major trading partners. The model also permits calculations of the effects of the FTA on economic welfare and returns to labor and capital in the individual countries/regions.

* Reprinted with permission from Ahmed Galal and Bernard Hoekman (eds.), *Regional Partners in Global Markets: Limits and Possibilities of the Euro-Med Agreements*, 1997, London and Cairo: Centre for Economic Policy Research and Egyptian Center for Economic Studies, Chapter 5.

A key issue in evaluating the Tunisian-EU FTA is how foreign direct investment (FDI) inflows may be affected. While changes in FDI inflows are not determined within the BDS CGE model, we can use the model nonetheless to investigate both how the incentives for FDI may be altered by the FTA and the ways in which potential changes in FDI associated with the FTA may impact on the Tunisian economy.

Our analysis focuses exclusively on the static effects of reductions in tariffs and NTBs in the Tunisian-EU FTA and on several possible changes in FDI. Our model is a static model and it therefore does not include various possible dynamic effects on longer run growth that may arise in response to the static changes. We also have not attempted to model other aspects of the effects of the FTA that some investigators have suggested may be more important than the changes in tariffs and NTBs themselves. Page and Underwood (1995) have discussed a number of such effects in connection with a survey of certain World Bank CGE studies of FTAs between the EU and both Tunisia and Morocco. These effects include the possible further benefits that may arise from harmonization of standards, product quality improvements, and increased trading efficiency. Such effects, especially because they would reduce the costs of trade not only with the EU but with other countries as well, are found in those studies to be more important than the reductions in tariffs and NTBs for the effects on welfare of the respective countries. We hope that these assessments are correct, but we did not include such changes in our own analysis because of the considerable uncertainties over how large they may really turn out to be.

The chapter proceeds as follows. In Section II, we outline some essential features of our CGE model and the data used to analyze the effects of the Tunisia-EU FTA. Since, as mentioned, our model-based approach is not altogether well suited to analyzing issues relating to FDI, we devote Section III to a brief summary of selected recent literature on the determinants of FDI, including especially the experiences of developing countries. This may be helpful in assessing how FDI may respond to the FTA, especially when investment incentives are offered. Thereafter, in Section IV, we discuss the details of the FDI incentives in Tunisia's 1994 Investment Code. The various model scenarios that we have run using our CGE model are described in Section V, and the aggregate and sectoral computational results of these scenarios are presented in Sections VI and VII. Finally, in Section VIII, we summarize our conclusions and consider the implications for Tunisia's trade and foreign investment policies.

II. The Michigan BDS CGE Trade Model[1]

Some Essential Model Features

The CGE model used in this chapter is an extension of the model first constructed by Brown and Stern (1989) to analyze the economic effects of the Canada-U.S. Trade Agreement (CUSTA), and later expanded by Brown *et al.* (BDS) (1992a,b, 1996a,b) to analyze the NAFTA, the extension of the NAFTA to some major trading countries in South America, and the formation of an East Asian trading bloc. The potential effects of integrating Czechoslovakia, Hungary, and Poland into the EU are also analyzed in Brown, Deardorff, Djankov, and Stern (1996). For our purposes here, we model the following eight countries/regions: Tunisia; Greece/Portugal/Spain (MEU); France/Italy (FR-IT); Other 7-EU countries (OEU); Other Europe (OEUR); Asia/Pacific (APAC); NAFTA; and South America (SAM).[2] All remaining countries of the world are consigned to a residual rest-of-world to close the model. The sectoral coverage in each country/region includes one agricultural sector, 21 product categories covering manufacturing, one mining sector, and six categories covering services, including government. All sectors are modeled as tradable.[3] The individual sectors and

[1] Readers who are not concerned with the technical details of the model may wish to proceed to the results of the analysis reported in the sections below.

[2] Other Europe includes: Austria; Finland; Norway; Sweden; Switzerland; Turkey; and Israel. Asia/Pacific includes: Hong Kong; Japan; Singapore; South Korea; Taiwan; India; Australia; and New Zealand. NAFTA includes Canada, Mexico, and the United States. South America includes: Argentina; Brazil; Chile; and Colombia. In 1995, the EU was expanded to include Austria, Finland, and Sweden, but as noted, we treat the EU as consisting of only 12 member countries.

[3] As will be noted below, treating all 29 model sectors as tradable enables us to analyze the effects and interaction of liberalization of both merchandise trade and services.

corresponding International Standard Industrial Classification (ISIC) categories are listed in Tables 1 and 2.

The agricultural sector in the model is characterized as being perfectly competitive and the nonagricultural sectors are taken to be monopolistically competitive with free entry.[4] Agricultural products are differentiated by country of production. The products of the manufacturing, mining, and services sectors are assumed to be differentiated by firm to correspond to the imperfectly competitive market structure. Domestic demands by sector reflect the overall demands in the economies, and we do not distinguish among different categories of demand such as consumption, investment, and government purchases. The level of total demand is determined by income.[5] The reference year for the data base of the model is 1990. The input-output relations used in the model refer to different years, depending on the availability of national input-output tables.[6]

---

[4] Issues of the modeling of market structure are discussed in Brown and Stern (1989), where a variety of different imperfectly competitive market structures are used in analyzing the economic effects of the CUSTA. As noted, for the current model, we use a structure of monopolistic competition, following Helpman and Krugman (1985), for all of the nonagricultural sectors. There is free entry of firms, each producing a different variety of a good/service and producing it with a fixed cost and constant marginal cost in terms of primary and intermediate inputs.

[5] Thus, we also do not allow an independent role for the government budget.

[6] It is always a problem to obtain completely up-to-date input-output tables because of ongoing changes in technology and productivity that would alter the input-output coefficients for particular sectors. However, our CGE model relies mainly on the intermediate input-value shares and the shares of primary factors as data. These shares tend to be more stable over time than physical input requirements. Indeed, to the extent that techniques change in response to price changes, a price increase will lead to an opposite change in quantity, leaving only a smaller change, if any, in input share. And to the extent that techniques change due to technological progress, input shares will again remain constant if that progress is neutral with respect to inputs in an appropriate sense. Therefore, the fact that prices and technologies undoubtedly do change over time does not necessarily mean that input-output tables lose their validity for our purposes. Nonetheless, it would of course be preferable to use newer data if those were available. For more discussion of this point, see Deardorff and Stern (1990, pp. 61–79).

Table 1. Tunisia: Basic data, 1990.

Sector	ISIC	(1) Output (Mill. $)	(2) Labor (000)	(3) Capital (Mill. $)	(4) Imports (Mill. $)	(5) Exports (Mill. $)
Agriculture, Forestry & Fisheries	(1)	2,668.6	542.4	3,343.5	317.9	176.9
Manufactures						
Food, Beverages & Tobacco	(310)	2,487.6	35.3	579.4	286.2	234.3
Textiles	(321)	525.6	76.9	734.4	818.0	121.0
Wearing Apparel	(322)	1,501.0	19.4	50.5	200.1	1,138.7
Leather Products	(323)	88.2	2.6	22.2	55.7	30.4
Footwear	(324)	139.1	12.1	50.5	12.0	48.3
Wood Products	(331)	141.9	6.6	13.5	104.0	5.1
Furniture & Fixtures	(332)	33.6	1.7	12.7	28.0	9.3
Paper & Paper Products	(341)	176.6	4.6	177.2	101.1	23.7
Printing & Publishing	(342)	82.9	5.0	29.5	24.5	2.2
Chemicals	(35A)	696.6	25.2	469.6	40.8	15.0
Petroleum & Related Products	(35B)	1,431.3	1.7	1,743.6	468.7	503.6
Rubber Products	(355)	163.1	5.0	23.5	298.3	65.6
Nonmetallic Mineral Products	(36A)	110.7	7.0	268.2	26.4	5.8
Glass & Glass Products	(362)	735.7	33.1	698.8	25.6	95.6
Iron & Steel	(371)	136.2	3.4	48.6	236.3	35.3
Nonferrous Metals	(372)	23.5	0.5	11.1	69.1	16.8
Metal Products	(381)	232.3	6.6	49.4	108.3	43.8

(*Continued*)

Table 1. (*Continued*)

Sector	ISIC	(1) Output (Mill. $)	(2) Labor (000)	(3) Capital (Mill. $)	(4) Imports (Mill. $)	(5) Exports (Mill. $)
Nonelectric Machinery	(382)	459.0	19.3	152.7	751.2	30.7
Electric Machinery	(383)	1,024.6	38.5	496.2	402.2	194.8
Transportation Equipment	(384)	196.8	5.8	111.9	442.4	43.7
Miscellaneous Manufactures	(38A)	148.2	5.3	39.4	273.7	90.0
Mining & Quarrying	(2)	682.7	1.6	69.1	251.6	529.9
Services						
Electricity, Gas & Water	(4)	549.1	12.5	1,349.9	133.1	6.9
Construction	(5)	1,573.0	63.6	317.9	4.1	12.4
Wholesale & Retail Trade	(6)	1,057.5	267.6	3,918.7	140.3	803.3
Transportation, Storage & Communications	(7)	1,275.9	52.3	3,470.8	432.5	536.2
Finance, Insurance & Real Estate	(8)	568.4	16.3	326.2	63.9	134.9
Community, Social & Personal Services	(9)	5,247.1	721.0	2,863.8	70.8	106.4
Total		24,166.8	1,992.9	21,442.8	6,186.8	5,060.6

Notes: Column (1) refers to gross output; Columns (1) and (2) are partly estimated for some sectors; Column (3) is based on cumulative annual sectoral investment, measured in constant prices, less depreciation; Columns (4) and (5) have been concorded from the Harmonized System to the ISIC sectoral categories.

Table 2. Tunisia: Tariff rates and services-sector tariff equivalents, pre-Uruguay Round (percentage).

Sector	ISIC	(1) Greece, Portugal, Spain	(2) France, Italy	(3) Other EU-7	(4) Other Eur.	(5) NAFTA	(6) Asia/Pac.	(7) South Amer.	(8) Rest of World
Agriculture, Forestry & Fisheries	(1)	21.9	19.7	22.1	28.1	20.2	13.8	19.9	18.0
Manufactures									
Food, Beverages & Tobacco	(310)	17.2	28.6	27.6	32.0	20.8	29.9	20.4	20.2
Textiles	(321)	38.2	37.3	37.9	31.1	32.2	30.2	29.5	34.2
Wearing Apparel	(322)	40.0	40.7	40.4	38.4	40.9	41.1	43.0	38.8
Leather Products	(323)	27.7	31.1	29.1	34.5	38.3	25.0	34.7	27.5
Footwear	(324)	39.0	39.6	42.4	42.7	43.0	42.1	0.0	41.9
Wood Products	(331)	27.9	23.4	30.4	22.1	21.8	38.9	22.0	21.5
Furniture & Fixtures	(332)	41.1	38.7	37.9	28.8	42.6	38.4	10.0	40.5
Paper & Paper Products	(341)	40.5	36.2	36.3	26.5	32.7	40.3	26.2	20.8
Printing & Publ.	(342)	19.7	25.0	26.6	26.8	12.1	40.7	0.0	25.5
Chemicals	(35A)	17.4	13.9	19.9	18.5	19.4	20.4	16.2	17.8
Petroleum & Related Products	(35B)	10.3	10.3	20.3	28.5	18.0	31.0	0.0	10.2
Rubber Products	(355)	33.3	30.9	33.4	33.8	36.4	32.2	28.7	24.9
Nonmetallic Mineral Products	(36A)	34.9	33.3	35.9	37.5	31.2	24.6	42.0	39.0
Glass & Glass Products	(362)	23.3	15.1	25.3	20.9	5.9	22.4	20.0	27.4
Iron & Steel	(371)	25.1	21.0	19.8	24.0	12.0	15.2	26.2	25.7

(Continued)

Table 2. (*Continued*)

Sector	ISIC	(1) Greece, Portugal, Spain	(2) France, Italy	(3) Other EU-7	(4) Other Eur.	(5) NAFTA	(6) Asia/Pac.	(7) South Amer.	(8) Rest of World
Nonferrous Metals	(372)	18.7	20.7	20.7	25.2	20.3	31.9	20.0	22.2
Metal Products	(381)	32.9	32.4	32.5	32.6	28.5	31.8	36.3	31.7
Nonelectric Machinery	(382)	16.8	18.0	15.8	15.5	18.1	13.1	13.4	16.9
Electric Machinery	(383)	26.7	28.6	22.7	36.8	18.8	19.4	27.8	27.3
Transportation Equipment	(384)	24.1	25.9	24.8	34.3	22.3	27.0	27.7	32.9
Miscellaneous Manufactures	(38A)	26.3	27.9	27.5	23.1	19.7	20.4	22.8	31.7
Mining & Quarrying	(2)	16.2	20.1	38.9	20.1	17.2	17.0	20.0	10.2
Services									
Electricity, Gas & Water	(4)	—	—	—	—	—	—	—	—
Construction	(5)	40.0	40.0	40.0	40.0	40.0	40.0	40.0	40.0
Wholesale & Retail Trade	(6)	34.4	34.4	34.4	34.4	34.4	34.4	34.4	34.4
Transportation, Storage & Commun.	(7)	193.9	193.9	193.9	193.9	193.9	193.9	193.9	193.9
Finance, Insurance & Real Estate	(8)	47.6	47.6	47.6	47.6	47.6	47.6	47.6	47.6
Community, Social & Personal Services	(9)	43.5	43.5	43.5	43.5	43.5	43.5	43.5	43.5

Note: The tariff rates on Sectors (1), (2), and (310)–(38A) are based on official Tunisian data and do not reflect exemptions and other duty-free allowances. They are weighted by bilateral imports. The *ad valorem* tariff equivalents in the services sectors (5–9) are "guesstimates" based on Hoekman (1995) and are not bilaterally weighted.

The data base and documentation as well as a full statement and description of the equations and parameters of the model are available from the authors on request.[7]

There are several important assumptions that either are built into the model or are implemented by the model for the present analysis. It is important that these be understood in interpreting the results to be reported below.

Full Employment — The analysis assumes throughout that the aggregate, or economy-wide, level of employment is held constant in each country. The effects of trade liberalization are therefore not permitted to change any country's overall rates of employment or unemployment. This assumption is made because overall employment is determined by macroeconomic forces and policies that are not contained in the model and would not themselves be included in a negotiated free trade agreement. The focus instead is on the composition of employment across sectors as determined by the microeconomic interactions of supply and demand resulting from the liberalization of trade.

Balanced Trade — It is assumed that trade remains balanced for each country, or more accurately that any initial trade imbalance remains constant, as trade barriers are changed. Thus, implicitly, the exchange rate (which as a nominal variable plays no role in the largely real analysis of the model) can be thought of as flexible. This reflects the reality of mostly flexible exchange rates, or at least adjustable exchange rates, among the countries involved. It also, like the full employment assumption, is appropriate as a way of abstracting from

---

[7] The sectoral data for merchandise trade, production, and employment come primarily from United Nations sources and to a lesser extent from national sources. The model parameters are constructed from the trade and input-output data for the countries included in the model and from published studies of trade and capital/labor substitution elasticities. More details on the data are provided below. See also Deardorff and Stern (1990, pp. 37–45).

the macroeconomic forces and policies that are the main determinants of trade balances.[8]

Rents and Revenues — Revenues from tariffs are assumed to be redistributed to consumers in the tariff-levying country and spent like any other income. Similarly, the rents from NTBs are also assumed to remain within the importing country and to be spent like other income. When tariffs and tariff equivalents are reduced, this means that income available to purchase imports falls along with their prices, and there is no overall bias towards expanding or contracting aggregate demand.

Fixed Relative Wages — While the economy-wide wage in each country is permitted to adjust so as to maintain full employment, the wages across sectors are held fixed relative to one another. This permits the analysis to focus on the labor-market adjustments that might be required, independently of any relative wage changes that may facilitate those adjustments.[9]

Fixed Labor Supply — The total labor supply in each country is assumed to be held fixed in the analysis. This is not to say that changes in labor supply will not occur in the course of the phase-in of trade liberalization, but only that such changes are assumed not to be the result of the negotiated agreement.

Role of Variety — The Dixit–Stiglitz aggregation function in its usual form uses a single parameter, the elasticity of substitution, to

[8] The results reported below for changes in total exports and imports may appear to contradict this assumption of balanced trade. This is because what are reported are measures of the changes in *quantities* traded, which are relevant for output and employment changes. They are not the *values* of trade, which undergo additional change due to changing relative prices. It is the values of exports relative to imports that are held fixed by the balanced trade assumption.

[9] We also do not distinguish workers according to their skill characteristics, and we therefore cannot determine how the wages and employment of different skill groups may be affected by the Tunisia-EU FTA.

determine both the degree of substitution among varieties of a good and the extent to which an increased number of varieties adds to welfare of consumers and reduces costs of intermediate inputs. This effect on welfare and cost could be quite important in an analysis of trade liberalization, since reduced trade barriers provide greater access to varieties produced abroad and could increase welfare on that account alone.[10]

The policy inputs into the model, which we discuss more fully below, are the pre-Uruguay Round tariffs and tariff equivalents applied to the bilateral trade of the countries/regions being modeled explicitly with respect to each other. Because our model is static, we will assume that the reduction of tariffs and NTB tariff equivalents takes place all at one time rather than being phased in over a period of several years as in fact will be the case. Therefore our analysis refers to the effects of the FTA that will occur in total, from before the reductions are initiated to the equilibrium that arises after all are completed. When the policy changes are introduced into the model, the method of solution yields percentage changes in sectoral employment and other variables of interest for each country/region. Multiplying the percentage changes by the actual 1990 levels given in the data base yields the absolute changes, positive or negative, that might result from the FTA.

We should further mention that we do not take account in our model of changes the cross-border movement of workers that might occur as the result of changes in real wages, and we also do not make any allowance for dynamic efficiency changes and economic growth. We will, however, make allowance for changes in inward foreign

[10] In earlier work we have noticed that the effect of variety in lowering costs can introduce an instability into the model, because an increase in demand for an industry can lead to entry, additional variety, lower costs to users, and hence additional demand. To avoid this happening in our model we therefore depart slightly from the Dixit–Stiglitz formulation, using an additional parameter to control these variety effects. In the results reported here, the effect of variety on welfare has been set to one-half of what would occur in the Dixit–Stiglitz model.

direct investment into Tunisia. We are aware that the Agreement between Tunisia and the EU involves much more than negotiated reductions and/or removal of tariffs and NTBs. That is, besides trade and related policies, the Agreement deals with the movement of capital, support for sectors experiencing adjustment problems and for structural reform, and a variety of labor and social issues.[11] While these other facets of the Agreement may be important, it is difficult to quantify the roles they will play. Our treatment of only the effects of liberalizing trade in goods, taking FDI into consideration, means therefore that our calculations of the consequences of the Tunisia-EU Agreement will be incomplete.

Policy Input Data

An indication of the basic data for Tunisia is provided in Tables 1 and 2. These data provide a sectoral breakdown, with 1990 as the reference year, of gross output, employment, capital stock, imports, exports, and bilateral tariffs.

The tariff data refer to the official tariff rates on Tunisian imports.[12] To obtain the sectoral tariff rates, we first aggregated the import data to the 6-digit Harmonized System (HS) classification and then matched the import and tariff data at this level. We then concorded the 6-digit HS import and tariff data to the 3-digit ISIC categories that we use in our CGE modeling framework. Tunisia's

---

[11] For details on the Agreement, see IMF (1996, pp. 77–79) and Hoekman and Djankov (1995, esp. pp. 14–25).

[12] There is an issue here as to whether the official tariff rates are representative of the rates actually applied on imports. That is, there may be a difference between the official rates and the actual collection rates which will reflect the various tariff exemptions that may be applied to particular categories of imports. Since data on collection rates were not available, we use the official rates. While the official rates may thus overstate Tunisia's import protection policies, a case can be made for using them insofar as the tariff exemptions may vary from year to year as government policies and the composition of imports are subject to change. The official rates are also representative of the rates that are bound by Tunisia's membership in the GATT/WTO. Further details on Tunisia's official rates are given in GATT (1994, esp. pp. 61–72).

bilateral tariff rates against the seven regions included in the model were calculated using bilateral imports as weights.[13] Since we disaggregated the EU-12 into Greece/Portugal/Spain, France/Italy, and the Other EU-7, we list separate weighted average sectoral tariffs for these disaggregated EU groupings. The differences among them reflect the different import compositions used in constructing the weighted averages. It is evident that Tunisia's weighted average official tariff rates show considerable dispersion, with some instances of rates below 10% and others in excess of 40%.

Besides tariffs, data on NTBs were needed. According to Nsouli *et al.* (1993, p. 69), 85% of Tunisia's imports in 1992 were effectively unrestricted. The remaining 15% were apparently subject to import licensing and annual import authorization.[14] We assumed for our purposes that these restrictions applied only to imports of agricultural products. Estimates based on Stanton (1994) suggest that the *ad valorem* equivalents of these agricultural NTBs were 5.5% on imports from the EU and 12.3% from all other regions. We have added these NTB *ad valorem* equivalents to the tariff rates for Sector 1 reported in Table 2.[15,16]

---

[13] Also included in Table 2 are "guesstimates" of the global *ad valorem* equivalents of Tunisian services barriers which have been calculated in Hoekman (1995). Given the tentative nature of these guesstimates, they will not enter into our FTA scenarios to be reported below.

[14] For information on Tunisia's existing nontariff restrictions, see GATT (1994, pp. 58–89). Tunisia also maintains export processing zones. We have no data on these zones, however, and have not included them in our analysis. For a brief description of the zones, see GATT (1994, Vol. II, pp. 40–41).

[15] In the absence of tariff equivalents, we typically model NTBs in terms of the percentage of trade subject to NTBs, using available or specially constructed NTB inventory data. These NTB measures are calculated by first making an inventory of existing NTBs classified by disaggregated import groupings, then determining the value of imports that are subject to any NTBs, and thereafter aggregating up to the sectors used in the model. Thus, a sector with a zero percent NTB trade coverage is taken to be completely exempt from NTBs, while, say, an NTB coverage of 25% is taken to mean that 25% of the imports in that sector are subject to one or more NTBs. The NTB coverage ratios are then used in the model to dampen the effects of tariff reductions undertaken when the NTBs are assumed to remain in place. It is

The EU maintains some quantitative restrictions on imports from Tunisia. These apply to such agricultural products as olive oil, oranges, potatoes, wine, apricot pulp, and sardines. In the absence of measures of the tariff equivalents of these restrictions, we decided to use a figure of 8% for the EU barriers on Sector 1 agricultural imports from Tunisia, based on the estimate in Harrison, Rutherford, and Wooton (1989). The EU also maintains certain seasonal restrictions on agricultural imports from Tunisia, which we assume to be included in the 8% tariff equivalent. With respect to manufactured goods, the EU has annual quotas limiting imports of cotton cloth and trousers from Tunisia. Since our textile and clothing sectoral aggregates cover a large variety of products and we do not have any information on the tariff equivalents involved, we have assumed that the EU quota restrictions here are not binding.[17]

important to emphasize that these measures of NTB trade coverage are *not* the same as the tariff equivalents of the NTBs. For further discussion, see Deardorff and Stern (1990, pp. 23–25). The most comprehensive available estimates of the NTB trade coverage by sectors for Tunisia are given in GATT (1994, esp. pp. 64, 66–68, and 167–172). These sectoral estimates are weighted apparently by total imports and cannot in themselves be used to calculate bilateral coverage ratios which we would ordinarily need for modeling purposes. In any case, as indicated below, we assume that the estimated tariff equivalents that we have already reflect the most significant existing NTBs, and that these NTBs will be eliminated in establishing the Tunisia-EU FTA. So long as this is the case, there is no need to use the NTB coverage ratios to dampen the effects of Tunisian tariff reductions.

[16] Tunisia's domestic tax system includes a value-added tax and a consumption tax. We chose not to represent these taxes in our modeling framework on the assumption that they would remain unchanged in the context of the Tunisia-EU FTA. For a brief overview of Tunisia's tax system, see Nsouli *et al.* (1993, esp. pp. 5–9 and 70–72).

[17] According to GATT (1994, pp. 89–96), the Tunisian Government has a variety of measures designed to restrain or promote exports in certain specified circumstances. Since information is not available that would permit assessment of the quantitative importance of these export-related measures and how they might be changed with implementation of the FTA, we have not taken them into account in our various modeling scenarios that will be noted below.

III. The Determinants of Foreign Direct Investment

An important reason why many developing countries are anxious to enter into FTAs with advanced industrialized industries is the belief that the FTA will stimulate inward foreign direct investment (FDI). Tunisia is no exception. In order to shed some light on this question, we reviewed some selected studies in an effort to identify what appear to be the main factors influencing FDI inflows into developing countries especially. These studies included UNCTAD (1993), UNCTC (1992), Bajo-Rubio and Sosvilla-Rivero (1994), Lucas (1993), and Haddad and Harrison (1993). Our reading of this literature suggested that macroeconomic factors appear to play a dominant role in influencing aggregate FDI inflows. It was especially striking in the studies we examined that FDI has not been shown to be responsive to the main microeconomic factor that one might have expected to influence capital flows: the return to capital. This may be because returns to capital do not in fact influence FDI, but there are alternative explanations as well. For example, FDI may respond so elastically to small variations in returns that the observed variations become too small to be picked up econometrically. Or, FDI may respond to variations in returns to capital separately by sector, so that measures of total FDI and average returns to capital hide the relationship. Finally, there was some evidence in the studies noted, although it was not overwhelming, that openness and trade barriers also affect aggregate FDI inflows.

As a general matter, the literature further suggested that incentives designed to encourage FDI inflows do not appear to matter very much, although once it is decided to engage in FDI, the presence of incentives may affect the magnitude and geographic location of the FDI.[18] As indicated earlier, Tunisia introduced a number of

[18] Effects may appear to be greater when FDI incentives are linked directly to exports, as in maquiladora-type export processing zones. These have been used extensively by East European countries in their arrangements with the EU, but is not clear that Tunisia is moving very far in that direction. By the same token, there is reason to believe that such arrangements have little spillover to the domestic economy.

investment incentives in 1994, hoping that this would result in an increase in inward FDI. While it is not possible to determine what effects these incentives will have, it may be interesting nevertheless to examine their potential impact within our CGE modeling framework, which we shall do below. But let us first consider some of the main features of Tunisia's Investment Code.

IV. Tunisia's 1994 Investment Code[19]

A new Investment Code was introduced in January 1994. It is global in character and covers all sectors except domestic trade and investments in mining, energy, and finance. Foreign investors are permitted 100% ownership, with some exceptions in industries that are not wholly exporting, and in agriculture where long-term leasing is permitted. Off-shore status can be granted to wholly exporting companies in the form of bonded factories or within a free trade zone. Common incentives are offered in all sectors, and there are additional incentives designed to promote exports, regional development, agricultural development, environmental protection, technology transfer and promotion, and development support activities and services (e.g., education, etc.). The incentives can be either fiscal in the form of tax reductions or waivers, or financial in the form of grants or subsidies.

The tax incentives offered are: 35% for all activities covered by the Investment Code; 50% for activities related to environmental protection and investments in development support activities and services; and 100% for wholly exporting activities, companies located in regional development areas, and agricultural development projects. All activities covered by the Code are eligible for suspension of the Value Added Tax (VAT) and consumption tax on locally manufactured capital goods and for reduction of tariffs to 10% and suspension of the VAT and consumption tax on imported equipment when no similar equipment is made locally. There are a variety of specific incentives for the priorities mentioned earlier for environmental protection, etc.

[19] Details on the 1994 Investment Code can be found in Ministry of International Cooperation and Foreign Investment (1994).

Additional tax incentives are available besides those mentioned above. They involve taking accelerated depreciation on capital goods and income tax exemptions for revenues derived from export activities. Companies with off-shore status have duty-free imports and can sell part of their production domestically subject to some restrictions. Partially exporting companies are allowed tax exemption and refunds of customs duties. There are special tax incentives for regional development projects, etc.

Besides the various incentives noted, foreign investors can employ foreign nationals up to 4% of their total employment, have certain personal tax advantages, are permitted free repatriation of profits, receive investment protection under treaty, are not subject to double taxation, are covered by foreign arbitration processes, are covered for non-commercial risks, and are given protection of industrial property rights.

This is evidently a broad and generous Code. The question then is how it will be implemented and whether it will lead to a significant increase in inward FDI. We have no way to determine how successful the Code may be in attracting FDI. But we can attempt to calculate, using our CGE model, how the common tax incentive of 35% might affect inward FDI and the consequences that this could have for the economy. We shall have more to say on this below.

Having set out the essential features of our CGE model and reviewed some considerations relating to the determinants of inward FDI and Tunisia's 1994 Investment Code, we turn now to a description of the model scenarios we have run and to our computational results.

V. Model Scenarios

It is possible to use our CGE model to analyze a variety of features of the Tunisia-EU FTA. These features can be analyzed individually as well as in combination. As discussed above, we have data on pre-Uruguay Round nominal tariff rates in agriculture, manufactures, and mining, as well as estimated *ad valorem* tariff equivalents of the agricultural NTBs. One question that immediately arises is what to assume about the reduction or elimination of the NTBs that may be negotiated as part of a FTA. Given that the NTBs are confined to the agricultural sector in our framework, we modeled the elimination of both bilateral tariffs and NTBs in agriculture.

A further issue is what to assume about services liberalization. Since it remains to be seen whether the FTA will involve the liberalization of both goods and services and since we do not have altogether reliable estimates of bilateral services barriers, we confined our attention to goods liberalization.

One other issue we should mention concerns whether or not to assume that labor and capital are mobile between sectors. It is common in the international trade literature for some purposes to treat labor as perfectly mobile and capital as completely immobile, that is, sector specific. This may capture some of the short- and medium-run effects of trade liberalization as compared to the long run when all factors of production are mobile. In what follows, we will implement scenarios of both types since this will help especially in determining how inward FDI may respond to the FTA.

In light of the foregoing considerations, we constructed the following five model scenarios:

Scenario A. Free Trade with Sectorally Specific Capital: Trade Only

A Free Trade Agreement (FTA), involving bilateral removal of tariffs and NTBs on goods only, between Tunisia and the 12-member EU, assuming perfect labor mobility and sector-specific capital.

Scenario B. Free Trade with Sectorally Mobile Capital: Trade Only

Same as A but with sectorally mobile capital.

Scenario C. Free Trade with Sectorally Mobile Capital: Trade and FDI

Same as B but including also a flow of capital into Tunisia equal to 10% of the Tunisian capital stock, taken proportionally from the capital stocks of the 12-member EU nations.

Scenario D. Free Trade with Sectorally Specific Capital: Trade and FDI

Same as A but also with an increase in the sectoral capital stocks of each sector in Tunisia that recorded a positive change in the nominal return to capital, r, in Scenario A. The elasticity of foreign direct investment with respect to this return to capital is assumed to be 5.0. Thus,

$$\text{FDI}(j) = \max\,\{5\Delta r(j)/r(j),\ 0\},$$

where FDI(j) is foreign direct investment into sector j as a fraction of sector j's (specific) capital stock.

Scenario E. Free Trade with Sectorally Specific Capital and Capital Tax: Trade and FDI

Same as D, but incorporating the Tunisian Investment Code as follows:

$$\text{FDI}(j) = \max\,\{5\alpha(j)\Delta r(j)/r(j),\ 0\},$$

where $\alpha(j)$ incorporates features of the Investment Code as follows:

i) To reflect excluded industries (page 1 of Code):

$$\alpha(j) = 0, \quad j = \text{ISIC } 2, 4, 6, 8$$

since the Code excludes the domestic trade, mining, energy, and finance sectors.

ii) To reflect tax exemptions on page 3 of Code for all other sectors:

$$\alpha(j) = \gamma(j)(1 + \tau) + (1 - \gamma(j))\,(1 + 0.35\tau),$$
$$j \neq \text{ISIC } 2, 4, 6, 8$$

where $\gamma(j)$ is the export share of production and τ is the tax rate for Tunisian capital income, which we have taken to be 35%.

The final scenario, Scenario E, is our attempt to incorporate features of the Tunisian Investment Code. To do this we augment the incentive to invest in each sector $(\Delta r(j)/r(j))$ by a factor $\alpha(j)$ representing the tax incentive. The latter appears in the last equation as the 0.35 multiplying the tax rate τ. Coincidentally, this tax incentive of 0.35 happens to be equal to the value of the tax rate τ, which is also 35%. The above formulation also includes adjustments to reflect the exclusion of certain industries from the Investment Code and the fact that wholly exporting firms get a tax break of 100%.

There is much more to the Investment Code than this, of course, but it appears to us that most other features of the Code either are likely to be quantitatively insignificant (e.g., provisions that apply only to capital goods manufactured locally), or are related to activities that we are unable to isolate in our model (e.g., environmental protection, regional development areas).

VI. Computational Results: Aggregate Effects

An overview of results on trade, terms of trade, welfare, and factor payments for each of the foregoing scenarios is reported in Table 3. Of considerable interest in evaluating the scenarios is the impact on economic welfare, that is, the "equivalent variation" measure of the change in real gross domestic product (GDP).

Scenario A

We begin with Scenario A, in which Tunisia becomes part of a free trade area (FTA) with the European Union. Since, as a consequence of the 1976 cooperation agreement between Tunisia and the European Communities (EC), EU trade restrictions against imports from Tunisia are already zero in all sectors except for agriculture and textiles/clothing, the Tunisian-EU FTA practically amounts to a unilateral removal of tariffs by Tunisia. However, because tariffs are eliminated only *vis-à-vis* the EU, these tariff reductions are discriminatory and need not necessarily lead to welfare improvement.

Table 3. Summary results of Tunisia-EU free trade: Changes in country imports, exports, terms of trade, welfare and return to labor and capital.

Country	Imports*	Exports*	Terms of Trade Percent Change	Equivalent Variation		Percent Change Real Wage	Real Return to Capital
				Percent of GDP	Millions $		
	(2)	(3)	(4)	(5)	(6)	(7)	(8)
A. Free Trade with Sector Specific Capital: Trade Only							
Tunisia	483.2	735.1	−5.0	−0.2	−26.8	2.5	6.6
Mediterranean EU	46.7	47.2	0.0	0.0	136.4	0.0	0.0
France-Italy	589.6	401.9	0.0	0.1	1542.0	0.0	0.0
Other EU	351.9	208.0	0.0	0.0	741.8	0.0	0.0
Other Europe	−31.4	−18.6	0.0	0.0	13.7	0.0	0.0
NAFTA	−28.2	2.1	0.0	0.0	54.3	0.0	0.0
Asia-Pacific	47.8	14.5	0.0	0.0	136.0	0.0	0.0
South America	0.0	−4.0	0.0	0.0	−0.6	0.0	0.0
B. Free Trade with Sectorally Mobile Capital: Trade Only							
Tunisia	911.6	1158.6	−4.9	3.3	430.3	−1.7	6.5
Mediterranean EU	52.8	58.7	0.0	0.0	172.3	0.0	−0.1
France-Italy	829.1	623.9	0.0	0.1	2186.3	0.0	−0.1
Other EU	481.3	317.8	0.0	0.0	1045.5	0.0	0.0
Other Europe	−8.5	−0.2	0.0	0.0	51.9	0.0	0.0
NAFTA	−15.5	13.9	0.0	0.0	−36.5	0.0	0.0
Asia-Pacific	71.4	26.1	0.0	0.0	147.6	0.0	0.0
South America	7.7	−1.7	0.0	0.0	17.0	0.0	0.0

(*Continued*)

Table 3. (*Continued*)

Country	Imports*	Exports*	Terms of Trade Percent Change	Equivalent Variation		Percent Change Real Wage	Real Return to Capital
				Percent of GDP	Millions $		
	(2)	(3)	(4)	(5)	(6)	(7)	(8)
C. Free Trade with Sectorally Mobile Capital: Trade & FDI							
Tunisia	533.3	1734.6	–7.0	–0.1	–15.0	4.6	7.1
Mediterranean EU	82.8	–9.4	0.0	0.0	284.3	0.0	–0.1
France-Italy	1037.0	493.8	0.1	0.2	3972.4	0.0	–0.1
Other EU	657.9	–1.9	0.0	0.1	1662.4	0.0	–0.1
Other Europe	–17.2	–11.0	0.0	0.0	189.2	0.0	0.0
NAFTA	–34.5	–3.6	0.0	0.0	115.8	0.0	0.0
Asia-Pacific	68.3	24.8	0.0	0.0	336.5	0.0	0.0
South America	4.5	–2.9	0.0	0.0	43.5	0.0	0.0
D. Free Trade with Sector Specific Capital: Trade & FDI							
Tunisia	501.5	917.7	–5.1	0.9	122.4	3.5	6.6
Mediterranean EU	54.4	41.0	0.0	0.0	123.8	0.0	0.0
France-Italy	659.9	424.5	0.0	0.1	1597.8	0.0	0.0
Other EU	394.9	136.0	0.0	0.0	642.6	0.0	0.0
Other Europe	–34.2	–23.7	0.0	0.0	21.4	0.0	0.0
NAFTA	–34.5	–1.9	0.0	0.0	55.6	0.0	0.0
Asia-Pacific	45.2	11.0	0.0	0.0	144.3	0.0	0.0
South America	1.0	–3.8	0.0	0.0	4.1	0.0	0.0

(*Continued*)

Table 3. (*Continued*)

Country	Imports*	Exports*	Terms of Trade Percent Change	Equivalent Variation		Percent Change Real Wage	Real Return to Capital
				Percent of GDP	Millions $		
	(2)	(3)	(4)	(5)	(6)	(7)	(8)
E. Free Trade with Sector Specific Capital and Capital Tax: Trade & FDI							
Tunisia	498.0	931.4	–5.1	1.0	130.8	3.6	6.6
Mediterranean EU	55.1	39.4	0.0	0.0	124.1	0.0	0.0
France-Italy	664.8	423.5	0.0	0.1	1600.9	0.0	0.0
Other EU	398.0	130.9	0.0	0.0	646.6	0.0	0.0
Other Europe	–34.7	–24.3	0.0	0.0	22.5	0.0	0.0
NAFTA	–34.7	–2.3	0.0	0.0	60.1	0.0	0.0
Asia-Pacific	44.3	10.5	0.0	0.0	143.9	0.0	0.0
South America	0.9	–3.8	0.0	0.0	4.5	0.0	0.0

*Exports and imports in millions of U.S. dollars, valued in U.S. dollar base period prices.

Indeed, in Scenario A, in which we assume that capital is unable to move among sectors, our results in Table 3 indicate that economic welfare in Tunisia declines by 0.2% of GDP due to this change.[20] This result is best understood in terms of the traditional concept of trade diversion. When Tunisia eliminates its relatively high tariffs against all EU-members but keeps its tariffs in place against other ("third") countries, a first effect is to cause substitution away from the imports from third countries. The reason is that imports from the EU now appear cheaper to buyers within Tunisia, who no longer have to pay the tariff. But these imports are not cheaper to the country as a whole, since, if they had been cheaper, they would have been purchased before when all imports faced the same tariffs. Therefore, the country as a whole loses from this substitution.

The way that this loss manifests itself within Tunisia is through the loss of tariff revenue. Initially, buyers were paying high prices for imports from the third countries, but a part of these high prices was staying within the country in the form of tariff revenues collected by the government. This tariff revenue was available to be used by the government and therefore contributed to economic welfare. In our model, government revenues are formally assumed to be redistributed to consumers in some non-distorting way, so that consumer incomes include both earned factor incomes plus this transfer from the government, both of which are spent on goods and services. When tariffs against the EU fall, consumers pay less for the imports that they now buy from the EU instead of from third countries, but they lose even more as the transfer of tariff revenue is reduced as well.

Now trade diversion is only one of two effects of a discriminatory tariff reduction such as this. To the extent that trade is also created, welfare can rise. Trade creation occurs, in this case, when buyers substitute imports from the EU for purchases of domestically produced goods. Since these two sources both now face zero tariffs, imports

---

[20] This is in contrast to the positive welfare effect cited by Page and Underwood (1995) in a World Bank study of a Tunisian-EU FTA. That study reported an increase in welfare (equivalent variation) of 1.7% due to trade liberalization alone, rising to 4.7% when effects of trade efficiency were included.

from the EU must be cheaper than their domestic alternatives in order to be bought, and the country therefore gains from switching to the more efficient source. Formally, there is no loss of tariff revenue to offset the gain experienced by the purchasers.

A limited amount of trade creation can occur to the extent that imports overall are made cheaper by the tariff reduction relative to domestic goods. But a greater scope for trade creation exists if the country is also able to increase exports, for then the revenues from increased exports can be spent on imports. Tariff reductions abroad (here only in agriculture), and a more general reallocation of factors toward export sectors, can therefore contribute to trade creation and cause the overall welfare effect of an FTA to become positive. In Scenario A, however, the sector-specificity of capital limits this reallocation, and it is perhaps not surprising that overall welfare falls in this short-to-medium run setting.

It is also evident in Table 3 that Tunisia's terms of trade — the relative price of its exports compared to its imports, or what it gets in return for its exports — fall by even more than welfare in Scenario A, and that is the case in all of the subsequent scenarios as well. This is a normal effect of a discriminatory and largely unilateral tariff reduction, especially for a country with relatively high tariffs like Tunisia. Tunisia is of course quite a small country, and it is customary to argue that small countries are unable to influence their terms of trade.[21] But this is not the case for a discriminatory tariff reduction. To the extent that trade diversion occurs as discussed above, Tunisia substitutes toward higher cost imports, and this is a direct worsening of its terms of trade. In other words, while it is largely true that a small country cannot influence world prices, it can nonetheless influence its

[21] This is not entirely the case in our model, however, even for a nondiscriminatory liberalization, because of product differentiation. In the agricultural sector, where we assume perfect competition, the Armington assumption of product differentiation by country of origin gives even small countries some leverage over their terms of trade. In other sectors, where product differentiation is at the level of the firm, that leverage is considerably reduced but it still exists to some extent. The effects on the terms of trade that appear in our scenarios, however, are better understood as a byproduct of trade diversion.

terms of trade by changing the composition of its import bundle. Thus Tunisia's terms of trade worsen, not because the prices of its exports fall or of its imports rise, but because it switches to higher priced imports from the EU. That is, it gets less in return for its exports because it switches to more costly imports. In quantitative terms, the terms of trade worsen by considerably more than overall welfare, however, because the country also benefits from the efficiency improvements that arise from trade creation.

The results in Scenario A also indicate that the real wage and the real return to capital both rise, by 2.5% and 6.6% respectively. This may at first appear to be inconsistent with the overall decline in welfare. However, recalling our discussion above that economic welfare derives both from earned incomes and from redistributed tariff revenue, this should not be so surprising. Furthermore, these changes in real factor returns, defined as the amount of goods that the wage and rent will buy, also include the effects of price changes and therefore contrast with the changes in nominal (money) factor returns which in this case, though not reported in Table 3, are both negative. By substantially reducing tariffs, Tunisia lowers the nominal domestic prices of both imports and import-competing goods, and this feeds through the economy to reduce other goods prices and factor prices as well. However, the falling prices of imports and other goods also mean that these lower nominal factor prices can be used to buy an increased amount of goods, and real factor prices therefore can rise.

As already noted, the return to capital rises in Scenario A relative to the wage. Evidently, according to these results, the structure of tariffs in Tunisia has been such as to protect labor more than capital, and the liberalization therefore causes a relative shift in favor of capital. However, both factors lose in nominal terms, which means in terms of the numeraire of world prices that are here essentially unchanged, capital simply losing less than labor. The reason is that domestic prices of goods and factors have been kept artificially high by the tariffs relative to world prices, and the liberalization therefore reduces them across the board. This will be important below when we look at capital flows.

Since Tunisia is small compared to its major trading partners, especially the EU member countries, the effects of the FTA with the EU would not be expected to have a significant impact on the EU countries. This is evident in Table 3 where it can be seen that EU total imports and exports rise by less than $1 billion and that there are negligible changes in the terms of trade, welfare as a percent of GDP, and real returns to labor and capital. Nonetheless, in terms of absolute changes in economic welfare, the gain for the EU-12 member countries amounts to $2.4 billion compared to the $26.8 million reduction in Tunisian welfare. France/Italy combined gain $1.5 billion. As noted, this asymmetry results from the fact that Tunisia is in effect cutting its tariffs unilaterally against the EU, given that Tunisia already has tariff-free access to the EU for most of its exports.

Scenario B

Scenario B is distinguished from Scenario A insofar as capital is no longer assumed to be sector-specific but is permitted instead to move among sectors. We still, however, keep capital internationally immobile. Capital therefore exits from those sectors where its return has fallen the most and migrates to sectors where the relative return, inside Tunisia, has increased. The movement of capital permits labor also to move among sectors by larger amounts, as we will note below in our discussion of sectoral effects.

The main effect of capital mobility is to cause greater changes in sectoral output, and therefore trade. This can be seen by comparing the export and import columns of Scenarios A and B in Table 3. Also, because trade creation is enhanced, the overall welfare effect of the FTA in Scenario B is now positive. Finally, the reallocation of capital in favor of the less protected capital-intensive sectors causes the ratio of the return to capital relative to labor to increase and actually leads to a fall in the real wage. That is, as capital migrates from previously protected labor-intensive sectors to capital-intensive sectors, labor is left with less capital to work with and its marginal product and real wage are reduced. This is apparently a reflection of the Stolper–Samuelson effect, even though in our model we have found on other occasions that the Stolper–Samuelson Theorem does not necessarily hold, due to the effects of scale and variety.[22]

The asymmetry of the effects of the FTA is further evident here. While Tunisian welfare rises in absolute terms by $430.3 million, the absolute increase in welfare for the 12-member EU together amounts to $3.4 billion. These effects are larger than in Scenario A because of the more complete adjustments represented with full mobility of both labor and capital.

Scenario C

In Scenario C we introduce an arbitrary international capital movement into the model, equal to 10% of the Tunisian capital stock.[23] The assumption is that it flows into Tunisia from the EU countries, in proportion to their own capital stocks.

Our original intent was to select the capital flow as approximating that which would undo the effect of the FTA on the nominal return to capital in Tunisia. The rationale for choosing this was two-fold. First, it is the relative nominal return in Tunisia compared to the rest of the world that would motivate capital to move; and second, we expected the FTA to raise the return to capital in Tunisia and to leave it essentially unchanged elsewhere. The latter expectation was borne out in the results of our model, as already noted in Scenarios A and B, but the former expectation was not. Instead, the removal of tariffs in Tunisia *vis-à-vis* the EU caused a small reduction, not an increase, in the nominal return to capital in Tunisia in those scenarios. Thus, if we were to rely on market signals to determine capital flows, our model would suggest that capital would flow out of Tunisia, rather than in.

---

[22] See Brown *et al.* (1993).

[23] This assumed capital inflow was $2,144 million in 1990 value. If, say, this was spread over a period of 10 years, it would amount to $214 million annually. This can be compared to the actual inflow of FDI in 1991, which according to GATT (1994, p. 52), was $133 million. Some 90% of this actual inflow went into energy-related sectors.

Of course, the model does not include certain considerations that might be expected to overcome these market signals and to draw capital into Tunisia in spite of them. Most frequently mentioned is the hope that an FTA between a small developing country and a larger, more advanced country or group of countries will lock into place certain market reforms in the developing country that accompany or precede liberalization. This in turn may reduce the risk that is associated with investment in the country and thus attract capital.[24] Our model does not include such effects, and therefore we thought it appropriate simply to impose an exogenous capital flow into Tunisia as a crude way of representing them. This is what is done in Scenario C. We have modeled the earnings on imported capital as being retained and reinvested in Tunisia, so that there is no effect on the balance of payments after the inflow itself is completed.

The results for Scenario C in Table 3 show a further worsening of the terms of trade, an increase in the expansion of exports and a decrease in the expansion of imports (needed to keep the trade balance unchanged when the prices of imports rise relative to exports), a rise (relative to Scenario B) in the wage-rental ratio, and a decline in overall welfare. All of these effects except the last are what one would expect from any capital inflow. The surprise may be the loss of welfare, which occurs because capital is flowing here in a direction opposite to market signals. That is, as noted above, the FTA drives the nominal return to capital in Tunisia down because it lowers prices in most sectors. Without evidence to the contrary, the model assumes that nominal returns on capital (adjusted for risk) were initially the same in Tunisia as elsewhere. Therefore, the natural market response to the FTA would have been for capital to flow out of Tunisia to other countries where it would be more productive. By instead forcing capital to flow into Tunisia in Scenario C, we are moving capital to a location where its productivity has been reduced by the FTA, and it is

[24] This argument was prominent in the discussions leading up to the NAFTA. Events starting in December 1994 unfortunately suggest that it may have been overly optimistic, at least for Mexico, and that perception may now stop it from working in other countries whether or not it would be justified.

now therefore below the return that is paid on it. The country is therefore paying more for this capital than it receives in increased output. This reduces welfare of the country as a whole.

Of course, if the risk premium story above were valid, so that a lower nominal return could be paid to foreign capital, then this result for welfare would be altered. The reduction in the risk premium could be much greater than any reduction in the marginal product of capital due to the FTA, and in that case the same capital flow would be welfare increasing. But we have no way of knowing how the risk premium might change, and therefore we are unable to quantify this possibility.

We again see the asymmetry *vis-à-vis* the EU in this Scenario. Tunisia has a welfare decline of $15.0 million, while the 12-member EU gains $5.9 billion in welfare. Compared to Scenario B, the capital flow from the EU to Tunisia has increased welfare somewhat in the EU. This is because Tunisia is assumed to pay a market return on the capital even though its productivity within Tunisia is less than that. The real return to capital in all three EU groupings falls by 0.1%.

Scenario D

We were reluctant to give up entirely on market-driven capital flows, however, and we therefore turned in Scenario D to an alternative formulation with sector-specific capital. With capital unable to move among sectors, perhaps because it has already been installed and is not easily converted to other uses, returns to capital rise in some sectors and fall in others. This was already mentioned in Scenario A. Our assumption in Scenario D is that capital flows into the sectors where the return has risen, but does not flow out of the sectors where returns have fallen.

Unfortunately we do not have any acceptable way to predict how much capital will respond to such signals. What we did therefore was simply to assume an arbitrary elasticity of capital with respect to its return, equal to 5.0. That is, an increase in the nominal return to capital in a sector is assumed to cause a capital flow into Tunisia that is five times as large relative to the Tunisian sectoral capital stock.

We have no way to establish whether this elasticity of 5.0 is plausible, and we therefore offer these results primarily for illustrative purposes.

What is shown in Table 3 is that the sector-specific capital flows cause largely very similar results to those of Scenario C, although the effects in this case are quite a bit smaller because the capital flow itself is smaller. Responding only to the sectors where the return to capital has increased, even with an elasticity of five, causes a capital flow of only 1.9% of the Tunisian capital stock, compared to the 10% in Scenario C.

The one effect that is noticeably different, however, is on economic welfare. Here, the small decline in welfare that we saw in Scenario A without the capital flow is turned into an also small but positive change in welfare by the sector-specific flow. The reason is simply that capital, in contrast to Scenario C, is now flowing only into sectors where it does earn a high enough return to pay for itself, and it thus creates a surplus for the economy.

Scenario E

Our final Scenario is intended to take account of the major features of the Tunisian Investment Code. The endogenous capital flows introduced in Scenario D are here expanded or contracted in response to various constraints and/or subsidies that are included in the Code. It is evident in Table 3 that the results differ hardly at all from those of Scenario D, although the fact that there is a slight increase in the welfare improvement from the FTA in the presence of the Code suggests that its features may have a small positive benefit. Apparently the Code is to some extent succeeding in directing capital to sectors where it can be most productive.

VII. Computational Results: Sectoral Effects

Sectoral results for Scenarios A, B, and D are given for Tunisia in Tables 4–6. The sectoral results for Scenarios C and E are available from the authors on request. The percent changes in total exports and imports are shown in columns (2) and (3) of each table. The percent

Table 4. Scenario A: Trade only with sectorally specific capital — sectoral effects on Tunisia of Tunisia-EU free trade (percent change unless otherwise noted).

Sector	Exports	Imports	Bilateral Imports							Output	No. Firms	Employment		Return to Capital
			MEU	FR-IT	OEU	OEUR	NAFTA	APAC	SAM			Percent	1000's	
	(2)	(3)	(4)	(5)	(6)	(7)	(8)	(9)	(10)	(11)	(12)	(13)	(14)	(15)
1 Agriculture	43.5	5.4	51.9	45.7	52.4	−20.3	−20.3	−20.3	−20.3	0.0	0.0	−0.9	−4.8	1.5
310 Food	18.2	17.4	22.0	53.0	50.1	−21.5	−21.5	−21.5	−21.5	−1.4	−1.3	−4.6	−1.6	0.0
321 Textiles	53.7	20.2	26.9	25.2	26.6	−44.6	−44.6	−44.6	−44.6	6.3	−4.7	−5.4	−4.2	−2.8
322 Clothing	14.8	66.5	66.0	67.9	67.1	−29.6	−29.5	−29.5	−29.5	3.7	3.6	6.5	1.3	7.7
323 Leather Products	58.3	23.7	21.0	28.5	24.0	−36.9	−36.9	−36.9	−36.9	18.2	2.4	9.4	0.2	9.7
324 Footwear	45.2	54.6	56.8	58.2	65.2	−32.4	−32.4	−32.4	−32.4	13.7	0.6	11.0	1.3	9.7
331 Wood Products	13.8	−6.7	62.5	49.2	70.0	−15.5	−15.4	−15.5	−15.5	12.5	1.9	7.9	0.5	11.4
332 Furniture, Fixtures	4.9	34.8	65.5	59.6	57.5	−30.9	−30.9	−30.9	−30.9	−7.6	−5.7	−12.8	−0.2	−8.3
341 Paper Products	17.6	19.9	61.4	51.0	51.1	−32.0	−32.0	−32.0	−32.0	−6.1	−2.0	−16.0	−0.7	−7.1
342 Printing, Publishing	14.4	13.3	18.5	31.5	35.7	−27.7	−27.7	−27.7	−27.7	−2.2	−0.9	−6.0	−0.3	−4.5
35A Chemicals	8.0	18.2	27.3	31.4	34.3	−18.3	−18.3	−18.3	−18.3	−3.5	−1.8	−4.8	−1.2	−1.6
35B Petroleum Products	8.8	8.4	10.4	10.2	38.4	−16.6	−16.6	−16.6	−16.7	1.7	−0.6	2.1	0.0	4.5
355 Rubber Products	7.6	30.1	42.2	36.3	42.2	−32.9	−32.9	−32.9	−32.9	−15.2	−13.5	−20.2	−1.0	−9.6
36A Nonmetal Min. Prod.	1.2	56.4	76.9	72.0	79.6	−18.6	−18.6	−18.6	−18.6	−6.8	−5.9	−8.0	−0.6	−3.6
362 Glass Products	6.0	22.2	42.6	20.0	48.4	−19.0	−19.0	−19.0	−19.0	−0.4	−0.8	−1.9	−0.6	1.1

(Continued)

Table 4. (*Continued*)

Sector	Exports	Imports	Bilateral Imports							Output	No. Firms	Employment		Return to Capital
			MEU	FR-IT	OEU	OEUR	NAFTA	APAC	SAM			Percent	1000's	
	(2)	(3)	(4)	(5)	(6)	(7)	(8)	(9)	(10)	(11)	(12)	(13)	(14)	(15)
371 Iron, Steel	6.9	5.8	33.8	23.2	20.1	−26.8	−26.8	−26.8	−26.8	−5.1	−6.5	−8.5	−0.3	−3.4
372 Nonferrous Metals	13.9	4.0	10.5	15.3	15.2	−31.0	−31.0	−31.0	−31.0	4.7	0.6	5.0	0.0	6.0
381 Metal Products	15.7	29.7	44.7	43.6	43.9	−31.1	−31.1	−31.1	−31.1	−5.2	−3.1	−9.3	−0.6	−6.8
382 Nonelec. Machinery	14.6	5.5	12.8	15.8	10.3	−26.7	−26.7	−26.7	−26.7	−2.2	−2.9	−5.4	−1.0	−4.9
383 Electrical Machinery	38.4	19.4	29.3	33.9	19.7	−31.2	−31.2	−31.2	−31.2	4.0	−1.3	−1.0	−0.4	0.7
384 Transport Equipment	18.0	12.8	15.7	19.7	17.2	−35.4	−35.4	−35.4	−35.4	−6.1	−6.8	−8.5	−0.5	−18.9
38A Misc. Mfrs.	33.5	11.9	18.4	22.1	21.0	−36.6	−36.5	−36.5	−36.5	13.5	2.0	11.6	0.6	11.0
2 Mining, Quarrying	21.0	−5.1	21.4	32.2	85.0	−20.1	−20.0	−20.1	−20.0	13.5	12.7	20.0	0.3	14.4
4 Utilities	22.1	−16.6	−16.8	−16.8	−16.8	−16.7	−16.7	−16.7	−16.8	1.8	0.3	2.4	0.3	3.5
5 Construction	22.9	−22.7	−22.7	−22.7	−22.7	−22.7	−22.7	−22.7	−22.7	−0.5	−2.8	−4.1	−2.6	−1.0
6 Wholesale Trade	3.6	−7.5	−7.5	−7.6	−7.5	−7.5	−7.5	−7.5	−7.5	1.3	0.4	14.1	37.8	8.2
7 Transportation	12.6	−10.5	−10.6	−10.6	−10.6	−10.5	−10.5	−10.5	−10.5	5.5	3.2	12.1	6.4	10.3
8 Financial Services	11.8	−11.5	−11.5	−11.5	−11.5	−11.5	−11.5	−11.5	−11.4	2.8	1.9	7.5	1.2	6.7
9 Personal Services	21.3	−19.6	−19.6	−19.6	−19.6	−19.5	−19.5	−19.5	−19.5	−2.0	−2.5	−3.5	−25.3	−0.5
Total	16.5	11.5	19.7	22.2	26.4	−24.9	−22.8	−29.6	−20.9	0.7	−1.8	0.0	0.0	3.5

Table 5. Scenario B: Trade only with sectorally mobile capital — sectoral effects on Tunisia of Tunisia-EU free trade (percent change unless otherwise noted).

Sector	Exports	Imports	Bilateral Imports							Output	No. Firms	Employment		Allocation of Capital
			MEU	FR-IT	OEU	OEUR	NAFTA	APAC	SAM			Percent	1000's	
	(2)	(3)	(4)	(5)	(6)	(7)	(8)	(9)	(10)	(11)	(12)	(13)	(14)	(15)
1 Agriculture	25.1	18.6	71.0	64.0	71.5	−10.3	−10.3	−10.3	−10.3	−4.1	0.0	1.8	9.7	−4.4
310 Food	5.3	34.1	39.6	75.0	71.8	−10.1	−10.1	−10.1	−10.1	−3.3	−3.8	6.6	2.3	−7.4
321 Textiles	−61.9	64.3	73.7	72.4	74.9	−24.4	−24.0	−24.1	−24.0	−85.9	−85.7	−85.1	−65.4	−86.2
322 Clothing	49.3	38.1	37.2	39.0	38.8	−41.7	−41.5	−41.5	−41.5	27.9	27.8	33.2	6.4	21.1
323 Leather Products	−3.3	39.8	36.8	45.4	40.6	−28.7	−28.6	−28.6	−28.6	−22.5	−27.0	−21.8	−0.6	−29.2
324 Footwear	31.7	69.3	71.5	73.1	81.0	−26.0	−26.0	−26.0	−26.0	9.1	3.5	13.3	1.6	1.0
331 Wood Products	10.0	−4.7	65.4	51.8	73.1	−14.0	−13.9	−13.9	−14.0	6.8	3.4	8.8	0.6	1.6
332 Furniture, Fixtures	0.1	57.7	94.1	87.1	84.7	−19.0	−19.0	−18.9	−19.0	−13.8	−14.7	−10.2	−0.2	−18.0
341 Paper Products	−6.8	50.2	104.4	91.2	91.3	−13.9	−13.9	−13.9	−13.9	−22.9	−25.0	−15.9	−0.7	−26.2
342 Printing, Publishing	1.5	39.4	46.4	62.4	67.6	−10.7	−10.7	−10.7	−10.7	−7.2	−8.9	−3.5	−0.2	−9.6
35A Chemicals	2.8	25.4	35.2	39.5	42.5	−13.3	−13.3	−13.3	−13.3	−7.6	−7.5	−3.4	−0.9	−11.5
35B Petroleum Products	6.2	15.6	17.9	17.7	47.5	−11.0	−11.0	−11.0	−11.1	2.1	−1.7	7.5	0.1	−0.8
355 Rubber Products	−19.9	53.1	67.5	61.2	67.1	−21.2	−21.1	−21.1	−21.1	−30.4	−28.8	−27.4	−1.4	−36.4
36A Nonmetal Min. Prod.	1.0	59.2	80.1	75.1	82.8	−17.1	−17.1	−17.1	−17.2	−7.2	−6.5	−4.1	−0.3	−13.2
362 Glass Products	5.2	28.6	50.0	26.2	56.1	−14.8	−14.8	−14.8	−14.8	1.9	−0.2	6.3	2.1	−4.0

(*Continued*)

Table 5. (*Continued*)

Sector	Exports	Imports	Bilateral Imports							Output	No. Firms	Employment		Allocation of Capital
			MEU	FR-IT	OEU	OEUR	NAFTA	APAC	SAM			Percent	1000's	
	(2)	(3)	(4)	(5)	(6)	(7)	(8)	(9)	(10)	(11)	(12)	(13)	(14)	(15)
371 Iron, Steel	4.3	7.2	36.2	25.3	22.1	−25.6	−25.6	−25.6	−25.6	−9.6	−11.5	−7.1	−0.2	−16.9
372 Nonferrous Metals	11.8	0.1	6.6	11.1	11.0	−33.5	−33.5	−33.5	−33.5	1.4	−1.9	5.9	0.0	−5.0
381 Metal Products	6.7	46.3	63.8	62.4	62.7	−22.0	−22.0	−22.0	−22.1	−8.4	−13.4	−8.6	−0.6	−15.3
382 Nonelec. Machinery	10.2	12.3	20.2	23.3	17.4	−21.9	−21.9	−21.9	−21.9	−3.7	−8.0	−5.2	−1.0	−10.2
383 Electrical Machinery	32.9	26.6	37.1	42.0	26.8	−27.1	−27.1	−27.1	−27.1	4.5	−2.8	0.9	0.4	−3.2
384 Transport Equipment	4.4	28.4	31.9	36.5	33.5	−26.3	−26.3	−26.3	−26.3	−14.9	−16.9	−15.3	−0.9	−17.6
38A Misc. Mfrs.	10.8	17.7	24.7	28.5	27.4	−33.2	−33.2	−33.2	−33.2	−4.7	−7.7	−0.9	0.0	−10.5
2 Mining, Quarrying	94.4	−27.4	−17.1	−10.5	26.2	−45.3	−45.4	−45.4	−45.4	63.1	63.2	69.8	1.2	50.0
4 Utilities	17.6	−14.0	−13.8	−13.9	−13.9	−13.8	−13.8	−13.8	−13.8	1.5	−0.7	13.1	1.6	−5.7
5 Construction	24.1	−20.9	−20.9	−20.9	−20.9	−20.8	−20.8	−20.8	−20.9	3.1	0.4	3.5	2.2	−5.3
6 Wholesale Trade	22.4	−17.2	−17.2	−17.2	−17.1	−17.1	−17.1	−17.1	−17.1	15.9	14.8	36.8	98.5	14.0
7 Transportation	34.4	−20.0	−20.2	−20.4	−20.3	−20.2	−20.2	−20.2	−20.2	17.9	16.5	26.1	13.7	12.2
8 Financial Services	11.9	−13.3	−13.3	−13.3	−13.3	−13.2	−13.2	−13.2	−13.2	1.3	0.8	10.5	1.7	−3.3
9 Personal Services	21.6	−17.1	−17.1	−17.2	−17.1	−17.1	−17.1	−17.1	−17.1	1.2	0.8	4.1	29.9	−4.6
Total	31.1	21.8	30.5	34.3	42.2	−20.6	−19.8	−23.7	−12.6	2.7	−20.1	0.0	0.0	1.4

Table 6. Scenario D: Trade & FDI with sectorally specific capital — sectoral effects on Tunisia of Tunisia-EU free trade (percent change unless otherwise noted).

Sector	Exports	Imports	Bilateral Imports							Output	No. Firms	Employment		Return to Capital
			MEU	FR-IT	OEU	OEUR	NAFTA	APAC	SAM			Percent	1000's	
	(2)	(3)	(4)	(5)	(6)	(7)	(8)	(9)	(10)	(11)	(12)	(13)	(14)	(15)
1 Agriculture	40.0	8.5	56.3	50.0	56.8	−18.0	−18.0	−18.0	−18.0	−0.1	0.0	−1.1	−6.1	2.1
310 Food	16.3	20.4	25.2	56.9	54.0	−19.5	−19.4	−19.4	−19.4	−1.1	−1.5	−5.0	−1.8	0.7
321 Textiles	53.0	22.1	29.0	27.3	28.6	−43.7	−43.7	−43.7	−43.7	7.1	−5.1	−5.7	−4.4	−2.2
322 Clothing	11.9	71.8	71.3	73.3	72.5	−27.3	−27.2	−27.2	−27.2	2.1	1.9	3.6	0.7	6.4
323 Leather Products	75.4	20.1	17.4	24.6	20.2	−38.8	−38.8	−38.8	−38.8	28.5	10.4	15.9	0.4	8.4
324 Footwear	60.0	44.5	46.5	47.8	54.3	−36.8	−36.8	−36.8	−36.8	20.1	7.2	12.4	1.5	5.6
331 Wood Products	23.9	−13.0	46.1	34.1	52.9	−24.0	−23.9	−24.0	−24.0	19.5	17.2	13.8	0.9	−1.0
332 Furniture, Fixtures	5.0	36.5	67.5	61.5	59.4	−30.0	−30.0	−30.0	−30.0	−6.2	−6.0	−12.6	−0.2	−7.3
341 Paper Products	17.6	21.2	63.3	52.7	52.8	−31.2	−31.2	−31.2	−31.2	−5.1	−2.2	−16.2	−0.7	−6.4
342 Printing, Publishing	13.6	15.7	21.0	34.3	38.6	−26.2	−26.2	−26.2	−26.2	−1.6	−1.2	−6.0	−0.3	−3.6
35A Chemicals	8.8	19.1	28.2	32.3	35.2	−17.8	−17.7	−17.7	−17.7	−1.3	−2.0	−3.5	−0.9	0.4
35B Petroleum Products	7.6	12.9	14.9	14.9	44.0	−13.2	−13.2	−13.2	−13.2	2.6	−0.9	2.5	0.0	5.9
355 Rubber Products	8.8	32.1	44.5	38.5	44.5	−31.8	−31.8	−31.8	−31.8	−13.4	−13.5	−18.3	−0.9	−7.6
36A Nonmetal Min. Prod.	1.2	58.0	78.6	73.7	81.3	−17.8	−17.8	−17.8	−17.8	−5.7	−6.1	−8.2	−0.6	−2.9
362 Glass Products	5.9	24.3	45.0	22.0	50.9	−17.6	−17.6	−17.6	−17.6	0.7	−0.8	−2.0	−0.6	2.0

(*Continued*)

Table 6. (*Continued*)

Sector	Exports	Imports	Bilateral Imports							Output	No. Firms	Employment		Return to Capital
			MEU	FR-IT	OEU	OEUR	NAFTA	APAC	SAM			Percent	1000's	
	(2)	(3)	(4)	(5)	(6)	(7)	(8)	(9)	(10)	(11)	(12)	(13)	(14)	(15)
371 Iron, Steel	6.7	7.6	36.1	25.4	22.2	−25.6	−25.5	−25.5	−25.5	−4.3	−7.0	−8.3	−0.3	−2.3
372 Nonferrous Metals	13.1	5.9	12.7	17.5	17.4	−29.7	−29.7	−29.7	−29.7	4.5	−0.2	3.5	0.0	5.9
381 Metal Products	15.6	31.5	46.7	45.6	45.9	−30.1	−30.1	−30.1	−30.1	−4.3	−3.2	−9.5	−0.6	−6.2
382 Nonelec. Machinery	14.5	7.0	14.4	17.4	11.8	−25.7	−25.7	−25.7	−25.7	−1.2	−3.1	−5.5	−1.1	−4.2
383 Electrical Machinery	37.9	21.2	31.2	35.9	21.5	−30.2	−30.2	−30.2	−30.2	4.9	−1.5	−1.2	−0.5	1.3
384 Transport Equipment	16.6	14.9	17.9	22.0	19.5	−34.1	−34.1	−34.1	−34.1	−6.5	−7.4	−9.1	−0.5	−19.8
38A Misc. Mfrs.	50.9	6.1	12.2	15.7	14.7	−39.9	−39.9	−39.9	−39.9	25.9	15.6	19.7	1.0	5.7
2 Mining, Quarrying	56.3	−15.2	1.6	10.8	54.9	−32.9	−32.9	−32.9	−32.9	39.4	38.8	40.1	0.7	4.9
4 Utilities	20.0	−14.3	−14.4	−14.5	−14.5	−14.4	−14.4	−14.4	−14.4	2.8	0.3	3.4	0.4	4.9
5 Construction	22.7	−21.6	−21.5	−21.6	−21.6	−21.5	−21.5	−21.5	−21.5	0.8	−2.8	−4.0	−2.5	0.0
6 Wholesale Trade	4.8	−7.1	−7.1	−7.2	−7.1	−7.1	−7.1	−7.1	−7.1	2.6	1.6	12.5	33.5	7.9
7 Transportation	27.9	−17.3	−17.5	−17.6	−17.5	−17.5	−17.5	−17.5	−17.5	14.4	12.8	16.0	8.4	5.7
8 Financial Services	8.8	−8.0	−8.0	−8.0	−8.0	−8.0	−8.0	−8.0	−8.0	2.9	1.6	7.3	1.2	7.6
9 Personal Services	18.6	−17.2	−17.2	−17.2	−17.2	−17.2	−17.2	−17.2	−17.2	−1.5	−2.6	−3.2	−22.8	0.7
Total	21.4	12.1	20.6	23.0	27.6	−25.5	−23.6	−29.3	−20.7	2.6	−0.6	0.0	0.0	3.4

changes in imports are decomposed bilaterally in columns (4) through (10). The percent changes in sectoral output and number of firms are listed in columns (11) and (12). The change in output per firm, and thus the extent to which economies of scale have been realized, can be determined by subtracting column (12) from (11). Columns (13) and (14) record the percentage and absolute changes in employment of labor, and column (15) records changes in the return to capital or in the employment of capital, depending on the individual scenario.[25] The sectoral results for the three EU regions and the other regions are in general very small and are therefore not reported here.

Scenario A

This Scenario refers to the bilateral removal of tariffs and NTBs between Tunisia and the EU, with labor assumed to be perfectly mobile, and with capital sector-specific and thus immobile. The results might best be interpreted as referring to the short-to-medium run effects of the Tunisia-EU FTA. As noted in column (2) of Table 4, there are sizable percentage increases in total Tunisian exports across all sectors. According to column (3), imports increase in all the goods sectors except wood products and mining and quarrying, and there are reductions in imports in all of the services sectors. These increases in goods imports reflect the unilateral reduction in Tunisian tariffs, whereas Tunisian services imports decline because the barriers in these sectors are assumed to remain intact. Since Tunisian goods imports will increase with the tariff removal, Tunisian exports will also increase in order for trade to balance.

---

[25] In interpreting the results for the changes in employment of labor and for the allocation of capital, we should note that the model was solved under the assumption that total employment of both labor and capital is constant, as indicated in the bottom line of the pertinent tables. However, because our solution algorithm solves a log-linear approximation to the true model, when the changes in logs of variables (which do average to zero) are converted to true percentages, they do not quite average to zero. This in turn means that the absolute changes in employment that are calculated from these percentages also fail to add exactly to zero.

There are substantial percentage increases in Tunisia's bilateral imports from the three EU groupings in all of the goods sectors and reductions in the services sectors, all of which reflect the relative price changes noted due to the assumed removal of Tunisian tariffs on goods imports. There are sizable negative percentage changes in Tunisia's imports from all of the non-EU regions noted in columns (7)–(10), which are indicative of the trade diversion that we have already mentioned in discussing the aggregate results reported in Table 3.[26]

As noted in column (11), there are increases in output in 14 of the 29 sectors, with the largest increases in leather products, footwear, wood products, miscellaneous manufactures, and mining and quarrying. The largest declines in output occur in rubber products, furniture and fixtures, paper products, and transport equipment. If we subtract the percent changes in number of firms in column (12) from the percent changes in output in column (11) to get changes in output per firm, there is evidence of positive scale effects in 20 sectors and negative scale effects in 8 sectors.

The changes in employment listed in columns (13) and (14) show expansion in 12 sectors and contraction in 17 sectors. The sectors with the largest absolute employment increases in number of workers are wholesale and retail trade and transportation services. The sectors with the largest absolute employment declines are agriculture, textiles, and community, social, and personal services.

Changes in the nominal return to capital are listed in column (15). There are positive changes in returns in 16 sectors, with the largest increases in mining and quarrying, wood products, miscellaneous manufactures, leather products and footwear, and clothing. The largest negative changes in returns to capital are in transportation

---

[26] Because Tunisia does not change tariffs on service imports or on goods imports from non-EU countries, all of these trade flows are affected symmetrically from within Tunisia. At first glance it appears that each of these levels of imports falls by the same percentage across trading partners. This is not quite the case, however, as a closer inspection of the results will reveal. Changes within the separate EU and other countries are very small here, but they sometimes lead to slight differences in these effects.

equipment, rubber products, furniture and fixtures, and paper products.[27]

Scenario B

In Scenario B, capital is now permitted to move among sectors rather than being sector-specific, that is, immobile among sectors as in Scenario A. The results of Scenario B might then be interpreted as the longer-run effects of the Tunisia-EU FTA when both labor and capital can move among sectors. Looking first at the percent changes in total exports in column (2) of Table 5 in comparison to Scenario A in Table 4, there are evidently now relatively larger increases especially in exports of clothing and mining and quarrying, which are two of Tunisia's most important export industries. There are four sectors that now show reductions in exports: textiles; leather products; paper products; and rubber products. As for total sectoral imports in column (3), the percentage increases are larger as compared to Scenario A since it is now possible for both capital and labor to be reallocated among sectors. Services sector imports also fall by sizable percentages in Scenario B. Bilateral imports from the three regions of the EU increase more in Scenario B than in Scenario A as indicated in columns (4)–(6). As for the regions outside the Tunisia-EU FTA, noted in columns (7)–(10), there appears to be somewhat less trade diversion when full mobility of capital and labor is permitted.

Allowing for full mobility of capital and labor has more pronounced effects on changes in sectoral output as compared to Scenario A. The sizable positive and negative changes in sectoral outputs suggest accordingly that there would be considerable intersectoral reallocation of capital and labor in response to the Tunisia-EU FTA, given

[27] As already mentioned, the sectoral effects on the EU regions are negligible in this scenario and those that follow. The effects on sectoral imports, output, employment, and the return to capital are mostly zeros, with the exception of some positive/negative effects of 0.1 or 0.2 for a few sectors. It was decided accordingly not to report these EU sectoral tables since they contain very little extra information beyond what is shown in the sectoral results for Tunisia.

Tunisia's relatively high manufacturing sector tariffs. This is evident from the results reported in columns (13)–(15).

Comparing columns (11) and (12), there are indications of positive scale economies in 23 sectors and negative scale economies in 5 sectors.

Scenario C

The results of this scenario, which are not reported here, suggest that the assumed infusion of FDI from the EU results in larger percentage expansions of exports and smaller percentage reductions as compared to Scenario B. Total imports show smaller percentage increases as compared to Scenario B, since there is a worsening in the terms of trade that limits the imports that can be financed with an unchanged balance of trade.[28]

The percentage changes in Tunisia's bilateral imports *vis-à-vis* the three EU regions are now also smaller as compared to Scenario B, which also reflects the change in terms of trade, and there is now more evidence of trade diversion with respect to the regions outside the EU. The percent changes in sectoral output tend to be larger with the assumed inflow of FDI, but this is not altogether uniform. The reallocation of labor and capital in this scenario is also substantial as was the case in Scenario B, even with the potential for proportional expansion in the sectoral capital stocks associated with an increased inflow of FDI.

Scenario D

This Scenario also considers an inflow of FDI but within the context of the sector-specific capital framework. That is, in Scenario A, we calculated the changes in the nominal returns to capital as the result of the removal of trade barriers in the Tunisia-EU FTA. Having identified sectors in which there was an increase in the nominal return to

[28] Recall that earnings on FDI are not repatriated, and therefore the trade balance remains unchanged.

capital (see the final column of Table 4), we then assumed that there would be an increase of FDI in these sectors only.[29] For this purpose, we assumed an elasticity of 5.0 for FDI inflows with respect to the return to capital.

If we compare the percentage changes in total sectoral exports and imports in columns (2) and (3) of Table 6 with those in Table 4, the results are not greatly different especially because the calculated FDI inflows turn out to be not substantial. That is, these FDI inflows constitute 1.9% of Tunisia's base-level total capital stock. Of course, some of the individual sectors are affected differentially because the FDI inflows are directed only at the sectors that show increases in the nominal return to capital. It is also difficult to see many important changes in the bilateral import results between Scenarios A and D.

While the investment inflows that occur in this scenario have only relatively small effects on the various magnitudes calculated by the model, it is of some interest to note which sectors of the Tunisian economy attract these inflows. This can be read from column (15) of Table 6, where increases in returns to capital correspond to sectors into which FDI is flowing. This includes more than half of the sectors, with the largest increases in returns to capital (and therefore the largest FDI inflows under our assumptions) in manufacturing sectors occurring in leather products, clothing, petroleum products, nonferrous metals, miscellaneous manufactures, and footwear. There are also increases in returns to capital and hence capital inflows into all of the services sectors, including especially wholesale trade, transportation, and financial services, some of which includes components of tourism.

Scenario E

This scenario is the same as Scenario D, but it incorporates some features of Tunisia's 1994 Investment Code. The results, which are not reported here, indicate that the inflow of FDI in this case is only slightly larger than in Scenario D, amounting to an increase of 2.1%

---

[29] Actually, the capital flows are based upon endogenous changes in returns to capital, which do not always increase in the same sectors as Scenario A.

in the base level of Tunisia's total capital stock. The detailed sectoral results are very close to the Scenario D results in Table 6.

Policies for Adjustment

The foregoing disaggregated results all indicate the need for substantial intersectoral adjustment by the Tunisian economy in response to implementation of the Tunisia-EU FTA. The question then arises what policies, if any, should be used to facilitate that adjustment. Since this is inherently a dynamic issue, our model does not say anything about it directly. However, the world has considerable experience in adjusting to the dislocations that are occasioned by trade liberalization, and that experience warns of the pitfalls of programs to facilitate adjustment, even if it does not tell us clearly how to avoid those pitfalls.

The greatest danger is that policies that are intended to reduce the burden of adjustment for industries whose output and employment must contract will instead permit them to avoid that adjustment entirely or delay it so that in fact the burden on the economy will be extended unnecessarily over time.[30] To avoid this, it is important that adjustment assistance policies be designed primarily to help workers accomplish the relocation and retraining that may be necessary to shift to expanding industries rather than merely to compensate them for the losses they incur in the contracting industries. Similar conditions apply to any assistance provided to owners of capital, although here the assistance might take the form of accelerated depreciation allowances and credits for investment in expanding sectors.[31]

---

[30] According to Hoekman and Djankov (1995, p. 16), the tariff reductions for the least competitive Tunisian industries will be backloaded towards the end of the 12-year phase-in period. Since the effective protection for these industries will be increased due to cheaper imports as tariffs on inputs are reduced in the early phase-in period, they point out that this could lead to inefficient investment and resistance to market opening down the road.

[31] According to the IMF (1996, p. 79), the Agreement provides for an industrial restructuring program that will cost an estimated $2.4 billion over five years and will be financed jointly by the Tunisian Government and contributions from the EU and the World Bank. It is interesting, though probably fortuitous, that the $2.4 billion corresponds to the estimated total welfare gain for the EU reported for our Scenario A in Table 3.

VIII. Conclusions and Implications for Policy

The objective of this chapter has been to investigate the potential economic effects on the Tunisian economy of the FTA between Tunisia and the EU as the result of bilateral removal of existing trade barriers coupled with possible changes in FDI inflows into Tunisia. For this purpose, we have carried out a number of trade and FDI scenarios using a specially constructed version of the Michigan Brown–Deardorff–Stern CGE Trade Model. Because the model is static, it has been assumed that all the changes in trade barriers and FDI occur at a single point in time rather than over a period of time as will be the case in actuality. Our computational results are therefore to be interpreted in a context of comparative static analysis, that is, moving from a pre-FTA starting point to a post-FTA equilibrium.

Our chief findings are as follows:

1. The static welfare benefits for Tunisia of the FTA with the EU involving the bilateral removal of existing trade barriers between Tunisia and the EU range from slightly negative to somewhat positive, depending on what is assumed about intersectoral capital mobility in Tunisia. Identifying capital mobility with the time horizon of the analysis, we expect the FTA to reduce Tunisia's aggregate welfare somewhat in the short run but raise welfare in the longer run.
2. Depending on the length of time allowed for phasing in of the FTA, Tunisia could experience significant adjustment problems in connection with the intersectoral movements of labor and capital that the FTA would induce.
3. Our FDI-related scenarios are intended to be primarily illustrative since there is no straightforward way to integrate FDI inflows into our CGE trade modeling framework. In any event, our results suggest that even an approximate doubling of the recent annual level of the FDI inflow into Tunisia in conjunction with the FTA would be unlikely to make a significant difference for Tunisian welfare. This applies as well when we make allowance

for FDI inflows in response to changes in sectoral rates of return and to features of Tunisia's 1994 Investment Code.

4. A question of concern is whether the success of the FTA between Tunisia and the EU depends on whether there is a substantial flow of FDI into Tunisia. Our results say that such FDI is not necessary for the FTA to become beneficial to Tunisia once enough time for adjustment has elapsed. Also, unless an FDI inflow is considerably larger than the flows that have been observed to date, and unless it is also systematically targeted primarily to sectors where it can yield a higher return than its cost, we would not expect the presence of FDI to make a noticeable difference to the economic success of the FTA. On the other hand, given the difficulty of observing the types of gain that the FTA is likely to yield, it may well be that a large visible flow of FDI is necessary for the FTA to be *viewed* as a success.

As noted earlier, we should reiterate that our CGE model does not make any allowance for dynamic efficiency changes and economic growth. Recent research suggests that static gains from trade, such as we have calculated here, may well be augmented by their effects over time on economic growth, so that the static changes, to the extent that they are positive, are really only lower bounds on what the economic benefits to an economy may turn out to be. On the other hand, the very few estimates of such effects that are available only suggest that the static gains will be increased by a small integer multiple, and this would not materially affect the conclusions we have reached here based on the estimates of the static model.[32]

There are other theoretical models that explore the possibility that trade liberalization may have a permanent positive effect on a country's rate of growth, by stimulating technological progress or by taking advantage of various "dynamic scale economies."[33] There is some empirical evidence for such an effect, but it is unclear whether the effects of trade on growth rates that have been found empirically

---

[32] See Baldwin (1992).

[33] See Grossman and Helpman (1991).

are transitory or permanent.[34] We therefore would hesitate to claim that the welfare effects found here will be significantly augmented by such considerations.

As noted above, we have also omitted from our analysis the possible reductions in trading costs with all countries that may be achieved through harmonization and other sources of increased trading efficiency discussed by Page and Underwood (1995) among others. This does not deny the potential importance of these other sources of benefit, but it remains to be seen whether and how effectively Tunisian policies and the Tunisian economic structure can be adapted to the realities and opportunities of the FTA.

Acting in the other direction, there may be some concern that the gains from the FTA with the EU could be reversed later by the EU backing out of the agreement. We see no reason to expect that to happen, based upon the history of the EU's other preferential trading arrangements. But we should also point out that Tunisia has benefited since the mid-1970s from preferentially low tariffs on most exports to the EU. The benefits to Tunisia from these preferences — which are not included in our analysis here since they are already present independently of the FTA — will be eroded if the EU continues to lower trade barriers multilaterally as a result of the Uruguay Round and future negotiations under the auspices of the World Trade Organization.

We have also left out a host of other considerations that have figured importantly in the negotiation of the Tunisia-EU FTA. Perhaps most importantly, we have not addressed any of the political considerations that may have served as major driving forces in the formation of the Tunisia-EU FTA. These forces include issues of democratization, as well as trying to diminish the potential influence of radical Islamic fundamentalism, as is evident in Algeria and Egypt.

[34] Levine and Renelt (1992), in a critical analysis of the empirical literature relating growth rates across countries to various determinants, find that the only robust conclusions are that growth responds to investment and that investment in turn responds to trade.

Overall, what the foregoing conclusions suggest to us is that Tunisia may not have a great deal to gain in economic terms from entering into the FTA with the EU. The reason is that the FTA amounts essentially to Tunisia eliminating its bilateral tariffs *vis-à-vis* the EU, since Tunisia already has had duty-free access to the EU except for some agricultural products and certain types of clothing exports. The trade diverting effects of such a discriminatory tariff reduction are likely to be harmful, especially in the short run. Further, the FTA does not in itself appear likely to generate an inflow of capital into Tunisia that would materially increase Tunisian welfare. The question thus arises as to whether Tunisia might pursue liberalization of its trade restrictions on a multilateral basis as well as preferentially with respect to the EU. This would avoid the trade diversion that our CGE model suggests might otherwise occur. Reducing its trade barriers multilaterally and reinforcing these actions with a liberalization of its foreign investment policies and maintenance of macroeconomic and political stability might in the end be the best path for Tunisia to follow.[35]

Study Questions

1. What are the static and dynamic effects that may arise from a free trade agreement? How important may be the non-trade effects of an FTA? What are the issues involved in modeling changes in foreign direct investment (FDI) in computational modeling? What are the principal features and data used in the Michigan Model?
2. What are the principal determinants of FDI especially in developing countries? How important are investment incentives?
3. What are the principal features of Tunisia's 1994 Investment Code?
4. What are the five model scenarios that were run and the principal aggregate results, especially with regard to international capital movements? What are the principal sectoral effects and

[35] A similar conclusion is reached by Hoekman and Djankov (1995, p. 31).

the potential need for intersectoral adjustments in the Tunisian economy?

5. What are the overall conclusions about the potential benefits to Tunisia of an FTA with the EU?

References

Bajo-Rubio, Oscar and Simón Sosvilla-Rivero. 1994. "An Econometric Analysis of Foreign Direct Investment in Spain," *Southern Economic Journal* 61, pp. 104–120.

Baldwin, Richard E. 1992. "Measurable Dynamic Gains from Trade," *Journal of Political Economy* 100, pp. 162–174.

Brown, Drusilla K. and Robert M. Stern. 1989. "Computable General Equilibrium Estimates of the Gains from U.S.-Canadian Trade Liberalization," in David Greenaway, Thomas Hyclak, and Robert J. Thornton, eds., *Economic Aspects of Regional Trading Arrangements.* London: Harvester Wheatsheaf.

Brown, Drusilla K., Alan V. Deardorff, and Robert M. Stern. 1992a. "A North American Free Trade Agreement: Analytical Issues and a Computational Assessment," *The World Economy* 15, pp. 15–29.

Brown, Drusilla K., Alan V. Deardorff, and Robert M. Stern. 1992b. "North American Economic Integration," *Economic Journal* 102, pp. 1507–1518.

Brown, Drusilla K., Alan V. Deardorff, and Robert M. Stern. 1993. "Protection and Real Wages: Old and New Trade Theories and Their Empirical Counterparts," Research Forum on International Economics, University of Michigan, Discussion Paper No. 331 (May).

Brown, Drusilla K., Alan V. Deardorff, and Robert M. Stern. 1996a. "Computational Analysis of the Economic Effects of an East Asian Preferential Trading Bloc," *Journal of the Japanese and International Economies*, forthcoming.

Brown, Drusilla K., Alan V. Deardorff, and Robert M. Stern. 1996b. "Expanding NAFTA: Economic Effects of Accession of Chile and Other Major South American Nations," *North American Journal of Economics and Finance*, forthcoming.

Brown, Drusilla K., Alan V. Deardorff, Simeon Djankov, and Robert M. Stern. 1996. "An Economic Assessment of the Integration of Czechoslovakia, Hungary, and Poland into the European Union," in Stanley Black, ed., *Europe's Economy Looks East.* New York: Cambridge University Press, forthcoming.

Deardorff, Alan V. and Robert M. Stern. 1990. *Computational Analysis of Global Trading Arrangements.* Ann Arbor: University of Michigan Press.

Dixit, Avinash K. and Joseph E. Stiglitz. 1977. "Monopolistic Competition and Optimum Product Diversity," *American Economic Review* 67, pp. 297–308.

General Agreement on Tariffs and Trade (GATT). 1994. *Trade Policy Review: Tunisia 1994*, Vols. I and II. Geneva: GATT (September).

Grossman, Gene M. and Elhanan Helpman. 1991. *Innovation and Growth in the Global Economy.* Cambridge, MA: MIT Press.

Haddad, Mona and Ann Harrison. 1993. "Are There Positive Spillovers from Direct Foreign Investment? Evidence from Panel Data for Morocco," *Journal of Development Economics* 42, pp. 51–74.

Harrison, Glenn W., Thomas F. Rutherford, and Ian Wooton. 1989. "The Economic Impact of the European Community," *American Economic Review* 79, pp. 288–294.

Helpman, Elhanan and Paul R. Krugman. 1985. *Market Structure and Foreign Trade: Increasing Returns, Imperfect Competition, and the International Economy.* Cambridge, MA: MIT Press.

Hoekman, Bernard. 1995. "Tentative First Steps: An Assessment of the Uruguay Round Agreement on Services," in Will Martin and L. Alan Winters, eds., *The Uruguay Round and the Developing Countries.* The World Bank, forthcoming.

Hoekman, Bernard and Simeon Djankov. 1995. "Catching Up With Eastern Europe? The European Union's Mediterranean Free Trade Initiative," Centre for Economic Policy Research, Discussion Paper No. 1300 (November).

Institut National de la Statistique (INS), Republique Tunisienne, Ministere du Plan et du Developpement Regional. 1990. *Statistiques du Commerce Exterieur.* Tunis: INS.

International Monetary Fund (IMF). 1996. *IMF Survey,* March 4. Washington, DC: IMF.

Levine, Ross and David Renelt. 1992. "A Sensitivity Analysis of Cross-Country Growth Regressions," *American Economic Review* 82, pp. 942–963.

Lucas, Robert E.B. 1993. "On the Determinants of Direct Foreign Investment: Evidence from East and Southeast Asia," *World Development* 21, pp. 391–406.

Ministry of International Cooperation and Foreign Investment, Tunisian Government. 1994. *Incentives for Investment in Tunisia.* Tunis: MCIIE.

Nsouli, Saleh, Sena Eken, Paul Duran, Gerwin Bell, and Zühtü Yücelik. 1993. *The Path to Convertibility and Growth: The Tunisian Experience,* Occasional Paper 109, International Monetary Fund. Washington, DC: IMF.

Page, John and John Underwood. 1995. "Growth, the Maghreb and the European Union: Assessing the Impact of the Free Trade Agreements on Tunisia and Morocco," presented at the International Economic Association, Eleventh World Congress, December 18–22, 1995, Tunis, Tunisia.

Stanton, Julie. 1994. "Estimates of Tariff Equivalents of Tunisia's Non-Tariff Barriers," unpublished manuscript, International Economics Division, World Bank.

United Nations Centre on Transnational Corporations (UNCTC). 1992. *The Determinants of Foreign Direct Investment: A Survey of the Evidence.* New York: United Nations.

United Nations Conference on Trade and Development (UNCTAD), Programme on Transnational Corporations. 1993. *Explaining and Forecasting Regional Flows of Foreign Direct Invesmtent.* New York: United Nations.

Suggested Further Reading

Konan, Denise Eby and Keith E. Maskus. 2006. "Quantifying the Impact of Services Liberalization in a Developing Country," *Journal of Development Economics* 81, pp. 142–162.

Lawrence, Robert Z. 2006. *A US-Middle East FTA: Expanding the Circle?* Washington, D.C.: Institute for International Economics.

Lawrence, Robert Z. and Ahmed Galal. 2005. *Anchoring Reform: US-Egypt Free Trade*. Washington, D.C.: Institute for International Economics.

Momani, Bessma. 2007. "A Middle East Free Trade Area: Economic Interdependence and Peace Considered," *The World Economy* 30, pp. 1682–1700.

Chapter 12

A North American Free Trade Agreement: Analytical Issues and a Computational Assessment*

Drusilla K. Brown, Alan V. Deardorff and Robert M. Stern†

I. Introduction

The successful pursuit of North American economic integration, beginning with the Autopact between the United States and Canada, has been underway for more than 25 years. The motivations

* Published in *The World Economy*, 15(11), January 1992, pp. 11–30. Reprinted with permission from Blackwell Publishing.

† This chapter was originally presented at "North American Free Trade: Economic and Political Implications," A Conference of the Fraser Institute, Center for Strategic and International Studies, University of Toronto Centre for International Studies, and the Stanford University Americas Program, Washington, D.C., June 27–28, 1991. Financial assistance was provided in part by the Fraser Institute and by a grant from the Ford Foundation in support of a program for research on trade policy in the Institute of Public Policy Studies at the University of Michigan. The authors would like to thank John Alfaro, Sundari Baru, and Seong-Hun Yun for assistance with the data and the computations, Judith Jackson for editorial and typing assistance, Andy Parks for assistance with data and concordances, and Tracy Murray for data on Maquiladora and GSP trade.

for seeking agreement have varied with each stage, ranging from an initial desire to settle the US-Canadian dispute over automobile industry market shares to the sweeping economic development ambitions of the current Mexican government. Concerns raised by the fear of economic dislocation associated with trade liberalization mirror the ambitions of the negotiating parties. An observer cannot avoid being struck by the intense political discussions in the United States over the proposed addition of Mexico to a North American Free Trade Area (NAFTA), as compared to the near US indifference to the 1987 US-Canada agreement. This was the case despite the considerably smaller trade flows involved between the United States and Mexico.

There are a number of issues raised by the addition of Mexico to the NAFTA that quite appropriately concern Canadians and Americans, such as the implication of an agreement for wages and employment of unskilled labor and the international allocation of capital. Similarly, for Mexico, the expected benefits of economic liberalization may not be sufficient to compensate for the accompanying cost of economic dislocation. While these concerns are undoubtedly important from an analytical point of view, the likely quantitative dimensions of the employment problems due to a trade agreement are not clear. Our purpose in this paper is to identify some of the important issues in analyzing the economic impact of a NAFTA and to provide some quantitative estimates of the effects of the elimination or reduction of trilateral tariffs, nontariff barriers (NTBs), and investment restrictions between Mexico, Canada, and the United States that might be implemented following the negotiation and legislative approval of an agreement.

We begin in Section II by identifying several issues that arise in undertaking an analysis of a NAFTA. In Section III, we present an overview of the computable general equilibrium model that we have developed to assess the possible economic effects of a NAFTA. Our computational results are presented in Section IV, and our conclusions are summarized in Section V.

II. Issues in Analyzing the Economic Impact of the NAFTA

Perhaps the overriding motivation for Canada in pursuing a US-Canada free trade agreement was a concern on the part of some government officials and academic economists that a high level of import protection had insulated some imperfectly competitive domestic industries from the competitive pressures associated with an open trading regime. The end result was that Canadian firms were foregoing economies of scale in production in order to provide a wide variety of products to the Canadian market. The United States, on the other hand, turned to the bilateral-liberalization option partly out of frustration with the multilateral negotiations, but it was also certainly aware of the potential political benefits of trade liberalization within the hemisphere. The subsequent negotiations between the United States and Canada proceeded relatively uneventfully, in part due to the fact that the US and Canadian economies are broadly similar in terms of factor endowments, quality of labor force, and standard of living.

The Mexican government's objectives in entering into the US-Canada FTA are considerably more ambitious, concomitantly raising many more difficult and controversial issues. Following the generally failed attempt at industrial policy during the 1970s, Mexico is now seeking to develop through a program of internal goods and factors markets deregulation along with a more liberal international trade policy. That is, Mexico seeks to grow economically by increasing the degree of international specialization in production.

Since Mexico is the relatively labor abundant country, we expect that trade liberalization will stimulate production of the labor-intensive sectors in Mexico and shift labor into the capital-intensive sectors in the United States and Canada. To the extent that intersectoral labor reallocation is substantial, the subsequent fall in wages in the United States, particularly of unskilled labor, is likely to aggravate the already growing income disparity between skilled and unskilled workers. In addition, concern has been expressed that capital may relocate to Mexico in order to take advantage of lower Mexican wages and more lax labor and environmental standards.

Despite concerns with the loss in economic welfare associated with the sometimes difficult movement of resources from one sector to another, we can nonetheless expect welfare in all three countries to rise as a consequence of a free trade agreement. First, there is a strong presumption that an agreement will improve the international allocation of production as each country specializes in the sectors in which it has a comparative advantage. We know, of course, from the theory of the second best that welfare gains from preferential liberalization are not assured. The NAFTA will eliminate any tariff-induced consumption distortions between domestic goods and imports from NAFTA partners, but a new consumption distortion between imports from NAFTA partners and non-NAFTA trade partners is introduced.

However, in the case of both Canada and Mexico, a very large fraction of trade already occurs within North America. Therefore, the volume of trade that could be potentially diverted is relatively small. This is much less the case, though, for the United States, which has sizable trade with both Europe and Asia. However, US tariffs are already quite low so that, again, the introduced consumption distortion is likely to be small.

Second, the transition costs once an agreement is in place are not expected to be large, particularly for the United States. The Mexican economy is so much smaller than the US economy, including sensitive sectors such as wearing apparel, that it is unlikely that even a substantial percentage increase in Mexican exports would noticeably alter US production levels in most sectors.

A trade agreement could be considerably more disruptive to the Mexican economy. As the smaller partner, Mexico will tend to specialize production in a narrower range of labor-intensive goods. However, the cost of transferring labor to the sectors in which Mexico has a comparative advantage must be weighed against the enormous burden that government regulations have imposed by limiting Mexico's economic growth. In addition, the Mexican government has indicated its intention to liberalize rules on foreign direct investment as part of its overall deregulation of markets. The capital inflow will reduce the difference in factor endowments in Mexico relative to its trade partners and, therefore, diminish the degree to which Mexico will specialize in the production of labor-intensive goods.

Third, all three countries in the NAFTA may experience an improvement in their terms of trade with the excluded countries, further raising economic welfare. Conventional general equilibrium theory of customs unions leads us to expect that the included countries will enjoy a terms-of-trade gain at the expense of the excluded countries. This result follows from the fact that the countries in the FTA will increase intra-NAFTA trade, thereby reducing supply to and demand from the rest of the world. Rest-of-world terms of trade tend to deteriorate as a result.

Fourth, international specialization is expected to narrow the wage gap between the United States and Mexico, thus reducing immigration pressure on the United States. In principle, it is possible that a narrowing of the wage gap will come about by lowering wages for US workers, but this outcome is not inevitable. We expect the marginal physical product of US labor to fall as production in the capital-intensive sectors expands. However, the value of US labor's marginal product may still increase due to the rise in the price of US goods on the world market. Thus, both US labor and capital may gain from the agreement.

Finally, the expected realization of economies of scale due to a more competitive environment within the NAFTA could potentially raise the real return to both capital and labor in all three countries.[1]

---

[1] A profit maximizing firm will hire each factor up to the point where the wage equals the marginal revenue product, which is given by

$$w^i = MR \times MP = P\left[1 - \frac{1}{e}\right] \times MP^i$$

for an imperfectly competitive firm, where w^i is the return to factor i. MR is marginal revenue for the firm, MP^i is the marginal product of factor i, and $e > O$ is the firm's perceived elasticity of demand. Trade liberalization tends to push down the return to the scarce factor by lowering its marginal product. However, if trade liberalization also leads each firm to perceive a more elastic demand curve, then the real return to each factor measured by w^i/P may rise even if factor i's marginal physical product falls.

Normally, the Stolper–Samuelson Theorem would lead us to expect that trade liberalization would lower the real return to at least one factor of production. However, in the case of increasing returns to scale, as firms move down their average total cost curves, the average product of both factors could rise. Thus, while the relative return of one factor may fall, the real return to both factors may rise.

III. The Computational Model

For the purpose of analysis, we have constructed a large scale computable general equilibrium model that is capable of evaluating the comparative static effects of changes in trade policy on factor prices, economic welfare, the intersectoral allocation of resources, and the international allocation of production. An overview of the model is provided below.

Countries in the model are aggregated into three broad groups. Each of the NAFTA members (the United States, Canada, and Mexico) is modeled individually, a group of 31 other major trading countries are aggregated to create a fourth country,[2] and the remaining countries are consigned to residual rest-of-world supply and demand equations. The countries of the model produce, consume, and trade 23 tradable aggregate products. In addition, there are six nontraded goods. The market structure in each sector is either perfectly competitive or monopolistically competitive, depending on the degree of scale economies in production. Product categories and market structure assignments are listed in Table 1.

Final demand equations in each country are obtained assuming a representative consumer who maximizes utility subject to a budget

[2] The 31 other countries include 16 industrialized countries — Australia, Austria, Belgium-Luxembourg, Denmark, Federal Republic of Germany, Finland, France, Ireland, Italy, Japan, the Netherlands, New Zealand, Norway, Sweden, Switzerland, and the United Kingdom — and 15 newly industrializing countries — Argentina, Brazil, Chile, Colombia, Greece, Hong Kong, India, Israel, Portugal, Singapore, South Korea, Spain, Taiwan, Turkey, and Yugoslavia.

Table 1. Industry structure.

Sector	Market Structure	Entry
Agriculture	Perfect Competition	Free
Food	Monopolistic Competition	Free
Textiles	Monopolistic Competition	Free
Clothing	Monopolistic Competition	Free
Leather Products	Monopolistic Competition	Free
Footwear	Monopolistic Competition	Free
Wood Products	Monopolistic Competition	Free
Furniture, Fixtures	Monopolistic Competition	Free
Paper Products	Monopolistic Competition	Free
Printing, Publishing	Monopolistic Competition	Free
Chemicals	Monopolistic Competition	Free
Petroleum Products	Monopolistic Competition	Free
Rubber Products	Monopolistic Competition	Free
Nonmetal Min. Prod.	Monopolistic Competition	Free
Glass Products	Monopolistic Competition	Free
Iron, Steel	Monopolistic Competition	Free
Nonferrous Metals	Monopolistic Competition	Free
Metal Products	Monopolistic Competition	Free
Nonelec. Machinery	Monopolistic Competition	Free
Electrical Machinery	Monopolistic Competition	Free
Transport Equipment	Monopolistic Competition	Free
Misc. Mfrs.	Monopolistic Competition	Free
Mining, Quarrying	Monopolistic Competition	Free
Utilities	Perfect Competition	Free
Construction	Perfect Competition	Free
Wholesale Trade	Perfect Competition	Free
Transportation	Perfect Competition	Free
Financial Services	Perfect Competition	Free
Personal Services	Perfect Competition	Free

constraint,[3] and intermediate demands are derived from the profit maximization decisions of representative firms in each sector. Products in both the perfectly competitive and monopolistically competitive

[3] Household income underlying the final demand equations is set at the level that will hold the trade balance equal to its level in the base data set. This procedure is, in principle, equivalent to setting income equal to factor payments plus tariff revenue.

industries are assumed to be characterized by some degree of product differentiation. In the case where markets are taken to be perfectly competitive, products are differentiated by country, while in the monopolistically competitive industries products are differentiated by firm.[4]

Turning to the factor markets, the variable input requirements are taken to be the same for the two market structures. Primary and intermediate input aggregates are required in fixed proportion to output.[5] In the monopolistically competitive industries, additional fixed inputs of capital and labor are required.[6] Capital and labor are assumed to be perfectly mobile between sectors and the returns to capital and labor are determined to equate factor demand to an exogenous supply of each factor.

Perfectly competitive firms set price equal to marginal cost, while monopolistically competitive firms maximize profits by setting price as an optimal mark-up over marginal cost. The number of firms in each industry is determined by the condition that there are zero profits.

International trade in goods is assumed to be subject to tariffs and nontariff barriers (NTBs). NTBs are incorporated by endogenously solving for the *ad valorem* tariff rate that will hold imports within each product category covered by NTBs at a predetermined level.

---

[4] In both cases, we adopt a modified version of the approach to product differentiation suggested by Dixit and Stiglitz (1977) and Spence (1976). Consumers and producers are assumed to use a two-stage procedure to allocate expenditure across differentiated products. At the first stage, expenditure is allocated across goods, without regard for the country of origin or the producing firm. At this stage the utility function is taken to be Cobb–Douglas, and the production function requires inputs in fixed proportion. In the second stage, expenditure on each monopolistically competitive good is allocated across competing firms without regard to place of production. However, in the case of perfectly competitive goods, individual firm supply is indeterminate. Therefore, expenditure on each good must be allocated across individual countries. The aggregation function in the second stage is CES.

[5] Expenditure on primary inputs is allocated between capital and labor, assuming that a CES function is used to form the primary input aggregate.

[6] It is assumed that fixed capital and labor are used in the same proportion as variable capital and labor so that the production function is homogeneous.

An *ad valorem* tariff variable in each product category is an average of the NTB tariff-equivalent rate and the nominal tariff rate, using the NTB coverage ratio to weight the NTB tariff equivalent.[7]

The bilateral trade-weighted tariff rates are reported in the last two columns of Tables 2, 3, and 4 for the United States, Canada, and Mexico, respectively. Tariffs in each case are aggregated up from the line-item level using bilateral trade as weights. US tariffs applying to imports from Mexico are then scaled down by a factor that reflects the value added applied to US exports to Maquiladora plants in Mexico.

Equilibrium prices are determined in world markets. In the perfectly competitive industries, total demand for each national variety must equal national output. For monopolistically competitive industries, total demand for the variety produced by each firm must equal supply by that firm. The *ad valorem* tariff variable discussed above then links equilibrium prices determined in the world system to prices paid by consumers in the country system.

The model is linear in form and thus can be solved by matrix inversion. The base year is 1989 for data on production, employment, and trade. Input-output coefficients for the production function were derived from the US input-output table for 1977, the Mexican table for 1980, and the Canadian table for 1976.

Some of the key parameters of the model are reported in Tables 2 to 4, for the United States, Canada, and Mexico. For the monopolistically competitive industries, the elasticity of demand, share of primary factors that are fixed, variable cost share of total cost, and the mark-up of price over marginal cost are all derivable from the theoretical structure of the model. Details are given in Brown and Stern (1989). The only data required are labor-share of primary input cost and primary input share of total cost, which were obtained from the input–output tables, and an indicator of the elasticity of substitution among different varieties of each good. The elasticity of substitution between all varieties of each good has been set equal to three.

[7] For additional details, see Deardorff and Stern (1990, pp. 23–24).

Table 2. Parameters of the model: United States.

ISIC Sector	Demand Elasticity	Variable *K* Share of Total *K*	Variable Input Cost Share	Labor Share of Primary Input Cost	Tariff on Canada Exports	Tariff on Mexico Exports
1 Agriculture	−2.9	1.00	1.00	0.24	1.6	4.0
310 Food	−3.0	0.12	0.75	0.47	3.8	2.6
321 Textiles	−2.9	0.11	0.73	0.71	7.2	2.8
322 Clothing	−3.0	0.12	0.66	0.79	18.4	6.2
323 Leather Products	−2.9	0.13	0.66	0.69	2.5	4.8
324 Footwear	−3.0	0.21	0.66	0.81	9.0	3.5
331 Wood Products	−3.0	0.11	0.66	0.59	0.2	1.3
332 Furniture, Fixtures	−3.0	0.19	0.66	0.76	4.6	1.4
341 Paper Products	−3.0	0.08	0.66	0.62	0.0	2.5
342 Printing, Publishing	−3.0	0.29	0.66	0.71	0.3	0.2
35A Chemicals	−2.9	0.02	0.66	0.54	0.6	1.2
35B Petroleum Products	−3.0	0.30	0.90	0.36	0.0	0.1
355 Rubber Products	−2.9	0.26	0.66	0.67	3.2	0.1
36A Nonmetal Min. Prod.	−3.0	0.24	0.66	0.62	0.3	1.0
362 Glass Products	−2.9	0.35	0.66	0.74	5.7	5.9
371 Iron, Steel	−3.0	0.07	0.66	0.81	2.7	1.6

(*Continued*)

Table 2. (*Continued*)

ISIC Sector	Demand Elasticity	Variable K Share of Total K	Variable Input Cost Share	Labor Share of Primary Input Cost	Tariff on Canada Exports	Tariff on Mexico Exports
372 Nonferrous Metals	–3.0	0.14	0.78	0.65	0.5	1.6
381 Metal Products	–3.0	0.21	0.66	0.68	4.0	2.2
382 Nonelec. Machinery	–2.9	0.27	0.66	0.69	2.2	0.9
383 Electrical Machinery	–3.0	0.28	0.66	0.76	4.5	2.3
384 Transport Equipment	–3.0	0.10	0.70	0.75	0.0	1.4
38A Misc. Mfrs.	–2.9	0.44	0.66	0.36	0.9	1.2
2 Mining, Quarrying	–3.0	0.48	0.66	0.25	0.0	0.1
4 Utilities		1.00	1.00	0.26		
5 Construction		1.00	1.00	0.81		
6 Wholesale Trade		1.00	1.00	0.60		
7 Transportation		1.00	1.00	0.62		
8 Financial Services		1.00	1.00	0.28		
9 Personal Services		1.00	1.00	0.86		

Table 3. Parameters of the model: Canada.

ISIC Sector	Demand Elasticity	Variable K Share of Total K	Variable Input Cost Share	Labor Share of Primary Input Cost	Tariff on US Exports	Tariff on Mexico Exports
1 Agriculture	−2.7	1.00	1.00	0.24	2.2	1.8
310 Food	−2.8	0.13	0.77	0.60	5.4	5.4
321 Textiles	−2.8	0.04	0.64	0.76	16.9	9.1
322 Clothing	−2.9	0.20	0.66	0.80	23.7	19.8
323 Leather Products	−2.9	0.08	0.66	0.83	4.0	16.8
324 Footwear	−2.9	0.19	0.66	0.86	21.5	22.5
331 Wood Products	−2.9	0.10	0.65	0.76	2.5	8.3
332 Furniture, Fixtures	−2.9	0.23	0.66	0.79	14.3	13.6
341 Paper Products	−2.9	0.14	0.65	0.63	6.6	9.9
342 Printing, Publishing	−2.9	0.36	0.65	0.71	1.1	3.9
35A Chemicals	−2.8	0.03	0.65	0.58	7.9	8.4
35B Petroleum Products	−2.8	0.33	0.91	0.36	0.4	0.0
355 Rubber Products	−2.9	0.19	0.66	0.78	7.3	0.0
36A Nonmetal Min. Prod.	−2.7	0.27	0.63	0.58	4.4	1.8
362 Glass Products	−2.9	0.34	0.65	0.66	6.9	4.2
371 Iron, Steel	−2.7	0.12	0.74	0.76	5.1	0.0

(*Continued*)

Table 3. (*Continued*)

ISIC Sector	Demand Elasticity	Variable K Share of Total K	Variable Input Cost Share	Labor Share of Primary Input Cost	Tariff on US Exports	Tariff on Mexico Exports
372 Nonferrous Metals	−2.7	0.16	0.80	0.77	3.3	0.0
381 Metal Products	−2.9	0.19	0.65	0.70	8.6	10.1
382 Nonelec. Machinery	−2.9	0.11	0.72	0.69	4.6	1.4
383 Electrical Machinery	−2.8	0.15	0.79	0.57	7.5	4.9
384 Transport Equipment	−2.8	0.15	0.79	0.70	0.0	0.9
38A Misc. Mfrs.	−2.9	0.11	0.65	0.69	5.0	8.3
2 Mining, Quarrying	−2.8	0.50	0.64	0.21	0.4	0.0
4 Utilities		1.00	1.00	0.32		
5 Construction		1.00	1.00	0.64		
6 Wholesale Trade		1.00	1.00	0.67		
7 Transportation		1.00	1.00	0.66		
8 Financial Services		1.00	1.00	0.34		
9 Personal Services		1.00	1.00	0.61		

Table 4. Parameters of the model: Mexico.

ISIC Sector	Demand Elasticity	Variable K Share of Total K	Variable Input Cost Share	Labor Share of Primary Input Cost	Tariff on US Exports	Tariff on Canada Exports
1 Agriculture	−1.5	1.00	1.00	0.26	2.0	1.1
310 Food	−2.8	0.10	0.69	0.25	9.3	1.6
321 Textiles	−2.8	0.23	0.64	0.33	11.6	11.7
322 Clothing	−2.9	0.26	0.66	0.27	19.8	19.4
323 Leather Products	−3.0	0.23	0.66	0.40	12.3	8.8
324 Footwear	−2.9	0.32	0.66	0.56	19.7	19.3
331 Wood Products	−2.9	0.21	0.66	0.34	13.6	15.0
332 Furniture, Fixtures	−2.9	0.32	0.66	0.26	14.7	14.2
341 Paper Products	−2.6	0.08	0.61	0.29	3.0	2.9
342 Printing, Publishing	−2.8	0.32	0.65	0.39	8.2	6.3
35A Chemicals	−2.8	0.17	0.64	0.35	7.1	9.8
35B Petroleum Products	−2.7	0.14	0.78	0.46	3.4	13.0
355 Rubber Products	−2.9	0.34	0.66	0.38	12.3	9.0
36A Nonmetal Min. Prod.	−2.9	0.42	0.66	0.24	14.6	14.7
362 Glass Products	−2.9	0.40	0.65	0.37	15.1	19.7
371 Iron, Steel	−2.9	0.01	0.66	0.38	7.5	3.8

(Continued)

Table 4. (*Continued*)

ISIC Sector	Demand Elasticity	Variable K Share of Total K	Variable Input Cost Share	Labor Share of Primary Input Cost	Tariff on US Exports	Tariff on Canada Exports
372 Nonferrous Metals	−2.9	0.14	0.66	0.27	7.9	4.2
381 Metal Products	−2.8	0.27	0.65	0.40	9.6	8.3
382 Nonelec. Machinery	−2.9	0.33	0.66	0.37	12.7	12.1
383 Electrical Machinery	−3.0	0.29	0.66	0.43	14.2	13.9
384 Transport Equipment	−2.8	0.06	0.64	0.41	13.7	11.0
38A Misc. Mfrs.	−3.0	0.34	0.66	0.28	14.0	11.9
2 Mining, Quarrying	−2.7	0.51	0.63	0.21	3.7	3.6
4 Utilities		1.00	1.00	0.54		
5 Construction		1.00	1.00	0.64		
6 Wholesale Trade		1.00	1.00	0.19		
7 Transportation		1.00	1.00	0.35		
8 Financial Services		1.00	1.00	0.18		
9 Personal Services		1.00	1.00	0.82		

IV. Computational Results

The negotiations to form a NAFTA are currently at a very early stage. Therefore, the specific aspects of an agreement are yet to emerge. Our purpose here is to explore computationally the economic implications of some likely liberalization scenarios. The model described above has been used to evaluate five experiments. These are: (A) removal of tariffs on trade among the United States, Canada, and Mexico, and expansion of US import quotas applied to Mexican exports of agriculture, food, textiles, and clothing by 25 percent; (B) same as experiment (A) plus Mexico is assumed to relax capital import restrictions, resulting in a capital inflow from outside of the NAFTA that expands Mexico's capital stock by 10 percent; (C) removal of tariffs on trade between the United States and Mexico, and expansion of US import quotas applied to Mexican exports of agriculture, food, textiles, and clothing by 25 percent; (D) same as experiment (C) plus Mexico is assumed to relax capital import restrictions, resulting in a capital inflow from outside of the NAFTA that expands Mexico's capital stock by 10 percent; and for purposes of comparison (E) removal of post-Tokyo Round tariffs on trade between the United States and Canada.

A summary of results for these five experiments is detailed in Table 5. The changes in the quantity of imports and exports measured in base period US dollars are reported in columns two and three, and the percent changes in the terms of trade are reported in column four. Note first, countries that enjoy an improvement in the terms of trade also tend to increase imports relative to exports. This outcome is simply a result of the fact that an increase in the price of exportables raises the volume of imports affordable without violating the balanced trade constraint.

However, the impact of a NAFTA on trade volumes is particularly lopsided for Mexico and the other 31 countries in scenarios (B) and (D). For example, under scenario (B) the quantity of Mexico's imports rise by $2.2 billion whereas exports rise by $12.4 billion. A deterioration in Mexico's terms of trade by 2.5 percent is playing a small role in the rise in exports relative to imports, but the imbalance

Table 5. Summary results of a North America Free Trade Area*: Changes in country imports, exports, terms of trade, welfare, and return to labor and capital (trade and welfare in millions of US dollars).

Country	Imports	Exports	Terms of Trade	Equivalent Variations		Percent Change	Percent Change
				Percent	Millions		
(A) *North American Free Trade: Tariffs and NTBs*							
United States	9374.8	8595.8	0.2	0.1	6449.1	0.2	0.2
Other	–830.0	–475.8	–0.9	–0.0	–15.3	–0.1	–0.1
Canada	5537.9	6107.7	–0.5	0.7	3508.4	0.4	11.4
Mexico	2951.7	2984.2	–0.1	1.6	1977.2	0.7	11.6
(B) *North American Free Trade: Tariffs, NTBs, and Foreign Direct Investment*							
United States	10451.6	10287.5	–0.0	0.3	13226.6	0.2	11.2
Other	6749.2	–4132.9	0.2	–0.0	–2081.2	–0.0	0.2
Canada	5579.2	6203.5	–0.5	0.7	3662.9	0.5	0.5
Mexico	2201.4	12353.0	–2.5	5.0	6298.5	9.3	3.3
(C) *US-Mexico Free Trade: Tariffs and NTBs*							
United States	3116.5	2936.7	0.0	0.1	3664.5	0.0	0.1
Other	–286.7	–124.0	–0.0	0.0	96.8	–0.0	–0.0
Canada	–5.6	28.5	–0.0	0.0	78.2	–0.1	–0.1
Mexico	2900.9	2933.7	–0.1	1.5	1922.7	0.7	0.6

(*Continued*)

Table 5. (*Continued*)

Country	Imports	Exports	Terms of Trade	Equivalent Variations		Percent Change	Percent Change
				Percent	Millions		
(D) *US-Mexico Free Trade: Tariffs, NTBs, and Foreign Direct Investment*							
United States	4193.7	4628.7	–0.1	0.2	10654.1	0.1	0.1
Other	7293.6	–3780.1	0.2	–0.0	–1947.6	0.0	0.2
Canada	35.9	124.4	–0.1	0.0	234.2	0.1	0.1
Mexico	2151.2	12302.8	–2.5	4.9	6255.3	9.3	3.3
(E) *US-Canada Free Trade: Tariffs Only*							
United States	6266.2	5651.8	0.1	0.1	2867.8	0.1	0.1
Other	–522.2	–326.4	–0.0	–0.0	–107.3	–0.1	–0.0
Canada	5491.6	6036.7	–0.5	0.6	3356.4	0.4	0.4
Mexico	3.7	8.6	–0.0	0.0	35.8	–0.1	–0.1

*Five experiments have been performed. These are:

(A) Removal of tariffs on trade among the United States, Canada, and Mexico, plus a 25 percent expansion of US import quotas imposed on Mexican exports of agriculture, food, textiles, and clothing;

(B) Same as experiment (A) plus relaxation of Mexico's capital import controls that results in a 10 percent increase in the capital stock in Mexico;

(C) Removal of tariffs on trade between the United States and Mexico, plus a 25 percent expansion of US import quotas imposed on Mexican exports of agriculture, food, textiles, and clothing;

(D) Same as experiment (C) plus relaxation of Mexico's capital import controls that results in a 10 percent increase in the capital stock in Mexico; and

(E) Removal of tariffs on trade between the United States and Canada.

*Exports and imports valued in US dollar base period prices.

is caused primarily by the capital flows assumed to occur in this scenario. In scenarios (B) and (D), Other 31 is assumed to install capital in Mexico, generating interest payments from Mexico to Other 31 of approximately $9.5 billion each year. The remittance of interest payments by Mexico must be offset by a surplus on the trade balance if the current account balance is to remain at the level prevailing in the base period. The opposite is the case for Other 31, which increases imports by $6.7 billion but reduces exports by $4.1 billion under scenario (B).

A second interesting point to note about the second, third, and fourth columns of Table 5 is that the formation of the NAFTA generally reduces the volume of trade between the NAFTA countries and the Other 31 countries in the model. The formation of the NAFTA reduces the demand for imports from and the supply of exports to the excluded countries, thereby lowering external trade and worsening the terms of trade of the Other 31.

The exceptions to this rule again occur in scenarios (B) and (D) in which Other 31 is assumed to relocate capital in Mexico. Recall that the change in Mexico's capital stock must also generate a surplus on Mexico's trade balance. The world goods market will be willing to absorb the increased supply of goods from Mexico only if the price of Mexico's goods falls on the world market. The opposite is the case for goods produced by the Other 31. Hence, Mexico's terms of trade tend to deteriorate substantially while Other's terms of trade improve. For example, under scenario (B) Mexico's terms of trade deteriorate by 2.5 percent, but Other's terms of trade improve by 0.2 percent.

The welfare effects of the various liberalization scenarios are reported in columns five and six of Table 5. Here we use the equivalent variation to measure welfare and express this value both nominally and as a percent of GDP.[8] Clearly, a NAFTA would be welfare improving for all three countries, but will have the largest impact on the Mexican economy. Mexican welfare rises by 1.6 percent of GDP under scenario (A) and, when capital flows are incorporated

---

[8] The equivalent variation is the change in income valued at base period prices that yields the same change in welfare that occurs with the assumed liberalization.

under scenario (B), Mexican welfare rises by 5 percent of GDP. Welfare gains for the United States and Canada are considerably smaller but not inconsequential.

It is worth pointing out that relaxing capital import restrictions by Mexico will not only ease the transition to the new NAFTA equilibrium but also dramatically enhances the static welfare benefits of trade liberalization. The capital inflow into Mexico substantially raises the equilibrium scale of production in Mexico, so that Mexican firms are led to realize economies of scale. The end result is to substantially raise the real return to both capital and labor. The percent changes in factor returns deflated by a consumer price index are reported in the last two columns of Table 5. The capital inflow into Mexico has the expected effect of raising the return to labor relative to the return to capital by six percent. But note that the rise in the wage-rent ratio occurs even though the return to capital rises by 3.3 percent. The rise in the return to both factors is made possible by increases in output per firm in Mexico, which, thus, tends to raise the average product of both factors.

These results also suggest that it is in Canada's interest to participate in the US-Mexican negotiations, though the gain to Canada of doing so is very small. The formation of a NAFTA raises Canada's welfare by $3.5 billion. In comparison, a US-Canada agreement combined with a US-Mexico agreement would raise Canada's welfare by a slightly smaller $3.4 billion. Canada, of course, has other political reasons for participating in the negotiations, such as taking the opportunity to impose restrictions on further accession to the NAFTA by other countries in central and South America.

Two other conclusions can be drawn by examining the last two columns of Table 5. First, the formation of a NAFTA has the expected effect of narrowing the wage gap between US and Mexican workers. In scenario (B), the wage paid to Mexican workers relative to US workers rises by over nine percent. Thus, the pressure for illegal immigration may be reduced.

However, the narrowing of the wage gap is not accomplished at the expense of US workers. Real wages rise in the US by 0.2 percent. This is partly a consequence of the improvement in the US terms of trade which raises the value of workers' marginal product on the world market and partly a consequence of the increase in the scale of production as a result of liberalization, the benefits of which accrue to both US workers and capital owners.

Sectoral results for the United States, Canada, and Mexico are reported in Tables 6, 7, and 8 respectively, for liberalization scenario (A). The sectoral results for the other scenarios are available from the authors on request. The percent changes in bilateral imports with each NAFTA trade partner are reported in columns four and five of each table. The bilateral trade changes between the United States and Canada exhibit a strong indication of increased intra-industry trade. Both the United States and Canada generally increase imports from each other in most product categories. The broad similarity between the US and Canadian economies in terms of factor endowments, labor force quality, and per capita income suggest that the benefits of liberalized US-Canada trade stem primarily from increased product variety rather than intersectoral specialization. Our use here of a model that combines both the roles of factor endowments and product variety in determining the pattern of trade allows this result to emerge.

In contrast, while Mexican imports from its two trade partners rise in every product category, Mexico's exports are heavily concentrated in a small range of sectors. For example, the United States reduces imports from Mexico in a wide range of industrial products. The notable exceptions are glass products (19.1%), nonferrous metals (27.6%), metal products (2.2%), and electrical machinery (102.2%). These results suggest a much stronger pattern of intersectoral specialization for Mexico which would be expected given Mexico's very different factor abundance as compared to the United States and Canada.

These results also suggest that Canada's fear that a US-Mexico agreement may seriously erode the position of Canadian firms in the US market is unfounded. There is not a single product category in which US imports from Mexico are displacing Canadian exports. Rather the opposite appears to be the case. Canadian exports to the United States of petroleum products, rubber products, non-metallic

Table 6. Sectoral effects on the United States of North American free trade: Tariffs and NTBs (percent change).

ISIC Sector	Exports	Imports	Bilateral Imports		Output	No. Firms	Elasticity	Capital	Employment
			Canada	Mexico					
1 Agriculture	0.07	2.03	4.28	10.81	−0.03	0.00	0.00	−0.03	−0.02
310 Food	1.87	1.71	9.98	12.22	0.11	−0.03	0.00	−0.03	0.00
321 Textiles	7.73	0.23	15.54	14.10	1.11	0.64	0.00	0.67	0.70
322 Clothing	10.01	1.47	46.59	24.90	0.65	0.12	0.00	0.15	0.20
323 Leather Products	1.16	1.93	11.75	14.47	0.04	−0.18	0.00	−0.21	−0.13
324 Footwear	11.16	2.52	29.17	10.53	0.24	−0.02	0.00	0.00	0.04
331 Wood Products	1.92	0.86	1.20	0.67	0.14	−0.01	0.00	0.00	0.02
332 Furniture, Fixtures	9.80	3.58	12.99	8.94	0.34	0.12	0.00	0.15	0.17
341 Paper Products	2.35	0.09	−0.00	5.12	0.21	0.05	0.00	0.04	0.08
342 Printing, Publishing	1.70	0.17	−0.37	−2.20	0.11	0.02	0.00	0.03	0.05
35A Chemicals	3.73	−0.48	−1.44	−3.76	0.62	0.43	0.00	0.42	0.44
35B Petroleum Products	−0.05	0.52	1.27	−4.73	0.02	−0.03	−0.00	4.02	−0.00
355 Rubber Products	6.15	0.54	9.85	−9.26	0.63	0.38	0.00	0.43	0.45
36A Nonmetal Min. Prod.	4.83	0.73	2.52	−0.12	0.14	0.05	0.00	0.05	0.08
362 Glass Products	−1.91	57.64	173.47	19.10	−11.45	−11.63	0.01	−11.58	−11.56
371 Iron, Steel	6.49	1.51	10.48	−4.84	0.28	0.14	0.00	0.14	0.16

(*Continued*)

Table 6. (*Continued*)

ISIC Sector	Exports	Imports	Bilateral Imports		Output	No. Firms	Elasticity	Capital	Employment
			Canada	Mexico					
372 Nonferrous Metals	−0.89	5.32	12.11	27.60	−1.01	−1.02	−0.00	−1.05	−1.01
381 Metal Products	6.02	2.71	13.25	2.25	0.29	0.14	0.00	0.16	0.18
382 Nonelec. Machinery	3.94	0.01	2.62	−24.56	0.72	0.54	0.00	0.58	0.59
383 Electrical Machinery	1.86	9.97	14.03	102.18	−0.80	−0.93	0.00	−0.90	−0.89
384 Transport Equipment	−0.18	2.13	7.47	−9.00	−0.17	−0.37	−0.00	−0.37	−0.34
38A Misc. Mfrs.	4.05	−0.76	−1.80	−7.92	0.87	0.73	0.00	0.77	0.81
2 Mining, Quarrying	−0.21	0.53	1.25	−1.76	−0.18	−0.23	−0.00	−0.22	−4.17
4 Utilities					−0.02			−0.02	0.01
5 Construction					0.05			0.04	0.06
6 Wholesale Trade					0.02			−0.00	0.03
7 Transportation					0.02			0.01	0.03
8 Financial Services					−0.00			−0.01	1.02
9 Personal Services					0.01			−0.01	0.01

Table 7. Sectoral effects on Canada of North American free trade: Tariffs and NTBs (percent change).

ISIC Sector	Exports	Imports	Bilateral Imports		Output	No. Firms	Elasticity	Capital	Employment
			US	Mexico					
1 Agriculture	0.38	3.23	4.74	3.65	–0.15	0.00	0.00	–0.15	–0.14
310 Food	4.99	4.61	12.35	15.12	0.26	–0.32	–0.00	–0.26	–0.23
321 Textiles	5.80	20.62	43.76	23.32	–3.80	–4.45	0.00	–4.44	–4.42
322 Clothing	31.01	11.27	56.59	25.52	0.66	–0.05	0.03	0.08	0.09
323 Leather Products	8.35	0.89	7.45	40.01	3.87	3.01	0.05	3.07	3.08
324 Footwear	26.80	7.51	45.33	45.97	3.04	1.69	0.05	1.94	1.96
331 Wood Products	0.95	4.41	6.33	18.88	0.44	–0.22	0.00	–0.16	–0.15
332 Furniture, Fixtures	11.38	21.00	35.70	38.93	–0.46	–1.31	0.02	–1.13	–1.11
341 Paper Products	–0.09	11.98	18.16	24.30	–0.29	–0.84	–0.00	–0.78	–0.75
342 Printing, Publishing	–0.51	2.67	3.33	8.34	–1.19	–1.40	–0.04	–1.33	–1.32
35A Chemicals	–1.68	12.83	21.36	15.07	–3.37	–4.01	–0.01	–4.00	–3.98
35B Petroleum Products	1.12	0.08	0.52	–5.73	0.70	0.11	0.01	0.30	0.32
355 Rubber Products	8.15	7.43	18.64	–11.61	0.92	0.21	0.06	0.33	0.35
36A Nonmetal Min. Prod.	2.48	4.45	11.67	1.27	0.99	0.22	0.05	0.42	0.44
362 Glass Products	159.80	–2.90	–1.86	8.77	157.93	156.45	–0.03	156.94	156.96
371 Iron, Steel	8.12	5.35	12.09	–10.36	2.71	1.49	0.16	1.62	1.64

(*Continued*)

Table 7. (*Continued*)

ISIC Sector	Exports	Imports	Bilateral Imports		Output	No. Firms	Elasticity	Capital	Employment
			US	Mexico					
372 Nonferrous Metals	9.58	−1.62	0.58	14.66	7.60	5.55	0.09	5.87	5.88
381 Metal Products	10.15	12.92	19.94	19.74	0.06	−1.45	0.02	−1.18	−1.16
382 Nonelec. Machinery	1.43	7.69	10.50	−25.74	−3.98	−4.83	0.02	−4.74	−4.73
383 Electrical Machinery	10.10	10.21	16.39	108.81	−0.16	−1.48	0.06	−1.28	−1.27
384 Transport Equipment	7.01	−2.92	−3.05	−12.65	5.41	3.82	0.05	4.06	4.06
38A Misc. Mfrs.	−2.06	7.42	11.75	8.47	−5.08	−6.07	0.02	−5.98	−5.96
2 Mining, Quarrying	0.94	0.57	0.90	−2.19	1.08	0.69	0.03	0.88	0.90
4 Utilities					0.17			0.16	0.20
5 Construction					0.13			0.12	0.13
6 Wholesale Trade					−0.21			−0.23	−0.20
7 Transportation					0.12			0.11	1.13
8 Financial Services					−0.14			−0.14	−0.12
9 Personal Services					−0.33			−0.34	−0.33

Table 8. Sectoral effects on Mexico of North American free trade: Tariffs and NTBs (percent change).

ISIC Sector	Exports	Imports	Bilateral Imports		Output	No. Firms	Elasticity	Capital	Employment
			US	Canada					
1 Agriculture	6.60	3.21	3.36	2.04	0.17	0.00	0.00	0.18	0.15
310 Food	7.39	12.11	20.45	4.27	–0.25	–0.62	0.01	–0.56	–0.67
321 Textiles	5.57	22.54	32.77	28.03	0.13	–0.15	0.03	–0.06	–0.13
322 Clothing	22.90	25.40	45.64	44.56	4.24	3.54	0.12	3.75	3.63
323 Leather Products	13.46	15.44	31.66	27.59	1.57	0.98	0.02	1.19	1.00
324 Footwear	10.53	38.33	48.90	52.62	0.84	0.05	0.01	0.32	0.28
331 Wood Products	0.58	29.56	36.68	40.79	–1.97	–2.25	0.02	–2.18	–2.23
332 Furniture, Fixtures	9.48	15.58	35.39	34.43	5.95	5.33	0.10	5.63	5.23
341 Paper Products	4.63	8.23	9.49	9.26	–1.14	–1.41	–0.02	–1.35	–1.47
342 Printing, Publishing	–1.74	10.63	23.29	17.08	–2.26	–2.67	–0.03	–2.52	–2.56
35A Chemicals	–4.74	15.83	21.59	24.87	–5.31	–5.28	–0.02	–5.27	–5.30
35B Petroleum Products	–4.72	4.60	4.74	14.73	–3.42	–2.73	–0.18	–2.63	–3.06
355 Rubber Products	–8.85	26.03	35.56	28.20	–7.40	–7.34	–0.02	–7.34	–7.39
36A Nonmetal Min. Prod.	–0.32	27.40	39.21	41.02	–1.85	–2.02	0.00	–1.92	–2.03
362 Glass Products	14.67	13.42	21.07	202.75	6.31	5.37	0.04	5.77	5.71
371 Iron, Steel	–5.39	13.10	23.20	16.69	–7.69	–7.42	–0.02	–7.40	–7.45

(Continued)

Table 8. (*Continued*)

ISIC Sector	Exports	Imports	Bilateral Imports		Output	No. Firms	Elasticity	Capital	Employment
			US	Canada					
372 Nonferrous Metals	23.76	4.25	9.69	11.40	21.31	19.74	0.12	19.98	19.89
381 Metal Products	1.91	18.22	25.97	24.86	−3.21	−3.82	0.04	−3.64	−3.69
382 Nonelec. Machinery	−23.08	19.19	32.00	27.05	−27.13	−27.98	−0.00	−27.68	−27.73
383 Electrical Machinery	100.17	−18.69	−2.30	−0.68	92.37	87.60	0.15	89.01	88.99
384 Transport Equipment	−8.63	18.56	22.91	23.66	−11.09	−10.67	−0.12	−10.69	−10.70
38A Misc. Mfrs.	−7.80	14.14	26.12	16.40	−10.95	−11.62	0.02	−11.37	−11.46
2 Mining, Quarrying	−1.98	5.43	6.13	6.59	−0.92	−0.93	−0.05	−0.89	−1.06
4 Utilities					−0.45			−0.44	−0.46
5 Construction					−0.33			−0.30	−0.34
6 Wholesale Trade					−0.22			−0.19	−0.37
7 Transportation					−0.40			−0.36	4.49
8 Financial Services					−0.34			−0.27	−0.66
9 Personal Services					−0.47			−0.45	−0.47

mineral products, iron and steel, non-electrical machinery, transport equipment, and mining and quarrying all rise while Mexican exports in these product categories fall. Gains by Mexican exporters to the United States appear to be primarily concentrated in agriculture, the semi-manufactured sectors, and some heavy industry. However, Canadian firms also expand exports to the United States in these product categories. Similarly, US producers displace Mexican producers in five different Canadian sectors, whereas the opposite occurs in only one (glass products), as can be seen in Table 7.

Mexico's increased exports to the US market are quite substantial in several product categories, such as clothing (24.9%), glass products (19.1%), nonferrous metals (27.6%), and electrical machinery (102.2%). The increases in US imports from Mexico in agriculture (10.8%), food (12.2%), and textiles (14.1%) are also substantial due to the assumed relaxation of US NTBs in these three product categories. However, the impact on total US imports is quite small due to Mexico's small share of the US market, as can be seen from column three of Table 6. The percent changes in total US imports of agriculture, food, textiles, and clothing under scenario (A) are only 2.0, 1.7, 0.2, and 1.5 percent, respectively.

Columns six and seven of Tables 6, 7, and 8 report the percent change in industry output and number of firms for each country. These results can also be used to calculate the percent change in firm output by taking the difference between these two columns. It is especially worth noting that firm output rises in the United States and Canada in every industry. The only exceptions in Mexico are chemicals, petroleum products, rubber products, and iron and steel, and in all four cases the decline in firm output is trivially small. This is the case despite the fact that firm perceived elasticity of demand falls in many sectors, as reported in column eight of each table.

The rationalization effect is sufficiently distinct that there are some sectors in Canada in which total industry production rises but employment of both capital and labor declines. For example, production of metal products rises by 0.1 percent in Canada even though capital and labor employment each fall by 1.2 percent (reported in the last two columns of Table 8). The industry expansion is possible due to the exit of 1.4 percent of the sector's firms, thus releasing fixed capital and labor for employment by the surviving firms.

Despite the distinctive increase in intra-industry trade, inter-sectoral specialization also emerges, particularly in Mexico. For example, employment of labor declines in 21 of the 29 industries in Mexico, shifting primarily toward the labor-intensive sectors: agriculture (0.2%), clothing (3.6%), leather products (1.0%), footwear (0.3%), furniture and fixtures (5.2%), and glass products (5.7%). However, the largest percentage changes in employment are in some of the industrial sectors, such as nonferrous metals (19.9%) and electrical machinery (89.0%).

Employment effects in the United States are more diffuse and are generally small, with percent employment declines generally less than one percent in each sector. The only exception is the glass products sector in which US employment declines by 11.6 percent. Note also that despite the sizable increase in US import quotas applied to Mexican exports of food, textiles, and clothing, US employment in these sectors still rises in order to satisfy the increase in Canadian demand for US-produced goods. US exports to Canada rise in food (12.4%), textiles (43.8%), and clothing (56.6%) due to the removal of Canada's relatively high tariffs in these product categories.

V. Conclusions

We have attempted to identify some important issues arising in the analysis of a NAFTA and to provide a computational assessment of some of the economic effects involved. While the various experiments that we have conducted are not exhaustive of all the possible changes that might be negotiated in connection with a NAFTA, they are nonetheless indicative of the order of magnitude on trade, output, number of firms, factor returns, and employment that could result from trilateral trade liberalization and increased investment.

Overall, our results suggest that the formation of a NAFTA will have positive benefits for all countries involved on several accounts, as follows:

1. The participating countries all enjoy an increase in aggregate welfare.
2. Although the inclusion of Mexico erodes some of Canada's benefits under the US-Canada FTA, the effect is minuscule.
3. The wage gap between the United States and Mexico will narrow, thereby reducing the incentive for illegal immigration. However, the real wage in the United States still rises as a result of trade liberalization.
4. A NAFTA will have beneficial scale effects in all three countries.
5. A reduction in barriers against foreign direct investment in Mexico will stimulate new capital formation, which has the beneficial effects of alleviating poverty in Mexico by raising the marginal product of labor and raising the average product of both capital and labor by increasing the scale of production in Mexico.
6. The inflow of capital into Mexico may come primarily from outside the NAFTA, not from the United States, suggesting the fear that US firms will relocate production in Mexico may be largely unfounded.
7. There appears to be relatively little intersectoral factor reallocation in the United States especially, so that the associated relocation costs are likely to be small.
8. While there are negative effects on the rest of the world, they appear to be relatively small.

Study Questions

1. What are the main issues that arise in analyzing the economic impact of the NAFTA from the standpoints of Canada, Mexico, and the United States? What are the potential economic effects to be expected?
2. What is the industry structure chosen for modeling purposes? The tariff rates and non-tariff barriers? The model parameters?

3. What are the computational experiments that are run, and what are the main computational results of the NAFTA with respect to Canada, Mexico, the U.S., and the rest of world? What are the implications of an increase in Mexico's capital stock? What are the employment and wage impacts of the NAFTA? Effects on sectoral outputs and trade?

References

Brown, D. K., A. V. Deardorff, and R. M. Stern (1991). "Some Estimates of a North American Free Trade Agreement," *Federal Reserve Bank of Minneapolis Quarterly Review* (Winter).

Brown, D. K. and R. M. Stern (1989). "US-Canada Bilateral Tariff Elimination: The Role of Product Differentiation and Market Structure," in R. C. Feenstra (ed.), *Trade Policies for International Competitiveness* (Chicago: University of Chicago Press).

Deardorff, A. V. and R. M. Stern (1990). *Computational Analysis of Global Trading Arrangements* (Ann Arbor: University of Michigan Press).

Dixit, A. and J. E. Stiglitz (1977). "Monopolistic Competition and Optimum Product Diversity," *American Economic Review* 76, pp. 297–308.

Hinojosa-Ojeda, R. and S. Robinson (1991). "Alternative Scenarios of US-Mexico Integration: A Computable General Equilibrium Approach," Working Paper No. 609 (Department of Agricultural and Resource Economics, University of California, Berkeley).

KPMG Peat Marwick/Policy Economics Group (1991). "Analysis of Economic Effects of a Free Trade Area Between the United States and Mexico: Executive Summary" (Washington, DC: US Council of the Mexico-US Business Committee).

Spence, M. E. (1976). "Product Selection, Fixed Costs, and Monopolistic Competition," *Review of Economic Studies* 43, pp. 217–236.

Suggested Further Reading

Brown, Drusilla K., Alan V. Deardorff, and Robert M. Stern. 1992. "A U.S.-Mexico-Canada Free Trade Agreement: Sectoral Employment Effects and Regional/Occupational Employment Realignments in the United States," National Commission for Employment Policy, *The Employment Effects of the North American Free Trade Agreement: Recommendations and Background Studies*, Special Report, October.

Brown, Drusilla K., Alan V. Deardorff, and Robert M. Stern. 1995. "Expanding NAFTA: Economic Effects of Accession of Chile and Other Major South American Nations," *North American Journal of Economics and Finance* 6, pp. 149–170.

Harris, Richard G. 2006. "The Economic Impact of the Canada-U.S. FTA and NAFTA Agreements for Canada: A Review of the Evidence," in John M. Curtis and Aaron Sydor (eds.), *NAFTA @ 10*, Trade Policy Research, Special Edition, Foreign Affairs and International Trade Canada. Ottawa: Minister of Public Works and Government Services Canada.

Hufbauer, Gary Clyde and Jeffrey J. Schott. 2005. *NAFTA Revisited: Achievements and Challenges*. Washington, D.C.: Institute for International Economics.

Lederman, Daniel, William Maloney, and Luis Servin. 2006. "NAFTA at Ten Years: Lessons for Development," in Richard Newfarmer (ed.), *Trade, Doha, and Development*. Washington, D.C.: The World Bank.

Chapter 13

Computable General Equilibrium Estimates of the Gains from US-Canadian Trade Liberalization*

Drusilla K. Brown and Robert M. Stern

I. Introduction

The purpose of this chapter is to provide some estimates of the economic effects of the elimination of bilateral US and Canadian tariffs that will be implemented as the result of the US-Canadian Free Trade Agreement (FTA) that was negotiated in 1986–1987 and received legislative approval subsequently. While we focus on bilateral tariff elimination, it should be emphasized that the FTA dealt with a number of nontariff barriers (NTBs) as well. These include, for example, the elimination of certain bilateral agricultural and related NTBs, removal of Canadian provincial wine restrictions, removal of US countervailing duties on shakes and shingles, removal of voluntary restraints on Canadian steel exports to the United States, and a lower threshold for bidding on government procurement contracts for

* Reprinted from *Economic Aspects of Regional Trading Arrangements*, David Greenaway, Thomas Hyclak and Robert J. Thornton (eds.), London: Harvester Wheatsheaf, 1989.

specified entities in the two nations. However, as is discussed later in the chapter, these changes in bilateral NTBs appear to be of comparatively minor importance.

Aspects of the agreement concerning the administrative governance of bilateral trade may ultimately prove to be the most interesting and significant. These include: new and possibly more liberal and transparent rules and procedures involving bilateral trade and investment in automobiles and parts, energy products, and services; certain clarifications and guarantees involving nondiscrimination in foreign direct investment; and some potentially very important arrangements for the settlement of trade and investment disputes that might arise in bilateral relations.

Bilateral removal of tariffs and certain NTBs can be analyzed in quantitative terms. But it is unfortunately very difficult to quantify the economic benefits that may arise from improvements in the rules and procedures governing international trade and investment transactions. Such benefits may nonetheless be substantial from the standpoint of both the United States and Canada, and must be factored into an overall assessment of the FTA.

To evaluate the FTA, we first review the various effects that the FTA might have on the United States and Canada. We next discuss the findings of previous studies of the effects of the FTA. We then describe the computational model that we have developed for the purpose of analyzing the effects of the FTA, and we follow with our empirical results. We conclude in the final section with a summary assessment.

II. Analyzing the Economic Impacts of the FTA

An indication of the size and sectoral characteristics of post-Tokyo Round bilateral Canadian and US tariffs and NTBs is given in Table 1. It is evident from this table that Canadian bilateral tariffs and NTBs are noticeably higher for most sectors as compared to the United States. If we assume that these tariffs and NTBs are to be removed in the course of the implementation of the FTA, what will the effects be?

Table 1. Comparison of post-Tokyo Round: Canadian and US trade barriers (%).

	Canada		United States	
	Tariff Rate	NTBs (tariff equivalent)	Tariff Rate	NTBs (tariff equivalent)
Agriculture	2.2	11.9	2.2	6.9
Forestry	0.0	0.1	0.2	0.2
Fishing and trapping	0.2	0.0	1.4	0.0
Metal mines	0.1	0.0	0.2	0.0
Mineral fuels	0.4	0.0	0.3	0.0
Nonmetal mines and quarries	0.5	0.0	0.1	0.4
Food and beverage	4.2	9.0	3.5	8.5
Tobacco products	16.0	0.0	10.1	0.6
Rubber and plastics products	8.9	0.0	8.4	0.4
Leather products	12.0	4.2	7.9	0.0
Textiles	8.9	0.0	7.3	0.4
Knitting mills	21.5	0.0	12.6	0.4
Clothing	17.2	0.0	10.7	0.4
Wood products	2.7	0.0	1.4	12.9
Furniture and fixtures	12.6	0.0	3.0	0.8
Paper and allied products	4.11	0.0	0.9	11.3
Printing and publishing	1.4	0.8	0.5	0.2
Primary metals	4.0	1.3	2.2	4.2
Metal fabricating	6.8	0.9	3.2	1.0
Machinery	4.7	0.9	2.5	3.0
Transportation and equipment	2.3	0.0	0.5	0.0
Electrical products	6.1	0.9	3.7	0.1
Nonmetallic mineral products	3.4	0.0	2.9	0.0
Petroleum and coal products	0.5	0.0	0.4	0.0
Chemical and chemical products	5.6	0.0	2.2	1.2
Misc. manufacturing	6.2	0.9	3.5	0.2
Weighted average	3.8	1.0	2.3	1.8

Source: Adapted from Magun, Rao, and Lodh (1987, pp. 25 and 141–153).

It is possible analytically to identify three main channels by which the removal of tariffs and NTBs would affect the two nations. These include: (1) inter-sectoral specialization effects; (2) rationalization effects; and (3) macroeconomic effects. In addition, the changes brought about by the FTA in the rules and procedures involving bilateral trade and investment may result in a reduction in the uncertainty of policies and therefore provide additional elements of potential benefit to the two nations.

Inter-Sectoral Specialization

A central issue in evaluating the FTA is how bilateral tariff removal may affect the allocation of factors of production among sectors of the economy. Depending on the relative levels of tariffs and NTBs in the two countries, some of the tradable goods sectors will expand whereas others will contract as the FTA liberalization takes effect. Productive resources will thus presumably be allocated more efficiently as compared to the pre-FTA position as each country specializes in the production of tradable goods in which it has a comparative advantage.

We might also expect a shift in production of tradable goods away from the production of nontradables (e.g., goods and services that are limited spatially because of transportation costs and other characteristics that require close proximity between production and consumption). The bilateral elimination of tariffs will result in reductions in consumer prices due to the lower costs of imported goods as well as reductions in the prices of imported inputs that firms use in the production process. Lower prices of inputs will result in lower costs to firms and possibly lower prices of goods to consumers as well. Both of the foregoing effects will result in a shift towards tradable goods whose prices will fall relative to nontradables.

In analyzing these various effects, there are some interesting and important modeling issues that arise when characterizing the US and Canadian economies and the relations between them and with third countries. For example, suppose that we assume a world in which the goods being produced and traded are homogeneous across firms and countries, there are constant returns to scale in production, and goods markets are perfectly competitive. Assume further that Canada is a small country economically speaking, so that the formation of an FTA would not affect equilibrium world prices.

In such a model, Canada would gain unambiguously from the formation of an FTA. As a result of preferential treatment, Canada would receive the world price plus the US tariff on any exports to the United States. These are more favorable terms of trade than Canada could obtain from sales either to any other market or to the US market in the absence of the FTA.

While this outcome may seem intuitively plausible, it involves an important difficulty. With preferential trading, the small country may trade only with the large country and will cease to trade with the rest of the world.

In order to avoid this implausible outcome, it has been common to assume that the products of the trading nations are differentiated nationally according to where they are produced. Allowance for "love of variety" in the utility functions of consumers guarantees that all bilateral trade flows will continue in the event that a preferential trading bloc is formed.

This formulation, however, has proved to have difficulties as well. Under national product differentiation, the relative sizes of the national tariffs and NTBs will determine how the two countries might be affected by an FTA. As we have seen, Canadian tariffs are noticeably higher than US tariffs. Consequently, the United States will penetrate Canadian markets more deeply in a number of sectors as compared to Canada's penetration of US markets. In these circumstances, the relative demand for the variety of each good produced by Canada will fall, leading to a decline in its price. Canada will thus experience a deterioration in its terms of trade, and it is conceivable that Canadian welfare could decline.

This feature of models in which goods are distinguished by country of origin arises because each country has a monopoly in the supply of the particular varieties of goods that it trades in world markets. Since market power can be exploited through the use of a tariff, optimal tariffs may therefore be relatively large, even for small countries. Preferential as well as multilateral trade liberalization may therefore result in significant changes in the terms of trade. These terms-of-trade changes, rather than efficiency gains from inter-sectoral reallocation of resources, may accordingly dominate the welfare conclusions.

If a model of this kind were to be used to analyze the US-Canadian FTA, the results would then be predisposed towards a terms-of-trade decline and welfare reduction of the country with the relatively higher tariffs. Thus, we would expect that Canada's welfare would decline while US welfare would rise.

In seeking alternatives to national product differentiation, one possibility might be to assume that there is product differentiation at the firm level. In this case, bilateral trade flows would be sustained with a preferential trading arrangement since no two firms in the world would sell the same variety. Another alternative is to assume that all firms supply a homogeneous product but that national markets are segmented so that firms make separate price and supply decisions for each national market. If firms behave as Cournot followers, taking output by other firms as fixed, then preferential trading would leave all of the bilateral trade flows intact.

It will be evident in these cases that the firms involved can exercise some degree of market power. This means that it is no longer possible to maintain the assumption of perfect competition, and that it is necessary accordingly to proceed in a framework in which there are imperfectly competitive firms. Once we make allowance for imperfect competition, this raises the possibility that there may be economies of scale and changes in product variety at the firm level that have to be taken into account.

Rationalization Effects

Proponents of a US-Canadian FTA have placed great emphasis on the gains that might be obtained from the realization of scale economies and the increased product variety that mutual market access will make possible. In addition, it is believed that the influx of tariff-free imports will improve the competitive environment for firms selling domestically, requiring these firms either to shut down and leave the industry or to increase their efficiency. Bilateral free trade can thus be expected to result in a rationalization of the production process by increasing output per firm and lowering average total cost.

According to this line of reasoning, there is a presumption that Canadian manufacturing firms especially will undergo rationalization as the consequence of the FTA. Canadian tariffs may have sheltered domestic firms historically, with the consequence that plants may be of suboptimal size and a large variety of products may be produced by individual firms. With the removal of bilateral tariffs and NTBs, Canadian firms will be induced by increased competitive pressures and profit considerations to take advantage of enhanced market opportunities by expanding output and reducing the number of product varieties. It is contended that the United States is less likely to gain from rationalization because the attainment of optimal plant size and concentration on a limited number of product varieties are more feasible in the US market because of its comparatively large size.

While there may well be rationalization as the result of a US-Canadian FTA, questions arise about the actual importance of rationalization and the economic factors that will govern its realization. The relatively low tariff rates noted in Table 1 suggest that US and Canadian firms already enjoy substantial access to each other's markets. Furthermore, Canadian firms have had to adapt to the multilateral tariff reductions implemented during the 1970s and 1980s as the result of the Kennedy and Tokyo Round negotiations. Finally, we may note that many Canadian firms are already being subjected to the efficiency-stimulating experience of having to compete with US firms in the US market. How large the benefits from rationalization will be as the result of the FTA is therefore unclear.

If there already exist significant pro-competitive effects in the trade relations between the United States and Canada, the issue is whether and how rationalization may occur in response to the bilateral removal of the existing relatively low tariffs. As we argue below, whether or not small tariff changes lead to rationalization will depend on the factor-intensity characteristics and cost structure of the firms and industries involved. This insight is potentially important because it implies that there may be a significant amount of *inter-industry* resource reallocation as the result of an FTA in contrast to the mainly *infra-industry* changes that have been emphasized in previous research.

Macroeconomic Effects

We have already mentioned that the bilateral elimination of tariffs and NTBs will lead to reductions in consumer prices, which may in turn result in an increase in the real disposable income of consumers. If this leads to increased consumer spending, if the economies are operating at less than full employment, and if domestic macroeconomic policies remain unchanged, then there will be an increase in real GNP, output, trade, and employment in both countries in the short-to-medium run. To the extent that these macroeconomic changes occur, they will reinforce the microeconomic benefits stemming from lower consumer prices, improvements in resource allocation, and the realization of economies of scale.

Reduction in the Uncertainty of Policies

In addition to the readily quantifiable effects of trade liberalization, there may be a number of potentially important benefits resulting from changes in the rules and procedures governing international trade and investment relations between the United States and Canada. These include the agreements that limit the use by Canada of investment performance requirements for foreign affiliates of US firms, the guarantee of national treatment and rights of establishment for foreign firms investing in most industries, the removal of Canadian duty remission schemes that had been condoned in the US-Canadian Auto Pact, and less nationalistic and potentially discriminatory Canadian energy and agricultural policies.

New dispute settlement procedures will also be established that are especially important to Canada. They are designed to depoliticize the investigation of trade and investment disputes and to reduce the likelihood that politically driven and therefore damaging actions will be taken by the United States. The costs of conducting trade and investment transactions may thus be materially reduced as the result of the FTA.

Having considered in general terms the economic effects that may result from the bilateral elimination of existing trade barriers, let us now review briefly what previous studies of a US-Canadian FTA have concluded.

III. What Do Previous Studies Suggest about the Effects of the FTA?

In order to determine the importance of existing restrictions and policies and thus to determine what the economic effects might be of removing the restrictions and bringing about changes in policies, it is necessary to rely on some kind of economic model. In choosing an economic model for purposes of analysis, it is imperative that the analyst make clear what the important assumptions and limitations of the model are. This includes a complete and careful statement of the theoretical foundations of the model being used, how the parameters of the model have been selected, and a description and documentation of the data used in implementing the model. These are obviously important matters that should be insisted upon by those who will be using the model in question and are depending on it to obtain numerical results that are to he trusted in evaluating the policy options involved.

Broadly speaking, there are two classes of models that can be used. The first is an econometric model that is based on historical relationships that can be presumed to remain unchanged in the relevant policy horizon. If an econometric model is constructed and it fits the data well, it can then be used to make forecasts of how important variables such as output, trade and employment might be affected by the FTA. It should then be possible *ex post* to compare the model forecasts with actual values to determine how accurate the forecasts may have been.

Unfortunately, many of the changes that will come about as the result of the FTA depend on a variety of complex microeconomic behavioral relations and intersectoral and inter-country interactions. Constructing an econometric model that adequately captures these intricate microeconomic relationships is not currently feasible. Nonetheless, as will be noted below, a number of efforts have been made to adapt existing macroeconometric models of the Canadian economy for the purpose of estimating the effects of the FTA. However, it is by no means clear how the results are to be interpreted since the models used do not have well articulated microeconomic structures.

Instead of using an econometric approach, an alternative is to construct a general equilibrium model that will incorporate the important behavioral and interaction effects and that can be solved computationally so as to yield numerical results relating to the potential impacts of the FTA. In recent years, there has been considerable progress made in developing and using general equilibrium computational models, and a number of such models have been adapted to analysis of the FTA.

It should be emphasized that these computational models do not provide predictions that can be compared against actual outcomes. Rather, the numerical results of the models are to be interpreted in the light of their assumptions, parameters, and data. This means that, in evaluating model results, tests should be conducted to determine how sensitive or robust the results are to changes in different aspects of the model.

The general equilibrium models that have been used to date to estimate the effects of a US-Canadian FTA include Harris and Cox (1985), Hamilton and Whalley (1985), Markusen and Wigle (1987), Wigle (1988), and Brown and Stern (1987). The Government of Canada's Department of Finance (1988) has used the Harris–Cox model, with adaptations of some key parameters and more recent data on tariffs and NTBs to provide some other estimates of the effects of the FTA.

The Harris–Cox and Department of Finance models refer only to the effects of the FTA on Canada since the United States and the rest of world are not modeled explicitly. The Hamilton–Whalley, Wigle, Markusen–Wigle, and Brown–Stern models identify separate effects of the FTA for Canada, the United States, and the rest of world.

Some key results are summarized in Table 2 together with estimates based on macroeconometric models of the Canadian economy that have been adapted especially for the purpose of analyzing the impact of the FTA on Canada. It should be noted that in each case the bilateral tariffs were assumed to be eliminated all at once rather than being phased in over a ten-year period as called for in the actual implementation of the FTA. Thus, in any given

Table 2. Summary of studies of estimated changes in real income resulting from a US-Canadian Free Trade Agreement.

	Change in real income		
	Canada (%)	United States (%)	Other countries ($ million)
General equilibrium models			
Harris and Cox (1985)	8.9		
Canadian Department of Finance (1988)	2.5		
Markusen and Wigle (1987)	0.6	0.1	Negative
Wigle (1988)	–0.1	0.1	
Hamilton and Whalley (1985)	0.6	–0.04	Negative
Brown and Stern (1987)	–0.3	0.03	–19.8
Macroeconometric models			
Informetrica (1985)	3.0		
Dungan (1985)	3.3		
Wharton Econometrics (1987)	3.1		
Magun *et al.* (1987)	3.3		
Magun *et al.* (1988)	2.5		

Note: The estimates reported are sensitive to the degree of response of exports and imports to changes in relative prices. The results in the Harris and Cox and Department of Finance analyses are sensitive to the price response of import-competing manufacturing firms to the reduction of domestic trade barriers. Estimates for a given study vary due to different assumptions about the extent of trade liberalization and the size of the rationalization gain resulting from freer trade. The complete citations for the studies noted are given in the references.
Source: Adapted in part from Government of Canada, Department of Finance (1988, p. 32).

year during the implementation process, the effects of the FTA would be a cumulative fraction of the ultimate effect over the entire period.

The estimate based on the Harris–Cox (1985) model suggests that the real income (welfare) gains resulting from the FTA could approach nearly 9 percent of Canadian GNP. The size of this gain depends crucially on the parameters that Harris and Cox use to represent rationalization effects and the assumed pricing rules for Canadian manufacturing firms.

Two imperfectly competitive market structures were adopted by Harris and Cox. Under the assumption of monopolistic competition, profit-maximizing firms set price as a mark-up over marginal cost. The size of the mark-up depends on the firm's perceived market power. Alternatively, firms within an industry may tacitly collude, by adopting a "focal price" which is charged by all firms. Harris and Cox set the focal price equal to the world price plus the import tariff. The actual price charged by each firm is assumed to be a weighted average of the monopolistically competitive and focal prices.

The effect of tariff liberalization on firm output can be determined by evaluating the impact on each component of the pricing rule. Tariff reductions increase import competition. For monopolistically competitive firms, increased competition raises the perceived elasticity of demand so that the profit-maximizing mark-up over marginal cost falls. The focal price of collusive firms also declines, since this price is equal to the world price plus the tariff. Free entry is assumed, which implies that a fall in price must be accompanied by an increase in firm output to satisfy the zero-profits condition.

The version of the Harris–Cox model used by the Canadian Department of Finance suggests an estimated real income gain of 2.5 percent, which is considerably less than the original Harris–Cox result. Rationalization effects nonetheless remain the driving force, resulting from the amalgamated pricing behavior being assumed for the imperfectly competitive Canadian-manufacturing firms.

The results obtained by Wigle and by Markusen and Wigle further illustrate the sensitivity of this approach to the precise theoretical and parametric specification. In both studies, monopolistically competitive and collusive behavior are modeled as in Harris and Cox. However, each industry is specified as *either* monopolistically competitive *or* collusive. Markusen and Wigle find that Canada's welfare would rise by 0.6 percent of national income, which is only one-quarter of the increase calculated by the Department of Finance, and that US welfare would rise by 0.1 percent. Wigle finds that bilateral tariff removal will result in a *decline* in welfare for Canada of 0.1 percent of national income and that welfare for the United States will rise by 0.1 percent. The decline in welfare for Canada appears to be the result of a deterioration in the terms of trade.

Hamilton and Whalley's results are considerably smaller than those obtained by Harris and Cox and the Department of Finance. Hamilton and Whalley use a model in which there is perfect competition and constant returns to scale, and they allow for national product differentiation. Brown and Stern use a somewhat different modeling approach, but they also assume perfect competition, constant returns to scale, and national product differentiation.

It is noteworthy that Hamilton and Whalley obtain a positive welfare gain for Canada equal to 0.6 percent of GNP and a welfare loss of 0.04 percent for the United States as the result of the bilateral removal of tariffs, whereas Brown and Stern report a welfare *loss* of 0.3 percent of GNP for Canada and a welfare *gain* of 0.03 percent for the United States. Given the relatively higher Canadian tariffs, it would have been expected that Canada might well experience a decline in its terms of trade and thus in welfare, which is what Brown and Stern found to be the case. It is therefore not clear why Hamilton and Whalley obtained the results noted.

The macroeconometric approach can be used for the purpose of analyzing the effects of the FTA by first determining the amount by which the import and export prices and volume of trade of the two countries may change. These factors are then entered as exogenous changes in the model and a solution is obtained for changes in the variables of interest.

Since the macroeconometric models used do not have well-articulated microeconomic structures, it cannot be readily determined how the aggregate results obtained correspond to the results based on the general equilibrium trade models. To illustrate this point, we may note, for example, that the Economic Council of Canada (Magun *et al.*, 1987, 1988) used the CANDIDE econometric model of the Canadian economy to carry out two simulations of the effects of the FTA. The first simulation considered only the macroeconomic impacts of the bilateral removal of tariffs and certain NTBs, while the second simulation involved an adjustment to take into account the possible rationalization (scale) effects that might occur in Canada. This necessitated decomposing the aggregate effects by sector on the basis of a Canadian input-output table and applying rationalization coefficients estimated for individual industries. The results thus reflect the structure of the CANDIDE macroeconometric model in combination with the Canadian input-output structure and scale economy parameters, but without explicit behavioral relations linking the various factors.

Several of the studies noted in Table 2 provide detailed results indicating how trade, output, employment and the returns to capital in individual sectors in Canada and the United States might be affected by the FTA. Considerable interest is attached to the sectoral results insofar as they indicate which industries may expand or contract as a consequence of the FTA.

However, because the studies noted in Table 2 vary substantially in terms of their modeling methodology and the particular assumptions made concerning market structure, pricing behavior, and the choice of elasticity and scale parameters, their sectoral details are bound to be different. We shall not dwell, therefore, on sectoral comparisons at this point. Instead, what we propose now is to turn to our own computational model that we have developed to estimate the economic effects of the US-Canadian FTA. When we present our sectoral results below, we shall have occasion to comment on how they differ from those in some of the studies noted in Table 2.

IV. The Computational Model

The review of previous modeling efforts reveals a number of modeling choices which cast doubt on the robustness of the results obtained. First, national product differentiation has been adopted in all of the general equilibrium trade models discussed above for the purpose of identifying the bilateral trade flows to receive preferential treatment. However, this assumption gives rise to terms-of-trade considerations that dominate the welfare conclusions of tariff liberalization. In view of the strong implications and artificial nature of this assumption, we have chosen to allow intra-industry trade to emerge naturally as the result of strategic firm behavior. National product differentiation is adopted only in perfectly competitive sectors in which firm behavior does not lead to intra-industry trade.

Second, the use of "focal pricing" to model collusive behavior by firms predisposes the model to the conclusion that tariff liberalization increases output per firm. However, this market structure has been strongly criticized as unsustainable in the presence of free entry. We have not adopted the focal pricing mechanism here, but rather adhere more closely to those market structures that are more robust theoretically.

Third, industry organization varies according to the degree of competition or market power, the degree of product differentiation, and the ease with which new firms can enter a market. Therefore, a variety of possible market structures have been integrated into the model to accommodate competitive differences.

The model has some features in common with previous general equilibrium models used to analyze the FTA. However, we capture a broader array of imperfectly competitive market structures in *both* nations and do so without relying on the *ad hoc* firm behavior and national product differentiation assumptions that have driven the results of previous work.

The model consists of four trading regions. Canada, the United States, and a group of thirty-two other countries are modeled explicitly,[1] while the rest of the world constitutes an abbreviated fourth region.

Sectoral coverage includes twenty-two tradable product categories based on three-digit ISIC industries and seven nontradable

---

[1] The thirty-two countries include sixteen industrialized countries — Australia, Austria, Belgium-Luxembourg, Denmark, Federal Republic of Germany, Finland, France, Ireland, Italy, Japan, the Netherlands, New Zealand, Norway, Sweden, Switzerland, and the United Kingdom — and sixteen newly industrializing countries — Argentina, Brazil, Chile, Colombia, Greece, Hong Kong, India, Israel, Mexico, Portugal, Singapore, South Korea, Spain, Taiwan, Turkey, and Yugoslavia.

categories based on one-digit ISIC industries.[2] Each industry in the model can be characterized by one of five market structures, including: perfect competition; monopolistic competition with free entry; monopolistic competition without entry; market segmentation with free entry; and market segmentation without entry.

An overview of the model is provided below. For those readers interested in the technical details, the equations and variables of the model are set out in the Appendix.

To elaborate on the different market structures, it will be recalled from our earlier discussion that, in order to identify bilateral trade flows that are to receive preferential treatment, one approach is to assume that products can be differentiated either by country of origin or by firm. Both the perfectly competitive and monopolistically competitive industries in our model arc characterized accordingly by some degree of product differentiation. In the case of perfect competition, products are assumed to be differentiated by *country*, while in the monopolistically competitive industries products are differentiated by *firm*.

In both cases, we adopt the approach to product differentiation suggested by Dixit and Stiglitz (1977) and Spence (1976). Consumers and producers are assumed to use a two-stage procedure for allocating expenditure across differentiated products. At the first stage, expenditure is allocated across goods, without regard for the country of origin or the producing firm. At this stage the utility function is taken to be Cobb–Douglas, and the production function requires inputs in fixed proportion.

The Appendix contains the proportionately differentiated version of the model, with the circumflex indicating proportionate change. Final and intermediate demands for tradable good j in country i are given by Equations (1) and (3), and final and intermediate demands for nontradable good j are given by Equations (2) and (4). Final and intermediate demand are aggregated to form total demand for a tradables and nontradables in Equations (5) and (6).

---

[2] Our country and sectoral coverage correspond to that used in various adaptations of the Michigan Model of World Production and Trade. See Deardorff and Stern (1986), Brown (1987), and Brown and Stern (1987).

In the second stage, expenditure on each good chosen in the first stage is allocated among the competing varieties. The aggregation function at this stage is CES. The demand for each variety, conditional on the level of the aggregate chosen in the first stage, is given in Equation (7). For perfectly competitive industries, Equation (7a) is demand in country i for the variety produced by country r. For monopolistically competitive industries, Equation (7b) gives demand in country i for the variety produced by a representative firm in country r. These equations differ in that entry in an industry will reduce the demand for other competing firms.

Perfectly competitive firms set price equal to marginal cost, as given in Equation (19a). However, monopolistically competitive firms maximize profits by setting price as a mark-up over marginal cost, as given in the second term in Equation (19b). It will be noted that the more elastic is demand, the smaller will be the difference between price and marginal cost.

Imperfectly competitive industries in which all firms produce a homogeneous product are modeled following Venables (1985). In this case, each firm behaves as a Cournot follower and assumes that national markets are segmented. The firm establishes a set of profit-maximizing prices, one for each national market, assuming that output by other firms is fixed. It can be shown, under these conditions, that a representative firm's sales to country r is given by Equation (7c).

Turning to the factor markets, the variable input requirements are taken to be the same for all market structures. Primary and intermediate input aggregates are required in fixed proportion to output. Expenditure on primary inputs is allocated between capital and labor, assuming that a CES function is used to form the primary input aggregate. This assumption implies conditional labor and capital demands given by Equations (10a) and (11a). In imperfectly competitive industries, an additional fixed input of capital is required, thus yielding conditional factor demands in Equations (10b), (10c), (11b), and (11c).

Capital and labor are assumed to be perfectly mobile between sectors. The return to capital is determined to equate demand to a fixed supply of capital, as given by Equation (27). The return to labor is fixed. However, total expenditure is set endogenously to maintain the demand for labor to a fixed supply of labor, as given by Equation (28).

The number of firms in each industry is determined by the zero-profit condition. In the free-entry versions of the monopolistic competition and market segmentation market structures, the number of firms is determined to guarantee that price equals average total cost, as given by Equations (24b) and (24c). In all other cases, the number of firms is assumed not to change.[3]

Equilibrium prices are determined in world markets. In the perfectly competitive industries, total demand for each national variety must equal national output as in Equation (31a). For monopolistically competitive industries, total demand for the variety produced by each firm must equal supply by that firm, as in Equation (31b). In the case of market segmentation, total supply by all firms to each national market must equal demand in that market, as given by Equation (31c).

Tariffs and exchange rates link equilibrium prices determined in the world system to prices paid by consumers or received by sellers in the country system. In the perfectly competitive and monopolistically competitive industries, the price determined in the world system is the price received by the seller denominated in the numeraire currency, which is the US dollar. The price paid by the consumer, then, is the world price, plus changes in the exchange rate and tariffs, as can be seen in Equations (14a) and (14b).

In the case of market segmentation, the price determined in the world system is the price paid by the consumer denominated in the numeraire currency. The price received by the seller is the world price, plus changes in the change rate, but minus the tariff-applied by the importing country, as is shown by Equation (14c).

The exchange rates for Canada and the group of other countries are determined to maintain the trade balance at its level in the base

[3] Under perfect competition, technology is characterized by constant returns to scale. Therefore, the number of firms is indeterminant. However, the threat of entry guarantees marginal cost pricing and zero profits.

period. This is shown by Equation (30i), where the trade balance is defined by Equation (29). With the US dollar taken as the numeraire, the price of the dollar is held constant as in Equation (30i′). In the case of the rest of the world, the currency is assumed to be pegged to a market basket of currencies, but an import licensing scheme is adopted to hold the current account at the base level. The tariff equivalent of an import license is calculated endogenously, as in Equation (34).[4]

The model is in linear form and thus can be solved by matrix inversion. The base year is 1976 for data on production, employment, and trade for the United States, Canada, and other countries, and the rest of the world. Input-output coefficients for the production function were derived from the US input-output table for 1972 and the Canadian table for 1976.

The market structure assignments by industry are listed in Table 3. These assignments represent our judgment of the industrial organization characteristics of each industry.[5] It may be that other analysts would choose different characteristics than the ones that we have selected. In this event, we could enter these alternative characteristics and solve the model accordingly.

The key parameters of the model are reported in Tables 4 (a), (b), and (c) for the United States, and Tables 5 (a), (b), and (c) for Canada. The bilaterally trade-weighted tariff averages for each industry involved in US-Canada trade are listed in the last column of Table 4 (a) and (b), and Table 5 (a) and (b).[6]

---

[4] See Deardorff and Stern (1986, pp. 22–23) for a discussion of the role of import licensing in the Michigan Model of World Production and Trade.

[5] We are indebted to Lynne Pepall for assistance in selecting the industry characteristics.

[6] These tariff averages do not correspond to those listed in Table 1 because of differences in industry classification and the year chosen for trade weighting. Also, we have not taken into account the *ad valorem* equivalents of the NTBs noted in Table 1. According to Magun *et al.* (1988, pp. 24–34), only minor modifications are to be made in existing NTBs in the course of implementation of the FTA. Nonetheless, some of our sector results for bilateral tariff removal will be overstated to the extent that the existing NTBs will serve to dampen the impact of the tariff removal.

Table 3. Industry structure of the model.

Sector	Market Structure	Entry
Tradable industries		
Agriculture	Perfect competition	Free
Food	Monopolistic competition	Free
Textiles	Monopolistic competition	None
Clothing	Monopolistic competition	Free
Leather products	Perfect competition	Free
Footwear	Monopolistic competition	Free
Wood products	Perfect competition	Free
Furniture and fixtures	Monopolistic competition	Free
Paper products	Monopolistic competition	Free
Printing and publishing	Monopolistic competition	Free
Chemicals	Monopolistic competition	None
Petroleum products	Market segmentation	None
Rubber products	Market segmentation	None
Nonmetallic min. products	Monopolistic competition	Free
Glass products	Market segmentation	None
Iron and steel	Market segmentation	Free
Nonferrous metals	Monopolistic competition	Free
Metal products	Monopolistic competition	Free
Nonelectrical machinery	Monopolistic competition	None
Electrical machinery	Monopolistic competition	Free
Transport equipment	Monopolistic competition	None
Misc. manufactures	Monopolistic competition	Free
Nontradable industries		
Mining and quarrying	Market segmentation	None
Utilities	Market segmentation	None
Construction	Perfect competition	Free
Wholesale trade	Monopolistic competition	Free
Transportation	Monopolistic competition	Free
Financial services	Monopolistic competition	None
Personal services	Perfect competition	Free

For the imperfectly competitive industries, the elasticity of demand, share of capital that is fixed, variable cost share of total cost, and the markup of price over marginal cost are all derivable from the theoretical structure of the model. Details are given in Brown and

Table 4. Parameters of the model: United States.

Sector	Labor Share of Primary Input Cost	Elasticity of Substitution	Tariff on Canadian Exports
(a) Perfect competition			
Tradable industries			
Agriculture	0.19	15.00	1.60
Leather products	0.87	15.00	2.50
Nontradable industries			
Wood products	0.62	15.00	0.20
Construction	0.79	15.00	
Personal services	0.90	15.00	

(*Continued*)

Table 4. (*Continued*)

Sector	Demand Elasticity	Variable K Share of Total K	Variable Input Cost Share	Labor Share of Primary Input Cost	Elasticity of Substitution	Tariff on Canadian Exports
(b) Monopolistic competition						
Tradable industries						
Food	−14.73	0.55	0.93	0.48	15.00	3.80
Textiles	−15.08	0.18	0.93	0.81	15.00	7.20
Clothing	−13.48	0.90	0.93	0.88	15.00	18.40
Footwear	−11.47	0.44	0.91	0.86	15.00	9.00
Furniture and fixtures	−14.37	0.19	0.93	0.79	15.00	4.60
Paper products	−14.62	0.40	0.93	0.70	15.00	0.00
Printing and publishing	−15.01	0.33	0.93	0.79	15.00	0.30
Chemicals	−15.56	0.64	0.94	0.56	15.00	0.60
Nonmetallic min. products	−14.67	0.58	0.93	0.66	15.00	0.30
Nonferrous metals	−13.80	0.13	0.93	0.74	15.00	0.50
Metal products	−14.78	0.40	0.93	0.74	15.00	4.00
Nonelectrical machinery	−15.97	0.47	0.94	0.76	15.00	2.20
Electrical machinery	−14.65	0.24	0.93	0.81	15.00	4.50
Transport equipment	−14.61	0.33	0.93	0.71	15.00	0.00
Misc. manufactures	−13.89	0.75	0.93	0.48	15.00	0.90
Nontradable industries						
Wholesale trade	−14.90	0.77	0.93	0.58	15.00	
Transportation	−14.88	0.75	0.93	0.61	15.00	
Financial services	−14.91	0.87	0.93	0.29	15.00	

(*Continued*)

Table 4. (*Continued*)

Sector	Mark-up Over MC			Variable K Share of Total K	Variable Input Cost Share	Labor Share of Primary Input Cost
	US	Other	Canada			
(c) Market segmentation						
Tradable industries						
Petroleum products	0.05	0.05	0.05	0.91	0.99	0.43
Rubber products	0.05	0.05	0.05	0.63	0.93	0.63
Glass products	0.05	0.05	0.05	0.57	0.93	0.69
Nontradable industries						
Iron and steel	0.05	0.05	0.05	0.24	0.93	0.77
Mining and quarrying	0.05			0.98	0.99	0.33
Utilities	0.05			0.98	0.99	0.28

Table 5. Parameters of the model: Canada.

Sector	Labor Share of Primary Input Cost	Elasticity of Substitution	Tariff on US Exports
(a) Perfect competition			
Tradable industries			
Agriculture	0.24	15.00	2.20
Leather products	0.83	15.00	4.00
Wood products	0.76	15.00	2.50
Nontradable industries			
Construction	0.64	15.00	
Personal services	0.61	15.00	

(*Continued*)

Table 5. (*Continued*)

Sector	Demand Elasticity	Variable K Share of Total K	Variable Input Cost Share	Labor Share of Primary Input Cost	Elasticity of Substitution	Tariff on Canadian Exports
(b) Monopolistic competition						
Tradable industries						
Food	−13.44	0.31	0.93	0.60	15.00	5.40
Textiles	−10.38	0.06	0.90	0.76	15.00	16.90
Clothing	−11.17	0.06	0.91	0.80	15.00	23.70
Footwear	−10.15	0.69	0.90	0.86	15.00	21.50
Furniture and fixtures	−14.35	0.26	0.93	0.79	15.00	14.30
Paper products	−19.91	0.67	0.95	0.63	15.00	6.60
Printing and publishing	−12.27	0.47	0.92	0.71	15.00	1.10
Chemicals	−12.95	0.49	0.92	0.58	15.00	7.90
Nonmetallic min. products	−15.43	0.69	0.94	0.58	15.00	4.40
Nonferrous metals	−14.08	0.30	0.93	0.77	15.00	3.30
Metal products	−13.11	0.41	0.92	0.70	15.00	8.60
Nonelectrical machinery	−11.27	0.08	0.91	0.69	15.00	4.60
Electrical machinery	−11.59	0.19	0.91	0.57	15.00	7.50
Transport equipment	−13.68	0.02	0.93	0.70	15.00	0.00
Misc. manufactures	−12.44	0.33	0.92	0.69	15.00	5.00
Nontradable industries						
Wholesale trade	−13.44	0.68	0.93	0.67	15.00	
Transportation	−14.07	0.58	0.93	0.66	15.00	
Financial services	−13.83	0.84	0.93	0.34	15.00	

(*Continued*)

Table 5. (*Continued*)

Sector	Mark-up Over MC			Variable *K* Share of Total *K*	Variable Input Cost Share	Labor Share of Primary Input Cost
	US	Other	Canada			
(c) Market segmentation						
Tradable industries						
Petroleum products	0.05	0.05	0.05	0.76	0.98	0.43
Rubber products	0.05	0.05	0.08	0.38	0.94	0.78
Glass products	0.05	0.05	0.15	0.40	0.89	0.66
Iron and steel	0.05	0.05	0.20	0.03	0.93	0.76
Nontradable industries						
Mining and quarrying			0.05	0.93	0.96	0.21
Utilities			0.07	0.88	0.93	0.32

Stern (1988). The only data required are labor's share of primary input cost and primary input share of total cost, which were obtained from the input-output tables, and an indicator of the elasticity of substitution among different varieties of each good. The elasticity of substitution is set at 15.[7]

Computational Results

We have used the model described above to investigate the economic welfare effects of bilateral tariff removal on the United States and Canada, assuming that the existing bilateral tariffs are to be removed all at once rather than in stages. An overview of the results is presented in Table 6. US imports increase by $6 billion and exports increase by $7.3 billion based on trade in 1976. Canada's imports rise by $8.3 billion and exports rise by $8.5 billion. Welfare, as measured by the equivalent variation,[8] increases for both countries as well.

Table 6. Summary of changes in a US-Canadian Free Trade Area.

Country	Imports*	Exports*	Exchange rate**	Terms of trade (%)	Equivalent variation
United States	6,018.4	7,348.0	–0.0	0.1	1,546.6
Other	–8,783.6	–3,415.5	0.4	–0.1	–142.7
Canada	8,272.6	8,544.0	–1.1	–0.2	2,077.0

Notes: * Dollar value of change in trade volume (millions US$).
** (+) indicates depreciation of currency.

[7] Values of the elasticity of substitution below 15 imply a value for fixed capital's share of total capital outside the interval (0,1).

[8] The equivalent variation is the income change valued at base period prices that yields the same change in welfare as the tariff reductions. The welfare calculation has two components. First, *ex ante* and *ex post* utility are calculated for each country using the explicit utility function and then converted to the equivalent variation. (See Shoven and Whalley (1984, p. 1014, Equation (13).) Second, changes in international debt are calculated by deflating the nominal trade balance by the change in the price level.

Canada's welfare rises by $2 billion, which is 1.1 percent of GDP in 1976, despite a deterioration in its terms of trade of 0.2 percent. US welfare rises by a smaller $1.5 billion which is less than 0.1 percent of US GDP in 1976. The other countries of the model experience a trivially small decline in welfare of $143 million.

The percentage changes in exports, imports and bilateral imports by sector are reported in the first three columns of Tables 7 and 8. US imports from Canada generally rise. The industries with the largest increases include textiles (101.0%), clothing (228.4%), footwear (130.3%), nonferrous metals (167.5%), and glass products (107.4%). The only sector that does not show a significant change in bilateral trade is transportation equipment (0.1%), which is already duty-free under the Automotive Pact. There are several industries in which US imports from Canada decline, including wood products (–2.0%), paper (–23.4%), printing and publishing (–7.5%), nonmetallic mineral products (–19.2%), and petroleum products (–11.4%). Canada's imports from the United States increase in every sector, with the largest changes occurring in textiles (179.9%), clothing (283.4%), footwear (254.6%), furniture and fixtures (179.5%), paper products (103.1%), metal products (114.4%) and rubber products (100.9%). Given that existing bilateral tariffs are highest in textiles, clothing and footwear, the computations suggest that there could be a dramatic increase in bilateral trade in these sectors unless this trade were to be restrained by some sort of intervention.

We mentioned in our previous discussion that there are two sources of welfare gain from liberalization. The first is inter-industry specialization. The import and export results indicate that the FTA would bring about substantial increases in intra-industry trade. However, considerable inter-industry specialization can also be expected.

The specialization results can be inferred from the percentage changes in industry output reported in the fourth column of Tables 7 and 8. The chemicals and transportation equipment industries are the only sectors in which output increases in both countries. There are only three sectors that contract in both countries: agriculture, food and nonelectrical machinery. Specialization will thus be occurring in

Table 7. Sectoral effects on the United States of US–Canadian bilateral tariff elimination (% change).

Sector	Imports from			Output	No. Firms		Elasticity	Capital	Employment
	Exports	World	Canada		US	World			
(a) Perfect competition									
Tradable industries									
Agriculture	−0.9	3.9	15.9	−0.4	0.0	0.0	0.0	−0.4	−0.5
Leather products	2.1	4.4	36.3	−0.6	0.0	0.0	0.0	−0.5	−0.6
Wood products	2.1	0.1	−2.0	0.6	0.0	0.0	0.0	0.6	0.5
Nontradable industries									
Construction				−0.0	0.0		0.0	0.1	−0.0
Personal services				−0.0	0.0		0.0	0.1	−0.0

(*Continued*)

Table 7. (*Continued*)

Sector	Exports	Imports from World	Imports from Canada	Output	No. Firms US	No. Firms World	Elasticity	Capital	Employment
(b) Monopolistic competition									
Tradable industries									
Food	7.7	7.2	46.2	0.0	0.0	−0.0	0.0	0.2	−0.0
Textiles	33.1	5.4	101.0	3.9	0.0	0.0	−0.0	0.8	3.9
Clothing	51.3	3.8	228.4	0.7	0.7	0.6	0.0	0.8	0.7
Footwear	82.1	4.4	130.3	−0.5	−0.6	−0.4	0.1	−0.4	−0.5
Furniture and fixtures	85.9	25.0	60.8	0.8	−0.8	−1.0	1.5	−0.3	0.8
Paper products	17.8	−21.2	−23.4	3.1	1.9	0.8	1.1	2.5	3.1
Printing and publishing	11.7	1.7	−7.5	0.2	0.0	0.0	0.2	0.2	0.2
Chemicals	9.3	14.8	84.2	0.8	0.0	0.0	9.6	0.6	0.8
Nonmetallic min. products	18.2	−2.2	19.2	0.9	0.9	0.7	0.0	1.0	0.9
Nonferrous metals	−0.0	62.6	167.5	−13.6	−13.6	−5.6	−0.0	−13.4	−13.6
Metal products	28.7	11.7	54.2	0.7	0.7	0.6	0.0	0.8	0.7
Nonelectrical machinery	3.4	12.1	35.1	−0.3	0.0	0.0	0.1	−0.1	−0.3
Electrical machinery	14.2	4.9	55.5	1.2	−0.4	−0.5	1.5	0.0	1.2
Transport equipment	−0.5	0.3	0.1	−0.0	0.0	0.0	1.9	0.0	−0.0
Misc. manufactures	3.9	6.0	33.5	−0.5	0.1	−0.2	−0.5	−0.3	−0.5
Nontradable industries									
Wholesale trade				−0.0	0.0		0.0	0.2	−0.1
Transportation				0.0	0.1		0.0	0.2	−0.0
Financial services				−0.0	0.0		0.0	0.1	−0.1

(*Continued*)

Table 7. (*Continued*)

Sector	Imports from			Output	No. Firms		Elasticity	Capital	Employment
	Exports	World	Canada		US	World			
(c) Market segmentation									
Tradable industries									
Petroleum products	0.3	−4.3	−11.4	0.4	0.0	−0.1	−0.1	0.5	0.2
Rubber products	28.3	15.1	72.0	0.1	0.0	−0.3	−0.2	0.2	0.1
Glass products	20.8	23.5	107.4	0.4	0.0	−0.1	−0.1	0.4	0.4
Iron and steel	9.3	10.3	53.8	−0.5	−0.5	−0.1	−0.1	−0.3	−0.5
Nontradable industries									
Mining and quarrying				−0.4	0.0	−0.1	−0.1	−0.3	−0.5
Utilities				−0.1	0.0	−0.1	−0.1	0.0	−0.3

Note: Percentage change in rental rate = −0.1 throughout.

Table 8. Sectoral effects on Canada of US–Canadian bilateral tariff elimination (% change).

Sector	Imports from			Output	No. Firms		Elasticity	Capital	Employment
	Exports	World	US		Canada	World			
(a) Perfect competition									
Tradable industries									
Agriculture	–3.6	23.8	33.7	–5.5	0.0	0.0	0.0	–5.5	–5.6
Leather products	10.8	4.7	27.7	4.9	0.0	0.0	0.0	5.0	4.9
Wood products	–4.2	28.4	34.5	–6.1	0.0	0.0	0.0	–6.1	–6.1
Nontradable industries									
Construction				1.1	0.0		0.0	1.2	1.0
Personal services				0.6	0.0		0.0	0.7	0.5

(*Continued*)

Table 8. (*Continued*)

Sector	Imports from			Output	No. Firms		Elasticity	Capital	Employment
	Exports	World	US		Canada	World			
(b) Monopolistic competition									
Tradable industries									
Food	16.3	40.5	82.7	−1.9	−2.7	−2.5	0.1	−2.4	−1.9
Textiles	19.5	82.2	179.9	−35.4	0.0	0.0	−5.1	−2.1	−35.4
Clothing	81.6	38.1	283.4	−6.4	−8.6	−6.8	0.7	−8.3	−6.4
Footwear	90.1	15.3	254.6	2.2	−1.4	−1.0	2.0	1.2	2.2
Furniture and fixtures	59.9	118.8	179.5	−2.5	−13.6	−12.1	9.3	−10.5	−2.5
Paper products	−23.5	96.8	103.1	−19.3	−19.1	−17.2	−1.0	−19.2	−19.3
Printing and publishing	−8.3	23.0	25.2	−3.2	−3.1	−2.7	−0.6	−3.1	−3.3
Chemicals	83.3	9.1	35.0	17.9	0.0	0.0	59.0	9.0	17.9
Nonmetallic min. products	−22.9	51.9	73.7	−16.8	−17.2	−13.5	−0.2	−16.8	−16.8
Nonferrous metals	151.6	34.8	52.5	152.4	150.3	-8.4	0.3	150.9	152.4
Metal products	31.1	83.6	114.4	−7.1	−9.0	−7.8	0.5	−8.1	−7.1
Nonelectrical machinery	25.2	15.3	25.7	−1.2	0.0	0.0	2.5	0.1	−1.2
Electrical machinery	27.0	60.6	94.8	−14.2	−18.1	−13.7	2.1	−17.3	−14.2
Transport equipment	−0.1	1.0	0.9	0.5	0.0	0.0	0.3	0.1	0.5
Misc. manufactures	31.2	12.1	37.8	7.3	−13.2	−5.3	17.1	−6.3	7.3
Nontradable industries									
Wholesale trade				0.5	0.3		0.0	0.7	0.5
Transportation				0.5	0.3		0.0	0.5	0.4
Financial services				0.5	0.0		0.0	0.5	0.4

(*Continued*)

Table 8. (*Continued*)

Sector	Imports from			Output	No. Firms		Elasticity	Capital	Employment
	Exports	World	US		Canada	World			
(c) Market segmentation									
Tradable industries									
Petroleum products	−11.9	0.1	9.7	−11.5	0.0	−1.2	−0.6	−8.5	−11.6
Rubber products	67.1	49.2	100.9	−1.2	0.0	−3.0	−1.9	0.1	−1.2
Glass products	81.1	39.8	64.7	−3.9	0.0	−4.5	−1.2	−1.5	−3.9
Iron and steel	34.2	44.0	92.4	28.5	7.2	−2.9	−0.9	7.9	28.5
Nontradable industries									
Mining and quarrying				−0.1	0.0	−0.5	−0.5	−0.8	−1.1
Utilities				0.3	0.0	−0.2	−0.2	0.4	0.1

Note: Percentage change in rental rate = −0.1 throughout.

the remaining seventeen tradable sectors. There are five sectors in which output in the United States declines while output in Canada rises. These include leather products, footwear, nonferrous metals, iron and steel, and miscellaneous manufactures. Nonferrous metals is the industry most dramatically affected, with a decline in output in the United States of 13.6 percent, and an increase in Canada of 152.4 percent. Canada's iron and steel industry may undergo a significant expansion, with output rising by 28.5 percent.

The United States, as the larger country, would evidently specialize in a broader range of product categories. Thus, output in the United States would increase while output in Canada would decline in twelve sectors, including: wood products, textiles, clothing, furniture and fixtures, paper products, printing and publishing, nonmetallic mineral products, metal products, electrical machinery, rubber products, glass products, and petroleum products. In most cases, the increase in US output is less than one percent. The exceptions are textiles (3.9%), paper products (3.1%), and electrical machinery (1.2%). The impact on Canadian producers appears, however, to be more noticeable. For example, Canadian textile production declines by 35.4 percent, paper products by 19.3 percent, nonmetallic mineral products by 16.8 percent, and electrical machinery by 14.2 percent.

The second source of welfare gain is the rationalization effect, which involves increasing output per firm, thereby realizing economies of scale in the industries with declining average cost. The change in output per firm can be determined by comparing the percentage change in industry output, in the fourth column of Tables 7 and 8, to the percentage change in the number of firms in each industry, in the fifth column of these tables. Of the twenty-four imperfectly competitive industries, output per firm in the United States rises in ten, falls in five, and remains unchanged in nine. In Canada, output per firm increases in sixteen industries and falls in eight.

The determinants of output per firm vary by industry. In cases in which there are barriers to entry, firm output depends only on industry output. Therefore, industries that are expanding in response to inter-industry specialization will also experience an increase in output per firm. The United States, as the larger of the two countries, will specialize in a broader range of product categories. Firms in these sectors will increase output. Indeed, half of the industries that rationalize in the United States fall into this category. Textiles, chemicals, petroleum products, rubber products, and glass products are all sectors that are characterized as having barriers to entry and that record increases in industry output.

On the other hand, firms in heavily protected industries, which contract with liberalization, will reduce output. This effect accounts for most instances of de-rationalization in Canada. Since trade liberalization will lead Canada to specialize in a smaller number of products, output in many industries will decline. For contracting industries in which there are barriers to entry, output per firm will fall. This effect accounts for five of the seven tradable sectors that de-rationalize in Canada. These include textiles, petroleum products, rubber products, glass products, and nonelectrical machinery.

However, if entry or exit of firms can occur, then firm output will depend on the interaction between the firm's perceived demand and average total cost curves, The zero-profit condition requires tangency between demand and average total cost. Therefore, if either curve changes shape, the point of tangency will occur at a new level of output. Relative factor prices determine the shape of average total cost.[9] However, the computational results indicate that the wage-rental ratio will be barely affected insofar as the return to labor is held fixed and the return to capital in both the United States and Canada declines by only 0.1 percent. Therefore, *demand*-side considerations are paramount.

In monopolistically competitive industries, liberalization affects the firm's demand curve in two ways. Domestic tariff reductions increase import competition for domestic firms selling to the domestic market. The increase in competition emerges in the model as an increase in the elasticity of demand by domestic consumers for the domestically produced good. Domestic firms are led to reduce the

[9] For a detailed discussion of the role of factor prices and factor intensities in determining output per firm, see Brown and Stern (1988).

mark-up of price over marginal cost and raise output, thereby reaping economies of scale. This is frequently referred to as the "pro-competitive" effect of tariff liberalization.

Foreign tariff reductions have the opposite effect. Domestic firms gain an improved competitive advantage in the foreign market. The greater market power emerges as a fall in the perceived elasticity of demand for exports. Firms respond to the fall in the perceived elasticity of demand by increasing the mark-up over marginal cost on exports and reducing output.

On balance, the firm's perceived elasticity of demand may rise or fall as a result of bilateral liberalization so that output per firm may rise or fall. The pro-competitive effect is apparently very strong in Canada, with output per firm increasing in nine of the eleven monopolistically competitive tradable industries in which entry can occur. The only exceptions are paper products and printing and publishing, for which output per firm falls.

Rationalization effects in the United States are slightly weaker. Output per firm remains unchanged in five of the eleven monopolistically competitive tradable sectors and falls in one.

There are instances in which the pro-competitive effect is so strong that exit occurs in both the United States and Canada even when the industry is expanding. For example, output of the footwear industry in Canada rises, but the number of firms declines. Expansion is brought about entirely by increasing output per firm. Footwear production in the United States declines, but the fall in the number of firms is so great that output per firm rises. Similarly, output in the furniture and fixtures and electrical machinery industries expands in the United States, but contracts in Canada. However, the number of firms falls in both countries and output per firm increases.

It is more common, however, that increases in industry output are accomplished by a combination of increasing the number of firms and increasing firm output. For example, in the United States, production of food, clothing, nonmetallic mineral products, and metal products expands entirely as a result of entry. Output per firm is virtually unaffected. Interestingly, these same four industries contract in Canada as a result of exit, but output per firm rises. Canada's relatively deep tariff reductions give rise to a strong pro-competitive effect on Canadian firms. This may account for the fact that rationalization occurs more frequently in Canada than in the United States.

The percentage changes in employment in the last column in Tables 7 and 8 more or less mirror the percentage changes in output noted in the fourth column of the tables. In the United States, the employment changes are less than one percent, with the exception of textiles (3.9%), paper products (3.1%), nonferrous metals (–13.6%), and electrical machinery (1.2%). This suggests that the United States would not experience major disruptions in labor markets, especially when it is recalled that the tariff reductions would be phased in over a ten-year period. On the other hand, in Canada, there are sizeable percentage increases in employment in leather products (4.9%), chemicals (17.9%), nonferrous metals (152.4%), miscellaneous manufactures (7.3%), and iron and steel (28.5%), and sizeable percentage reductions in employment in agriculture (–5.6%), wood products (–6.1%), textiles (–35.4%), clothing (–6.4%), paper products (–19.3%), nonmetallic mineral products (–16.8%), metal products (–7.1%), electrical machinery (–14.2%), and petroleum products (–11.6%).

Our computational results thus suggest that there will be a significant increase in inter-industry specialization, especially in Canada, as a result of the FTA. Strong pro-competitive effects emerge in many Canadian industries in which entry and exit occur due to Canada's relatively deep tariff reductions. There may be sizeable labor reallocation effects in Canada, although the phasing in of the tariff removal would mitigate some of the adjustment problems that might occur otherwise. In the aggregate, nonetheless, our results indicate that economic welfare would be increased in Canada and in the United States with the bilateral removal of tariffs.

V. Summary Assessment of the FTA

It seems appropriate to ask in conclusion how our results compare to those obtained in other studies. As noted in Table 2, the two classes of studies of the effects of the US-Canadian FTA include those based on general equilibrium models and those based on macroeconometric models. It is important to note that our present study as well as most previous ones suggest that the FTA will be beneficial to both Canada and the United States, although there is some disagreement as to how large the benefits may be.

A welfare gain as the result of bilateral tariff removal in the range of one to two percent of national income for Canada but less than one percent for the United States seems plausible. Significantly larger welfare gains for Canada obtained by some studies were revised downward in light of new information concerning the proper specification of key parameters.

Some models obtained negative welfare results for one or other of the countries. However, this can be traced to be doubtful assumption that infra-industry trade is generated by national product differentiation. It is nonetheless comforting to know that even under such a pessimistic assumption the possible welfare loss is only a small fraction of one percent of national income.

It is difficult to interpret the results based on the macroeconometric models because these models do not capture the essential microeconomic behavior that governs the responses of firms to the changes in relative prices and competitive pressures that the FTA would engender. We are skeptical accordingly of the detailed industry results that are obtained, for example, in the Economic Council of Canada studies by Magun *et al.* (1987, 1988).

We noted in our earlier discussion that the FTA entails some minor bilateral modifications in certain existing NTBs, and, more importantly, a variety of potentially far-reaching changes in the rules and procedures governing bilateral trade and investment relations that would reduce the uncertainty of policies and lower the costs of transactions. We have not been able to quantify the effects of these changes. But when their potential is viewed in conjunction with the benefits that will be realized as the result of the bilateral elimination of tariffs, our overall assessment of the FTA is that it will enhance economic welfare in both the United States and Canada. It is very likely that the economies of the rest of the world will benefit as well since they are affected in only a minor way by the bilateral tariff elimination and they may benefit from the improvements in the bilateral trading environment that carry over to the multilateral trading system.

Appendix

Country equations ($i = 1,\ldots,m$)

Goods Demand

Final demand for tradable good j $\qquad j = 1,\ldots,n$

$$\hat{C}_{ij}^{T} = \hat{E}_i \hat{P}_{ij}^{T} \tag{1}$$

Final demand for nontradable good j $\qquad j = n+1,\ldots,n'$

$$\hat{C}_{ij}^{N} = \hat{E}_i \hat{P}_{ij}^{N} \tag{2}$$

Intermediate demand for tradable good j by industry k $\qquad j = 1,\ldots,n;\ k = 1,\ldots,n'$

$$\hat{Z}_{ijk}^{T} = \hat{S}_{ik} \tag{3}$$

Intermediate demand for nontradable good j by industry k $\qquad j = n+1,\ldots,n';\ k = 1,\ldots,n'$

$$\hat{Z}_{ijk}^{N} = \hat{S}_{ik} \tag{4}$$

Aggregate demand for tradable good j $\qquad j = 1,\ldots,n$

$$\hat{D}_{ij}^{T} = v_{ij}\hat{C}_{ij}^{T} + \sum_{k=1}^{n} v_{ijk}\hat{Z}_{ijk}^{T} + \sum_{k=n+1}^{n'} v_{ijk}\hat{Z}_{ijk}^{N} \tag{5}$$

Aggregate demand for nontradable good j $\qquad j = n+1,\ldots,n'$

$$\hat{D}_{ij}^{N} = v_{ij}\hat{C}_{ij}^{N} + \sum_{k=1}^{n} v_{ijk}\hat{Z}_{ijk}^{T} + \sum_{k=n+1}^{n'} v_{ijk}\hat{Z}_{ijk}^{N} \tag{6}$$

Demand for tradable good j produced by country r:

Perfect competition $j = 1,\ldots,n$

$$\hat{D}_{ij}^{r} = \hat{D}_{ij}^{T} + \sigma_{ij}(\hat{P}_{ij}^{T} - \hat{P}_{ij}^{r}) \tag{7a}$$

Monopolistic competition $j = 1,\ldots,n$

$$\hat{D}_{ij}^{r} = \hat{D}_{ij}^{T} + \sigma_{ij}(\hat{P}_{ij}^{T} - \hat{P}_{ij}^{r}) - \sum_{s=1}^{m} \theta_{ij}^{s} \hat{n}_{sj} \tag{7b}$$

Supply of good j to country r by a representative firm:

Market segmentation $j = 1,\ldots,n$

$$\hat{S}_{ij}^{T} = \hat{D}_{rj}^{T} + \frac{\hat{p}_{ij}^{r} - M\hat{C}_{ij}}{\bar{M}_{ij}^{r}} \tag{7c}$$

Demand for tradable good j produced by rest of world:

Perfect competition $j = 1,\ldots,n$

$$\hat{D}_{ij}^{E} = \hat{D}_{ij}^{T} + \sigma_{ij}(\hat{P}_{ij}^{T} - \hat{P}_{ij}^{E}) \tag{8a}$$

Demand for tradable good j produced by a representative firm in rest of world:

Monopolistic competition $j = 1,\ldots,n$

$$\hat{D}_{ij}^{E} = \hat{D}_{ij}^{T} + \sigma_{ij}(\hat{P}_{ij}^{T} - \hat{P}_{ij}^{E}) - \sum_{s=1}^{m} \theta_{ij}^{s} \hat{n}_{sj} \tag{8b}$$

Supply of good j to rest of world by a representative firm:

Market segmentation $j = 1,\ldots,n$

$$\hat{S}_{ij}^{E} = L_{E} + \frac{\hat{P}_{ij}^{E} - M\hat{C}_{ij}}{\bar{M}_{ij}^{E}} \tag{8c}$$

Primary Factor Demand

Primary input demand by industry *j*:

Perfect competition $j = 1,\ldots,n'$

$$\hat{V}_{ij} = \hat{S}_{ij} \tag{9a}$$

Primary input demand by a representative firm in industry *j*:

Monopolistic competition $j = 1,\ldots,n'$

$$\hat{V}_{ij} = \hat{S}_{ij} - \hat{n}_{ij} \tag{9b}$$

Market segmentation $j = 1,\ldots,n'$

$$\hat{V}_{ij} = \hat{S}_{ij} - \hat{n}_{ij} \tag{9c}$$

Labor demand by industry *j*:

Perfect competition $j = 1,\ldots,n'$

$$\hat{L}_{ij} - \hat{V}_{ij} - \bar{\sigma}_{ij}\theta_{ij}^{K}(\hat{w}_{ij} - \hat{r}_{ij}) \tag{10a}$$

Labor demand by a representative firm in industry *j*:

Monopolistic competition $j = 1,\ldots,n'$

$$\hat{L}_{ij} = \hat{V}_{ij} - \bar{\sigma}_{ij}\theta_{ij}^{K}(\hat{w}_{ij} - \hat{r}_{ij}) \tag{10b}$$

Market segmentation $j = 1,\ldots,n'$

$$\hat{L}_{ij} = \hat{V}_{ij} + \hat{n}_{ij}\theta_{ij}^{K}\theta_{ij}^{VK}(\hat{w}_{ij} - \hat{r}_{ij}) \tag{10c}$$

Capital demand by industry *j*:

Perfect competition $j = 1,\ldots,n'$

$$\hat{K}_{ij} = \hat{V}_{ij} + \bar{\sigma}_{ij}\theta_{ij}^{L}(\hat{w}_{ij} - \hat{r}_{ij}) \tag{11a}$$

Capital demand by a representative firm in industry *j*:

Monopolistic competition $j = 1,\dots,n'$

$$\hat{K}_{ij} = \theta_{ij}^{VK}[\hat{V}_{ij} + \bar{\sigma}_{ij}(1-\theta_{ij}^{K}\theta_{ij}^{VK})(\hat{w}_{ij} - \hat{r}_{ij})] + \hat{n}_{ij} \tag{11b}$$

Market segmentation $j = 1,\dots,n'$

$$\hat{K}_{ij} = \theta_{ij}^{VK}[\hat{V}_{ij} + \bar{\sigma}_{ij}(1-\theta_{ij}^{K}\theta_{ij}^{VK})(\hat{w}_{ij} - \hat{r}_{ij})] + \hat{n}_{ij} \tag{11c}$$

Goods Prices

Consumer price of tradable good *j* $j = 1,\dots,n$

$$\hat{P}_{ij}^{T} = \theta_{ij}^{M}\hat{P}_{ij}^{M} + (1-\theta_{ij}^{M})\hat{P}_{ij}^{i} \tag{12}$$

Consumer price of imported good *j*:

Perfect competition $j = 1,\dots,n$

$$\hat{P}_{ij}^{M} = \sum_{r\neq 1}^{m+1} \theta_{ij}^{rM}\hat{P}_{ij}^{r} \tag{13a}$$

Monopolistic competition .....$j = 1,\dots,n$

$$\hat{P}_{ij}^{M} = \sum_{r\neq 1}^{m+1} \theta_{ij}^{rM}\hat{P}_{ij}^{r} \tag{13b}$$

Market segmentation .....$j = 1,\dots,n$

$$\hat{P}_{ij}^{M} = \hat{P}_{wj}^{i} + \hat{R}_{i} \tag{13c}$$

Consumer (seller) price of good *j* imported from (exported to) country *r*:

Perfect competition r I; $r = 1,\dots,m+1$; $j = 1,\dots,n$

$$\hat{P}_{ij}^{r} = \hat{P}_{wj}^{r} + \hat{R}_{i} + \hat{t}_{ij}^{r} \tag{14a}$$

Monopolistic competition r I; $r = 1,\ldots,m+1$; $j = 1,\ldots,n$

$$\hat{P}_{ij}^{r} = \hat{P}_{wj}^{r} + \hat{R}_{i} + \hat{t}_{ij}^{r} \tag{14b}$$

Market segmentation r I; $r = 1,\ldots,m+1$; $j = 1,\ldots,n$

$$\hat{P}_{ij}^{r} = \hat{P}_{wj}^{r} + \hat{R}_{i} + \hat{t}_{rj}^{i} \tag{14c}$$

Consumer price of good j produced domestically:

Perfect competition ....$j = 1,\ldots,n$

$$\hat{P}_{ij}^{i} = \hat{P}_{ij}^{*} \tag{14a$'$}$$

Monopolistic competition ....$j = 1,\ldots,n$

$$\hat{P}_{ij}^{i} = \hat{P}_{ij}^{*} \tag{14b$'$}$$

Market segmentation ....$j = 1,\ldots,n$

$$\hat{P}_{ij}^{i} = \hat{P}_{wj}^{i} + \hat{R}_{i} \tag{14c$'$}$$

Price received by seller of good j:

Perfect competition ....$j = 1,\ldots,n$

$$\hat{P}_{ij}^{*} = \hat{P}_{wj}^{i} + \hat{R}_{i} \tag{15a}$$

Monopolistic competition $j = 1,\ldots,n$

$$\hat{P}_{ij}^{*} = \hat{P}_{wj}^{i} + \hat{R}_{i} \tag{15b}$$

Market segmentation $j = 1,\ldots,n$

$$\hat{P}_{ij}^{*} = \sum_{r=1}^{m+1} \delta_{ij}^{r} \hat{P}_{ij}^{r} \tag{15c}$$

Price of nontradable good j:

Perfect competition $\quad j = n+1,\ldots,n'$

$$\hat{P}_{ij}^{N} = M\hat{C}_{ij} \tag{16a}$$

Monopolistic competition $\quad j = n+1,\ldots,n'$

$$\hat{P}_{ij}^{N} = M\hat{C}_{ij} + \frac{\hat{\eta}_{ij}}{\eta_{ij}+1} \tag{16b}$$

Market segmentation $\quad j = n+1,\ldots,n'$

$$\hat{P}_{ij}^{N} = M\hat{C}_{ij} \tag{16c}$$

Primary input price aggregate in industry j:

Perfect competition $\quad j = n+1,\ldots,n'$

$$\hat{P}_{ij}^{V} = \theta_{ij}^{K}\hat{r}_{ij} + \theta_{ij}^{1}\hat{w}_{ij} \tag{17a}$$

Monopolistic competition $\quad j = n+1,\ldots,n'$

$$\hat{P}_{ij}^{V} = \theta_{ij}^{K}\theta_{ij}^{VK}\hat{r}_{ij} + (1-\theta_{ij}^{K}\theta_{ij}^{VK})\hat{w}_{ij} \tag{17b}$$

Market segmentation

$$\hat{P}_{ij}^{V} = \theta_{ij}^{K}\theta_{ij}^{VK}\hat{r}_{ij} + (1-\theta_{ij}^{K}\theta_{ij}^{VK})\hat{w}_{ij} \tag{17c}$$

Supply

Marginal cost in industry $j \quad j = 1,\ldots,n'$

$$M\hat{C}_{ij} = b_{ij()}\hat{P}_{ij}^{V}\sum_{k=1}^{n} b_{ikj}\hat{P}_{ik}^{T} + \sum_{k=n=1}^{N'} B_{IJK}\hat{p}_{IK}^{n} \tag{18}$$

Supply of tradable good *j*:

Perfect competition $j = 1,\ldots,n$

$$\hat{P}^{*}_{ij} = \hat{MC}_{ij} \tag{19a}$$

Monopolistic competition $j = 1,\ldots,n$

$$\hat{P}^{*}_{ij} = \hat{MC}_{ij} + \frac{\hat{\eta}_{ij}}{\eta_{ij} + 1} \tag{19b}$$

Market segmentation $j = 1,\ldots,n$

$$\hat{S}^{T}_{ij} = \sum_{r=1}^{m+1} \delta^{r}_{ij} \hat{S}^{r}_{ij} + \hat{n}_{ij} \tag{19c}$$

Supply of nontradable good *j* $j = n + 1,\ldots,n'$

$$\hat{S}^{N}_{ij} = \hat{D}^{N}_{ij} \tag{20}$$

Elasticity of Demand

Elasticity of demand for tradable good *j* produced by a representative firm in country *r*:

Perfect competition $j = 1,\ldots,n$

$$\hat{\eta}^{i}_{rj} = 0 \tag{21a}$$

Monopolistic competition $r = 1,\ldots,m;\ j = 1,\ldots,n$

$$\hat{\eta}^{i}_{rj} = \frac{(\sigma_{ij} - 1)\theta^{r}_{ij}}{n_{rj}\eta^{i}_{rj}} (\hat{D}^{r}_{ij} + \hat{P}^{r}_{ij} - \hat{D}^{T}_{ij} - \hat{P}^{T}_{ij}) \tag{21b}$$

Market segmentation $j = 1,\ldots,n$

$$\hat{\eta}^{i}_{rj} = 0 \tag{21c}$$

Elasticity of demand for a representative producer of tradable good *j*:

Perfect competition $j = 1,\ldots,n$

$$\hat{\eta}_{rj} = 0 \tag{22a}$$

Monopolistic competition $j = 1,\ldots,n$

$$\hat{\eta}_{ij} = \sum_{i=1}^{m+1} (\hat{D}^{i}_{rj} + \hat{\eta}^{r}_{ij} - \hat{S}^{T}_{ij} + \hat{n}_{ij}) \frac{\delta^{r}_{ij}\eta^{r}_{ij}}{\eta_{ij}} \tag{22b}$$

Market segmentation $j = 1,\ldots,n$

$$\hat{\eta}_{rj} = 0 \tag{22c}$$

Elasticity of demand for a representative producer of nontradable good *j*:

Perfect competition $j = n+1,\ldots,n'$

$$\hat{\eta}_{rj} = 0 \tag{23a}$$

Monopolistic competition $j = n+1,\ldots,n'$

$$\hat{\eta}_{ij} = \frac{(1-\sigma_{ij})}{n_{ij}\eta_{rj}} \hat{n}_{ij} \tag{23b}$$

Market segmentation $j = n+1,\ldots,n'$

$$\hat{\eta}_{rj} = 0 \tag{23c}$$

Number of Firms

Number of firms in tradable industry *j*:

Perfect competition $j = 1,\ldots,n$

$$\hat{\eta}_{rj} = 0 \tag{24a}$$

Monopolistic competition — free entry $j = 1,\ldots,n$

$$\hat{P}^{*}_{ij} = \theta^{FC}_{ij}(\hat{r}_{ij}\hat{S}^{T}_{ij} + \hat{n}_{ij}) + \theta^{VC}_{ij} M\hat{C}_{ij} \tag{24b}$$

Monopolistic competition — no entry $j = 1,\ldots,n$

$$\hat{\eta}_{ij} = 0 \tag{24b$'$}$$

Market segmentation — free entry $j = 1,\ldots,n$

$$\hat{P}^{*}_{ij} = \theta^{FC}_{ij}(\hat{r}_{ij}\hat{S}^{T}_{ij} + \hat{n}_{ij}) + \theta^{VC}_{ij} M\hat{C}_{ij} \tag{24c}$$

Market segmentation — no entry $j = 1,\ldots,n$

$$\hat{\eta}_{ij} = 0 \tag{24c$'$}$$

Number of firms in nontradable industry j:

Perfect competition $j = n+1,\ldots,n'$

$$\hat{\eta}_{ij} = 0 \tag{25a}$$

Monopolistic competition — free entry $j = n+1,\ldots,n'$

$$\hat{P}^{N}_{ij} = \theta^{FC}_{ij}(\hat{r}_{ij}\hat{S}^{T}_{ij} + \hat{n}_{ij}) + \theta^{VC}_{ij} M\hat{C}_{ij} \tag{25b}$$

Monopolistic competition — no entry $j = n+1,\ldots,n'$

$$\hat{\eta}_{ij} = 0 \tag{25b$'$}$$

Market segmentation — free entry $j = n+1,\ldots,n'$

$$\hat{P}^{N}_{ij} = \theta^{FC}_{ij}(\hat{r}_{ij}\hat{S}^{T}_{ij} + \hat{n}_{ij}) + \theta^{VC}_{ij} M\hat{C}_{ij} \tag{25c}$$

Market segmentation — no entry $j = n+1,\ldots,n'$

$$\hat{\eta}_{ij} = 0 \tag{25c$'$}$$

Factor Market Equilibrium

Wage paid to labor $\qquad j = 1,\ldots,n'$

$$\hat{w}_{ij} = 0 \tag{26}$$

Return to capital

$$0 = \sum_{j=1}^{n'} h_{ij}^{K} \hat{K}_{ij} \tag{27}$$

National expenditure

$$0 = \sum_{j=1}^{n'} h_{ij}^{K} \hat{L}_{ij} \tag{28}$$

World Equations

Trade balance:

Perfect competition $\qquad i = 1,\ldots,m$

$$dB_i^T = \sum_{j=1}^{n}\left(X_{ij}\hat{P}_{wj}^{i} + \sum_{r\neq i}^{m} X_{ij}^{r}\hat{D}_{rj}^{i} + X_{ij}^{E} L_E \right) - \sum_{j=1}^{n}\left[M_{ij}^{E}(\hat{P}_{wj}^{`E} + \hat{D}_{ij}^{E}) + \sum_{r\neq i}^{m} M_{ij}^{r}(\hat{P}_{wj}^{r} + \hat{D}_{ij}^{r}) \right] \tag{29a}$$

Monopolistic competition $\qquad i = 1,\ldots,m$

$$dB_i^T = \sum_{j=1}^{n}\left(X_{ij}\hat{P}_{wj}^{i} + \sum_{r\neq i}^{m} X_{ij}^{r}(\hat{D}_{rj}^{i} + \hat{n}_{ij}) + X_{ij}^{E} L_E \right) - \sum_{j=1}^{n}\left[M_{ij}^{E}(\hat{P}_{wj}^{E} + \hat{D}_{ij}^{E}) + \sum_{r\neq i}^{m} M_{ij}^{r}(\hat{P}_{wj}^{r} + \hat{D}_{ij}^{r} + \hat{n}_{rj}) \right] \tag{29b}$$

Market segmentation $i = 1,\ldots,m$

$$\begin{aligned} dB_i^T &= \sum_{j=1}^{n}\sum_{r\neq i}^{m+1} X_{ij}^r(\hat{S}_{ij}^r + \hat{P}_{wj}^r + \hat{n}_{ij} - \hat{t}_{rj}^i) \\ &\quad - \sum_{i=1}^{n}\left\{\sum_{r\neq i}^{m} M_{ij}^r[\hat{S}_{rj}^i + \hat{n}_{rj} + \hat{P}_{wj}^i - \hat{t}_{ij}^r]\right. \\ &\quad \left. + M_{ij}^E\left[(1+\varepsilon_j^E)(\hat{P}_{wj}^i - \hat{t}_{ij}^E) + \varepsilon_j^E\sum_{r=1}^{m}\theta_{RE}^r\hat{R}_r\right]\right\} \end{aligned} \tag{29c}$$

Exchange rate:

Balanced trade $i = 1,\ldots,m-1$

$$dB_i^T = 0 \tag{30i}$$

$$\hat{R}_m = 0 \tag{30i'}$$

Pegged exchange rates $i = 1,\ldots,m$

$$\hat{R}_i = \sum_{r=1}^{m}\theta_{Ri}^r\hat{R}_r \tag{30ii}$$

Goods market clearing condition:

Perfect competition $j = 1,\ldots,n;\ i = 1,\ldots,m$

$$\hat{S}_{ij}^T \hat{S}_{ij}^T = D_{Ej}^i L_E + \sum_{r=i}^{m} D_{rj}^i \hat{D}_{rj}^i \tag{31a}$$

Monopolistic competition $j = 1,\ldots,n;\ i = 1,\ldots,m$

$$\hat{S}_{ij}^T \hat{S}_{ij}^T = D_{Ej}^i L_E + \sum_{r=i}^{m} D_{rj}^i(\hat{D}_{rj}^i + \hat{n}_{ij}) \tag{31b}$$

Market segmentation $j = 1,\ldots,n;\ i = 1,\ldots,m$

$$D_{ij}^T \hat{D}_{ij}^T = \sum_{r=1}^{m} S_{rj}^i (\hat{S}_{rj}^i + \hat{n}_{rj}) + \varepsilon_j^E S_{Ej}^i \left(\hat{P}_{wj}^i - t_{ij}^E + \sum_{r=1}^{m} \theta_{RE}^r \hat{R}_i \right) \quad (31c)$$

Goods market clearing condition for rest of world:

Perfect competition $j = 1,\ldots,n$

$$dS_i^E = \sum_{i=1}^{m} D_{ij}^E \hat{D}_{ij}^E \quad (32a)$$

Monopolistic competition $j = 1,\ldots,n$

$$dS_i^E = \sum_{i=1}^{m} D_{ij}^E \hat{D}_{ij}^E \quad (32b)$$

Market segmentation $j = 1,\ldots,n$

$$M_j^E L_E = \sum_{i=1}^{m} S_{ij}^E (\hat{S}_{ij}^E + \hat{n}_{ij}) \quad (32c)$$

Net supply of rest of world:

Perfect competition $j = 1,\ldots,n$

$$dS_j^E = S_j^E \varepsilon_j^E \left(\hat{P}_{wj}^E + \sum_{i=1}^{m} \theta_{RE}^i \hat{R}_i \right) \quad (33a)$$

Monopolistic competition $j = 1,\ldots,n$

$$dS_j^E = S_j^E \varepsilon_j^E \left(\hat{P}_{wj}^E + \sum_{i=1}^{m} \theta_{RE}^i \hat{R}_i \right) \quad (33b)$$

Market segmentation $j = 1,\ldots,n$

$$dS_j^E = \sum_{i=1}^{m} S_{Ej}^i \varepsilon_j^E \left(\hat{P}_{wj}^i - t_{ij}^E + \sum_{i=1}^{m} \theta_{RE}^i \hat{R}_i \right) \quad (33c)$$

Import licensing equivalent for rest of world:

Perfect competition

$$0 = \sum_{j=1}^{n} \left[(dS_j^E + S_j^E \hat{P}_{wj}^E) - \left(M_j^E L_E + \sum_{i=1}^{m} M_{Ej}^i \hat{P}_{wj}^i \right) \right] \tag{34a}$$

Monopolistic competition

$$0 = \sum_{j=1}^{n} \left[(dS_j^E + S_j^E \hat{P}_{wj}^E) - \left(M_j^E L_E + \sum_{i=1}^{m} M_{Ej}^i \hat{P}_{wj}^i \right) \right] \tag{34b}$$

Market segmentation

$$0 = \sum_{j=1}^{n} \left\{ \left[dS_j^E + \sum_{i=1}^{m} X_{Ej}^i (\hat{P}_{wj}^i - \hat{t}_{ij}^E) \right] - \sum_{i=1}^{m} M_{Ej}^i (\hat{P}_{wj}^E - \hat{t}_{Ej}^i + L_E) \right\} \tag{34c}$$

Variables of the Model

C_{ij}^T = Final demand for tradable good *j* in country *i*

C_{ij}^N = Final demand for nontradable good *j* in country *i*

Z_{ijk}^T = Intermediate demand by industry *k* for tradable good *j* in country *i*

Z_{ijk}^N = Intermediate demand by industry *k* for nontradable good *j* in country *i*

D_{ij}^T = Total demand for tradable good *j* in country *i*

D_{ij}^N = Total demand for nontradable good *j* in country *i*

D_{ij}^r = Perfect competition: demand by country *i* for tradable good *j* produced by country *r*

= Monopolistic competition: demand by country *i* for tradable good *j* produced by a representative firm in country *r*

S_{ij}^r = Market segmentation: sales of good *j* by a representative firm in country *i* to country *r*

V_{ij} = Perfect competition: primary input demand by industry *j* in country *i*
= Monopolistic competition: primary input demand by a representative firm in industry *j* in country *i*
= Market segmentation: primary input demand by a representative firm in industry *j* in country i

K_{IJ} = Perfect competition: capital demand by industry *j* in country *i*
= Monopolistic competition: capital demand by a representative firm in industry *j* in country *i*
= Market segmentation: capital demand by a representative firm in industry *j* in country *i*

p_{ij}^{T} = Price index of tradable good *j* in country *i*

P_{ij}^{N} = Price index of nontradable good *j* in country *i*

P_{ij}^{M} = Price index of imports of good *j* in country *i*

P_{ij}^{r} = Perfect competition: price paid by consumers in country *i* for the variety of good *j* produced in country *r*
= Monopolistic competition: price paid by consumers in country *i* for the variety of good *j* produced by a representative firm in country *r*
= Market segmentation: price received by a typical producer in country *i* for sales of *j* to country *r*

P_{ij}^{*} = Perfect competition: price received by sellers of good *j* in country *i*
= Monopolistic competition: price received by a representative seller of good *j* in country *i*
= Market segmentation: sales weighted average price received by a representative seller of good *j* in country *i*

P_{ij}^{N} = Perfect competition: price of nontradable good *j* in country *i*
= Monopolistic competition: price of nontradable good *j* produced by a representative firm in country *i*
= Market segmentation: price of nontradable good *j* produced by a representative firm in country *i*

P_{ij}^{V} = Primary input price index in industry *j* in country *i*

MC_{ij} = Marginal cost in industry *j* in country *i*

S_{ij}^T = Industry supply of tradable good j by country i
S_{ij}^N = Industry supply of nontradable good j by country i
η_{ij}^i = Monopolistic competition: elasticity of demand in country i for the product of a representative firm in industry j
η_{ij} = Monopolistic competition: market elasticity of demand for the product of a representative firm in industry j in country i
n_{ij} = Number of firms in industry j in country i
w_{ij} = Wage paid to labor in industry j in country i
r_{ij} = Return to capital in industry j in country i
E_i = Total expenditure in country i
B_i^T = Trade balance of country i
R_i = Exchange rate of country i
P_{wj}^i = Perfect competition: seller price of good j produced by country i denominated in the numeraire currency
= Monopolistic competition: seller price of good j produced by a representative firm in country i denominated in the numeraire currency
= Market segmentation: consumer price of good j in country i denominated in the numeraire currency
S_j^E = Net supply of good j by rest of world
L_E = Import licensing equivalent for rest of world
t_{ij}^r = Tariff imposed by country i on imports of j from country r

Parameters of the Model

m = Number of countries
n = Number of tradable goods
n' = Number of goods
v_{ijo} = Final demand share in industry j in country i
v_{ikj} = Industry k's share of total demand in industry j in country i
σ_{ij} = Elasticity of substitution among varieties of good j in country i
θ_{ij}^r = Country r's share of the market for good j in country i
θ_{ij}^M = Import share of the market for good j in country i

θ_{ij}^{rM} = Country *r*'s share of imports of good *j* by country *i*

$\bar{M}_{ij}^{r}$ = Market segmentation: mark-up over marginal cost by representative firm in country *i* on sales of good *j* to country *r*

$\bar{\sigma}_{IJ}$ = Elasticity of substitution between capital and labor in industry *j* in country *i*

θ_{IJ}^{K} = Capital's share of primary input cost in industry *j* in country *i*

θ_{IJ}^{L} = Labor's share of primary input cost in industry *j* in country *i*

θ_{ij}^{VK} = Variable capital's share of total capital in industry *j* in country *i*

δ_{ij}^{r} = Market segmentation: fraction of sales by a representative firm in industry *j* in country *i* sold to country *r*

b_{ijo} = Primary input share of variable cost in industry *j* in country *i*

b_{ijk} = Intermediate input *k*'s share of variable cost in industry *j* in country *i*

O_{ij}^{FC} = Fixed cost share of total cost in industry *j* in country *i*

O_{ij}^{VC} = Variable cost share of total cost in industry *j* in country *i*

H_{ij}^{K} = Share of capital employed in industry *j* in country *i*

h_{ij}^{E} = Share of labor employed in industry *j* in country *i*

X_{ij} = Exports of good *j* by country *i*

X_{ij}^{r} = Exports of good *j* to country *r* by country *i*

M_{ij} = Imports of good *j* by country *i*

M_{ij}^{r} = Imports of good *j* from country *r* by country *i*

ε_{i}^{E} = Elasticity of supply of good *j* by rest of world

O_{Ri}^{r} = Weight of country *r*'s currency in market basket of currencies to which country *i* pegs

Study Questions

1. What are the components covered in the U.S.-Canada free trade agreement, and to what are these components subject to being modeled quantitatively?
2. What are three main channels by which trade liberalization will affect the two nations: (a) inter-sectoral specialization effects;

(b) rationalization effects; and (c) macroeconomic effects? What effects will changes in rules and procedures have?

3. What do previous studies suggest about the effects of a U.S.-Canada FTA? How does the computational model used in this chapter relate to previous studies? How is imperfect competition incorporated into this model? What are the data inputs required for the model?
4. What are the principal economic effects shown by the model for the United States, Canada, and the rest of world?

References and Further Reading

Brown, Drusilla K. (1987), "Tariffs, the terms of trade and national product differentiation," *Journal of Policy Modeling* 9, pp. 503–526.

Brown, Drusilla K. and Robert M. Stern (1987), "A modeling perspective," in Robert M. Stern, Philip H. Tresize, and John Whalley (eds.), *Perspectives on a US-Canadian Free Trade Agreement*, Washington, D.C.: The Brookings Institution.

Brown, Drusilla K. and Robert M. Stern (1988), "Computational analysis of the US-Canada Free Trade Agreement: The role of product differentiation and market structure," National Bureau of Economic Research Conference on Trade Policies for International Competitiveness, Cambridge, MA, April 29–30, 1988.

Deardorff, Alan V. and Robert M. Stern (1986), *The Michigan Model of World Production and Trade: Theory and Applications*, Cambridge, MA: MIT Press.

Dixit, Avinash and Joseph E. Stiglitz (1977), "Monopolistic competition and optimum product diversity," *American Economic Review* 76, pp. 297–308.

Dungan, Peter (1985), "The macroeconomic impacts of free trade with the United States: Lessons from the FOCUS-PRISM models," Institute for Policy Analysis, University of Toronto, Working Paper, DP 85–86 (November).

Government of Canada, Department of Finance (1988), *The Canada-US Free Trade Agreement: An Economic Assessment*, Ottawa.

Hamilton, Bob and John Whalley (1985), "Geographically discriminatory trade arrangements," *Review of Economics and Statistics* 57, pp. 446–455.

Harris, Richard G. and David Cox (1985), "Summary of a project on the general equilibrium evaluation of Canadian trade policy," in John Whalley (ed.), *Canada–United States Free Trade* 11, Research Studies, Royal Commission on the Economic Union and Development Prospects for Canada, Toronto: University of Toronto Press.

Informetrica (1985), "Economic impacts of enhanced bilateral trade: National and provincial results," prepared for the Department of External Affairs, Government of Canada.

Magun, Sunder, Someshwar Rao, and Bimal Lodh (1987), "Impact of Canada-US free trade on the Canadian economy," Economic Council of Canada, Discussion Paper No. 331 (August).

Magun, Sunder, Someshwar Rao, Bimal Lodh, Laval Lavallee, and Jonathan Peirce (1988), "Open borders: An assessment of the Canada-US Free Trade Agreement," Economic Council of Canada, Discussion Paper No. 344 (April).

Markusen, James and Randall M. Wigle (1987), *US-Canada Free Trade: Effects on Welfare and Sectoral Output/Employment Levels in the Short and Long Run*, London: Mimeo/Ontario: University of Western Ontario.

Shoven, John B. and John Whalley (1984), "Applied general equilibrium models of taxation and international trade: An introduction and survey," *Journal of Economic Literature* 22, pp. 1007–1051.

Spence, Michael E. (1976), "Product selection, fixed costs, and monopolistic competition," *Review of Economic Studies* 43, pp. 217–236.

Venables, Anthony J. (1985), "Trade and trade policy with imperfect competition: The case of identical products and free entry," *Journal of International Economics* 19 (August), pp. 1–20.

Wharton Econometrics (1987), *Canada-US Free Trade: Opportunities, Risks and Prospects* (September), University of Pennsylvania.

Wigle, Randall M. (1988), "General equilibrium evaluation of Canada-US trade liberalization in a global context," *Canadian Economic Journal* 21, pp. 539–564.

Suggested Further Reading

Brown, Drusilla K. and Robert M. Stern. 1992. "Some Conceptual Issues in Analyzing the Canada-U.S. Free Trade Agreement," *North American Journal of Economics and Finance* 3, pp. 1–20.

Gaston, Noel and Daniel, Trefler. 1997. "The Labour Maket Consequences of the Canada-U.S. Free Trade Agreement," *Canadian Journal of Economics* 30, pp. 18–44.

Romalis, John. 2007. "NAFTA's and CUSFTA's Impact on International Trade," *Review of Economics and Statistics.*

Trefler, Daniel. 2004. "The Long and Short of the Canada-U.S. Free Trade Agreement," *American Economic Review* 94, pp. 870–895.

Trefler, Daniel. 2005. "Successful Economies, Failed Economics: What the Canada-U.S. Free Trade Agreement Teaches Us about International Economics," in David Laidler and Bill Robson (eds.), *The Macdonald Commission Report 20 Years On.* Toronto: C.D. Howe Institute.

Chapter 14

The Effects of the Tokyo Round on the Structure of Protection*

Alan V. Deardorff and Robert M. Stern†

In this chapter, we use the Michigan Model of World Production and Trade to analyze the structure of protection in the United States and abroad as it was altered by reductions in tariffs and selected nontariff barriers (NTBs) negotiated in the Tokyo Round. We employ a methodology developed in Deardorff and Stern (1983b) that accounts for the protective effects of trade barriers in many countries simultaneously, both directly and indirectly through the exchange rate changes that these barriers may induce. In addition to calculating the effects of the Tokyo Round on the structure of protection, we examine how our measures of protection correspond to alternative specifications of our data inputs and assumed technology, and to a

* Reprinted with permission from *The Structure and Evolution of Recent U.S. Trade Policy*, Robert E. Baldwin and Anne O. Krueger (eds.), Chicago: University of Chicago Press for the NBER.

† The authors would especially like to thank Robert Baldwin for his valuable comments on various versions of this paper. Useful comments were also received from NBER conference participants and seminars at the University of Michigan, Georgetown University, and the University of Colorado.

number of economic variables and other characteristics of our model, including the resource flows that are calculated directly by the model.

The paper is organized as follows. We describe the Michigan Model briefly in Section I, our methodology in Section II, and data and results in Sections III and IV. Some concluding remarks are given in Section V.

I. Description of the Model

The Michigan Model is a disaggregated, microeconomic model that we have developed in the past several years to analyze the effects of changes in tariffs and NTBs and a variety of other important variables.[1] The equations of the model are listed in the Appendix. While a full description of the model is given in Deardorff and Stern (1981), some brief comments describing the model may nonetheless be useful here for those not familiar with our previous work.

The model incorporates supply and demand functions and market-clearing conditions for twenty-two tradable and seven nontradable industries in thirty-four countries.[2] There is also an aggregated sector representing the rest of the world. Exchange rates are assumed to be flexible in all the industrialized countries except New Zealand and pegged in most developing countries.

Supply and demand functions interact on both national and world markets to determine equilibrium prices, quantities traded and produced, plus the flexible exchange rates. Labor demand functions also

---

[1] In our early applications of the model, we examined proposed Tokyo Round tariff reductions in Deardorff, Stern, and Baum (1977) and the effects of exchange rate changes in Deardorff, Stern, and Greene (1979).

[2] The industries are identified by names and International Standard Industrial Classification (ISIC) number in the accompanying tables. The model originally covered the eighteen major industrialized countries: Australia, Austria, Canada, the members of the European Economic Community, Finland, Japan, New Zealand, Norway, Sweden, Switzerland, and the United States. We have since added sixteen major developing countries: Argentina, Brazil, Chile, Colombia, Greece, Hong Kong, India, Israel, South Korea, Mexico, Portugal, Singapore, Spain, Taiwan, Turkey, and Yugoslavia.

determine employment in each industry and country. We abstract from such macroeconomic determinants of aggregate employment as levels of government spending, taxes, and the money stock. Instead, aggregate expenditure is adjusted endogenously to hold aggregate employment constant in each country.

Supply and demand functions were derived from maximization of profit and utility functions. These in turn were selected to permit a rich variety of behavior, but also to have parameters that could be either readily observed from available data or inferred from published econometric estimates. The model uses a base of 1976 data on trade, production, and employment for all thirty-four countries, plus tariffs in the industrialized countries. To describe technology, we use the 1972 input-output table for the United States and the 1970 national tables for the individual EEC-member countries and for Japan. The U.S. table is applied to the remaining industrialized countries. We use the 1970 input-output table for Brazil and apply this table to the other developing countries. Estimates of import demand elasticities and elasticities of substitution between capital and labor were obtained from the literature.

For want of a better measure, we represent existing NTBs in developed countries in terms of the fractions of 1976 trade that were covered by any kind of NTB in particular sectors and countries. We then model these sectors as less sensitive to tariff changes than would otherwise be the case. Specifically, the model includes, for each industry and country, an endogenous tariff-equivalent variable that reduces changes in imports to a fraction of what they would be without NTBs. That fraction is taken to be the fraction of trade not covered by NTBs in 1976. In addition, the model includes several shift parameters in supply and demand functions that can be used to represent aggregate negotiated changes in NTBs as described below.

For developing countries, we have data on trade, production, and employment but no data on tariffs and NTBs. This is not serious since they will make few, if any, changes in policies as a result of the Tokyo Round. We do, however, capture elements of their existing NTBs by modeling a system of import licensing in most of these countries.

II. Conceptual Framework

Our conceptual framework[3] derives from the theory of effective protection, which is defined by Corden (1966, p. 22) as "the percentage increase in value added made possible by the tariff structure." Since our model treats prices as endogenous, it is well suited to the measurement of value added. But, more importantly, our model incorporates general equilibrium relations and takes into account the rather moderate degree of substitution between imports and home-produced goods that characterizes behavior in international trade.[4] We can thus provide a more realistic indication of the degree to which industries are protected than is possible using the simple partial equilibrium formula that was so popular in early studies of effective protection. Further, because of the multilateral and flexible exchange rate features of the model, we can capture the protective effects of both domestic and foreign tariffs, as well as the effects of changes in exchange rates.

To proceed more formally, let us define the value added per unit of an activity which produces a good j as:

$$v_j = p_j^O - \sum_{i=1}^{n} a_{ij} p_i^I, \qquad (1)$$

where v_j is value added per unit in production of good j. p_j^O is the price that producers receive for their output of good j. p_j^I is the price they must pay for intermediate inputs of good i, and a_{ij} is the number of units of good i used in producing one unit of good j. Our objective is to calculate the "change in per unit value added" (CPVA) that will result from the implementation or change of some measure of protection. From Equation (1), in proportional terms, this is

$$CPVA_j = \frac{\Delta v_j}{v_j} = \left(\frac{1}{1-\sum_{i=1}^{n} b_{ij}}\right)\left[\frac{\Delta p_j^O}{p_j^O} - \sum_{i=1}^{n} b_{ij}\frac{\Delta p_i^I}{p_i^I}\right], \qquad (2)$$

[3] This section is based in large measure on Deardorff and Stern (1983b).

[4] The role of imperfect substitutability in trade modeling has been addressed also in de Melo and Robinson (1981).

where

$$b_{ij} = \frac{p_i^I a_{ij}}{p_j^O} \tag{3}$$

is the share of input i in the value of production of a unit of good j. The changes (Δs) in Equation (2) can refer to the results of any protective policy one wishes to examine. Most often, they refer to the results of implementing an entire structure of tariffs, starting from a base of free trade. But they could just as easily be used to measure the effects of changing particular tariffs or groups of tariffs, or installing or removing a system of nontariff barriers.

Calculation of all of the price changes that appear on the right-hand side of Equation (2) would normally be very difficult, though, of course, that is what our computational model is designed to do. In most previous studies of the structure of protection, however, the problem has been considerably simplified by assuming that all traded goods are infinitely elastically supplied at given world prices p_i^w. It follows, for imported goods, that the domestic prices p_i^D of both outputs and inputs are given by the world price plus the tariff. For *ad valorem* tariffs t_i, this gives us

$$p_i^D = (1 + t_i) p_i^w . \tag{4}$$

The price changes that result when these tariffs are levied, starting from tariffs of zero, are just the tariffs themselves, since the world prices are constant. Equation (2) then provides the following simpler measure of protection:

$$ERP_j = \frac{\Delta v_j}{v_j} = \frac{t_j \sum_{i=1}^{n} b_{ij} t_i}{1 - \sum_{i=1}^{n} b_{ij}}. \tag{5}$$

This is the formula used by Corden (1966) and many others to measure the protection due to a tariff structure. For convenience, we shall use the term "effective rate of protection" to refer only to this simple calculation, and reserve the term "change in per unit value added" or CPVA, for the more accurate measure of protection defined in Equation (2).[5]

As our derivation of (5) indicates, and as Corden himself acknowledges, the validity and usefulness of (5) depend on a number of assumptions, of which the following three will be of particular interest to us here:[6]

1. Goods are infinitely elastically supplied or demanded on world markets, so that tariff-exclusive prices are independent of the tariffs themselves.
2. Exchange rates are held constant.
3. Foreign tariffs are either constant or irrelevant.

Each of these assumptions plays an identifiable role in causing differences between ERP and CPVA. These differences were explained and verified using our model in Deardorff and Stern (1983b). Since they are important for interpreting the computational results, we shall review them here as well.

Exogeneity of Tariff-Exclusive Prices

For this to be true, two further assumptions are necessary. First, the country must be sufficiently small as a participant in world markets, so that its changes in supply and demand do not affect world prices. For some countries this may be approximately true, but for the United States it most certainly is not. Thus, if the United States were to levy tariffs and consequently reduce its demand for imports, the

[5] Corden (1971) has gone well beyond the simple formula of Equation (5) in considering many of the general equilibrium complications that our model is designed to incorporate. We will associate the simple formula with his name only for ease of reference.

[6] It is also common to assume fixed production coefficients. Our model is capable of handling either fixed or variable coefficients, and, as will be noted below, we have done the calculations both ways.

world prices in affected sectors would fall and the U.S. domestic price would not rise by the full amount of the tariff. The precise implication of this phenomenon for calculation of protection in Equation (2) depends on how the country's importance to world markets is distributed among outputs and inputs. But we would expect, in general, that by dampening the domestic price changes that occur, country size would tend to reduce somewhat the levels of protection.

The second assumption needed for price exogeneity is that domestic and foreign goods are perfect substitutes. If they are not, then even if the price of an import rises by the full amount of the tariff, the price of a corresponding domestic good will not. Thus, imperfect substitutability will further dampen the price changes in Equation (2) and reduce levels of protection below what would be calculated by the ERP.

Imperfect substitutability is also what warrants the distinction we made in Equations (1) and (2) between input and output prices. Outputs are, by definition, domestically produced, while inputs will in general come from both imported and domestic sources. If the two are imperfect substitutes, with the prices of domestic goods varying by less than the price of imports as just suggested, then the prices of outputs will also vary by less than the prices of inputs. When, as we impose a structure of tariffs, all are tending to rise, this means that the positive term in (2) is dampened by more than the negative terms, and the level of effective protection is reduced algebraically compared to (5).

All prices are endogenous in our computational model. World prices are determined simultaneously by the interaction of all countries together, and no country is assumed *ex ante* to be small. Further, domestic and traded goods are distinct, with finite elasticities of substitution between them based on empirically estimated import elasticities. Thus from what we have said so far, we would expect our calculations of CPVA based on Equation (2) to be both smaller in absolute value and more often negative than the effective rate of protection based on the Corden formula (5). This was confirmed by our numerical results in Deardorff and Stern (1983b).

Exogeneity of Exchange Rates

While Corden defined effective protection under the assumption of a fixed exchange rate, he recognized the inevitability of an eventual exchange rate change in response to the imposition or elimination of a complete structure of tariffs. He thus suggested a simple adjustment of all effective rates to take this into account. Such an ad hoc procedure is not necessary for us here, since our computational model can be solved for endogenous exchange rates along with everything else. Nor need the effect of the exchange rate change be quite so trivial as it was for Corden, since different sectors can be affected differently by exchange rates in our model.[7]

In general terms, both we and Corden expect exchange rate adjustment to alter the protection calculation as follows. When a country imposes tariffs in most industries, its trade balance is expected to improve. If the exchange rate is flexible, its currency will appreciate to restore equilibrium, and this will reduce the domestic prices of both imports and exports, leading to negative protection in those sectors which were least protected by the tariffs themselves. Thus, exchange rate flexibility reduces and makes more negative our measures of CPVA based on Equation (2) as compared to analogous rates based on fixed currency values. Naturally, the opposite is true of the CPVA due to a general tariff reduction rather than an increase.

Exogeneity of Foreign Tariffs

Nothing in the concept of effective protection limits it to a country's own tariffs, though these are obviously the only policies that can be taken into account in the simplified formula (5). Industries also experience protective and antiprotective effects from the tariffs levied by other countries, and one might want to include them with a country's own tariffs in a complete analysis of the structure of protection worldwide. Whether to do so is largely a matter of choice, depending less

[7] We have explored the sectoral impact of exchange rate changes in several papers, beginning with Deardorff, Stern, and Greene (1979).

on economic reasoning than on the question one wishes to answer. For our purpose here of analyzing the effects of the Tokyo Round of multilateral trade negotiations, the world view is clearly the most appropriate.

Presumably a country's own tariffs tend to protect its industries and foreign tariffs tend to play the opposite role. Therefore, we expect levels of protection to be even smaller and more negative when allowance is made for foreign tariffs. It thus appears that the modifications of the simple analysis that we have discussed here — endogenizing prices and exchange rates and allowing for foreign tariffs — all tend to reduce, either absolutely or algebraically, the levels of protection that we should expect.

Traded versus Nontraded Goods

The treatment of nontraded goods has always been a source of difficulty in calculations of effective protection. The problem is that the prices of nontraded goods are not pegged to any world prices as in Equation (4). Corden (1966) describes two alternative procedures for handling them, neither of which is wholly satisfactory. One alternative is to include them with the traded inputs in both summations of Equation (5), letting their tariffs in the numerator be zero. This would be valid only if the nontraded goods were themselves infinitely elastically supplied, so that their prices would be unaffected by the tariffs on traded goods. Since this is manifestly implausible, especially if the nontraded goods are themselves produced with traded inputs, Corden prefers the second alternative of including nontraded goods with value added, and thus excluding them from both summations in (5). This second alternative, which differs from the first only in the denominator, leaves us with no clear idea of which sectors are actually being protected by the levels of effective protection that we measure.

An important advantage of using our computational model to estimate protection via Equation (2) instead of (5) is that none of this difficulty arises. From the model we have estimates of how all prices are affected by tariffs, and these include the prices of nontraded goods. Thus, we can include nontraded with traded goods in calculating (2), and the results refer clearly to the protection of value added actually employed directly in each sector. Protection of value added in non-traded sectors is handled in the same way.

Using the simple formula (5) to estimate effective protection of nontraded sectors, one would of course find their levels of protection to be negative. This results from the rise in the prices of traded inputs that are used in the nontraded sectors. In a general equilibrium context, however, this can be reversed. Tariffs on most tradable goods, especially if levied by all countries at once, tend to act like a consumption tax on tradables, raising their prices relative to nontradables. As demanders substitute toward nontradables their prices also tend to rise, and since the output price in (2) gets a larger weight than even the combined prices of the inputs, the nontradables in general may be protected positively. This phenomenon, that tariffs may afford positive protection to nontradable industries, is an important implication of a general equilibrium model that deserves to be studied further.

III. Data

The Tokyo Round of Multilateral Trade Negotiations (MTN) was concluded in April 1979. It marked the seventh round of multilateral reductions in trade barriers negotiated under the auspices of the General Agreement on Tariffs and Trade (GATT) since World War II. Tariffs on industrial products had last been reduced on a major scale in the Kennedy Round, which was concluded in 1967 and implemented over the subsequent five years. The Tokyo Round tariff reductions began in 1980 and will be phased in over a seven-year period. An even more noteworthy accomplishment of the Tokyo Round is the negotiation of a series of codes covering such NTBs as customs valuation, government procurement, import-licensing procedures, subsidies and countervailing duties, and product standards.

In Deardorff and Stern (1983a), we used our model to analyze the effects of the Tokyo Round negotiations on trade, employment, economic welfare, exchange rates, and domestic prices for the thirty-four countries and twenty-nine sectors covered by the model. To obtain the tariffs for use in the model, we began at the line-item level of the Brussels Tariff Nomenclature and aggregated by ISIC sector in each country, using own-country imports as weights for each of the twenty-two tradable sectors. This was done for both the pre-Tokyo Round tariff rates and the offer rates that were negotiated. The differences between these rates thus represent the negotiated changes in tariffs.

As mentioned above, because of the lack of information, we were unable to represent most existing NTBs in our model in an explicit manner to capture their protective effects. What we did was to calculate the fraction of trade covered by any kind of NTB in particular sectors and countries and to model these sectors as less sensitive to tariff changes than would otherwise be the case. This may not be too great a drawback for present purposes. Except for certain bilateral agricultural concessions and the liberalization of government procurement, whose effects we did model explicitly together with the tariff reductions,[8] the NTB codes that were negotiated do not lend themselves readily to quantification. Moreover, most of the existing NTBs affecting trade in agricultural products, textiles and clothing, footwear, iron and steel products, consumer electronic products, automobiles, and shipbuilding were exempted from the negotiations.

IV. Results

The weighted average nominal tariffs by sector for pre- and post-Tokyo Round are shown in columns (1) and (4) of Tables 1–3 for the

[8] The bilateral agricultural concessions were modeled as a relaxation of import quotas in each of the countries. For government procurement, we had information on the amounts of nondefense procurement that governments had tentatively agreed to open to foreign bidding. We assumed these amounts would be spent in proportion to the sector breakdown of each government's expenditures. Estimated government imports by sector were then determined by applying import shares from the private sector. This procedure will tend somewhat to overestimate the effects of procurement liberalization since, due to data limitations, no allowance has been made for existing government imports.

Table 1. Protection measures in the United States (Percent levels and changes in protection. Numbers in parentheses are column ranks).

	ISIC	Pre-Tokyo Round			Post-Tokyo Round			Change due to Tokyo Round		
		Nominal Tariffs	Effective Rate of Protection (Corden)	CPVA (Change Per Unit Value Added)	Nominal Tariffs	Effective Rate of Protection (Corden)	CPVA (Change Per Unit Value Added)	Nominal Tariffs	Effective Rate of Protection (Corden)	CPVA (Change Per Unit Value Added)
		(1)	(2)	(3)	(4)	(5)	(6)	(7)	(8)	(9)
Traded goods:										
Agr., for., & fish.	(1)	2.20(18)	2.09(18)	−1.96(29)	1.80(17)	1.91(18)	−0.21(27)	−0.40(4)	−0.18(12)	1.74(1)
Food, bev., & tob.	(310)	6.30(10)	13.41(5)	−0.01(20)	4.70(7)	10.16(4)	−0.05(24)	−1.60(12)	−3.26(22)	−0.0(23)
Textiles	(321)	14.40(2)	28.33(2)	0.12(5)	9.20(2)	18.02(2)	0.1G(3)	−5.20(22)	−10.31(29)	0.04(7)
Wearing apparel	(322)	27.80(1)	50.63(1)	0.14(4)	22.70(1)	43.30(1)	0.12(5)	−5.10(21)	−7.33(28)	−0.02(21)
Leather products	(323)	5.60(11)	5.62(14)	0.11(6)	4.20(9)	4.95(12)	0.30(1)	−1.40(10)	−0.67(16)	0.19(2)
Footwear	(324)	8.80(5)	13.14(6)	0.06(9)	8.80(3)	15.37(3)	0.07(7)	0.0 (1)	2.23(1)	0.01(13)
Wood products	(331)	3.60(16)	4.58(15)	0.10(7)	1.70(18)	1.72(19)	0.05(9)	−1.90(14)	−2.86(20)	−0.05(26)
Furniture & fixt.	(332)	8.10(6)	12.33(8)	0.02(14)	4.10(11)	5.52(11)	−0.01(22)	−4.00(19)	−6.81(26)	−0.04(22)
Paper & paper prod.	(341)	0.50(22)	−1.14(28)	−0.02(23)	0.20(22)	−0.86(28)	0.00(14)	−0.30(3)	0.27(4)	0.03(9)
Printing & publ.	(342)	1.11(21)	1.32(20)	−0.00(18)	0.70(21)	0.90(20)	0.00(15)	−0.40(5)	−0.43(14)	0.00(15)
Chemicals	(35A)	3.80(14)	5.76(13)	−0.24(26)	2.40(16)	3.66(15)	−0.12(26)	−1.40(11)	−2.11(18)	0.12(4)
Pet. & rel. prod.	(35B)	1.40(19)	4.27(16)	−0.02(22)	1.40(19)	4.69(13)	−0.00(20)	0.0 (2)	0.42(3)	0.02(11)
Rubber products	(355)	3.60(15)	2.37(17)	0.15(3)	2.50(14)	1.95(16)	0.15(4)	−1.10(9)	−0.42(13)	0.01(16)
Nonmet. min. prod.	(36A)	9.10(4)	15.93(4)	0.31(2)	5.30(5)	9.23(6)	0.18(2)	−3.80(18)	−6.70(25)	−0.13(28)

(*Continued*)

Table 1. (*Continued*)

	ISIC	Pre-Tokyo Round			Post-Tokyo Round			Change due to Tokyo Round		
		Nominal Tariffs (1)	Effective Rate of Protection (Corden) (2)	CPVA (Change Per Unit Value Added) (3)	Nominal Tariffs (4)	Effective Rate of Protection (Corden) (5)	CPVA (Change Per Unit Value Added) (6)	Nominal Tariffs (7)	Effective Rate of Protection (Corden) (8)	CPVA (Change Per Unit Value Added) 9)
Glass & glass prod.	(362)	10.70(3)	16.87(3)	0.08(8)	6.20(4)	9.77(5)	0.03(11)	−4.50(20)	−7.10(27)	−0.04(24)
Iron & steel	(371)	4.70(13)	7.81(11)	0.04(12)	3.60(12)	6.1S(9)	0.05(10)	−1.10(8)	−1.63(17)	0.01(14)
Nonferrous metals	(372)	1.20(20)	1.03(21)	0.03(13)	0.70(20)	0.50(21)	0.05(8)	−0.50(6)	−0.53(15)	0.02(10)
Metal products	(381)	7.50(8)	12.70(7)	−0.02(21)	4.80(6)	7.S6(7)	−0.01(21)	−2.70(16)	−4.84(23)	0.01(12)
Nonelec. machinery	(352)	5.00(12)	6.25(2)	−0.16(25)	3.30(13)	4.06(14)	−0.05(25)	−1.70(13)	−2.20(19)	0.08(6)
Elec. machinery	(383)	6.60(9)	9.38(10)	−0.26(27)	4.40(8)	6.34(8)	−0.22(28)	−2.20(15)	−3.04(21)	0.03(8)
Transport equip.	(384)	3.30(17)	1.50(19)	−0.43(28)	2.50(15)	1.94(17)	−0.28(29)	−0.80(7)	0.14(8)	0.15(3)
Misc. manufact.	(38A)	7.80(7)	11.11(9)	0.34(1)	4.20(10)	5.79(10)	0.11(6)	−3.60(17)	−5.32(24)	−0.23(29)
Nontraded goods:										
Mining & quarrying	(2)		−0.70(26)	−0.09(24)		−0.47(26)	0.02(12)		0.23(5)	0.10(5)
Elec., gas, & water	(4)		−0.20(23)	0.05(10)		−0.16(23)	0.01(13)		0.04(11)	−0.05(25)
Construction	(5)		−4.69(29)	−0.01(9)		−2.88(29)	−0.02(23)		1.81(2)	−0.01(17)
Wh. & ret. trade	(6)		−0.77(27)	0.02(15)		−0.55(27)	0.00(16)		0.21(6)	−0.02(20)

Table 2. Protection measures in the European Community (Percent levels and changes in protection. Numbers in parentheses are column ranks).

	ISIC	Pre-Tokyo Round			Post-Tokyo Round			Change due to Tokyo Round		
		Nominal Tariffs	Effective Rate of Protection (Corden)	CPVA (Change Per Unit Value Added)	Nominal Tariffs	Effective Rate of Protection (Corden)	CPVA (Change Per Unit Value Added)	Nominal Tariffs	Effective Rate of Protection (Corden)	CPVA (Change Per Unit Value Added)
		(1)	(2)	(3)	(4)	(5)	(6)	(7)	(8)	(9)
Traded goods:										
Agr., for., & fish.	(1)	7.10(13)	6.18(17)	−0.44(18)	4.86(12)	4.10(17)	−0.53(22)	−2.24(14)	−2.08(14)	−0.09(23)
Food, bev., & tob.	(310)	12.44(2)	20.96(2)	−0.20(14)	10.06(3)	17.83(3)	−0.07(13)	−2.38(16)	−3.13(21)	0.13(8)
Textiles	(321)	9.78(8)	11.42(11)	−1.52(28)	7.17(8)	8.79(10)	−1.14(29)	−2.62(18)	−2.63(17)	0.38(3)
Wearing apparel	(322)	16.77(1)	23.49(1)	−0.50(19)	13.37(1)	19.26(2)	−0.41(19)	−3.40(21)	−4.23(26)	0.09(11)
Leather products	(323)	3.65(18)	1.35(21)	−0.70(22)	2.01(21)	−2.19(28)	−1.07(28)	−1.63(8)	−3.54(73)	−0.37(28)
Footwear	(324)	11.67(3)	17.90(4)	−0.74(23)	11.63(2)	20.08(1)	−0.64(24)	−0.04(2)	2.17(1)	0.10(10)
Wood products	(331)	3.31(19)	2.00(20)	0.38(3)	2.51(18)	1.68(20)	0.11(6)	−0.79(4)	−0.32(10)	−0.27(27)
Furniture & fixt.	(332)	8.50(9)	18.20(3)	−0.83(24)	5.60(9)	11.30(8)	−0.52(21)	−2.90(19)	−6.90(29)	0.31(5)
Paper & paper prod.	(341)	7.32(12)	11.13(12)	0.54(1)	5.37(11)	8.29(12)	0.11(7)	−1.95(10)	−1.85(20)	−0.43(29)
Printing & publ.	(342)	3.23(20)	−0.64(22)	0.07(11)	2.06(20)	−1.03(26)	0.09(10)	−1.17(5)	−0.39(11)	0.02(15)
Chemicals	(35A)	11.49(4)	17.00(5)	−0.88(25)	7.95(5)	11.71(6)	−0.67(25)	−3.55(22)	−5.29(27)	0.20(7)
Pet. & rel. prod.	(35B)	1.16(22)	3.11(19)	0.37(4)	1.16(22)	3.39(18)	0.11(8)	0.0 (1)	0.28(4)	−0.26(26)
Rubber products	(355)	5.28(16)	3.76(18)	−0.63(20)	3.54(17)	2.29(19)	−0.52(20)	−1.74(9)	−1.47(12)	0.10(9)
Nonmet. min. prod.	(36A)	5.19(17)	8.95(15)	0.03(12)	3.66(16)	6.52(15)	0.02(11)	−1.53(6)	−2.43(16)	−0.01(16)

(*Continued*)

Table 2. (*Continued*)

	ISIC	Pre-Tokyo Round			Post-Tokyo Round			Change due to Tokyo Round		
		Nominal Tariffs	Effective Rate of Protection (Corden)	CPVA (Change Per Unit Value Added)	Nominal Tariffs	Effective Rate of Protection (Corden)	CPVA (Change Per Unit Value Added)	Nominal Tariffs	Effective Rate of Protection (Corden)	CPVA (Change Per Unit Value Added)
		(1)	(2)	(3)	(4)	(5)	(6)	(7)	(8)	(9)
Glass & glass prod.	(362)	9.89(7)	15.30(7)	−0.29(17)	7.70(7)	12.16(5)	−0.20(17)	−2.19(13)	−3.14(22)	0.09(12)
Iron & steel	(371)	6.21(15)	15.43(6)	−0.25(15)	4.67(14)	11.59(7)	−0.18(15)	−1.54(7)	−3.84(25)	0.08(13)
Nonferrous metals	(372)	2.56(21)	9.92(14)	0.07(10)	2.13(19)	8.29(11)	−0.04(12)	−0.43(3)	−1.63(13)	−0.11(24)
Metal products	(381)	7.88(10)	10.75(13)	−0.26(16)	5.46(10)	7.07(13)	−0.19(16)	−2.42(17)	−3.68(24)	0.07(14)
Nonelec. machinery	(382)	6.45(14)	7.35(6)	−0.88(^{2}–6)	4.37(15)	4.71(16)	−0.57(23)	−2.07(12)	−2.64(18)	0.31(4)
Elec. machinery	(383)	9.92(6)	13.51(9)	−0.66(21)	7.89(6)	10.79(9)	−0.40(18)	−2.03(11)	−2.72(19)	0.26(6)
Transport equip.	(384)	10.23(5)	14.65(8)	−1.38(27)	7.95(4)	12.31(4)	−0.99(26)	−2.27(15)	−2.34(15)	0.39(2)
Misc. manufact.	(38A)	7.70(11)	12.13(10)	−1.88(29)	4.67(13)	6.55(14)	−1.02(27)	−3.03(20)	−5.58(28)	0.86(1)
Nontraded goods:										
Mining & quarrying	(2)		−0.72(24)	−0.10(13)		−0.51(22)	−0.14(14)		0.22(5)	−0.04(18)
Elec., gas, & water	(4)		−0.80(25)	0.20(7)		−0.61(23)	0.14(4)		0.19(9)	−0.05(21)
Construction	(5)		−4.10(29)	0.21(6)		−2.96(29)	0.17(3)		0.14(2)	−0.04(20)
Wh. & ret. trade	(6)		−1.76(28)	0.26(5)		−1.37(27)	0.20(2)		0.39(3)	−0.06(22)
Transp., stor., & comm.	(7)		−0.94(27)	0.12(9)		−0.74(25)	0.09(9)		0.20(7)	−0.03(17)
Fin., ins., & real est.	(8)		−0.66(23)	0.45(2)		−0.46(21)	0.34(1)		0.19(8)	−0.11(25)
Comm., soc., pers. serv.	(9)		−0.53(26)	0.1$(8)		−0.61(24)	0.13(5)		0.21(6)	−0.04(19)

Table 3. Protection measures in Japan (Percent levels and changes in protection. Numbers in parentheses are column ranks).

	ISIC	Pre-Tokyo Round			Post-Tokyo Round			Change due to Tokyo Round		
		Nominal Tariffs (1)	Effective Rate of Protection (Corden) (2)	CPVA (Change Per Unit Value Added) (3)	Nominal Tariffs (4)	Effective Rate of Protection (Corden) (5)	CPVA (Change Per Unit Value Added) (6)	Nominal Tariffs (7)	Effective Rate of Protection (Corden) (8)	CPVA (Change Per Unit Value Added) (9)
Traded goods:										
Agr., for., & fish.	(1)	18.40(2)	21.17(4)	0.86(1)	18.40(2)	21.40(4)	0.77(1)	0.0(1)	0.23(14)	−0.08(26)
Food, bev., & tob.	(310)	25.40(1)	49.80(2)	−0.18(20)	25.40(1)	50.31(1)	−0.14(20)	0.0(2)	0.51(7)	0.03(10)
Textiles	(321)	3.30(14)	−3.55(24)	−0.37(24)	3.30(12)	−2.41(24)	−0.39(24)	0.0(3)	1.14(2)	−0.02(18)
Wearing apparel	(322)	13.S0(4)	41.62(3)	−0.13(18)	13.50(4)	42.20(3)	−0.09(16	0.0(4)	0.58(4)	0.04(9)
Leather products	(323)	3.00(15)	−15.56(28)	−0.05(16)	3.00(13)	−14.75(28)	−0.12(19)	0.0(5)	0.81(3)	−0.07(24)
Footwear	(324)	16.40(3)	51.99(1)	0.06(4)	15.70(3)	50.02(2)	−0.02(13)	−0.70(14)	−1.98(21)	−0.08(27)
Wood products	(331)	0.30(21)	−30.94(29)	−0.32(22)	0.30(21)	−30.59(29)	−0.27(22)	0.0(6)	0.35(11)	0.05(8)
Furniture & fixt.	(332)	7.80(6)	16.45(5)	0.03(8)	5.10(7)	10.26(5)	0.00(10)	−2.70(19)	−6.18(27)	−0.02(20)
Paper & paper prod.	(341)	2.10(17)	1.22(15)	−0.04(14)	2.10(16)	1.75(14)	−0.05(14)	0.0(7)	0.53(6)	−0.00(14)
Printing & publ.	(342)	0.20(22)	−1.58(23)	−0.01(12)	0.10(22)	−1.51(23)	−0.01(12)	−0.10(9)	0.07(17)	0.01(11)
Chemicals	(35A)	6.20(10)	8.69(11)	−0.04(13)	4.80(8)	6.39(11)	−0.11(17)	−1.40(15)	−2.31(2^{2})	−0.07(25)
Pet. & rel. prod.	(35B)	2.80(16)	5.21(13)	0.51(2)	2.20(15)	4.14(13)	0.17(2)	−0.60(13)	−1.08(20)	−0.34(29
Rubber products	(355)	1.50(18)	−5.17(27)	−0.78(26)	1.10(18)	−4.99(27)	−0.60(25)	−0.40(11)	0.15(16)	0.18(3)
Nonmet. min. prod.	(36A)	0.60(20)	−0.92(19)	−0.16(19)	0.50(20)	−0.54(19)	−0.11(18)	−0.10(10)	0.38(10)	0.05(7)

(*Continued*)

Table 3. (*Continued*)

	ISIC	Pre-Tokyo Round			Post-Tokyo Round			Change due to Tokyo Round		
		Nominal Tariffs (1)	Effective Rate of Protection (Corden) (2)	CPVA (Change Per Unit Value Added) (3)	Nominal Tariffs (4)	Effective Rate of Protection (Corden) (5)	CPVA (Change Per Unit Value Added) (6)	Nominal Tariffs (7)	Effective Rate of Protection (Corden) (8)	CPVA (Change Per Unit Value Added) (9)
Glass & glass prod.	(362)	7.50(7)	12.02(9)	−0.05(15)	5.10(6)	8.10(7)	−0.07(15)	−2.40(18)	−3.92(25)	−0.02(19)
Iron & steel	(371)	3.30(13)	4.77(14)	−0.48(25)	2.80(14)	4.34(12)	−0.65(27)	−0.50(12)	−0.43(19)	-0.17(28)
Nonferrous metals	(372)	1.10(19)	1.18(16)	−0.08(17)	1.10(19)	1.73(15)	0.09(4)	0.0 (8)	0.55(5)	0.17(4)
Metal products	(381)	6.90(9)	12.52(7)	−0.33(23)	5.20(5)	9.23(6)	−0.23(21)	−1.70(17)	−3.29(24)	0.10(6)
Nonelec. machinery	(382)	9.10(5)	15.57(6)	−0.13(21)	4.40(10)	6.74(9)	−0.27(23)	−4.70(22)	−8.83(29)	−0.04(22)
Elec. machinery	(383)	7.40(8)	12.49(8)	−1.10(28)	4.30(11)	6.73(10)	−0.86(28)	−3.10(20)	−5.76(26)	0.24(2)
Transport equip.	(384)	6.00(12)	8.42(12)	−1.73(29)	1.50(17)	0.03(16)	−1.58(29)	−4.50(21)	−8.39(28)	0.15(5)
Misc. manufact.	(38A)	6.00(11)	10.00(10)	−0.87(27)	4.60(9)	7.30(8)	−0.62(26)	−1.40(16)	−2.70(23)	0.25(1)
Nontraded goods:										
Mining & quarrying	(2)		−1.49(22)	0.06(5)		−0.99(22)	0.01(9)		0.50(9)	−0.05(23)
Elec., gas, & water	(4)		−1.11(21)	−0.00(11)		−0.79(21)	−0.00(11)		0.33(12)	−0.00(15)
Construction	(5)		−5.07(26)	0.06(6)		−3.64(25)	0.06(5)		1.43(1)	0.00(12)
Wh. & ret. trade	(6)		−0.59(18)	0.04(7)		−0.39(18)	0.03(6)		0.21(15)	−0.00(17)
Transp., stor., & comm.	(7)		−1.04(20)	0.02(10)		−0.54(20)	0.02(7)		0.50(8)	0.00(13)
Fin., ins., & real est.	(8)		−0.21(17)	0.16(3)		−0.16(17)	0.14(3)		0.05(18)	−0.03(21)
Comm., soc., pers. serv.	(9)		−3.96(25)	0.02(9)		−3.69(26)	0.02(8)		0.27(13)	−1.00(16)

United States, EEC, and Japan.[9] The rank order by sector is shown in parentheses. Thus, the sectors with the highest nominal tariffs in the United States were wearing apparel, textiles, leather products, nonmetallic mineral products, and glass and glass products. In the EEC, the highest nominal tariffs were in wearing apparel, food products, footwear, chemicals, and transport equipment. In Japan, the highest nominal tariffs were in food products, agriculture, footwear, wearing apparel, and nonelectric machinery.

Levels of the effective rate of protection based on formula (5) for pre- and post-Tokyo Round are shown in columns (2) and (5) of Tables 1–3, together with the sector rankings.[10] We used here the first of Corden's alternatives for handling nontraded goods mentioned above. That is, they are included in both summations in (5) but with zero tariffs. These simplified effective rates are noticeably higher than the nominal rates, especially in the United States and the EEC, although in Japan several of the effective rates were negative. Further, the nontraded sectors all have negative effective rates.

In columns (3) and (6) of Tables 1–3, we report the "change in per unit value added" (CPVA) for pre- and post-Tokyo Round based on our model, using Equation (2). These calculations were obtained by reducing the tariffs from their given levels to zero and then using the negative of the resulting price changes in Equation (2) to calculate the CPVAs by sector. The calculations in column (6) reflect as well the agricultural concessions and liberalization of government procurement. Since the results in columns (3) and (6) are based on a full model solution, they take into account all of the interactions both within and among all thirty-four countries in the model.

---

[9] To make the reporting of our results somewhat less burdensome, we decided to concentrate only on the United States, EEC, and Japan. For this purpose, the EEC member countries have been combined using weighted averages for the particular measures noted. It should be noted, however, that all of our calculations have been done using the full thirty-four-country model and that detailed results are available for each country.

[10] In calculating these effective rates, we did not attempt to make any adjustments to the input-output coefficients to correct for any biases in using actual rather than free trade conditions.

The most noticeable feature of these results, which was also noted in Deardorff and Stern (1983b), is that our model calculations of CPVA are an order of magnitude smaller than the nominal tariffs and the simple effective tariffs based on the Corden formula. Also, there are many more sectors with negative protection in our calculations. We discussed earlier several reasons why we expect smaller and more negative values for our measure of protection than have traditionally been calculated. The most important of these reasons, based on our model, appears to be the imperfect substitutability between domestic and foreign goods.[11]

Given the importance of imperfect substitutability, some further explanation of how it works may be useful. When tariffs are increased, they raise the prices of imports. If domestic goods were perfect substitutes for imports, their prices also would rise by the same amount. But if substitution is imperfect, an equal rise in domestic prices would leave demand unchanged while increasing supply. Equilibrium requires instead that domestic prices rise by less than import prices to stimulate both supply and demand by equal amounts. This smaller rise in domestic prices means that protection, as calculated from Equation (2), is reduced from what it would be if substitution were perfect.

Note further that domestic prices are only part of what appears in the numerator of (2). Import prices also enter, but negatively, to the extent that imports are used as inputs. Thus, imperfect substitution reduces substantially the protective effect of tariffs on output prices, but does not reduce by nearly as much the antiprotective effect of tariffs on input prices. Together, these two mechanisms can account for much of the reduction in measures of protection going from columns (2) to (3) and (5) to (6) in the tables.

A related phenomenon, not mentioned so far, is the effect of tariffs on exports. If domestic and foreign goods were perfect substitutes, then a given industry could not both export and import.

---

[11] In Deardorff and Stern (1983b), we examined the effects of country size, exchange rate flexibility, and foreign tariffs, all of which had relatively much smaller effects than imperfect substitutability.

But with imperfect substitution such two-way trade can and does take place. Now, producers for export enjoy no increase at all in their output price when tariffs are raised and, if anything, suffer a fall in price if world markets weaken. Thus, producers for export experience only antiprotective effects of tariffs. When they are averaged in with producers for domestic markets, as they are in the calculations we report, they account still further for the smallness of our measures of CPVA.

Regarding nontraded goods, we find that in most cases they are protected positively rather than negatively in a general equilibrium model.

Finally, in columns (7) to (9) of Tables 1–3, we report the changes due to the Tokyo Round in nominal tariffs, simple effective tariffs based on Equation (5), and our model calculations of CPVA based on Equation (2). The calculations in column (9) are of most immediate interest since they provide an indication of which sectors will tend to expand or contract relatively in response to the tariff reductions and NTB concessions that were negotiated among the major industrialized countries.

Thus, in the United States, the largest percentage increases in value added due to the Tokyo Round were recorded in agriculture, leather products, transport equipment, chemicals, and mining and quarrying; while the largest percentage declines were in miscellaneous manufactures, nonmetallic minerals, finance, insurance, and real estate, wood products, and electricity, gas, and water. For the EEC, the largest percentage increases in value added due to the Tokyo Round were in miscellaneous manufactures, transport equipment, textiles, nonelectric machinery, and furniture and fixtures; and the largest declines were in paper and paper products, leather products, wood products, petroleum and related products, and finance, insurance, and real estate. For Japan, the largest increases were in miscellaneous manufactures, electrical machinery, rubber products, nonferrous metals, and transport equipment; and the largest declines were in petroleum and related products, iron and steel, footwear, agriculture, and chemicals.

To make comparisons involving the columns in these tables, we calculated both simple and rank correlations for each pair of columns in each table. Based on these correlations (which are not reported here), it does not seem to matter very much whether one uses nominal tariffs or effective tariffs to measure protection. The two are highly correlated for each group of columns. On the other hand, our measure of CPVA is generally not significantly correlated with either of the other two measures of protection. Thus, one needs something like the approach based on our model to evaluate correctly the positions of individual sectors due to protection or changes therein. Otherwise, the effects of general equilibrium and imperfect substitution are not taken into account. Corden's simple formula does not even provide a poor approximation for this purpose.

The similarity of pre- and post-Tokyo Round structures of protection also is apparent from the correlations, regardless of how protection is measured. This can be seen by comparing columns (1) and (4), (2) and (5), and (3) and (6). Likewise, the change in protection due to the Tokyo Round is for the most part strongly negatively correlated with the levels of protection, again regardless of how both are measured. This is evident by comparing columns (1) and (4) with (7), (2) and (5) with (8), and (3) and (6) with (9). Thus, the effects of the Tokyo Round were in the direction of undoing the protection that previously existed, but were not strong enough to cause the overall pattern of protection to change significantly.

Besides calculating the effects of the Tokyo Round as just noted, we made several additional calculations of interest. These involved alternative measures of CPVA, correlation analysis designed to explain the nature of tariff reductions in the Tokyo Round, evaluation of indicators of resource pull, some further comparisons of the structures of protection in pre- and post-Tokyo Round, and the effects of the Tokyo Round on the developing countries. Let us consider each of these in turn.

Alternative Measures of CPVA

Our basic measure of the CPVA due to the Tokyo Round is calculated from our model assuming simultaneous changes in both tariffs and quantifiable NTBs in all (developed) countries at once. Also, our basic solution assumes a technology of fixed coefficients among intermediate inputs. To investigate the importance of these assumptions, we conducted alternative runs of the model in which we calculated CPVA for tariff changes only, for own-country tariff and NTB changes only, and for a version of the model with a Cobb–Douglas technology. The results were as follows.

For most developed countries, it made little difference whether the tariff and NTB changes for all countries were accounted for or only the own-country effects were calculated. This may be a surprise, since one might expect the effects of foreign tariff reductions to be quite different from one's own. The reason that this is not the case is that the patterns of tariff reduction were quite similar in most countries. This means that foreign tariff reductions do tend to offset the effects of domestic ones, but in the same industries, thus merely dampening their effects and not changing their pattern very much.[12] This pattern of correlated tariff reductions may bear out earlier observations of previous negotiations, namely, that trade liberalization has usually been balanced, presumably to avoid major industry dislocation.

Further, it does not seem to matter very much for the structure of protection whether negotiated changes in NTBs are or are not included in calculating the effects of the Tokyo Round. All correlations between the two sets of results are large and quite significant except for Norway and Sweden, where correlations are negative, and to a lesser extent Finland, Switzerland, and Mexico. These are all countries where NTB concessions were substantial, especially compared to country size.

Finally, the introduction of a Cobb–Douglas technology into the model in place of fixed coefficients made virtually no difference for the results, especially in the major industrialized countries.[13]

---

[12] It is noteworthy that this is not the case in Japan, where the correlation between own-country and all-country protection measures is not significant, and New Zealand, where the correlation is negative. In correlations run between pairs of developed country vectors of tariff reductions, these two countries stand out as unusual.

[13] It should be noted that our model is not able to incorporate differences between the capital-to-intermediate good elasticity, on the one hand, and the labor-to-intermediate good elasticity, on the other. Our experiment using Cobb–Douglas technology should thus be interpreted with this limitation in mind.

Both simple and rank correlations were above 0.90 and highly significant for CPVA measures from the two runs, except in a few developing countries.

Explanations of the Pattern of Changes in Tariffs and Protection

We correlated both nominal tariff changes and CPVA with a number of variables that we thought might help to explain *why* tariffs were reduced as they were in the Tokyo Round. The ideas here stem from interest in the political economy of protection. Ideally, policymakers and their constituents understand the economy well enough so that it is the actual *effects* of protection that guide their lobbying and policy choices. These effects are what we try to capture in our CPVA measure. However, if either our measure is inaccurate or, more likely, if policymakers are unable to perceive where true economic interest lies, then they may view nominal tariffs as the more appropriate indicator of protection, and it is this that will be correlated with the variables explaining protection.

One problem here is that the variables we look at are likely to influence both the level of protection and its change. Thus, for example, import penetration seems a likely source of protectionist pressure, and this could show up as small Tokyo Round tariff reductions and hence a large protective effect of the Tokyo Round. On the other hand, this same import penetration would also account for high pre-Tokyo Round tariffs and, if in general tariffs are reduced by some across-the-board proportion, it would also show up as large tariff reductions and a small or negative protective effect. Therefore, we do not know *a priori* whether a determinant of protection will show up in our results as a large or as a small protective effect due to the Tokyo Round. Our results are important in indicating the pattern of changes that are likely to have occurred, but they do not tell us anything about the validity or otherwise of various political theories of protection.

A final problem with the interpretation of these correlations concerns the mechanism of causation. The CPVA is calculated endogenously in our model and depends on everything in it. It is not at all an exogenous indicator of the results of the Tokyo Round negotiations. Thus it may be, as we have found before, that virtually *any* pattern of tariff reductions will tend to benefit traded sectors at the expense of nontraded ones, and thus give us a positive correlation between CPVA and import or export shares independently of whether the negotiations in fact favored sectors with large trade shares. Again, our results telling who has benefited are valid.

But whether this benefit was the deliberate outcome of the political process or instead a built-in economic effect of the way an economy responds to trade liberalization, we cannot say.

With these remarks as caveats, let us turn now to our findings. The patterns we report are based on correlations that were run between pairs of variables, both for individual countries and industries, across groups of countries and industries, and overall.

Initial Tariffs. As just explained, an across-the-board tariff reduction would reduce large tariffs the most, and a harmonization formula (e.g., the Swiss formula) should have this effect to an even greater extent. When we correlated nominal tariff changes with initial (pre-Tokyo Round) nominal tariff levels, this was confirmed. That is, the correlation between the two was negative and significant, although not terribly large. Thus, tariffs in the Tokyo Round were in fact reduced the most in those sectors where they were initially highest.[14] Interestingly, this relationship does *not* carry over to the estimated effects of the Tokyo Round as measured by the CPVA. Here the only significant correlations are positive, but these are few enough to be not particularly meaningful. Thus, it appears that initial tariffs are a poor guide to the protective effects that actually occurred as the general equilibrium implications of the Tokyo Round worked themselves out.

---

[14] This finding was least true for Japan, where neither simple nor rank correlations, though negative, were significant. Since our data on tariff offers reflected the unilateral tariff reductions made by Japan prior to the conclusion of the Tokyo Round negotiations, our comparisons for Japan may not reflect accurately the forces involved there.

Initial Protection. When we correlated CPVA due to the Tokyo Round with the CPVA due to initial tariffs, we did find a strong relationship. The simple correlation is negative and significant (–0.61). Previously protected sectors appear therefore to be the greatest losers from the Tokyo Round. It may well be that this result is the automatic bias in favor of traded goods that we normally observe for trade liberalization. Presumably those sectors that were initially the most protected were also rather lightly involved with trade as a result.

Trade Shares. We correlated both tariff changes and CPVA due to the Tokyo Round with various import and export shares. Since trade shares are zero for nontraded sectors, and since tariff changes were zero for the developing countries, the only meaningful correlations here are those for the traded sectors of the developed countries. We looked first at each sector's share of its country's imports and exports. We found nothing significant for import shares, yet small but significant correlations with export shares. The latter were negative for tariff changes, but positive for CPVA. This indicates that tariffs tended to be reduced in most sectors with large export shares, but that these sectors were also the most likely to benefit from reductions overall. This suggests that it is not really the country's own tariff reductions that are providing the benefit here, but rather those of its trading partners. We have already seen how the tariff changes tend to be correlated across countries, so this makes some sense. The failure of the import shares to show a significant correlation is somewhat surprising, given our expectation of benefits from relying on trade. Indeed, when nontraded sectors are included, the correlation does become positive and significant, making it clear that traded sectors benefit more than nontraded ones, but within the traded sector group we find no such relationship.

Looking at countries' shares of *world* exports and imports by sector, similar results were found. No significant correlations appeared for import shares, but significant correlations were noted for export shares of world markets. Again though, they are small and of opposite sign for tariff changes and CPVA. These indicate that tariff reductions were largest where they were also presumably the least meaningful, that is, in those sectors and countries with the most dominant export positions in world markets. Furthermore, since the benefits of general trade liberalization go substantially to exporters, it is the dominant export sectors and countries that benefit the most.

Net Exports. We also looked for correlations with net export positions and found results that parallel those for exports above.

Final Demand Shares. In light of the observation that tariffs are highest on final goods and lowest on primary and semiprocessed goods, we might then expect some relationship between our results and the shares of final demand in total demand by industry. However, we did not find anything significant here either, except for a slight tendency for tariffs to be reduced most in sectors with large final demand shares. Thus, we find no evidence that protection has become any more or less cascaded against imports of final goods as the result of the Tokyo Round.

Labor Shares. To see whether the Tokyo Round favored labor-intensive industries, we correlated tariff changes and CPVA with shares of labor in both value added and gross output. Nothing meaningful was found.

Employment. As another check on the connection between protection and labor, we correlated our results with employment, both levels and shares. While nothing much significant was found, the results had one odd feature. Simple correlations were not significant, but in several instances rank correlations, though small, were. These rank correlations show some evidence, admittedly weak, that tariffs were reduced most in those sectors where both employment levels and shares were large, while at the same time the Tokyo Round had its most beneficial effects, measured by CPVA, in these same sectors.

NTBs. We correlated CPVA with our data on quantitative restrictions on trade and found nothing significant.

Indicators of Resource Pull Effects of Protection

Corden's formula in Equation (5) for the effective rate of protection was intended to provide a better indicator of the effect of protection on resource allocation than was provided by nominal tariffs. Our measure of CPVA is intended to be even better. To check that the various measures do in fact perform this way, we correlated them with estimates calculated from the model of changes in employment, changes in outputs, and changes in the returns to capital by sector and country. The results of these correlations demonstrate clearly the superiority of our measure of CPVA over both nominal and effective tariffs in determining resource flows.[15]

Looking first at employment changes, in percentage terms, we found a strong positive relationship between these and our CPVA measure. The rank correlation across developed country traded sectors was 0.97 and was almost as high when developing countries and nontraded goods were included. Simple correlations were smaller, but still significant at the 99 percent level. Corden's effective tariff changes showed no significant correlation with employment changes in developed country traded sectors. Nominal tariff changes did even worse, since they showed a small but significant negative correlation with employment changes, even for developed country traded goods. The reason, again, is the similarity of tariff reductions among the developed countries, which leads employment to expand in precisely those sectors where tariffs are being reduced the most. Here, presumably, it is the fact that our measure of protection captures worldwide tariff changes that makes it work so well.

Output changes, again in percentage terms by sector and country, were similarly well explained by our CPVA measure and not at all by nominal and effective tariff changes. The only difference in

[15] de Melo and Robinson showed that across-the-board tariff changes are likely to have different effects on resource allocation than tariffs changed individually by sector. Our results, which involve comparisons of across-the-board tariff changes for the individual measures noted, are in agreement with their conclusion but show it to be the case even more strongly.

comparison with the employment change results just noted is that nominal tariffs no longer showed any significant correlation of any sign.

Finally, we calculated the change in the return to capital by sector and country due to the Tokyo Round as an indicator of the incentives for long-run resource movement. This was calculated as the change in value added net of wages, as a percent of the (fixed) value of the capital stock. From this definition it may not be surprising that the CPVA will be related to it, since their definitions overlap. However, the relationship is not at all trivial, since changes in employment change the wage bill in a direction that could conceivably cancel out improvements in the return to capital. Nonetheless, our correlations showed the strongest connection yet between CPVA and changes in the return to capital, both simple and rank correlations being close to unity wherever we measured them. Once again, both nominal and effective tariffs failed to show any significant correlations with this variable worth noting.

We conclude therefore that our measure provides a vastly superior indicator of resource flows than the alternatives. Given that our basis for comparison is the pattern of resource flows calculated by our own model, the success of our measure may not be surprising. But the failure of even the Corden measure to correspond at all with these calculated flows is surprising indeed, since the Corden formula is intended to yield an approximation to the same economic magnitude of the change in per unit value added. Nonetheless, the Corden measure seems to provide no guidance at all, and nominal tariffs are actually misleading as to the pattern of resource flows as we have calculated them.

Further Comparison of the Pre- and Post-Tokyo Round Structure of Protection

We have already noted that changes in protection were negatively correlated with their levels prior to the Tokyo Round. This was also true for the structure of protection remaining after completion of the Tokyo Round. Both of these results are consistent with the view that the Tokyo Round tended to reduce tariffs across the board, without much effect on the cross-industry and cross-country pattern of protection. This was verified even more strongly when we correlated the structures of protection for the pre- and post-Tokyo Round with each other. Here, both simple and rank correlations were in the 90 percent range throughout and highly significant.

It was also of interest to examine whether the efforts to "harmonize" the tariff reductions using the Swiss formula had the desired effect of making structures of protection more uniform. To check this we calculated coefficients of variation of our CPVA measures of pre- and post-Tokyo Round protection across industries, across countries, and overall. These turned out to have remained roughly the same before and after the Tokyo Round, suggesting that if levels of protection are indeed more uniform, it is only because they are closer to zero. This is in marked contrast, incidentally, to the pattern of nominal tariffs. The coefficients of variation for these fell consistently due to the Tokyo Round for all countries, almost all industries, and overall. Thus, while the general adherence to the Swiss formula resulted in some harmonization of nominal tariffs, this may not be particularly meaningful in terms of harmonizing levels of protection.[16]

The Terms of Trade of the Major Developing Countries

Our final concern was to investigate whether the structure of changes in tariffs and NTBs in the Tokyo Round was biased in favor of, or against, the major developing countries. As an indicator of this, we correlated the changes in world prices that our model ascribes to the Tokyo Round with various measures of trade performance of the developing countries. These measures were import shares, export shares, and trade balances. None of the results was significant, with some minor exceptions. This suggests that the

[16] With only twenty-two tradable industries in our model, it is certainly possible that harmonization did occur but is obscured by our level of aggregation. Since we did find evidence of harmonization of nominal tariffs, however, such harmonization of true protection must have been relatively weak.

effects of the Tokyo Round were *not* significantly biased either for or against the major developing countries as far as changes in world prices are concerned.[17]

V. Conclusion

In this chapter, we analyzed the protective effects of the changes in tariffs and NTBs that were negotiated in the Tokyo Round, using the Michigan Model of World Production and Trade. Since prices are endogenous in the model, we are able to calculate the changes in value added by sector for all the major industrialized and developing countries that participated in the Tokyo Round negotiations. We take into account the direct effects of changes in both domestic and foreign tariffs and NTBs, as well as the direct effects of exchange rate changes that may result from trade liberalization.

Clearly a general equilibrium model like ours is needed to analyze how individual sectors may be affected by trade liberalization. It will not be very helpful in this regard to look at changes in nominal tariffs or even effective rates of protection calculated under simplified conditions. As our results show, calculations from the model of changes in value added by sector are very good indicators of the sectoral resource shifts that tend to take place within a general equilibrium model.

Among the many findings noted in the paper, the following are especially noteworthy:

1. As just mentioned, the change in per unit value added (CPVA) as calculated using our model, provided substantially different information about the structure of protection than is available from either nominal or effective tariffs. This information is also

[17] As we point out in Deardorff and Stern (1983a), the Tokyo Round tariff reductions will be beneficial to some developing countries involved currently in the exports of manufactures. But since many existing NTBs affecting a variety of manufactured exports from developing countries were left intact (e.g., textiles and apparel, footwear, etc.), the Tokyo Round may be of limited consequence for these countries.

superior in that it is closely related to the flows of resources that changes in protection bring about, while other measures are not very useful in this respect.

2. The Tokyo Round reduced protection most in those sectors that were previously most protected. Nonetheless, the pattern of protection remains substantially unaltered from what it was before.
3. The greatest benefits of the Tokyo Round will tend to be felt in those sectors with the greatest export interests. This is true even though these are also the sectors in which nominal tariffs tended to be reduced the most, and this reflects the fact that the pattern of tariff reductions was quite similar across most countries.
4. We found no evidence that levels of protection have become more uniform as a result of the Tokyo Round. Nor did we find, within the constraints of our model and the level of aggregation of our data, any significant evidence that protection is becoming any more or less cascaded against imports of final goods, or that the Tokyo Round has been biased against the exports of the major developing countries.

Appendix. Equations of the Model

Country System Equations

Supply functions for export (X) and home (H) markets:

$$S_{ij}^{I} = S_{ij}^{I}(p_{ij}^{I}, p_{i1}^{H}, \ldots, p_{in}^{H}, p_{i1'}^{M}, \bar{w}_i, \bar{K}_{ij}^{I};\ I = X, H; \quad i = 1, \ldots, m;\ j = 1, \ldots, n \text{ or } n'. \tag{A.1}$$

Demand functions for imported (M) and home-produced (H) goods:

$$D_{ij}^{I} = D_{ij}^{I}(p_{ij}^{J}, [p_{ij}^{I}].E_i, S_{i1}^{H}, \ldots, S_{in}^{H}, \ldots, S_{in}^{X}, \bar{G}_{ij}); \quad I, J = M, H;\ i = 1, \ldots, m;\ j = 1, \ldots, n \text{ or } n';\ [\,]\ \text{if}\ j \le n. \tag{A.2}$$

Export and import prices:

$$p_{ij}^{I} = [t_{ij}^{Meq}]R_i p_i^{W}; \qquad \text{(A.3)}$$
$$I = X, M;\ i = 1,\dots,m;\ j = 1,\dots,n;\ [\,]\ \mathit{if}\ \ I = M.$$

Consumer expenditure and tariff revenue:

$$E_i = \bar{E}_i^{0} + \sum_{j=1}^{n} (t_{ij}^{Meq} - 1) R_i p_j^{W} D_{ij}^{M}; \qquad \text{(A.4)}$$
$$i = 1,\dots,m.$$

Market equilibrium for home goods:

$$S_{ij}^{H} = D_{ij}^{H}; \qquad \text{(A.5)}$$
$$i = 1,\dots,m;\ j = 1,\dots,n'.$$

Tariff equivalents (a: quotas; or b: import licensing):

$$t_{ij}^{Meq} = t_{ij}^{Meq}(\bar{t}_{ij}^{M}, D_{ij}^{M}, \bar{Q}_{ij}^{M}); \qquad \text{(A.6a)}$$
$$i = 1,\dots,m;\ j = 1,\dots,n.$$

$$D_{ij}^{M} = L_{ij}\left(\sum_{k=1}^{n} p_k^{W} S_{ik}^{X} + \bar{B}_i^{K} \right); \qquad \text{(A.6b)}$$
$$i = 1,\dots,m;\ j = 1,\dots,n.$$

Employment by industry:

$$D_{ij}^{L} = D_{ij}^{L}([S_{ij}^{X}], S_{ij}^{H}, [\bar{K}_{ij}^{X}], \bar{K}_{ij}^{H}); \qquad \text{(A.7)}$$
$$i = 1,\dots,m;\ j = 1,\dots,n\ \mathit{or}\ n';\ [\,]\ \mathit{if}\ \ j \le n.$$

Net exports:

$$N_{ij}^{X} = S_{ij}^{X} - D_{ij}^{M}; \qquad \text{(A.8)}$$
$$i = 1,\dots,m;\; j = 1,\dots,n.$$

World System Equations

Market equilibrium for traded goods:

$$\sum_{i=1}^{m} N_{ij}^{X} + N_{j}^{row}\left(p_1^W,\dots,p_n^W, R_1,\dots,R_m\right) = 0; \qquad \text{(A.9)}$$
$$j = 1,\dots,n.$$

Trade balances:

$$B_i^T = \sum_{i=1}^{n} p_i^W N_{ij}^{X}; \qquad \text{(A.10)}$$
$$i = 1,\dots,m.$$

Exchange rates (a: fixed; or b: flexible):

$$R_i = \prod_{j \neq i} (R_j)^{\theta_{ij}^R} \bar{R}_{ij}^{O} \qquad \text{(A.11a)}$$
$$i = 1,\dots,m.$$

$$B_i^T + \bar{B}_i^K = 0, \left(R_m = \bar{R}_m^O\right); \qquad \text{(A.11b)}$$
$$i = 1,\dots,m-1.$$

Notation (m = number of countries; n = number of tradable goods; n' = number of goods total)

Endogenous Variables:

S_{ij}^{I} = supply of good j by country i, sector $I = X, H$.

D_{ij}^{I} = demand for good j in country i from sector $I = M, H$.

$p_{[i]}^{I}$ = price of good j on world market ($I = W$) [or, in country i, price of export ($I = X$), import ($I = M$), or home sector ($I = H$)].

E_i = final expenditure in country i.

B_i^T = balance of trade of country i.

R_i = exchange rate of country i (price of world currency).

D_{ij}^{L} = demand for labor by industry j in country i.

I_{ij}^{Meq} = tariff equivalent on good j in country i.

$N_{[i]j}^{I}$ = net exports of good j by the rest of world (I = row) [or by country i ($I = X$)].

Exogenous Variables:

$\bar{K}_{ij}^{I}$ = capital stock of industry j, country i, sector $I = X, H$.

$\bar{w}_i$ = money wage in country i.

$\bar{t}_{ij}^{M}$ = one plus tariff on good j in country i.

$\bar{G}_{ij}$ = government procurement parameter in industry j, country i.

$\bar{E}_i^{O}$ = exogenous component of expenditure in country i.

$\bar{R}_i^{O}$ = exogenous exchange rate of country i.

$\bar{B}_i^{K}$ = capital inflow into country i.

$\bar{Q}_{ij}^{M}$ = quota parameter for good j, country i.

θ_{ij}^{R} = pegged exchange rate weight.

Explanation of Functions and Regimes

(A.1): Supplies, $S_{ij}^{I}(\bullet)$, depend on price of output, prices of all home and imported inputs, an exogenous country-wide wage, and exogenous capital stocks that are specific to the home and export sectors of each industry.

(A.2): Demands, $D^I_{ij}(\bullet)$, depend on home and import prices, aggregate expenditure, outputs in all sectors (reflecting demands for inputs), and a shift parameter for government procurement.

(A.6a): With quotas covering part of an industry, the tariff equivalent, $t^{Meq}_{ij}(\bullet)$, depends on the nominal tariff, other determinants of import demand, and a shift parameter representing the quota.

(A.6b): With import licensing, tariff equivalents are determined implicitly to hold import demands at licensed levels. The licensing function, $L_{ij}(\bullet)$, allocates changes in net foreign exchange earnings, from exports and capital flows, to imports in proportion to their existing levels.

(A.7): Employment equals labor demand, $D^L_{ij}(\bullet)$, and depends on output and sector-specific capital.

(A.9): The rest of world contributes net supplies to world markets, $N^{row}_j(\bullet)$, that depend on world prices and exchange rates, the latter reflecting pegging by the rest of world to currencies in the model.

(A.11a): Some currencies in the model are pegged, either to particular currencies or to baskets of currencies expressed as geometric weighted averages.

(A.11b): Other currencies are flexible and determined so as to maintain zero balance of payments. One currency (the *m*th usually the U.S. dollar) is numéraire and its value is exogenous.

Functional Forms

The behavioral functions in (A.1), (A.2), (A.6), (A.7), and (A.9) are expressed as log-linear functions of the changes in the variables involved. They were derived from the first-order conditions for utility and profit maximization. The assumed utility and production functions were nested composites of the Cobb–Douglas, CES, and fixed-coefficient functional forms. Coefficients are calculated from data on production, trade, employment, and input-output transactions, plus published estimates of demand and substitution elasticities. Details are contained in Deardorff and Stern (1981).

Study Questions

1. What is the theory of effective protection, and how is effective protection dealt with conceptually in the Michigan Model of World Production and Trade in terms of the change in per unit value added (CPVA)?
2. In interpreting differences between effective rates of protection (ERP) and CPVA, what is the role of exogeneity of tariff-exclusive prices, exchange rate, foreign tariffs, and traded versus nontraded goods?
3. What were the main accomplishments of the Tokyo Round negotiations, and how are they taken into account in the computational modeling?
4. What are the major findings of the computational analysis? How do the results change with different modeling assumptions?
5. To what extent do nominal tariff changes and CPVA explain the pattern of changes in tariffs and protection, the resource pull effects of protection, changes in the structure of protection, and the terms of trade?
6. What are the overall conclusions about the effects of the Tokyo Round with regard to the use of measures of CPVA, the pattern of protection, effects on export interests, the effects on imports of final goods, and the bias against the exports of the major developing countries?

References

Corden, W. M. 1966. The structure of a tariff system and the effective protective rate. *Journal of Political Economy* 74, pp. 221–237.

_____. 1971. *The Theory of Protection*. Oxford: Oxford University Press.

Deardorff, A. V., and R. M. Stern. 1981. A disaggregated model of world production and trade. *Journal of Policy Modeling* 3, pp. 127–152.

_____. 1983a. Economic effects of the Tokyo Round. *Southern Economic Journal* 49, pp. 605–624.

_____. 1983b. Tariff and exchange rate protection under fixed and flexible exchange rates in the major industrialized countries. In *Economic Interdependence and Flexible Rates*, eds. J. Bhandari and B. Putnam. Cambridge: MIT Press.

Deardorff, A. V., R. M. Stern, and C. F. Baum. 1977. A multi-country simulation of the employment and exchange-rate effects of post-Kennedy Round tariff reductions. In *Trade and Employment in Asia and the Pacific*, eds. N. Akrasanee *et al.* Honolulu: University Press of Hawaii.

Deardorff, A. V., R. M. Stern, and M. N. Greene. 1979. The sensitivity of industrial output and employment to exchange-rate changes in the major industrialized countries. In *Trade and Payments Adjustment under Flexible Exchange Rates*, eds. J. P. Martin and M. A. M. Smith. London: Macmillan.

de Melo, J., and S. Robinson. 1981. Trade policy and resource allocation in the presence of product differentiation. *Review of Economics and Statistics* 63, pp. 169–177.

Suggested Further Reading

Deardorff, Alan V. and Robert M. Stern. 1981. "A Disaggregated Model of World Production and Trade Applied to the Tokyo Round," *Journal of Policy Modeling* 3, pp. 127–152.

Deardorff, Alan V. and Robert M. Stern. 1983. "The Economic Effects of Complete Elimination of Post-Tokyo Round Tariffs," in William R. Cline (ed.), *Trade Policy in the 1980s*. Washington: Institute for International Economics.

Deardorff, Alan V. and Robert M. Stern. 1985. "Input-Output Technologies and the Effects of Tariff Reductions," *Journal of Policy Modeling* 7, pp. 253–279.

Deardorff, Alan V. and Robert M. Stern. 1985. "Structure of Tariff Protection: The Effects of Foreign Tariffs and Existing NTBs," *Review of Economics and Statistics* 67, pp. 539–548.

Part III

SERVICES TRADE

Chapter 15

Empirical Analysis of Barriers to International Services Transactions and the Consequences of Liberalization*

Alan V. Deardorff and Robert M. Stern

I. Introduction

Barriers to trade interfere with the ability of firms from one country to compete with firms from another. This is true of trade in goods, where a tariff or nontariff barrier (NTB) typically drives a wedge between the price of the good on the world market and its domestic price. This wedge, or "tariff equivalent," provides a convenient and often observable measurement of the size of the impediment. In the case of services, however, no such simple measurement is often observable. It remains true, though, that the concept of a tariff equivalent — now thought of as the equivalent tax on foreign suppliers in their competition with domestic suppliers — is a useful way of quantifying a barrier to trade even though it may be much harder to observe. Both the role of barriers to trade in services and the possible

* Originally published in *Handbook of International Trade in Services*, edited by Aaditya Mattoo, Robert M. Stern, and Gianni Zanini (2008). By permission of Oxford University Press.

Table 1. International services transactions by modes of supply, 1997.

Mode of Supply[a]	Category	Value ($bn)	Cumulative Share (%)
Mode 1	Commercial services (excl. travel)	890	41.0
Mode 2	Travel/Tourism	430	19.8
Mode 3	Gross output of foreign affiliates	820	37.8
Mode 4	Compensation of employees	30	1.4
Total		2170	100.0

[a]Modes 1, 2, and 4 are derived from balance-of-payments accounts. Mode 3 is derived from data on the operations of foreign affiliates in host countries.
Source: Karsenty (2000).

meaning of a tariff equivalent can be better understood in the context of each of the standard four "modes of supply" that arise for traded services and are shown in Table 1 for 1997. The four modes of supply are:

- Mode 1 — services that are traded internationally across borders;
- Mode 2 — services that require the consumer to be in the location of the producer;
- Mode 3 — services that require commercial presence in the form of foreign direct investment;
- Mode 4 — services that require the temporary cross-border movement of workers.

To clarify further, Mode 1 refers to "separated" services such as telecommunications, which are traded internationally across borders in a manner similar to cross-border trade in goods. Here, foreign suppliers of a service provide it to domestic buyers through international means of communication and perhaps transportation, with a unit of the service itself often unobservable as it crosses national borders. A French telecoms company, for example, may provide telephone services to a customer in Mexico, in competition with a Mexican-based provider. A trade barrier in this case might consist of Mexican restrictions on the French firm's access to phone lines in Mexico, discriminatory taxes on its operations, or regulations on the ways that Mexican consumers are allowed to access the foreign firm's services. A tariff equivalent of all such impediments would be defined as the tax on the French firm's operations in Mexico that, if it replaced all other impediments, would cause it to operate at the same level and have the same effects on the domestic telecoms providers and consumers within Mexico. As in the case of traded goods, a single tariff equivalent may not capture all of these effects simultaneously, especially if competition is imperfect. And even with perfect competition, such a tariff equivalent is unlikely to be observable as a simple price difference. There is no world price of Mexican telephone services, for example, with which to compare what Mexican firms are charging, since the nature and cost of a service depend in part on the location of the consumer. Nonetheless, a tariff equivalent is a conceptually useful way of quantifying barriers to trade in services as well as goods, and many studies have sought to express their results in this form.

Mode 2 of services trade refers to services that require the consumer to be in the location of the producer, as in the cases of tourism and education. Here again, the service provided is likely to be differentiated by the location or identity of the provider, so that a world price of the service may not be meaningful. It would be meaningless, for example, to try to compare the "world price" of a visit to the Taj Mahal or an MBA degree from the Wharton School with the prices of these services within, say, Brazil. But it remains the case that Brazilian restrictions on their citizens' travel to India or the U.S. to consume these services will alter the markets for other tourist attractions and educational institutions within Brazil. Such restrictions again can in principle be quantified as equivalent to a tax on Brazilians' visits abroad for these purposes.

Mode 3 of international services provision is arguably the most general and the most important: provision through a commercial presence that is the result of foreign direct investment (FDI). Almost any service can be provided by firms from one country to consumers in another if the firms are allowed to establish a physical presence there. This is true even of tourism — think of Euro-Disney. In this case there may well be a foreign price with which one could easily compare, but the comparison is unlikely to be meaningful. It would be a mistake to infer a trade barrier from the higher price of admission to Euro-Disney in Paris as compared to Florida, or the absence of a trade barrier from the lower price of a McDonald's hamburger in Argentina than in New York. In all such cases, prices depend on local costs of labor and raw materials as much as they do on trade barriers. However, and once again, foreign service providers may well face impediments, both to their establishment and to their ongoing operations, the effects of which would be similar to a tax if only we could infer what it is.

The final mode of supply, Mode 4, refers to the temporary cross-border movement of workers. Examples are the movement of computer programmers, engineers, management personnel, and lesser skilled construction workers who are granted temporary visas to work in a host country. Most movement that is actually permitted consists of workers within industries that produce traded goods or that produce services that are primarily thought of as traded through other modes. Thus, we do not think of many industries as producing services that are primarily traded through Mode 4. On the other hand, labor itself is a service that could be traded in this way, and occasionally it has been, in the form of guest-worker programs and the like. The fact that Mode 4 service-provision figures appear to be relatively small in the data on services trade in Table 1 is therefore symptomatic of the very high barriers that exist for Mode 4, except within industries where it facilitates other kinds of trade. Mode 4 is the one mode in which the tariff equivalent of barriers could most easily be measured, as simply the differences across countries in the real wages of particular kinds of labor.

For all of the modes, then, one objective of empirical measurement is to deduce some sort of tariff equivalent of the barrier to trade in particular services. Since direct price comparisons seldom serve that purpose, however, researchers have pursued other means of inferring the presence and size of barriers to trade. Some of these methods have been quite direct: they simply ask governments or participants in markets what barriers they impose or face. The answers are usually only qualitative, indicating the presence or absence of a particular type of barrier, but not its quantitative size or effect. Such qualitative information takes on a quantitative dimension, however, when it is tabulated by sector, perhaps with subjective weights to indicate severity. The result is a set of "frequency measures" of barriers to trade, recording what the barriers are and where, and perhaps also the fraction of trade within a sector or country that is subject to them. Frequency measures do not directly imply anything like the tariff equivalents of trade barriers, but in order to use them for quantitative analysis, analysts have often converted them to that form in rather ad hoc ways that we will indicate below.

Other, more indirect measurements of trade barriers in service industries have also been used, alone or in combination with frequency measures. These may be divided into two types: measurements that use information about prices and/or costs; and measurements that observe quantities of trade or production and attempt to infer how trade barriers have affected these quantities. In both cases, as we will discuss, if one can also measure or assume an appropriate elasticity reflecting the response of quantity to price, a measured effect on either can be translated into an effect on the other. Thus both price and quantity measurements are also often converted into, and reported as, tariff equivalents.

In what follows, we begin with a conceptual framework for understanding international services transactions and the barriers that may affect them. We then turn to a discussion of the characteristics of services barriers, and we provide some examples of barriers for the banking sector and for foreign direct investment in services sectors. This is followed with a discussion of methods of measurement of services barriers, including frequency measures and indexes of restrictiveness, price-effect and quantity-effect measurements, gravity-model estimates, and financial-based measurements. In each case, we provide information and examples of how the measurements are constructed and an evaluation of their merits and limitations. We also provide in the Appendix brief summaries of studies that have used these methods. We consider thereafter how the various measurements can be used in assessing the economic consequences of the liberalization of services barriers. Since this chapter is designed for instructional purposes, we conclude with a presentation of guideline principles and recommended procedures for measuring services barriers and assessing the consequences of their liberalization. Finally, we include an Appendix containing discussion of selected technical issues and summaries of literature pertinent to methods of measurement of services barriers. Study questions are also included.

II. Conceptual Framework

In this section, we use demand-and-supply analysis to show how the introduction of a services barrier will affect the domestic price of a service, the quantity demanded, and the quantity supplied by domestic and foreign firms. We show, using diagrammatic analysis, how the service barrier can be measured as a tariff equivalent. Three cases are presented:

- Figure 1 — domestic and foreign firms are highly competitive and their services are highly substitutable.
- Figure 2 — the services of the domestic and foreign firms are not readily substitutable and have distinctive prices.
- Figure 3 — there is a single domestic firm with monopoly power and the entry of foreign firms is restricted.

The effects of a service barrier, and thus the tariff equivalent, in these various cases will depend on the competitiveness of domestic and foreign firms and the degree of substitution between the services that they provide.

Figure 1 illustrates the functioning of a domestic market for a service when there are domestic and foreign suppliers present. It is assumed here that the suppliers are highly competitive and that their services are readily substitutable. Other cases will be considered below. The foreign suppliers may be serving the domestic market through any of the four modes of supply already discussed, although the degree of substitution between the foreign and domestic services may vary for the different modes.

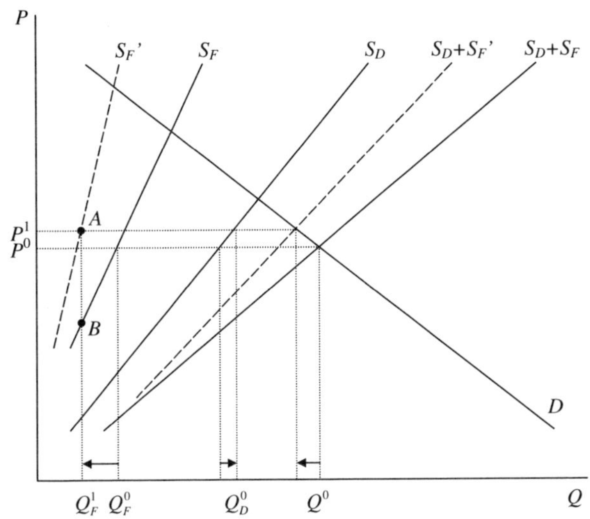

Figure 1. Perfect competition and perfect substitution between domestic and foreign services firms.

The horizontal axis in Figure 1 measures the quantity of the service supplied to and demanded by domestic purchasers. This could include amounts purchased abroad, as in the case of Mode 2, which are nonetheless regarded here as competing with domestic supplies. The demand schedule for the service is downward sloping with respect to the price, P, which is the same for all suppliers. The supply schedules for the two sets of suppliers, domestic and foreign, are upward sloping and shown by S_D for domestic firms and S_F for foreign firms.[1] In the absence of any impediments to trade, the relevant total supply schedule in this market is the horizontal sum, labeled $S_D + S_F$. Price is determined where the total supply schedule intersects the demand schedule at P^0, with the quantity Q^0 divided between domestic firms, Q^0_D, and foreign firms, Q^0_F.

Let us suppose now that a barrier is introduced that inhibits the ability of the foreign firms to serve this market. This may raise foreign

[1] Domestic supply is shown as further to the right (larger quantity for given price) than foreign supply, but this is not needed for any of the implications of the analysis.

firms' costs, shifting their supply schedule upward, or it may reduce or constrain the quantity that they supply, shifting the schedule to the left. Either way, S_F is shifted up and to the left, as is the total supply schedule, $S_D + S_F$, to the positions shown as S'_F and $S_D + S'_F$. The effect is to raise the price of the service to P^1, reduce the total quantity purchased, and increase the quantity sold by domestic firms. Sales by the foreign firms fall from Q^0_F to Q^1_F, which is the decline in imports of the service due to the barrier.

The tariff equivalent of this barrier may be defined as the *ad valorem* tax on foreign service providers that would have caused the same effects as this barrier. Such a tax, by increasing the cost of sales by foreign firms, would cause their supply schedule to shift up by the amount of the tax. Therefore, a tax that shifts S_F up so as to pass through point A is the tariff equivalent. That is, the tariff equivalent is the percentage by which point A lies above point B. What should be noted in the case of Figure 1 is that the tariff equivalent is not measurable from any observable price or price change. That is, the increase in the price of the service on the domestic market is considerably smaller than the tariff equivalent of the barrier that caused it.

There is, however, one special case in which the tariff equivalent would equal the price change. This occurs when the foreign supply schedule is horizontal (i.e., infinitely elastic) at some price P^0 so that the effect of the barrier is to raise foreign firms' cost to P^1. Then the two foreign supply schedules are horizontal at these prices, and the tariff equivalent would be just the amount by which they are shifted upward. To the extent that empirical measurements of tariff equivalents are based on observed prices, a horizontal foreign supply schedule will represent a special case that may exist for a small country that faces a given world price for the service.

Figure 2 shows a case in which the services provided by domestic and foreign firms are not readily substitutable and can therefore have different prices. In this case we must consider markets for the two services separately, as is done in the two panels of Figure 2, and we must also allow for the two services being imperfect substitutes. This is done by having each of the two demand schedules depend on the price in the other market, as indicated. Once again, the figure shows

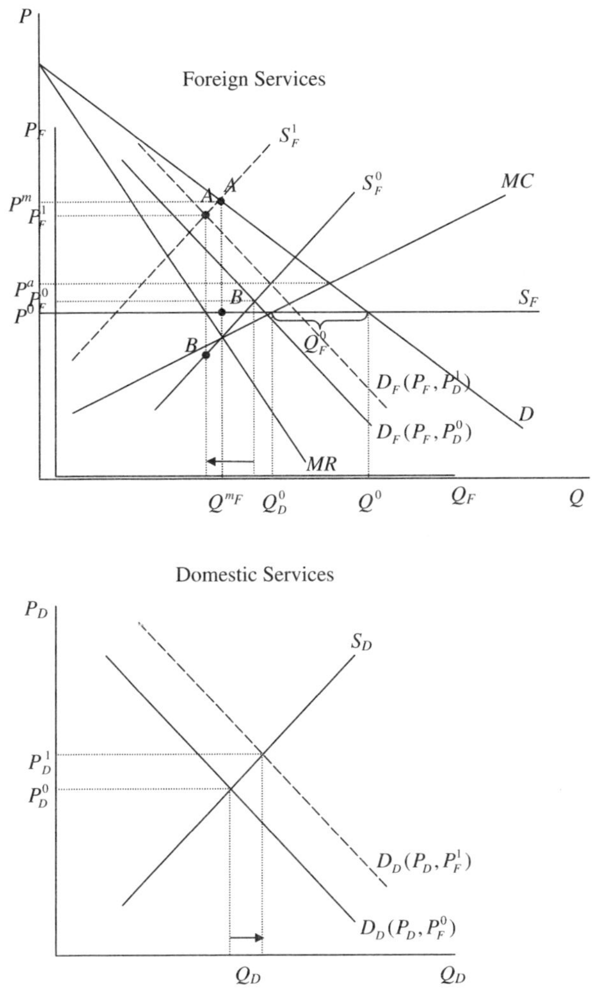

Figure 2. Imperfect competition and substitution between domestic and foreign services firms.

supply and demand schedules, quantities, and prices without any trade barrier with superscript 0, and those in the presence of a trade barrier with superscript 1. The introduction of a barrier shifts the foreign supply schedule to the left and up, as before, to S_F^1 and leads to higher prices in both markets, P_F^1 and P_D^1, which now cause both demand schedules to shift somewhat to the right. As in the case of Figure 1, with close substitution of the services, the domestic quantity supplied increases while the foreign quantity supplied declines. And here again, the tariff equivalent can be observed in the figure as the percentage by which S_F^1 lies above S_F^0, that is, the percentage by which point *A* is above point *B*.

So far we have assumed that markets are highly competitive. But this is clearly inappropriate in many service markets where an incumbent domestic firm may have a monopoly or only a very limited number of competitors. In such markets, a barrier to service trade may be a limit on entry by new firms that, though not explicitly discriminatory, favors the domestic incumbent firm and implicitly limits trade more than domestic supply. We therefore now consider, in Figure 3, the case in which there is a single domestic incumbent firm together with competing foreign suppliers. If there is unimpeded entry of firms, the market price will be P^0. In this case, the single domestic firm whose costs are increasing along *MC* will produce Q^0_D. Total sales are Q^0, and the foreign firms will sell $Q^0_F = Q^0 - Q^0_D$ in the

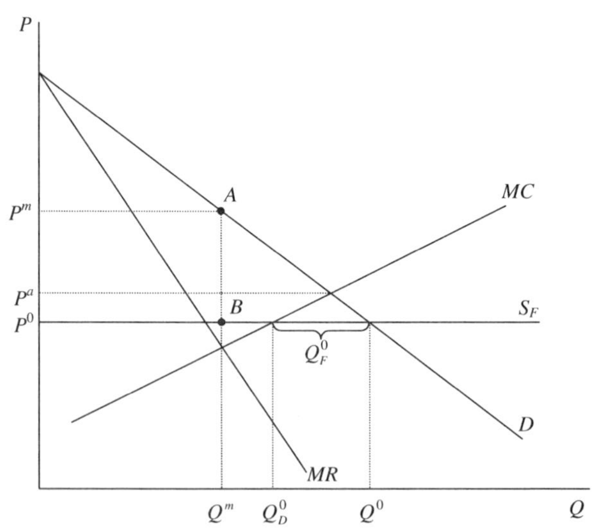

Figure 3. Domestic services firm with monopoly power and restrictions on foreign firms.

domestic market. Let us now suppose that a barrier is introduced that raises the cost of the foreign firms when they sell in the domestic market. This would cause the domestic firm's sales to rise along *MC* and foreign sales to decline. If the foreign cost rises above P^a (the intersection of domestic *MC* and demand), however, then foreign sales will fall to zero. The domestic firm can thus charge a price that just barely undercuts the foreign cost, so that the domestic firm will be able to monopolize the market. The tariff equivalent of the barrier in the case of Figure 3 is therefore the amount by which it increases foreign cost, up to the limit of $P^m - P^0$. However, if the foreign supply schedule were instead upward sloping rather than horizontal, then both the analysis and the identification of the tariff equivalent would be accordingly more difficult to measure. But the general conclusion is that the tariff equivalent of an entry restriction will be measured by the excess of the monopoly price over the competitive price that would have obtained if both trade and entry were free.

Figures 1–3 clearly do not exhaust all of the possible cases. The real world is bound to involve further mixtures of imperfect substitution between the products of domestic and foreign services firms and the degree of competition between these firms that have not been considered here. Also, many service industries have numerous special features, both in the ways that they operate and in their amenability to measurement, and simple theoretical models do not take these factors into account. Empirical work is therefore essential to address the measurement of the various services barriers that impede international services transactions. In what follows, we review and summarize many of the studies that have been done.

III. Characteristics of Services Barriers

As noted by Hoekman and Primo Braga (1997, p. 288), border measures such as tariffs are generally difficult to apply to services because customs agents cannot readily observe services as they cross the border. It is also the case, as discussed above, that many services are provided in the country of consumption rather than cross-border. Typically, therefore, services restrictions are designed in the form of government regulations applied to the different modes of services transactions. Thus, for example, regulations may affect the entry and operations of both domestic and foreign suppliers of services and in turn increase the price or the cost of the services involved. Services barriers are therefore more akin to NTBs than to tariffs, and their impact will depend on how the government regulation is designed and administered.

These regulations can take many forms, and are usually specific to the type of service being regulated. Therefore, since services themselves are so diverse, services barriers are also diverse, making them somewhat difficult to classify in general terms. There are, however, two distinctions that tend to apply across many types of services and service barriers: regulations that apply to entry or establishment of firms *versus* their operations; and regulations that are nondiscriminatory *versus* discriminatory.[2] That is, most barriers to trade in services can be placed in one of the four cells of the following simple 2 × 2 classification:

	Entry/establishment	Operations
Non-discriminatory		
Discriminatory		

For example, a limit on the number of firms that may be licensed without regard to their nationality would fall into the upper left cell, while such a limit that favors domestically owned firms would be in the lower left. Likewise, a regulation that all service providers in an industry to perform certain extra tasks would raise cost or operations

[2] These distinctions are suggested by the Australian Productivity Commission, whose website can be consulted for more details (www.pc.gov.au/research/memoranda/servicesrestriction/index.html). See also Hoekman and Braga (1997, p. 288), who classify and provide examples of services barriers as follows: (1) quotas, local content, and prohibitions; (2) price-based instruments; (3) standards, licensing, and procurement; and (4) discriminatory access to distribution networks.

in a nondiscriminatory fashion and lie in the upper right cell, while a regulation that requires special performance by foreign providers that is not expected of domestic firms would be in the lower right. Of course, a policy could in principle be discriminatory in favor of foreign firms rather than against them, but that would not be typical.

In terms of our conceptual framework, the entry *vs.* operations distinction may be thought of as determining whether the regulation shifts the supply schedules of services to the left or up. That is, regulations that restrict or impede the establishment of service providers within a market will usually reduce their numbers and therefore the quantity supplied at any given price. Regulations of ongoing operations, on the other hand, may not reduce the number of suppliers, but they will increase their costs, causing them to supply a given quantity only at a higher price. This distinction is not perfect, however, and in any case it does not need to be, since as long as the supply schedules are upward sloping, shifts to the left and up have the same qualitative effects, as we have seen. The distinction is useful mainly for classifying different types of barriers.

Likewise, the nondiscriminatory *vs.* discriminatory distinction above determines whether a regulation shifts the supply curve of only foreign service providers (when it is discriminatory), or instead raises costs and shifts supply for both foreign and domestic suppliers. As we have noted, however, a regulation that impedes establishment of all new service providers, in spite of being nondiscriminatory, can nonetheless limit trade and competition by favoring a domestic incumbent. It is also important to note that some regulations may be designed to achieve certain social objectives, such as health and safety or environmental requirements, and may not be protectionist in intent.

Of course, actual regulations differ greatly across service industries and are often based on characteristics of the particular service being provided. Thus, within each cell of the table above we may think of additional distinctions being made, usually distinctions that are peculiar to the service sector under consideration.

To illustrate, we use the case of banking services based on a study by McGuire and Schuele (2000) done under the auspices of the Australian Productivity Commission. Table 2 lists groupings of restrictions that apply especially to Modes 3 and 4 of international

Table 2. Restriction categories for banking services.

Restriction Category	Relevant for Foreign Index	Total Weight	Relevant for Domestic Index	Total Weight
Restrictions on commercial presence				
Licensing of banks	Yes	0.200	Yes	0.190
Based inversely on the maximum number of new banking licenses issued with only prudential requirements				
Direct investment	Yes	0.200	Yes	0.190
Based inversely on the maximum equity participation permitted in an existing domestic bank				
Joint venture arrangements	Yes	0.100	No	n.a.
New bank entry only through joint venture with a domestic bank				
Movement of people	Yes	0.020	No	n.a.
Based inversely on years that executives, specialists and/or senior managers can stay				
Other restrictions				
Raising funds by banks	Yes	0.100	Yes	0.143
Banks are restricted from accepting deposits from the public and/or raising funds from domestic capital markets				
Lending funds by banks	Yes	0.100	Yes	0.143
Banks are restricted in types or sizes of loans and/or are directed to lend to housing and small business				

(*Continued*)

Table 2. (*Continued*)

Restriction Category	Relevant for Foreign Index	Total Weight	Relevant for Domestic Index	Total Weight
Other business of banks — insurance and securities services	Yes	0.200	Yes	0.095
Banks are excluded from insurance and/or securities services				
Expanding the number of banking outlets	Yes	0.050	Yes	0.048
Based inversely on the number of outlets permitted				
Composition of the board of directors	Yes	0.020	No	n.a.
Based inversely on the percentage of the board that can comprise foreigners				
Temporary movement of people	Yes	0.010	No	n.a.
Based inversely on the number of days temporary entry permitted to executives, specialists and/or senior managers				
Total weighting or highest possible score		1.000		0.808

Source: McGuire and Schuele (2000, Tables 12.1 and 12.3, pp. 204–205, 208).

banking services transactions. These restrictions relate to commercial presence and "other restrictions" applied to banking services, together with a brief indication of what these restrictions represent and how an index of them has been constructed.[3] As McGuire and Schuele note (p. 206): "The commercial presence grouping covers

[3] See the Productivity Commission website for detailed listings by country of the categories of domestic and foreign restrictions on establishment and ongoing operations for some selected services sectors, including: accountancy, architectural, and engineering services; banking; distribution; and maritime services.

restrictions on licensing, direct investment, joint venture arrangements, and the movement of people. The 'other restrictions' grouping covers restrictions on raising funds, lending funds, providing other lines of business (insurance and securities services), expanding banking outlets, the composition of the board of directors and the temporary movement of people." Thus the top half of Table 2 corresponds roughly to regulations of entry/establishment in the small table above, while the bottom half corresponds roughly to regulations of operations. For each type of restriction, separate columns also indicate whether they apply to foreign and domestic firms, hence being discriminatory if they apply only to the former. An indication of the restrictiveness of these regulations is also provided in Table 2 and will be discussed below.

Just as different sub-classifications may be needed for different types of services, so too may the appropriate classification depend on the purpose for which the classification will be used. This point is made especially by Hardin and Holmes (1997) in their discussion of barriers affecting FDI (Mode 3). Focusing, in effect, on the lower left cell of our table above — the establishment of a commercial presence in many sectors in host countries — they define (p. 24) an FDI barrier as "... any government policy measure which distorts decisions about where to invest and in what form." In considering ways of classifying such FDI barriers, they note (pp. 33–34)[4]:

> The appropriate classification system may vary, depending on the purpose of the exercise. For example, if the purpose is to check and monitor compliance with some policy commitment, then the categories should reflect the key element of the commitment. ... If the primary interest is instead the resource allocation implications of the barriers, some additional or different information may be useful.
>
> Barriers to FDI may distort international patterns and modes of ... trade. They may also distort allocation of capital between different economies, between foreign and domestic investment, between different sectors, and between portfolio and direct investment. ... [T]he classification system ... should highlight the key characteristics of the barriers that will determine their size and impact. Market access and national treatment are ... relevant

[4] See also Holmes and Hardin (2000).

> categories from a resource allocation perspective. ... [N]ational treatment is generally taken to refer to measures affecting firms after establishment. A ... way to classify barriers is therefore ... according to what aspect of the investment they most affect: establishment, ownership and control; or operations. In addition..., some further information may be useful ... on distinctions ... between direct versus indirect restrictions on foreign controlled firms; and rules versus case-by-case decisions.[5]

The main types of FDI barriers that have been identified by UNCTAD (1996) are noted in Table 3, which divides barriers into three groups, the first of which concerns entry and the last operations. The middle group — ownership and control restrictions — illustrates the weakness of any simple classification system since it seems to include elements of both. Further information on the barriers most commonly used to restrict FDI especially in the APEC economies is provided in Hardin and Holmes (1997, esp. pp. 37–40 and 45–55). As they note (p. 40), some common characteristics appear to be[6]:

> application of some form of screening or registration process involving various degrees of burden for the foreign investor; restrictions on the level or share of foreign ownership, particularly in some service sectors, and often in the context of privatizations; widespread use of case-by-case judgments, often based on national interest criteria; widespread use of restrictions on ownership and control (e.g., restrictions on board membership), particularly in sectors such as telecommunications, broadcasting, banking; and relatively limited use of performance requirements on input controls in services sectors.

It is evident from the foregoing discussion that services barriers exist in a variety of forms, depending on the types of services involved,

[5] Direct restrictions include limitations on the total size or share of investment in a sector and requirements on inputs used (e.g., local content). Indirect restrictions include net benefit or national interest criteria and limitations on membership of company boards. The distinction between rules and case-by-case decisions relates to issues of clarity in specification and transparency as compared to the exercise of administrative discretion.

[6] Hardin and Holmes (pp. 40–43) also provide information on investment incentives, which are widely used and for the most part are not subject to multilateral disciplines.

Table 3. Barriers to FDI.

Restrictions on market entry	Bans on foreign investment in certain sectors Quantitative restrictions (e.g., limit of 25 percent foreign ownership in a sector) Screening and approval (sometimes involving national interest or net economic benefits tests) Restrictions on the legal form of the foreign entity Minimum capital requirements Conditions on subsequent investment Conditions on location Admission taxes
Ownership and control restrictions	Compulsory joint ventures with domestic investors Limits on the number of foreign board members Government appointed board members Government approval required for certain decisions Restrictions on foreign shareholders' rights Mandatory transfer of some ownership to locals within a specified time (e.g., 15 years)
Operational restrictions	Performance requirements (e.g., export requirements) Local content restrictions Restrictions on imports of labor, capital and raw materials Operational permits or licenses Ceilings on royalties Restrictions on repatriation of capital and profits

Source: UNCTAD (1996).

the country imposing the barriers, and the sectors to which the barriers are applied. To help further the understanding of the different services barriers, it would be useful accordingly to organize the available information by country and sector, according to the four modes of international services transactions and whether or not they are protectionist in intent. As already noted, these modes cover: cross-border services (Mode 1); consumption abroad (Mode 2); FDI (Mode 3); and the temporary movement of workers (Mode 4). Using this information, the next and difficult step will be to devise methods of measurement of the various barriers and to integrate these measures within a framework designed to assess their economic effects.

It should be emphasized, finally, that not all regulations of services should be viewed as protectionist, even when they do serve to reduce service imports. Many regulations serve legitimate purposes, such as protecting health and safety or preventing fraud and other misconduct. Such a regulation, if applied in a nondiscriminatory manner, is not protectionist and should not be viewed as a barrier to service trade, even though it may maintain a higher standard than prevails abroad and thus reduce imports compared to what they would be without the regulation. On the other hand, nondiscrimination is not by itself enough to absolve a regulation from being protectionist if it, say, enforces a standard that has no legitimate purpose but happens to be met by domestic providers and not by foreign ones. Distinguishing legitimate from illegitimate regulations may not be easy, especially since it usually requires the sort of detailed knowledge of the industry that can only be gotten from industry insiders who are unlikely to be disinterested.

IV. Methods of Measurement of Services Barriers

Measurements of trade barriers, in markets for both goods and services, can be either direct or indirect. Direct measurements start from the observation of an explicit policy or practice, such as an import quota or a regulation of a foreign provider of services, and then attempt in some fashion to measure its economic importance. Indirect measurements try instead to infer the existence of barriers using observed discrepancies between actual economic performance and what would be expected if trade were free. Direct measurements have the advantage that one knows what one is measuring, and the disadvantage that they can only include those barriers that are in fact explicit and recognized. Indirect measurements have the advantage that their quantitative importance is known, at least in the dimension used to identify them, but the disadvantage that they may incorporate unrecognized frictions other than the policy impediments that one seeks to identify.

In the case of trade in goods, direct measurements of NTBs typically take the form of inventories of identified trade restrictions, such as those compiled in the United Nations Conference on Trade and Development (UNCTAD) TRade Analysis and INformation System (TRAINS).[7] Since NTBs usually cover only some industries or products, a first step in quantifying them is often to measure the fraction of trade that they cover in different sectors and countries. These fractions may then be used directly in empirical work, even though they do not themselves say anything about how effective the NTBs have been in restricting trade.[8] Indirect measurements, on the other hand, can be fairly straightforward in the case of goods, based either on their observed prices before and after they cross an international border or on the quantities that cross it. For example, one can often infer both the presence of an import barrier and its effect on price by simply comparing the price of a good inside a country to that outside, since in the absence of any barrier one would expect competitive market forces to cause these prices to be the same. Indirect measurements based on quantities are more difficult, since they depend on a theoretical benchmark for comparability that is likely to be much less certain. Nonetheless, as we note in our discussion below, such quantity-based measurements of NTBs have been used with some success.

For trade in services, direct measurements must be carefully done since regulation in service industries is so common that merely to document its presence would not be informative. A common approach is therefore to complement the documentation of regulations by incorporating information about the restrictiveness of the regulations, and then use this information to construct an index of restrictiveness that can be compared across countries. We will provide further detail of how this may be done below, together with examples from the literature.

Indirect measurements of restrictiveness are also possible with traded services, although simple price comparisons are seldom of much use. This is because many services are differentiated by location in a way that renders comparison of their prices inside and

[7] TRAINS is available on-line at www.unctad.org.

[8] In fact, they are somewhat perverse for this purpose, since the more restrictive is an NTB, the less will be the trade that it permits.

outside of a country meaningless. For example, the cost of providing telephone service to consumers on the Texas side of the US-Mexican border need bear no particular relationship to the cost, for the same firm, of providing it across the border in Mexico, where wages are much lower but costs of infrastructure may be much higher. So even if trade in the service were completely unimpeded, we would not expect these prices to be the same, and we therefore cannot infer a trade barrier in either direction from the fact that they are not. Similar arguments can be made about most traded services.

Indirect measurements of barriers to trade in services are therefore less common than for trade in goods, although they do exist. As we will discuss below, there has been some success using the so-called gravity model as a benchmark for quantities of trade in services, and the results of these models have therefore been the basis for indirect measurement of barriers in the quantity dimension. Financial data have also been the basis for inferring barriers from differences in the markups of price over cost, as we will also discuss.

With indirect measurements of the presence of services barriers less common, however, there is therefore the need for some other approach to quantifying the effects of barriers that have been identified. In this connection, indexes of restrictiveness can be constructed that are typically measured on a scale of zero to one, and they do not purport to say how much a barrier either raises price or reduces quantity. To get such information, another step is needed. Commonly, this step involves using econometric analysis to relate an index of restrictiveness to observed prices or quantities, thus translating the measures of the presence of barriers into an estimate of their economic effect in particular on services markets.

In what follows, then, we first discuss the construction of measures of the presence of barriers, commonly referred to as frequency-based measurements, and the use of these measurements to construct indexes of restrictiveness. This is followed by a discussion of how the effects on prices and quantities can be derived. We then turn to methods that attempt to infer the presence of services barriers indirectly, first from a gravity model of the quantities of trade, and second from financial data within service firms.[9]

Frequency Studies and Indexes of Restrictiveness

Studies of frequency-based measures start by identifying the kinds of restriction that apply to a particular service industry or to services in general. For particular industries, this requires considerable industry-specific knowledge, since each industry has, at a minimum, its own terminology, and often also its own distinctive reasons for regulatory concern. Regulations often serve an ostensibly valid purpose — protecting health and safety, for example — and knowledge of the industry is also necessary to distinguish such valid regulations from those that primarily offer protection. Thus, a frequency study is best carried out by an industry specialist, or it must draw upon documents that have been prepared by such specialists. Industry studies therefore often build upon the documentation provided by industry trade groups, such as the International Telecommunications Union in the case of telecoms, bilateral air service arrangements in the case of passenger air travel, or the TradePort website in the case of maritime services.

For broader studies of restrictions in services, covering multiple industries, some source must be found that incorporates such expertise across sectors. An early approach to doing this was in the studies by PECC (1995) and Hoekman (1995, 1996) that we discuss below. These studies used information that countries had submitted to the General Agreement on Trade in Services (GATS), to be used as the basis for commitments to be made for services liberalization in the Uruguay Round negotiations. Such measures are therefore not ideally suited for documenting trade barriers. Better information requires that someone deliberately collect the details of actual barriers and regulatory practices, as in the data collected by Asia Pacific Economic Cooperation (APEC) and used by Hardin and Holmes

[9] Interested readers may also consult Warren and Findlay (2000), Whalley (2004), and Dee (2005), which cover many of the same issues of measurement and services as we do.

(1997), whose study we also discuss below. In all cases, the goal is not just to assemble a complete list of barriers, but also to know the restrictiveness of these barriers in terms such as the numbers of firms or countries to which they apply and other characteristics. This latter information is then used to construct an Index of Restrictiveness. Typically, each barrier is assigned a score between zero and one, with a score of one being the most restrictive and a score of zero being the least restrictive. These scores are then averaged, using weights that are intended to reflect the relative importance of each type of barrier.

There are several ways in which the weights on different barriers in a restrictiveness index may be assigned. Most commonly, these reflect the judgments of knowledgeable investigators as to the importance of each type of barrier. This may well be the best approach if the investigator really is knowledgeable, as in the case when an index is being constructed for a specific, narrowly defined industry.

An alternative that has been used by Nicoletti *et al.* (2000) and subsequently by Doove *et al.* (2001) is to apply factor analysis to the data once they are assembled. This enables them to distinguish those barriers that vary most independently among their data, and then to apply the largest weights to them. This is a purely statistical technique that is not, in our view, necessarily an improvement on the use of judgmental weights.

A third approach is not to construct an index at all, but rather to use the scores or proxy measures for each barrier separately in an empirical analysis. The difficulty here is that these scores may be interrelated, so that their independent influence on any variable of interest may be impossible to ascertain using standard statistical methods. If this can be done, however, the advantage is that it allows for the fact that barriers may differ in their importance for different aspects of economic performance, and this approach allows these differences to make themselves known. Ideally, one would prefer an approach that allows the weights in an index of restrictiveness to be estimated simultaneously with the importance of that index for a particular economic outcome. Thus the construction of the index would be interlinked with its use for estimating effects on prices and quantities, for example, which we will discuss below.

First, however, we discuss a few of the main studies that have constructed frequency measurements and indexes of restrictiveness.

PECC and Hoekman

PECC (1995) and Hoekman (1995, 1996) use information contained in the country schedules of the GATS, referring to all four modes of supply of services, to construct frequency ratios that measure the extent of liberalization promised by countries in their commitments to the GATS, as part of the Uruguay Round negotiations completed in 1993–1994. The frequency ratios are constructed based on the number of commitments that were scheduled by individual countries designating sectors or sub-sectors as unrestricted or partially restricted. The ratios that are calculated equal the number of actual commitments in relation to the maximum possible number of commitments.[10] Hoekman focused on commitments relating to market access and national treatment. As he notes (1996, p. 101), there were 155 sectors and sub-sectors and four modes of supply specified in the GATS. This yields $620 \times 2 = 1{,}440$ total commitments on market access and national treatment for each of 97 countries.[11] The frequency ratio for a country or a sector is then defined as the fraction of these possible commitments that were in fact made, implying an index of trade restrictiveness equal to one minus this fraction.

There are some important limitations to these calculations that are worth mentioning. Thus, as Holmes and Hardin (2000, pp. 58–59) note, Hoekman's method may be misleading or biased because it

[10] In counting commitments, the commitment for a sector or sub-sector to be unrestricted is counted as one, whereas a listing of the restrictions that will continue to apply, so that the commitment to liberalization is only partial, is counted as one-half.
[11] As noted in Hardin and Holmes (1997, p. 70), the GATS commitments are based on a "positive list" approach and therefore do not take into account sectors and restrictions that are unscheduled. In PECC (1995), it is assumed that all unscheduled sectors and commitments are unrestricted, which will then significantly raise the calculated frequency ratios compared to Hoekman (1996), who treats unscheduled sectors as fully restricted.

assumes that the absence of positive country commitments in the GATS schedules can be interpreted as indicating the presence of restrictions, which may not be the case in fact. Also, the different types of restrictions are given equal weight.[12]

Hardin and Holmes

Hardin and Holmes (1997) and Holmes and Hardin (2000) have attempted to build on and improve Hoekman's methodology, though focusing only on restrictions on FDI in services (Mode 3). In particular, they use information on the actual FDI restrictions taken from Asia Pacific Economic Cooperation (APEC), rather than just the GATS commitments. Rather than treating all restrictions equally, they devise a judgmental system of weighting that is designed, as in the case of the banking restrictions noted in Table 2, to reflect the efficiency costs of the different barriers. The components of their index and the weights assigned to the different sub-categories are given in Table 4. It can be seen, for example, that foreign equity limits are given greater weights than the other barriers noted. Their results for 15 APEC countries for the period 1996–1998 are summarized in Table 5.[13] It is evident that communications and financial services are most subject to FDI restrictions, while business, distribution, environmental, and recreational services are the least restricted. Korea, Indonesia, China, Thailand, and the Philippines have relatively high restrictiveness indexes, while the United States and Hong Kong have the lowest indexes.

McGuire and Schuele

Table 2 indicated the restriction categories and weights applied to banking services in the study by McGuire and Schuele (2000), which

---

[12] More information is needed accordingly on the restrictions that may apply to both scheduled and unscheduled services sectors in order to obtain a comprehensive measure of all existing restrictions.

[13] Details on the construction of the indexes and their sensitivity to variations in the restrictiveness weights are discussed in Hardin and Holmes (1997, esp. pp. 103–111).

Table 4. Components of an index of FDI restrictions.

Type of Restriction	Weight
Foreign equity limits on all firms	
No foreign equity permitted	1.000
Less than 50 percent foreign equity permitted	0.500
More than 50 percent and less than 100 percent foreign equity permitted	0.250
Foreign equity limits on existing firms, none on greenfield	
No foreign equity permitted	0.500
Less than 50 percent foreign equity permitted	0.250
More than 50 percent and less than 100 percent foreign equity permitted	0.125
Screening and approval	
Investor required to demonstrate net economic benefits	0.100
Approval unless contrary to national interest	0.075
Notification (pre or post)	0.050
Control and management restrictions	
All firms	0.200
Existing firms, none for greenfield	0.100
Input and operational restrictions	
All firms	0.200
Existing firms, none for greenfield	0.100

Source: Holmes and Hardin (2000, p. 62).

is based on a variety of data sources (pp. 202–203), including the GATS schedules of commitments and a number of other reports and documentation pertaining to actual financial-sector restrictions in 38 economies for the period 1995–1998. McGuire and Schuele (pp. 204–205) have assigned scores for different degrees of restriction, ranging between 0 (least restrictive) and 1 (most restrictive). The various categories are weighted judgmentally in terms of how great the costs involved are assumed to be with respect to the effect on economic efficiency. Thus, it can be seen in Table 2 that restrictions on the licensing of banks are taken to be more burdensome than restrictions on the movement of people. Also, the scores are given

Table 5. FDI restrictiveness indexes for selected APEC economies and selected sectors, 1996–1998 (percentage).

Sectors	Australia	Canada	China	Hong Kong	Indonesia	Japan	Korea	Malaysia
Business	0.183	0.225	0.360	0.015	0.560	0.062	0.565	0.316
Communications	0.443	0.514	0.819	0.350	0.644	0.350	0.685	0.416
Postal	1.000	1.000	1.000	1.000	1.000	1.000	1.000	1.000
Courier	0.175	0.200	0.275	0.000	0.525	0.050	0.550	0.075
Telecommunications	0.300	0.325	1.000	0.200	0.525	0.100	0.550	0.375
Audiovisual	0.295	0.530	1.000	0.200	0.525	0.250	0.640	0.215
Construction	0.175	0.200	0.400	0.000	0.525	0.050	0.750	0.775
Distribution	0.175	0.200	0.275	0.050	0.525	0.050	0.625	0.075
Education	0.175	0.200	0.525	0.000	0.525	0.200	0.550	0.075
Environmental	0.175	0.200	0.275	0.000	0.525	0.117	0.700	0.075
Financial	0.450	0.375	0.450	0.233	0.550	0.358	0.875	0.608
Insurance and related	0.275	0.425	0.475	0.400	0.575	0.450	0.838	0.600
Banking and other	0.625	0.325	0.425	0.067	0.525	0.267	0.913	0.617
Health	0.175	0.200	0.275	0.000	0.525	0.050	0.550	0.317
Tourism	0.175	0.200	0.283	0.000	0.525	0.050	0.617	0.542
Recreation	0.175	0.200	0.275	0.000	0.525	0.050	0.550	0.175
Transport	0.204	0.235	0.455	0.093	0.525	0.114	0.573	0.122

(*Continued*)

Table 5. (*Continued*)

Sectors	Mexico	New Zealand	Papua New Guinea	Philippines	Singapore	Thailand	United States
Business	0.289	0.086	0.300	0.479	0.261	0.775	0.005
Communications	0.739	0.434	0.475	0.758	0.518	0.838	0.345
Postal	1.000	1.000	1.000	1.000	1.000	1.000	1.000
Courier	0.775	0.075	0.300	0.475	0.250	0.775	0.000
Telecommunications	0.705	0.425	0.300	0.975	0.571	0.804	0.200
Audiovisual	0.475	0.235	0.300	0.580	0.250	0.775	0.180
Construction	0.450	0.075	0.300	0.475	0.250	0.775	0.000
Distribution	0.325	0.075	0.300	0.475	0.250	0.775	0.000
Education	0.450	0.075	0.300	0.475	0.250	0.775	0.000
Environmental	0.075	0.075	0.300	0.475	0.250	0.775	0.000
Financial	0.554	0.200	0.300	0.954	0.378	0.875	0.200
Insurance and related	0.575	0.125	0.300	0.975	0.250	0.775	0.000
Banking and other	0.533	0.275	0.300	0.933	0.506	0.975	0.400
Health	0.408	0.075	0.300	0.475	0.250	0.775	0.000
Tourism	0.275	0.075	0.300	0.808	0.317	0.775	0.000
Recreational	0.075	0.075	0.300	0.475	0.250	0.775	0.000
Transport	0.283	0.131	0.300	0.975	0.250	0.780	0.025

Notes: The higher the score, the greater the degree to which an industry is restricted. The maximum score is 100%. Because of data constraints on the value of output by sector, the indexes shown are based on simple averages of the sub-sectors involved in the individual countries.

Source: Adapted from Holmes and Hardin (2000, pp. 63–64).

separately for the restrictions applicable only to foreign banks and the "domestic" restrictions applicable to all banks. The differences between the foreign and domestic measures can then be interpreted as indicating the discrimination imposed on foreign banks. Finally, it will be noted that the foreign scores sum to a maximum of 1 and the domestic scores to a maximum of 0.808, because some of the restrictions noted apply only to foreign banks and not to domestic banks.

Based on detailed information available, the scores for banking restrictions in individual countries can be constructed. Using the category weights in Table 2, it is then possible to calculate "indexes of restrictiveness" of the foreign and domestic regulations by country. These indexes are depicted graphically for selected Asia-Pacific countries, South Africa, and Turkey in Figure 4 and for Western Hemisphere countries in Figure 5. India, Indonesia, Malaysia, and the

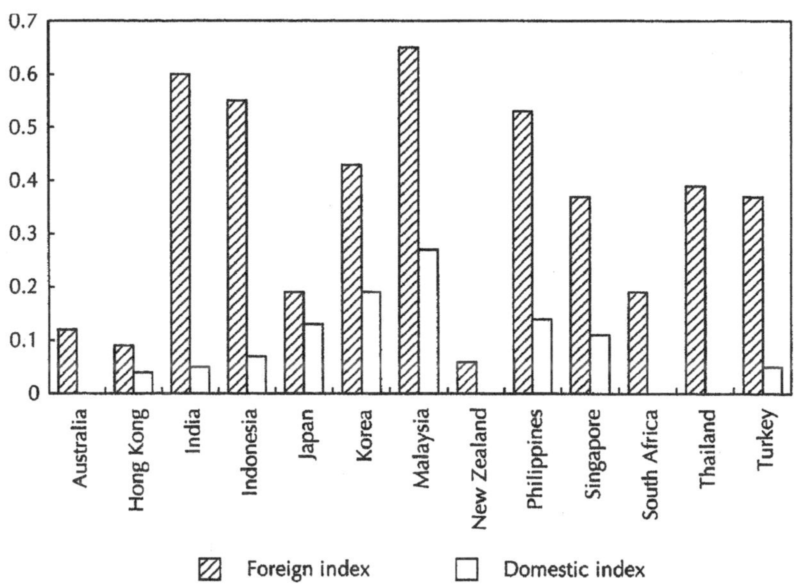

Figure 4. Restrictiveness indexes for selected Asia-Pacific economies, South Africa, and Turkey.

Note: The higher the score the more restrictive an economy; scores range from 0 to 1. *Source*: McGuire and Schuele (2000, p. 211).

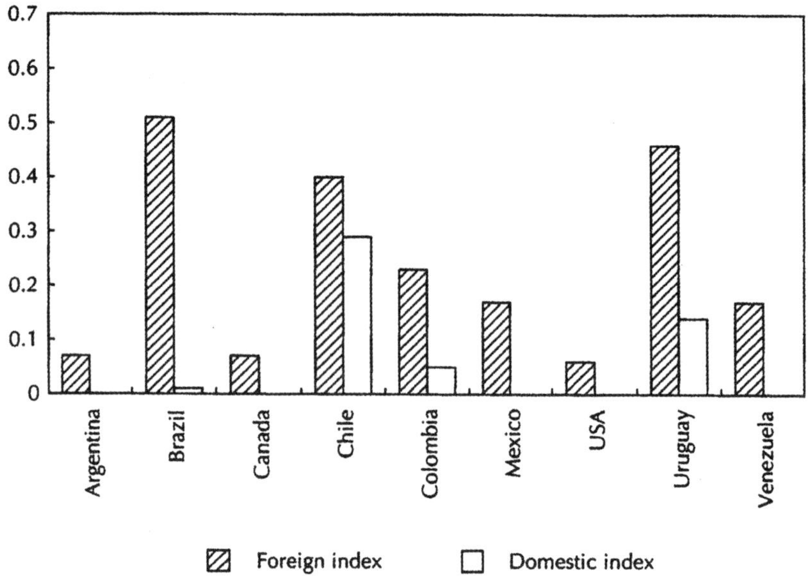

Figure 5. Restrictiveness indexes for selected Western Hemisphere economies.
Note: The higher the score the more restrictive an economy; scores range from 0 to 1.
Source: McGuire and Schuele (2000, p. 211).

Philippines can be seen to have relatively high foreign index scores; Korea, Singapore, Thailand, and Turkey have moderate foreign index scores; and Australia, Hong Kong, Japan, New Zealand, and South Africa have the lowest foreign index scores. The domestic index scores are indicative of the restrictions applied both to domestic and foreign banks, and it appears that the domestic index scores are highest for Japan, Korea, Malaysia, and the Philippines.

While the absolute values of the foreign and domestic index scores are not reported, the differences in the scores can be interpreted visually as a measurement of the discrimination applied to foreign banks. Thus, in Figure 4, India, Indonesia, Korea, Malaysia, the Philippines, Singapore, Thailand, and Turkey appear to have the highest discrimination against foreign banks. In Figure 5, Brazil, Chile, and Uruguay have the highest foreign index scores; Colombia, Mexico, and Venezuela have moderate scores; and Argentina, Canada, and the

United States have the lowest scores. Chile and Uruguay have the highest domestic index scores, while Argentina, Canada, Mexico, the United States, and Venezuela have domestic index scores of zero. Brazil, Colombia, and Uruguay have the most discriminatory regimes against foreign banks.[14] McGuire and Schuele (2000, pp. 212–213) further found that countries with less restricted banking sectors tended to have higher GNP per capita.

The frequency measures and indexes of restriction that we have discussed thus far are especially useful in identifying the types of barriers and the relative degrees of protection afforded to particular services sectors across countries. In the Appendix, we review briefly some other studies that are based on measurements of this type. It is evident accordingly that there exists a considerable amount of information on barriers covering a wide variety of services sectors, including financial services, telecommunications, accountancy, distribution, air transport, and electricity supply. As such, the compilation of such measurements and construction of such indexes are important first steps that can provide the basis for the next step, which involves using available methodologies to assess the economic effects of maintaining or eliminating the barriers.

Price-Impact Measurements[15]

As discussed above, the nature of services tends to prevent the use of price and quantity differences across borders to measure their presence or size. Therefore, in order to construct measurements of the price and/or quantity effects of barriers to trade in services, some other approach is needed.

The simplest is just to make an informed guess. For example, having constructed a frequency ratio for offers to liberalize services trade

---

[14] The detailed scores for the components of the domestic and foreign banking restrictions are broken down by individual countries and are available on the Productivity Commission website.

[15] See Bosworth, Findlay, Trewin, and Warren (2000) for a useful methodological discussion of the construction and interpretation of price-impact measurements of impediments to services trade.

in the GATS as discussed above, Hoekman (1995, 1996) then assumed that failure to liberalize in a sector would be equivalent to some particular tariff level that he selected using knowledge of the sector. These maximum tariff equivalents ranged from a high of 200 percent for sectors in which market access was essentially prohibited in most countries (e.g., maritime cabotage, air transport, postal services, voice telecommunications, and life insurance) to 20–50 percent for sectors in which market access was less constrained. He then applied his frequency-ratio measurements of liberalization to these maximum tariffs to construct tariff equivalents that differed by country based on their offers in the GATS. Thus, for example, assuming a benchmark tariff equivalent of, say, 200 percent for postal services, and a frequency ratio of 40 percent to reflect a country's scheduled market access commitments, the tariff equivalent for that sector and country is set at $200 - 0.4(200) = 120$ percent.

Using the value of output by sector for a representative industrialized country, it is then possible to construct weighted average measurements by sector and country. The resulting weighted-average tariff equivalent "guesstimates" for 1-digit International Standard Industrial Classification (ISIC) sectors for selected countries are indicated in Table 6. It can be seen that the tariff equivalents are highest for ISIC 7 (Transportation, Storage & Communication), reflecting the significant constraints applied within this sector. There is also considerable variation within the individual sectors for the relatively highly industrialized countries listed in Table 6.

It should be emphasized that Hoekman's measurements are designed to indicate only the *relative* degree of restriction. We refer to them as "guesstimates," which are not to be taken literally as indicators of absolute *ad valorem* tariff equivalents. That is, the tariff equivalent benchmarks are just judgmental and are not distinguished according to their economic impact. Further, the benchmarks include only market-access restrictions and cover all of the different modes of service delivery.

An improved approach that has been used in more recent studies is to combine other data together with an index or proxy measures of restrictiveness in order to estimate econometrically the effects of

Table 6. Constructed *ad valorem* tariff equivalent "guesstimates" by 1-digit ISIC services sectors for selected countries (percentage).

Country	ISIC 5 Construction	ISIC 6 Wholesale & Retail Distr.	ISIC 7 Transp., Storage & Communic.	ISIC 8 Business & Fin. Services	ISIC 9 Social & Personal Services
Australia	12.0	7.4	183.4	24.8	25.4
Austria	5.0	4.6	98.7	20.1	13.9
Canada	6.0	9.0	117.7	25.9	40.2
Chile	40.0	34.4	182.2	45.2	42.9
European Union	10.0	10.0	182.0	27.2	23.6
Finland	19.0	14.6	181.0	23.8	31.7
Hong Kong	32.0	31.5	149.8	39.0	42.9
Japan	5.0	4.6	142.0	28.9	32.3
Korea	16.0	21.4	164.9	36.3	40.7
Mexico	24.0	21.3	152.3	40.9	29.8
New Zealand	5.0	13.4	181.5	30.5	36.1
Norway	5.0	13.4	122.2	25.7	24.0
Singapore	12.0	34.4	138.8	35.9	33.7
Sweden	12.0	13.4	184.2	22.5	26.9
Switzerland	5.0	8.0	178.1	27.7	32.3
Turkey	5.0	34.4	31.6	35.4	35.9
United States	5.0	4.6	111.4	21.7	31.7

Source: Hoekman (1995, pp. 355–356).

barriers. For example, suppose that an index of restrictiveness has been constructed for a group of countries, and that price data are also available for the services involved in this same group. Using knowledge and data on the economic determinants of these prices, an econometric model can be formulated to explain them. Then, if the restrictiveness index and/or proxy measures of restrictiveness are included in this equation as additional explanatory variables, the estimated coefficient(s) will measure the effect of the trade restrictions on prices, controlling for the other determinants of prices that have been included in the model.

Use of this method of course requires data on more than just the barriers themselves, including prices and other relevant determinants of prices. However, these additional data may be needed for only a subset of the countries for which the restrictiveness measures have been constructed, so long as one can assume that the effects of restrictions may be common across countries. The coefficients relating restrictiveness to prices can be estimated for a subset of countries for which the requisite data are available, and the estimated coefficients can then be applied to the other countries as well.

An example of this approach may be found in the study of the international air passenger transport industry by Doove *et al.* (2001, Chapter 2), which is summarized in the Appendix. They built on work by Gonenc and Nicoletti (2001), who had constructed an index of restrictiveness for this industry in the manner already discussed, and who had also used an econometric model to estimate the effects of restrictiveness for a group of 13 OECD countries. Doove *et al.* extended the index of restrictiveness to a larger set of 35 OECD and non-OECD countries and applied this estimated coefficient to calculate price effects.

The estimating equation used for this was the following:

$$p = \alpha + \beta BRI + \gamma E + \varepsilon, \tag{1}$$

where p represents the price of air travel over a particular route; BRI is the index of restrictiveness for that route; and E is a vector of variables for the determinants of prices, including indexes of market structure both for the route and at the route ends, measurements of airport conditions, government control, and propensity for air travel. The coefficients, α, β, and γ, are to be estimated econometrically, while ε is the disturbance term. The price variable p in this equation is of some interest, since it demonstrates the not uncommon need to model particular features of a service industry. It is based on a separate analysis of international airfares, relating them to distance and to other route-specific variables. The price that is entered in Equation (1) is then the percentage that the actual airfare lies above the price predicted from this analysis.

Thus, holding this predicted price constant as unaffected by a particular trade restriction, the estimated coefficient β measures the percentage by which the price — air fare in this case — is increased by a restrictiveness of one, compared to the price at a restrictiveness of zero. Applying this estimated coefficient to the values of the index of restrictiveness for the larger set of countries, Doove *et al.* (2001) produced the price-effect estimates reported in Table 7. As can be seen, these tend to be largest for developing economies and for business travel.

Other studies have been done using variations on this technique. These variations include the use of separate indexes of restrictiveness or proxy measures for different types of trade barriers, including individual modes of supply. A number of these other studies of price impacts of services restrictions are summarized in the Appendix. These studies cover several sectors, including international air services, wholesale and retail food distributors, banks, maritime services, engineering services, telecommunications, and industrial electricity supply in both developed and developing countries. These various sectors are evidently distinctive in terms of their economic characteristics and the regulatory measures that affect their operations. Specialized knowledge of the sectors is thus essential in designing the conceptual framework and adapting the available data to calculate the price impacts of the regulatory measures involved.

Quantity-Impact Measurements

Another approach, appropriate for some service industries, is to model the determination of quantity rather than price, and then to include the trade restrictiveness index in a quantity equation. The result, analogous to that for prices above, is an estimate of effects of trade barriers on quantities. This can in turn be converted into an effect on prices by use of an assumed or an estimated price elasticity of demand.[16]

For example, Warren (2000b) has assessed the quantitative impact of barriers in telecommunications services, chiefly mobile telephony

[16] That is, having estimated that barriers reduce the quantity of a service by some percentage, this is divided by the elasticity of demand to obtain the percentage price increase to which it corresponds.

Table 7. International air passenger transport: Bilateral restriction indexes and price impacts.

	Number of Agreements/ Routes	Bilateral Restriction Index[a]	Price Impacts[b]		
			Business	Economy	Discount
Asia Pacific economies					
Australia	24	0.62	146.0	54.8	14.6
India	20	0.77	164.4	81.3	21.8
Indonesia	16	0.73	139.7	53.0	20.4
Japan	29	0.73	121.1	41.4	18.1
Korea	18	0.72	181.5	89.9	20.4
Malaysia	22	0.71	199.1	95.6	18.4
New Zealand	15	0.39	82.1	66.8	11.7
Philippines	20	0.79	207.5	70.1	20.9
Singapore	30	0.70	141.5	57.5	16.8
Thailand	25	0.68	124.5	71.3	16.2
Americas economies					
Argentina	12	0.74	161.7	62.0	17.5
Brazil	19	0.70	195.5	63.9	15.5
Canada	29	0.60	114.5	56.9	11.4
Chile	17	0.61	125.2	49.5	12.9
Mexico	19	0.82	224.7	92.2	18.4
Uruguay	32	0.52	96.9	38.5	12.3
USA	32	0.40	52.9	33.2	8.9
European economies					
Austria	28	0.32	47.2	20.6	6.1
Belgium	31	0.36	63.3	22.0	6.9
Denmark	30	0.34	53.1	21.1	7.0
Finland	22	0.23	33.6	11.5	3.8
France	32	0.35	57.0	20.8	8.3
Germany	32	0.37	56.5	20.3	8.1
Greece	26	0.31	72.1	24.9	7.2
Ireland	23	0.21	32.2	20.1	4.5
Italy	25	0.29	49.9	18.5	6.4
Luxembourg	23	0.24	36.9	15.0	4.2
Netherlands	31	0.39	104.0	20.0	10.0
Norway	28	0.32	62.1	16.4	4.4
Portugal	21	0.14	45.5	20.3	6.1

(Continued)

Table 7. (*Continued*)

	Number of Agreements/ Routes	Bilateral Restriction Index[a]	Price Impacts[b]		
			Business	Economy	Discount
Spain	31	0.36	68.0	25.4	8.9
Sweden	29	0.32	45.5	20.3	6.1
Switzerland	32	0.75	102.5	42.6	13.8
Turkey	20	0.56	98.8	32.2	10.7
United Kingdom	32	0.30	46.3	21.5	7.6

[a] Unweighted average of the route-level bilateral restriction indexes for each economy based on the number of agreements/routes shown in the preceding column. Ranges from 0 to 0.97, with a higher score indicating more restrictions.
[b] Percentage increase in airfares compared to the benchmark regime.
Source: Doove *et al.* (2001, p. 39).

and fixed network services, for 136 countries. For this purpose he estimated equations such as the following, which was for mobile telephony:

$$Q^m_i = \alpha + \beta_1 Y_i + \beta_2 Y_i^2 + \beta_3 PD_i + \beta_4[P^m_i] + \varepsilon_i. \tag{2}$$

Here, for each country i, Q^m_i is the number of cellular telephone subscribers per 100 inhabitants, Y_i is GDP per capita, and PD_i is population density. $[P^m_i]$ is a policy variable, which for mobile telephony took two forms: an index of market access for investment in the industry based on number of competitors, privatization, and policies towards competition; and a broader average of several trade and investment-related indexes.

Combining these quantitative estimates of the effects of removing existing barriers with an estimate of the price elasticity of demand for the telecommunications services involved, tariff equivalents in the form of price wedges were calculated. The tariff equivalents for domestic and for foreign providers of telecommunication services in the major nations are shown in Table 8. The estimates for the advanced industrialized countries are relatively low in comparison to

Table 8. Tariff equivalents of barriers to telecommunication services in major nations (percentage).

	Domestic	Foreign
Australia	0.31	0.31
Austria	0.85	0.85
Belgium	0.65	1.31
Brazil	3.81	5.68
Canada	1.07	3.37
Chile	1.68	1.68
Hong Kong	1.26	1.26
Colombia	10.55	24.27
Denmark	0.20	0.20
Finland	0.00	0.00
France	0.34	1.43
Germany	0.32	0.32
Ireland	1.46	2.67
Italy	1.00	1.00
Japan	0.26	0.26
Korea	4.30	8.43
Mexico	6.24	14.43
Netherlands	0.20	0.20
New Zealand	0.27	0.27
Singapore	2.10	2.72
Spain	2.03	3.93
Sweden	0.65	0.65
Switzerland	1.23	1.23
Turkey	19.59	33.53
United Kingdom	0.00	0.00
United States	0.20	0.20

Source: Adapted from Warren (2000b).

the much higher estimates for the newly industrializing countries shown. There are cases of developing countries (not shown) that in some cases have very large tariff equivalents, including some with several hundred percent, e.g., China (804 and 1,000 percent), Colombia (11 and 24 percent), India (861 and 1,000 percent), Indonesia (71 and 128 percent), South Africa (14 and 21 percent), and Venezuela (10 and 15 percent).

Gravity-Model Estimates

Because the modeling of prices that is needed to estimate a price effect above is necessarily very sector specific, the techniques described so far have limited use for quantifying barriers across sectors. Likewise, they are not useful for comparing the overall levels of service trade barriers across countries. For that, one needs a more general model of trade to use as a benchmark, and the natural choice is the so-called gravity model. This model relates bilateral trade volumes positively to the incomes of both trading partners, and also negatively to the distance between them.[17] It has become a very popular tool in recent years for eliciting the effects of a wide variety of policy and structural influences on trade in a manner that controls for the obvious importance of income and distance.

Francois (1999) has fit a gravity model to bilateral services trade for the United States and its major trading partners, taking Hong Kong and Singapore to be free trade benchmarks. The independent variables, in addition to distance between trading partners, included per capita income, gross domestic product (GDP), and a Western Hemisphere dummy variable. The differences between actual and predicted imports were taken to be indicative of trade barriers and were then normalized relative to the free trade benchmarks for Hong Kong and Singapore. Combining this with an assumed demand elasticity of 4, tariff equivalents can be estimated. The results for business/financial services and for construction are indicated in Table 9. Brazil has the highest estimated tariff equivalent for business/ financial services (35.7 percent), followed by Japan, China, Other South Asia, and Turkey at about 20 percent. The estimated tariff equivalents are considerably higher for construction services, in the 40–60 percent range for China, South Asia, Brazil, Turkey, Central Europe, Russia, and South Africa, and in the 10–30 percent range for the industrialized countries. Further details are given in the Appendix on the limitations of the use and interpretation of gravity models.

---

[17] Typically, the log of the volume of total bilateral trade between two countries is regressed on the logs of their national incomes, the log of distance between them, and other variables such as per capita income and dummy variables to reflect a common border, common language, etc.

Table 9. Estimated tariff equivalents in traded services: Gravity-model based regression method (percentage).

Countries/Regions	Business/Financial Services	Construction
North America[b]	8.2	9.8
Western Europe	8.5	18.3
Australia and New Zealand	6.9	24.4
Japan	19.7	29.7
China	18.8	40.9
Taiwan	2.6	5.3
Other Newly Industrialized Countries	2.1	10.3
Indonesia	6.8	9.6
Other South East Asia	5.0	17.7
India	13.1	61.6
Other South Asia[a]	20.4	46.3
Brazil	35.7	57.2
Other Latin America	4.7	26.0
Turkey[a]	20.4	46.3
Other Middle East and North Africa	4.0	9.5
CEECs & Russia	18.4	51.9
South Africa	15.7	42.1
Other Sub-Saharan Africa	0.3	11.1
Rest of World (ROW)	20.4	46.3

[a] Turkey and Other South Asia are not available, separately, in the U.S. data, and have been assigned estimated ROW values.
[b] North America values involve assigning Canada/Mexico numbers to the United States.
Source: Francois (1999).

Financial-Based Measurements

Hoekman (2000) has suggested that financial data on gross operating margins calculated by sector and country may provide information about the effects of government policies on firm entry and conditions of competition.[18] As he notes (p. 36):

> In general, a large number of factors will determine the ability of firms to generate high margins, including market size (number of firms), the business

[18] Gross operating margins are defined as total sales revenue minus total average costs divided by total average costs.

> cycle, the state of competition, policy enforcement, the substitutability of products, fixed costs, etc. Notwithstanding the impossibility of inferring that high margins are due to high barriers, there should be a correlation between the two across countries for any given sector. Data on operating margins provide some sense of the relative profitability of activities, and therefore, the relative magnitude (restrictiveness) of barriers to entry/exit that may exist.

The country-region results of Hoekman's analysis, averaged over firms and sectors for 1994–1996, are indicated for agriculture, manufacturing, and services in Table 10. Sectoral results for services only are given in Table 11. Services margins are generally higher than manufacturing margins by 10–15 percentage points, and the services

Table 10. Average gross operating margins of firms listed on national stock exchanges, 1994–1996 by country/region (percentage).

Country/Region	Agriculture	Manufacturing	Services
Australia	8.4	15.5	16.6
Canada	32.1	22.6	32.9
Chile	39.1	40.8	44.0
China	30.6	28.1	49.5
European Union	22.9	23.8	31.6
Hong Kong	25.9	12.8	18.1
Indonesia	41.8	34.3	41.3
Japan	38.4	26.4	28.7
Republic of Korea	11.2	25.7	25.8
Malaysia	22.6	6.0	21.6
Mexico	38.4	39.3	37.2
New Zealand	33.3	16.6	26.8
Philippines	18.1	28.6	42.3
Singapore	0.0	11.1	22.0
Taiwan	19.6	25.1	41.3
Thailand	38.2	27.3	52.6
United States	36.6	21.2	42.3
Rest of Cairns Group[a]	36.3	31.1	39.0

[a] Includes Argentina, Brazil, and Colombia.

Source: Hoekman (2000). Based on calculations using Disclosure, *Worldscope* (1998) data.

Table 11. Average gross operating margins of services firms listed on national stock exchanges, 1994–1996, by country/region and by sector (percentage).

Country/Region	Recreation	Business Services	Construction	Consulting	Finance	Health	Hotels	Retail Trade	Wholesale	Transport/ Utilities
Australia	17.9	13.8	15.3	7.0	41.0	b	27.3	7.9	9.1	c
Canada	60.1	51.7	14.4	19.2	44.5	2.3	67.8	12.0	16.0	36.5
Chile	b	b	68.7	b	55.2	b	b	21.3	27.9	46.8
China	b	b	45.9	67.1	34.0	b	77.5	24.4	25.5	46.9
European Union	42.5	32.1	19.3	22.1	51.6	22.3	23.7	23.6	19.9	32.6
Hong Kong	b	6.5	12.9	11.5	25.4	b	31.3	10.1	6.9	31.0
Indonesia	b	81.1	22.9	25.3	53.6	b	68.2	26.4	24.8	45.3
Japan	28.1	31.6	14.2	28.6	40.5	40.1	27.2	32.9	15.6	20.6
Republic of Korea	b	41.2	15.3	b	b	b	b	26.7	14.9	31.2
Malaysia	13.3	c	18.3	14.7	28.3	24.3	38.7	11.2	10.8	30.7
Mexico	19.6	b	25.7	37.3	33.3	b	49.6	28.4	25.0	51.0
New Zealand	b	b	13.8	b	57.6	b	26.9	6.6	19.7	35.6
Philippines	19.9	b	40.2	b	53.9	b	55.8	43.9	40.3	42.3
Singapore	46.7	8.6	10.6	7.7	46.3	29.2	28.2	5.4	7.9	28.0
Taiwan	79.9	36.3	21.6	11.1	64.8	b	74.5	21.5	23.2	38.9
Thailand	85.4	35.8	38.1	c	60.3	40.6	55.5	44.2	25.6	56.7
United States	46.8	56.2	20.2	c	56.3	37.0	48.5	34.6	27.0	43.4
Other Cairns[a]	b	b	28.9	26.2	69.8	29.3	64.6	24.2	22.9	52.4

[a] Includes Argentina, Brazil, and Colombia.
[b] Data not available.
[c] Reflects negative gross operating margin.
Source: Hoekman (2000). Based on calculations using Disclosure, *Worldscope* (1998) data.

margins vary considerably across countries. Australia, Hong Kong, and Singapore have the lowest services margins — in the neighborhood of 20 percent — while Chile, China, Indonesia, Philippines, Taiwan, Thailand, and the United States have services margins in excess of 40 percent. The sectoral results indicate that the margins for hotels and financial services are relatively high, and the margins for wholesale and retail trade are lower. The margins for several developing countries appear to be relatively high in a number of sectors. Overall, as Hoekman suggests (p. 39):

> ... business services, consultancy, and distribution do not appear to be among the most protected sectors. ... [B]arriers to competition are higher in transportation, finance, and telecommunications. These are also basic 'backbone' imports that are crucial for the ability of enterprises to compete internationally.

Diversity of Methods

As should be clear from the foregoing, studies of services barriers have used a wide variety of approaches. This is not surprising given the wide variety of the service industries themselves and the variation across them in the data that may be available. In our concluding section, below, we will outline the steps that seem to have been most commonly used and/or successful in the largest number of studies, as a guide to those who intend to replicate their work in other industries and countries. However, it will often be the case that one or more of these steps cannot be followed in particular cases. Research on services barriers must therefore often make do with whatever information may be available. As illustrated by the studies discussed here, this may require creative exploitation of seemingly heroic assumptions in order to extract any information at all.

V. Measuring the Economic Consequences of Liberalizing Services Barriers

While the various measurements of services barriers that we have reviewed are of interest in themselves, they need to be incorporated into an explicit economic modeling framework in order to determine how the existence or removal of the barriers will affect conditions of competition, productivity, the allocation of resources, and economic welfare within or between sectors and countries. In this regard, a modeling framework can be devised for individual sectors or on an economy-wide basis using computable general equilibrium (CGE) modeling.

Sectoral Modeling

An example of sectoral modeling is provided by Fink, Mattoo, and Rathindran (2003), who analyze the impact of policy reform on sectoral performance in basic telecommunications. Their data cover 86 developing countries globally for the period 1985–1999. They address three questions, covering the impact of: (1) policy changes relating to ownership, competition, and regulation; (2) any one policy reform coupled with the implementation of complementary reforms; and (3) the sequencing of reforms.

Their findings are: (1) privatization and the introduction of competition significantly increase labor productivity and the density of telecommunication mainlines; (2) privatization and competition work best through their interactions; and (3) there are more favorable effects from introducing competition before privatization. They further conclude that autonomous technological progress outweighs the effects of policy reforms in increasing the growth of teledensity.

What is especially noteworthy about this type of study is its focus on both the policy and market structure of the sector and the econometric framework that is designed to measure the determinants of teledensity and telecommunications productivity. The assessment of particular services barriers may therefore be most effectively addressed when incorporated into a sectoral modeling framework.[19]

---

[19] See also Fink *et al.* (2002) and the Appendix for a summary of their study of the importance of restrictive trade policies and private anti-competitive practices relating to international maritime services.

Computational General Equilibrium (CGE) Modeling

In contrast to sectoral modeling, CGE modeling provides a framework for multi-sectoral and multi-country analysis of the economic effects of services barriers and related policies. Most CGE modeling research to date has been focused on barriers to international trade in goods rather than trade in services and FDI. The reasons for this stem in large part from the lack of comprehensive data on cross-border services trade and FDI and the associated barriers, together with the difficult conceptual problems of modeling that are encountered. Some indication of pertinent CGE modeling work relating to services is provided in Hardin and Holmes (1997), Brown and Stern (2001, pp. 272–274), and Stern (2002, pp. 254–256). The approaches to modeling can be divided as follows: (1) analysis of cross-border services trade liberalization in response to reductions in services barriers; (2) modeling in which FDI is assumed to result from trade liberalization or other exogenous changes that generate international capital flows in the form of FDI in response to changes in rates of return; and (3) modeling of links between multinational corporations' (MNCs) parents and affiliates and distinctions between foreign and domestic firms in a given country/region.

The third type of CGE modeling study just noted comes closest to capturing the important role played especially by MNCs and their foreign affiliates in providing Mode 3-type services. This, for example, is the focus of the study by Brown and Stern (2001), some details of which are presented in the Appendix. Brown and Stern analyze the effects of removal of services barriers under alternative conditions of international capital mobility and changes in the world capital stock due to increased investment. Their results, presented in Table A-7, suggest that the welfare effects of removing services barriers are sizable and vary across countries depending on how international capital movements and changes in domestic investment respond to changes in rates of return. The largest potential benefits are realized for all of the major developed and developing countries when allowance is made for changes in investment that augment the stock of capital.

VI. Guideline Principles and Recommended Procedures for Measuring Services Barriers and for Assessing the Consequences of Their Liberalization

As a summary of what we have reported in detail here about the methodologies for measuring services barriers and using these measurements to assess the consequences of liberalization in services, we conclude first with several principles to be kept in mind during this process and then with more detailed procedural steps that we recommend should be followed:

Principles:

1. Most barriers to trade and investment in services take the form of domestic regulations, rather than measures at the border.
2. No single methodology is sufficient for documenting and measuring barriers to trade in services. Instead, investigators need to draw upon all available information, including both direct observation of particular barriers and indirect inference of barriers using data on prices and quantities.
3. Because of the special role of incumbent firms in many service industries, regulations do not need to be explicitly discriminatory against foreign firms in order to have discriminatory effects.

Procedures:

1. Collect the details of domestic regulations and related policies affecting services firms in the countries and/or sectors being examined, including the manner in which they apply to foreign versus domestic firms, plus quantitative details of their application, such as any percentage or dollar limits that they impose.
2. Ideally, this information should be collected by systematic surveys of governments and/or firms. However, it may also be possible to infer it less directly from documents prepared for other purposes, such as the commitments that governments

made to the GATS in the Uruguay Round and subsequent negotiations.

3. For each type of regulation or policy, define degrees of restrictiveness and assign scores to each, ranging from zero for least restrictive to one for most restrictive.
4. Construct a measure of restrictiveness by: weighting the scores from step 3 based on judgments of the relative importance of each policy; using a statistical methodology such as factor analysis that will serve to identify the weights; or designing proxy measures, such as dummy variables, to represent particular restrictions. The resulting measures can then be used directly for reporting the presence and importance of barriers across industries and countries, as well as for providing an input to subsequent analysis.
5. Convert the measures of restrictiveness from step 4 into a set of tariff equivalents by one or more of the following methods. Depending on the quality of information that goes into their construction, these tariff equivalents may be superior to the measures themselves for reporting about barriers and analyzing their effects.

    a. Assign judgmental tariff-equivalent values to each of the component measures, representing the percentage taxes on foreign suppliers to which each component is thought to correspond at their most restrictive levels (index = 1).
    b. Use data on prices and their determinants as the basis for a regression model that includes an index or other measures of restrictiveness and that estimates the effect on prices.
    c. Use data on quantities produced or traded as the basis for a regression model that includes an index or other measures of restrictiveness and that estimates the effect on quantities. This estimate can then be converted to tariff equivalents using an assumed or estimated price elasticity of demand.

6. Use an index or other measures of restrictiveness or the tariff equivalents constructed above as inputs into a model of production and trade in order to ascertain the effects of changes in the

barriers to which they correspond. The appropriate model for this purpose depends on whether sectoral or economy-wide policy changes are to be analyzed. For economy-wide policy changes, the model should be a general equilibrium one, incorporating the full effects of barriers across sectors and countries. Ideally, too, the model should be designed to capture the effects of service regulations in the form that they have been observed and quantified as above.

Appendix Literature Summaries of Methods of Measurement

In this Appendix, we provide a somewhat more technical discussion of the various methods of measurement of services barriers, focusing especially on available studies that have been completed and that can be consulted for more information on methodology and data and possible adaptation in further research.

Frequency Studies and Indexes of Restrictiveness

In what follows, we summarize several studies that complement our discussion in the main text:

- Mattoo (1998) analyzed market access commitments in **financial services**, covering direct insurance and banking. His results indicated that Latin America was the most restricted in direct insurance and Asia the most restricted in banking services.
- Marko (1998) constructed frequency measures for the basic **telecommunications** markets, using Hoekman's (1995) methodology. Marko found that 58 percent of the basic telecommunications services market for the 69 signatories of the February 1997 Agreement on Basic Telecommunications was covered by partial or full GATS commitments.
- McGuire (1998) showed that Australia's impediments in **financial services**, including banking, securities, and insurance, were much lower as compared to other economies in Asia.

- Colecchia (2000) provided a methodological, pilot study of the barriers on **accountancy services** for Australia, France, the United Kingdom, and the United States, using OECD information on regulatory regimes for 1997. The United Kingdom was found to be the most liberal, the United States the least liberal.
- Kalirajan (2000) constructed restrictiveness indexes for 38 economies, using GATS schedules and a variety of other information on barriers to **distribution services** as of June 1999. The indexes covered the services of commission agents, wholesalers, retailers, and franchisers. The findings were that: (1) Belgium, India, Indonesia, France, Korea, Malaysia, the Philippines, Switzerland, and Thailand were the most restrictive economies and Singapore and Hong Kong the most open; and (2) the countries that were the most discriminatory against foreign firms included Malaysia, the Philippines, Venezuela, Brazil, the United States, and Greece. The detailed domestic and foreign restrictiveness indexes were broken down by country and are available on the Productivity Commission website.
- Kemp (2000) constructed restrictiveness indexes for the four modes of providing **educational services**, using GATS data on commitments for market access and national treatment for the five sub-sectors of educational services and covering 29 countries. While only a quarter of GATS member countries scheduled commitments, the evidence suggested that consumption abroad, which is the major mode of educational trade in terms of foreign-student tuition, fees, and expenditures, was comparatively the least restricted mode.
- McGuire, Schuele, and Smith (2000) developed indexes for restrictions on foreign **maritime service** suppliers and all maritime service suppliers covering 35 economies during the period 1994–1998, using a variety of GATS and other data sources. They found that: (1) Brazil, Chile, India, Indonesia, Korea, Malaysia, the Philippines, and the United States had the most restricted markets against foreign maritime suppliers; and (2) Chile, the Philippines, Thailand, Turkey, and the United States were the most discriminatory in favoring domestic suppliers. The detailed

domestic and foreign indexes of restrictiveness were broken down by country and are available on the Productivity Commission website.

- Nguyen-Hong (2000) constructed restrictiveness indexes for **accountancy**, **architectural**, **and engineering services** for 34 economies and **legal services** for 29 economies. The indexes were compiled from WTO, OECD, APEC, and a variety of other sources. The findings were that: (1) legal and accounting were the most highly restricted services; (2) Indonesia, Malaysia, Austria, Mexico, and Turkey were the most restrictive for the four professions, and Finland and the Netherlands the most open; (3) nationality requirements were the most extensive in legal and accountancy services; (4) residency requirements were common in accountancy services; (5) partnerships and practices between accountants and lawyers were commonly restricted; and (6) recognition of foreign qualifications and licenses was subject to a variety of restrictions among countries. The detailed domestic and foreign restrictiveness indexes were broken down and are available on the Productivity Commission website.
- Warren (2000a) used data for 136 countries from the International Telecommunications Union (ITU) to construct five indexes for the regulation of **telecommunications** policies that discriminate against: (1) all potential providers of cross-border telecommunications services; (2) foreign providers of cross-border services; (3) all potential providers of fixed network services; (4) all potential providers of cellular services via FDI; and (5) foreign providers of mobile services via FDI. He found: (1) significant variation across countries in all five indexes; (2) most countries relied only on foreign carriers to provide competition in mobile markets; (3) countries were less prepared to use majority-owned foreign carriers in their fixed network markets; (4) countries that liberalized their mobile networks were more likely to liberalize their fixed networks; (5) countries that limited commercial presence via FDI were more liberal in permitting cross-border entry; and (6) GATS-based indexes that tended to reflect legal conditions, as calculated by Marko (1998), were not altogether well correlated with ITU-based indexes that were designed to reflect

economic conditions. The detailed domestic and foreign indexes by country are available on the Productivity Commission website.

- Doove, Gabbitas, Nguyen-Hong, and Owen (2001) constructed restrictiveness indexes for international air passenger transport, telecommunications, and electricity supply. The index for **air transport** was an average of the bilateral restrictiveness indexes applicable to pairs of countries. The data covered 875 airline routes for 35 economies and referred to the late 1990s. The bilateral restrictions included designation, capacity, fares, and charter services, with weights derived using factor analysis in an OECD study by Gonenc and Nicoletti (2001). The bilateral restrictions were generally not covered under the GATS, so that discriminatory restrictions on third countries may have been applied. The results are shown in column (2) of Table 7 and indicate substantial variation across countries as a consequence of the agreement-specific bilateral restrictions.

  The restrictiveness index for **telecommunications** covered 24 OECD member countries and 23 non-OECD countries, using data for 1997. The telecommunications industry has been undergoing rapid technological change in recent decades, and there has been widespread regulatory reform and structural reform undertaken in many countries. Doove *et al.* built upon the OECD study by Boylaud and Nicoletti (2000), who focused on the four major telecommunications sectors: trunk (domestic long distance); international (international long distance); mobile (cellular); and leased-line services. The regulatory measures covered include: market share of new entrants; index of governmental control of the public telecommunications operators (PTOs); degree of internationalization of domestic markets; time to liberalization; and time to privatization. These measurements were incorporated into an econometric framework for the individual sectors in order to estimate the price impacts involved that are noted in Table A-1.

  Electricity supply has also been undergoing significant deregulation and structural reform. Building upon OECD work by Steiner (2000), Doove *et al.* assembled data for 50 economies for 1996. The regulatory measures covered were: unbundling of electricity

Table A-1. Price impact of regulation on telecommunications prices, 1997 (percent of notional price existing under benchmark regulatory regime).

Economy	Trunk	International	Mobile	Leasing	Industry-wide
OECD					
Australia	21	33	23	4	19
Austria	10	51	17	11	20
Belgium	41	207	18	5	52
Canada	33	95	8	0	27
Denmark	63	12	16	3	39
Finland	5	34	50	17	22
France	41	95	16	9	34
Germany	40	176	17	8	38
Greece	37	35	10	19	27
Iceland	31	199	96	11	54
Ireland	17	56	16	10	22
Italy	32	41	10	3	21
Japan	39	34	14	5	23
Luxembourg	17	108	105	22	59
Netherlands	32	30	13	5	23
New Zealand	30	24	15	1	21
Norway	26	67	42	14	31
Portugal	22	15	8	6	15
Spain	28	30	7	4	18
Sweden	53	b	54	15	b
Switzerland	13	165	49	16	40
Turkey	35	b	17	24	b
United Kingdom	78	63	6	2	47
United States	61	32	8	1	38
Unweighted mean	34	73	26	9	31
Standard deviation	17	61	27	7	13
Additional OECD[a]					
Czech Republic	36	20	6	ne	22
Hungary	69	44	2	ne	38
Korea	18	16	9	ne	14
Mexico	54	16	7	ne	40
Poland	18	30	9	ne	17
Unweighted mean	39	25	7	na	26
Standard deviation	23	12	3	na	12

(*Continued*)

Table A-1. (*Continued*)

Economy	Trunk	International	Mobile	Leasing	Industry-wide
Non-OECD					
Argentina	64	21	6	ne	45
Brazil	27	15	16	ne	23
Chile	41	35	7	ne	32
China	b	b	b	ne	b
Colombia	28	22	20	ne	25
Hong Kong	49	47	24	ne	43
India	68	41	b	ne	b
Indonesia	41	52	56	ne	46
Malaysia	23	34	23	ne	24
Peru	32	12	7	ne	24
Philippines	30	23	8	ne	23
Russia	63	b	b	ne	b
Singapore	25	196	35	ne	44
South Africa	35	26	b	ne	b
Taiwan	25	54	40	ne	32
Thailand	41	111	18	ne	42
Uruguay	42	37	8	ne	33
Vietnam	b	b	b	ne	b
Unweighted mean	40	48	21	na	34
Standard deviation	15	47	15	na	9
All 47 Economies					
Minimum	5	12	2	0	14
Maximum	78	207	105	24	59
Unweighted mean	36	58	22	9	31
Standard deviation	17	54	22	7	12

ne: not estimated.

na: not applicable.

[a] OECD economies not included in Boylaud and Nicoletti (2000).

[b] Excluded.

Source: Doove *et al.* (2001, pp. 72–73).

generation from transmission; third party access; presence of a wholesale electricity market; degree of private/public ownership; time to liberalization; and time to privatization. The price impacts of regulation were estimated and are indicated in Table A-2.

Table A-2. Price impacts of regulation on industrial electricity prices, 1996.[a]

Economies in Original Study	Percent	Extended Coverage	Percent
Australia	0.0	Argentina	0.0
Belgium	15.4	Austria	13.2
Canada	8.8	Bolivia	16.5
Denmark	8.5	Brazil	15.6
Finland	0.0	Chile	0.0
France	16.0	China	17.2
Germany	8.3	Colombia	0.0
Greece	16.6	Czech Republic	13.6
Ireland	13.9	Hong Kong	15.6
Italy	17.1	Hungary	13.3
Japan	10.2	Iceland	35.3
Netherlands	15.5	India	17.2
New Zealand	0.0	Indonesia	16.8
Norway	0.0	Korea	15.4
Portugal	17.9	Luxembourg	13.8
Spain	9.5	Malaysia	16.6
Sweden	0.0	Mexico	17.3
United Kingdom	0.0	Peru	0.0
United States	7.5	Philippines	17.6
		Poland	13.6
		Russia	17.1
		Slovak Republic	14.8
		Singapore	15.6
		South Africa	15.6
		Switzerland	21.9
		Taiwan	16.1
		Thailand	16.3
		Turkey	20.7
		Uruguay	32.2
		Venezuela	27.2
		Vietnam	32.0

[a] Percentage increase in pre-tax industrial electricity prices relative to the estimated price under the benchmark regulatory regime.
Source: Doove *et al.* (2001, p. 105).

Price-Impact Studies

We summarize below a number of other pertinent studies of price-impacts that may be consulted for further technical details and results:

- Johnson *et al.* (2000) noted that **international air services** are regulated by means of bilateral agreements and are largely excluded from the GATS. They developed a partial-equilibrium, spatial econometric model that was used to analyze the effects on prices, quantities, and economic welfare, in Australia and foreign countries, of the entry of a new airline (Ansett) into the Australian market, as well as plurilateral reform for an "open club" for airlines among Australia, China, Hong Kong, and Japan. They showed that there were significant benefits realized from the entry of new competitors into the airline markets. Also, members of an open club gained, but at the expense of non-members.
- Kalirajan (2000) used firm-level accounting data for wholesale and retail **food distributors** in 18 economies to indicate the relationship between trade restrictiveness and distributors' price-cost margins. The results suggested that the restrictions were primarily cost creating rather than rent creating and were accounted for mainly by restrictions on establishment. Using the restrictiveness indexes, coefficient estimates, and sample means, the estimated cost impacts noted in Table A-3 range between 0 and 8 percent.
- Kalirajan *et al.* (2000) developed and estimated a model applied to 694 banks in 27 economies for 1996–1997 to assess the impact of non-prudential restrictions on the interest margins of **banks**. The net interest margin is the difference between a bank's lending and deposit rates. A two-stage procedure was used for estimation purposes. In the first stage, bank-specific variables were used to explain the interest margins in all the economies, and, in a second stage, cross-country estimation was used to take economy-wide variables into account. The foreign and domestic restrictiveness indexes calculated in McGuire and Schuele (2000)

Table A-3. Estimated cost impacts of foreign and domestic barriers to establishment in wholesale and retail food distributors (percent).

Economy	Cost Impact of Foreign Barriers to Establishment	Cost Impact of Domestic Barriers to Establishment
Australia	0.57	—
Belgium	4.87	6.69
Canada	3.09	0.98
Chile	1.32	1.92
France	5.16	7.10
Greece	0.25	—
Hong Kong	0.06	—
Indonesia	3.66	—
Ireland	2.70	—
Japan	2.26	6.79
Malaysia	8.23	3.97
Netherlands	2.73	—
New Zealand	0.77	—
Singapore	0.03	—
South Africa	0.47	—
Switzerland	5.24	8.32
United Kingdom	2.76	—
United States	2.26	—

— Zero.
Source: Kalirajan (2000, p. 52).

entered into the second-stage estimation. The foreign restrictiveness index was found to be a significant determinant of interest rate spreads, while the domestic restrictiveness index was not significant. The price impacts of the restrictions were calculated from the second-stage results and are presented in Table A-4. Chile, Indonesia, Malaysia, the Philippines, Singapore, South Korea, and Thailand have the highest price impacts due to the restrictions on foreign banks.

- Kang (2000) investigated the impact of restrictions on **maritime services**, using a partial-equilibrium econometric model that incorporated cross-country and bilateral trade data as determinants of demand for these services. Shipping margins for manufactured

Table A-4. Estimated price impacts of foreign and domestic trade restrictiveness indexes (TRI) on net interest margins of banks (percent).

Economy	Price Effect Using the Foreign TRI_i	Price Effect Using the Domestic TRI_i[b]
Argentina	5.34	0.00
Australia	9.30	0.00
Canada	5.34	0.00
Chile	34.00	23.67
Colombia	18.35	3.73
European Union[a]	5.32	0.00
Hong Kong	6.91	2.97
Indonesia	49.32	5.26
Japan	15.26	9.99
Malaysia	60.61	21.86
Philippines	47.36	10.79
Singapore	31.45	8.39
South Korea	36.72	14.93
Switzerland	5.95	0.00
Thailand	33.06	0.00
United States	4.75	0.00

[a] The European Union grouping excludes Finland, Ireland and Luxembourg.
[b] Uses the coefficient estimate for the foreign trade restrictiveness index as a proxy.
Source: Kalirajan *et al.* (2000, p. 229).

goods were derived from FOB/CIF value differentials and were used as a proxy for price. The shipping margins were to be explained by bilateral restrictions, distance, and the scale of bilateral trade. Indexes for 23 countries were adapted from McGuire, Schuele, and Smith (2000), and the remaining data were from the 1995 database of the Global Trade Analysis Project (GTAP). The foreign index of restrictiveness was decomposed into measures affecting commercial presence and into other restrictions such as on cabotage and port services. Allowance was also made for different bilateral relationships as between industrialized and developing economies. The most important conclusion reached was that a low degree of restrictions in any trading partner was necessary in order to have low shipping charges. Further, low-income countries stood to gain the most from eliminating restrictions on shipping services.

- Nguyen-Hong (2000) estimated the influences of restrictions on the price-cost margins of 84 **engineering service** firms in 20 economies, using 1996 company accounting data compiled from a variety of private and official sources. A model of firm behavior was developed to include the determinants of the observed price-cost margins, and a linear version using ordinary least squares was implemented with cross-section data. The index of foreign barriers to establishment was highly significant and had a positive and statistically significant impact on price-cost margins. The index of domestic barriers to establishment had a negative and significant impact. The price and cost impacts of the restrictions were calculated, using the actual indexes of restrictiveness, estimated coefficients, and the sample means of the independent variables. The price impacts, which are summarized by country in Table A-5, exceed 10 percent for Austria, Mexico, Malaysia, Indonesia, and Germany. The cost impacts are relatively small, ranging between 0.7 and 6.8 percent. The price and cost impacts were also calculated by types of barriers.
- Trewin (2000) used time-series data on the total costs of providing **telecommunications services** for 37 countries obtained from the International Telecommunications Union (ITU) for the period 1982–1992. He used a frontier cost method as a means of estimating the minimum possible costs that are expended from a given combination of inputs. The distance of an observation above the cost frontier is a measurement of the degree of technical inefficiency. The measurements of restrictiveness calculated by Marko (1998) and Warren (2000a) were used in the estimation process. The results suggested that countries that provide higher levels of FDI face lower costs. Making allowance for the quality-cost aspects of telecommunication services reinforced the importance of the cost impacts of restrictions. When the sample was divided between low and high income countries, the average efficiency of the high income set was more than three times better than the low

Table A-5. Estimated price and cost impacts of restrictions on engineering services (percent).

	Price Impact[a]		Cost Impact	
	Foreign Barriers to Establishment	Foreign Barriers to Ongoing Operations	All Foreign Barriers	Domestic Barriers to Establishment
Austria	11.1	3.5	14.5	6.8
Mexico	13.9	0.2	14.2	1.9
Malaysia	11.3	0.7	12.0	5.3
Indonesia	9.9	0.3	10.2	3.2
Germany	4.7	5.5	10.2	2.9
Spain	5.1	3.7	8.7	3.9
United States	5.1	2.2	7.4	3.8
Sweden	5.9	0.9	6.8	0.7
Japan	3.1	3.4	6.6	2.2
Canada	3.1	2.2	5.3	2.7
Singapore	4.9	0.2	5.0	0.8
Hong Kong	3.6	1.5	5.1	2.3
South Africa	3.5	0.2	3.7	0.7
Netherlands	3.5	0.2	3.7	5.2
Australia	2.1	0.7	2.8	2.1
United Kingdom	2.3	0.2	2.5	1.4
Finland	1.8	0.5	2.3	0.7
Denmark	0.3	0.8	1.1	0.7
France	0.3	0.6	0.9	0.7
Belgium	0.3	0.2	0.5	0.7

[a] The price impact for all foreign barriers is the sum of the price impacts for foreign barriers to establishment and ongoing operations, respectively.
Source: Nguyen-Hong (2000, p. 63).

income set. The results are listed in Table A-6. It can be seen, in the high income set, that Luxembourg is close to the efficiency frontier whereas Portugal and Korea are relatively high cost countries.

- Doove *et al.* (2001) constructed restrictiveness indexes and estimates of price impacts for international air passenger transport,

Table A-6. Coefficient estimates of technical efficiency in telecommunications services.

Low Income	Technical Efficiency	High Income	Technical Efficiency
Chile	3.82	Australia	1.67
China	6.31	Austria	1.31
Hungary	2.61	Belgium	1.55
Iceland	1.16	Canada	1.34
Indonesia	11.96	Denmark	1.43
Ireland	3.22	Finland	1.24
Malaysia	4.31	France	1.74
Mexico	15.41	Germany	1.66
PNG	7.75	Greece	1.11
Philippines	3.06	Hong Kong	1.44
Poland	2.30	Italy	1.71
Thailand	5.25	Japan	1.21
Turkey	4.07	Korea	1.98
		Luxembourg	1.03
		Netherlands	1.43
		New Zealand	1.83
		Norway	1.75
		Portugal	2.08
		Singapore	1.57
		Spain	1.75
		Sweden	1.40
		Switzerland	1.42
		United Kingdom	1.67
		United States	1.48
Mean	5.48	Mean	1.54

Note: A coefficient estimate equal to 1.00 indicates full technical efficiency in relation to the minimum-cost frontier.
Source: Trewin (2000, p. 112).

telecommunications, and electricity supply. Their indexes of bilateral restrictions on **international air passenger transport** referred to 35 economies in the Asia-Pacific, Americas, and European regions. Focusing on the discount segment of the air passenger market, they implement a procedure for estimating the price effects of the applicable restrictions, using fare data primarily for the end years of the 1990s. The results, which were shown in Table 7, indicated that the higher price effects range from 12 to 22 percent in the Asia-Pacific economies, 9 to 18 percent in the Americas, and generally below 10 percent in the European economies. The price impacts for business and economy airfares were considerably higher but should be interpreted tentatively due to data constraints.

Measurements of the impact of **telecommunications** regulations were derived for 24 OECD and 23 other countries, using data for 1997. Price-impact measurements of regulation were calculated for four major sectors of telecommunications, including trunk, international, mobile, and leasing services and are listed by country and type of service in Table A-1. While the results suggested that countries with more stringent regulatory regimes tended to have higher telecommunications prices, the authors noted that there were several cases in which the results appeared to be counter-intuitive and sensitive to small changes in the data. The reported results should therefore be treated with caution, pending further clarification and improvement of the model and data that were used.

Measurements of regulation and impacts on **industrial electricity** prices for 50 economies, using 1996 data, were developed. The estimated price impacts are listed by country in Table A-2. The impacts ranged from 0 to 35 percent, with a mean of 13 percent and a standard deviation of 13 percent. The authors noted, however, that the estimated price impacts were quite sensitive to the methodology and data used and therefore should be treated as ordinal rankings rather than absolute values.

- Fink *et al.* (2002) analyzed the importance of restrictive trade policies and private anti-competitive practices for **international maritime services**. For this purpose, they used data on U.S. imports carried by liners from 59 countries that accounted for about 65 percent of the total value of U.S. maritime imports in 1998. While restrictions on the provision of port services were found to be significant, private anti-competitive practices involving collusion among international maritime cartels were shown to have a considerably greater influence on maritime transport prices.

Gravity-Model Estimates

Deardorff and Stern (1998, p. 24) have noted that measurements based on the gravity model are useful mainly in identifying *relative* levels of protection across sectors and countries. But gravity models have some important drawbacks. That is, by attributing to trade barriers all departures of trade from what the included variables can explain, there is a great burden on the model being used. Thus, the worse the model, the more likely it is that trade barrier estimates will have an upward bias.

An additional problem exists when this technique is used to infer barriers for separate industries. The theoretical basis for the gravity equation, as in Anderson (1979) and Deardorff (1998), applies to total trade, not to trade in individual sectors. The gravity equation makes sense at the sectoral level only if all countries are equal in their capacity to produce in a sector, which of course would be a denial of the role of comparative advantage. Thus, if a country were in fact to have a comparative advantage in a particular service sector, so that its output would be high and its cost of serving its domestic market itself would be low, then it will import less from abroad than would be expected based on income and distance alone. Thus comparative advantage may show up as an implicit barrier to trade, when in fact none exists.

Computable General Equilibrium (CGE) Modeling

In the study by Brown and Stern (2001), each MNC is assumed to produce a differentiated product and to allocate production to its various host-country locations. The monopolistically competitive firms employ capital, labor, and intermediate inputs in their production, and they set prices as an optimal mark-up of price over marginal cost. The number of firms is permitted to vary to hold MNC profits at zero. Consumers are assumed to allocate their expenditure between goods and services that are produced by firms domestically and varieties that are imported from each national source. Labor is taken to be freely mobile among domestic sectors but not across borders.

Capital, however, is mobile internationally, although not perfectly so, because there is a risk premium that will vary depending on the size of a country's capital stock.

Barriers to FDI are assumed to take the form of an increased cost of locating investment in a host country. For this purpose, Brown and Stern use the cost-price margins estimated by Hoekman (2000), which have been discussed above and are listed in Tables 10 and 11, as indicative of barriers to FDI. Since the cost-price gap is smallest in most sectors in Hong Kong, a country thought to be freely open to foreign firms, the excess in any other country above the Hong Kong figure is taken to be due to barriers to the establishment of foreign firms.

Using the aforementioned modeling structure with three sectors (agriculture, manufactures, and services) and 18 countries/regions, Brown and Stern calculate the economic effects of removal of services barriers according to the following three scenarios[20]:

Scenario A: Removal of services barriers, with perfect international capital mobility and fixed world capital stock.

Scenario B: Removal of services barriers, with risk-premium elasticity = 0.1 to allow for imperfect capital mobility, and fixed world capital stock.

Scenario C: Removal of services barriers, with risk-premium elasticity = 0.1 to allow for imperfect capital mobility, and world capital stock increased by 3 percent.

When barriers are lowered, international capital in the form of FDI will then be attracted to countries with the relatively highest rates of return and away from other countries.

The welfare effects, as a percentage of GNP and in billions of dollars, resulting from the assumed removal of the services barriers for each of the three scenarios are listed in Table A-7 for the

[20] See also studies undertaken at the Australian Productivity Commission by Dee and Hanslow (2001) and Verikios and Zhang (2001) for computational results based on a related modeling framework and with estimates of services barriers taken from Kalirajan *et al.* (2000) and Warren (2000a,b).

Table A-7. Welfare effects of elimination of services barriers (percent and billions of dollars).

Country	Scenario A: Perfect Int'l Capital Mobility and Fixed World Capital Stock		Scenario B: Risk-Premium Elasticity = 0.1 and Fixed World Capital Stock		Scenario C: Risk-Premium Elasticity = 0.1 and World Capital Stock Increased by 3%	
	% GNP	$Bill.	% GNP	$Bill.	% GNP	$Bill.
Industrialized Countries						
Australia	1.8	6.0	1.5	5.0	4.9	16.8
Canada	14.8	84.0	12.9	73.7	14.9	85.0
European Union	0.5	42.4	0.5	38.0	2.5	202.4
Japan	–2.0	–103.7	–1.7	–88.4	0.5	25.7
New Zealand	9.1	5.2	7.5	4.3	10.5	6.0
United States	0.5	35.0	0.3	23.2	3.1	222.5
Developing Countries						
Asia						
China	3.8	26.9	3.2	22.9	6.0	42.8
Hong Kong	6.6	6.6	5.4	5.5	13.4	13.5
Indonesia	15.6	30.8	13.1	25.8	16.9	33.3
Korea	–2.8	–12.3	–2.3	–10.1	1.4	6.4
Malaysia	2.3	2.1	1.9	1.8	4.7	4.4
Philippines	2.3	1.6	1.9	1.3	8.3	5.7
Singapore	1.7	1.0	1.3	0.7	4.3	2.5
Taiwan	7.6	20.7	6.8	18.5	7.7	21.2
Thailand	–2.2	–3.6	–1.8	–2.9	4.4	7.1
Other						
Chile	–2.0	–1.3	–1.6	–1.0	2.7	1.7
Mexico	–4.3	–11.7	–3.2	–8.8	0.2	0.5
Rest of Cairns	–3.7	–39.6	–3.2	–34.1	0.6	6.2
Total		**90.3**		**75.6**		**703.7**

Source: Brown and Stern (2001, pp. 277–278).

countries/regions covered by the model.[21] When services barriers are lowered, international capital in the form of FDI will then be attracted to countries with the highest rates of return and away from other countries.

It is evident in Table A-7 that the welfare effects of removing the services barriers are sizable and that they vary markedly across countries. For the industrialized countries in Scenario A with perfect international capital mobility, the largest increases are for Canada, \$84.0 billion (14.8% of GNP); the European Union (EU), \$42.4 billion (0.5% of GNP); and the United States, \$35.0 billion (0.5% of GNP). Because it loses capital, Japan has a decline of \$103.7 billion (2.0% of GNP). Among the developing countries, the largest increases are for Indonesia, \$30.8 billion (15.6% of GNP); China, \$26.9 billion (3.8% of GNP); and Taiwan, \$20.7 billion, (7.6% of GNP). It is also evident that there are declines in welfare for a number of developing countries, in particular, Korea, Thailand, Chile, Mexico, and the Rest of Cairns Group. What is reflected in the results is that welfare is affected by whether or not a country attracts or loses capital as a result of services liberalization. Countries that lose capital become "smaller" in the economic sense of the word. As the economy contracts, surviving firms produce less than before. The fall in firm output generally occurs in order to avoid a large loss in variety of domestically produced goods. The subsequent economy-wide reduction in scale economies is usually the source of the welfare loss.

The results in Scenario A are sensitive to the assumption of perfect capital mobility. As noted above, countries that import capital are assumed to pay a risk premium that is a function of capital imports.

---

[21] See Brown and Stern (2001, pp. 277–278) for the results for the absolute changes in imports and exports, the percentage change in the terms of trade, and the percentage change in the real wage. The sectoral results for the three aggregated sectors for Scenario C are reported in Brown and Stern (pp. 281–282). They show that output increases economy-wide in just about every sector in all countries/regions, and there is a wide prevalence of the realization of economies of scale. There are also generally significant increases in activity by foreign-owned affiliates, especially in the countries that record large increases in output.

The elasticity of the risk premium with respect to the volume of capital imports can be set exogenously in the model. Thus, in Scenario B, Brown and Stern assume that capital imports that result in a 1 percent increase in the capital stock generate an interest-rate risk premium of 0.1 percent. That is, the risk-premium elasticity is 0.1 percent. It is apparent from the results for Scenario B in Table A-7 that the introduction of a risk premium that reflects a decrease in international capital mobility has the effect of reducing the welfare effects of services liberalization as compared to Scenario A, in which there was perfect capital mobility.

In both Scenarios A and B, there is a rise in the real return to capital. Therefore, it is likely that, over time, there will be an increase in the world's capital stock as savers and investors respond to the increased incentive to accumulate capital. To take this into account, in Scenario C, with the risk premium elasticity remaining at 0.1 percent, Brown and Stern allow for an increase in the world's capital stock by 3 percent. This is the amount necessary to hold the real return to capital equal to the level in the base period. As can be seen in Table A-7, the welfare effects of services liberalization are now positive for all of the countries shown. For the world as a whole, welfare rises by $703.7 billion. Canada's welfare increases by $85.0 billion (14.9% of GNP); the EU by $202.4 billion (2.5% of GNP); and the United States, $222.5 billion (3.1% of GNP). There are also sizable absolute and percentage increases for the developing countries, in particular China, Indonesia, Taiwan, and Hong Kong. It is further noteworthy that welfare increases for all of the countries/regions shown.

It is evident accordingly that these welfare effects associated with an increase in the world's capital stock in response to an increase in the rate of return to capital are considerably larger than what is commonly seen in CGE models in which capital is assumed to be internationally immobile.[22] This may not be surprising because it has been apparent from previous CGE analyses of trade liberalization that

[22] Compare, for example, the results of the Michigan Model reported in Brown, Deardorff, and Stern (2003).

have made allowance for international capital flows that the largest welfare gains stem from these flows rather than from the removal of tariffs and other trade barriers that distort consumer choice in goods trade.[23]

The understanding of the consequences of liberalizing services barriers thus is enhanced when allowance is made for the behavior of multinational firms whose foreign affiliates are already located in or attracted to host countries. When services liberalization occurs and the real return to capital is increased, so that there are FDI (Mode 3) international capital flows and the world capital stock expands, most countries stand to gain significantly in terms of economic welfare.

Study Questions

I. *Introduction*

1. What is the difference between a tariff and nontariff barrier (NTB)?
2. What is a tariff equivalent, and how is it measured?
3. What are the four modes of supply of traded services? To what extent can barriers to traded services be measured as tariff equivalents?
4. What are "frequency measures" of barriers to trade in services? Price and/or quantity measurements?

II. *Conceptual Framework*

1. How can the demand and supply of services be depicted under conditions of competition and perfect substitution? What is the effect of an impediment to the foreign supply of services and the determination of the tariff equivalent of the impediment?
2. What are the effects when the services provided are imperfect substitutes? What are the effects when there are impediments to entry of firms?

---

[23] See Brown, Deardorff, and Stern (1992) and Dee and Hanslow (2001).

III. *Characteristics of Services Barriers*

1. Why are services barriers more akin to NTBs than tariffs?
2. What are the two dimensions of the government regulation of services, and how may the supply curve for services be affected?
3. In the case of banking services, what are the principal foreign and domestic services restrictions that may be present, and how may the different degrees of restriction be scored and weighted? How can the discrimination against foreign banks be measured? What is an "index of restrictiveness," and how is it calculated?
4. What are the main types and most prevalent characteristics of barriers to FDI in services?

IV. *Methods of Measurement of Services Barriers*

Frequency Studies and Indexes of Restrictiveness

1. What are direct and indirect measurements of barriers to trade in goods and services? How may price comparisons be used?
2. What are the steps involved in carrying out frequency studies and constructing indexes of restrictiveness for specific services sectors or across multiple sectors? How are indexes of restrictiveness scored, weighted, and used in assessing economic performance?
3. How may commitments in the GATS be used in constructing frequency measurements and indexes of restrictiveness? What is the "positive list" approach? What are the drawbacks of using data on GATS commitments? How are the data on actual FDI restrictions in the APEC countries weighted? Which services sectors appear to be the most subject to FDI restrictions? Which APEC countries?
4. What is the distinction between foreign and domestic restrictiveness indexes? Which countries appear to have the greatest degree of discrimination against foreign banks?
5. How useful are restrictiveness indexes, and how can they be used in assessing the impacts of services barriers?

Price-Impact and Quantity-Impact Measurements

1. How did Hoekman calculate "guesstimates" of the tariff equivalents of services barriers? What are the limitations of Hoekman's methodology?
2. How can restrictiveness indexes be used in econometric estimation of the price effects of the restrictions? What additional information is needed to construct these estimates?
3. How can the quantitative impact of barriers on services trade be calculated and the associated tariff equivalents?

Gravity-Model Estimates

1. What is a gravity model, and how can it be used to determine the levels of services trade barriers across countries? What are the advantages and limitations of gravity-model estimates of services barriers?

Financial-Based Measurements

1. What are financial-based measurements, and how can they be used to determine the levels of services trade barriers across countries? What are the advantages and limitations of these measurements?

V. *Measuring the Economic Consequences of Liberalizing Services Barriers*

1. What are the three approaches to the CGE modeling of services liberalization?
2. What are the characteristics and assumptions of the Brown and Stern CGE model of services liberalization? How do they measure services barriers?
3. What are the computational scenarios that Brown and Stern investigate, and what are the results? What are the effects of international capital mobility and an increase in the world's capital stock?

References

Anderson, James E. 1979. "A Theoretical Foundation for the Gravity Equation," *American Economic Review* 69, pp. 106–116.

Bosworth, Malcolm, Christopher Findlay, Ray Trewin, and Tony Warren. 2000. "Price-Impact Measures of Impediments to Services Trade," in Christopher Findlay and Tony Warren, eds., *Impediments to Trade in Services: Measurement and Policy Implications*. London and New York: Routledge.

Boylaud, O. and G. Nicoletti. 2000. "Regulation, Market Structure and Performance in Telecommunications," Working Paper No. 237ECO/WKP (2000), 10, Economics Department, OECD, Paris, April 12.

Brown, Drusilla and Robert M. Stern. 2001. "Measurement and Modeling of the Economic Effects of Trade and Investment Barriers in Services," *Review of International Economics* 9, pp. 262–286.

Brown, Drusilla K., Alan V. Deardorff, and Robert M. Stern. 1992. "Estimates of a North American Free Trade Agreement: Analytical Issues and a Computational Assessment," *The World Economy* 15(1), pp. 11–29.

Brown, Drusilla K., Alan V. Deardorff, and Robert M. Stern. 2003. "Multilateral, Regional, and Bilateral Trade-Policy Options for the United States and Japan," *The World Economy* 26(6), pp. 803–828.

Colecchia, Alessandra. 2000. "Measuring Barriers to Market Access for Services: A Pilot Study on Accountancy Services," in Christopher Findlay and Tony Warren, eds., *Impediments to Trade in Services: Measurement and Policy Implications*. London and New York: Routledge.

Deardorff, Alan V. 1998. "Determinants of Bilateral Trade: Does Gravity Work in a Neoclassical World?" in Jeffrey A. Frankel, ed., *The Regionalization of the World Economy*. Chicago: University of Chicago Press.

Deardorff, Alan V. and Robert M. Stern. 1998. *Measurement of Nontariff Barriers*. Ann Arbor: University of Michigan Press.

Dee, Philippa. 2005. "A Compendium of Barriers to Services Trade," World Bank, unpublished.

Dee, Philippa and Kevin Hanslow. 2001. "Multilateral Liberalization of Services Trade," in Robert M. Stern, ed., *Services in the International Economy*. Ann Arbor: University of Michigan Press.

Dee, Philippa, Alexis Hardin, and Leanne Holmes. 2000. "Issues in the Application of CGE Models to Services Trade Liberalization," in Christopher Findlay and Tony Warren, eds., *Impediments to Trade in Services: Measurement and Policy Implications*. London and New York: Routledge.

Disclosure. 1998. *Global Researcher — Worldscope Database*. Bethesda, Maryland: Disclosure.

Doove, Samantha, Owen Gabbitas, Duc Nguyen-Hong, and Joe Owen. 2001. "Price Effects of Regulation: Telecommunications, Air Passenger Transport and

Electricity Supply," Productivity Commission Staff Research Paper, AusInfo, Canberra (October).

Fink, Carsten, Aaditya Mattoo, and Ileana Cristina Neagu. 2002. "Trade in International Maritime Services: How Much Does Policy Matter?" *World Bank Economic Review* 16, pp. 81–108.

Fink, Carsten, Aaditya Mattoo, and Randeep Rathindran. 2003. "An Assessment of Telecommunications Reform in Developing Countries," *Information Economics and Policy* 15, pp. 443–466.

Francois, Joseph. 1999. "Estimates of Barriers to Trade in Services," Erasmus University, unpublished manuscript.

Gonenc, R. and G. Nicoletti. 2001. "Regulation, Market Structure and Performance in Air Passenger Transportation," OECD Economic Studies, No. 32, OECD, Paris.

Hardin, Alexis and Leanne Holmes. 1997. *Services Trade and Foreign Direct Investment.* Staff Research Paper, Industry Commission. Canberra: Australian Government Publishing Services.

Hoekman, Bernard. 1995. "Assessing the General Agreement on Trade in Services," World Bank Discussion Paper No. 307. Revised version published in 1996, in Will Martin and L. Alan Winters, eds., *The Uruguay Round and the Developing Countries*, Cambridge University Press.

Hoekman, Bernard. 2000. "The Next Round of Services Negotiations: Identifying Priorities and Options," *Federal Reserve Bank of St. Louis Review* 82, pp. 31–47.

Hoekman, Bernard and Carlos A. Primo Braga. 1997. "Protection and Trade in Services: A Survey," *Open Economies Review* 8, pp. 285–308.

Holmes, Leanne and Alexis Hardin. 2000. "Assessing Barriers to Services Sector Investment," in Christopher Findlay and Tony Warren, eds., *Impediments to Trade in Services: Measurement and Policy Implications.* London and New York: Routledge.

Johnson, Martin, Tendar Gregan, Geraldine Gentle, and Paul Belin. 2000. "Modeling the Benefits of Increasing Competition in International Air Services," in Christopher Findlay and Tony Warren, eds., *Impediments to Trade in Services: Measurement and Policy Implications.* London and New York: Routledge.

Kalirajan, Kaleeswaran. 2000. "Restrictions on Trade in Distribution Services," Productivity Commission Staff Research Paper, AusInfo, Canberra (August).

Kalirajan, Kaleeswaran, Greg McGuire, Duc Nguyen-Hong, and Michael Schuele. 2000. "The Price Impact of Restrictions on Banking Services," in Christopher Findlay and Tony Warren, eds., *Impediments to Trade in Services: Measurement and Policy Implications.* London and New York: Routledge.

Kang, Jong-Soon. 2000. "Price Impact of Restrictions on Maritime Transport Services," in Christopher Findlay and Tony Warren, eds., *Impediments to Trade in Services: Measurement and Policy Implications.* London and New York: Routledge.

Karsenty, Guy. 2000. "Just How Big Are the Stakes? An Assessment of Trade in Services by Mode of Supply," in Pierre Sauvé and Robert M. Stern, eds., *Services 2000: New Directions in Services Trade Liberalization*. Washington, D.C.: Brookings Institution.

Kemp, Steven. 2000. "Trade in Education Services and the Impacts of Barriers on Trade," in Christopher Findlay and Tony Warren, eds., *Impediments to Trade in Services: Measurement and Policy Implications*. London and New York: Routledge.

Marko, M. 1998. "An Evaluation of the Basic Telecommunications Services Agreement," CIES Policy Discussion Paper 98/09, Centre for International Economic Studies, University of Adelaide.

Mattoo, Aaditya. 1998. "Financial Services and the WTO: Liberalization in the Developing and Transition Economies," for presentation at the Workshop, "Measuring Impediments to Trade in Services," Productivity Commission, Canberra, April 30–May 1, 1998.

McGuire, Greg. 1998. *Australia's Restrictions on Trade in Financial Services*. Staff Research Paper, Productivity Commission, Canberra.

McGuire, Greg and Michael Schuele. 2000. "Restrictiveness of International Trade in Banking Services," in Christopher Findlay and Tony Warren, eds., *Impediments to Trade in Services: Measurement and Policy Implications*. London and New York: Routledge.

McGuire, Greg, Michael Schuele, and Tina Smith. 2000. "Restrictiveness of International Trade in Maritime Services," in Christopher Findlay and Tony Warren, eds., *Impediments to Trade in Services: Measurement and Policy Implications*. London and New York: Routledge.

Nguyen-Hong, Duc. 2000. "Restrictions on Trade in Professional Services," Productivity Commission Staff Research Paper, AusInfo, Canberra (August).

Nicoletti, G., S. Scarpetta, and O. Boylaud. 2000. "Summary Indicators of Product Market Regulation with an Extension to Employment Protection Legislation," Working Paper No. 226, Economics Department, ECO/WKP(99)18, OECD, Paris, April 13 (revised).

Pacific Economic Cooperation Council (PECC). 1995. *Survey of Impediments to Trade and Investment in the APEC Region*. Singapore: PECC.

Steiner, F. 2000. "Regulation, Industry Structure and Performance in the Electricity Supply Industry," Working Paper No. 238, ECO/WKP (2000), Economics Department, OECD, Paris, April 12.

Stern, Robert M. 2002. "Quantifying Barriers to Trade in Services," in Bernard Hoekman, Aaditya Mattoo, and Philip English, eds., *Development, Trade, and the WTO: A Handbook*, Washington, D.C.: The World Bank.

Trewin, Ray. 2000. "A Price-Impact Measure of Impediments to Trade in Telecommunications Services," in Christopher Findlay and Tony Warren, eds., *Impediments to Trade in Services: Measurement and Policy Implications*. London and New York: Routledge.

United Nations Conference on Trade and Development (UNCTAD). 1996. *World Investment Report 1996: Investment, Trade and International Policy Arrangements*. New York and Geneva: UNCTAD.

Verikios, George and Xiao-guang Zhang. 2001. "Global Gains from Liberalizing Trade in Telecommunications and Financial Services," Productivity Commission Staff Research Paper, AusInfo, Canberra (October).

Warren, Tony. 2000a. "The Identification of Impediments to Trade and Investment in Telecommunications Services," in Christopher Findlay and Tony Warren, eds., *Impediments to Trade in Services: Measurement and Policy Implications*. London and New York: Routledge.

Warren, Tony. 2000b. "The Impact on Output of Impediments to Trade and Investment in Telecommunications Services," in Christopher Findlay and Tony Warren, eds., *Impediments to Trade in Services: Measurement and Policy Implications*. London and New York: Routledge.

Warren, Tony and Christopher Findlay. 2000. "How Significant Are the Barriers? Measuring Impediments to Trade in Services," in Pierre Sauvé and Robert M. Stern, eds., *Services 2000: New Directions in Services Trade Liberalization*. Washington, D.C.: Brookings Institution.

Whalley, John. 2004. "Assessing the Benefits to Developing Countries of Liberalization in Services Trade," *The World Economy* 27(8), pp. 1223–1253.

Suggested Further Reading

Arnold, Jens Matthia, Beata Javorcik, and Aaditya Mattoo. 2006. "The Productivity Effects of Services Liberalization: Evidence from the Czech Republic," World Bank Policy Research Working Paper No. 4109.

Hoekman, Bernard. 2006. "Liberalizing Trade in Services: A Survey," World Bank Policy Research Working Paper No. 4030.

Hoekman, Bernard. 2007. "Trade in Services at 25: Theory, Policy, and Evidence," in Bernard Hoekman, ed., *Theory, Policy, and International Cooperation*. Edward Elgar.

Jensen, Jesper, Thomas Rutherford, and David Tarr. 2007. "The Impact of Liberalizing Barriers to Foreign Direct Investment in Services: The Case of Russian Accession to the World Trade Organization," *Review of Development Economics* 11, pp. 482–506.

Mattoo, Aaditya, Randeep Rathindran, and Arvind Subramanian. 2006. "Measuring Services Trade Liberalization and its Impact on Economic Growth: An Illustration," *Journal of Economic Integration* 21, pp. 64–98.

Part IV

INTERNATIONAL TRADE AND LABOR STANDARDS

Chapter 16

Pros and Cons of Linking Trade and Labor Standards*

Drusilla K. Brown, Alan V. Deardorff and Robert M. Stern

I. Introduction

Until about ten years ago, international discussions of national economic policies were compartmentalized. International trade policies were the province of the General Agreement on Tariffs and Trade (GATT) and were discussed and negotiated primarily by specialists on trade. Policies involving labor markets, including labor standards, were similarly discussed only among specialists on labor, with international initiatives centered in the International Labor Organization (ILO). Similar compartmentalization existed for intellectual property issues in the World Intellectual Property Organization (WIPO), and also for environmental issues, which unlike the others were spread among several international bodies.

This all began to change in the early 1990s, for several reasons to be mentioned below. Some of this compartmentalization has already

* This article was published in *The Political Economy of Policy Reform: Essays in Honor of J. Michael Finger*, edited by Douglas Nelson, © Elsevier (2004). Reprinted with permission.

disappeared, and more of it seems to be on the way out, as important constituencies now favor integrating the issues under a single institutional framework. Because the successor to the GATT, the World Trade Organization (WTO), is the only international organization with meaningful enforcement powers, it has become the favored place for integrating these diverse policy issues. Intellectual property rights issues have already been taken over by the WTO in the Uruguay Round Agreement on Trade-Related Intellectual Property Rights (TRIPS). Some advocates of labor and environmental rights have asked that these issues also be taken over by the WTO, and that they be enforced by the same mechanism that it uses for policing trade policies. This chapter reviews the arguments for and against such integration in the case of labor standards.

We will first try to put the debate into context by reviewing the issues and the events that have led to the current situation. We will next turn to the arguments in favor of putting labor standards into the WTO, then address the arguments against doing so. Finally we will offer our own advice to developing countries as to the position that they should take in this debate, and how more broadly they should deal with this and other issues in multilateral trade negotiations. We conclude with an epilogue, noting that the linkage issues were not discussed at the November 2001 WTO Ministerial Meeting in Doha, Qatar, but that these issues might well re-emerge under different circumstances in the future.

II. Background and Issues

We are ourselves all specialists in the economics of international trade, and we are therefore much better versed in the history, institutions, and economic case for trade than we are knowledgeable about labor standards. However, precisely because of the debate we will be describing, we have had occasion in recent years to become more familiar with labor issues and to write several joint and individually authored papers on the subject.[1] It is from these perspectives that

[1] See Brown *et al.* (1996, 1998, 2001a,b), Brown (2000, 2001), and Stern (1999).

we will first provide a brief overview of the issues that arise in both trade and labor, and of how they have been dealt with in the world's institutions.

The core problem of international trade policy is that countries and their governments have a variety of incentives to restrict trade, usually imports, and that such restrictions are economically harmful both to other countries and to those within the restricting countries who do not benefit directly from protection. Left to their own devices governments may be unable to resist these incentives, with the result that all countries in the world are made worse off. The incentives may be macroeconomic, as they were in the Great Depression of the 1930s when countries raised tariffs to divert demand from other countries toward themselves. Or they may be microeconomic and political, as is often the case today when countries protect individual industries or groups of workers from import competition.

The GATT was created at the end of World War II to prevent countries from restricting trade for these and other purposes, although it did allow tariffs to be raised in several specified circumstances. One of those circumstances was, as a last resort, if one country violated GATT's rules. After other remedies were exhausted, an offending country could become the target of retaliatory tariffs, the purpose being to provide enforcement of GATT rules. This "dispute settlement mechanism" (DSM) of the GATT was rather weak, for institutional reasons, but these weaknesses were removed in the WTO. A major difference between the WTO and its GATT predecessor is the strength of the WTO DSM, which employs several layers of procedure that lead ultimately, if offending behavior is found and not reversed, to "trade sanctions." That is, the ultimate remedy against a country breaking GATT/WTO rules is for other countries to restrict imports from it by use of increased tariffs.

Given the understanding that trade restrictions are economically harmful, even to the country that imposes them, this feature of the WTO is somewhat perverse, for it seeks to prevent harmful behavior by use of more of the same. The rationale must be that the sanctions will seldom be used, and that the threat of them will almost always be enough to force eventual compliance with the rules. Experience so far suggests that most WTO cases do not, indeed, result in trade sanctions. However, their use in some recent disputes between the United States and the European Union involving bananas, beef hormones and possibly corporate tax exemptions has been sufficiently disturbing that one may easily wish that some other enforcement mechanism were available. The main reason for the absence of any other mechanism, presumably, is that the GATT and WTO have had jurisdiction only over trade and have had to find their remedies within that jurisdiction. Had the WTO been able, say, to impose monetary fines on countries for breaking its rules, then that would undoubtedly have been preferable.

Turning now to labor standards, here the core problem is to improve the well-being of workers around the world. The need arose, or at least was recognized, when workers moved off the land and into factories, where working conditions were often both poor and out of the workers' control. The motivation for improvement was provided in part by humanitarian concern for the workers, and in part by fear of social unrest if the growing number of industrial workers were to give vent to their unhappiness. There was also a perceived need to coordinate improvement in working conditions across countries, so as to avoid undermining the international competitiveness of countries that achieved such improvement by themselves. All of these concerns contributed to the creation of the ILO in 1919, which today has 175 member states.

The ILO has done many things, including most notably the adoption of a series of Conventions that spell out a long list of labor standards. At the core of this list are eight "Fundamental ILO Conventions" in four areas: freedom of association, abolition of forced labor, equality, and elimination of child labor. Additional conventions address a much wider variety of issues, including basic human rights, conditions of work such as wages and hours, security of employment, and many more.[2]

These conventions have been adopted by many of the member countries, with the notable exception of the United States, which has

[2] See Brown *et al.* (1996) for more details on ILO conventions.

adopted only a few. However, regardless of whether a member country has adopted a convention, the ILO has relatively little that it can do to enforce adherence to it. Its "enforcement" powers consist primarily of several mechanisms for monitoring and reporting abuses of the standards, but there is little that it can do to a country, even if the country flaunts a standard, except to publicize the fact. The strongest action it can take is to censure a country for noncompliance, and this is hardly ever done. Most would agree that in the vast majority of countries the conventions serve at best as goals that the member countries may be striving to achieve in the future, rather than as descriptions of current practice. This is true even in those countries that have adopted them.

It is this lack of "teeth" in the ILO that has led to interest, on the part of many who wish to advance labor rights, in incorporating them somehow into the WTO. The objective is clear: to be able to apply the WTO enforcement mechanisms, which it already applies to violations of rules on trade policy, to violations of labor rights as well. Interest in doing this has been advanced by several events.

One of these events was the expansion of GATT and later WTO procedures to deal with what many regarded as domestic policies. As GATT gradually expanded its coverage beyond "border measures" such as import tariffs to other policies that might affect trade, it began to deal with domestic policies such as government procurement and product standards, whose primary purpose may have had nothing to do with trade but whose effects could impinge on trade and on foreign producers. The effect of this expansion was no doubt good for trade, but it blurred the distinction between trade policies and other policies. Some individuals and groups whose interests lay outside of trade, including certainly some environmentalists, began to object strenuously to this expansion of the GATT/WTO onto their turf, and they wished to see its activities curtailed. But others, including advocates of labor rights, saw an opportunity, if they could only harness the procedures of trade policy to their own cause.

A second event contributing to the desire for linkage was the precedent set by the TRIPS Agreement that was negotiated as part of the new WTO. In spite of its name, TRIPS really is not limited to issues involving trade, but instead covers the entire intellectual property regimes of the WTO member countries. It requires specific standards of intellectual property protection (patents, copyrights, trademarks, etc.) that must be enforced in these countries, including in sectors such as pharmaceuticals that some developing countries had previously exempted from such protection. Furthermore, the rules of TRIPS are covered under the same DSM as the rest of the WTO provisions, meaning that trade sanctions can be used for their enforcement, again as a last resort. Since the economic case for TRIPS was questionable,[3] its connection with trade was tenuous, and it was evident in any case that TRIPS was primarily a response to political pressure from multinational enterprises (MNEs) seeking to extend their markets, TRIPS provided both the example and part of the justification for labor interests to extend the WTO to labor standards as well.

Finally and more broadly, the rapid expansion of international trade and investment during the last half of the twentieth century accelerated in the 1990s and contributed to increasing concern over "globalization."[4] This concern has included a wide variety of symptoms and issues on the part of an even wider variety of constituencies. But certainly a major part of it was the perception that globalization had hurt workers, at least in industrialized countries and relative to owners of capital and more valuable skills. Although this perception is only partially justified, according to most careful economic studies that have been done,[5] it is popularly believed and attributed to the increasing political and economic power of corporations, especially MNEs relative to workers. The WTO itself is believed by many to have been created solely for the benefit of corporations, and the example of TRIPS does little to contradict this perception. This too, then, has fed the desire to countervail against the corporate interests within the WTO by bringing labor interests on board as well.

---

[3] See Deardorff (1990).

[4] See Deardorff and Stern (2002).

[5] See for example Freeman (1995).

In fact, although it is true that the WTO does serve many corporate interests, and that its creation may well have depended on this fact, it is *not* primarily an agent of corporate control. Instead, the benefits that it provides to the world are spread very broadly and extend especially to the poorest countries and the poorest people within those countries, including labor. What most of the rules of the WTO do, and those of the GATT before it, is to foster international competition, permitting sellers from many countries to compete with domestic sellers in the member countries. This is certainly beneficial for the owners — mostly corporate — of the firms that due to low cost, high quality, or effective strategy are best able to compete with other firms, but it can drive other less able firms, often also corporate, out of business. Lobbyists for protection have always included plenty of corporations seeking to secure their domestic markets, and the WTO is not their friend. Naturally, the corporations who succeed best in an environment of open markets tend to become large and to qualify for the moniker, MNE, or "transnational corporation." But in fact, no matter how large these firms become, as long as open international markets force them to compete with enough others like themselves, none of them has the power that their opponents ascribe to them.

The real beneficiaries of the world trading system that has grown up under the GATT and WTO are ordinary people in all countries. The thriving world economy has naturally created the most visible benefits for those who can afford the most consumption, and this means the populations of the industrialized countries whose standards of living today are unprecedented and owe a great deal to trade, whether they know it or not. But in our view, the most important beneficiaries from the world trading system are probably workers in developing countries, even though they remain (with some exceptions) far poorer than their counterparts abroad.[6]

Without liberal trade, the United States and its people would have remained well off, just not quite as well off as they are today. The same is probably true of Europe, Japan, and other industrialized countries. But without liberal trade, the pressures of population

[6] In this connection, see Brown, Deardorff, and Stern (2002).

growth and resource depletion in developing countries would have driven many of them even further into poverty. Instead, trade has permitted wages in many developing countries to rise, albeit far less than we would hope eventually to see.

This could not have happened, very likely, without the GATT. Without it, the rich countries would almost certainly have yielded to the above-mentioned incentives to restrain trade, if not in good times then surely when crises and recession caused them to turn inward, as they did in the 1930s. It was the GATT that prevented this, first by limiting the circumstances under which countries could restrict trade, and second by facilitating successive rounds of negotiations to reduce trade barriers. Successful corporations gained hugely from this process, and it was they who more than anyone else drove the process forward. Indeed, developing countries often resisted the liberalization of trade and even sought exemption from liberalizing themselves, to their own cost as many later learned. But by fostering as much liberalization as it did, and by restraining the rich countries from throwing around their economic weight, the GATT has left most developing countries far better off today than they would otherwise have been.

Those who see the world economy as a contest between capital and labor find this very hard to accept. To them, anything that benefits capital must hurt labor, as though the world economy provides only a certain total of benefit for all and the only question is which group gets it. From that perspective, because they perceive the WTO as promoting the interests of capital, they either want it destroyed or want labor to be given equal power within it. This is certainly part of the motivation for linking labor rights to trade through formal inclusion in the WTO.

To most economists, this is just not the way the world economy works. Economic benefit arises only from the efficient application of both capital and labor, which together produce the economic pie. The purpose of the WTO is to help make this pie as large as possible, which is best accomplished through the forces of competition in free markets that guide resources into their most productive uses. Incidentally, this same competition also determines how the pie is divided among different groups, including capital and labor, developed and developing, and rich and poor. This division is not what many, including economists, would most like to see. But it is important not to try to alter this division with policies that will so reduce the size of the pie that even the poor will be made worse off. It is from that perspective that economists like ourselves tend to respond to proposals to link trade and labor standards.

It is also the case that linking even seemingly unrelated issues in a round of negotiations can have the added benefit of deepening agreements in both policy dimensions when linkage improves enforcement power. For example, Spagnolo (1999) considers the case in which two governments are attempting to cooperate over two separate policy issues, e.g., tariffs and labor standards. Both of these policy issues are characterized by a prisoner's dilemma; that is, both countries would gain if they could find a sustainable mechanism to cooperate on lower tariffs and higher labor standards, but an inferior outcome emerges in the absence of cooperation.

In a repeated prisoner's dilemma game, cooperation can be self-enforcing if the benefit of defecting in any round of the game is smaller than the cost of lost cooperation in all succeeding rounds. Thus, one strategy for sustaining cooperation in a repeated prisoner's dilemma game is a trigger strategy: cooperate as long as the other party cooperates, but make clear that if the other party ever defects, then there will be no future cooperative behavior. When policy issues become linked in an international agreement, defection on either tariff or labor standards commitments will cause the entire agreement to collapse. Consequently, defection from a linked agreement results in the loss of benefits from cooperation on *both* tariffs and labor standards. Employing linkage to raise the cost of defecting from either tariff or labor standards commitments should help to sustain compliance in both dimensions.

It is also possible that linking trade and labor standards in a single round of negotiations might produce additional bargaining efficiencies by transferring some enforcement power from the trade dimension to the labor dimension. In this connection, Limao (2000) considers a case in which the international community has found it relatively easy to achieve a nearly optimal agreement on tariffs but has had greater difficulty finding a self-enforcing agreement on labor standards. If tariffs and labor standards are linked together, the likely agreement would consist of less trade liberalization but tighter labor standards than would have occurred in a partitioned agreement. Nevertheless, world welfare is higher than in the absence of linkage because the gains from improving the relatively inadequate labor standards are larger than the losses from raising the already close-to-optimal tariff levels.

III. Arguments in Favor of Linking

Trade Sanctions as an Enforcement Device

The most direct argument for linking labor standards to trade in the WTO should be obvious from the discussion above. Anyone who favors raising the level and enforcement of labor standards around the world would presumably prefer additional tools to make that happen, and trade can provide such a tool. Trade sanctions have long been used to pressure countries to alter their behavior, albeit with mixed success. The hope is that by threatening a country with restriction or taxes on exports, the country would be motivated to avoid that by improving its labor standards. Experience suggests that when such tools are used in a hostile environment, they often fail. But here, by using them within the agreed upon DSM of the WTO to enforce labor standards that many countries have also accepted within the ILO, it seems plausible that compliance might be more forthcoming. If so, then the trade sanctions themselves would seldom actually be applied, and the goal of improving labor standards would be achieved.

Setting Efficient Labor Standards

Implicit in this argument is the belief that countries cannot be trusted to set labor standards optimally for their own populations, and therefore that they need external inducement to do the right thing. Where governments are corrupt and/or non-democratic, this may not be questioned. However, for reasonably well-functioning democracies the case for external pressure must be argued with care. That is, governments have a strong interest in adopting economic policies, including labor standards, that promote economic efficiency.

Inefficient policy-making even in a democracy may occur for a couple of different reasons. First, we might make a political economy argument. Just as with trade policies, labor policies are also set in response to many conflicting incentives, political and economic. Consequently, the public may be better served by governments that are externally constrained. For example, owners of capital are likely to have disproportionate power compared to labor, and they thus may be able to influence government to set or to enforce weak labor standards. Just as political forces favoring trade protection may be more effectively and beneficially resisted by membership in the GATT/WTO, forces favoring weak labor standards may also be resisted if labor standards are made part of the WTO. Governments may welcome the assistance, even if they cannot say so.

Second, even governments that are able to choose nationally optimal labor standards policies, may still over- or under-regulate labor markets when viewed from the point of view of worldwide economic efficiency. A discrepancy between efficiency and nationally optimal policies will emerge when labor standards alter the volume of trade to such an extent that world prices are disturbed.

For example, a large capital-abundant country, when considering a change in an existing labor standard, may at least consider the domestic costs and benefits of the standard at the margin. In addition, such a country may also consider the impact that the labor standard has on its international terms of trade. A large capital-abundant country may realize that a tightened labor standard may also result in a larger volume of labor-intensive imports that can be purchased on world markets only if the world price of labor-intensive goods also rises. That is, tightened labor standards tend to turn the terms of trade against large capital-abundant countries.

As a consequence, when policy-makers in our hypothetical country consider the economic effects of a tightened labor standard, they require that the domestic benefits exceed the domestic costs by enough to offset the national cost of the deterioration in the terms of trade. However, from a world-efficiency point of view, terms-of-trade effects are zero-sum. That is, terms of trade losses for one country are gains for another, and thus should be ignored in any evaluation of the benefits and costs of the labor standard under consideration. This analysis suggests, then, that large capital-abundant countries may set their labor standards at a point where the marginal benefit exceeds marginal cost, thus under-regulating their labor markets.

Bargaining Inefficiencies in the WTO

In fact, both the political economy and the terms-of-trade externality considerations are a part of a more general argument in favor of incorporating labor standards into the WTO. Bagwell and Staiger (2001) have noted that when we negotiate over border controls and labor standards separately, bargaining inefficiencies are likely to emerge. The inefficiency arises due to the fact that border controls and labor standards can be considered to be policy substitutes. That is, either can be used to accomplish protectionist objectives.

The protectionist content of labor standards has already been alluded to above. Weak labor standards in a capital-abundant country benefit import-competing producers by lowering their labor costs. The consequent increase in domestic production also lowers import demand. Thus, lax labor standards are able in principle to accomplish the twin trade policy goals of protecting domestic import-competing interests and exercising monopoly control over the terms of trade.

Given the parallels between border controls and labor standards, protectionist urges may be deflected onto labor standards. In a single-dimensional negotiating environment in which we agree to constrain the use of trade policies, governments are motivated to replace inefficient trade policies with inefficient labor policies. That is, following a round of trade negotiations in which trade barriers have been reduced, policy makers may then relax labor standards in order to return the volume of imports closer to their pre-negotiation level. Bargaining efficiency can be achieved only when border controls are negotiated simultaneously with the protectionist content of labor standards, thereby constraining policy makers from replacing protectionist border controls with protectionist labor standards.

Bargaining Complementarities

A fourth and final argument in favor of linking does not necessarily concern whether trade sanctions will be used to enforce labor standards, but rather deals with whether issues of labor standards should be included in a new multilateral round of negotiations under the auspices of the WTO. Developing countries are resisting this, as are most trade economists, while Europeans tend to favor it and in the United States, Republicans and Democrats are divided on the issue. The alternative to including labor standards in a new round is, of course, to leave labor standards as they are now, confined to the ILO.

Arguments against doing this will be discussed in the next section, but an argument in favor needs to be stated here, and it is a simple application of a more general principle. The principle is that when countries negotiate on multiple issues, all can gain by linking those negotiations. The reason is simple: this permits countries to exchange concessions on one issue for gains on others, thus permitting a more efficient outcome that benefits all. For example, it may be that although developing countries would prefer not to give ground on labor standards, they also are seeking more market access in textiles and clothing than developed countries are willing to provide. If their desire for market access exceeds their unwillingness to raise labor standards, then they may gain by giving up something on labor standards in exchange for market access. Alternatively, if their concern about raising labor standards is the greater, then they might be willing to sacrifice some market access for that.[7] Either way, depending on their preferences, linking the two issues permits them to achieve what they

[7] Note that what actually matters is not just one party's relative preferences, but these compared to the relative preferences of the other negotiating party. See Bagwell and Staiger (2001) and Staiger (2001) for a case that can be made that permits WTO member countries to trade off between changes in tariffs and changes in national labor standards as a way of providing secure market access for foreign exporters.

will regard as a better outcome, something that they could not do if negotiations on the two issues were to remain separate.[8]

This is actually a familiar principle for trade specialists, who have long recognized the benefits of negotiating over diverse trade issues within a single round, rather than handling each of them separately. Even when only tariffs were being negotiated, this permitted countries to exchange their own tariff cuts in some sectors for their trading partners' cuts in others. This facilitated the substantial reductions in tariffs that were achieved through the early rounds of negotiation under the GATT. The Tokyo Round extended the scope of negotiations beyond tariffs, although these tradeoffs were hampered by the use of separate codes for each of the new issues, codes that countries could sign onto or not as they chose. The Uruguay Round achieved much more by returning to the all-or-nothing package approach of previous rounds, permitting countries to exchange, say, concessions on agricultural subsidies for concessions on trade in industrial products.

In fact, the principle was most evident on two issues of great importance to developing countries: market access in textiles and clothing, and intellectual property rights. Developing countries eventually accepted the TRIPS agreement, despite what they viewed as its cost to them, as the price to pay for eventual ending of the Multi-Fiber Arrangement (MFA). Of course, this example also illustrates the dangers of accepting tradeoffs of this sort: many developing countries today are unhappy with the deal that they made.

IV. Arguments Against Linking

A first argument against linking trade and labor standards is simply to question the efficacy of labor standards themselves. Nobody questions the ultimate desirability of improving conditions for workers. However, one may easily question whether simply imposing better conditions will in fact make all workers better off. The concern is analogous to the traditional economists' argument against a minimum

[8] See Horstmann *et al.* (2000).

wage, but it applies to all manner of labor standards. If higher standards are imposed, then the cost of hiring labor will rise and fewer workers will be employed. The result will be better conditions for some, but worse for others. Economists will also point out, in this situation, that those who gain would be unable to compensate the losers, even in principle, because the outcome is inefficient. But that may be beside the point, since the harm to the losers in itself may be enough to condemn the policy in most minds.

Of course, this argument applies with different force for different labor standards, depending on the likely numbers of winners and losers, and also on whether labor markets really work this way. Many would accept this argument as applied to a minimum wage in developing countries, and indeed most who favor linking trade and labor standards reject trying to raise wages in developing countries above market levels.

But other labor standards, such as the Fundamental ILO Conventions mentioned above, may be less likely to harm workers, may actually enhance labor market efficiency, or may embody issues of principle that should override simple economic costs and benefits. Thus, freedom of association may be viewed as necessary in order for labor markets to work properly, given what otherwise would be an extreme asymmetry between the market powers of employers and employed. Forced labor, too, is hardly a case of a properly functioning labor market, which ought to have voluntary participation from both sides. Child labor, on the other hand, may be a case of principle, which should be prohibited even if the children and their parents believe that the work makes them better off. For both cases, however, we would plead that enforcement of labor standards not be accepted too uncritically, and that what truly happens to all affected workers (not just those who remain employed) should be taken into account.

Suppose, now, that we accept that certain labor standards do need to be imposed on labor markets. What, then, can be wrong with using trade sanctions to enforce these standards? The answer depends in part on whether the threatened sanctions turn out to be used or not. In any system of sanctions (trade or otherwise), the purpose is to achieve the standards, not to apply the sanctions. But the system will not likely work unless the sanctions are sometimes applied.

If they are, then the world suffers the costs of distorted trade that we trade economists routinely teach to our students. Is that the only cost of using trade sanctions? If so, then the case against them would be weak, since costs of distorted trade are unlikely to be very large in comparison with the gains that are sought by imposing the labor standards. However, there is a more important cost. That is, trade sanctions, if applied, are likely to hurt most the workers who were intended to benefit from the labor standards. For example, suppose that a country prevents its workers from organizing in its export industries, and that the world responds by restricting those exports. Then these workers, who were presumably already suffering from their lack of union representation, now lose their jobs as well.

All of this assumes that trade sanctions, if permitted, will only be applied where the failure of labor standards justifies their use. However, there is good reason to worry that this will not be the case. Trade sanctions are restrictions on trade, and, when used, they benefit the firms and workers that compete with the restricted imports. We know from long experience that whenever conditions for restricting trade are accepted as legitimate or written into law — as, for example, in antidumping and countervailing duty statutes — industries become very aggressive and creative in asserting that these conditions have been met. Who could be better placed to identify abuses of labor standards abroad than the domestic competitors of supposedly offending foreign firms? But also, who could have better reason to identify abuses where there are none, since they will then be rewarded with protection? It is this concern, that trade sanctions will be co-opted for protectionist purposes, that most worries both trade specialists like ourselves and developing country trade negotiators.

It is also this concern about protectionism that makes us doubtful of the alternative argument that trade sanctions will seldom be used, only threatened. If in fact this were the case, then the harm we have ascribed to the sanctions themselves would not arise (although the caveat remains that forcing higher labor standards may be harmful).[9] But the forces of protectionism have shown themselves to be both strong and insistent, sure to exploit any loophole in WTO rules that may be provided. It seems likely that whenever abuses of labor standards are alleged, no amount of response by raising standards will be enough to satisfy those who will seek to exploit the situation by seeking protection. This will include not only those who benefit from the trade sanctions that are applied, but also those who benefit from easier competition with the industries where standards are raised. The prospect that somehow these protectionist interests will drop their case when valid abuses have been corrected seems distinctly unlikely. Trade sanctions are likely to become the norm, not the exception.

These ideas have been formalized by Limao (2000), who points out that linkage of trade and labor standards within a single negotiating environment can enhance the political power of those who seek protection, thereby making it more difficult to sustain a cooperative agreement. He examines the case in which there is a powerful lobby that advocates in favor of producers in the import-competing sector. In such a situation, linkage can destroy enforcement power.

Consider, for example, a situation in which a powerful import-competing lobby is affecting trade policy. The lobby may reward policy makers for defecting from an international agreement. Obviously, the larger the import-competing sector, the larger the reward the lobby will be willing to pay for obtaining additional protection on its behalf, because the economic rents reaped from protection are roughly proportional to industry output. In a linked agreement, the lobby calculates the reward that it is willing to pay based on the size of the industry once defection from the international agreement has occurred. Thus, when the lobby calculates its willingness to pay for defection from a labor agreement, it realizes that the defection will also trigger a collapse of the linked trade agreement.

[9] See Srinivasan (1998) and Pahre (1998) for a discussion of how the "hijacking" of the concern for labor standards by protectionist forces may influence the adoption of higher standards and affect the economic welfare of the countries. See also Singh (2001).

As a consequence, the industry base benefiting from relaxed labor standards will be larger than it would have been in the absence of linkage.

A similar consideration applies when calculating the benefits of defection from a trade agreement. In other words, from the point of view of the lobby, there are complementarities between trade and labor standards that increase the payoff from defection. Such complementarities within a linked agreement raise the cost of compliance, making cooperation more difficult to sustain.

V. Advice for Developing Countries

Given these arguments, what position should developing countries take in engaging in multilateral negotiations? Should they continue to resist bringing labor standards into the WTO, or should they not?

On balance, our view is that the dangers of using trade sanctions to enforce labor standards outweigh the benefits, both in terms of likely protectionism and in harm to affected workers. Therefore, we would prefer that labor issues be left out of the WTO. For the same reasons, we concur with the position that most developing countries have taken, arguing against the inclusion of labor standards in the WTO. It is true that by giving up something in labor standards, developing countries might be able to get other benefits that would be worth even more. But experience with TRIPS suggests that they might regret this later on.

However, we also believe that whatever their position on labor standards, the overriding interest of developing countries is in the continued successful functioning of the WTO system. Even though the WTO is not explicitly intended to help developing countries, we believe that it offers them their best protection from being victims of developed country trade policies, for reasons touched on earlier. With that in mind, whatever position developing countries take on labor standards should not get in the way of the ability of the WTO to continue to do its job.

In particular, while developing countries should be advised to continue to resist inclusion of labor standards on the multilateral negotiating agenda, circumstances could arise such that the only way to get agreement on a negotiating round would be to permit labor standards to enter it in a small way. Developing countries might accept this and then do their best to deal with the issue in their own interests during the round.

There are several different channels through which labor standards might enter the WTO, some more problematic than others. It has been suggested, for example in OECD (1996), that poorly protected labor standards might constitute dumping under GATT 1994 Article VI, or be interpreted as a subsidy under GATT 1994 Article XVI. But the most direct approach would be to add poorly protected labor rights to the list of general exceptions articulated in Article XX. However, a complaint under these three articles would likely generate a long, detailed, and potentially intrusive discussion as to what constitutes poorly protected worker rights, and whether harm has been done to domestic interests.

Bagwell and Staiger have alternatively suggested that labor standards be dealt with under the Nullification and Impairment clause. In their conceptualization of international trade negotiations, countries can be thought of as agreeing to a certain level of market access. Changes in domestic policies that reduce that access can then become the basis of a nullification and impairment complaint. They recommend that Article XXIII be amended to require countries that loosen labor standards in their import-competing industries to compensate foreign suppliers with an offsetting tariff reduction that restores the volume of trade to the previously agreed upon level. In order to create symmetry, countries that tighten labor standards in their import-competing industries, which have the effect of expanding import demand, are then also entitled to raise import tariffs to offset the impact on the volume of trade.

The virtue of the Bagwell–Staiger mechanism is that it removes any incentive to alter labor standards so as to gain a strategic advantage internationally. The international trade implications for labor standards would be neutralized by equal and offsetting changes in tariffs. As a consequence, governments become free to consider only the efficiency effects of labor standards and need not be concerned with the implications for international competitiveness.

An additional virtue of the Bagwell–Staiger approach is that it focuses the attention of the WTO on the implications of heterogeneous labor standards on international competitiveness. That is, the Nullification and Impairment clause, as envisioned by Bagwell and Staiger, can be used to prevent a "race to the bottom" in international labor standards that may otherwise occur if trade policy is largely controlled by import-competing interests.

By contrast, the General Exceptions provision is more likely to be used to focus attention on moral and humanitarian concerns with the nature of production in developing countries. However, as we have discussed above, trade sanctions are not a very attractive device for expressing humanitarian concerns. Trade sanctions are likely to hurt the very people we are trying to help in focusing on worker rights. Furthermore, reliance on the General Exceptions provision requires us to attempt to agree on universally accepted language on worker rights that can be codified in international trade law. Some statements about labor standards may be attractive as general goals, but they vary too much across countries to be defined as rights that should be enforced by trade sanctions.

VI. Epilogue

This paper was initially written prior to the conclusion of the WTO Ministerial Meeting convened in Doha, Qatar, in November 2001 for the purpose of designing the agenda for a new round of multilateral trade negotiations. Following 9/11, the United States and other WTO members had an incentive to downplay the disputes that had led to the failure of the Seattle Ministerial Meeting in December 1999 and to adopt a more cooperative position in launching a new trade round in 2002. It was also the case that the Bush Administration did not favor linking trade and labor standards in the WTO. Thus, for now, the issue of linkage is moot, and the ILO will continue to have the institutional responsibility for the oversight of international labor standards. But the fact remains that there is continued support for linkage on the part of organized labor, as well by many human and labor rights NGOs in the United States and some other industrialized countries. The issues that we have discussed in this paper may well therefore re-emerge in the future when economic and political conditions change and linkage issues will again be prominent in the policy dialogue.

Study Questions

1. To what extent are international organizations compartmentalized or having overlapping jurisdictions? What were the traditional roles of the GATT and now of the WTO? How does dispute settlement differ between these two organizations? What is the rationale in using sanctions in dispute settlement cases?
2. What are the Fundamental ILO Conventions? What kinds of enforcement powers, if any, does the ILO have in dealing with abuses of labor standards? What are the origins of the movement to include labor standards in the WTO? Who gains and loses from globalization and from the WTO?
3. What are arguments in favor of linking trade and labor standards in the WTO? What are the arguments against linking? Should developing countries resist bringing labor standards into the WTO? What changes would be needed in the WTO if there was linkage? What is the current status of the relations between trade and labor standards in the global trading system and in the negotiations of preferential trading arrangements?

References

Bagwell, Kyle and Robert W. Staiger. 2001. "The WTO as a Mechanism for Securing Market Access Property Rights: Implications for Global Labor and Environmental Issues," *Journal of Economic Perspectives* 15, pp. 68–88.

Brown, Drusilla K. 2000. "International Trade and Core Labour Standards: A Survey of Recent Literature," Labour Market and Social Policy Occasional Papers No. 43. Paris: OECD.

Brown, Drusilla K. 2001. "Labor Standards: Where Do They Belong on the International Trade Agenda?" *Journal of Economic Perspectives* 15, pp. 89–112.

Brown, Drusilla K., Alan V. Deardorff, and Robert M. Stern. 1996. "International Labor Standards and Trade: A Theoretical Analysis," in Jagdish Bhagwati and Robert Hudec (eds.), *Fair Trade and Harmonization: Prerequisites for Free Trade?* Cambridge, MA: MIT Press.

Brown, Drusilla K., Alan V. Deardorff, and Robert M. Stern. 1998. "Trade and Labor Standards," *Open Economies Review* 9, pp. 171–194.

Brown, Drusilla K., Alan V. Deardorff, and Robert M. Stern. 2001a. "Child Labor: Theory, Evidence and Policy," prepared for Swedish Ministry of Foreign Affairs, Expert Group on Development Issues (EGDI); Research Seminar in International Economics, Discussion Paper No. 474, August 17.

Brown, Drusilla K., Alan V. Deardorff, and Robert M. Stern. 2001b. "U.S. Trade and Other Policy Options and Programs to Deter Foreign Exploitation of Child Labor," in Magnus Blomström and Linda Goldberg (eds.), *Topics in Empirical International Economics: A Festschrift in Honor of Robert Lipsey.* University of Chicago Press.

Brown, Drusilla K., Alan V. Deardorff, and Robert M. Stern. 2002. "CGE Modeling and Analysis of Multilateral and Regional Negotiating Options," in Robert M. Stern (ed.), *Issues and Options for U.S. Japan Trade Policies.* Ann Arbor: University of Michigan Press, pp. 23–65.

Deardorff, Alan V. 1990. "Should Patent Protection Be Extended to All Developing Countries?" *The World Economy* 13, pp. 497–507.

Deardorff, Alan V. and Robert M. Stern. 2002. "What You Should Know about Globalization and the World Trade Organization," *Review of International Economics*, forthcoming.

Freeman, Richard B. 1995. "Are Your Wages Set in Beijing?" *Journal of Economic Perspectives* 9, pp. 15–32.

Horstmann, Ignatius J., James R. Markusen, and Jack Robles. 2000. "Multi-Issue Bargaining and Linked Agendas: Ricardo Revisited or No Pain No Gain," in process (December).

Limao, Nuno. 2000. "Trade Policy, Cross-Border Externalities and Lobbies: Do Linked Agreements Enforce More Cooperative Outcomes?" mimeo.

OECD. 1996. *Trade, Employment and Labour Standards.* OECD, Paris.

Pahre, Robert. 1998. "Labor Standards, Trade Sanctions, and the Hijacking Hypothesis," in Alan V. Deardorff and Robert M. Stern (eds.), *Constituent Interests and U.S. Trade Policies.* Ann Arbor: University of Michigan Press.

Singh, Nirvikar. 2001. "The Impact of Labor Standards: A Survey of Economic Theory," prepared for Swedish Ministry of Foreign Affairs, Expert Group on Development Issues (EGDI), in process.

Spagnolo, Giancarlo. 1999. "Issues Linkage, Delegation, and International Policy Cooperation," Cambridge, DEA Working Paper No. 9913.

Srinivasan, T. N. 1998. "Trade and Human Rights," in Alan V. Deardorff and Robert M. Stern (eds.), *Constituent Interests and U.S. Trade Policies.* Ann Arbor: University of Michigan Press.

Staiger, Robert W. 2001. "The International Organization and Enforcement of Labor Standards," prepared for Swedish Ministry of Foreign Affairs and Expert Group on Development Issues (EGDI), in process.

Stern, Robert M. 1999. "Labor Standards and International Trade," INTAL, *Integration and Trade*, May/June (in English and Spanish).

Suggested Further Reading

Ederington, Josh. 2002. "Trade and Domestic Policy Linkage in International Agreements," *International Economic Review* 43, pp. 1347–1368.

Limao, Nuno. 2005. "Trade Policy, Cross-Border Externalities and Lobbies: Do Linked Agreements Enforce More Cooperative Outcomes?" *Journal of International Economics* 67, pp. 175–199.

Chapter 17

The Effects of Multinational Production on Wages and Working Conditions in Developing Countries*

Drusilla K. Brown, Alan V. Deardorff and Robert M. Stern†

I. Introduction

This chapter is designed to assess the empirical evidence on the effects of multinational production on wages and working conditions in developing countries. It is motivated by the controversies that have emerged especially in the past decade or so concerning whether or not multinational firms in developing countries are

† We wish to thank Robert Baldwin, Elliot Berg, Rob Howse, Rachel McCulloch, Ian Robinson, André Sapir, participants in the NBER pre-conference meeting, and participants in the NBER/CEPR/SNS Stockholm conference, as well as seminar participants at the University of Michigan and the University of Leuven, for their helpful comments on earlier versions of our paper. We also thank Gladys Mitchell for research assistance and Judith Jackson for editorial and typing assistance.

exploiting their workers in "sweatshop" conditions by paying low wages and subjecting them to coercive, abusive, and unhealthy and unsafe conditions in the workplace. Thus, in Section II, we address these controversies in the context of the efforts and programs of social activist groups and universities and colleges involved in the "Anti-Sweatshop" Campaign in the United States and the related issues of the social accountability of multinational firms and the role of such international institutions as the International Labor Organization (ILO) and World Trade Organization (WTO) in dealing with labor standards and trade. We then turn more broadly in Section III to a conceptual treatment of the effects of foreign direct investment (FDI) on wages in host countries and the effects of outsourcing and subcontracting by multinational firms. Thereafter, the empirical evidence on multinational-firm wages in developing countries is reviewed in Section IV, together with evidence on the relationship between FDI and labor rights. Conclusions are presented in Section V.

II. Political Economy Issues

As mentioned, our paper has been motivated by the controversies as to whether multinational firms are exploiting and mistreating their workers by employing them under "sweatshop" conditions. What this means is exploiting the workers by paying low wages and subjecting them to violations of certain universal social norms or standards governing their employment. In this connection, Moran (2002) has stressed the importance of distinguishing low-wage, relatively unskilled labor-intensive industries such as apparel and footwear from industries that employ more highly skilled workers and produce relatively more skill-intensive products such as electronics and automotive products. Many social activists and activist organizations that are critical of multinational wages and working conditions in developing countries do not make this distinction. Rather, much of the criticism by social activists in the United States especially has been directed at multinational operations in the apparel and footwear industries that are allegedly producing under "sweatshop" conditions.[1] We turn next accordingly to consider the salient anti-sweatshop issues.

The Anti-Sweatshop Campaign in the United States

Elliott and Freeman (2001, pp. 15–16) note that:

> Sweatshops have characterized apparel production since industrial revolution days, and so too have campaigns to improve labor conditions in the industry. ... Many of the issues are the same, but a major difference between anti-sweatshop campaigns at the turn of the 21st century and those at the turn of the 20th century is that sweatshops then were largely local whereas today they are found mostly in poor developing countries. This means that U.S.-based activists cannot lobby the U.S. government to improve labor standards. Instead they must target U.S.-based corporations who operate or source in developing countries or pressure the world trading community to demand changes in less developed countries.[2]

Elliott and Freeman (2001, pp. 48–49) provide a timeline of U.S. anti-sweatshop activities from 1990 to spring 2000,[3] and a list of

[1] Graham (2000, pp. 101–102) has noted that products originating in the footwear, apparel, toy-making, and sporting goods industries combined accounted for less than 10 percent of world merchandise exports in 1997. He then states: "If indeed sweatshop conditions are concentrated in these industries, they do not represent the greater part of globalized economic activity." It would be more meaningful, however, to consider how important the exports of these goods are for developing countries, rather than for the world as a whole. Graham's source, WTO (1998), does not report trade by level of development. But its geographic data are suggestive: WTO (2000) reports textile exports as a percent of manufactured exports to be only 2.3 percent for Latin America, 3.6 percent for Africa, and 6.9 percent for Asia excluding Australia, Japan, and New Zealand.

[2] Robert Baldwin has pointed out to us that the unfavorable perception of FDI, and industrialization in general, may be related historically to the change from a household to a factory system of production. Thus, one does not usually think of a family engaged in household production as working under sweatshop conditions. It is mainly when workers are assembled to produce in factories that it is believed that they may be subjected to sweatshop conditions, even though their wages may be higher and children may have more access to education and better medical care.

[3] See also Varley (1998, pp. 12–13).

transnational labor rights activist organizations (Appendix Exhibit A). As they note (pp. 16–17), during this period, multinationals such as Levi Strauss, Gap, Phillips-VanHeusen, and others were singled out for condoning undesirable labor practices. And Wal-Mart, a major retailer, was cited as selling clothing made by child labor in Bangladesh and Honduras. Many of the firms involved in producing or sourcing abroad have responded to the criticisms by adopting codes of conduct that are designed presumably to guide their operations.[4] In 1996, the Clinton Administration established the Apparel Industry Partnership (AIP) to address sweatshop issues globally by bringing together apparel firms, unions, and NGOs by means of a code of conduct and a monitoring system that were introduced in April 1997 and that would be applicable to the firms involved. Subsequently, in November 1998, the AIP established the Fair Labor Association (FLA) to implement and monitor the code. Some groups, in particular the Union of Needletrades, Industrial and Textile Employees (UNITE), were critical of the AIP/FLA program, complaining as Elliott and Freeman note (p. 17) that "...the code failed to require payment of a living wage; had weak language with respect to union rights in nondemocratic countries; and had a weak monitoring and verification system." Nonetheless, by fall 2000, 140 colleges and universities had become affiliated with the FLA, and, as of the end of 2001, the number had grown to 192.[5]

It was during this period that student activism on sweatshops took hold at a number of American campuses. A group called Students Against Sweatshops was established at Duke University in August 1997. With assistance from UNITE, the United Students Against Sweatshops (USAS) was established on a national basis in summer 1998. In expressing their dissatisfaction with the FLA, the student members of the USAS orchestrated sit-ins during 1999 at a number of prominent universities and colleges. On October 19, 1999, the USAS announced the creation of the Worker Rights Consortium (WRC)

---

[4] We have more to say on this below.

[5] The list of colleges and universities affiliated with the FLA can be found at www.fairlabor.org/htm/affiliates/university.html.

and urged institutions to withdraw from the FLA and join the WRC, which purportedly had a stronger code of conduct, a focus on worker complaints and education on worker rights, and a requirement for disclosure of the name and location of factories producing licensed apparel. As of June 2000, 50 institutions had become affiliated with the WRC. The number had grown to 92 as of December 13, 2001, and 49 of these institutions continued to remain affiliated with the FLA.[6]

Elliott and Freeman (2001, p. 18) note that a number of additional organizations were created that formulated codes of conduct and mechanisms for monitoring adherence to the codes. These organizations include such U.S. groups as: Social Accountability International, which administers its SA8000 code on a global and multi-industry basis; the Collegiate Licensing Company (CLC); the Worldwide Responsible Apparel Production (WRAP); and Verité, which monitors human rights especially. There is also the Europe-based Ethical Trade Initiative, and there are NGOs based in developing countries. There are a number of private monitoring groups, including PriceWaterhouseCoopers (PWC) and Ernst and Young. In addition, many American academic institutions have established codes of conduct,[7] although they depend for the most part on the monitoring to be carried out by the FLA or WRC.[8] It is of interest therefore to compare the main features of the FLA and WRC.

Comparison of the FLA and WRC

As noted above, the FLA was established in 1998 as an outgrowth of the Apparel Industry Partnership (AIP) sponsored by the Clinton

---

[6] The list of institutions affiliated with the WRC can be found at www.workersrights.org/as.asp.

[7] See, for example, the University of Michigan code of conduct in University of Michigan Advisory Committee on Labor Standards and Human Rights (2000, pp. 7–8).

[8] It is noteworthy that the University of Chicago decided against joining either organization. According to the *University of Chicago Magazine* (2000), they opted to rely on Barnes & Noble, which operates the University bookstore locations, to require that all merchandise sold complies with FLA standards.

Administration. Its focus is on improving working conditions in the global apparel industry.[9] In considering the relative merits and membership in the FLA and WRC, the University of Michigan Advisory Committee on Labor Standards and Human Rights (2000, pp. 30–33) noted for example the following positive features of the FLA: (1) the FLA membership includes most of the largest apparel producers, is well funded, may be cost effective in avoiding the proliferation of codes of conduct and monitoring, and may provide economies of scale in coordinating its membership and carrying out monitoring; (2) the FLA focuses on the apparel industry as a whole, and its charter gives universities the option to pursue more flexible strategies if so desired. Some of the concerns expressed about the FLA were that it might be dominated by corporate interests that would favor a weak code of conduct on such issues as health and safety, women's rights, compensation, and hours and overtime, and that it would be reluctant to provide public disclosure of factory locations.

With regard to the WRC, the Michigan Advisory Committee Report (2000, pp. 29–31) cited the following attractive features:[10] (1) emphasis on disclosure, transparency, and public information on conditions in apparel factories; (2) emphasis on the investigation of complaints as a means of focusing attention on factories where problems are reported rather than relying on monitoring per se; (3) commitment to involve workers and their representatives in the development and implementation of WRC policies; (4) insistence on including a living-wage standard in the WRC code of conduct to focus the attention of universities and licensees on wage issues; (5) concentration on university-licensed apparel rather than on the entire apparel industry as a means of enhancing the leverage of universities; and (6) independence from the FLA and other groups as a means of providing a check on the quality and reliability of other monitoring efforts. Some concerns expressed about the WRC were: (1) its adversarial approach towards licensees, with the consequence that licensees may view the WRC with suspicion, make them hesitant in

[9] The code of conduct of the FLA can be found at www.fairlabor.org.

[10] The code of conduct of the WRC can be found at www.workersrights.org.

self-reporting their activities, undermine the credibility and legitimacy of the WRC investigation of reported complaints, and disrupt university-business relationships with licensee partners; (2) the WRC objective of educating workers and encouraging them to act on their own rights may compromise the impartial and independent investigation of worker complaints; (3) there may be an over-reliance on complaint investigation insofar as it presumes that workers are aware of their rights and willing to take risks in filing complaints; and (4) that the independence and credibility of the WRC may be compromised because of the presence on its Governing Board of UNITE or other U.S. unions with a documented history of trade protectionism and discouragement of apparel job creation in developing countries.[11]

From the perspective of many American colleges and universities, it should be evident from the foregoing discussion that there are some important differences between the FLA and WRC in terms of their objectives and mode of operation. Two issues that stand out are deserving of further comment: (1) the living wage; and (2) conditions of work, including the right of association and collective bargaining.

The Living Wage

As noted in www.fairlabor.org, the FLA code relating to wages and benefits is:

> **Wages and Benefits.** Employers recognize that wages are essential to meeting employees' basic needs. Employers shall pay employees, as a floor, at

[11] In this regard, it is of interest to note the statement in the *University of Chicago Magazine* (2000):

> It is the WRC's apparent intention to move beyond a monitoring function to an advocacy role — supporting particular social, political, and environmental positions — that troubles the University administration and faculty. ... As ... outlined by the faculty in the 1967 Kalven Committee Report on the University's Role in Political and Social Action: 'A university ... is a community but only for the limited, albeit great, purposes of teaching and research. It is not a club, it is not a trade association, it is not a lobby.'

> least the minimum wage required by local law or the prevailing industry wage, whichever is higher, and shall provide legally mandated benefits.

As noted in www.workersrights.org, the WRC code relating to wages and benefits is:

> 1. *Wages and Benefits*: Licensees recognize that wages are essential to meeting employees' basic needs. Licensees shall pay employees, as a floor, wages and benefits which comply with all applicable laws and regulations, and which provide for essential needs and establish a dignified living wage for workers and their families. [A living wage is a "take home" or "net" wage, earned during a country's legal maximum work week, but not more than 48 hours. A living wage provides the basic needs (housing, energy, nutrition, clothing, health care, education, potable water, childcare, transportation and savings) of an average family unit of employees in the garment manufacturing employment sector of the country.]

It is evident that the WRC concept of what constitutes a living wage is much more explicit than the FLA basic-needs criterion of the payment of the minimum wage or prevailing industry wage, whichever is higher. As noted by Elliott and Freeman (2001, p. 50), the WRC is apparently willing to postpone the implementation of its living-wage standard pending the completion of further research. This is essentially similar to the position of the FLA, which called for a wage study that was carried out by the U.S. Department of Labor (2000) and a request for follow-up on this study with possible annual updates.[12] In any event, the question at issue is how to define and measure what constitutes a living wage or basic needs and how this relates to the wages that workers are actually receiving.

The information on wages that we will present in Section IV below suggests that there is pervasive evidence that workers employed in multinational firms and subcontracting in developing countries are being paid wages that are on average higher than compared to alternative employment domestically. Of course, these wages are low in absolute terms in comparison with wages of workers in developed countries. Granting this, many observers have argued that workers'

---

[12] See www.fairlabor.org/html/faqs.html.

wages in developing countries may not be sufficient to satisfy basic needs. Hence the pressure for higher wages.

In this connection, for example, a group of students from the Columbia University School of International and Public Affairs carried out a study in 1999 for the National Labor Committee to calculate a living wage for maquila workers in El Salvador — see Connor *et al.* (1999). They found that most maquila workers earned the legal monthly minimum wage of 1,260 colones, which was estimated to be barely sufficient to meet basic food requirements. According to the formula used, it was estimated that maquila workers in El Salvador required a living wage of 4,556 colones to cover the basic needs of a family of 4.3 people living on one wage and allowing for 12.5 percent to be saved for the future. It was recommended that the process for setting wages according to a living-wage formula be standardized and multinational firms should adopt industry-wide standards for paying a living wage.

Moran (2002, Ch. 4, pp. 10–12) has pointed out the extraordinary complexities involved in calculating a living wage:

(1) There is a need to determine the nutritional standards, types of housing, expenditure categories, savings, and provisions for contingencies to be included in the living-wage formula and to make allowance for inter-country differences in purchasing-power-parity and macroeconomic conditions.
(2) Estimates of family size as a basis for wage adequacy may be arbitrary and discriminatory since average family size may vary, and there may be differences among wage earners depending on their age, gender, and family relationships.

Using South Asia as an example, Srinivasan (2001) also questions the relevance of attempting to calculate and administer a living wage. He notes that:

(1) in South Asia, over half of the labor force is self-employed and the proportion of regularly employed wage-paid workers is small;
(2) workers employed by multinationals are generally well paid, unionized, have legal protection of their rights, and receive mandated

benefits, so that payment of a living wage to these workers may be redundant;

(3) focusing on paying a living wage to workers employed by multinationals diverts attention from the far more serious and relevant problem of poverty and from the need to promote rapid economic growth to help eradicate poverty; and

(4) the goal of the living-wage proponents would be better served if they would lobby to eliminate barriers in developed countries on imports of labor-intensive manufactures and other trade barriers more generally, and relax immigration restrictions on unskilled workers. By the same token, efforts should be made in developing countries themselves to eliminate bureaucratic corruption, remove barriers to trade, and dismantle domestic policies that are inimical to the poor.

While living-wage proponents may grant many of the foregoing objections, they commonly argue nonetheless that multinationals can well afford to pay higher wages to workers in developing countries because those wages are typically but a tiny fraction of the selling price of the product. In this connection, some examples noted in Moran (2002, Ch. 4, pp. 15–16) are of interest: in 2000, the piece rate plus benefits of jeans produced in Nicaragua was $0.66 compared to the U.S. retail sales price of $21.99; in 2000, the unit labor cost, inclusive of benefits, for a ladies jacket made in Hong Kong was $0.84 compared to the U.S. retail price of $99; in 2001, the unit wage was $0.40 for a sport shoe produced in Indonesia that sold for $100 in the United States; and, in 2001, Nike reported that the labor cost of Nike shoes was $2.43 compared to a retail price of $65.

What are we to make of these comparisons? One can argue that the comparisons are inappropriate because they do not take into account the costs of further processing, transportation, advertising, and distribution. There is also a presumption that the multinational firms may be capturing oligopoly rents because of brand preferences, private labels, and name recognition that they have established. While it is conceivable that some of the largest multinationals may be capturing oligopoly rents, it is unclear how pervasive this is especially for firms competing at the retail level. But suppose for the sake of argument that some multinationals are mandated or may opt to divert some of their profits to pay higher wages to their workers in developing countries. It is by no means clear exactly how this would be done and what would prevent the companies from shifting their operations to locations with already higher wages and higher productivity.

The difficulty of paying higher wages would be even more pronounced if subcontracting firms were obliged to do so. Thus, as Moran notes (p. 16), in the examples cited above, the local wage bill ranged from 20 percent of the pre-tax profit for the firm producing footwear in Indonesia, 46 percent for the jeans production in Nicaragua, and 250 percent for the Nike shoes. Since subcontracting firms are generally independently owned, mandating higher wages for them in these circumstances would almost surely motivate them to search out less costly production locations.

The view that mandating higher wages for workers in developing countries can be accomplished with minimum disruption to employment within and between countries has been colored by the research finding of Card and Krueger (1995) that increases in the minimum wage in the United States in the early 1990s did not reduce teenage employment. In our judgment, contrary to Card and Krueger, there is reason to believe that labor-intensive manufacturing in developing countries is relatively sensitive to changes in wage levels. This is particularly true for the production of apparel and footwear, which are prototype "footloose" industries. This is borne out, for example, by the experiences of Japan and the Asian Tigers — Hong Kong, Singapore, South Korea, and Taiwan — insofar as increased labor costs in these countries in the course of their economic expansion from the 1960s onward resulted in a shift of the location of labor-intensive industries to China and Southeast Asia and to some extent to South Asia. Also worth mentioning are the experiences of Mauritius and Madagascar noted by Moran (2002, Ch. 4, p. 9), which suggest that labor-intensive producers were sensitive to changes in relative wage levels in deciding where to expand or contract employment and change the location of production.[13] More recently, there have been news reports about maquiladora factories closing down in Mexico and moving to Asia or Eastern Europe, and garment and shoe-manufacturing orders being lost in Indonesia to competitors in China and Vietnam where wages are lower and quality and delivery schedules more reliable.[14]

A common response to this argument — that mandating a living wage will cause employers to change locations — is to say that the living wage should be mandated in all countries, not just a few, so that there is no place for employers to go. But this misses the point. Wages vary across countries due to differences in labor productivity, which typically rises with the level of development. However the living wage may be defined, it will be above the productivity-based market wages in some countries and below that in others. If employers are required to pay the living wage, they will tend to move to countries where the living wage is justified by productivity.[15]

We conclude therefore that efforts to define and measure the living wage are fraught with insuperable difficulties,[16] and that it is likely that the imposition of a living wage that exceeds existing market-determined wage levels will result in employment shifts in

---

[13] See also Cooper (2001) for a journalistic account of the experiences of the two countries.

[14] See *The New York Times* (June 29, 2002, p. A3) and *The Wall Street Journal* (August 14, 2002, p. A11).

[15] In an econometric study of the effects of labor costs on foreign direct investment (FDI), while controlling for labor productivity, Kucera (2001, p. 28) has noted that "... coefficients of the wage share [of value added] variable are more and significantly negative for LDCs ..." and that "... a 10 percent increase in wage share would be associated with a 6.6 to 8.5 percent decline in FDI inflows in LDCs, compared with a 4.3 to 5.8 percent decline for all countries."

[16] The most comprehensive effort to define and measure the living wage is to be found in U.S. Department of Labor (2000). Their conclusion (p. vi) is: "For the countries considered, there appears to be little conclusive evidence on the extent to which wages and non-wage benefits in the footwear and apparel [industries] meet workers' basic needs."

developing countries that would be detrimental to economic efficiency and welfare.[17]

The Right of Association and Collective Bargaining

As noted in www.fairlabor.org, the pertinent FLA code is:

> **Freedom of Association and Collective Bargaining.** Employers shall recognize and respect the right of employees to freedom of association and collective bargaining.

The pertinent WRC code noted in www.workersrights.org is:

> 9. *Freedom of Association and Collective Bargaining*: Licensees shall recognize and respect the right of employees to freedom of association and collective bargaining. No employee shall be subject to harassment, intimidation or retaliation in their efforts to freely associate or bargain collectively. Licensees shall not cooperate with governmental agencies and other organizations that use the power of the State to prevent workers from organizing a union of their choice. Licensees shall allow union organizers free access to employees. Licensees shall recognize the union of the employees' choice.

---

[17] Neumark (2002) has studied the effects of living wage ordinances that have been adopted in many cities across the United States. These ordinances typically mandate a minimum wage floor that is often considerably higher than the traditional minimum wages set by state and federal legislation. Among the most significant findings are the following: (1) living wage ordinances have sizable positive effects on the wages of low-wage workers; (2) employment is reduced among the affected workers; (3) a detectable number of families may be lifted above the poverty line, even allowing for employment reductions; and (4) unionized municipal workers especially may gain from narrow living wage laws covering city contractors. Thus, while there is some evidence that living wages may provide some assistance to the working poor, Neumark notes that such ordinances may not be the best policy for helping the urban poor and that a range of other issues needs to be addressed, including budget implications, the incidence of the measures, effects on taxes and local development, the provision of city services, productivity, compliance and enforcement, and equity and overall economic welfare. See also the variety of comments on Harvard's living-wage debate in *Harvard Magazine* (2001).

The right of association and collective bargaining is arguably the most contentious of issues in countries with low-wage labor and specialization in labor-intensive industries like apparel and footwear. As Moran (2002, Ch. 3, p. 14) notes, the problems include: (1) the representation of workers and anti-union discrimination; (2) the right to strike; and (3) the threat to close plants that form unions.

Many employers have initiated worker-management associations designed to foster good relations with employees, and, according to Moran (p. 15), there is evidence for example in the Philippines, Dominican Republic, and Costa Rica of relatively high wages and good treatment of workers. By the same token, there have been allegations and evidence offered of cases of discrimination against workers seeking to organize unions in a number of countries.[18] This has been a problem especially when there already exists a government sponsored or government favored union, or when unions are prohibited by the government. Moreover, workers have been dismissed in some cases for participating in strikes, and replacement workers have been hired. Further, the threat to close plants that form unions has been alleged to occur at times.

There are divergent views on the issues of the right of association and collective bargaining. Thus, it can be argued that encouragement of unions and collective bargaining may enhance the efficiency of labor markets and increase the productivity of workers, especially when there are monopsonistic employers.[19] There may also be significant political and social spillover effects as democratic institutions and social harmony are strengthened. Further, it may be the case that governments are weak so that there is nobody to protect the workers but the workers themselves. On the other hand, as noted in the above discussion of the living wage, it may be the case in many low-income countries that labor unions are already concentrated in the formal

---

[18] A recent example is a strike by about 800 workers making collegiate apparel for Nike in the Korean owned factory, Kukdong International Mexico, located in Atlixco, Mexico, after some of their fellow workers had been fired in connection with their involvement in labor-rights disputes. For more information, see Verité (2001).

[19] See, for example, Freeman (1993).

manufacturing sector, and there may be substantial numbers of workers employed in public enterprises. As a consequence, the fostering of unions could be harmful to workers and families in the informal and in the rural/agricultural sectors that would have to absorb the workers displaced from these organized sectors. This is where much of the labor force is self-employed, often doing "home work" on a piece-rate basis, and the numbers of regularly employed wage-paid workers may be limited.[20]

The point just made should not be construed as condoning the suppression of unions and worker rights. Rather, the issue is whether the right of association and collective bargaining should be considered to be the prime objective, as emphasized by the WRC, to enhance the welfare of workers in low-income countries. That is, account needs to be taken of the wages and benefits that workers are actually receiving together with the treatment that they are being accorded in the workplace. Thus, as Moran (2002) in particular has stressed, there is considerable evidence suggesting that market forces combined with judicious government policies can provide the basis for enhancing worker welfare in poor countries. There may well be cases in which workers are mistreated in terms of not receiving their rightful wages or are subjected to poor working conditions.[21] In these instances, corrective measures should be taken by government in conformity with domestic law.

The ACIT and SASL Initiatives

We have had occasion in the preceding discussion to review the issues that are pertinent to the Anti-sweatshop Campaign that has focused

[20] In this connection, Srinivasan (1998, p. 239) has remarked: "... where the freedom to form unions has been exercised to a considerable extent, namely in the organized manufacturing and public sectors in poor countries, labor unions have been seen promoting the interests of a small section of the labor force at the expense of many. ... [I]t should be recognized ... that unionized labor often constitutes a small labor aristocracy in poor countries."

[21] For documentation, see, for example, Business for Social Responsibility Education Fund *et al.* (2000) and Verité (2000).

attention on the wages and working conditions in multinational firm operations in the apparel and footwear industries in low-income countries. Much of this campaign is being played out in the efforts of organizations like the WRC and the FLA to provide codes of conduct and monitoring of firms engaged in the production and marketing of apparel and related items bearing university and college logos.

As mentioned above, the strategy of the WRC and associated student groups has been one of confrontation with university/college administrations in the form of protests and sit-ins that were resolved in most cases by agreeing to membership in the WRC. At the same time, the FLA has been active in its efforts to engage and induce universities and colleges to become FLA members. As noted above, the FLA had 192 members at the end of 2001. The WRC had 92 members, and 49 of them were also members of the FLA.

Following the failure of the WTO Ministerial Meeting in Seattle in December 1999, Jagdish Bhagwati of Columbia University and Robert M. Stern of the University of Michigan convened a group of academic international trade economists and lawyers that met in January 2000 at the Georgetown University Law Center. The objective of the meeting was an effort to review what had happened in Seattle and the role that academic trade specialists might play in bringing their expertise to bear on the important issues of trade policy and engaging the attention of policy makers and the public. After the Georgetown meeting, it was decided to establish the Academic Consortium on International Trade (ACIT) with the foregoing objectives in mind. An ACIT Steering Committee was established and comprised: Robert E. Baldwin, University of Wisconsin; Jagdish Bhagwati, Columbia University; Alan V. Deardorff, University of Michigan; Arvind Panagariya, University of Maryland; T. N. Srinivasan, Yale University; and Robert M. Stern, University of Michigan, as Head of the Steering Committee. An ACIT website (www.Fordschool.umich.edu/rsie/acit) was created as a repository for academic papers, reports, policy statements, and news articles dealing with trade policy and related issues.

One of the most contentious issues at the Seattle Ministerial Meeting was that of trade and labor standards. This is a topic that most of the members of the ACIT Steering Committee had addressed individually and jointly in their published theoretical and policy-oriented writings. These writings explored the analytical complexities, political economy, empirical evidence, and the policies of national governments and international organizations involving trade and labor standards. The ACIT group concluded that much of the social activism in the United States regarding labor standards was motivated by protectionist considerations especially on the part of organized labor. The interests of low-income, developing countries were seen therefore to be especially at risk, particularly if efforts were made to mandate higher labor standards, including higher wages, by means of trade sanctions or other pressures on low-income countries.

It was with these concerns in mind that the ACIT Steering Committee decided to address the decisions taken by university and college administrators to design codes of conduct on their own and/or to become affiliated especially with the WRC to deal with issues of sweatshop labor. The ACIT Steering Committee prepared a letter that was sent in September 2000 to around 600 university and college presidents, stating that the actions taken or to be taken on sweatshop issues at many institutions were possibly not well informed and therefore ill advised. This letter is available on the ACIT website and in Broad (2002, pp. 222–223). It was first circulated to academic trade specialists and other members of the academic community, and some 352 (primarily) economists and other academics indicated that they wished to be signatories of the letter. The list of signatories is available on the ACIT website.

It is noteworthy that only a small number of university presidents or administrators acknowledged receipt of the letter. These included Columbia, Duke, UC-Berkeley, Harvard, and some smaller institutions. But what is perhaps more significant is that the ACIT letter received considerable press and media coverage, much of which can be found on the ACIT website.

It stands to reason that some members of the academic community would take issue with the position expressed in the ACIT letter. Thus, a group calling itself Scholars Against Sweatshop Labor (SASL) was formed, and they prepared a letter that was endorsed by

434 signatories (73 percent economists) and thereafter sent in October 2001 to more than 1,600 university and college presidents. The SASL letter is reproduced on the SASL website (www.umass.edu/per/sasl/) and in Broad (2002, pp. 224–227). The list of signatories is also included on the SASL website. There are several points in the SASL letter that are worthy of comment:

- *Are colleges and universities making decisions about codes of conduct without adequate consultation?*

  SASL assertion: "Colleges and universities that have adopted codes of conduct have generally done so after careful consultation with appropriate faculty and/or outsider experts."
  Evaluation: The SASL ignores the fact that the adoption of a code of conduct at many institutions was in response to campus sit-ins and protests, and that there was not a broad representation of alternative views and faculty expertise and campus-wide student involvement.

- *Worldwide consultation and monitoring*

  SASL assertion: "… the three organizations (WRC, FLA, and Social Accountability International) bring different strengths to the task of establishing and monitoring effective labor standards worldwide. Ongoing cooperation and competition between these groups should also raise the general performance standard for all three."
  Evaluation: As we have noted in our earlier discussion, the primary focus of the WRC on workers' rights and collective bargaining and a living wage, the influence of protectionist labor unions, and the adversarial approach to the business community may serve to limit the effectiveness of the WRC.

- *Wages, labor costs, and employment opportunities in the global garment industry*

  SASL assertion: "While caution is clearly needed in setting minimum decent standards for workplace conditions, workers rights, and wage levels, there is still no reason to assume that a country or region that sets reasonable standards must experience job losses." Evaluation: The fact remains that workers in low-income developing countries are generally being paid wages that are higher than in alternative employment. Mandatory increased wages and more stringent labor standards may improve the position of some workers in the affected industries, but it is almost certain to disadvantage other workers not covered by the mandated changes and may induce firms to seek out lower cost production locations.

In our judgment, many of the points raised in the ACIT letter remain valid and have apparently been accepted in the SASL statement. We remain critical, however, of the SASL statement on the grounds that it: (1) glosses over the ways in which the Anti-sweatshop Campaign led by student activists has intimidated the administrations of many academic institutions; (2) apparently accepts the objectives and operation of the WRC; and (3) downplays the possibly detrimental effects of labor-market interventions in low-income countries. The question remains then as to what the most effective ways may be to address the issues of multinational wages and working conditions in developing countries. One way that we favor and will now consider is the provision of voluntary codes of conduct designed to promote the social accountability of multinationals.

Social Accountability of Multinational Firms

Having just reviewed the issues involved in the Anti-Sweatshop Campaign and the efforts of activist organizations and academic institutions in the United States to address these issues, we now focus on the options that multinational firms may choose to pursue on matters of their social accountability. In this connection, it might be argued, with externalities aside, that in a competitive environment all that matters to a firm is profit maximization and, to society, the resultant optimal allocation of resources and increased consumer welfare. In this context, competitive firms need not concern themselves with their social accountability, although questions might arise about the distribution of income. But when there are market failures, including the possible exercise of market power by imperfectly competitive firms, there will be grounds for intervention at the firm or industry level, designed to achieve the social optimum.

Market failures aside, it appears to us that the thrust of the Anti-Sweatshop Campaign and other antiglobalization activities represents an effort primarily to alter the distribution of income between rich and poor countries. Under the circumstances, if there is a desire to reduce international income and related inequalities, the optimal policy is to provide direct income transfers and technical assistance from the rich to the poor countries. Furthermore, maintaining and extending open markets for the imports from developing countries will be similarly beneficial. It will be suboptimal therefore in terms of resource misallocation if multinational firms are mandated or pressured by interest groups to effect income transfers in the guise of higher wages to workers in developing countries. And more seriously, there is the real possibility that such measures will transfer income not from rich countries to poor countries, but only from workers in poor countries to workers in rich countries.

If the preceding reasoning is accepted, it might be argued that the Anti-Sweatshop Campaign aimed at multinationals is misdirected.[22] The evidence to be presented in Section IV below generally bears this out. Nonetheless, multinational firms have come under increased scrutiny by activist organizations for their alleged violations of social norms especially in low-wage, labor-intensive industries. It is essential therefore for multinational firms to devise modes of response to allegations of the mistreatment of workers so as to ward off consumer reactions that may be detrimental to their sales and profitability. This is especially the case for firms whose image in the eyes of consumers is derived from a recognized brand name or private label.

As already mentioned, it has become commonplace especially for large multinationals to devise codes of conduct. Thus, as noted in Moran (2002, Ch. 5, p. 5), the Organization for Economic Cooperation

---

[22] This has led Graham (2000) to entitle his book, *Fighting the Wrong Enemy: Antiglobal Activists and Multinational Enterprises.*

and Development (OECD) had 246 corporate codes in its inventory in the year 2000 covering a variety of industries.[23] This included (p. 7) 37 firms in the textile and apparel industry, 25 of which were U.S. firms. But what should be noted is that a written code of conduct in itself may not be sufficient. What is needed to complement such codes is a monitoring or certification system that is designed to assure code compliance. This is of course what the FLA is intended to do for the apparel industry, and both it and the WRC for university/college suppliers. As we have noted earlier, there are several additional nongovernmental organizations that have been established to carry out monitoring and certification, and there are a number of private monitoring groups as well.

Moran (2002, Ch. 5, p. 9) notes that: "movement toward meeting the prerequisites for credibility and legitimacy [in monitoring and certification] has not been smooth." Some of the issues that have proven troublesome include: circumscribing the availability of information on plant locations on confidentiality grounds; the use of business and auditing firms to conduct inspections; public disclosure of alleged code violations and efforts at remediation; and comprehensiveness of scheduling of monitoring and follow up.[24] It is no doubt too much to expect that a system of monitoring and compliance will be perfect. Nonetheless, as Moran (p. 12) has concluded: "There has ... been considerable movement, albeit contentious movement, toward meeting the conditions needed to create a credible 'voluntary' system for certifying plants that comply with good worker standards and identifying plants that do not."

If this judgment is correct, it suggests that many multinational firms have found it in their interests to devote resources as a kind of

---

[23] See also Varley (1998, pp. 505–594) for the texts of a subset of 46 (out of a total of 121) codes of conduct collected for a variety of multinational firms. The Investor Responsibility Research Center (IRRC) has posted profiles of these 46 firms and eight others on its website (www.irrc.org). We should mention as well UN Secretary-General Kofi Annan's Global Compact, which has been signed onto and endorsed by many multinational firms and a number of labor unions and NGOs.

[24] See Varley (1998, esp. Chs. 11 and 12) for a discussion entitled "Corporations Grapple with Codes of Conduct" and "The Compliance Conundrum."

insurance against the possibility of unfavorable publicity regarding their operations that could prove damaging to them in the eyes of consumers and thereby reduce their sales and profitability.[25] By the same token and apart from the issues of code monitoring and compliance, it should be recognized, as Moran (2002) has stressed in his study *Beyond Sweatshops*, that the improvement of wages and working conditions is an ongoing process as economies evolve, bringing about endogenous changes in the structure and composition of output and conditions of employment, including a movement towards more technologically advanced industries. For this to happen, as already mentioned, it is necessary for governments to adopt domestic policies that will enhance economic efficiency and welfare and thereby provide the basis for improvements in workers' skills and the conditions of work.

The Role of the International Labor Organization (ILO) and the World Trade Organization (WTO)

We have focused thus far on the efforts and issues involving the design of codes of conduct, monitoring, and compliance applicable to multinational firm operations in these countries. These various issues have

[25] Bhagwati (2001) makes the case more strongly in arguing that: "… the truly, indeed the only, compelling reason for corporations to assume social responsibility is that it is the right thing to do. For, in so doing, they will *accelerate* the social good that their economic activities promote, and for which there is now much evidence." Ruggie (2002), who served as an advisor to UN Secretary-General Kofi Annan in helping to develop the Global Compact, notes that the Global Compact is based on a learning approach to induce corporate change rather than a regulatory arrangement involving a legally binding code of conduct with explicit performance criteria and independent monitoring of company compliance. Ruggie notes further that the Global Compact comprises a network form of organization that comprises the UN, business, labor, and civil society organizations. The hope is that the Global Compact will assist companies in internalizing the relevant principles of social policy embodied in the Global Compact and thereby induce the companies to shape their business practices accordingly. Whether or not this objective can be attained, Ruggie concludes, will depend on the viability of the inter-organizational networks being developed.

also been addressed at the multilateral level, and there has been a continuing debate on whether or not, and how, to deal with trade and labor standards in the ILO and WTO.

The crux of the argument is that the ILO is an international organization that was established around 80 years ago for the purpose of improving labor conditions in its member countries. The ILO mandate is carried out by specifying conventions covering a variety of labor issues and conditions of work to which member countries agree to adhere. These conventions include the so-called core labor standards, which cover forced labor, freedom of association, the right of collective bargaining, equal pay for men and women, discrimination in the workplace, the minimum age of employment, and ban on the most egregious types of child labor. These core and other labor standards have been incorporated in various forms into most of the codes of conduct of NGOs, colleges and universities, and multinational firms. The *modus operandi* of the ILO is to monitor member-country compliance with the various conventions, call attention to departures from the conventions, and provide technical and financial assistance for developing countries to help them upgrade their labor standards. The ILO thus functions as a clearing house to provide information on labor issues and as a facilitator to improve labor conditions. It carries out its mandate without the use of or threat of sanctions against noncomplying member countries.

The WTO is an international organization whose main purpose is to design and implement rules governing the conduct of international trade among its member countries. In contrast to the ILO, the WTO does have sanctioning authority that permits member countries to impose trade restrictions in cases in which trading partners are found via the WTO dispute settlement process to be in violation of particular WTO rules. The trade sanctions can remain in place until such time as the violation is corrected by a change in policy. As tariffs have been increasingly reduced in periodic multilateral trade negotiations, there have been efforts to probe more deeply into the domestic nontariff regulatory policies of member countries that may impede trade. It is in this context that proposals have been made to link labor standards and trade, on the grounds that countries with allegedly low labor standards may have an unfair advantage in their trade that is detrimental to their trading partners. In Brown, Deardorff, and Stern (2002), we have explored the pros and cons of linking trade and labor standards in the WTO. In the final analysis, we oppose such linkage on the grounds that it may be subject to capture by protectionist interests in the developed countries and be detrimental therefore to the trade and welfare of developing countries. In our judgment, issues of labor standards should continue to be the responsibility of the ILO.

This concern about protectionist influence relates as well to the Anti-Sweatshop Campaign discussed earlier, especially in view of the support that UNITE and other organizations with a protectionist orientation have provided to activist organizations such as the WRC. Of course, there are many activist organizations that are motivated by concerns over human rights and international inequalities in the distribution of income. In our view, while these concerns are commendable, they are for the most part misdirected against the operations of multinational firms. There is a real danger therefore that well-intentioned efforts to raise the wages and working conditions of workers in developing countries may work to the detriment of these workers and their families. Instead of focusing on codes of conduct, monitoring, and compliance, society would be better served if efforts were directed by activist groups and universities/colleges to the reduction or removal of existing trade barriers and domestic impediments to economic efficiency in both developed and developing countries.

III. Conceptual Considerations

The preceding discussion was designed to focus on the sweatshop and related issues as a specific example of interest to many concerned about the impact of multinational firms on wages and working conditions in developing countries. With this in mind, we now turn our attention more broadly to a review of what economic theory has to say about the effects of FDI and multinational firms on wages and working conditions in host countries. We begin with a brief discussion of the motivations for FDI and multinational firm activity. One lesson of that is that multinationals exist for a variety of reasons and perform a variety of functions, so that we cannot identify them with any single activity whose effects we should explore. Rather, we need to consider them in several roles, each of which may have different implications for wages and working conditions.

We look broadly at four such roles. The first is as a conveyer of additional capital to the host country, either as an addition of the world's capital stock or in place of capital that would otherwise be in the source country. For this purpose we address the question in the context of the general equilibrium models with perfect competition that are familiar in international trade theory. Second, we consider the possibility that FDI carries with it, instead of or in addition to capital, technologies that may be superior to those previously available, technologies that may also "spill over" to domestic workers and/or firms in the host country. Again, FDI as a source of improved technology can be analyzed in the context of perfectly competitive general equilibrium trade models. Third, we acknowledge that, even with unchanged capital and technology, multinational production may involve different sets of production activities than simpler national firms, and we look at how the choice of activities may matter for labor markets. This may happen, for example, within multinationals that use their parent-firm location to provide headquarters support for activities in subsidiaries abroad, or more generally it may involve production processes that are fragmented across countries, even to be done in different unaffiliated firms through subcontracting. Fourth and finally, we note that, because of their size, multinationals may have the power to set prices and/or wages to a degree that perfectly competitive firms could not. We examine several ways that their price-setting behavior could matter for wages, including monopsony pricing of labor, efficiency wages, and rent sharing.

Throughout this section we focus for convenience only on wages, rather than explicitly considering the full package of wages, other compensation, and the hours and working conditions that firms ask of and provide to their workers. In practice, of course, all of these are determined together, either in the competitive interactions of firms and workers, or in negotiation between them. In general, therefore, when we say that an event such as FDI raises or lowers wages, one should think here of the whole package of wages and working conditions as improving or worsening to an extent that is determined by these interactions.[26]

Motivations for FDI

FDI consists of the acquisition of physical capital in another, or "host," country, usually in the form of a production facility or a retail establishment owned at least in part by a parent firm in the home, or "source," country.[27] When done among developed countries, FDI often takes the form of acquisition of an existing facility, but most FDI into developing countries is "greenfield" investment — that is, newly constructed establishments — which therefore add to the physical capital of the host country.[28] Strictly speaking, such capital need not be financed from the home country, and it therefore need not in any sense be a movement of capital from the home country to the host country, although in practice it is often interpreted that way. For our purpose, however, of examining the effects of FDI on the host country, this distinction is not important. What matters is primarily the fact of, and the nature of, the addition to capital in the host country.

FDI also often carries with it a technology that may not have been previously available in the host country. That, as well as the additional

---

[26] Lim (2001, p. 41) notes that "higher wages are usually correlated with better labor standards."

[27] It should be noted that FDI may span a variety of industries, including extractive, manufacturing, and service industries. The literature tends to focus especially on FDI in manufacturing, but our discussion is intended to encompass FDI covering the range of different industries. According to Kucera (2001, p. 17): "As of 1997, 50.1 percent of FDI flows into LDCs went to manufacturing (down from 66.8 percent in 1988), compared to 41.3 percent to services ... and 4.6 percent to the primary sector." The remaining FDI was "unspecified."

[28] See Graham (2000, p. 85). Kucera (2001, p. 4) notes that: "For less developed countries, the value of M&As (mergers and acquisitions) in relation to total FDI inflows increased from about 15 to 30 percent from 1993 to 1999. ..."

possibility that such technology may spread to workers and firms outside the foreign-owned establishment, is something we will consider in a later subsection. To start, we will focus only on the role played in the host country by the additional capital.

To some extent, that role may depend on the motivation for the FDI itself. Broadly speaking, there are two types of FDI: that intended to serve the host-country market and that intended to produce for export.[29] Obviously, there exists some FDI that serves both purposes, but if so, one purpose is usually dominant and the other incidental. The distinction can be important because the firms that engage in FDI usually have alternative means available for achieving either of these objectives, and their choice of FDI is an indication of market conditions that favor FDI over these other means.[30]

In the case of serving the host-country market, the alternatives are to export the product from the home country or, especially in the case of services, to franchise or otherwise license its production by a local firm in the host country. Since the firm's competitive advantage originated with production in its home country, the choice of FDI instead of these alternatives indicates that there must be extra costs associated with them. For exports, these extra costs include transport costs, tariffs, and other trade barriers; for licensing, they include costs of controlling quality or protecting technology. In both cases, FDI is likely to be a higher-cost method of producing the product than the alternative, chosen only because these other costs are even higher. This second-best nature of FDI in such cases may undermine the benefits that one would otherwise expect from freely functioning markets. For example, "tariff-jumping" FDI may involve production that is so inefficient that it lowers the welfare of the host country. Likewise, concerns about control of technology may induce firms to use only outmoded machines for serving a host-country market.

In the case of FDI for export, the alternatives are, first, not to involve the host country at all, producing either at home or in a third

[29] These types of FDI are also frequently referred to, respectively, as "horizontal" and "vertical" FDI, as noted in Kucera (2001, pp. 4–5).

[30] The points made here and in the next two paragraphs draw on Moran (2002).

country; and second, again, the possibility of licensing production to a host-country firm. Here there is no reason to produce in the host country at all unless it can be done for lower cost (or higher quality), so the presumption is that the host country offers an advantage in the form of cheaper and/or higher quality inputs, such as labor or some natural resource. The decision to own the facility rather than to license it could, again, reflect distrust of local firms that outweighs the cost advantage that local firms presumably have due to their familiarity with host-country conditions. However, it may be more likely, since the local market is now less important, that the firm can achieve cost or quality advantages itself by using its own personnel. The result here is a presumption that FDI for export will reduce the cost of providing the product to the home or to the world market, and we would expect this cost reduction to be beneficial, at least from a global perspective.

What is it that allows a multinational to achieve such a cost reduction that a local firm, unaffiliated with the multinational, could not? The answer may only be that the multinational has better access to capital, which is why we start by considering the effects of capital flows on wages. Or the multinational may have a technology that is not available in the developing country, or even outside the multinational itself, as we examine second. But a third possibility is that the multinational produces an input in one country, perhaps the source country location of the parent firm, that contributes to the productivity of other activities that it performs in the host country. One or both of these activities may also have the nature of a public good, expanding productivity of multiple affiliates in multiple countries, but that is not essential for our concern here with effects on host-country labor markets. What is important is that the multinational provides the motivation for locating a fragment of its production activity in the source country, an activity that without the multinational would not be viable. This fragmentation is the third source of cost reduction that we examine below.

Effects of International Capital Flows

The simplest story one can tell about FDI is in a one-sector model. Suppose that all countries produce the same good, using inputs of capital and labor in a neoclassical, constant-returns-to-scale, production function: $X = F(K,L)$, where X is output and K and L are factor inputs of capital and labor respectively. FDI from abroad then increases a host country's capital stock and raises its output. With competitive factor markets paying factors the value of their marginal products, the increased capital stock will raise the marginal product of labor and thus its wage. There is no possibility here of FDI hurting the host country's labor, and if the amount of FDI is large enough to matter at all, it will surely help it. Of course, the flip side of this is in the source country where, if the FDI entails a drop in the capital stock there, the opposite occurs. But that is not our concern here.

One need not go far to find a different theoretical answer, however. In standard Heckscher–Ohlin (HO) trade theory, with two sectors producing two goods in each of two countries, the factor price equalization (FPE) theorem tells us that an increase in the capital stock of a country will leave both factor prices unchanged in either of two circumstances.[31] First, if the host country is small so that any change in its outputs will not affect world prices, then an increase in its capital stock, whatever its source, will leave its factor prices unchanged as long as the country continues to produce both goods. And second, even if the host country is large, if the increase in its capital stock matches an equal decline in the capital of another country, as it would if FDI actually moves capital from place to place, then if that other country also produces both goods both before and after the change, factor prices will again stay the same.

Considering the obvious importance of international trade in the world today, one might think that this two-sector HO model ought easily to be preferred over the one-sector model and that we should forget about FDI affecting wages. But the case just considered is actually very special, and there are many other possibilities within the general HO framework that do not yield this result.

First, the simple specific factors model with mobile labor and two kinds of immobile capital (which can be thought of as a three-factor,

[31] It is this implication of the FPE theorem that causes Leamer and Levinsohn (1995) to rename it the factor-price-insensitivity theorem.

two-good case of the general HO model) has the property that an increase in either capital stock raises the wage even in a small country. Second, with specialization, the HO model behaves much more like the one-sector model, with each country producing a single, albeit different, good. Third, without complete specialization but with multiple "cones of diversification,"[32] a movement of capital from a capital-abundant to a labor-abundant cone will cause prices of goods to change in a way that causes internationally unequal factor prices to move closer together. In this last case, far different on its face from the one-sector model, FDI again causes the wage to rise in the host country and to fall in the source country, with opposite changes in returns to capital.

Perhaps the richest variant of the HO model for use in describing developing countries is a two-factor (capital and labor) model with many cones of diversification. In this model, FDI that raises the capital stock of an initially poor, small country sufficiently will cause it to grow from cone to cone, with the wage remaining constant as it advances within a cone, but then rising as it moves up to the next cone. This sort of progress, which has been explored theoretically by Krueger (1977) and Deardorff (2000) and has been documented empirically by Moran (2002), may offer the best hope for developing countries to escape poverty if they can accumulate capital (or skill, although this is outside these simple models), either on their own or with the help of FDI.

So far we have considered models with only two factors, capital and labor. Equally important is the distinction between skilled and

[32] This refers to the property of HO models with more goods than factors that equilibria can involve FPE for groups of countries whose factor endowments lie within a cone-shaped subset of factor space. If there is only one such cone, then all countries either completely specialize (and are thus outside the cone) or share common factor prices. If there are multiple cones, then countries whose factor endowments are within the same cone (and thus are in that sense similar in their factor endowments) diversify and share a common set of factor prices, but they have different factor prices than countries in another cone. A popular model of trade between developed and developing countries has two such cones, with capital-abundant developed countries in one and capital-scarce developing countries in the other.

unskilled labor, but to address this along with capital flows requires allowing for three factors of production. This opens up more possibilities than we can consider here, and we therefore look only at a single case, but it is one that seems particularly appropriate for today's world.

The model is another variant of the HO model, this one introduced by Feenstra and Hanson (FH) (1996). They assumed a continuum of goods, each produced with capital and a fixed-coefficient aggregate of skilled and unskilled labor. The skill/unskilled intensities varied along the continuum, while the shares of capital versus aggregate labor did not. In their equilibrium, factor endowments differed between their two countries, North and South, sufficiently that factor prices were unequal and each country produced a different range of goods — i.e. they were in different cones. In particular, FH assumed that the return to capital was higher in South than in North, and that the ratio of the skilled wage to the unskilled wage was also higher in South than in North.[33]

FH used this model to derive a result that is very relevant here. When capital moves from North to South, it expands the range of goods that can be produced in South and contracts that range in North. The goods whose production location moves are the least skill-intensive previously produced in North, and they become the most skill-intensive now produced in South. As a result, the average skill intensity of production rises in both countries. This also raises the relative demand for skilled labor in both, causing the skilled wage to rise in both places and the unskilled wage to fall. This is the first sign we get, in theory, of FDI causing a fall in any wage in the host country. It does so because, rather than moving into producing the goods that use the cheapest factor in that less developed country — unskilled labor — FDI instead expands production of relatively skill-intensive products there. As we will see in our look at the empirical evidence below, this is exactly what a great deal of FDI into developing

[33] This is nicely consistent with having both wages realistically lower in South than in North, although FH also allowed international differences in technology that could lead to this result.

countries actually does. Why does it do this? In the FH model it happens because production of the least skill-intensive goods is already, in the initial equilibrium, being done exclusively in the South. In those industries, there is nothing to move. So if capital is going to move to South at all, in order to take advantage of the higher return to capital there, it must produce something else, and more skill-intensive goods are all that are available.

This is an interesting result that strikes us as important, and we will hark back to it frequently later in the paper. However, there is a qualification that Feenstra and Hanson do not mention. Their is a two-country model, with both countries of significant size. We are often concerned, not with a massive flow of capital from the developed to the developing world, but rather with flows into particular developing countries that might better be viewed as small. What effects would FDI have into a small country that is embedded in what is otherwise the FH framework? The answer is that it would not affect relative wages in the small country at all.

The reason is essentially that a small developing country in the FH framework is within the cone of diversification of the South, and its factor prices are constrained by those of the South as well. This is not to say that factor prices will be equalized. The small country will be able to specialize completely in the only one of the continuum of goods that fully employs its skilled and unskilled labor, and thus the FPE theorem does not apply. However, to keep producers from shifting to any other good in the continuum within the cone, the ratio of the skilled wage to the unskilled wage must remain the same as in all of the other countries of the larger South.[34] As a result, as FDI

[34] This can be seen in the FH model by differentiating the (log of the) cost function with respect to the index of the good, z in the FH notation. This derivative depends on the factor prices only through the ratio of the two wages, q_i/w_i. If a small country had a wage ratio differing from that of the larger South at the z that can fully employ its two kinds of labor, then its cost function would cut South's from above or below, and firms would seek to produce only goods of higher or lower z. Labor markets would not both clear.

Table 1. Effect of FDI as capital flow on host-country wage.

Model (sectors × factors)		Small Country[a]	Two-Country Model[b]
One-sector (1 × 2)		+	+
HO (2 × 2) diversified		0	0
HO (2 × 2) specialized		+	+
Specific Factors (2 × 3)		+	+
HO (3+ × 2) two-cone, diversified		0	+
Feenstra–Hanson (∞ × 3)	Skilled labor	+	+
two-cone, diversified	Unskilled labor	+	−

[a] The small country is defined by facing world prices that are fixed independently of what it produces.

[b] In the two-country model, FDI here takes the form of an increase in the capital stock of the host country and an equal decrease in the capital stock of the other country.

expands the capital stock of the small country, wages of both skilled and unskilled labor rise in the same proportion, while the return to capital falls.

All of the theoretical results discussed so far are collected in Table 1, which shows the direction of change in the real wage of labor in the host country due to capital-inflow FDI. Each of the models considered is identified by the number of sectors and factors that it assumes. Also indicated is whether the host country is diversified or specialized into production of a single good and whether, where relevant, the world equilibrium has two cones of diversification. Results are reported for both the case of a small country, which takes prices as given from a much larger world economy of the sort indicated, and for a two-country model. In the latter case, the FDI is assumed to take the form of an increase in the capital stock in the host country together with an equal decline in the capital of the source country.

The results, clearly, are somewhat varied, in that there are several cases where wages do not change and even one where a particular wage — that of unskilled labor — falls. However, most of the cases show labor earning a higher wage as a result of an inflow of FDI, and we regard this as the normal case, in the absence of knowledge that circumstances are otherwise.[35]

Effects of Technology Flows

It is arguably the case that multinationals who engage in FDI possess technologies that others do not, particularly other firms in their host countries. They must, after all, have some sort of advantage in order to overcome the disadvantage of operating in an unfamiliar environment. And if this is the case, then FDI is not fully captured by the simple inflow of capital considered above. Indeed, some FDI may actually involve no addition to a host country's capital stock at all, if the capital already exists and is simply acquired by the multinational through merger or acquisition. In that case, FDI may consist purely of the introduction of an improved technology into the host country.

This is not necessarily technology transfer, if the secrets of the technology remain with the acquiring firm and its source-country personnel. But the technology will still be applied to factors in the host country, and it will increase the output that they produce, even if the advantage would be lost if the firm pulled out. Thus we can model this as an improvement in technology and ask its effects. If technology transfer does take place, willingly on the part of the firm or otherwise, then these effects will be just that much larger and longer lasting.

Graham (2000, Appendix A) argues that an improvement in technology must raise wages. After all, he says, technology raises productivity, and workers are paid their marginal product, which will be larger as a result of the improved technology. However, this ignores the interaction of supply and demand. A competitive industry with an improved technology will expand output and employment until the value of labor's marginal product equals its wage, but this

[35] It is not inevitable that even some labor must gain. For example, in a one-sector model with three factors — labor, capital, and land — if capital is a complement for land and a substitute for labor, a rise in the capital stock could reduce the wage of all labor.

could happen in several ways: by a fall in the price of the good, as output expands relative to demand; by a fall in the marginal product of labor, as employment expands relative to other factors such as capital; and by a rise in the wage, as workers are induced to leave other industries or to give up leisure. Only the third of these mechanisms entails an increase in the wage, and it will not happen at all in some contexts, such as that of FPE. Thus there really is no assurance that an improvement in technology due to FDI will raise the host country wage at all. It will depend on the circumstances, just as did the effect of a capital inflow above.

Consider first a single multinational firm that brings an improved technology into a host country. Will it pay a higher wage than what prevails in the local market? It may, for any of several reasons that we will discuss below, but the increased marginal product of labor is not one of those reasons. If the marginal revenue product of labor is initially higher than the prevailing wage, then the firm will expand its use of labor to the point where this would not be true for an additional unit of labor. But even then it has no reason, on account of the technology alone, to pay more than the market wage. This argument applies as well to larger numbers of firms as long as they do not alter the technology of all firms operating in the sector — a case we consider next. Of course, with more firms expanding employment, the effect on the market wage itself may become significant, the wage rising as labor is pulled up its supply curve, but if this happens it is due to the expanded demand for labor, independently of whether its cause was an improvement in technology.

Suppose next that FDI brings to a host country an improved technology for a whole sector of the economy, either because multinationals themselves take over the whole sector or because spillovers of the technology raise productivity in local firms as well. Like the case of an increased capital stock above, several possibilities arise depending on country size and patterns of specialization. In the simplest case of a one-sector economy, the effect of technology depends on its factor bias. Hicks neutral improvement will raise all factor prices in the same proportion, while improvement that is biased toward use of one factor or another will raise one factor price more than another and

Table 2. Effect of FDI as technology flow on host-country wage.

Model (sectors × factors)	Nature of Technology Change	Effect on Wage
One-sector (1 × 2)	Neutral	+
	Labor using	+
	Labor saving	+ or –
HO (2 × 2) diversified	In labor-intensive sector	+
	In capital-intensive sector	–
HO (3+ × 2) two-cone, diversified	In labor-intensive sector of cone	+
	In capital-intensive sector of cone	–

may even cause one factor price to fall. Thus it is possible, if the new technology is biased strongly enough away from using labor, for it to reduce the wage, although this seems an unlikely outcome.

With multiple sectors, on the other hand, as has been discussed at length in the "trade and wages" literature, the effects of a technological improvement on wages depend on the relative factor intensity of the sector in which it occurs.[36] In a small, two-sector, diversified economy, for example, improvement in the capital-intensive sector will lower the wage, while improvement in the labor-intensive sector will raise it. With more sectors and multiple cones, it is again the factor intensity of the sector where technological change takes place that matters for factor prices, though here it is factor intensity relative to other sectors in the same cone, not relative to all sectors. All of these theoretical results are summarized in Table 2.

Fragmentation

So far we have treated multinationals as providing capital and/or technology to developing countries and then using it within the same industries that already exist, either there or in the source countries. In fact, an increasing amount of multinational firm activity involves changes in the organization of production so that portions of a previously

[36] See Krugman (2000) and the references cited therein.

integrated activity can be done elsewhere. This phenomenon, which has gone under many different names, we will here call "fragmentation." It may take the form of a source-country firm building a subsidiary abroad to perform some of the functions that it once did at home, such as making particular parts for its product or completing particular steps in its production process. Or it may take the form of subcontracting such activities to local firms in the host country, to which it provides detailed specifications and even fragments of its technology. In both cases, this activity may be included in what is often called "outsourcing." And in both cases too, it may or may not be accompanied by an increase in the host-country capital stock or by an improvement in technology. What is distinctive about fragmentation is that a portion of the activity that was previously done in the source country now becomes possible to do in the host country instead. Fragmentation may not require any expansion of the multinational firm's direct operations, and it therefore may not be recorded as FDI, but it is nonetheless the existence of the multinational firm that makes it possible.

By the same token, it is often the potential for fragmentation that makes a multinational firm possible, or at least provides the economies that make multinational firms more efficient than national ones. It is not unusual for some fragments of a firm's activities to serve the needs of multiple other fragments, creating a form of economies of scale. For example, research and development need only be done once for all of the subsidiaries of a multinational firm. Indeed, it is this feature of many multinationals that Markusen (1984) and Helpman (1984) used as the basis for their seminal models of multinationals.[37] For our purposes here, it is what a multinational does and not so much why it does it that is important. Once a fragment of production is located in a host country, it matters little for that country's labor market whether it is there because of multiplant economies or for some other reason.

---

[37] See also references cited in Carr *et al.* (2001) for more extensive modeling of multinational firms based on this assumption.

Fragmentation is both motivated and constrained by the same things that matter for international trade in general. A fragment of a production process will be moved abroad only if it can be done there more cheaply, which means that fragmentation is responsive to the same determinants of comparative advantage as any other trade. In particular, it is likely to occur only if factor prices differ across countries. Even then, it will not occur if the extra costs that are associated with fragmentation outweigh the gain from lower cost of the activity itself. These extra costs may include transportation, communication, and other costs needed to coordinate the activity with what is still being done in the home country.

Both the causes and the effects of fragmentation in general equilibrium have been examined by Deardorff (2001a,b), among others. There is some tendency for fragmentation, like trade more generally, to cause internationally unequal factor prices to move closer together. However, no general conclusion in this regard seems to be possible, and the effects of any particular instance of fragmentation may do this, or its opposite, depending on the factor intensities of the fragments.

Thus, to take a not implausible example similar to the movement of capital studied by Feenstra and Hanson (1996), suppose that an industry has previously functioned entirely within a developed country where the relative wage of skilled labor is relatively low due to its abundance. Now it becomes possible to split off a portion of that production process, one that is less skill-intensive than the industry as a whole. In the absence of factor price equalization, this fragment of production will cost less in the developing country, to which it will now move if the cost savings more than cover any increased cost of transportation, communication, etc. How it will affect factor prices there, however, depends on just how unskilled-labor-intensive it is. If it is more skill-intensive than the average of existing production there — as it may well be, since all activities in the developing country are less skill-intensive than those at home — then it will put upward pressure on the relative wage of skilled labor in the developing country. Since this relative wage was already higher than in the developed country, this particular example of fragmentation may be moving the two countries' factor prices further apart.[38] Of course, this is just one example, and fragmentation could equally well cause an even less skill-intensive fragment to be outsourced, in which case the effect on factor prices would be the reverse. The lesson is only that anything can happen, depending on factor intensities of fragments relative to factor endowments of the country. And there seems to be no reason to expect any one pattern of these factor intensities more than any other.

Imperfect Competition

We have assumed so far that firms engaged in FDI are perfectly competitive in all markets. Since these are multinational firms, large almost by definition, many would undoubtedly question this assumption. In fact we believe that the assumption is not that bad in many cases, since even large, multinational firms face considerable competition, both from others like themselves and from smaller actual and potential entrants. But it is surely worth asking whether market power can cause a firm engaging in FDI to pay wages higher or lower than we would expect from perfect competitors.

Imperfect competition can take many forms, of course, and there probably exist market structures that will yield just about any theoretical result that one wants to get. We won't play that game, but will merely assume that the firms we consider have some market power. That is, they face market prices that depend on the quantities they buy or sell, and we ask how this matters. Formally, our firms are now monopolists or monopsonists, or perhaps monopolistic competitors without our considering effects on entry.

The most obvious place for market power to matter for wages is in the labor market itself. Suppose that FDI creates a monopsonist buyer of labor in the host country. If it faces an upward-sloping supply curve of labor, such a firm will employ less labor and pay lower wages than it would under perfect competition, since it recognizes

[38] What happens to factor prices in the other country depends on the factor intensities of the industry before and after fragmentation occurs, relative to factor endowments there. See Deardorff (2001a).

that the wage needed to elicit an additional unit of labor must be paid to all employees. Does this mean that such FDI actually lowers wages? Probably not, since the labor supply curve reflects whatever residual options the workers have, such as subsistence farming, and without the FDI the wage from these other sources would be no better, and perhaps even lower. However, it is not difficult to construct a scenario in which monopsonist FDI lowers wages. Suppose that prior to the FDI labor was employed by a competitive local industry with a more primitive and therefore low-productivity technology than the multinational's. If the FDI, due to its superior technology, displaces those local firms, and if the resulting monopsonist multinational pays less than workers' (now higher) marginal product because of its market power, then wages might go down. This is only a possibility, of course; wages might just as well rise. It depends on the parameters of the problem.

Monopsony in labor markets is possible, and historically it may even have been quite common. But today's multinationals often tend to be attracted especially to urban areas where they must compete in labor markets with many other firms, so monopsony today is arguably less of a concern.

More obviously, many multinationals appear to have market power in output markets. One thinks immediately of prominent brands like Nike and McDonalds, but they are hardly alone. In fact, a great deal of production by and for multinationals is of inputs that are produced by many competing firms, so we would not regard market power in output markets as the norm. But it surely exists.

Suppose, then, that FDI is undertaken by a multinational firm that is a monopoly as a seller of its product, either to the world market or to the local, host-country market. How will this firm's behavior differ from that of a perfect competitor? The answer, of course, is that it will produce a smaller quantity and charge a higher price than a perfect competitor, meaning that its price will be above its marginal cost of production. On its face, this says nothing about the wages this firm will pay, and in fact, since we have now assumed no market power in the labor market, it will simply pay the market wage.

What is notable, however, is that, unlike a perfect competitor, this firm does not pay a wage that is equal to the value of its labor's marginal product. Instead, its wage is equal to its marginal-revenue product, taking into account that the output of an additional worker would have to be sold on the product market by charging a lower price on all inframarginal units. Put simply, because the monopolist charges a monopoly price for its product, the value of what a worker produces at the margin, valued at the monopoly price, is higher than the wage. Of course there are many reasons why the market price of a Nike shoe is much higher than the cost of the labor that produces it, including payments to many other inputs in both production and distribution, but the fact that the shoe is sold for a monopoly price contributes to this. This does not mean that Nike's market power in the shoe market has permitted it to pay a lower wage to labor. It has not. But it does contribute to the perception that Nike could afford to pay its workers more. And indeed it could, if it were somehow willing or compelled to accept a smaller monopoly profit.

Under the heading of imperfect competition, we should also consider the possibility that labor markets may depart from the perfectly competitive norm on the supply side, rather than (or as well as) on the demand side. That is, labor markets may be unionized, or they might have the potential for being unionized if multinational firms were not present. Here is perhaps the clearest case we can see for FDI and multinational firms to reduce wages, since any market power that workers may be able to acquire by organizing is bound to be diminished if the firms that they bargain with have the option, as multinationals, of producing elsewhere. Unions are in fact notoriously weak in developing countries, and they were already weak, in most cases, before the arrival of multinational firms. But as these countries' incomes rise, it is plausible that unions would gain in strength, and that they would gain faster, other things equal, if multinational firms were not present. Other things would not be equal, however, and without FDI the growth of income that permits the growth of unions might not occur.

The presence of unions matters in another way, however, when it is combined with product-market power by the employers.

Bargaining over wages will result in workers sharing a part of the firm's monopoly profits, as discussed and documented by Katz and Summers (1989).[39] If a multinational has greater profit than a domestic employer, then it may well pay higher wages for this reason, offsetting the effects of its greater bargaining power.

Payment of Above-Market Wages

Except for this last-mentioned possibility of bilateral monopoly involving a multinational and a union, the theories we have considered so far do not allow for or explain a phenomenon that we will see below to be quite common: that multinational firms pay higher wages than do local, host-country firms. To a partial extent, this phenomenon is an artifact of the data. If multinational firms draw on different parts of the labor market than average local firms, then they may pay higher wages just because on average they require different sorts of workers, in terms of education, skill, or location. However, the evidence below will show that multinationals continue to pay higher wages than local firms even after accounting for these effects and several others. Standard competitive models, and even most familiar models of imperfect competition, do not explain this. Nor does the suggestion, often made, that workers are somehow more productive in multinational firms, since as we have seen in looking at the role of technology, this does not provide a valid theoretical reason for firms to pay higher wages than are needed to attract their workers.

Relatively standard explanations for this behavior do exist, however, in the macroeconomic literature on "efficiency wages" that was developed to explain both downward wage rigidity and unemployment. There are several versions of this theory, summarized for example in Yellen (1984), all of them providing reasons why workers will become more productive or efficient as a result of being paid more. That is, in efficiency wage theory, the high wage is not the result of higher productivity, but its cause.

---

[39] See also Budd *et al.* (2002) and references cited therein.

The simplest and apparently oldest version of efficiency wage theory applies best to developing countries, where market wages may be insufficient to sustain workers' health. Firms may therefore pay higher than the market wage in order to improve the health of their workers and thus their productivity. Other versions of the theory depend on somewhat more complex modeling of interactions between firms and workers. They can be summarized by saying that firms pay higher than market wages in order to: (1) reduce shirking (or elicit greater effort); (2) reduce turnover and the costs of retraining; (3) attract and retain the most able and productive workers from a heterogeneous workforce; and (4) improve worker morale in a context where social pressures can make workers more productive.

An alternative explanation for payment of above-market wages is possible in precisely the context that anti-globalization protest is serving to create. In the preceding section, we discussed the Anti-Sweatshop Campaign and other public pressures that have been brought to bear on multinationals for allegedly mistreating their workers. This pressure may well be creating a reluctance on the part of at least the most visible multinationals to be seen providing wages and working conditions that could become a source of embarrassment and lost sales, even when these are at levels generally prevailing in local markets. In response to that pressure, then, they may pay above equilibrium wages even when they do not expect this to improve the productivity of their workers. It is unlikely that much of the empirical evidence for high wages by multinationals could be due to this, since the data mostly predate the anti-globalization movement. However, it is plausible that multinationals may currently be responding to that pressure, and that future studies of wages paid by multinationals will reflect that.

In all of these stories, it is clear that the workers who receive the above-market wages are better off than those who do not (although in the case of efficiency wages this gain may be partially offset by any extra effort that they provide in return). And if FDI expands employment in firms that pay above-market wages, a larger number of workers will enjoy these benefits. However, it is not necessarily clear that all members of the country's labor force are, on average, better off. The efficiency wage models, in particular, were developed in part to help explain unemployment. Indeed it is likely that above-market wages, whatever their cause, will be accompanied by increased unemployment of workers who are waiting and hoping to get these desirable jobs.

Years ago, Harris and Todaro (1970) proposed a model in which a given above-equilibrium wage was paid in the urban sector of an economy, inducing migration from the rural sector and urban unemployment to the point that the expected wage of these migrants equaled the lower rural wage. This expected wage included not only the high wage of employed workers, weighted by the probability of employment, but also the zero wage of the unemployed weighted by the probability of not finding a job. This same model could be applied within an urban sector, where certain firms pay higher than market wages for any of the reasons we have discussed. They too will attract a larger pool of workers than they can employ, workers who will accept either unemployment or lower-than-market wages in return for the chance of eventually getting one of these high paid jobs. Equilibrium workers as a group, both employed and unemployed, are not better off than those who continue to work elsewhere in the economy for the market wage. And of course there is the additional unhappy consequence of greater inequality among workers, some of whom have these high paying jobs and others of whom do not.

In this framework, the market offers potential workers the same expected wage that they can earn somewhere else, far from the high-wage sector. Therefore, simply adding more firms that pay above-market wages may not change that equilibrium expected wage. Instead, although the market looks very different from the usual competitive model, the underlying forces that will change average wages economy-wide will be the same forces of supply and demand that we have discussed earlier.

In the case of efficiency wages, the firms get something in return for their higher wages that they could not necessarily get elsewhere — higher productivity from their employees — and that together with the low market wage, to which the wage premium is added, is what attracts them to produce in these countries in the first place. But when above-market wages are being paid for other reasons, such as pressures from NGOs, enforcement of minimum wage laws, or even fear of government sanctions, the benefit of avoiding public censure may be obtained as well by producing somewhere else, rather than by paying higher wages in poor countries. Whatever may be the level of wages and working conditions that will satisfy a critical public, firms may choose to produce in countries where that level is already the equilibrium due to workers' higher productivity. If so, then an additional effect of the pressure to pay higher wages will be a loss of employment in low-wage countries.

Leamer (1999) has provided an account of wage differentials that differs somewhat from the efficiency wage story, although it too rests on the degree of effort exerted by workers. His model has the advantage of being amenable to general equilibrium analysis. In his model, "effort" determines total factor productivity in a two-sector, two-factor context that is otherwise that of the HO model. Since the return to effort is, in effect, higher in the more capital-intensive sector, equilibrium has that sector paying higher wages and requiring greater effort from its workers than the labor-intensive sector. This model has a long list of striking implications, only one of which need concern us here.

In Leamer's effort model, an increase in a country's capital stock, which could (but need not) be due to FDI, has remarkably different implications in closed and open economies. In a closed economy, increased capital lowers the relative price of the capital-intensive good. This lowers the return to effort and leads to a reduction in effort levels in both sectors. In a small open economy, on the other hand, increased capital may, in one type of equilibrium, leave factor prices and effort levels unchanged, through a variant of FPE. But, in another type of equilibrium, it may lead instead to new production of capital-intensive goods, thus creating higher-effort, higher-wage jobs.

All of the cases we have considered in this theoretical overview — capital flow, technology flow, and fragmentation — have failed to yield unambiguous conclusions about the effects of FDI and multinational firms on equilibrium wages in host countries. Even when we examined reasons for multinationals to pay above-equilibrium wages, there was no assurance that they would do so. There seems to be a presumption, at least in the case of capital flows, that FDI will raise at least some wages, but even this is not certain, and it becomes even less so when we recognize other forms of multinational activity such as fragmentation. It is therefore an empirical question whether the actual operations of multinationals have raised or lowered wages in developing countries. It is to that empirical question that we now turn.

IV. Effects on Wages and Working Conditions: What are the Facts?

In keeping with the broad conceptual focus in the preceding section, we turn now to a review of the empirical evidence on wages and working conditions associated with multinationals.[40] We first consider the effects on wages and thereafter the relationship between FDI and labor rights broadly conceived.

Foreign Ownership and Wages

The published evidence on the effects of foreign ownership on wages in developing countries is based on ad hoc observations and surveys as well as a number of studies using econometric methods.

Lim (2001, pp. 39–40) provides a useful summary of some evidence that foreign-owned and subcontracting firms in manufacturing industries tend to pay higher wages than domestic firms:[41]

- Affiliates of U.S. multinational enterprises pay a wage premium that ranges from 40 percent in high-income countries to 100 percent,

---

[40] In his conference comment, André Sapir suggested that we should have focused more narrowly on the production, trade, wages, and working conditions in the apparel industry and on the respective roles of multinational firms and subcontractors. While Sapir's suggestion is well taken, the approach that we took was designed to provide a broader context for the conceptual and empirical issues involved.

[41] See also Kristof and WuDunn (2000). Much of the available information evidently refers to wages in manufacturing. It would be useful accordingly to obtain information on wages paid by foreign-owned and subcontracting industries in extractive industries such as mining and in service industries in different developing countries.

or double the local average in low-income countries.[42] Graham (2000)

- Workers in foreign-owned and subcontracting apparel and footwear factories in Vietnam rank in the top 20 percent of the population by household expenditure. Glewwe (2000).
- In Nike subcontractor factories in June/July 2000, annual wages were \$670 compared with an average minimum wage of \$134. In Indonesia, annual wages were \$720 compared with an average annual minimum of \$241. Lim (2000).
- In Bangladesh, legal minimum wages in export processing zones are 40 percent higher than the national minimum for unskilled workers, 15 percent higher for semi-skilled workers, and 50 percent higher for skilled workers. Panos (1999).
- In Mexico, firms with between 40 and 80 percent of their total sales going to exports paid wages that were, at the low end, 11 percent higher than the wages of non-export oriented firms; for companies with export sales above 80 percent, wages were between 58 and 67 percent higher. Lukacs (2000).
- In Shanghai, a survey of 48 U.S.-based companies found that respondents paid an average hourly wage of \$5.25, excluding benefits and bonuses, or about \$10,900 per year. At a jointly-owned GM factory in Shanghai, workers earned \$4.59 an hour, including benefits; this is about three times higher than wages for comparable work at a non-U.S. factory in Shanghai. Lukacs (2000).

According to a report on Nike contract factories in Vietnam and Indonesia by students from The Amos Tuck School at Dartmouth College, Calzini *et al.* (1997, p. 2):

- For factory workers living on their own, Nike contract factory wages allow workers to generate discretionary income in excess of basic expenditures such as food, housing, and transportation.

---

[42] It may be noted further, according to OECD (2001, Fig. 8) that compensation per employee of firms under foreign control in the OECD countries was substantially higher than the average for national firms.

- For workers living in extended-family households, Nike contract factory wages are used to augment total household income to raise overall living standards.
- Nike contract factory workers consistently earn wages at or above government-mandated minimum wage levels.
- Given the employment opportunities available, Nike contract factories offer an economically attractive alternative for entry-level workers. Nike contract factory jobs provide workers a consistent stream of income in contrast to common alternatives such as farming or shop-keeping. There are significantly more applicants than factory positions available.
- In Indonesia, non-cash benefits provided help to offset recurring expenses for food, housing, and transportation.
- In Vietnam, overtime wages are perceived by workers to be an attractive means to supplement base income levels.

Moran (2002, Ch. 1, 2) provides extensive evidence on wages and related benefits of FDI and foreign-originated subcontracting in low-skill and low-wage sectors in developing countries as follows:

- The ILO (1998) finds, based on worker surveys, that wages paid in export-processing zones (EPZs) are higher than in the villages from which workers are typically recruited.
- The U.S. Department of Labor (2000) finds that footwear and apparel manufacturers in selected countries pay higher wages and offer better working conditions than those available in agriculture.
- The International Youth Foundation (2002) surveyed three footwear and two apparel factories in Thailand and found that 72 percent regarded their wages as "fair" and 60 percent were able to accumulate savings.
- Bhattacharya (1998) reports that garment workers in Bangladesh earn 25 percent more than the country's average per capita income.
- Razafindrakoto and Roubaud (1995, p. 226) find that EPZ workers in Madagascar earned 15–20 percent more than the average worker in the rest of the economy even after controlling for

education level, extent of professional experience, and tenure in employment.
- Workers in the Philippine EPZ reported themselves to be better off after finding employment in the EPZ during the 1990s. As reported by the World Bank (1999, Appendix C), 47 percent of workers earned enough to have some savings, as compared to 9 percent before employment in the zone. In addition, employees received social security, medical care, paid vacation, sick leave, maternity leave, and other employee benefits.

Let us next consider some econometric-based evidence on the wage effects of multinationals. The earliest evidence grew out of a literature examining the role of FDI in transmitting technology internationally. The impact of FDI on wages was used as an indication that technological know-how raises labor productivity. For example, Aitken, Harrison, and Lipsey (1996) explored the impact of foreign ownership in Mexico, Venezuela and the United States. They found that the presence of foreign ownership significantly raises wages within the plant in all three countries, but the impact spills over into locally-owned plants only in the United States.

For all three countries, manufacturing survey data were analyzed. In the case of Mexico, 2,113 plants were surveyed concerning factor usage, sales, equity ownership, and input and output prices. Data were also available on industry and location. For Venezuela, data were available on foreign ownership, assets, employment, input costs, and location for all plants employing more than 50 workers. The log of the industry/region average wage was regressed on the proportion of employment in foreign-owned firms within the industry-region, a measure of the capital stock, royalty payments, and average output and input prices. Aitken *et al.* found that a 10 percent increase in the share of foreign investment in regional/industry employment raised wages on the order of 2.5 percent in Mexico and Venezuela. However, when the analysis was restricted to domestic-owned firms, the foreign investment variable was insignificant.

The empirical analysis was then performed at the plant level, incorporating information on plant size and age. As with the industry-level analysis, the extent of foreign ownership raised wages of both skilled and unskilled workers, with the impact on skilled workers about 50 percent higher than for unskilled workers. However, as will be seen in the case for Indonesia noted below, about one-third of the wage-premium paid by foreign-owned firms was accounted for by larger plant size.

In order to identify the source of the FDI wage premium, Aitken *et al.* analyzed a cross-section of firms for Venezuela and the United States in 1987 and Mexico in 1990. They took as a point of departure that foreign-owned firms in all three countries paid about 30 percent more than domestic firms for both skilled and unskilled labor. Controlling for industrial sector, they first found that this accounted for a significant portion of the FDI wage premium. That is, foreign firms tended to locate in higher-paying sectors of the economy. For the United States, industry effects accounted for about half of the premium. In Mexico the figure was two-thirds and for Venezuela the figure was one-third. They then considered location. In the case of the United States, foreign-owned firms actually tended to locate in low-wage regions. As a consequence, controlling for region made the FDI wage premium larger. However, foreign affiliates were located in high-wage regions of Venezuela and Mexico. Nevertheless, even after controlling for region, foreign-owned firms paid more than domestic firms. Finally, Aitken *et al.* controlled for plant size and capital intensity. Foreign-owned firms tended to operate larger facilities, giving rise to economies of scale that may raise wages. However, as with location and industry, the foreign ownership variable retained some explanatory power. Unfortunately, Aitken *et al.* did not report regression results in which they controlled simultaneously for industry, location, plant size, and capital intensity. As a consequence, it is not possible to tell whether foreign ownership serves as a proxy for the omitted variables in each equation. Nevertheless, the Aitken *et al.* results support the view that foreign-owned firms pay premium wages.

Further supporting evidence is found by Feenstra and Hanson (1997) in their study of the impact of foreign-owned capital on the skilled-labor wage premium in Mexico for the period 1975–1988.

They found in particular that foreign capital impacts the demand for skilled labor disproportionately. FDI constitutes a significant and growing portion of the capital stock in Mexico. In 1987, FDI accounted for 13.7 percent of total fixed investment in Mexico, a level sufficient to affect the demand for labor. A surge in investment in the border region occurred following liberalization measures enacted by Mexico between 1982 and 1985. Rules prohibiting majority foreign ownership were relaxed, and the average tariffs were lowered from 23.5 to 11.8 percent. In the immediate aftermath, the share of FDI in total investment in Mexico rose nearly six-fold. At the same time, the wages of skilled and unskilled workers began to diverge after nearly 20 years of convergence.

In order to test whether FDI in the maquiladoras contributed to the growing wage disparity in Mexico during the 1980s, Feenstra and Hanson analyzed labor-market census data for nine 2-digit ISIC categories in 32 states for the three periods, 1975–1980, 1980–1985, and 1985–1988. The nonproduction wage bill as a fraction of the total wage bill was regressed on a measure of alternative wages for skilled and unskilled workers, the state's domestic capital stock, and the ratio of maquiladoras in a state to the number of domestically-owned establishments. They found that the fraction of establishments that are foreign-owned significantly raised the relative return to skilled labor. Between 1985 and 1988, FDI accounted for 52.4 percent of the increase in the wage share of nonproduction workers in the border region.

Although Feenstra and Hanson's results are informative, they focus primarily on the impact that foreign ownership has on the demand for labor in local factor markets, thereby providing little evidence on the specific labor practices of multinational firms. The evidence presented above supports the view that multinational firms are improving the lives of at least some workers by raising overall labor demand. However, in order to respond to some of the challenges raised by the issue of sweatshop labor, we might also want to know whether foreign-owned firms play a positive role by altering industry characteristics or by paying above-market wages.

To this end, Lipsey and Sjöholm (2001) analyzed the wages paid by foreign-owned plants in Indonesia.[43] They were specifically interested in whether foreign-owned firms pay more for local workers than do domestic firms and, if so, why. Can the difference be attributed to plant characteristics, worker characteristics, or industry characteristics? Further, do the labor practices of multinationals affect the wages paid by local firms? Lipsey and Sjöholm analyzed survey evidence for all plants in Indonesia that had more than 20 employees. In 1996, 19,911 plant managers responded to the survey, providing data on value-added, energy inputs, location, and labor characteristics for blue-collar and white-collar workers.

Lipsey and Sjöholm used the plant-level data to estimate a standard wage equation. The log of the average plant-level wage was regressed on average education level (as measured by proportion of workers with primary, junior, senior, and university education), plant characteristics including size, proportion of workers that are female, energy inputs, other inputs, and binary variables for foreign ownership, government ownership, sector, and location.

Three separate wage equations were estimated. First, Lipsey and Sjöholm controlled only for ownership and education level. They found that foreign-owned firms paid 33 percent more for blue-collar workers and 70 percent more for white-collar workers than locally owned firms. So the next question was, what is it about foreign-owned firms that produces the premium? When the region and sector dummy variables were added to the regression equation, the premium fell to 25 percent for blue-collar workers and 50 percent more for white-collar workers. Finally, controlling for plant size, energy inputs per worker, other inputs per worker and the proportion of employees that is female, the foreign-ownership premium fell to 12 percent for blue-collar and 22 percent for white-collar workers. So, about one-third of the foreign-ownership premium for labor of a specific quality was accounted for by region and industry, one-third by inputs and

[43] Hill (1990) and Manning (1998) also find that foreign firms pay higher wages than domestic firms in Indonesia.

plant size, leaving one-third of the premium unexplained. Thus, foreign-owned firms are raising wages for blue-collar and white-collar workers above and beyond the impact of increased productivity associated with more inputs per worker and a more efficient scale of production.

Lipsey and Sjöholm suggested several reasons why foreign-owned firms might pay a higher wage for the same quality of labor and in the same industrial setting. One possibility, of course, is that they are responding to social pressure to combat desperately poor working conditions. However, foreign-owned firms may have less knowledge of the local market, want to invest in the skills of their employees, or fear the loss of competitive advantage to locally-owned firms. Alternatively, workers may prefer domestic-owned firms, requiring foreign firms to pay a premium.

Lipsey and Sjöholm also considered whether the presence of FDI raises the wages in domestically-owned plants. They regressed the log of wages in domestically-owned plants on worker, plant, and industry characteristics, but also included a variable indicating the proportion of industry value-added produced in foreign-owned plants. In contrast to the results obtained by Aitken *et al.* in the case of Mexico and Venezuela, the presence of foreign-owned firms in an industry significantly affected the wages paid by domestically-owned firms in Indonesia. This was the case whether industries were defined at the 2-, 3- or 5-digit level.

Given these findings that foreign-owned firms pay higher wages even after controlling for scale, worker quality, industry, age of facility, inputs and industry and regional characteristics, one might wonder whether firms are motivated by humanitarian concerns or public pressure. Similarly, foreign-owned firms could be more likely to conform with laws regulating minimum wages, overtime pay, and benefits. However, if humanitarian concern or public and legal pressure are the motivating factors, we might expect that the impact would be most pronounced for the most poorly paid workers. However, this is not the case. That is, the largest bonus for working with foreign capital apparently accrues to skilled/white-collar workers in the form of higher wages. Thus, while foreign capital may raise wages on average, it may also tend to worsen the distribution of income between skilled and unskilled workers.

Alternatively, it has been suggested (as discussed above) that foreign firms pay premium wages for unobservable characteristics such as intelligence, flexibility or discipline. Employees who reveal these capabilities after they are hired are likely to be retained with higher-than-average compensation.

However, it is important to note first that there is considerable evidence that the FDI wage premium is a consequence of total factor and labor productivity gains associated with foreign ownership. In this connection, a positive correlation between productivity gains and foreign ownership was found by: Aitken and Harrison (1993) for Venezuela; Haddad and Harrison (1993) for Morocco; Harrison (1996) for Cote d'Ivoire; and Luttmer and Oks (1993) for Mexico.

Furthermore, Budd and Slaughter (2000) and Budd, Konings, and Slaughter (2002) present evidence that multinationals share profits with local and foreign workers. They find, in particular, that affiliate wages are positively correlated with parent profits. They argue that such profit sharing is profit-maximizing in a model in which both workers and firms are risk-averse. Profit sharing will also emerge if wages are set in a bargaining framework in which the firm's ability to pay depends positively on profitability.

Foreign Direct Investment and Labor Rights

In addition to the controversy about the effects of multinationals on wages, it is often argued that they are attracted to markets where worker rights are poorly protected. That is, multinationals are alleged to seek out havens safe from union activism, and there is no shortage of governments willing to accommodate the interests of foreign capital. The allegation stems in part from the view that foreign firms have lower labor costs in locations with weak labor protections. Indeed, several studies find that FDI is attracted to regions with low labor cost after controlling for productivity.

Studies of the role of labor costs in foreign investment decisions provide ambiguous evidence, with some studies finding a positive correlation and others a negative correlation. (See for example: Schneider and Frey (1985); Jun and Singh (1997); Wheeler and Mody (1992); Billington (1999); Cooke and Noble (1998); and Head, Ries, and Swenson (1999).) However, these studies all suffer from the weakness that they do not control for labor productivity. As a consequence, studies that find a positive correlation between wages and FDI, without controlling for productivity, suffer from the weakness that wages are probably a proxy for productivity rather than labor costs.

In contrast, Culem (1988), in an analysis of bilateral FDI flows among a selection of industrialized countries between 1969 and 1982, found that FDI was significantly adversely affected by high labor costs once output per worker was introduced as an explanatory variable. Similarly, Friedman, Gerlowski and Silberman (1992) found that the allocation of FDI across individual states in the United States between 1977 and 1988 was significantly affected by the relative labor costs of individual states, after controlling for state-level labor productivity.

However, in a recent survey of managers of transnational corporations reported by Hatem (1997), several other factors were considerably more important than labor cost when selecting a site for FDI. Market size, political and social stability, labor quality, the legal and regulatory environment, and infrastructure were all rated as more important than the cost of labor. Labor rights that promote political stability and enhance labor quality may in fact make a particular location attractive to foreign investors.

For this reason, it is useful to separate the role that worker rights play in raising labor costs relative to labor productivity from those that improve the efficient functioning of a production facility. For example, Head, Ries, and Swenson (1999) found that the unionization rate in a U.S. state lowered the inflow of Japanese investment. Cooke and Noble (1998) found similar adverse effects of unionization in developing countries. However, Friedman, Gerlowski and Silberman (1992) found that Japanese firms were more likely to locate a plant in a U.S. state with a high unionization rate after controlling for wages and productivity. Thus, it seems that, as long as the union does not raise wages above worker productivity, Japanese firms appear to believe that unions play a positive role in the plant.

Of course, worker rights are not limited to collective bargaining. The empirical evidence on worker rights more broadly defined is unambiguous. No matter how worker rights are defined, foreign investors do *not* appear to be attracted to countries with poorly protected worker rights. Similarly, political and social stability have a positive impact on the choices of foreign investors.

Cooke and Noble (1998) found that U.S. outward FDI was positively correlated with the number of ILO conventions ratified. OECD (2000) found that FDI was positively correlated with the right to establish free unions, the right to strike, the right to collective bargaining, and protection of union members. Rodrik (1996) found that U.S. outward FDI between 1982 and 1989 was positively correlated with a Freedom House democracy index but was deterred by a high index of child labor. This was the case even though countries with a high democracy index and a low child-labor index had higher labor costs.

The work on FDI and worker rights has been criticized on two counts. Martin and Maskus (2001) in particular note the problems with relying on ILO conventions ratified and the Freedom House indicators of democracy. Furthermore, the studies listed above did not control for other determinants of FDI. Kucera (2001) has attempted to improve on the existing literature on worker rights and labor costs by using multiple definitions of each type of worker rights.

Following Rodrik, Kucera first regressed the log of wages per employee on value added per employee in manufacturing, GDP per capita, manufacturing share of GDP, the urbanization rate, and multiple measures of freedom of association and collective bargaining, child labor, and gender inequality. Data were for the period 1992–1997 in a sample of 127 countries, including 27 "high income economies" and 100 LDCs. First, like Rodrik (1999), Kucera found that wages were positively correlated with all of the measures of political freedom. Surprisingly, the unionization rate had an insignificant negative impact on wages. However, other measures of free association and collective bargaining rights had a positive impact on wages. These measures may be more meaningful since they are based on observed rights violations. The evidence on child labor and wages was quite curious. First, wages were positively correlated with labor-force participation rates for 10–14 year olds. The coefficient on the secondary non-enrollment rate was also positive. Kucera noted that it is difficult to interpret such results. Finally, in countries where the female proportion of the labor force was higher than average, wages were lower than average. However, this effect was not generally statistically significant.

Kucera then turned to estimate the impact of worker rights on FDI. Each country's share of world FDI inflows was regressed on wages relative to value-added in manufacturing, population, per capita GDP, international trade's share of GDP, exchange rate growth, urbanization, literacy, and the measures of worker rights. He found several very interesting results for the cross-section of all countries as well as for the LDCs separately:

(1) FDI is attracted to countries with a higher civil liberties index even though labor costs are higher. An increase in the civil-liberties index of one unit (on a 10-point scale), controlling for wages, is associated with an 18.5 percent increase in FDI flows. When the negative impact of increased wages in democracies is factored in, a one-unit increase in the civil-liberties index raises FDI inflows by 14.3 percent. So even though democracies pay higher wages for a given level of worker productivity, they still provide an attractive location for foreign investors.
(2) Unionization rates are positively correlated with FDI, controlling for wages relative to labor productivity in equations that also include regional dummies.
(3) FDI is higher in countries with fewer episodes in which rights to free association and collective bargaining are repressed.
(4) FDI is negatively correlated with labor-force participation rates for 10–15 year olds. Otherwise results are mixed and not statistically significant.
(5) Measures of gender discrimination are not statistically significant.

In short, there is no solid evidence that countries with poorly protected worker rights attract FDI. If anything, investors apparently prefer locations in which workers and the public more generally function in a stable political and social environment in which civil liberties are well established and enforced.[44] This evidence is also consistent with FDI causing improvements in worker rights and working conditions. As we noted in our theoretical discussion earlier in the paper, the same forces that may lead multinational firms to pay higher wages are likely in equilibrium to improve working conditions as well.

V. Conclusions

The popular press is rife with anecdotes about foreign workers who labor for multinational firms for low wages and for excruciating long hours under horrific conditions in low-income countries to produce goods for Western consumers. This negative impression that multinationals are exploiting and mistreating their workers is reinforced by calculations that labor costs are typically a tiny fraction of the retail-selling price of the goods being produced, and that the multinationals therefore can and should pay higher wages to their workers.

It is true that, as a theoretical matter, multinationals can have an array of positive and negative impacts on host-country workers. However, as an empirical matter, some anecdotal evidence notwithstanding, there is virtually no careful and systematic evidence

[44] A caveat to this conclusion is that it is based in large measure on cross-section regression analysis and may therefore not apply directly to individual countries such as mainland China, which is a major recipient of FDI even though it may lack the worker protection and civil liberties found in many other developing countries. However, in a separate communication based on the regression residuals in his analysis, Kucera has informed us that: "All in all, the results suggest that China does not receive so much FDI because of its weak FACB [freedom of association and collective bargaining] rights." It should also be mentioned that most empirical studies do not clearly distinguish FDI for export purposes and FDI to serve the host-country market. Further, most studies treat manufacturing in the aggregate and thus lack the sectoral detail of interest, especially for the relatively labor-intensive industries such as apparel and footwear that are the focus of the anti-sweatshop activists.

demonstrating that, as a generality, multinational firms adversely affect their workers, provide incentives to worsen working conditions, pay lower wages than in alternative employment, or repress worker rights. In fact, there is a very large body of empirical evidence indicating that the opposite is the case. Foreign ownership raises wages both by raising labor productivity and expanding the scale of production, and, in the process, improving the conditions of work. Furthermore, there appears to be some evidence that foreign-owned firms make use of aspects of labor organizations and democratic institutions that improve the efficiency characteristics of their factory operations.

It is undoubtedly the case that public pressure can and ought to be brought to bear on some multinational firms and their suppliers who are abusing social norms to the detriment of their workers. But great care needs to be exercised since, generally, measures that are punitive or provide firms an incentive to alter the location of production are unwarranted and may adversely affect the very workers they are intended to benefit.

Study Questions

1. What are "sweatshops"? How are they viewed historically and currently? What is the Fair Labor Association (FLA)? UNITE? USAS? Worker Rights Consortium (WRC)? What are the main features of the FLA and WRC? What is a "living wage," how may it be measured, and what effects may its mandatory imposition have? What are the issues involved in determining the right of association and collective bargaining in low-income countries?
2. What are the positions on "sweatshop" issues of the Academic Consortium on International Trade (ACIT) and the Scholars Against Sweatshop Labor (SASL)?
3. What is meant by the social accountability of multinational firms? Is the Anti-Sweatshop Campaign aimed at multinationals misdirected? How may multinational firms strive for social accountability? What are the meanings of code monitoring and compliance? How feasible and effective are voluntary codes of conduct?

4. What are the objectives and modes of operation of the International Labor Organization (ILO) and the World Trade Organization (WTO)? Should issues of labor standards and trade be the responsibility of the ILO or the WTO?
5. What are the motivations of foreign direct investment (FDI)? How may capital inflow FDI affect the real wages of labor in the host country? What are the effects on real wages in host countries of: technology flows; fragmentation of production (outsourcing); market power (monopoly/monopsony); and payment of above-market or "efficiency" wages?
6. What is the ad hoc evidence on the effects of multinational production on wages in developing countries? The econometric-based evidence?
7. What is the evidence between FDI and labor rights in developing countries?
8. What is the evidence overall on the effects of multinational production on wages and working conditions in developing countries? What are the policy implications involved?
9. What should be the policy of the University of Michigan regarding the production and sale of apparel and related items with the UM logo?

References

Aitken, Brian and Ann Harrison. 1993. "Does Proximity to Foreign Firms Induce Technology Spillovers?" PRD Working Paper (World Bank).

Aitken, Brian, Ann Harrison, and Robert E. Lipsey. 1996. "Wages and Foreign Ownership: A Comparative Study of Mexico, Venezuela, and the United States," *Journal of International Economics* 40, pp. 345–371.

Bhagwati, Jagdish. 2001. "Thinking Responsibly about Social Responsibility," *World Link* (February).

Bhattacharya, Debapriya. 1998. *Export Processing Zones in Bangladesh: Economic Impact and Social Issues.* Geneva: International Labor Office, Working Paper No. 80.

Billington, Nicholas. 1999. "The Location of Foreign Direct Investment: An Empirical Analysis," *Applied Economics* 31, pp. 65–76.

Broad, Robin (ed.). 2002. *Global Backlash: Citizen Initiatives for a Just World Economy.* Boulder and New York: Rowman and Littlefield Publishers, Inc.

Brown, Drusilla K., Alan V. Deardorff, and Robert M. Stern. 2002. "Pros and Cons of Linking Trade and Labor Standards," forthcoming in Douglas R. Nelson, *The Political Economy of Policy Reform.*

Budd, John W., Jozef Konings, and Matthew J. Slaughter. 2002. "International Rent Sharing in Multinational Firms," NBER Working Paper 8809, Cambridge: National Bureau of Economic Research.

Budd, John W. and Matthew J. Slaughter. 2000. "Are Profits Shared Across Borders? Evidence on International Rent Sharing," NBER Working Paper 8014, Cambridge: National Bureau of Economic Research.

Business for Social Responsibility Education Fund, Investor Responsibility Research Center, and Dara O'Rourke. 2000. *Independent University Initiative: Final Report.*

Calzini, Derek, Jake Odden, Jean Tsai, Shawna Huffman, and Steve Tran. 1997. "Survey of Vietnamese and Indonesian Domestic Expenditure Levels, Nike Inc.," *Field Studies in International Business*, The Amos Tuck School, Dartmouth College.

Card, David and Alan Krueger. 1995. *Myth and Measurement: The New Economics of the Minimum Wage.* Princeton: Princeton University Press.

Carr, David L., James R. Markusen, and Keith E. Maskus. 2001. "Estimating the Knowledge-Capital Model of the Multinational Enterprise," *American Economic Review* 91, pp. 693–708.

Connor, Melissa *et al.* 1999. "The Case for Corporate Responsibility: Paying a Living Wage to Maquila Workers in El Salvador," A Study for the National Labor Committee, Program in Economic and Political Development, School of International and Public Affairs, Columbia University. Available at: www.nlcnet.org/elsalvador/sipareport.htm.

Cooke, William and Deborah Noble. 1998. "Industrial Relations Systems and U.S. Foreign Direct Investment Abroad," *British Journal of Industrial Relations* 34, pp. 581–609.

Cooper, Helene. 2001. "Madagascar's Textile Sector Draws Fresh Life from U.S. Trade Move," *The Wall Street Journal* on-line (WSJ.com).

Culem, Claude. 1988. "The Locational Determinants of Direct Investments among Industrialized Countries," *European Economic Review* 32, pp. 885–904.

Deardorff, Alan V. 2000. "Patterns of Trade and Growth Across Cones," *De Economist* 148(June), pp. 141–166.

Deardorff, Alan V. 2001a. "Fragmentation across Cones," in Sven W. Arndt and Henry Kierzkowski (eds.), *Fragmentation: New Production Patterns in the World Economy.* Oxford: Oxford University Press.

Deardorff, Alan V. 2001b. "Fragmentation in Simple Trade Models," *North American Journal of Economics and Finance* 12, pp. 121–137.

Elliott, Kimberly Ann and Richard B. Freeman. 2001. "White Hats or Don Quixotes? Human Rights Vigilantes in the Global Economy," NBER Working Paper 8102 (January).

Feenstra, Robert C. and Gordon H. Hanson. 1996. "Foreign Investment, Outsourcing, and Relative Wages," in Robert C. Feenstra, Gene M. Grossman, and Douglas A. Irwin (eds.), *The Political Economy of Trade Policy: Essays in Honor of Jagdish Bhagwati*. Cambridge, MA: MIT Press.

Feenstra, Robert C. and Gordon H. Hanson. 1997. "Foreign Direct Investment and Relative Wages: Evidence from Mexico's Maquiladoras," *Journal of International Economics* 42, pp. 371–393.

Freeman, Richard B. 1993. "Labor Market Institutions and Policies: Help or Hindrance to Economic Development?" *Proceedings of the World Bank Annual Conference on Development Economics 1993*, pp. 117–144.

Friedman, J., D. Gerlowski and J. Silberman. 1992. "What Attracts Foreign Multinational Corporations? Evidence from Branch Plant Location in the United States," *Journal of Regional Science* 32, pp. 403–418.

Glewwe, Paul. 2000. "Are Foreign-Owned Businesses in Viet Nam Really Sweatshops?" in University of Minnesota Extension Service Newsletter, No. 701 (Summer).

Graham, Edward M. 2000. *Fighting the Wrong Enemy: Antiglobal Activists and Multinational Enterprises*. Washington, D.C.: Institute for International Economics.

Haddad, M. and Ann Harrison. 1993. "Are There Positive Spillovers from Direct Foreign Investment? Evidence from Panel Data for Morocco," *Journal of Development Economics* 42, pp. 51–74.

Harris, John R. and Michael P. Todaro. 1970. "Migration, Unemployment and Development: A Two-Sector Analysis," *American Economic Review* 60, pp. 126–142.

Harrison, Ann. 1996. "Foreign Investment in Three Developing Countries: Determinants and Consequences," in M. Roberts and J. Tybout (eds.), *Industrial Evolution in Developing Countries: Micro Patterns of Turnover, Productivity and Market Structure*. New York: Oxford University Press.

Harvard Magazine. 2001. "Ways and Means: Harvard's Wage Debate," November–December (www.Harvard-magazine.com/on-line/110182.html).

Hatem, Fabrice. 1997. *International Investment: Towards the Year 2001*. United Nations.

Head, C. Keith, John Ries, and Deborah Swenson. 1999. "Attracting Foreign Manufacturing: Investment Promotion and Agglomeration," *Regional Science and Urban Economics* 29, pp. 197–218.

Helpman, Elhanan. 1984. "A Simple Theory of International Trade with Multinational Corporations," *Journal of Political Economy* 92, pp. 451–471.

Hill, Hal. 1990. "Indonesia's Industrial Transformation Part II," *Bulletin of Indonesian Economic Studies* 26, pp. 75–109.

ILO. 1998. *Labor and Social Issues Relating to Export Processing Zones*. Geneva: ILO.

International Youth Foundation. 2002. *Needs Assessment for Workers and Communities*. Research conducted by the Chulalongkorn University Social Research Unit, sponsored by the Global Alliance for Workers and Communities.

Jun, Kwang and Harinder Singh. 1997. "The Determinants of Foreign Direct Investment: New Empirical Evidence," *Transnational Corporations* 5, pp. 67–105.

Katz, Lawrence F. and Lawrence H. Summers. 1989. "Industry Rents: Evidence and Implications," *Brookings Papers on Economic Activity*, in *Brooking Papers on Economic Activity Microeconomics 1989*, C. Winston and W. N. Baily (eds.). Washington, D.C.: Brookings Institution Press, pp. 209–275.

Kristof, Nicholas D. and Sheryl WuDunn. 2000. "Two Cheers for Sweatshops," *The New York Times Magazine* (September 24) (http://www.fordschool.umich.edu/rsie/acit/ProViews.html).

Krueger, Anne O. 1977. *Growth, Distortions, and Patterns of Trade Among Countries.* Princeton Studies in International Finance, No. 40 (Princeton).

Krugman, Paul R. 2000. "Technology, Trade, and Factor Prices," *Journal of International Economics* 50, pp. 51–71.

Kucera, David. 2001. "The Effects of Core Worker's Rights on Labour Costs and Foreign Direct Investment: Evaluating the 'Conventional Wisdom.'" Decent Work Research Programme EP/130/2001, International Labour Organization.

Leamer, Edward E. 1999. "Effort, Wages and the International Division of Labor," *Journal of Political Economy* 107, pp. 1127–1162.

Leamer, Edward E. and James Levinsohn. 1995. "International Trade Theory: The Evidence," in Gene M. Grossman and Kenneth Rogoff (eds.), *Handbook of International Economics*, Vol. III. Amsterdam: North-Holland.

Lim, Linda Y.C. 2000. "My Factory Visits in Southeast Asia and UM Code and Monitoring," September 6 (http://www.fordschool.umich.edu/rsie/acit/ProViews.html).

Lim, Linda Y.C. 2001. *The Globalization Debate: Issues and Challenges.* Geneva: International Labour Organization.

Lipsey, Robert E. and Fredrik Sjöholm. 2001. "Foreign Direct Investment and Wages in Indonesian Manufacturing," NBER Working Paper No. 8299 (May).

Lukacs, Aaron. 2000. *WTO Report Card III: Globalization and Developing Countries*, Trade Briefing Paper. Washington, D.C.: Center for Trade Policy Studies, Cato Institute.

Luttmer, E. and D. Oks. 1993. *Productivity in Mexican Industries.* Washington, D.C.: World Bank.

Manning, Chris. 1998. *Indonesian Labour in Transition: An East Asian Success Story?* Cambridge: Cambridge University Press.

Markusen, James R. 1984. "Multinationals, Multiplant Economies, and the Gains from Trade," *Journal of International Economics* 16, pp. 205–226.

Martin, Will and Keith Maskus. 2001. "The Economics of Core Labor Standards: Implications for Global Trade Policy," *Review of International Economics* 9, pp. 317–328.

Moran, Theodore. 2002. *Beyond Sweatshops: Foreign Direct Investment in Developing Countries.* Washington, D.C.: Brookings Institution, forthcoming.

Neumark, David. 2002. *How Living Wage Laws Affect Low-Wage Workers and Low-Income Families.* San Francisco: Public Policy Institute of California.

OECD. 2000. *International Trade and Core Labour Standards.* Paris: OECD.

OECD. 2001. "Measuring Globalization," in *The Role of Multinationals in OECD Economies*, Vol. I: Manufacturing Sector. Paris: OECD.

Panos. 1999. *Globalization and Employment: New Opportunities, Real Threats.* Panos Briefing No. 33 (May).

Razafindrakoto, Mireille and Francois Roubaud. 1995. "Les Entreprises Franches a Madagascar: Economie d'enclave ou promesse d'une novelle prosperité? Mouvel exclavage ou opportunité pour le developpement du Pays?" *Economie de Madagascar*, No. 2.

Rodrik, Dani. 1996. "Labor Standards in International Trade: Do They Matter and What Do We Do About Them?" in Robert Lawrence, Dani Rodrik, and John Whalley (eds.), *Emerging Agenda for Global Trade: High Stakes for Developing Countries.* Washington, D.C.: Overseas Development Council.

Rodrik, Dani. 1999. "Democracies Pay Higher Wages," *Quarterly Journal of Economics* 114, pp. 707–738.

Ruggie, John Gerard. 2002. "The Theory and Practice of Learning Networks: Corporate Social Responsibility and the Global Compact," *JCC* 5, pp. 27–36.

Schneider, Friedrich and Bruno Frey. 1985. "Economics and Political Determinants of Foreign Direct Investment," *World Development* 13(2), pp. 161–175.

Srinivasan, T. N. 1998. "Trade and Human Rights," in Alan V. Deardorff and Robert M. Stern (eds.), *Constituent Interests and U.S. Trade Policies.* Ann Arbor: University of Michigan Press.

Srinivasan, T. N. 2001. "Living Wage in Poor Countries," manuscript.

The New York Times. 2002. "Mexico is Attracting a Better Class of Factory in Its South," June 29, p. A3.

The Wall Street Journal. 2002. "Newly Aggressive Labor Groups Pressure Corporate Indonesia," August 14, p. A11.

U.S. Department of Labor, Bureau of International Labor Affairs. 2000. *Wages, Benefits, Poverty Line, and Meeting Workers' Needs in the Apparel and Footwear Industries of Selected Countries.* Washington, D.C.

University of Chicago Magazine. 2000. "Student Activists Raise Signs Over Sweatshops," June (http://www.fordschool.umich.edu/rsie/acit/NeuViews.html).

University of Michigan. 2000. *The Final Report of the Advisory Committee on Labor Standards and Human Rights* (May). Available at: www.Fordschool.umich.edu/rsie/ACIT.

Varley, Pamela (ed.). 1998. *The Sweatshop Quandary: Corporate Responsibility on the Global Frontier.* Washington, D.C.: Investor Responsibility Research Center.

Verité. 2000. *Pilot Project for Licensing Labor Code Implementation*, Final Report (October 3).

Verité. 2001. *Comprehensive Factory Evaluation Report.* Prepared by Verité on *Kukdong International Mexico, S.A. de C.V.*, Atlixco, Puebla, Mexico (February 5–7).

Wheeler, David and Ashoka Mody. 1992. "International Investment Location Decisions: The Case of U.S. Firms," *Journal of International Economics* 33, pp. 57–76.

World Bank. 1999. *The Philippines: The Case of Economic Zones.* Washington, D.C.

World Trade Organization. 1998, 2000. *International Trade Statistics 2001.* Geneva.

Yellen, Janet L. 1984. "Efficiency Wage Models of Unemployment," *American Economic Review Papers and Proceedings* 74, pp. 200–205.

Suggested Further Reading

Flanagan, Robert J. 2003. *International Labor Standards: Globalization, Trade and Public Policy.* Stanford: Stanford University Press.

Harrison, Ann E. and Jason Scorse. 2004. "Globalization's Impact on Compliance with Labor Standards," in Susan M. Collins and Dani Rodrik (eds.), *Brookings Trade Forum 2003.* Washington, D.C.: Brookings Institution Press.

Kucera, David. 2002. "Core Labour Standards and Foreign Direct Investment," *International Labour Review* 141(1–2), pp. 31–69.

Kucera, David and Ritash Sarna. 2006. "Trade Union Rights, Democracy, and Exports: A Gravity Model Approach," *Review of International Economics* 14, pp. 859–882.

Lipsey, Robert E. 2004. "Foreign Direct Investment and the Operations of Multinational Firms: Concepts, History and Data," in E. Kwan Choi and James Harrigan (eds.), *Handbook of International Trade*, Volume 1. Oxford: Blackwell.

Chapter 18

U.S. Trade and Other Policy Options and Programs to Deter Foreign Exploitation of Child Labor*

Drusilla K. Brown, Alan V. Deardorff and Robert M. Stern

I. Introduction

The chapter explores issues of child labor exploitation in developing countries and the variety of trade and other policy options and programs that are available to the United States and other major industrialized countries to deter such exploitation. Child labor exploitation is by no means a new issue, but in recent years it has obviously become a highly emotionally charged one. It has evoked considerable discussion and controversy in the United States and elsewhere as labor unions and human rights and other public interest groups have advocated the pursuit of improved labor standards and conditions of work in developing countries. While we have explored the conceptual and policy issues involving international

* Reprinted with permission from *Topics in Empirical International Economics: A Festschrift in Honor of Robert Lipsey*, Magnus Blomström and Linda Goldberg (eds.), University of Chicago Press.

labor standards[1] and trade in a number of previous papers — Brown, Deardorff, and Stern (1996, 1998a,b) and Stern (1997, 1998) — our focus in this paper is more narrowly on child labor. It will be evident in what follows that there are numerous complexities involved in understanding the causes and consequences of child labor and therefore in devising appropriate measures that will effectively and beneficially reduce employment of children.

We begin in Section II with a discussion of the determinants of child labor and selected information on the global, national, and sectoral employment of children. In Section III, we discuss the range of policies and programs used in the United States to help effect a reduction in foreign child labor. With the foregoing as background, we turn in Section IV to conceptual considerations, using a framework that we have developed to analyze the economic determinants of child labor and the expected consequences of alternative measures that are designed to reduce child labor. Conclusions and implications for further research and policy are presented in Section V.

II. Determinants, Magnitudes, and Characteristics of Child Labor

Determinants of Child Labor

It is useful to begin by considering what is meant by child labor. As Grootaert and Kanbur (1995, p. 188) point out, it is by no means obvious how to define a "child." In western societies, chronological age is customarily used. However, in other societies, the concept of a child is not merely a matter of chronological age. Rather, how children are viewed will often be determined by societal factors, including: (1) the level of economic development; (2) the level and composition of social expenditures; (3) cultural considerations; and

[1] So-called core international labor standards, according to OECD (1996, p. 26), include: (1) prohibition of forced labor; (2) freedom of association; (3) the right to organize and bargain collectively; (4) elimination of child labor exploitation; and (5) nondiscrimination in employment.

(4) the phase of demographic transition. Thus, it is common and taken for granted in many developing countries that children may be involved in a variety of work-related activities, ranging from helping out with domestic tasks in the home, working in home enterprises or on farms, or working in wage employment outside the home. Attending school rather than working is of course another option, but this will vary depending on family circumstances and the conditions and availability of schooling.

In considering the potential supply of child labor, Grootaert and Kanbur (1995, p. 191) note that the household will allocate a child's time devoted to different activities depending on such factors as: (1) the size, age, and gender structure of the household; (2) the level and variability of family income in relation to work at home and in the market; (3) income and substitution effects between the labor of the child and parents; (4) parental education; (5) accessibility of schooling; (6) family wealth holdings; and (7) the complex of government economic and social policies that bear upon family decision making. The contribution that children may make to family income will in turn influence decisions on household size, both when children are young and when they may later become the source of support for aging parents.

On the demand side, Grootaert and Kanbur (1995, pp. 192–193) note that the level and flexibility of the wages of adults and children and the degree of monopsony power will influence the employment decisions that firms may make and determine the mix between adult and child labor. The demand for child labor will also depend on the relative importance and the degree of segmentation of the formal and informal sectors in the economy. While children are more likely to be employed in the informal sector, there may be an interaction between the formal and informal sectors as firms decide to break up into smaller units or to subcontract parts of their production to households or informal enterprises in an effort to avoid the costs of conforming to social legislation. In these circumstances, the demand for child labor may increase.

There may be sectors in which children are apprenticed for long periods of time in exchange for benefits that may come later as they are trained and acquire on-the-job experience. The issue of course is whether the apprenticed children will in fact benefit at a later time, or whether instead their employers are simply exploiting them. An extreme form of exploitation occurs when children become the objects of forced or bonded (indentured) labor and can remain subjugated for long periods of time without adequate recompense and with resulting permanent damage to their long-run health and welfare.

The nature of production technology may also condition the demand for child labor according to Grootaert and Kanbur (1995, pp. 195–196) in cases where children may be preferred because of their pliability, small stature, and nimbleness of their fingers (e.g., as in the case of carpet weaving, operation of sewing machines in making clothing, and electronic assembly). By the same token, there have been technological changes that have reduced the demand for child labor, examples being mechanization of spinning and weaving, the green revolution and mechanization of agriculture, expanded use of electrical power, and more efficient equipment for transporting heavy loads.

Child Labor: What are the Facts?

Child labor is a pervasive phenomenon especially in developing countries, but there is a wide range of uncertainty about the actual magnitudes involved. Since child labor is prevalent especially in agriculture and in the informal sectors, it is obviously difficult to design and implement surveys that will guarantee a high degree of accuracy within and across countries. Thus, as reported in Grootaert and Kanbur (1995, pp. 188–189):

> The ILO recently produced statistics on child labour based on a uniform definition — economically active population under the age of 15 (Ashagrie, 1993). That attempt highlighted the difficulties that arise in terms of data availability; a number of sources had to be used, including a set of specially designed questionnaires sent to 200 countries and territories (with an uneven response rate across regions). On the basis of returns from 124 countries, the ILO obtained an acknowledged underestimate of 78.5 million economically active children under 15 years of age in 1990; 70.9 million of them were aged 10–14 (a participation rate of 13.7 percent).

Similarly, UNICEF reports 80 million children aged 10–14 whose work is characterized as "so long or onerous that it interfered with their normal development." However, the total number of working children worldwide is thought to be far greater. The ILO places the figure closer to 100–200 million (Bureau of International Labor Affairs, 1994, p. 2). An even larger estimate of child labor is found when the work of younger children is included. For children aged between 5 and 14, the ILO estimates that 250 million are working, of which 120 million are working full-time (U.S.-DOL, 1998, p. 1).[2]

Child Labor and Poverty

Basu (1998, p. 7) reports cross-country data on participation rates for children, 10–14 years of age, taken from ILO (1996b) for the period from 1990 to 1995, with projections to 2010. In 1995, the regional participation rates were: Africa, 26.2%; Asia, 12.8%; and Latin America & Caribbean, 9.8%; and the participation rates for selected countries were: Brazil, 16.1%; China, 11.6%; Ethiopia, 42.3%; and India, 14.4%. While these participation rates are sizable and perhaps represent understatements, it is especially noteworthy that they have shown marked declines from their 1950 levels which, by region, were: Africa, 38.4%; Asia, 36.1%; and Latin America, 19.4%; and, by country: Brazil, 23.5%; China, 47.8%; Ethiopia, 53.0%; and India, 35.4%. According to Basu (p. 8), this striking decline in child-labor participation rates over these 4½ decades may be attributed to overall economic growth,[3] changes

[2] See Kruse and Mahony (1998) for estimates of children and youth working under conditions that violate U.S. federal and state child labor laws.

[3] Note that there is some risk in relying too much on economic growth to alleviate the financial burden that poverty places on children. That is, countries differ dramatically in terms of the income level at which child labor begins to decline. On the negative side, for example, Turkey continues to have a relatively high labor-force participation rate by children despite a standard of living that is closing in on those achieved by other industrialized countries. In comparison, China has virtually no industrial employment by children. The *one-child* policy has no doubt raised the value of children in the family. Mandatory, publicly funded, high quality education almost certainly has played a role, as well.

in technology, improved labor market conditions for adult workers, and greater availability and accessibility of schooling for children.[4] Basu also points out (pp. 12–13) the widespread use of child labor historically in the industrialized countries in the 18th and first half of the 19th centuries and the decline that occurred thereafter, which was due to the same set of factors just mentioned.

The importance of poverty as a major cause of child labor is formally documented in work by Krueger (1997), who finds a strong negative correlation between per capita income and labor force participation by children. Labor force participation by children under the age of 14 is clearly highest in the world's poorest countries, reaching as high as 49% in Burundi, 45% in Uganda and 42% in Rwanda. By comparison, Krueger finds virtually no children under 14 years of age working in countries in which GDP per capita exceeds $5000.

Child Labor in International Trade

Since issues of foreign child labor are addressed in the United States in the context of trade with developing countries, it is of interest to inquire about the employment of children in the export industries of developing-country U.S. trading partners. Though the United States has made much of the possibility of using trade sanctions to prohibit goods produced by children, it appears to be the case that few child workers can be found in the export sectors. According to the Bureau of International Labor Affairs (1994, p. 2):

> Only a very small percentage of all child workers, probably less than five percent, are employed in export industries in manufacturing and mining.

[4] Inadequate educational opportunities are often cited as a cause of child labor. Pakistan, for example, is one of the few countries targeted with complaints of child labor that does not have publicly-funded or compulsory education. According to Khan (1996), children who work in tanneries in Kasur had a drop-out rate of 63 percent and on average had only one year of schooling. Reasons given by the children for dropping out included physical abuse by teachers, teachers forcing students to do domestic chores at their homes, boring classes and economic reasons. By contrast, the high standards of formal education in China are frequently cited as a primary reason that children are not generally found in the workforce.

> And they are not commonly found in large enterprises; but rather in small and medium-sized firms and in neighborhood and home settings. Those export industries which most commonly employ children include garments, carpets, shoes, small-scale mining, gem-polishing, food-processing, leather tanning, and furniture. In some cases, government policies to promote exports of low-skilled, labor intensive products, such as garments and carpets, may have resulted in an increase in the demand and use of child labor.

Rather, as noted in the Bureau of International Labor Affairs (1994, p. 2), children are usually found in family-based agriculture, in services such as domestic servants, restaurants, and street vending, prostitution, and in small-scale manufacturing such as carpets, garments, and furniture. Due to the informal nature of the type of work usually undertaken by children, their work is not always regulated by national law.[5]

The Working Conditions of Children

In addition to the incidence of child labor, it is worthwhile to consider the conditions under which children work. There is a wealth of information provided by various sources concerning the nature of child labor. For example, the Bureau of International Labor Affairs (1995, pp. 2–5) describes work for children employed in commercial agriculture:

> ... Large numbers of children may be found toiling in the fields and fisheries from daybreak until dusk. Many of these children work for commercial farms and plantations or fishing operations. Plantations, which produce commodities exclusively for export, employ 20 million persons, or 2 percent of the persons working in the agricultural sector in developing countries. Children make up an estimated 7 to 12 percent of the work force on plantations. ... Among the products produced by children are cocoa, coffee,

---

[5] Selected sectoral estimates of child labor for Africa and Asia based on micro-data collection undertaken to study household behavior are reported in Grootaert and Kanbur (1995, p. 190). These data indicate labor force participation rates ranging from 20–60 percent, depending on the age and gender of the children and the type of work performed.

coconuts, cotton, fruit and vegetables, jasmine, palm oil, rubber, sisal, sugar cane, tea, tobacco, and vanilla. Children also dive for fish, work on fishing platforms and boats, and work in factories that process fish. ... The great majority of children in agriculture work as part of a family unit. ... Workdays can be extremely long. ... Children in agriculture face many safety and health risks. ... Regular exposure to dangerous chemical fertilizers and pesticides poses another threat to children.

Children delivered into bonded labor for the purposes of intergenerational debt servitude perhaps suffer most of all. Human Rights Watch (1996, p. 54) has documented bonded child labor in the Indian footwear industry. They estimate that between 2,000 and 20,000 bonded child laborers as young as 6 or 7 years old are trafficked from the rural villages of Rajasthan to Mumbai annually. Further, Human Rights Watch (1996, pp. 104–105) estimates that 10 to 20 percent of child laborers in the Indian hand-knotted carpet industry are bonded workers. Generally, these children are trafficked from Bihar or Nepal. A similar situation exists in Nepal. Brokers, known as *naikes*, offer rural families loans in exchange for their children. The children are then sent to Kathmandu to discharge the families' debts by working in carpet factories.

Intergenerational servitude is clearly a form of child labor that is most easily characterized as *exploitative*. Children are removed from the home, have their housing and food provided by the employer and earn little or nothing for their work. Wages are remitted back to the families either in the form of a lump-sum payment when the child is taken or paid as earned. As a consequence, it is necessarily the case that the standard of living enjoyed by the child falls short of the child's total earnings. Thus, on balance, the child is subsidizing the living standard of his or her family.

Furthermore, working conditions for bonded child laborers can be quite horrific. The Bureau of International Labor Affairs (1995, pp. 2–5) reports that

... Forced and bonded child labor can be found in all sectors of the economy. Bonded children working in the carpet industries of India, Pakistan, and Nepal may work up to 20 hours a day. They often sleep, eat and work in the same small, damp room, and are sometimes locked in at

> night. ... Many of the children suffer from skin ailments, chronic colds, respiratory problems, spine deformities, and weakened eyesight. ... In the jungle of south-eastern Peru, children recruited by contractors to work for nine months in gold mines find they must continue to work well beyond that period to pay [what] ... they owe the contractors. ... The forced labor of children occurs in the fishing industries of Indonesia, Sri Lanka, the Philippines, India, and Pakistan. ... Forced child labor is also widespread in the informal service sector, particularly in the employment of child domestic servants and in the sex industry. ... A different form of child labor in the service sector is the use of young boys, usually kidnapped from southern Asia, as camel jockeys in Persian Gulf States.

Similarly, Human Rights Watch (1996, pp. 104, 109) documents cases in the Indian hand-knotted carpet industry in which children are "forced to work long hours ... for no wages or nominal wages ... some being ill-treated, beaten, tortured, abused, branded, and kept half-fed, half-clad." Children working with sharp instruments frequently cut themselves. The wounds may be treated by "...putting sulphur from match heads into the cuts and then lighting them on fire, thereby sealing the wound" and avoiding infection. As adults, these former child workers suffer from badly damaged hands and eyes and stunted growth.

III. Policies and Programs for Reducing Foreign Child Labor

Having discussed the determinants, magnitudes, and characteristics of child labor, we now consider the policies and programs used in the United States to deter the foreign employment and exploitation of child labor. These include: (1) U.S. trade policies; (2) economic and technical assistance provided though the ILO; (3) supra-national measures; (4) codes of conduct for U.S. firms engaged in foreign production; and (5) consumer labeling. We discuss briefly each of the foregoing.

U.S. Trade Policies

As indicated above, elimination of child labor exploitation is considered to be a core international labor standard, the others being:

prohibition of forced labor; freedom of association; the right to organize and bargain collectively; and nondiscrimination in employment. For some time, the United States has had in effect a number of policies and programs designed to achieve these core standards and other standards that bear upon conditions of work. These are summarized in Table 1. The most recent measure is one sponsored by Congressman Sanders (I, VT) in October 1997 as a rider to the Fiscal Year 1998 Treasury Appropriations Act, which was approved by voice vote in Congress and signed by President Clinton. Section 1307 of the U.S. Tariff Act of 1930 provides authority for the U.S. Customs Service to prohibit "...importation of products made, in whole or in part, with use of convict, forced, or indentured labor under penal sanctions." The Sanders Amendment makes it "...explicit that merchandise manufactured with 'forced or indentured child labor' falls within the prohibition of this statute."[6] With funding made available by the Congress, the U.S. Customs Service is currently involved in devising and implementing monitoring and inspection procedures to take action to ban imports embodying forced child labor in response to complaints that are filed.[7]

The United States also uses preferential tariff treatment of exports to induce developing country trade partners to reduce child labor under the U.S. Generalized System of Preferences (GSP). Since 1984, the GSP program specifies a number of labor rights violations that might be cause for suspension of GSP. Evidence of a change in policies is a condition for the preferences to be reinstated.[8]

---

[6] For further details, see: <http://www.customs.ustreas.gov/enforce, childfi2.htm>. See also the *Journal of Commerce*, October 14, 1997, NEWS, p. 1A, "Customs walks tightrope on new child labor law."

[7] According to the *New York Times*, November 6, 1997, p. 12, "Ban Sought on South Asian Rugs in Campaign Against Child Labor," the International Labor Rights Fund filed a complaint to ban imports of South Asian carpets under the provisions of the Sanders Amendment. This complaint is presently under investigation by the Customs Service. See also *The Wall Street Journal*, September 9, 1998, p. A1, "Citrus Squeeze: U.S. Child Labor Law Sparks a Trade Debate over Brazilian Oranges."

[8] Further details can be found in Brown, Deardorff, and Stern (1996, pp. 234–236).

Table 1. Evolution of labor standards in U.S. trade policy legislation.

Year	Act	Labor Standards Provisions
1890	McKinley Act	Prohibited imports made by convict labor
1930	Tariff Act, Section 1307	Prohibited imports of goods made by convict labor, forced labor, or indentured labor under penal sanction
1933	National Industrial Recovery Act (judged unconstitutional by U.S. Supreme Court in 1935)	Imports permitted only if produced according to U.S. domestic fair labor standards, including the right to organize and bargain collectively, limits on maximum hours of work, and minimum wages
1974	Trade Act	Directed the President to seek the adoption of fair labor standards in the Tokyo Round of GATT negotiations
1983	Caribbean Basin Economic Recovery Act	Criteria for eligibility as a beneficiary country extended to include the degree to which workers are afforded reasonable workplace conditions and enjoy the right to organize and bargain collectively
1984	Generalized System of Preferences Renewal Act	Criteria for eligibility as a beneficiary country extended to include whether or not the country has taken, or is taking, steps to afford its workers internationally recognized worker rights defined as including freedom of association, the right to organize and bargain collectively, freedom from forced labor, minimum age for the employment of children, and acceptable conditions of work with respect to wages, hours of work and occupational safety and health
1985	Overseas Private Investment Corporation Amendments Act	The Corporation is to insure, reinsure, guarantee or finance a project in a country only if the country is taking steps to adopt and implement internationally recognized worker rights as defined for GSP purposes above

(*Continued*)

Table 1. (*Continued*)

Year	Act	Labor Standards Provisions
1986	Anti-Apartheid Act	Made it incumbent on U.S. firms employing more than 25 persons in South Africa to follow a Code of Conduct that includes fair labor standards
1987	U.S. participation in Multilateral Investment and Guarantee Agency of World Bank	Made U.S. participation conditional on countries affording internationally recognized worker rights to their workers
1988	Trade Act (Omnibus Trade and Competitiveness Act)	Made the systematic denial of internationally recognized worker rights (as defined above) by foreign governments an unfair trade practice and liable for U.S. countermeasures where such denials cause a burden or restriction on U.S. commerce
1997	Sanders Amendment to 1930 Tariff Act, Section 1307	Merchandise manufactured with forced or indentured child labor falls within the prohibition of this statute

Source: Adapted in part from Alam (1992, p. 25).

Economic and Technical Assistance Provided Through the ILO

The United States provides a significant amount of economic and technical assistance to developing countries through its bilateral foreign aid programs and its contributions to multilateral institutions. But for our purposes here, we wish to call attention to the U.S. assistance to address issues of child labor that is channeled through the ILO. Thus, as noted in U.S.-DOL (1998), President Clinton proposed in his Fiscal Year 1999 budget:

> … a new initiative to fight abusive child labor. The initiative builds on the administration's record of reporting on child labor, aiding the private sector in the development of codes of conduct and labeling efforts, pressing successfully for a greater ILO focus on exploitative child labor, leveraging change in the domestic garment industry though the use of 'hot

> goods' [sic] laws, and using U.S. laws to suspend trade benefits in response to persistent exploitative child labor practices.

What is especially noteworthy in particular is the U.S. assistance provided to the ILO International Programme for the Elimination of Child Labor (IPEC)[9]:

> The President's FY 99 ... budget proposes that the U.S. contribute a total of $30 million — *a 10-fold increase* — to IPEC in support of programs aimed at reducing the most intolerable forms of child labor — forced or indentured work, work by very young children, and work in the most hazardous occupations. The U.S. funds will support multi-dimensional programs including key elements such as in-country ownership, innovative partnerships between governments, workers, and NGOs, development of reasonable educational alternatives, monitoring, creative use of media, and documentation.

U.S. contributions/pledges to IPEC as of March 1998 are indicated in Table 2. The total U.S. assistance of $8.1 million contributed to IPEC since its inception in 1992 will be increased significantly by the funds appropriated in the FY 99 U.S. budget. There are presently 20 donor countries providing IPEC support to 29 developing countries, with an additional 24 developing countries preparing to participate. The U.S.-supported IPEC programs noted in Table 2 evidently address many different aspects of child labor. As noted in U.S.-DOL (p. 3), this range of programs: "...suggests that interventions need to be made on all fronts and that no single type of intervention is sufficient in itself. It is exactly this type of broad based multi-sectoral action that ILO-IPEC is promoting." It is also noteworthy that IPEC strives to involve trade unions and NGOs in its programmatic activities. Thus (p. 6): "In recent years, a broad social alliance involving governments, NGOs, workers, and employers' organizations, media, academic institutions and various other actors has emerged in many

[9] IPEC (ILO, 1996a) identifies three conditions that characterize "intolerable" child labor: children working under forced labor conditions and in bondage; children in hazardous working conditions and occupations; and very young children under the age of 12.

Table 2. U.S. contributions/pledges to IPEC as of March 1998.

Country	Program	Amount	Comments
Bangladesh	Project to phase children out of garment factories and place them in schools	\$867,273	Approx. 10,000 children have been phased out of factories and placed in 315 schools
	Phase 2 of project: funding for continuation of monitoring and verifications project	\$840,779	Monitoring continues
Philippines	Statistical survey on child labor in the Philippines	\$268,465	Completed
Africa	Regional workshop on child labor in commercial agriculture	\$170,381	Completed
	Protection of children from hazardous work in plantations in selected countries in Africa (pledged)	\$1,000,000	Project proposal underway
	Fund Uganda participation in IPEC (pledged)	\$1,500,000 over 3 years	
Brazil	Combating child labor in the shoe industry of Vale dos Sinos	\$308,958	Ongoing
Thailand	1) Northern program to prevent children from being lured into exploitative child labor and prostitution (Phase I)	\$484,923	Completed
	2) Phase II of program above	\$261,070	Project underway
Pakistan	Soccer Balls: Phasing children out of soccer ball industry; providing educational opportunities; internal and external monitoring	\$755,744	Project underway

(*Continued*)

Table 2. (*Continued*)

Country	Program	Amount	Comments
Nepal	Elimination of girls' trafficking and commercial sexual exploitation of children. This includes children trafficked into India	$192,809	Project underway
Central America	Combating child labor in selected Central American countries (specifics TBD) (pledged)	$1,000,000	Awaiting project proposal

Source: U.S.-DOL (1998).

countries — often as [a] result of the catalytic and facilitating role IPEC has played."

Supra-National Measures

It should be clear from the preceding discussion that the ILO is the main international organization that is concerned with labor standards. Established in 1919, the methods and principles set out in the ILO constitution deal with all conceivable aspects of labor standards. In particular, the ILO is primarily concerned with: (1) the definition of worker rights, especially through the adoption of ILO Conventions and Recommendations[10]; (2) measures to secure the realization of worker rights, especially by means of international monitoring and

[10] It is interesting that formal ratification of ILO Conventions differs considerably among ILO members, apparently because particular conventions may be at variance with national laws and institutional practices. Thus, for example, as Rodrik (1996, pp. 15–16) notes, the United States has ratified only 11 of the 176 ILO Conventions, whereas several other industrialized and developing countries have ratified a significantly larger number. Ratification of ILO Conventions may therefore not be an accurate indicator of existing national regulations governing labor standards, and there are many cases in which ratified Conventions are in fact not enforced.

supervision, but not by imposition of trade sanctions; and (3) assistance in implementing measures, especially through technical cooperation and advisory services.

Since the establishment of the GATT following World War II, the United States has attempted unsuccessfully on several occasions, most recently in the Uruguay Round, to place labor standards on the multilateral negotiating agenda. When the Uruguay Round accords were signed in April 1994, the United States put the international community on notice that it intended to pursue issues of labor standards in future multilateral negotiations. Subsequently, efforts were made to develop a so-called social clause dealing with core labor standards that would be monitored by the ILO and that included trade sanctions for noncompliance that might be incorporated into the newly created World Trade Organization (WTO). The United States, with support from some members of the European Union, Canada, and Japan, sought to add this issue to the agenda of the WTO Ministerial Meeting held in Singapore in December 1996. As a result, there was considerable debate and controversy at the Singapore Ministerial over whether labor standards should be brought under WTO auspices. But, in the end, this was not done. As reported in *The Financial Times*, December 16, 1996, p. 4:

> ... hardest to resolve was the issue of labour standards, where the U.S. threatened to veto the entire declaration if no mention was made. Ministers eventually agreed to uphold internationally recognised core labor standards. ... But trade sanctions to enforce them were rejected and there is no provision to follow-up such work in the WTO, which is asked simply to maintain its (minimal) collaboration with the International Labour Organization.[11]

---

[11] In considering whether or not the WTO is an appropriate forum for dealing with trade and alleged violations of core labor standards, it is pertinent to note the conclusion reached in OECD (1996, pp. 16–17):

> Existing WTO provisions have not been designed for promoting core standards. Some of the suggestions under discussion would imply a reinterpretation of WTO practices and procedures while others would require to a greater or lesser extent renegotiation and amendment of WTO articles. ... a consensus among WTO Members on the appropriateness and effectiveness of using WTO procedures to promote core labour standards and on the institutional changes required would have to be reached. Such a consensus does not exist at present.

In the U.S. Congress, the Republicans have been opposed to linking labor standards and trade. The Clinton Administration made an effort in the fall of 1997 to induce Republicans to approve fast-track negotiating authority by downplaying its support for including labor standards in future trade agreements. However, organized labor, environmental interest groups, and labor and human rights public interest groups mounted an intensive campaign to oppose fast-track unless the legislation included protection of labor rights and the environment. When it became clear in mid-November 1997 that there were insufficient Democratic votes to obtain fast-track approval in the House of Representatives, the legislation was withdrawn. Fast-track legislation was re-introduced in the fall of 1998 and again failed to pass. The link between trade and labor standards thus remains a highly visible and controversial issue of public discourse on future trade legislation.

On a global level, it seems evident that the ILO has been ceded responsibility for dealing with issues of international labor standards. With regard to child labor, as noted above, the United States has greatly increased its support for the ILO's International Programme for the Elimination of Child Labor (IPEC). In our judgment, it would be desirable for the United States to enlarge further its financial and technical support for the ILO and to encourage efforts to increase the effectiveness of the ILO's role in monitoring and bringing about improvements in labor standards.[12]

Codes of Conduct

On the domestic side, the Clinton Administration has sought to work with U.S. firms to develop codes of conduct that would limit imports

[12] See Brown (1998) for a transactions cost politics analysis of the handling of child labor issues as between the ILO and the WTO and a conclusion that supports giving the ILO sole authority and responsibility for dealing with child labor and other labor standards. In contrast, Bagwell and Staiger (1998) provide an analytical structure in which they develop a negotiating strategy designed to accommodate national sovereignty over labor standards in a context that resembles the negotiating procedures spelled out in the GATT/WTO. They do not address the question of which of the two international organizations may be best suited to deal with labor standards.

of goods produced by children as a matter of corporate policy. As noted by the Bureau of International Labor Affairs (1996, p. 12):

> Corporate codes of conduct are policy statements that define ethical standards for companies. Corporations voluntarily develop such codes to inform consumers about the principles that they follow in the production of goods and services they manufacture or sell. Corporate codes of conduct usually address many workplace issues — including child labor — and, according to some observers are part of a broader movement toward corporate social responsibility.

Codes of conduct have become more widespread in recent years, especially in the apparel industry. However, how meaningful and effective codes of conduct will be depends above all on their credibility. Of particular importance are: (1) the transparency of the codes of conduct; (2) monitoring; and (3) enforcement (pp. 9–10):

> First, codes of conduct cannot be effectively implemented without transparency. It is critical that all actors affected by a code — buying agents, contractors, subcontractors, union representatives and the workers themselves — be aware of its provisions. Research conducted for this report suggests that codes of conduct in the headquarters of U.S. apparel importers are not necessarily well known in the overseas facilities that produce their goods.
>
> Second, while a credible system of monitoring — to verify that a code is indeed being followed in practice — is essential, there is no agreement on the best way to conduct monitoring. Some companies only monitor their largest contractors or contractors that produce private-label merchandise for them and rely on buyer agents or self-monitoring for other facilities. Several methods of monitoring are currently being used and developed, including monitoring by outside auditors and local and international NGOs. The most effective type of monitoring may vary according to the characteristics of the importing company, such as whether it has a strong presence abroad or whether it is vertically integrated. It appears that the closer a company is to the production, the more leverage it has to ensure that the conditions of manufacturing facilities comply with its policies. There also appears to be some dispute among retailers, manufacturers, overseas contractors and other parties as to who has the ultimate responsibility for monitoring.

> Third, the issue of enforcement presents some complex issues. If a company discovers child workers in a facility, the quickest and perhaps easiest way to resolve the problem is to require their immediate dismissal. A small number of companies have strived to come up with more comprehensive solutions to the problem — such as providing financial support for the education of the children.[13]

It is evident from the foregoing that many difficulties may arise in designing and implementing codes of conduct. For the reasons mentioned above, firms in industries like apparel that rely importantly on foreign production may have a strong incentive to articulate and carry out codes of conduct. By doing so, the firms can reassure consumers that they are seriously making efforts to upgrade foreign labor standards and working conditions for both adults and children.[14]

Consumer Labeling

Several American and European importers have recently attempted to go beyond a corporate code of conduct to communicate standards of

[13] Programs intended to subsidize educational expenses by the family can sometimes have disappointing results. For example, the Carpet Export Promotion Council (CEPC) is a quasi-governmental body which oversees the mandatory registration of all Indian carpet exporters and issues export licenses. Since 1995 the CEPC has been providing funding for twelve schools, two of which are part of Project Mala in the village of Amoi. The program provides children with three years of non-formal vocational education, medical check-ups, a mid-day meal, and a $2.90 monthly stipend. However, it was found that the stipend was used by the family to retire debt rather than for the intended purpose of furthering the child's education. The monthly stipend was replaced with a contribution to a special account that could be used by the student at the end of the three-year program only for specified purposes.

[14] According to the *New York Times*, April 9, 1997, p. A11, "Apparel Industry Group Moves to End Sweatshops: Agreement to Bring Worldwide Inspection," a Presidential task force comprising human rights groups, labor unions, and apparel industry giants reached an agreement that seeks to end sweatshops by means of a code of conduct on wages and working conditions for foreign apparel factories that American companies use. Subsequently, it turned out that it was not possible for all parties concerned to reach agreement on the link between wages and the basic needs of workers. For this reason, some of the participating labor unions and labor rights groups declined to support the agreement.

employment to consumers. Many firms have adopted the strategy of labeling products with statements that are intended to give the impression that child labor was not employed during production.

Product labeling as a strategy for improving labor market conditions has a century-long history in the United States. The length of the work day and working conditions for women and children were targets of labeling efforts toward the end of the 19th century. Product labeling as a market-based avenue in which consumers could express their views on desirable labor market conditions subsequently received analytical support from Freeman (1994).

Product labeling intended to combat illegal child labor began in earnest in the 1990s. A brief summary of existing programs in hand-knotted carpets, footwear and soccer balls is provided in Table 3. A thorough description of each program can be found in the Bureau of International Labor Affairs (1997). The programs differ dramatically in their structure, underlying philosophy and objective. However, all state either on the product label or in the program's literature that the objective is to produce goods that are not manufactured with illegal child labor.

Rugmark is one of the most widely publicized and rigorous of the product labeling programs. Like most labeling programs, the founders include a combination of governmental agencies, international agencies, human rights activists, labor activists and industry interests in both the importing and exporting countries. Initial funding for the program in India was provided by the German Development Agency. The program in Nepal has received funding from UNICEF and the German Development Agency as well as from the Asian American Free Labor Institute which is now part of the AFL-CIO's American Center for International Labor Solidarity.

Rugmark's primary goals are to eliminate child labor in the carpet industry and to rehabilitate former child weavers. However, *Rugmark* is distinguished by its rigorous licensing and monitoring procedures. A license applicant must submit a list of all looms and their locations on which carpets are produced. The number of looms is compared to the applicant's production level as a device for ensuring that all of the applicant's looms are identified. *Rugmark* agents

Table 3. Product labeling programs claiming nonuse of illegal child labor.

Program	Country	Year	Fees	Monitoring	Child Development	Label	Penalty
Hand-Knotted Carpets							
Rugmark (private)	India Nepal Pakistan	1994 1995 in process	Importers: 1–1.75%, Exporters: 0.25% of carpet value	Licensing, random inspection, carpet tracking, loom registration	5 schools for weavers' children and former child weavers funded from importer fees	On carpet	License revoked after second violation
Kaleen (quasi-gov't)	India	1995	Exporters: 0.25% of carpet value	Registration of carpet and looms, random inspection	Contributes to fund 12 schools in rugmaking region	On carpet	License revoked after third violation
STEP (Swiss industry group)	India Nepal Pakistan	1995	Importers: $2.40 per square meter	None, few site visits	Support to child care center, health ed., two schools	Retailer display	Deregistered after one violation
Care and Fair (German industry group)	India Nepal Pakistan	1994	Importers: $125 + 1% of carpet value, Exporters: 0.25% of carpet value	Self-monitoring	Support to 35 projects in India and Nepal, one school in Pakistan	Retailer display	Placed on list of noncompliant firms
Jackciss (carpet weaving collective)	Pakistan	1987		Supervisors inspect	Builds or contributes to schools where non-existent	On carpet	

(*Continued*)

Table 3. (*Continued*)

Program	Country	Year	Fees	Monitoring	Child Development	Label	Penalty
Leather Footwear							
Abrinq Foundation (non-profit)	Brazil	1990	None	Commitment letter, background check, self-monitoring	Individual members undertake child devel. projects	On product, retailer display	30-day period to correct followed by decertification
Pro-Child Institute (non-profit)	Brazil	1995	\$50–\$200/ month	Commitment letter, self-monitoring		On shoes	30 days to correct violation followed by decertification
Soccer Balls							
Reebok (firm)	Pakistan	1996		Centralized production in one facility, guarded entrance and exit, external monitoring by human rights activist	Educational project targeting displaced child workers	On balls	

(*Continued*)

Table 3. (*Continued*)

Program	Country	Year	Fees	Monitoring	Child Development	Label	Penalty
Baden Sports (firm)	China Pakistan	1977		Centralized production, automation, switch production from Pakistan to China		On balls	
Dunkin' Donuts (firm)	Pakistan			Detailed records on sites and workers, random inspection by labor rights activists		On balls	
Seneca (firm)	Pakistan			Centralized production facility			
Franklin Sports (firm)	Pakistan			Centralized production			

Source: Bureau of International Labor Affairs (1997).

then inspect a random sample of the applicant's looms. If child workers are found on two separate inspections, the application is rejected. Otherwise, the applicant is accepted.

All of the looms of a licensee are assigned an individual identification number. Each purchase order received by the licensee must be registered with *Rugmark* and is assigned a serial number. The licensee must maintain detailed records concerning each carpet's production. During the production process, the site is subject to random inspection in order to determine whether child labor is employed. If children are found working during two separate inspections, the licensee is decertified.

Rugmark employs an array of devices to maintain the credibility of the inspection process. Inspectors are university graduates who are paid significantly above the region's average wage. Inspectors work in pairs that are changed daily and are not informed of each day's inspection assignments until the morning of the inspection. As of June 1997, *Rugmark* India had 18,400 registered looms.

During the preceding year, *Rugmark* had conducted 22,800 inspections, finding 1,060 children on 635 looms. Of the children found, 15 to 30 percent were bonded child laborers. Typically, inspectors find a child worker on one out of every thirteen looms inspected.

Funds garnered from importer licensing fees are used to educate and support former child weavers and the children of adult weavers. *Rugmark* maintains a primary school in Bhadohi which enrolls 250 weaver's children and a rehabilitation center for former child weavers. The latter program provides education, vocational and human rights awareness training, shelter and medical care to 37 former child weavers (21 of whom are former bonded laborers).

Welfare of Former Child Workers

Labeling as a strategy for reducing child labor is of course not without its critics. Some elements of the *Rugmark* program have been designed to address various potential weaknesses. First and foremost, any campaign that removes a child from the workplace is vulnerable to the charge that the welfare of the child has not necessarily been improved. For example, the decline of the carpet industry appears to have eliminated jobs for children in Kathmandu. Technological change and changing comparative advantage are two possible explanations. However, the consequences for at least some children are quite negative. According to UNICEF (1995, p. 7) there are some reports that 5,000–7,000 young girls have been trafficked from carpet factories in Kathmandu into the Indian sex trade. More generally, work may simply be the difference between life and death for some children. Eliminating jobs could easily leave child workers with greatly worsened choices.

Some of the labeling programs that appear to have the greatest success in credibly eliminating child workers have in fact the worst record in demonstrating that children's lives have been improved. The recent public outcry over child labor used to stitch soccer balls has led some soccer ball retailers to make changes in their production practices. It appears that firms such as *Reebok* and *Baden Sports* have earnestly set about to eliminate children from their suppliers' facilities. *Reebok* has worked with its Pakistani supplier and is planning an educational project for children in the Sialkot region. The program will target displaced child workers.

However, *Baden Sports*, exasperated with the inability to gain a credible commitment to use only adult labor from its Pakistani suppliers, moved production to China and substituted machine-stitched balls for hand-stitched ones. While *Baden Sports* can quite credibly claim that their soccer balls are not sewn by children, the relocation of their production facility undoubtedly did nothing for their former child workers and their families. Arguably, the former Pakistani workers and their families have been made worse off by the switch in location and the change in the production process.

Furthermore, the outcry against child labor in soccer ball manufacturing was glibly caught in the concern that American children were playing soccer with balls sewn by children. However, of the array of possible employment in which impoverished children might engage, soccer ball stitching is probably one of the most benign. In 1996, 75 percent of the world's hand-stitched soccer balls were made in Sialkot, Pakistan. This is a region that has been known for over 80 years for its skilled sporting goods craftsmen. Children generally work alongside other family members in the home or in small workshops. Bonded child labor is not considered to be an issue. Nor are the children exposed to toxic chemicals, hazardous tools or brutal working conditions. Rather, the only serious criticism concerns the length of the typical child stitcher's work-day and the impact on formal education. Seventy percent of these children work 8 to 9 hours a day and some work as much as 10 to 11 hours per day. Many have never attended school.

Centralizing the production process in a single facility can also adversely impact families. Some soccer balls are sewn by mothers in between other household tasks and thus provide supplemental income to the family. However, such practices are not tenable when stitching is centrally located at some distance from the family home. In addition, since children are not permitted in the factories, mothers must obtain child-care which may be costly.

It thus appears to us that the case for eradicating child labor in soccer ball stitching is not compelling. A more appropriate policy response would be improvement of educational opportunities and/or a subsidy paid for children who attend school that can replace the child's earnings as a contribution to family income.[15]

---

[15] An educational subsidy program targeted at the children of Brazilian orange pickers has produced very suggestive results. Citrovita Agro Industrial Ltd., the largest juice producer in the town of Catanduva, funds an educational center for underprivileged youth. In addition, the local government gives needy parents whose children maintain a specified school-attendance record a stipend of $45 per month per child. The stipend roughly equals the child's foregone earnings as an orange picker while in school. In the year since the program has been in effect, truancy in Catanduva has dropped from 18 percent to less than 1 percent. The success of the program in Catanduva clearly stems from two characteristics. First, the subsidy is paid only *in lieu* of work by the child. And, perhaps more importantly, the program designers are willing to accept the parents' decision as to how the subsidy is spent. As a consequence, the community has replaced work with school as a way for the child to bring resources into the household.

The rehabilitation programs maintained by *Rugmark* for child carpet weavers are clearly an attempt to increase the likelihood that the options for children are improved while eliminating or reducing work. However, many child-welfare projects associated with labeling programs have encountered difficulties in providing services to children. *Rugmark* officials acknowledge that many former child laborers are not placed in transition and rehabilitation facilities. In the case of *Rugmark*, the agency has been unable to locate the child's parents and obtain permission to remove the child from work. In addition, both of *Rugmark*'s facilities have a waiting list that equals the current enrollment. Many children reach the legal age to work before a space in the facility becomes available.

Rehabilitation projects for other labeling programs face even greater difficulties. For example, the *Kaleen* labeling program in India imposes a fee on licensees equal to 0.25 percent of their carpet export value that is contributed to a Child Welfare Fund. Only 12 percent of licensees consistently pay the fee. Furthermore, as of 1997, the fund had accumulated approximately $500,000 of which only 6.3 percent has been spent on child welfare programs. A similar problem plagues *Care and Fair*, a Hamburg-based association of carpet importers. During the program's first year of operation, 1995, $700,000 was collected for child welfare programs. Currently, the fund has $2.5 million in unspent funds. The culprit in this case appears to be India's strict regulation of foreign contributions to welfare programs.

Label Credibility

Product labeling programs have also been criticized on grounds of the credibility of the claims made on their labels. In order to address these criticisms, elaborate monitoring procedures have been adopted. *Rugmark*, for example, has endeavored to design a monitoring scheme that at least makes a good faith effort to monitor its licensees. The evidence suggests that their efforts have had some effect. *Rugmark* executives argue that when the program was first put in place, children were found on one out of every six or seven looms inspected. Currently, child workers are found on one in twelve or thirteen looms. Hence, the credibility of their monitoring program has had a positive impact on licensee compliance.

However, other organizations believe that credible monitoring is simply an impossible task. For example, the Secretary General of *Care and Fair* argues that there are "...280,000 looms in India spread over 100,000 square kilometers..." (Bureau of International Labor Affairs, 1997, p. 46). Thus it is argued that credibly monitoring such a large number of geographically dispersed looms is simply not tenable. To the extent that these efforts succeed, they do so by raising awareness of the plight of child workers locally and in the west.

In fact, there is some evidence that *Rugmark* has had some difficulty with effective monitoring in spite of the great care put into their monitoring program. Difficulties have been noted by U.S. Labor Department observers during site visits. In one village, *Rugmark* inspectors were unable to find any of the looms or loom owners listed by a *Rugmark* licensee. It is also frequently the case that a loom targeted for inspection is unattended, making it impossible for the inspector to determine whether the weaver is an adult or a child (Bureau of International Labor Affairs, 1997, p. 34).

Monitoring carpet weaving in Nepal is considerably more straightforward. Most carpet manufacturing is undertaken in large centrally located facilities.

The nature of the soccer ball also lends itself well to credible monitoring. *Reebok* has had considerable success concentrating all of its soccer ball manufacturing into a single facility. *Reebok* has enlisted the services of two human rights activists to monitor their subcontractors' conduct with regard to child labor. *Reebok* has gone so far as to hire a guard who searches employees entering and leaving the facility in order to guarantee that no soccer ball kits are removed for stitching in locations where children might be working. In nine inspections over a five-month period, no child workers were found at the *Reebok* plant.

Reebok also employs what is sometimes referred to as *natural* monitoring. Large posters printed in the local language stating *Reebok*'s policy on child labor are posted in the plant. *Reebok* estimates that the cost of benefits and transportation will increase the stitching cost by 15 percent, or about 10 cents per ball (U.S.-DOL, 1998, pp. 104–105).

In some cases, however, a poorly designed or absent monitoring scheme appears largely to have the intent of distorting the product quality signal provided by the more rigorous labeling efforts. For example, the Carpet Export Promotion Council (CEPC) of India sponsors the *Kaleen* label and has a monitoring procedure that resembles that employed by *Rugmark*. However, the outcome is quite different. The CEPC retains the Academy of Management Studies to undertake monitoring. They inspect 10–11 percent of looms each year. This is in stark contrast to the monitoring intensity maintained by *Rugmark*. Virtually all of *Rugmark*'s looms will be inspected once or twice a year.

The outcome of the monitoring efforts is also uninspiring. During the first year of *Kaleen* inspections (October 1995–October 1996), 22 percent of the looms targeted for inspection were either sold or could not be found by the inspectors. Of the looms inspected, 43 percent were idle. As a consequence, the inspector could not determine whether the operator was typically an adult or a child. Therefore, the actual annual inspection rate is only about 4.5 percent. Finally, out of 9,400 *Kaleen* inspections, only 100 illegal child weavers were found. By contrast, 22,800 inspections by *Rugmark* monitors located 1,060 children, which is about five times the discovery rate achieved by *Kaleen*.

Other programs have provisions for de-certification of licensees but no monitoring program at all. For example, the *Abrinq Foundation for Children's Rights* in Brazil has no formal monitoring procedure. Rather, they rely on reports of violations by employees, subcontractors, suppliers, buyers or other affiliates. However, it was generally found that *Abrinq* licensees do not publicize their policies regarding child labor. Not surprisingly, no reports have been made and no licensees have ever been decertified.

Monitoring in Labeling Programs

The intensity with which labeling programs are monitored and enforced is the single greatest source of disagreement among labeling program architects. The central issue generally debated turns on whether or not monitoring can be carried out credibly. In some cases the answer appears to be a qualified "yes" as with the soccer ball industry. In other cases, monitoring is characterized by some as "a joke" as with the geographically dispersed rug-making industry.

However, it may be more interesting to evaluate the issue of monitoring from the point of view of the welfare of the children involved. As we discussed above, programs that remove children from work without addressing the alternatives available to the displaced child workers are unlikely to actually improve the welfare of children. The only case in which one can feel confident that a displaced child has been made better off is one that forecloses options chosen by parents which reflect the low standing that the child has in the household. As a consequence, a program that seeks to remove children from work must have a feature that raises revenue that can be used to replace the child's lost income or at least to improve the educational opportunities available to the family. With a few exceptions, most labeling programs have such a child-welfare component.

In this connection, then, it is useful to evaluate monitoring in light of the implications for the revenue raised by a monitoring program. Without exception, labeling programs generally follow a trigger-strategy as a punishment device for licensees who are found to have violated agency rules governing child workers. Generally, if after one or two inspections, children are found working, the licensee is decertified and no longer permitted to use the agency's label.

Consider a very simple two-period model of the labeling and employment choices facing a firm. The set of decisions and payoffs facing a prospective licensee is depicted in Figure 1. At the initial node, a firm must choose whether or not to join a labeling program. In the event that the firm chooses not to label, the firm sells into a perfectly competitive market of non-labelers. Hence, the price received, P, equals the average total cost of producing with child labor, ATC_C, and the payoff is zero.

Alternatively, the firm may choose to join a labeling program. Once accepted, the firm must decide whether to comply with the terms of the label, hiring only adult labor, or to cheat and continue to

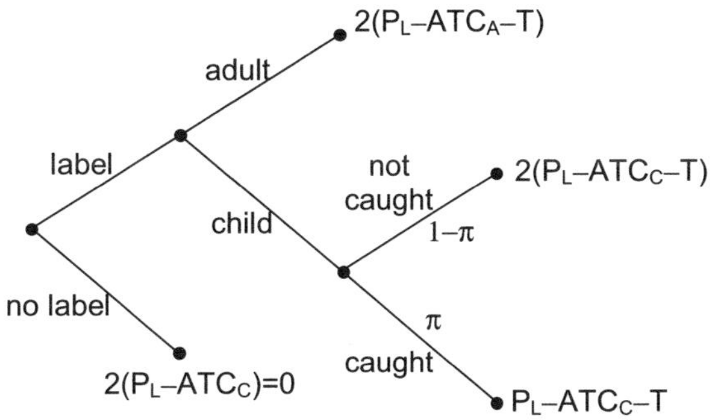

Figure 1. Decisions and payoffs facing a prospective licensee.

employ children. In the event that the firm chooses to hire only adults, it receives the going price of a labeled good, P_L, but must pay a certification fee of T to the labeling agency and must bear the additional cost of hiring adult labor. Therefore, the payoff is given by $2(P_L - T - ATC_A)$ where ATC_A is the average total cost of the adult-only production process. Here, we have ignored discounting which needlessly complicates the analysis.

In the event that the firm chooses to cheat, continuing to employ children, the payoff depends on whether the cheating is detected. With probability $1 - \pi$ the cheating will go undetected so that the firm will receive the price for a labeled product, P_L, but at a production cost of ATC_C. Hence the payoff from undetected cheating is given by $2(P_L - T - ATC_C)$. However, with probability π the cheating will be detected. The firm will receive the cheating profits in the first period, but will subsequently be decertified. At this point, the firm will simply revert back to employing both adults and children and receive the unlabeled price, P. Hence, the firm receives the cheaters payoff in the first period but the payoff in the second period is zero.

The optimal monitoring regime adopted by the labeling agency, and, therefore, the behavior of the firm, depend on the size of the labeling premium offered by the customer. Three cases are depicted in Figure 2. Here we have drawn a unit-value isoquant showing the various combinations of adult and child labor that are technologically

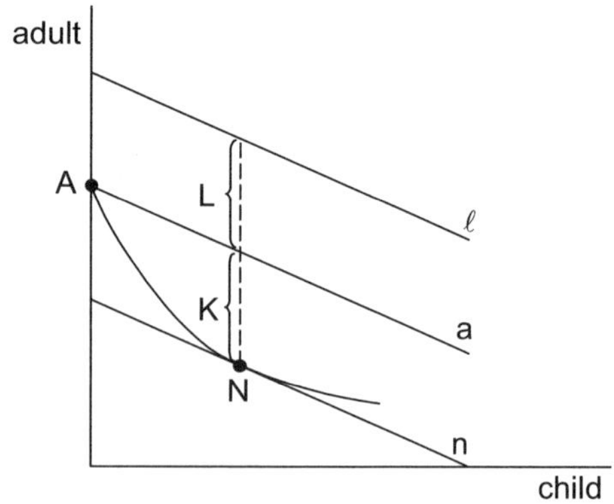

Figure 2. Firm behavior and the size of the labeling premium offered.

feasible. The isoquant intersects the adult labor axis indicating that it is feasible to produce with adult labor only.

In the absence of labeling, cost-minimizing firms will choose to produce at a point like N in Figure 2, where the unit-value isoquant is tangent to the unit value isocost line, "n". If, alternatively, the firm chooses to use adult labor only, then it must produce at a point like A, the cost of which is given by the isocost line denoted by "a".

Case 1: First, suppose that the labeling premium falls short of the additional cost of hiring adult labor only. In this case we have $P_L - ATC_A < 0$. That is, the firm cannot break even using adult labor only. Clearly, we cannot satisfy the participation constraint with compliance. The certifying agency will have to live with certain cheating.

Therefore, the firm will earn labeling profits in both periods, $2(P_L - T - ATC_C)$, with probability $1 - \pi$ and labeling profits in only one period, $P_L - T - ATC_C$, with probability π. Since we know that $ATC_C = P$, the participation constraint becomes $T < P_L - P$. That is, the certifying agency can collect nearly all of the labeling premium which can then be directed toward child welfare programs.

The revenue earned by the certifying agency is given by Revenue = $nT + (1 - \pi)nT$ where n is the number of certified firms. The second period revenue is smaller than the first period revenue since the cheaters detected in the first period have been decertified and are no longer labeling. Clearly, the only effect of monitoring in this case is to reduce the number of firms contributing to the child welfare fund in the second period. Therefore, there should be no effective monitoring. That is, $\pi = 0$.

Equilibrium in this case, therefore, is characterized by monitoring which has no credibility. The consumer may respond to the lack of credibility of the certifying agency by setting $P_L = P$. But there is actually no real reason for them to do so if their true interests lie with the welfare of child workers. Virtually all of the labeling premium paid is contributed to a child welfare fund.

Case 2: Consider next the possibility that the labeling premium is just barely sufficient to cover the additional cost of employing adults only. In this case, $P_L - ATC_A = 0$. Clearly, cheating with labeling will continue to be the equilibrium outcome. Firms that do not label will just break even. This is the case as well for firms that label and comply with rules regulating the employment of children. However, the expected payoff to cheating will be $[2(1 - \pi) + \pi](P_L - ATC_C)$ which is positive. Even with intensive monitoring, all firms will earn a higher payoff by hiring adults and children.

Case 3: This brings us to the final case. In order to satisfy the incentive compatibility constraint that induces a firm to comply with child labor restrictions, the expected value of lost profits due to de-certification in the second period must be larger than the gains from cheating in the first period. That is:

$$\begin{aligned} 2(P_L - T - ATC_A) &> 2(1 - \pi)(P_L - T - ATC_C) + \pi(P_L - T - ATC_C) \\ &> (2 - \pi)(P_L - T - ATC_C). \end{aligned}$$

It is worth noting that even with intensive monitoring, the certifying agency will be unable to tax away all of the extra normal profits earned by the compliant firms generated by the labeling premium. Solving for the certifying fee, T, under the assumption that monitoring is perfect, we have

$$T < (P_L - ATC_A) - (ATC_A - ATC_C).$$

The first term on the right is the extra-normal profit that the labeling firm receives above and beyond the cost of using the adult-only technology. This is the payoff that a compliant firm receives in the second period if it does not cheat in the first period. The second term on the right is the payoff from cheating in the first period. In order to deter cheating, the certifying agency must allow the compliant firm to retain enough of the extra-normal profits in the second period in order to compensate the firm for the foregone profits from cheating in the first period.

In terms of Figure 2, compliant firms must earn revenue given by the isocost line "l". That is, the extra-normal profits given by the line segment L must be as large as the gain from cheating given by the line segment K.

It remains to be determined, however, whether any monitoring is desirable. Once again, it turns out the equilibrium will be characterized by zero monitoring and universal cheating. If the certification fee is set sufficiently low to satisfy the incentive compatibility constraint, then revenue raised from each firm is less than L in Figure 2. However, if cheating is tolerated, then the certification fee can be set just short of L + K and the firms will still choose to label.

The results obtained from this simple model suggest that zero monitoring and universal cheating are optimal from the point of view of the welfare of children when the certifying agency adopts a trigger strategy as a punishment device.

Monitoring Reforms

The foregoing analysis suggests that labeling as a strategy for raising revenue for former child workers will be hampered by two effects. First, some of the labeling premium paid by consumers must be captured by the firm in order to defray the more expensive and less efficient use of adult labor. Second, an additional part of the labeling premium can be captured by the firm in order to prevent firms from cheating, thereby creating extra-normal profits.

There is nothing to be done about the need to compensate firms for higher production costs when no children are employed. However, from a theoretical point of view, at least, it is possible to reform the labeling program to eliminate much or all of the extra-normal profits earned to deter cheating.

The choice to set the certification fee to be equal to $P_L - ATC_C$ guarantees that a participating firm will not be able to break even employing only adults, thereby undermining the ultimate objective of reducing the number of working children. Therefore, the certifying agency may want to constrain the certification fee T to be smaller than $P_L - ATC_A$. That is, the labeling agency is only trying to capture the line segment L in Figure 2 for the child welfare fund.

With labeling programs as currently configured, the extra-normal profits given by L must be retained by the firm in order to deter cheating. However, if an applicant is required to post a bond equal to L which it forfeits if caught employing children, then the certifying agency can retain the extra-normal profits L for the child welfare fund.

Introducing a bond into the licensing procedure addresses the problem raised by the need to pay compensation in order to deter cheating by licensees. However, it does not address the second problem that bedevils labeling agencies: the entry of labeling agencies that purport to monitor the employment of children but, in fact, do not. Legitimate certifying agencies such as *Rugmark* have had difficulty distinguishing themselves from their less meticulous competitors.

There is a substantial literature on self-regulation, of which product labeling is an example.[16] In all cases the regulating agency arises due to the lack of information that consumers have concerning product quality. Consumers are able to acquire information concerning

---

[16] See, for example, Donabedian (1995), Donnenfeld, Weber and Ben-Zion (1985), Gehrig and Jost (1995), Bagwell and Staiger (1989), and Palma and Deneckere (1995).

the reliability of the regulating agency by evaluating the quality of previously certified products. However, it is difficult to apply such logic to the labor practices of foreign firms since the consumer never has an opportunity to gain information on the labor quality characteristics by consuming goods produced. For this reason, producers employing children may be unable to regulate themselves. It seems inevitably the case that legitimate certifying agencies such as *Rugmark* will have to acquire credibility from an international or governmental agency.

IV. Conceptual Considerations and Analysis of Alternative Measures to Reduce Child Labor

In order to shed some light on what the effects of various policies regarding child labor might be, we use this section of the paper to examine the issue in the context of a theoretical model. The model consists essentially of a microeconomic model of a family — parent and child — labor supply that is imbedded in a standard Heckscher–Ohlin (H–O) general equilibrium model of production and trade. For both, we draw upon more detailed work that has been done elsewhere, contenting ourselves here with giving only the flavor of some of the results that can be obtained together with the intuition behind them.

The H–O Model

We use a "two-cone" version of the H–O model as most closely and simply capturing the large differences that exist between the developed and developing parts of the world.[17] That is, while we assume that countries everywhere share the same constant-returns-to-scale technologies for several goods from primary inputs of capital and labor, the factor endowments of countries are sufficiently diverse as to prevent factor price equalization (FPE) among all of them. Instead, the world is divided into two "cones" of factor proportions. In the

[17] See Deardorff (1979).

more capital-abundant cone of the "North," we find the factor endowments of the rich developed countries. Within that cone, these countries have FPE among themselves, and they produce and collectively export goods from the capital-intensive end of the factor-intensity spectrum. At the same time, the less capital-abundant countries of the "South" occupy a more labor-abundant/-intensive cone. They too have FPE among themselves, and they specialize in labor-intensive goods. Factor prices can differ markedly between these two parts of the world, with the South having much lower wages (and higher returns to capital) than the North.

For the most part, too, the South produces different goods than the North, while within the South countries specialize further among the various labor-intensive goods depending on their factor endowments relative to other countries in the southern cone. The countries with the smallest endowments of capital per worker, which will be the focus of our attention here, will pay the same wages as other countries in the same cone, due to FPE among them. However, they will tend to produce and export a different selection of goods, concentrating on the most labor-intensive of the larger group of labor-intensive goods produced in the South.

For simplicity and concreteness of results, we allow only two factors in our discussion, capital and labor. Implicitly one may think of human capital as being present in the model but aggregated together with capital. One could also allow some exogenous variation in the amount of "effective" labor per worker, especially across countries. More importantly, we explicitly allow the labor factor in the South to encompass both adult and child labor as perfect substitutes, with children contributing only a constant fraction of the effective labor input of an adult.

Before moving on to the micro model of labor supply, several familiar properties of this H–O trade model may be noted. First, as long as world prices of all goods remain unchanged, factor prices of countries within a cone will not change with their factor endowments or factor supplies. This is the lesson of FPE,[18] and it applies within a

---

[18] Causing Leamer and Levinsohn (1995) to call it the "Factor Price Insensitivity Theorem."

cone of a multi-cone model as much as in the more familiar textbook model with a single cone. Second, if prices of goods change, as they will when large changes in factor supplies cause changes in world supplies of goods, then factor prices change in accordance with the Stolper–Samuelson Theorem. However, that Theorem must be interpreted within the context of a cone of specialization. That is, when the relative price of a good goes up, the effect on factor prices in a cone — the South, say — depends on whether that good is produced there at all, and, if it is produced, on the factor intensity of the good relative to others in the same cone.[19] If the good is not produced, then its higher relative price simply lowers the real wages of all factors in the cone. But if it is produced, then it raises the real return to the factor used intensively in its production, relative to other goods in the same cone.

These familiar properties of the H–O model, in their perhaps unfamiliar guises appropriate to the multi-cone model, will be useful later on as we discuss the general equilibrium and world-market implications of various policies for dealing with child labor.

Parent and Child Labor Supply

Unlike most applications of the H–O trade model, ours will assume variable labor supply, and in particular we will make a distinction between supply of adult labor and supply of child labor. Our model of a family has just two people, a parent and a child, with a single utility function that is intended to reflect the interests of both. Both members of the family can potentially contribute to that utility by three means: leisure, home work, and market work. The model is static, but the leisure of the child can be taken to include time spent in school, and the contribution of the child's leisure to family utility can therefore implicitly encompass the future return to education. Home work represents whatever the family member can

[19] See Davis (1996).

contribute directly to the family's welfare by working in the home (or implicitly on the family's land) to produce goods and services for their own consumption. It does not include work they may do at home to produce goods for sale or in a subcontracting arrangement with a firm. Such work, although done at home, is part of market work, which of course may also be done elsewhere in a factory or on a plantation.

Family utility depends on these three arguments — leisure, home consumption, and market consumption — each of which may be contributed by one or both family members. These three arguments in the utility function are not, in general, perfect substitutes, and indeed we will further specify the pattern of substitution among them below. The contributions of parent and child to each of these arguments, however, are taken to be perfect substitutes for each other, though not one-for-one. Thus, each hour of home work by the parent will yield some fixed amount of home consumption, while each hour of home work by the child will yield a similarly fixed, but presumably smaller, amount of home consumption. Likewise, working in the market, each family member earns a fixed wage, again the child's wage presumably being smaller than the parent's. The contributions of each family member's leisure time to family utility are similarly fixed per hour, although here we presume (and hope) that the family places a higher value on the child's leisure than on the parent's. If they do not, then we may get what we take to be the pathological (but perhaps all too common) case of true exploitation of child labor.

We will not attempt in this paper to explore this model in full detail and rigor, but it is perhaps useful in spite of that to lay it out formally.

The Model

Notation

C_h, C_m = Consumption of home-produced and market-purchased goods

T_i, H_i, L_i	=	Time allocated to leisure, home production, and market labor supply by family member $i = p, c$ for parent and child respectively
v_i, a_i, w_i	=	Productivity of time allocated to leisure (in terms of utility), home production (in terms of home-produced consumption), and market labor (the wage) for family member i
C, T	=	Effective total consumption (CES aggregate) and leisure
$\bar{T}_p, \bar{T}_c$	=	Time available for parent and child respectively (excludes biologically necessary leisure)
$\rho_j = \dfrac{\sigma_j - 1}{\sigma_j}$	=	CES utility parameters, $j = U, C$.

Equations

The family is assumed to choose T_i, H_i, L_i, $i = p, c$, to solve the following maximization problem:

$$\max \quad [C^{\rho_U} + T^{\rho_U}]^{1/\rho_U} \tag{1}$$

$$\text{s.t.} \quad C = [C_h^{\rho_C} + C_m^{\rho_C}]^{1/\rho_C} \tag{2}$$

$$T = v_p T_p + v_c T_c \tag{3}$$

$$C_h = a_p H_p + a_c H_c \tag{4}$$

$$C_m = w_p L_p + w_c L_c \tag{5}$$

$$H_p + L_p + T_p = \bar{T}_p \tag{6}$$

$$H_c + L_c + T_c = \bar{T}_c \tag{7}$$

If home and market consumption are relatively close substitutes, such that $\sigma_C > 1$ as we assume, and if consumption and leisure are not close substitutes, such that $\sigma_U < 1$ as we also assume, then this formulation yields a backward-bending supply curve of labor. That is, if we raise both wages keeping their proportions fixed, total labor supply first rises with the wage for low wages but falls thereafter with further increases in wages.

Exactly who does what within this family depends both on the level of the wages and on the productivities of the parent and child in satisfying their various needs. Because the formulation here is linear, it is convenient to think in terms of parents and children each having comparative advantage in one or another activity, very much like a Ricardian trade model with three goods. That is, we can order the three activities — leisure, home production, and market work — by the ratio of the parent's and the child's productivity, to get a chain of comparative advantage. It follows, exactly as in a Ricardian trade model, that neither family member will engage in any activity in which it has a comparative disadvantage unless the other family member is already devoting all of their time to it as well.

To illustrate, we will assume throughout most of our discussion that the following ordering prevails:

$$\frac{v_c}{v_p} > \frac{a_c}{a_p} > \frac{w_c}{w_p}. \tag{8}$$

The motivation here is: (1) that the child is less productive than the adult at both home production and market work, so that the second and third ratios are both less than one; (2) that the family sees greater value in the child's leisure than in the parent's, partly out of care for the child and partly because the child's leisure includes the benefits of education; and (3) that the child's greatest comparative disadvantage is in market work. With this assumed ordering, the child will never engage in market work unless the parent is already devoting all of its time to market work as well. But this can happen, if wages of both are low and productivity of home production is even lower.

In general, under the assumption in (8), the only patterns of intra-family specialization that can be observed are those depicted in the table below.

T Leisure	H Home Production	L Market Work
C, P	P	P
C	P	P
C	C,P	P
C	C	P
C	C	C, P

Which of these patterns is chosen then depends upon all of the parameters, including the market wage rates.

For our purposes here, we care most about the implications of the model for labor supply. There are two aspects of this that will be of interest: how the total labor supply of the family varies when wages of parent and child move together; and how they vary when the wage of only one family member changes while the other is fixed. The first case is depicted in Figure 3.

Here it is assumed that the parent's and child's wages move together, as they would (and will below) if the child's productivity in market work is some fixed fraction of an adult's while both become more or less valuable with varying market conditions.

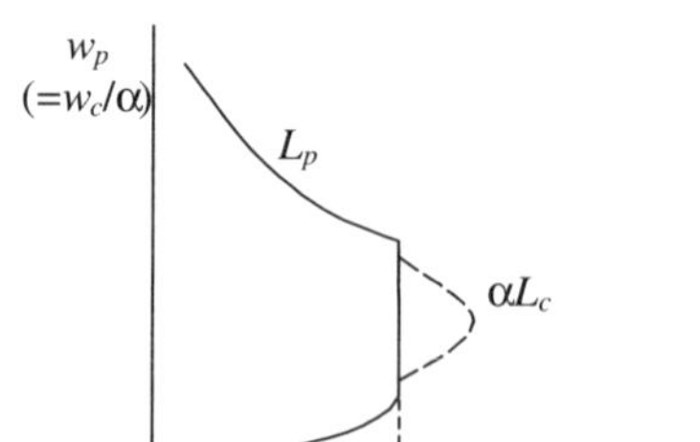

Figure 3. Family labor supply as wages vary together.

Letting $\alpha = w_C/w_P < 1$ be that fraction, we graph the family's total effective labor supply in units of the parent's labor, $L_S = L_P + \alpha L_C$, as a function of the parent's wage. For both wages very low, even the parent provides very little market labor, since they can use their time more productively at home. As the wages rise, the parent increases its labor supply, but because of the child's comparative disadvantage in market work, the child remains at home, engaged in leisure and probably home production. Only when the rising wage has drawn the parent into market work full-time does the family even consider putting the child to work as well, and even then the wages must rise a bit more before that happens. Now as wages rise further, we finally do see child labor, its amount increasing, for a time, with the wage.

With the assumed elasticities of substitution, however, there comes a point at which further increases in (both) wages cause the family to reduce labor supplied to the market, and with the assumed pattern of comparative advantage it is the child's labor that is withdrawn first. Only when the wages have risen to the point that the child no longer works in the market does the parent's labor supply begin to decline as well.

We can also ask how labor supplies vary if we change one wage holding the other fixed. Of greatest interest below will be changes in the child's wage, so that is the case we consider here. Suppose, starting from some point on the labor supply curve in Figure 3, that the child's wage now changes while the parent's does not. Of course, if the child is not working initially, then a small change in the child's wage will not change that. Most interesting therefore are cases in which we start with the child working. Two such cases are shown in Figure 4.

Here we have magnified the portion of the family labor supply curve along which the child works, shown as the solid curve L_S. Then for two points selected on this curve, marked A and B, we draw portions of the labor supply curves that would be observed if only w_C were then to change. In both cases, the broken curves show what would happen if w_C were to vary as it does along L_S but w_P were to remain fixed at w_A and w_B respectively. In both cases, because a fall in the child's wage is now not accompanied by the income loss of a fall

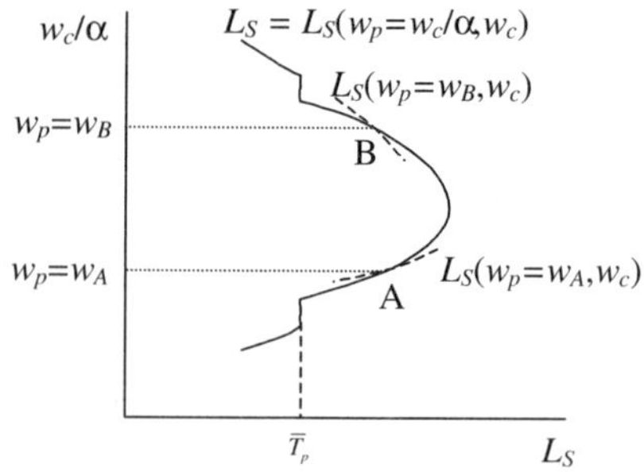

Figure 4. Family labor supply as child's wage varies.

in the parent's wage as well, the family cuts back more on the child's labor supply than it does along L_S. Thus, where the labor supply was positively sloped at A, its response to a fall in only the child's wage is more elastic than if both wages fall together. If the labor supply was negatively sloped at B, the response become less elastic.

From this we see something like a tradeoff between the income of the family and the effect that can be obtained on child labor by changing the wage. If the family is very poor, as at point A, then a reduction in the child's wage rate will discourage the family from having the child work, at the cost, of course, of reducing the family's income still further. On the other hand, if wages are somewhat higher to start with, as at B, so that the family has reached the point where further wage increases will reduce child labor, a fall in the child's wage will have the perverse effect of causing it to work more. As we will see, this case may have some relevance for policy.

Not depicted above but always true under the assumed pattern of comparative advantage is the effect of a change in the parent's wage on child labor. Starting again from a situation in which the child is working, a rise in the parent's wage has the same effect on the family as an increase in its wealth, since it simply raises the income from the maximum number of hours that the parent is already working. Because the utility function is homothetic in consumption and leisure, this can only reduce the amount of market labor that the family asks the child to provide, and increase the child's leisure. By the same token, a fall in the parent's wage will increase child labor supply if it is already positive, and may well put the child to work if it was not already there.

What our model cannot tell us very clearly is the effect of any of these changes on the welfare of the child alone. We have chosen to model the utility only of the family unit, not of the individuals within it. Certainly a rise in either wage benefits the family as a whole, even though a rise in the child's wage may put the child to working longer hours. That this may nonetheless benefit the child, however, is quite possible, since the family enjoys greater market consumption as a result.

The Bad Parent

The case we have considered so far, with assumption (8), provides the most favorable interpretation of child labor. Here, children work only if their parents are already working the maximum that they biologically can, and the family acknowledges the high cost to the child of working, in foregone leisure. It nonetheless sends the child to work if the need for what it can earn is large enough due to low wages overall and a low productivity at home. Based on the evidence we have described earlier in the paper, we believe that this captures reasonably well a large fraction of the child labor observed in the world.

But it does not capture all of it. As we have discussed above, many children are trapped in situations so harsh that it is implausible that they are benefiting at all from the arrangement. When children are essentially sold, as bonded laborers or in other similar arrangements, and when they live apart from their families with their wages given to the family, not to them, then it seems clear that the parents are benefiting at their expense.

Our model can capture at least an aspect of that behavior by simply reducing the value that the family unit places on the child's leisure, v_c. Reduced sufficiently, this will alter the ordering in Equation (8), putting the child's comparative advantage in leisure below that of both kinds of work. The patterns of specialization that one may observe are now altered from those laid out above. It is now easy to generate a scenario in which it is the child who works the maximum that is physically possible, either at home (Cinderella) or in the market (as essentially slave labor). Indeed, if we completely reverse the ordering of Equation (8), the same graphs of labor supply that we used above will apply, but with the identification of parent and child labor supply reversed. It is worth noting that, even in this case, a reduction in the wage of the child worker may cause its parent to make it work more, not less, though only if it is not already working the maximum.

Policies Toward Child Labor

We turn now to a discussion of several policies that might be used to discourage child labor, in the hope that our model may help to illuminate their effects. We will consider three policies: a complete ban on child labor; a non-prohibitive tax on child labor; and a subsidy to education. In each case we consider first the effects if the policy is applied "in the small," to a small enough part of the developing world that it will not change world prices, and second if it is applied "in the large," to all LDCs as a group.

Ban on Child Labor

Suppose first, then, that child labor is simply and effectively banned within a single small LDC. If that does not alter wages of parents, then under the assumptions of our model the families of child workers are unambiguously made worse off. They lose the income of the children, and we know from their choice to put the children to work in the first place that they view the benefits of that income as outweighing its costs. We can question whether the children themselves are worse off, of course, but only if we doubt the goodwill of the parents.

But won't the ban in fact alter the parent's wage? With less labor supplied by children, then one might expect the wages of the remaining workers to be driven up. That would be true in a closed economy, but in the small open economy assumed here it is not. As long as factor price equalization holds, the wages of parents — which are determined by unchanged world prices of goods — will not be changed by the ban on employing their children.

Thus it is only when we expand the ban on child labor to much or all of the developing world that we can expect to find this effect. In that case, the ban reduces labor supply in enough of the world to reduce the supply on world markets of the most labor-intensive goods, and the prices of these will rise as a result. It is through this mechanism — the Stolper–Samuelson Theorem in action — that we can expect to see the ban on child labor improving the wages of their parents. This is hopeful, but there is still no assurance that families or their children will be made better off. This will depend on many things, including the elasticity of demand for labor-intensive goods.

A Non-Prohibitive Tax on Child Labor

We next consider a non-prohibitive tax on child labor, not because anyone has proposed this as a desirable policy, but because many policies that have been proposed and used have effects similar to such a tax. A campaign of opprobrium, for example, leveled against employers of child labor, implicitly raises the cost to them of that employment, but it may not raise it enough to stop them doing it. A well advertised program of labeling can have a similar effect, by causing unlabelled merchandise to sell at a discount.

Suppose then that such a tax is implemented, again, to start with, in the small. The productivity of child labor is not altered by the tax, and therefore potential employers will continue to be willing to employ them for a wage equal to that productivity minus the tax. In other words, the effect of the tax is simply to lower the wage received by child workers. Since it does not alter the wage of their parents (FPE again), the scenario is exactly that of Figure 4. The tax may therefore either increase or decrease the hours worked by children, depending on which portion of the labor supply curve they were in. But unambiguously the welfare of the children's families is reduced. Thus the tax almost certainly does not make the children better off (except perhaps in the case of the bad parent), and it may even cause them to work more.

As in the case of the ban on child labor, the tax may possibly become beneficial if it is levied in the large, on enough of the developing world to alter world prices. But note in this case that labor supply may rise, not fall, in which case the effect on world prices would be the opposite of a ban, and could lower prices of unskilled-labor-intensive goods and the implied unskilled wage.

Of course, the analysis of a tax is not complete without accounting for how the revenue from it is used, but that is an issue only if it really is a tax. If costs are increased by other means, as suggested above, then there is no revenue, even potentially, to offset the adverse effects on the child workers and their families.

A Subsidy to Education

We have noted earlier in the paper and, with approval, the recent moves that have been made toward pulling children out of work instead of pushing them into work. By offering families a cash subsidy to send their children to school, one can obviously alter in an important way the calculus of their decision making. In the model above, this would alter Equation (5) to include the market consumption that can be financed by the subsidy:

$$C_m = w_p L_p + w_c L_c + s_e T_c \tag{5'}$$

where s_e is the education subsidy. If $s_e > w_c$, then the effect is extreme, since the family would never then send the child to work. Even with a smaller subsidy, however, the change in incentives can have important effects, and it seems clear that this can only reduce child labor. Furthermore, and unlike the other policies, this subsidy can only benefit the families, not harm them.

This is true in the small, when wages are fixed by FPE, and it is equally true in the large. For once again, by reducing the supply of child labor, the education subsidy has the potential, if used broadly enough, of reducing the overall supply of unskilled labor and raising the world prices of goods these workers produce, as well as their wage.

This all sounds fine, but of course we have not accounted for the very real cost of financing the subsidy. As usual in matters of this sort, unless there is a market failure being corrected, a subsidy will itself distort markets and cause a net reduction in economic welfare. In this case, since the gains to the poor families of the child workers seem clear, this means that these gains are smaller than the cost of the subsidies. It probably would not be hard to dream up market failures to justify this cost, but we do not view that as necessary. Redistribution of world income toward the poor is sufficiently difficult that one should not condemn a policy like this on the grounds of a little economic inefficiency. On the contrary, if the world can harness the righteous indignation over child labor to the cause of truly helping these children and their families, the effort seems to us to be truly worthwhile.

V. Conclusions and Implications for Policy

In Section III we noted five kinds of policies and programs that have been suggested or used for deterring the employment of children. We conclude by revisiting them, providing our assessment of their desirability from the perspectives both of our analysis in Section IV and from broader considerations. To avoid repetition, we address the policies and programs in three groups.

Trade Policies

As might be expected from trade economists, we have a very low opinion of the use of trade restrictions to deter exploitation of foreign child labor. Our objections arise only partly from the usual distortions that trade intervention brings about, or from our concern that the real motivation for such policies is the protection of domestic interests in the developed countries rather than the welfare of the exploited children. As usual, if such protection is the real aim of policies, then there are better ways for all concerned to achieve it than by restricting trade.

More importantly, however, is the welfare of the exploited children themselves, and whether they are truly helped by, say, a boycott of the goods they are employed to produce. If such a boycott were truly complete, then the effect would be that of a ban on child labor, as discussed above. Such a ban would indeed reduce the employment of children, but except perhaps in the case of bad parents, it would hurt the children rather than helping them. Furthermore, if trade restrictions effect only a partial boycott — being implemented by only some importing countries rather than all — or if they merely lower the net prices of imported goods that continue to be produced with child labor, then the effect will be similar to a tax on child labor that we also discussed. Here, as we saw, the children are hurt while their employment may actually rise.

ILO Assistance and Other Supra-National Measures

We already noted with approval the funds that have been contributed by the United States and other developed countries to the ILO's IPEC for improving labor standards. These funds can be used in a variety of ways, and they are not without their pitfalls, as we have noted along the way. But they provide the best means we have seen for truly alleviating the plight of working children, and not just removing them from view. To the extent that such funds are used to subsidize education among poor youth, and in particular to provide them and their families an incentive to remove them from more arduous activities, these programs act much like the subsidy to education that we discussed above. The gains are clear and unambiguous, and we strongly recommend that such efforts be expanded. It is notable that the amount of money contributed to these programs by the United States, though laudable, is miniscule compared to what the U.S. contributes to many other domestic and even international initiatives.

Codes of Conduct and Labeling

Both codes of conduct and consumer labeling (which in effect simply helps producers to gain a marketing advantage from their codes of conduct) are not, in our view, unambiguously desirable. To the extent that they only reduce the demand for child labor or, equivalently, raise its perceived cost to potential employers, these initiatives cater more to the sensitivities of western firms and their customers than to the children that are said to be their focus. Indeed, simply to stop employing an impoverished child should be viewed in many cases as a greater form of exploitation than employing them — again, however, with perhaps the exception of children of bad parents in forced or bonded labor.

The focus of a code of conduct and of any labeling that results should not be the negative one of not employing children, but the positive one of actually helping them. As we have discussed, the better codes and labeling schemes have in fact devoted some of their revenues to educating children, and that is the truly positive role that they can play. So far, this role has been a very limited one, limited by the licensing fees that labelers can collect and by the generosity of corporations. What is really needed, we believe, is for the public to recognize the true problems of child poverty, not child labor, and for them to contribute, in whatever ways can be designed, to programs that will help children in poverty. If the desire for profits by corporations can be harnessed to this end, that is all to the good, but the focus *must* be on getting resources from those who have them, to those who have not.

Study Questions

1. What are the principal determinants of child labor? What are the global estimates of the numbers of child labor and the changes in child labor that have occurred? To what extent are children employed in export industries in developing countries? What is the evidence on the working conditions of child labor?
2. What are the U.S. policies and programs that are designed to deter the foreign employment and exploitation of child labor: trade policies; ILO programs; supra-national measures; codes of conduct for multinational firms; and consumer labeling?

3. What are modeling features used to analyze the supply of parent and child labor and policies designed to reduce child labor?
4. To what extent may trade policies be effective in reducing child labor? ILO programs and/or WTO measures? Codes of conduct and labeling?

References

Alam, Asad. 1992. *Labor Standards and Comparative Advantage*. Unpublished doctoral dissertation, Columbia University.

Ashagrie, Kebebew. 1993. "Statistics on Child Labour," *Bulletin of Labour Statistics* 3: 11–24.

Bagwell, Kyle and Robert W. Staiger. 1989. "The Role of Export Subsidies When Product Quality is Unknown," *Journal of International Economics* 27: 69–89.

Bagwell, Kyle and Robert W. Staiger. 1998. "The Simple Economics of Labor Standards and the GATT," in Alan V. Deardorff and Robert M. Stern (eds.), *Social Dimensions of U.S. Trade Policies*. Ann Arbor: University of Michigan Press, forthcoming.

Basu, Kaushik. 1998. "Child Labor: Cause, Consequence and Cure, with Remarks on International Labor Standards," *Journal of Economic Literature*, forthcoming.

Basu, Kaushik and Pham Hoang Van. 1998. "The Economics of Child Labor," *American Economic Review* 88: 412–427.

Brown, Drusilla K. 1998. "A Transactions Cost Politics Analysis of International Child Labor Standards," in Alan V. Deardorff and Robert M. Stern (eds.), *Social Dimensions of U.S. Trade Policies*. Ann Arbor: University of Michigan Press, forthcoming.

Brown, Drusilla K., Alan V. Deardorff, and Robert M. Stern. 1996. "International Labor Standards and Trade: A Theoretical Analysis," in Jagdish Bhagwati and Robert Hudec (eds.), *Harmonization and Fair Trade: Prerequisites for Free Trade?* Cambridge: MIT Press.

Brown, Drusilla K., Alan V. Deardorff, and Robert M. Stern. 1998a. "Issues of Environmental and Labor Standards in the Global Trading System," in Stanley W. Black (ed.), *Globalization, Technological Change, and Labor Markets*. Amsterdam: Kluwer Academic Press.

Brown, Drusilla K., Alan V. Deardorff, and Robert M. Stern. 1998b. "Trade and Labor Standards," *Open Economies Review* 9: 171–194.

Bureau of International Labor Affairs, U.S. Department of Labor. 1994. *By the Sweat and Toil of Children*, Volume I, *The Use of Child Labor in American Imports*,

A Report to the Committee on Appropriations, United States Congress. Washington, D.C.: U.S. Department of Labor.

Bureau of International Labor Affairs, U.S. Department of Labor. 1995. *By the Sweat and Toil of Children*, Volume II, *The Use of Child Labor in U.S. Agricultural Imports & Forced and Bonded Child Labor*, A Report to the Committee on Appropriations, U.S. Congress. Washington, D.C.: U.S. Department of Labor.

Bureau of International Labor Affairs, U.S. Department of Labor. 1996. *By the Sweat and Toil of Children*, Volume III, *The Apparel Industry and Codes of Conduct: A Solution to the International Child Labor Problem?* Washington, D.C.: U.S. Department of Labor.

Bureau of International Labor Affairs, U.S. Department of Labor. 1997. *By the Sweat and Toil of Children*, Volume IV, *Consumer Labels and Child Labor.* Washington, D.C.: U.S. Department of Labor.

Davis, Donald R. 1996. "Trade Liberalization and Income Distribution," in process, July.

Deardorff, Alan V. 1979. "Weak Links in the Chain of Comparative Advantage," *Journal of International Economics* 9: 197–209.

Donabedian, Bairj. 1995. "Self-Regulation and the Enforcement of Professional Codes," *Public Choice* 85: 107–118.

Donnenfeld, Shabtai, Shlomo Weber, and Uri Ben-Zion. 1985. "Import Controls under Imperfect Information," *Journal of International Economics* 19(3/4): 341–354.

Freeman, Richard B. 1994. "A Hard-Headed Look at Labor Standards," in *International Labor Standards and Global Economic Integration: Proceedings of a Symposium.* Washington D.C.: U.S. Department of Labor, Bureau of International Labor Affairs.

Galasso, Emanuela. 1998. "Intra-Household Allocation and Child Labor in Indonesia," manuscript.

Gehrig, Thomas and Peter J. Jost. 1995. "Quacks, Lemons and Self Regulation: A Welfare Analysis," *Journal of Regulatory Economics* 7: 309–325.

Grootaert, Christiaan. 1998. "Child Labor in Côte d'Ivoire: Incidence and Determinants," in Christiaan Grootaert and Harry Patrinos (eds.), *The Policy Analysis of Child Labor: A Comparative Study.* The World Bank, in process.

Grootaert, Christiaan and Ravi Kanbur. 1995. "Child Labour: An Economic Perspective," *International Labour Review* 134: 187–203.

Human Rights Watch. 1995. *Contemporary Forms of Slavery in Pakistan.* New York: Human Rights Watch.

Human Rights Watch. 1996. *The Small Hands of Slavery: Bonded Child Labor in India.* New York: Human Rights Watch.

International Labour Organization (ILO). 1996a. Directorate of Labour Welfare and the International Programme for the Elimination of Child Labour (IPEC), *Child Labour in the Football Manufacturing Industry.* Geneva: ILO.

International Labour Organization (ILO). 1996b. *Economically Active Populations: Estimates and Projections, 1950–2010.* Geneva: ILO.

International Labour Organization (ILO). 1996c. *International Programme on the Elimination of Child Labour (IPEC) Brochure.* Geneva: ILO.

Khan, Fawad Usman. 1996. *Child Protection from Exploitative and Hazardous Labour.* Kasur, Pakistan.

Krueger, Alan. 1997. "International Labor Standards and Trade," in *Annual World Bank Conference on Development Economics 1996.* Washington, D.C.: The World Bank, pp. 281–302.

Kruse, Douglas and Douglas Mahony. 1998. "Illegal Child Labor in the United States: Prevalence and Characteristics," Working Paper 6479, National Bureau of Economic Research.

Leamer, Edward E. and James Levinsohn. 1995. "International Trade Theory: The Evidence," in Grossman and Rogoff (eds.), *Handbook of International Economics*, Vol. III. Amsterdam: North-Holland.

Organization for Economic Cooperation and Development (OECD). 1996. *Trade, Employment and Labour Standards: A Study of Core Workers Rights and International Trade.* Paris: OECD.

Palma, Andre de and Raymond Deneckere. 1995. "The Market for Audit Services and Mandatory Rotation," manuscript.

Rodrik, Dani. 1996. "Labor Standards in International Trade: Do They Matter and What Do We Do About Them?" in Robert Lawrence, Dani Rodrik, and John Whalley (eds.), *Emerging Agenda for Global Trade: High Stakes for Developing Countries.* Washington, D.C.: Overseas Development Council.

Stern, Robert M. 1997. "Issues of Trade and International Labor Standards in the WTO System," in Symposium on The Emerging WTO System and Perspectives from East Asia, *Joint U.S.-Korea Academic Studies*, Vol. 7. Washington, D.C.: Korea Economic Institute of America.

Stern, Robert M. 1998. "Labor Standards and International Trade," INTAL, *Integration and Trade*, forthcoming.

UNICEF. 1995. *Girls in Especially Difficult Circumstances: An Action Research Report.* Kathmandu: UNICEF.

U.S. Department of Labor (U.S.-DOL). 1998. "The Role of Governments and Non-Governmental Organizations in Combating Child Labor: ILO-IPEC Experience," Public Hearing, February 13, processed.

Suggested Further Reading

Brown, Drusilla K., Alan V. Deardorff, and Robert M. Stern. 2003. "Child Labor: Theory, Evidence and Policy," in Kaushik Baushik, Henrik Horn, Lisa Roman, and Judith Shapiro (eds.), *International Labour Standards.* Blackwell Publishers.

Edmonds, Eric V. 2007. "Child Labor," in T. Paul Shultz and John Strauss (eds.), *Handbook of Development Economics*, Volume 4. Blackwell.
Edmonds, Eric V. and Nina Pavcnik. 2005. "The Effect of Trade Liberalization on Child Labor," *Journal of International Economics* 65, pp. 401–419.
Edmonds, Eric V. and Nina Pavcnik. 2005. "Child Labor in the Global Economy," *Journal of Economic Perspectives* 19, pp. 199–220.
Edmonds, Eric V. and Nina Pavcnik. 2006. "International Trade and Child Labor: Cross-Country Evidence," *Journal of International Economics* 68, 115–140.

Chapter 19

Labor Standards and International Trade*,†

Robert M. Stern

I. Introduction

The interaction of labor standards and international trade is by no means a new issue. Nonetheless it has assumed new importance due to the increasingly vocal arguments by labor interests and social activists in the United States and other industrialized countries that "unfair" labor practices and conditions that may exist in their developing country trading partners need to be offset by appropriate trade policy measures in order to "level the playing field." Thus, for example, issues of lax enforcement of labor standards in Mexico were at the center of the public debate in the United States especially in 1992–1993 when the North American Free Trade Agreement

* Published in INTAL, *Integration and Trade*, May/June 1999, pp. 15–38. Reprinted with permission.

† This paper was awarded the first prize of $10,000 in October 1998 in an essay contest on the topic, "Labor Standards and Income Distribution and Their Relation to Trade." The contest was sponsored by the Institute for the Integration of Latin America and the Caribbean (INTAL), which is part of the Integration and Regional Programs Department of the Inter-American Development Bank.

(NAFTA) was being negotiated and later submitted for approval by the U.S. Congress. Efforts were also made (unsuccessfully) by the United States and some members of the European Union (EU) at the December 1996 World Trade Organization (WTO) Ministerial Meeting in Singapore to extend the WTO to include rules governing trade-related labor standards. Labor standards were again at issue in the fast-track authority that the Clinton Administration requested from Congress in November 1997 and then withdrew because of insufficient support from House Democrats.

The concern of labor and social activists is that the increased imports from countries in which labor standards are ostensibly not enforced at a sufficiently high level will be detrimental to wages and working conditions in the industrialized importing countries. As will be noted in our discussion that follows, there is a wide disparity of views on issues of international labor standards. The purpose of this chapter is to explore these different views and the available options for addressing the issues involved. The chapter is structured as follows. Section II deals with the definition and scope of labor standards. Theoretical aspects of the economic effects of labor standards are considered in Section III, while Section IV summarizes the available empirical evidence. Global, regional, national/unilateral, and other arrangements for the monitoring and enforcement of labor standards are discussed in Section V. Conclusions and implications for policy are presented in Section VI.

II. Definition and Scope of Labor Standards

Labor standards are multi-faceted and may vary from country to country depending on the stage of development, per capita income, and political, social, and cultural conditions and institutions. It may be difficult therefore to distinguish unambiguously those labor standards that everyone would consider to be universal rights from other labor standards that will depend on given national circumstances. Nonetheless, efforts have been made to identify and achieve consensus on a group of so-called core labor standards that ideally should apply universally. For example, according to OECD (1996, p. 26), core labor standards include: (1) prohibition of forced labor; (2) freedom of association;

(3) the right to organize and bargain collectively; (4) elimination of child labor exploitation; and (5) nondiscrimination in employment.

Agreement on the universality of these core labor standards derives ostensibly from the widespread acceptance and ratification of United Nations Covenants and Conventions as well as acceptance (though not necessarily ratification) of the pertinent Conventions of the International Labour Organization (ILO) that deal with human rights and labor standards.[1] Besides the aforementioned core standards, there are other labor standards that are less universally accepted, and that relate to "acceptable conditions of work," which include: a minimum wage; limitations on hours of work; and occupational safety and health in the workplace.[2]

Some of the difficulties that may arise in interpreting and implementing core standards and distinguishing between core and other standards can be illustrated in the attempt by Fields (1995, p. 13) to articulate what he considers to be: "...a set of *basic labour rights for workers throughout the world:*

i) No person has the right to enslave another or to cause another to enter into indentured servitude, and every person has the right to freedom from such conditions.
ii) No person has the right to expose another to unsafe or unhealthy working conditions without the fullest possible information.
iii) Children have the right not to work long hours whenever their families' financial circumstances allow.
iv) Every person has the right to freedom of association in the workplace and the right to organise and bargain collectively with employers."

[1] According to OECD (1996, pp. 31–34), there are seven fundamental ILO Conventions that form the basis of consensus among the ILO's constituents. These include: prohibition of forced labor (No. 29); freedom of association and protection of the right to organize (No. 87); right to organize and collective bargaining (No. 98); equal remuneration for men and women for work of equal value (No. 100); abolition of forced labor (No. 105); nondiscrimination in employment and occupation (No. 111); and minimum age of employment of children (No. 138).

[2] See Brown, Deardorff, and Stern (1996, Appendix Table 1) for the definitions and principles of the core and other labor standards that are articulated in U.S. trade law, based on Lyle (1991, pp. 20–31).

It would be no easy matter to make operational Fields's proposed basic worker rights. Thus, for example, it is unclear how to interpret what is meant by "the fullest possible information" about working conditions or "families' financial circumstances" in the case of child labor. Further, countries may differ in the extent to which labor unions and collective bargaining are guaranteed as an absolute right.

To illustrate further, Aggarwal (1995, pp. 4–5) has proposed that a distinction be drawn between standards related to *labor processes* and standards related to *labor outcomes*. This distinction would apply some definition of what constitutes a "minimum" standard to the determination of basic worker rights in terms of labor processes. Presumably, the point of taking labor processes, rather than outcomes, into account is to make allowance for differences and changes over time in the level of economic development and related factors. What remains ambiguous, however, as Aggarwal acknowledges, is the difficulty of deciding whether the identification and guarantee of labor processes provide an effective pre-condition for attaining the minimum criteria associated with achieving labor outcomes.

While, as already mentioned, there is concern in the United States especially that many of its developing country trading partners appear to be violating certain basic worker rights,[3] it has been pointed out, for example, by Bhagwati (1995, pp. 754–755, and 1997) that the United States is itself open to criticism when it comes to the realization of several labor standards. He argues accordingly that it is "morally obtuse" for the United States to seek to impose on poor countries particular requirements relating to worker rights, while not extending these efforts to its own problems in implementing the proposed international standards.[4]

---

[3] See, for example, Reich (1994).

[4] A similar argument is made by Srinivasan (1994, 1995, 1996, 1997), who argues that humanitarian concerns need to be reflected in the willingness of citizens in developed countries to assume responsibility and to provide financial assistance to enhance the welfare of workers, including children, in developing countries.

The foregoing discussion is by no means intended to deny the desirability of improving working conditions through higher labor standards. The issue, rather, is how this can best be accomplished. More will be said on this below in discussing existing institutions and mechanisms for the monitoring and enforcement of labor standards. It may be useful first though to discuss the central theoretical issues and the available empirical evidence involved in analyzing the economic effects of labor standards.

III. Economic Effects of Labor Standards: Theoretical Considerations

In this section, two main issues are considered: (1) the diversity of labor standards and the case for free trade; and (2) the effects of standards and the international harmonization of standards on economic welfare and the terms of trade of individual nations.

Diversity of Standards and the Case for Free Trade

As noted in the preceding discussion, labor standards may vary across nations depending on their level of development, per capita incomes, and a host of political, social, and cultural conditions and institutions. The issue is whether such diversity of standards alters the case for free trade. This has been investigated in depth by Srinivasan (1995, 1997), based on a theoretical model in which standards use productive resources and also affect consumer welfare. The upshot of Srinivasan's theoretical analysis is that the diversity of labor standards between nations will reflect differences in factor endowments and levels of income, and that such diversity is consistent with the case for free trade. If minimum international labor standards are to be attained, it will therefore be necessary to have arrangements for international income transfers and domestic tax/subsidies. This will be the case as well when consumers in countries with high standards have a moral preference to raise standards in their trading-partner countries with lower standards. Further, if there are market failures that prevent the attainment of minimum labor standards, income transfers and domestic tax/subsidies will be required to achieve optimal conditions for resource allocation and consumer welfare.[5] Finally, the use of trade intervention could hinder the attainment of higher labor standards, and it may accordingly be in the collective interests of countries to cooperate in setting labor standards. The implications of Srinivasan's conclusions will be examined below in considering the different options for dealing with international differences in labor standards.

International Harmonization of Standards

Brown, Deardorff, and Stern (BDS, 1996) analyze the effects of standards on economic welfare and the terms of trade and do not concern themselves directly with issues of the diversity of standards and the case for free trade. They employ a variety of theoretical models in which different national characteristics may determine the outcome of the introduction of labor standards.[6]

A general conclusion emerging from the BDS analysis is that economic welfare is best served when countries act to correct their domestic (labor) market failures. But, since these market failures will likely differ between countries, there is no obvious case on welfare grounds for pursuing universal standards and the international harmonization of standards that this may imply. This conclusion is consistent with that of Srinivasan, namely that diversity of working conditions between nations is the norm and is by no means in itself "unfair" so long as the extant labor standards are consistent with

---

[5] Srinivasan points out that the case for promoting labor unions and collective bargaining, which is considered to be a core labor standard, is by no means obvious in many developing countries, especially where unions are concentrated in the organized manufacturing and public sectors rather than in agriculture where a relatively large proportion of the population may be employed.

[6] See Bloom and Noor (1994) for research along related lines. Casella (1996) develops a model in which labor standards respond endogenously to changing levels of income. Further theoretical analysis of labor standards is to be found in Golub (1997), Maskus (1997), and OECD (1996, esp. pp. 215–232).

efficient resource use.[7] Further, despite the good intentions of government, it may turn out that the imposition of labor standards will fail to correct a market failure if the preferences of workers are heterogeneous with respect to what they consider to be acceptable levels of, say, health and safety conditions in the workplace.[8]

In considering the economic consequences that may result from pursuing the international harmonization of labor standards, BDS conclude that in cases in which low-income countries are relatively labor abundant, harmonization of child labor and certain other standards will reduce the effective labor endowment of these countries and thereby the supply of labor-intensive production on the world market. This could improve (worsen) the terms of trade of the low (high) income countries, although this is not what the high-income countries may intend.

BDS further assess arguments for having standards imposed on low-income countries. They note that low-income countries might conceivably benefit in case a government is unable for domestic political reasons to enact legislation on its own, although this presumes that the policy in question will indeed correct a market failure. It is also possible that requiring the guarantee of such standards as the right of workers to organize may serve to reinforce development of democratic institutions. Finally, they ask if there is any justification for high-income countries to take countervailing actions against the ostensibly unfair labor standards of their trading partners. They answer in the negative so long as resources are being employed efficiently. If, nonetheless, a high-income country imposes a tariff or quota on labor-intensive imports from a low-income country, this will obviously be harmful to the economic interests of workers in the low-income country.

[7] An exception arises here in cases of slave labor and what may be considered to be egregious treatment of child labor.

[8] See Maskus, Rutherford, and Selby (1996) for a computable general equilibrium (CGE) model analyzing the effects of changes in Mexico's labor standards. They demonstrate conditions in which improved labor standards may enhance the welfare of Mexican workers. See also Maskus (1997).

In general then, BDS conclude that the case for international harmonization of labor standards appears rather weak, and it is quite possible that harmonization could have unintended adverse consequences for the very people who are in the greatest need for assistance. It is difficult therefore to generate much theoretical support for pursuit of core labor standards that would have universal application.

Labor Standards as Private/Public Goods

We have already indicated that there may be a strong moral basis motivating the pursuit of higher labor standards.[9] Thus, in his analysis noted above, Srinivasan made allowance for moral considerations so that consumers could express their concern by a willingness to pay relatively higher prices for goods and services that reflected higher labor standards. In this connection, there is an issue of whether labor standards are to be considered as *public* or *private* goods. As long as the same standards appear in the utility functions of more than one individual, the standards are public goods. Suppose, on the other hand, that individual consumers have a sense of virtuousness and derive pleasure from believing that the good they are consuming embodies some acceptably high level of labor standards. In this case, individual consumers care only about their own satisfaction and not about others, so that labor standards can be treated as private goods.

[9] Granting this, it is nevertheless important to stress that concern about labor standards ought to be motivated by concern for the welfare of the workers involved, and not for the workers with whom they compete in the advanced industrialized countries. It is this latter view that motivates many of the advocates of labor standards. What these advocates may not realize or acknowledge is that taking actions against alleged violators of labor standards will normally make the "exploited" workers worse off, not better off. That will be true whether the sanctions are applied by government policy or by individual consumers responding to labeling. Therefore, if we wish to make workers and their families better off, we must find a way to *raise* their incomes, not take their incomes away.

This view of higher standards as private goods has been expressed most forcefully by Freeman (1994a), who argues that a market solution based on labeling may be an especially effective way to raise labor standards internationally. He makes the point that labeling has the advantage that consumers pay more for what they consider morally acceptable, and at the same time foreign suppliers are compensated for their increased costs. Labeling also undercuts protectionist influences.[10]

It is not altogether clear, however, that labor standards should be considered to be private goods that lend themselves to a market-based treatment dependent on supplying all relevant information to consumers. If instead, labor standards take the form of public goods, Freeman (p. 30) acknowledges that some type of government intervention may be called for.[11] In their theoretical analyses, Srinivasan and Brown, Deardorff, and Stern considered cases of domestic market failure in which a governmentally imposed tax/subsidy arrangement would be introduced to correct the distortion and permit the first-best optimum to be attained. While tax/subsidy (price-based) arrangements have a clear theoretical appeal, it is important to recognize in dealing with issues of labor standards that governments often prefer to use nonprice measures, i.e., legal regulation and enforcement.[12]

---

[10] However, as just noted, labeling does not in itself raise the incomes of foreign workers and their families.

[11] Freeman's argument for consumer labeling may therefore be limited insofar as it rests on treating labor standards as private goods. He does not make clear, moreover, what role the government should play, if any, in providing information to consumers and facilitating labeling and preventing private labeling arrangements from being co-opted by producing interests.

[12] It should be noted that this discussion refers to national or federal standards. John H. Jackson has pointed out to the author that there may be significant differences between U.S. states and regions in the impacts that national standards may have and yet the national standards remain operative. What helps this to work is that there is free movement of labor within the United States coupled with various programs of income support and transfers. As noted in the theoretical discussion above, one or both of these elements would be needed for an international system of labor standards to function effectively.

Freeman (p. 29) cites a number of regulatory examples in U.S. law, including prohibition of slavery, restrictions on child labor, occupational health and safety standards, and discrimination in the workplace. As he argues, the choice of different policy measures will depend on given empirical and institutional circumstances, and it is likely that some combination of price-based and regulatory approaches will produce the best results.

Political Economy Aspects of International Labor Standards

In discussing the sources of support for governmental action on labor standards, it is important to identify the constituent interest groups involved. Thus, in the United States for example, it would appear that organized labor, import-competing firms, and human-rights and public-interest groups are the main proponents of stricter labor standards applied to low-income countries. These interest groups may often recommend policies, including sanctions and import restrictions, which are presumably designed to change the behavior of trading-partner governments. By the same token, interest groups are influential in many low-income countries, especially among unionized workers in manufacturing sectors, employees of state enterprises, and owners/managers of import-competing firms. These groups may seek to protect and enhance their own ends and to resist foreign intrusion in setting standards. Krueger (1997, p. 283) characterizes the protectionist motivation as the "prevailing *political economy* view of international labor standards."[13,14] The issue then is how governments choose to respond to the various interest groups. This will be addressed in Section V.

---

[13] While Krueger's characterization may apply to unions and import-competing firms, it may not apply to the activities of human-rights and public-interest groups which are not motivated by protectionist considerations.

[14] See Noor (1996) for development of a theoretical model in which labor standards may enhance protection in an industrialized country. Also, see T. N. Srinivasan's comment on Stern (1997).

IV. Economic Effects of Labor Standards: Empirical Evidence

Labor Standards and Trade

In our earlier discussion, we distinguished "core" and "other" labor standards. The question then is the extent to which international differences in the various standards affect trade performance.

Rodrik (1996) represents an especially noteworthy effort to determine whether labor standards matter for trade. Using a variety of measures of labor standards and factor endowments, based on information for the 1980s and 1990s Rodrik first investigated whether labor standards affect labor costs. Making allowance for the effects of worker productivity in a sample of 36 countries, he found that per capita income was strongly correlated with labor costs and hence higher labor standards. Turning next to the effects on trade, he found that only the factor endowment (comparative advantage) variables were statistically significant and that none of the labor standard indicators were statistically significant.

Another study of interest is Aggarwal (1995), who investigated in detail the relationships of labor standards and the pattern of U.S. imports from ten major developing countries that accounted for 26.5 percent of U.S. imports in 1994. Aggarwal's major findings (p. 7) were as follows:

> Sectors typically identified as having egregious labor conditions do not occupy the only or even the primary share of these countries' exports.
>
> Comparisons across more export-oriented and less export-oriented sectors indicate that core labor standards are often lower in less export-oriented or non-traded sectors such as agriculture and services.
>
> Similarly, within an export-oriented sector, labor conditions in firms more involved in exporting are either similar to or better than those in firms that are less involved in exporting.
>
> Changes in technology and the structure of international trade are leading developing countries to compete in a race upward in terms of product quality rather than a race downward with respect to price.

> ... Wages and working conditions in developing countries have been exhibiting positive trends. In general, these have been in line with productivity changes.[15]

Finally, we may cite some of the main conclusions from the OECD study of *Trade, Employment and Labour Standards* (1996, pp. 12–13):

> ... empirical research suggests that there is no correlation at the aggregate level between real-wage growth and the degree of observance of freedom-of-association rights;
>
> ... there is no evidence that low-standards' countries enjoy a better global export performance than high-standards' countries;
>
> ... a detailed analysis of US imports of textile products (for which competition from low-standards' countries is thought to be most intense) suggests that imports from high-standards' countries account for a large share of the US market. Moreover, on average, the price of US imports of textile products does not appear to be associated with the degree of enforcement of child labour standards in exporting countries. ...

While the studies cited above may not constitute the final word on the relationships between labor standards and trade, the conclusion seems inescapable that there is little compelling empirical evidence suggesting that low labor standards have an impact on trade.[16]

---

[15] Aggarwal also had occasion to note that: the impact of imports from developing countries is small relative to imports from industrialized countries; countries with lower labor standards do not exhibit higher rates of import penetration than countries with relatively higher labor standards; and imports from developing countries do not appear to have larger displacement effects on U.S. employment and wages in sectors associated with poor labor standards relative to other sectors. See also Erickson and Mitchell (1996) who focus on the pattern and labor content of U.S. trade and find relatively small adverse wage effects and displacement of U.S. workers.

[16] Alan Krueger has suggested to the author that this is consistent with his view that the demand for international labor standards in the United States does not emanate from disguised protectionism. On this matter, however, see the discussion below of Krueger's research.

Labor Standards and Foreign Direct Investment (FDI)

It is often alleged that multinational enterprises may be attracted to locate in countries with lower labor standards to take advantage of lower costs. The available empirical evidence actually indicates the opposite to be the case.

Thus, Rodrik (1996) investigated the determinants of U.S. FDI abroad during 1982–1989, including measures of foreign exchange distortions, population, and income growth in host countries together with the various indicators of labor standards. He found (p. 22) that countries that scored lower in guaranteeing civil liberties and political rights and that had difficulty in providing for and enforcing standards affecting child labor received *less* foreign investment during 1982–1989 than would have been predicted on the basis of other country characteristics. Taken at face value, he concluded that these results indicate that low labor standards may be a hindrance, rather than an attraction, for foreign investors. Aggarwal (1995, p. 7) reached a similar conclusion: "U.S. foreign direct investment is not typically concentrated in countries or industries with poor labor standards." Finally, as reported in OECD (1996, p. 13): "...while core labour standards may not be systematically absent from the location decisions of OECD investors in favour of non-OECD destinations, aggregate FDI data suggest that core labour standards are not important determinants in the majority of cases."

Thus, the empirical evidence suggests rather convincingly that low labor standards are not reflected in the existing trade performance of the major developing countries and that FDI is more attracted to countries with high rather than low standards.

Labor Standards and the Role of Interest Groups

As mentioned above, there is a view that is widespread that support for international labor standards reflects protectionist interests in the United States and other industrialized countries. In an effort to test this proposition empirically, Krueger (1997) analyzed the determinants of support in the U.S. House of Representatives for the Child Labor Deterrence Act of 1995. If this type of legislation were approved, it would prohibit imports of goods produced abroad by child labor under specified circumstances, including by children under 15 years old and subject to a review of child labor practices by the U.S. Secretary of Labor. The Act was co-sponsored by Senator Tom Harkin (D-IA) and Congressman Barney Frank (D-MA), with 35 co-sponsors in the House and 7 in the Senate.[17] Krueger (p. 289) found that "...Congressmen from districts with a high concentration of high school dropouts are *less* likely to co-sponsor the Child Labor Deterrence Act. ...This finding is contrary to what I would expect from a simple political economy model...." Krueger also found that higher rates of unionization were associated with support for the Act as were representatives who were Democrats and also had voted against NAFTA and the Uruguay Round negotiations.

In interpreting his results, Krueger (p. 293) suggested that the demand for international child labor standards should be considered to be a "normal" good, following Freeman (1994a). That is, voters with higher socioeconomic attainment will select Congressmen who favor limitations on employment of child labor. He further argued that unionized workers who tend to be more highly skilled and thus may not benefit directly from a ban on imported goods made with child labor may in this case be acting to pursue policies that strengthen worker rights more generally rather than pursuing their own narrow self-interest. He goes on more broadly to state (pp. 293–294): "Indeed, in many instances I am surprised that the AFL-CIO used its limited political capital to press for international labor standards that are of little benefit to its members, when instead it could

[17] As noted in footnote 38, the U.S. 105th Congress has subsequently enacted the Bonded Child Labor Elimination Act, and it was signed by President Clinton on October 10, 1997.

pursue policies that are of much greater direct benefit to its membership."[18]

While Krueger's results are suggestive, they are by no means definitive. In particular, as Srinivasan (1996, 1997) has noted, a Congressman may have chosen not to sponsor the legislation and yet may be supportive of it. Further, less educated and less skilled individuals tend to vote less and to work in nontradable service industries. The interests of these workers may thus have been given less weight in a Congressman's deciding whether or not to be a co-sponsor. Finally, Krueger's results suggest support for the legislation from Congressmen from districts with a higher rate of unionization and voting records opposing NAFTA and the GATT negotiations.

Another noteworthy empirical study is by Freeman (1993) who investigated the evidence in developing countries for and against government intervention designed to introduce/remove labor-market distortions and, alternatively, to enhance labor-market institutions.[19] He labels these two views, respectively, the "World Bank Distortion View" and the "International Labour Organization (ILO) Institutional View." These views differ insofar as removing interventions is believed to enhance economic efficiency and welfare in the

[18] Krueger also examined other aspects of child labor, including the relationship between employment of children and GDP per capita and the experiences with compulsory schooling laws. He found that employment of young children was negatively related to GDP per capita. That is, child labor is more prevalent in low-income regions and negligible in high-income regions. This is a clear demonstration of the fact that restrictions on child labor can be looked at as a normal good, in this case less of it being condoned as per capita incomes rise. Evidence on the effects of compulsory schooling laws suggested that there may be definite benefits from such laws in high-income countries, but that there is widespread noncompliance with existing laws in many low-income countries. These findings suggest that reliance on child labor in low-income countries will diminish as family incomes rise, and that realization of the benefits of compulsory schooling laws depends on increasing economic opportunities and financial support for poor families so as to reduce their dependence on employment of their children.

[19] See also Freeman (1994b) which contains empirical studies of labor-market institutions and policies in several industrialized countries.

former, whereas in the latter introducing interventions is believed to lead to these same results. To investigate the validity of these alternative views, Freeman examined evidence on labor-market policies and institutions for selected developing countries mainly during the 1980s. His empirical findings suggest that neither the distortion nor the institutional view is clearly supported by the available data. In particular, real and relative wages in developing countries turned out to be much more flexible in response to changing market conditions than the strict distortionist view would suggest.[20] Freeman's overall conclusion was that the costs and benefits of the labor-market policies that may be adopted will depend on individual country circumstances.[21]

This selective review of labor standards and the role of interest groups suggests some ambiguities with respect to the issues. While there may thus be scope for different views, in this writer's judgment the weight of the theoretical and empirical analysis argues strongly against taking an activist position to mandate and enforce international

[20] See Squire and Suthiwart-Narueput (1997) for data on real minimum wages for selected developing countries for 1970–1990 and for an analysis of how noncompliance with official minimum wages may reduce distortionary costs.

[21] Linda Lim in commenting on Stern (1997) has pointed out that, in spite of the absence of formal worker rights and standards in such Southeast Asian countries as Malaysia, Singapore, and Indonesia, wages and working conditions have improved markedly. In contrast, the experiences in Thailand and the Philippines have been much less favorable even though these nations encouraged worker rights and minimum wages. She also noted that both Malaysia and Singapore have attracted considerable inflows of FDI and that workers have benefited in the firms involved. See also the comment by Mari Pangestu on Stern (1997) and evidence on Indonesian economic growth and accompanying improvement in social indicators noted in IMF (1997).

Studies of labor-market institutions and regulatory reform in Brazil, Chile, Uruguay, and Venezuela suggest that labor standards are not universally complied with especially in the informal sectors, and that labor-market regulations are considerably more restrictive than in the United States. Nonetheless, in Chile especially, there has been high sustained growth and increasing real per capita incomes for an extended period. Details on these Latin American labor-market characteristics and experiences are provided in Márquez (1995).

labor standards.[22] Nonetheless, because issues of labor standards will continue to have a high profile in the current policy environment, it is essential to consider the alternative arrangements that exist for their monitoring and enforcement. This will be done in the following section. We will conclude with some recommendations that may serve the interests and needs of the United States and other high-income countries as well as the low-income countries.

V. Monitoring and Enforcement of Labor Standards

Labor standards are presently dealt with in a variety of settings: global; regional; national/unilateral; and other, including private, arrangements. We shall discuss briefly each of these in turn.

Global Arrangements

The main international organization that is concerned with labor standards is the ILO, which was established as part of the Treaty of Versailles of 1919 following the end of World War I. The methods and principles set out in the ILO constitution deal with all conceivable aspects of labor standards. As stated in ILO (1988, p. 4), ILO action designed to promote and safeguard worker rights takes three main forms: (1) definition of rights, especially through adoption of

[22] There is evidently a marked difference in world view between most advocates of labor standards and trade (and most other) economists. Labor standards advocates seem to see the world in terms of a struggle between capital and labor for the rewards from production, without much regard to the size of the output that they will have to share. They see the outcome as depending on power, not on economics. Trade economists see the world in terms of how resources are allocated to production with a view to maximizing the total output. They see the distribution of that output between capital and labor as depending on scarcity and productivity, not on power. Therefore labor standards advocates favor the use of intervention to tilt the balance of power in favor of labor, believing then that labor will get a larger share of a fixed pie. Trade economists see those same policies as shrinking the pie while altering the slices not by changing power but by changing the markets within which scarcity determines the rewards to capital and labor.

ILO Conventions and Recommendations; (2) measures to secure the realization of rights, especially by means of international monitoring and supervision but not by imposition of trade sanctions; and (3) assistance in implementing measures, particularly through technical cooperation and advisory services.

What might be considered to be ILO core labor standards has already been mentioned. It is interesting that formal ratification of ILO Conventions differs considerably among ILO members, apparently because particular Conventions may be at variance with national laws and institutional practices. Thus, for example, as Rodrik (1996, pp. 15–16) notes, the United States has ratified only 11 ILO Conventions in all, whereas several other industrialized and developing countries have ratified a significantly larger number. Ratification of ILO Conventions may therefore not be an accurate indicator of existing national regulations governing labor standards, and there are many cases in which ratified Conventions are in fact not enforced.[23]

It is interesting in this connection, as Charnovitz (1986, pp. 566–567) has noted, that issues of alleged unfair competition involving labor standards were addressed in Article 7 of Chapter II of the 1948 (still-born) (Havana) Charter of the International Trade Organization (ITO). Since the GATT was conceived with a more narrow mandate as compared to the ITO, it did not address labor standards, except in Article XX(e) that provides for prohibition of goods made with prison labor. Charnovitz (p. 574) notes further that as early as 1953 the United States proposed (unsuccessfully) adding a labor standards article to the GATT. This would have empowered GATT members to take measures against other countries under the provisions of GATT Article XXIII (Nullification and Impairment). The United States continued, again unsuccessfully, to push for negotiation of a GATT article on labor standards in both the Tokyo and Uruguay Rounds of Multilateral Trade Negotiations in the 1970s and 1980s. But the international community was put on notice in April 1994 at the Marrakesh signing of the Uruguay Round accords that

[23] A detailed discussion of the observance of core labor standards in 75 selected countries is provided in OECD (1996, pp. 39–70).

the United States intended to pursue issues of labor standards in future multilateral negotiations.

In the interim, there have been efforts at drafting a so-called social clause dealing with core labor standards and including trade sanctions for noncompliance that might eventually be incorporated into the WTO. As noted in Aggarwal (1995, p. 38), in June 1994, the ILO began a research program dealing with the integration of social welfare and trade policy. A central objective was to develop a stronger enforcement mechanism. The ILO Secretariat proposed that the ILO and WTO work jointly on the oversight of international core labor standards, with the ILO concentrating on international monitoring and the WTO responsible for enforcement by means of trade-related sanctions. But because of disagreements among the country representatives of the ILO Working Party on the Social Dimensions of the Liberalization of International Trade, it was decided in early 1995 to suspend further discussion of the use of trade sanctions for alleged noncompliance with core labor standards. Instead, as noted in OECD (1996, p. 7), the ILO has undertaken a program of research on the effects of trade liberalization on core standards and a review of ILO means of action for the promotion of standards.

The United States, with some support from France and southern European Union members, Canada, and Japan, nonetheless continued to pursue the issue of trade and labor standards in the context of the WTO, and there was a concerted effort to add the issue to the agenda for the WTO Ministerial Meeting held in Singapore in December 1996.

In considering whether or not the WTO is an appropriate forum for dealing with trade and alleged violations of core labor standards, it is pertinent to note the conclusion reached in the OECD *Report on Trade, Employment and Labour Standards* (1996, pp. 16–17):

> Existing WTO provisions have not been designed for promoting core standards. Some of the suggestions under discussion would imply a reinterpretation of WTO practices and procedures while others would require to a greater or lesser extent renegotiation and amendment of WTO articles. Extending the WTO's Trade Policy Review Mechanism procedure to include labour standards would fall into the former category while other

> proposals would fall into the latter. In all cases, a consensus among WTO Members on the appropriateness and effectiveness of using WTO procedures to promote core labor standards and on the institutional changes required would have to be reached. Such a consensus does not exist at present. However, while some countries continue to call for discussion of the issue in the WTO and others are opposed, this remains an issue for international consideration. The debate on this issue and on the associated conceptual and practical difficulties will continue.[24]

Rodrik (1996) makes a case for using the Uruguay Round safeguard procedures for investigating complaints arising from imports from countries with unacceptable labor standards that may be disruptive to domestic producing interests. He stresses the need for including the views of consumers and public interest groups in the importing countries as well as the views of foreign producers. Srinivasan (1996, 1997) has pointed out an important problem with Rodrik's argument, namely that there are all kinds of government regulations, besides labor standards, that influence production costs (e.g., building codes and zoning laws). Thus, in principle, objections might arise concerning imports that may not conform to any one or more domestic regulations. Singling out labor standards is then not convincing. It is not obvious, moreover, that the safeguard procedures, which are designed to be temporary, can be implemented with the broad representation that Rodrik recommends. Finally, as Anderson (1996) has observed, the U.S. experiences with antidumping and countervailing duty procedures certainly suggest how difficult it may be to avoid the temporary safeguard procedures from being captured by producing interests.

[24] John Martin has suggested to the author that since the WTO has already been assigned a role in dealing with trade-related intellectual property rights (TRIPs) as a result of the Uruguay Round negotiations, it may be reasonable to include labor standards in the WTO as well. However, the inclusion of TRIPs in the WTO can be considered as an effort by the industrialized countries to capture the monopoly rents associated with intellectual property rights and thus ostensibly to prevent the "piracy" of these rights. This is a very different matter from dealing with intercountry differences in labor standards which may reflect variations in per capita income levels and a host of structural and institutional factors.

It is also worth noting that Freeman (1994a, p. 32) is somewhat inclined to support the inclusion of labor standards in trade agreements:

> Unlike trade economists who view any interference with free trade as the work of the devil, I would be pragmatic in this area. ... If trade negotiations are the only way to raise forcefully the standards flag in an international setting, why not? If trade sanctions can improve labor standards, that benefit must be weighed against the cost of lost trade. If trade sanctions can overturn an evil dictatorial regime and save human lives, go for it. Perhaps the standards issue will induce international trading groups to consider innovative ways that international trade might be used to finance improvements in standards.

Krueger (1997, p. 288) has expressed a similar view:

> Labor standards strike me as a legitimate subject of bargaining in trade negotiations. Presumably, a well-intentioned government will not accept an agreement unless, in total, it is expected to make the country better off. ... Because the demand for labor standards tends to rise with national income, many countries will choose on their own to strengthen and enforce their standards following trade agreements.

While the views expressed by Freeman and Krueger may be justified on pragmatic and political grounds, there are better and less costly ways to effect improvements in labor standards. There is also the further important question of whether and how labor standards should be dealt with in the WTO multilateral context. The welfare gains from trade liberalization have long been a central feature of nondiscrimination in the GATT system. It would be a major departure from precedent if countries with allegedly low labor standards were now to be denied improved market access on these grounds.[25]

The debate on whether labor standards should be placed under the WTO's purview was apparently resolved in the negative

[25] The point therefore is not that the recommendations of Freeman and Krueger are to be interpreted as "the work of the devil." Rather, trade agreements and trade sanctions are not effective and equitable means for raising international labor standards.

at the December 1996 WTO Ministerial Meeting. Thus, as reported by Williams in *The Financial Times* (December 16, 1996, p. 4):

> Predictably hardest to resolve was the issue of labour standards, where the U.S. threatened to veto the entire declaration if no mention was made. Ministers eventually agreed to uphold internationally recognised core labour standards,.... But trade sanctions to enforce them were rejected and there is no provision for follow-up work in the WTO, which is asked simply to maintain its (minimal) collaboration with the International Labour Organisation.

The U.S. position at the Singapore Ministerial Meeting could be interpreted in part as pre-election posturing by the Democrats especially since the Republicans have opposed linking labor standards and trade. Thus, the Republican-controlled 104th Congress was reluctant to grant fast-track negotiating authority to the Clinton Administration so long as the intention was to include labor issues as part of any future trade negotiations.[26] The Republican opposition was continued in the first session of the 105th Congress in 1997, and the Clinton Administration made an effort to mute its position on trade and labor standards in order to induce Republicans to approve fast-track negotiating authority. However, organized labor, environmental interest groups, and human rights organizations mounted an intensive campaign to oppose fast-track unless the legislation included explicit protection of labor rights and the environment.[27] When it became clear in mid-November 1997 that there were insufficient Democratic votes to obtain fast-track approval in the House of

---

[26] See, for example, U.S. House of Representatives (1995).

[27] Thus, as reported by Greenhouse in *The New York Times*, February 20, 1997, p. C3: "Putting the labor movement on a potential collision course with President Clinton, AFL-CIO leaders voted to oppose extending the North American Free Trade Agreement to other countries unless it includes protections on labor and the environment that the Administration has previously rejected." This is a good example of the point made earlier that advocates of labor standards apparently care more about protecting their own interests rather than the interests of supposedly exploited foreign workers.

Representatives, the legislation was withdrawn and presumably will be reintroduced in 1998. The link between trade and labor standards will therefore remain a highly visible and controversial issue of public discourse on future trade legislation in the United States especially.

Regional Arrangements

European Union (EU)

Issues of worker rights have been a focus of attention in the EU because of concerns over low-wage competition from some EU member countries, persistent unemployment, and wage stagnation. Sapir (1995b) notes that the first efforts to address the harmonization of social policies in Europe can be traced back to early stages of European integration prior to 1958. According to De Boer and Winham (1993, p. 17), the issue of a Community-wide Social Charter was first broached in 1972. Subsequently, with the issuance in 1985 of the white paper signaling the intention to remove remaining barriers to trade and creation of a Single Market, a Community Charter of Fundamental Social Rights for Workers was drafted in 1988. This Charter, which is quite comprehensive and encompasses the "core" and "other" labor standards noted in our earlier discussion,[28] was adopted by all EU members except the United Kingdom. It was hoped to incorporate the Social Charter into the Maastricht Treaty in December 1991, but this was opposed once again by Britain. The Social Charter was subsequently approved by the other 11 EU members, but on a voluntary basis and not as part of the Maastricht Treaty.[29]

[28] The highlights of the Charter of Fundamental Social Rights are summarized in De Boer and Winham (1993, pp. 36–37), and the full text is to be found in Commission of the European Communities (1990).

[29] It is interesting to note, with the advent of a Labor Government in the United Kingdom in the May 1, 1997 election, that Britain has indicated that it will give its approval to the Social Charter and thus will no longer be the only EU member country not to accept the Charter.

In his evaluation of the EU Social Charter, Sapir (1995a, pp. 742–743; 1996) concluded that harmonization of social policies was not a pre-condition of successful European trade liberalization and integration. He noted further that: "In the mid-1990s, differences in labour standards between member states remain substantial and 'social harmonisation' remains a distant reality. ... whatever harmonisation has been achieved in Europe, it could not have occurred without redistributive mechanisms between countries. In the absence of such mechanisms, the harmonisation of social policies cannot be contemplated internationally."[30]

NAFTA

At the time that NAFTA was being negotiated, some observers urged that NAFTA include a Social Charter for North America as a possible means of protecting the interests of workers.[31] Instead of including a Social Charter, however, and since the NAFTA had already been signed by the member countries in the summer of 1992, the newly elected Clinton Administration opted to pursue a separate side agreement covering labor issues as well as an agreement covering environmental issues.[32] Aggarwal (1995, p. 34) has summarized the main features of the labor side agreement as follows:

> First, the NAFTA supplemental agreement contains a more comprehensive list of labor standards than the five typically present in U.S. trade programs [which are noted below]. The agreement commits each party to the promotion of eleven broad labor conditions ranging from freedom of association to migration policies. Second, the agreement does not attempt to apply U.S. standards or ... common uniform criteria in its evaluation of labor conditions

---

[30] For information on the degree of convergence (or lack of it) between the EU and the European Free Trade Area (EFTA) on labor standards, see the chapter on "Labour Standards and Economic Integration" in OECD (1994).

[31] A useful reference is Lemco and Robson (1993).

[32] At the time, the negotiation of these side agreements may have been helpful in obtaining Congressional approval of the NAFTA. However, as noted below, the resort to such side agreements does not carry over necessarily to other regional or multilateral trade agreements.

> in other countries. Instead, the agreement contains different enforcement mechanisms for different standards. The complaint process consists of three stages — filing a petition with the domestic National Administrative Office (NAO), Ministerial consultations, and lastly consultation with the Evaluation Committee of Experts (ECE). Complaints pertaining to freedom of association, the right of collective bargaining, and/or the right to strike can only be taken to the second stage of the complaint process. More importantly, sanctions cannot be utilized to encourage enforcement of laws pertaining to these rights. Of the eleven labor principles, only the implementation of those pertaining to child labor, minimum employment standards, and occupational health and safety can be supported by sanctions.[33]

Because it required some time to establish the institutional framework following the implementation of NAFTA in January 1994, there has been limited experience to date in administering the labor side agreement. As of November 1997, the U.S. NAO has received seven submissions alleging non-compliance by Mexico with its labor laws. These submissions have involved issues of freedom of association being denied to Mexican workers. No action was recommended on two submissions, the third was withdrawn, and the others are pending. Mexico has received one submission about U.S. noncompliance with its labor laws, involving closure of a subsidiary of the Sprint Corporation in San Francisco. This case is pending.

It is interesting to ask whether the NAFTA labor side agreement might serve as a model for an agreement that might in the future be incorporated into the WTO, an expanded NAFTA, or other regional trading arrangements. As far as a global agreement is concerned, the NAFTA side agreement goes beyond what are considered to be core labor standards and emphasizes the observance of existing national laws governing labor standards in the NAFTA member countries rather than the intercountry harmonization of these laws that proponents of labor standards favor. Further, not all standards are subject to sanctions and those that are (i.e., child labor, minimum employment standards, and occupational safety and health) are precisely ones that have engendered much of the ongoing controversy in the global context. Whether an agreement on labor rights and standards should be made a condition of

[33] See also OECD (1996, pp. 178–183).

expanding NAFTA to include Chile and other nations in the Western Hemisphere or made applicable to other existing regional trading arrangements also appears problematic on both conceptual and empirical grounds. By the same token, if future Congressional approval of fast-track negotiating authority is to be obtained, it almost certainly will have to acknowledge the importance of labor standards. This could be accomplished by stressing in the negotiating authority the desirability of enhancing labor standards as an objective to be sought by the sovereign nations involved, and that trade sanctions are not to be used to impose labor standards that may not be appropriate for the economic circumstances of low-income countries.

National/Unilateral Arrangements

As noted in Brown, Deardorff, and Stern (1996, p. 229), since the 1980s it has become increasingly common to include international labor standards criteria in U.S. foreign economic legislation.[34] The most important of these actions have been in establishing eligibility for trade preferences in the 1983 Caribbean Basin Economic Recovery Act and the 1984 renewal of the Generalized System of Preferences (GSP), and making the foreign denial of worker rights actionable under Section 301 of the 1988 Trade Act. The 1988 Trade Act also expanded the requirements of the Departments of State and Labor to submit periodic reports to Congress on human rights abuses and foreign adherence to internationally recognized worker rights. The stipulations on labor standards in the GSP were made mandatory. GSP eligibility has in fact been revoked at times for a number of developing countries until they showed evidence that the offending actions had been or were in the process of being eliminated. Apparently prompted by the U.S. experience, the EU has adopted similar labor standards criteria for its GSP program to become effective in 1998.

[34] The standards include: (1) freedom of association; (2) the right to organize and bargain collectively; (3) freedom from forced labor; (4) a minimum age for employment; and (5) acceptable conditions of work, including a minimum wage, limitations on hours of work, and occupational safety and health rights in the workplace.

While there may be instances in which countries have improved their labor standards in order to maintain GSP eligibility, these cases may not be important economically, considering the size of the countries involved and the limited benefits that the GSP offers because of the restricted product coverage. Also, in the future the value of GSP will be eroded as the result of implementing the tariff reductions negotiated in the Uruguay Round. Nonetheless, it may appear that the experiences with quid-pro-quo actions under the GSP program can possibly provide some useful insights into the design and implementation of policies and procedures governing trade-linked labor standards in other contexts. This may be misleading, however, since the removal of GSP eligibility is essentially decided unilaterally by the United States and the EU, both of which are obviously very powerful entities in the global trading system.[35] Unilateral U.S. action can also be taken under Section 301 of the U.S. Trade Act. One should be wary therefore of arrangements in which developing countries may be coerced into taking actions detrimental to their own interests in response to pressures from their more powerful trading partners.[36]

Other Arrangements

There are a number of other arrangements that deserve mention in addition to those already discussed above.

For example, as noted in OECD (1996, pp. 161–169), the OECD, ILO, UNICEF, and other UN agencies have been active in promoting cooperative programs of economic development in which practical measures backed up often by multilateral and bilateral financial assistance can be devised to deal with some of the underlying causes of poverty in poor countries that may be reflected in the employment of children and the absence or relatively weak enforcement of core labor standards. The OECD and ILO have also developed international codes

[35] Further discussion of labor standards and trade preferences can be found in OECD (1996, pp. 182–190).

[36] Srinivasan (1997) characterizes the GSP as "'crumbs from the rich man's table' which the developing countries should do well without."

of conduct applicable to multinational enterprises (MNEs) that may assist in improving labor standards and working conditions in MNE affiliates in host developing countries. Individual firms can attempt to develop codes of conduct on their own, as Aggarwal (1995, p. 39) has noted has been done by such U.S. MNEs as Levi Strauss, Liz Claiborne, Nike, Reebok, Sears, Timberland, and Walmart. These cooperative efforts and codes of conduct are essentially voluntary in nature, and, of course, there is no guarantee that they will be effective in all circumstances in low-income countries, as some firms have already discovered. Nonetheless, they serve an important role insofar as they help to focus attention on the importance of the root causes of underdevelopment and the types of business practices that may help low-income countries to raise per capita incomes and improve conditions of work.

Finally, also worth mentioning is the importance of consumer labeling in providing a market-based method for helping to improve labor standards when these standards can be treated as private goods. The advantage of labeling is that it provides information about production processes being used and allows consumers in making their consumption choices to reflect the satisfaction that they derive from the presumed realization of higher labor standards internationally.[37]

---

[37] Aggarwal (1995, pp. 39–40) cites the example of the Child Labor Coalition, which was formed in 1989 by several religious, human rights, and union groups for the purpose of informing consumers in high-income countries about child labor conditions used in producing goods such as rugs in South Asia. The Coalition has sponsored the so-called Rugmark campaign which provides producers with a certifying label that they can attach to their exports indicating that they do not employ child labor. According to de Jonquieres and Williams (1996), the United States has proposed in the ILO that the Rugmark labeling system be extended to clothing and other products. See also U.S. Department of Labor (1996) for a report on codes of conduct for the U.S. apparel industry based on a survey of 42 companies and visits to six countries that are major apparel exporters to the U.S. market. These voluntary codes of conduct in the apparel industry have become increasingly common since the early 1990s, although monitoring and enforcement of the codes often present difficulties in many instances. The most recent example is the U.S. Presidential task force agreement to "end" apparel sweatshops worldwide and give a seal of approval to companies that comply with the code of conduct. For details, see Greenhouse in *The New York Times*, April 9, 1997, p. A11.

When labor standards are considered to be public goods, there will be a need for governmental policies. What is important is that these various private and public actions can be carried out without the coercion that may be involved when efforts are made internationally to influence governments to change their domestic labor-market policies.[38]

VI. Conclusions and Implications for Policy

The motivation for this chapter has been to consider whether international labor standards should be incorporated into the rules and mandate of the WTO which oversees the international trading system and into regional and national trade policies and trade agreements. A case could possibly be made for devising WTO rules and disciplines to improve core labor standards in low-income countries and, by the same token, to prevent the United States and other high-income countries from abusing their economic power in seeking measures that would be detrimental to the cost competitiveness and economic welfare of low-income countries.[39] However, it is difficult to make this case convincingly because of the diversity of labor standards in countries with differing national characteristics, policies, and institutions. Furthermore, the literature review summarized above suggests that there are no compelling theoretical and empirical grounds to

[38] It should be noted, however, that in a "quiet maneuver" led by Representative Bernard Sanders, (Ind-VT) and Senator Tom Harkin (D-IA), the 105th U.S. Congress enacted the Bonded Child Labor Elimination Act, and it was signed by President Clinton on October 10, 1997. The Act is designed to prohibit imports of goods made by indentured child laborers, that is, children who are sold into bondage by their parents and who must work for an extended period of time to gain their freedom. It is not yet clear how this Act is to be enforced, and, as already stated, it is unlikely to effect significant improvement in the conditions of poverty that are characteristic of the families involved. For more details, see Greenhouse (1997b).

[39] Bernard Hoekman has suggested to the author that some existing features in the WTO such as the agreements on pre-shipment inspection and trade-related intellectual property rights could be helpful in facilitating the provision of information to international traders and consumers.

support the international enforcement and harmonization of labor standards.[40]

What then should be done on the global level? Issues of international labor standards have historically been the province of the ILO, which is often criticized because it lacks a mechanism for enforcement of discipline to raise labor standards and because it espouses an interventionist social agenda. While these criticisms may be true, they miss the point. If one looks at the economic development of the United States, Western Europe, Japan and other advanced industrialized countries over the past century, it is evident that the real incomes of workers have increased dramatically and that the conditions of work have improved concomitantly. To achieve these improvements in labor standards has required an active role for government together with broad public support in individual nations. In recent decades, there have been similar improvements in a substantial number of developing countries, especially in East and Southeast Asia as well as in Latin America. What the historical record suggests therefore is that policies are needed currently to provide technical and financial assistance to low-income countries to promote economic progress, which in turn will help these countries to enhance the economic welfare of their citizenry.

With sufficient encouragement and increased financial support, the ILO can provide a multilateral forum that would serve to strengthen its role and authority in pursuing improved labor standards internationally. While the United States and many of the EU member countries wanted to link labor standards and trade in the

---

[40] Issue can therefore be taken with the point made in the OECD Report (1996, p. 14) that: "Even though efforts to improve observance of core labour standards may be facilitated by economic growth and freer trade, there are reasons to doubt that market forces alone will automatically improve the standards. Hence, the importance of more direct promotion mechanisms." The key words here are "automatically" and "direct." As already discussed and as Srinivasan also notes in his comment on Stern (1997), it may well be that labor-market failures are present in many countries. But if this is the case, the optimal policies are domestic in character, and it is by no means obvious why international policies are preferred and how they can better overcome the domestic market failures at issue.

December 1996 WTO Ministerial Meeting, their efforts were unsuccessful. The challenge then is to reinforce the institutional role for which the ILO has been designed.[41]

If the responsibility for monitoring and helping developing countries to improve their labor standards is centered in the ILO, there is no obvious case to be made for the United States and other industrialized countries to incorporate labor standards issues into their national and regional trade policies and trade agreements. It has to be acknowledged nonetheless that adherence to certain specified labor standards has been made a condition in U.S. preferential trade arrangements, especially in the GSP and in the labor side agreement in the NAFTA. There is not much evidence, however, that actual or threatened withdrawal of GSP has had much impact on developing country labor standards. Further, the actions initiated to date under the NAFTA labor side agreement have primarily involved alleged noncompliance with the right of freedom of association.

---

[41] In considering the spectrum of international organizations that have been created over the years, Srinivasan (1995, 1997) points out that these organizations have been specialized according to function. For example, he notes the particular rules and mandates that apply to such organizations as the: ILO; GATT/WTO; UNCTAD; World Bank; International Monetary Fund; Universal Postal Union; and Berne and Paris conventions. The issue then is whether it is desirable and efficient to require that individual organizations assume responsibilities for rules for which the organizations were not designed. More specifically, he argues that issues of labor standards are best left to the ILO and should not be mandated to the GATT/WTO, which has been designed to articulate, monitor, and enforce the rules governing the international trading system. For similar views, see Bhagwati (1995), Charnovitz (1995), and Pangestu (1996). Charnovitz (1995) in particular offers suggestions for reinvigorating the ILO and changes especially in U.S. policies that would serve to strengthen the ILO.

Some observers might take issue with the above characterization of the GATT/WTO, arguing that it constitutes a forum for discussion and negotiation on trade-related matters, and, in this light, should include issues of labor standards. But even if this were the case, there is a genuine possibility that the WTO could become overloaded if it were to take on labor standards as well as other new issues like the environment and competition policy.

The experience of the NAFTA thus does not provide much guidance for dealing with issues of labor standards in other regional trading arrangements, such as those currently existing in Latin America and Asia. The same may be true of the experience of the EU, except insofar as income transfers among EU member countries may have helped to harmonize standards to some extent. The review of the empirical evidence on labor standards and U.S. trade suggests that there is no case to be made that low foreign labor standards are harmful to American firms and workers. Moreover, foreign direct investment appears to be more attracted to countries with high rather than low labor standards. Thus, as already stated, the policies of the United States and other industrialized countries should be directed to maintaining open markets and encouraging the economic growth of their developing country trading partners. This is the surest way to achieve higher labor standards since there is pervasive historical evidence that standards are improved with higher levels of per capita incomes. This suggests accordingly that national governments in developing countries should institute pro-active policies designed to improve working conditions and workers' rights as their economies expand and more resources can be channeled towards social betterment.

Study Questions

1. What is the focus of social activists regarding labor standards in developing countries?
2. What are "core" labor standards? ILO Conventions? What are Fields' proposed basic worker rights? What is the distinction between labor processes and labor outcomes, i.e., between "core" and "other" labor standards?
3. Does the diversity of labor standards across countries alter the case for free trade? What are market failures, and how should they be corrected? What is the case to be made for universal labor standards and the international harmonization of standards?
4. What determines whether labor standards are "public goods" or "private goods"? What is the prevailing *political economy* view of international labor standards?

5. What does the empirical evidence suggest about the effects of trade on the U.S. skilled/unskilled wage differential? What is biased technical change? What is the evidence on the effects of multinational production on wages and working conditions in developing countries? How is trade affected by variations in labor standards? Foreign direct investment (FDI)? Does the support for international labor standards reflect protectionist interests in the United States and other industrialized countries?
6. What are the methods and principles of the ILO in dealing with labor standards? Why do countries differ in their ratification and enforcement of the ILO core labor standards? What has been the U.S. position on incorporating labor standards into the GATT/WTO? The position of the developing countries?
7. How has the EU addressed issues of social harmonization? What are the main features of the labor side agreement in the NAFTA? What submissions have been filed? How are labor issues addressed in U.S. bilateral free trade agreements (FTAs)? How do other nations deal with labor issues in their FTAs? How are labor issues addressed in U.S. and EU preferential trade agreements? Can these various arrangements be carried over for inclusion in the WTO?
8. What are voluntary codes of conduct that have been designed by multinational enterprises? What are the advantages and limitations of consumer labeling?
9. What should be done at the global level in addressing issues of international labor standards? What does economic history suggest about long-term increases in real incomes of workers and conditions of work? How have trade-linked programs involving labor standards affected developing countries?

References

Aggarwal, Mita. 1995. "International Trade, Labor Standards, and Labor Market Conditions: An Evaluation of the Linkages," USITC, Office of Economics Working Paper No. 95-06-C (June).

Anderson, Kym. 1996. "Social Policy Dimensions of Economic Integration: Environmental and Labour Standards," in T. Ito and A. O. Krueger (eds.), *Regionalism vs. Multilateral Trade Agreements.* Chicago: University of Chicago Press for the NBER.

Bhagwati, Jagdish. 1995. "Trade Liberalisation and 'Fair Trade' Demands: Addressing the Environmental and Labour Standards Issues," *The World Economy* 18, pp. 745–759.

Bhagwati, Jagdish. 1997. "Fast Track: Not So Fast," *Wall Street Journal*, September 10.

Bloom, David E. and Waseem Noor. 1994. "Labor Standards and the Emerging World Economy," processed, Columbia University.

Brown, Drusilla K., Alan V. Deardorff, and Robert M. Stern. 1996. "International Labor Standards and Trade: A Theoretical Analysis," in Jagdish N. Bhagwati and Robert E. Hudec (eds.), *Fair Trade and Harmonization: Prerequisites for Free Trade?* Cambridge: MIT Press.

Casella, Alessandra. 1996. "On Standards and Trade: A Review of Simple Results," in Jagdish Bhagwati and Robert Hudec (eds.), *Fair Trade and Harmonization: Prerequisites for Free Trade?* Cambridge: MIT Press.

Charnovitz, Steve. 1986. "The Influence of International Labor Standards on the World Trading Regime: A Historical Review," *International Labour Review* 126, pp. 565–584.

Charnovitz, Steve. 1995. "Promoting Higher Labor Standards," *The Washington Quarterly* 18, pp. 167–190.

Commission of the European Communities. 1990. *The Community Charter of Fundamental Social Rights for Workers.* European File 6/90. Brussels: Commission of the European Communities.

De Boer, Elizabeth and Gilbert R. Winham. 1993. "Trade Negotiations, Social Charters, and the NAFTA," in Jonathan Lemco and William B.P. Robson (eds.), *Ties Beyond Trade: Labor and Environmental Issues under the NAFTA.* Canadian-American Committee: C.D. Howe Institute (Canada) and National Planning Association (U.S.A.).

de Jonquieres, Guy and Frances Williams. 1996. "Balancing Fair Trade and Fair Work," *The Financial Times* (June 20), p. 8.

Erickson, Christopher L. and Daniel J.B. Mitchell. 1996. "Labor Standards and International Trade: Background Analysis," presented at conference on "The Multilateral Trading System in a Globalizing World," sponsored by the East-West Center (August 7–9).

Fields, Gary. 1995. *Trade and Labour Standards: A Review of the Issues.* Paris: OECD.

Freeman, Richard B. 1993. "Labor Market Institutions and Policies: Help or Hindrance to Economic Development?" in *Proceedings of the World Bank Annual Conference on Development Economics 1993*, pp. 117–144.

Freeman, Richard B. 1994a. "A Hard-Headed Look at Labor Standards," in U.S. Department of Labor, Bureau of International Labor Affairs, *International Labor*

Standards and Global Economic Integration: Proceedings of a Symposium. Washington, D.C.: U.S. Department of Labor.

Freeman, Richard B. 1994b. "Lessons for the United States," in Richard B. Freeman (ed.), *Working Under Different Rules*. New York: Russell Sage Foundation.

Golub, Stephen S. 1997. "International Labor Standards and International Trade," International Monetary Fund, Working Paper 97/37 (April).

Greenhouse, Steven. 1997a. "Apparel Industry Group Moves to End Sweatshops," *The New York Times*, April 9, 1997, p. A11.

Greenhouse, Steven. 1997b. "Congress Set to Ban Imports of Goods Made by Child Slave Labor," *The New York Times*, October 1.

Greenhouse, Steven. 1997c. "Union Leaders Oppose Expanding Free-Trade Treaty Without Modifications," *The New York Times*, February 20, p. C3.

International Labour Organization (ILO). 1988. *Human Rights: A Common Responsibility*. International Labour Conference, 75th Session, 1988. Geneva: ILO.

International Monetary Fund (IMF). 1997. "Indonesian Economic Growth Accompanied by Improved Social Indicators," *IMF Survey* (August 18).

Krueger, Alan. 1997. "International Labor Standards and Trade," in *Annual World Bank Conference on Development Economics 1996*. Washington, D.C.: The World Bank, pp. 281–302.

Lemco, Jonathan and William B.P. Robson (eds.). 1993. *Ties Beyond Trade: Labor and Environmental Issues under the NAFTA*. Canadian-American Committee: C.D. Howe Institute (Canada) and National Planning Association (U.S.A.).

Lyle, Faye. 1991. "Worker Rights in U.S. Policy," *Foreign Labor Trends*, 91–54, U.S. Department of Labor, Bureau of International Labor Affairs. Washington, D.C.: U.S. Government Printing Office.

Márquez, Gustavo (ed.). 1995. *Reforming the Labor Market in a Liberalized Economy*. Washington, D.C.: Inter-American Development Bank.

Maskus, Keith E. 1997. "Should Core Labor Standards Be Imposed Through International Trade Policy?" Policy Research Working Paper, WPS 1817, The World Bank Development Research Group (August).

Maskus, Keith E., Thomas J. Rutherford, and Steven Selby. 1996. "Implications of Changes in Labor Standards: A Computational Analysis for Mexico," *North American Journal of Economics and Finance* 6, pp. 171–188.

Noor, Waseem. 1996. "Labor Standards: A Guise for Protectionist Policy?" processed, Columbia University.

Organization for Economic Cooperation and Development (OECD). 1994. *OECD Employment Outlook*. Paris: OECD.

Organization for Economic Cooperation and Development (OECD). 1996. *Trade, Employment and Labour Standards: A Study of Core Workers' Rights and International Trade*. Paris: OECD.

Pangestu, Mari. 1996. "Asia to West: Stop Playing the Labor Game," *The Asian Wall Street Journal Weekly*, July 1, p. 18.

Reich, Robert. 1994. "Keynote Address," in U.S. Department of Labor, Bureau of International Labor Affairs, *International Labor Standards and Global Economic Integration: Proceedings of a Symposium*. Washington, D.C.: U.S. Department of Labor.

Rodrik, Dani. 1996. "Labor Standards in International Trade: Do They Matter and What Do We Do About Them?" in Robert Lawrence, Dani Rodrik, and John Whalley (eds.), *Emerging Agenda for Global Trade: High Stakes for Developing Countries*. Washington, D.C.: Overseas Development Council.

Sapir, André. 1995a. "Symposium: Does Free Trade Require Fair Trade and Harmonisation? Introduction," *The World Economy* 18, pp. 741–744.

Sapir, André. 1995b. "The Interaction Between Labour Standards and International Trade Policy," *The World Economy* 18, pp. 791–803.

Sapir, André. 1996. "Trade Liberalization and the Harmonization of Social Policies: Lessons from European Integration," in Jagdish N. Bhagwati and Robert E. Hudec (eds.), *Fair Trade and Harmonization: Prerequisites for Free Trade?* Cambridge: MIT Press.

Squire, Lyn and Sethaput Suthiwart-Narueput. 1997. "The Impact of Labor Market Regulations," *World Bank Economic Review* 11, pp. 119–143.

Srinivasan, T. N. 1994. "International Labor Standards Once Again!" in U.S. Department of Labor, Bureau of International Labor Affairs, *International Labor Standards and Global Economic Integration: Proceedings of a Symposium*. Washington, D.C.: U.S. Department of Labor.

Srinivasan, T. N. 1995. "International Trade and Labour Standards," in Pitou van Dijck and Gerrit Faber (eds.), *Challenges to the New World Trade Organization*. Amsterdam: Martinus Nijhoff/Kluwer.

Srinivasan, T. N. 1996. "Post-Uruguay Round Issues for Asian Member Countries," *Asian Development Review* 14, pp. 1–43.

Srinivasan, T. N. 1997. "Trade and Human Rights," in Alan V. Deardorff and Robert M. Stern (eds.), *Representation of Constituent Interests in the Design and Implementation of U.S. Trade Policies*. Ann Arbor: University of Michigan Press, forthcoming.

Stern, Robert M. 1997. "Issues of Trade and International Labor Standards in the WTO System," in *The Emerging WTO System and Perspectives from East Asia*, Joint U.S.-Korea Academic Studies, Vol. 7. Washington, D.C.: Korea Economic Institute of America. With comments by T. N. Srinivasan, Linda Lim, and Mari Pangestu.

U.S. Department of Labor, Bureau of International Labor Affairs. 1996. *The Apparel Industry and Codes of Conduct: A Solution to the International Child Labor Problem*. Washington, D.C.: U.S. Department of Labor.

U.S. House of Representatives, One Hundred Fourth Congress, First Session, Joint Hearing Before the Subcommittee on Trade of the Committee on Ways and Means and the Subcommittee on Rules and Organization of the House of the

Committee on Rules. 1995. *Fast-Track Issues.* Washington, D.C.: U.S. Government Printing Office (May 11 and 17).

Williams, Frances. 1996. "Singapore Deals Give a Boost to WTO," *The Financial Times*, December 16, p. 8.

Suggested Further Reading

Academic Consortium on International Trade (http://www.fordschool.umich.edu/rsie/acit/).

Brown, Andrew G. and Robert M. Stern. 2008. "What Are the Issues in Using Trade Agreements for Improving International Labor Standards?" *World Trade Review* 7, pp. 331–357.

Busse, Matthias. 2002. "Do Labor Standards Affect Comparative Advantage in Developing Countries?" *World Development* 30, pp. 1921–1932.

Elliott, Kimberly Ann and Richard B. Freeman. 2003. "Vigilantes and Verifiers," in *Can Labor Standards Improve Under Globalization?* Washington D.C.: Institute for International Economics, pp. 49–72 and 143–150.

Engerman, Stanley. 2003. "The History and Political Economy of International Labor Standards," in Kaushik Basu, Henrik Horn, Lisa Roman and Judith Shapiro (eds.), *International Labor Standards.* Malden, MA: Blackwell Publishing Ltd.

Kucera, David (ed.). 2007. *Quantitative Indicators of Labour Standards: Comparative Methods and Applications.* Dordrecht, The Netherlands: Springer.

National Research Council. 2004. *Monitoring International Labor Standards: Techniques and Sources of Information.* Washington, D.C.: The National Academies Press.

Stern, Robert M. 2003. "Labor Standards and Trade Agreements," *Revue d'Economie du Developpement* 17, pp. 125–150.